Buster Keaton

Buster Keaton

A Filmmaker's Life

James Curtis

 ALFRED A. KNOPF · NEW YORK · 2022

THIS IS A BORZOI BOOK
PUBLISHED BY ALFRED A. KNOPF

Copyright © 2022 by James Curtis

www.aaknopf.com

Knopf, Borzoi Books, and the colophon
are registered trademarks of Penguin Random House LLC.

The Library of Congress Cataloging-in-Publication Data has been applied for.
ISBN: 978-0-385-35421-9
eISBN: 978-0-385-35422-6

Front-of-jacket photograph: Wolf TracerArchive/Photo 12/Alamy
Spine-of-jacket photograph: Hulton Archive/Getty Images
Back-of-jacket photograph: ullstein bild/Getty Images
Jacket design by John Gall

Manufactured in the United States of America
First Edition

In memory of James Karen

One of the reasons I love him so much is because he lives comedy as well as practices it. The real comedian has to live his work and be happy about that.

—STAN LAUREL

Contents

Buster Keaton

Rivers, Manitoba

T HE MAN IN THE PORK PIE HAT is unhappy. His head down, arms akimbo, he paces grimly as a documentary crew captures him on film.

"What happened?" he is asked from off camera. "Didn't he tell you what he was going to do?"

"No, I didn't know he shifted gags on me."

"What did you expect it was going to be?"

Buster Keaton strikes a match, shielding it from the wind as he lights a cigarette. "I thought I was going to be fouled up with the map 'cause I decided that last night. And he decided not to. I didn't know it."

The setting is a trestle spanning the Little Saskatchewan Valley, a bridge that, when it was built, was the longest of its kind in Western Canada. On its single track, Keaton, in his by-now-familiar costume of hat, coat, vest, and string tie, is to be piloting a "speeder," a little two-cylinder track car that carries him along at speeds of up to thirty miles an hour. The question is what he should be doing as he crosses the trestle, which rises some ninety feet above the valley floor. His director, animator Gerald Potterton, has asked that he cross while doing his laundry, the idea being that he never leaves the moving vehicle from the time he boards it on the coast of Nova Scotia until he reaches Vancouver and the Pacific Ocean, a journey of more than 3,800 miles. Keaton, however, thinks he should be bunched up in a map so that his character isn't aware he is in danger.

The idea had taken form the previous day. "Beautiful trestle bridge," said Potterton as he entered Keaton's private car, a seven-compartment sleeper on loan from Canadian National Railways. Gerry Potterton and a company of nine were in the middle of making a twenty-four-minute color subject for the National Film Board called *The Railrodder*. Simultaneously, a 16mm documentary on the making of the film was being shot under the title *Buster Keaton Rides Again*. Potterton and his cameraman, Robert Humble, had made an advance trip in August in which the men identified likely settings for their breezy travelogue, and the historic trestle just outside Rivers offered the chance for any number of gags.

Keaton had an idea: "Now, I get out the map. Once I get it pretty well open and the wind catches it, it's going to wrap around me. So I cross that trestle wrapped up in a paper, standin' up in the car, fightin' the paper."

Potterton was apprehensive. "I'll tell you the locality is fine . . ." he hedged, hoping to change the subject. Keaton was a master of physical comedy, and racing along a trestle in an open car didn't begin to approach some of the signature stunts he had done over his long career. But he was also just days from his sixty-ninth birthday and, though solidly built, in fragile health.

"It might be the funniest way to do it," Keaton mused.

"There's another thing come along," said Potterton, pointing out the window. "See those little houses over here?"

"Yeah."

"Well, in those houses live little speeders, about six of them."

"Oh, I see."

"Imagine this: a long shot of the bridge, and suddenly, from left to right, three or four of these other little box speeders all come over—*ch-ch-ch-ch-ch-ch-ch-ch*—"

"That's a single-track trestle?"

"Yeah, single track. Yeah. They go across—*ch-ch-ch-ch-ch-ch*—slight hold, and they all reverse, going like mad—*ch-ch-ch-ch*—and you're there, waving them on."

"You mean I chase them off."

"Chase them off. Next shot, you cut to those little houses. The four guys come in very quickly, stop, take them off the tracks, and you just—*whoosh!*—shoot through. And that's the sequence."

"And they all look out at the same time."

"Yes, exactly."

Keaton, though, was not easily dissuaded. "I don't know why," he said, "but I like that—cleaning house, I get out the map to look at it just as I hit the trestle. Gettin' on it and gettin' scared is not gonna mean anything."

"I'll get my pad because I want to draw it, and I'll show you what we're going to do." Potterton begins to sketch the scene. "This is the shot with the bridge. We get the valley like that, this damn great big bridge . . ."

"Why aren't these two gags the same thing?" wondered Keaton, acting it out. "I don't know. I put my broom down and everything else. 'Now I wonder where I am?' Out with the map, and once I get it opened, I'm helpless. Well, now your shot goin' across that trestle is all the funnier—I'm chasin' 'em but fightin' the paper at the same time."

"Yeah."

"I'm fightin' the paper and goin' past, and four heads come out and look. I don't know I've chased 'em out. I don't know I've crossed a dangerous place either. They don't feel like bein' run into, so it'll all work out."

It was a test of wills between a fledgling director and a world-renowned comedian, the sort of match that in Hollywood wouldn't end well for a young man with just one live-action short to his credit. But Keaton was never one to throw his weight around, even at times when the quality of the picture was at stake. He would grouse, pace, complain, but in the end he would do what he was told, even when he knew it was wrong.

Buster Keaton was a gentle soul, so quiet and unassuming it was easy to forget he had been making the world laugh since the age of five. On-screen, he was a tabula rasa of emotionless energy onto which audiences could project their own aspirations, triumphs, and misfortunes. To James Agee, his unsmiling face ranked with Lincoln's as an early American archetype—"haunting, handsome, almost beautiful, yet it was irreducibly funny." The French called him "Malec," the Poles "Zbysco," and in Iceland he was known as "Glo-Go." At some point the Great Stone Face ceased being a work of nature as defined by Nathaniel Hawthorne and attached itself to him so thoroughly it could easily have been his legal name.

Keaton's authority on the set of *The Railrodder* comes not only from his stature as one of the screen's great silent clowns—in the opinion of many, greater even than Charlie Chaplin—but also as a world-class filmmaker with a string of nineteen short comedies and twelve masterful features to his credit. Just prior to the start of shooting, in fact, the *Railrodder* company, along with NFB staff and friends, squeezed into the Film Board's Theatre 3 in Quebec's Saint-Laurent borough to witness the showing of a movie Keaton had co-written and directed in 1926. *The General,* another story about trains and the tracks that carry them, was Keaton's masterpiece, easily the most ambitious comedy feature of the entire silent era, a film that would eventually come to dominate the *Sight & Sound* critics' poll as the greatest comedy of all time. And thirty-three-year-old Gerald Potterton was charged with directing the man who made it.

"What makes it tough," Keaton tells the documentarians, "is that I can't match scenes . . . 'cause I didn't have it in my mind that way. I don't know. . . . If I went back now to protect this chase in close-ups, I wouldn't have the slightest idea what I was doin' at the time I should be doin' it. So we can't make scenes match."

Cut to Gerry Potterton. "Don't forget there's still two other shots to go to complete the sequence, Buster. There's a long shot of the bridge, of him going over. That's the whole center of the gag is that long shot of the bridge."

"The bridge is not your gag," Keaton insists. "The bridge is only suspense, a thrill. There's no gag to the bridge at all. Not a goddamn thing. It's only a dangerous place to be when there might be a collision. That's the only thing that's funny."

Back in the railcar that doubles as a dressing room, club car, and occasional overnight accommodations, he is playing solitaire.

"Well," his wife says, "I know the main reason they didn't want you going over the trestle all wrapped up in newspapers and things . . ."

"If they took a good look, the scene we did is a worthless scene. The scene can't be used. So it's a nice scene to have sometime when you're going to show it to friends or somethin' like that. You don't use it in the picture."

"[Gerry] said it was too dangerous."

"I sez, 'Who suggested the gags?' He says, 'You did.' I sez, 'I generally know what I'm doin'.'" Impatiently: "That is not dangerous. That's child's play, for the love of Mike."

"Don't tell me about that."

"I told them. I do worse things in my sleep than that."

"I know."

"In my own backyard with a swimmin' pool I take more chances than that."

Jo Kirkpatrick, the unit business manager, holds up a prop map, fully eight feet square. "Here's the map," she says. "It's terribly strong."

"I'd like that to look like it was a big sail goin' [across the bridge]."

"And you won't fall off?"

"No, certainly not. I took more chances washin' clothes doin' it because my feet were sliding all over the place in that car."

He returns to his cards.

"Any time you're shootin' gags or laying 'em out in advance, you'll so often run into guesswork. 'Well, maybe his way is better than doin' it mine.' Then you try to sell yourself one way or the other because there is a certain amount of guess. Has to be. But every now and then there ain't no guesswork. This is one of 'em."

Two days later, they are back at the trestle to do the scene Keaton's way. "I was quite happy with him doing his washing," said Potterton, laughing. "I *liked* him doing his washing." Still, he had to admit the logic in Keaton's reasoning: "With the map, it did work with the idea that he was out there in the middle of the Manitoba wilderness, that he's looking at it. He takes that big map out to see where he's going." The bit with the washing would remain, but Keaton is no longer zipping across the bridge when he does it. "That whole gag was built on the premise that after all this clear running from east to west, suddenly there are guys coming towards him on the line, the little workmen on that bridge, and the gag was that he would be completely unaware of those guys as they were waving to each other, *Go back! Go back to your little sheds!* The idea was that he would shoot by, sit down, perfectly unaware that he'd been in mortal danger."

It was a theme that had followed Keaton from his earliest work on-screen—his utter cluelessness in the presence of disaster, as if an impending holocaust existed on a completely separate plane. He is guileless, but he is also an adult, not an overgrown child as so many comics present themselves. He was, as Walter Kerr would write, the most silent of silent comedians, immobile as in a sense of alert repose, but whose intuitions about the nature of man in the universe were as perceptive as they were simple. "His pictures are motion pictures. Yet, though there is a hurricane eternally raging about him, and though he is often fully caught up in it, Keaton's constant drift is toward the quiet at the hurricane's eye."

Part One

LOW COMEDY

1

The Smallest Comedian

WHEN MYRA CUTLER laid eyes on Joe Keaton for the first time, she was all of sixteen years old. It was August 1893, not long before the opening of the Cherokee Outlet, and the Cutler Comedy Company was stopping in Edmond, just north of Oklahoma City. Migration toward the border of Old Oklahoma was surging, prices were rising, and shortages were common. Among those traveling with the Cutlers were Sam and Violet Bryant, whose marquee product was Dr. Bryant's Magic Liniment, a potent mixture of cayenne pepper and gasoline that sold for fifty cents a bottle, three for a dollar. ("Feel it penetrate?" Sam would ask.) It was Violet, the singing star of the show, who introduced Joe to his future wife, thus sealing Myra's fate as his eventual partner in vaudeville.

The Bryants were drawn by the land run that was set to take place on September 16, putting more than six million acres up for grabs in the northwest corner of what would become, fourteen years later, the forty-sixth state of the union. An original boomer, Joe Keaton had taken part in the Run of '89, securing a quarter section for himself, which he later sold for $900. "Having been through the game," he said, "I wanted to try it again." But with more than 100,000 would-be homesteaders competing for just 42,000 available parcels, Joe found himself lost amid the dust and general chaos of the event. Acting as his father's agent, Joe had to settle for purchasing another man's claim. Then he signed on with the Cutlers as a general utility man, earning three dollars a week, board, and transportation. The following month, he made his first stage appearance in a tent pitched on the courthouse square in Perry, Oklahoma.

Joseph Hallie Keaton, a transient of sorts who considered Edmond his home, was born in Prairie Creek township, a farming community sixteen miles south of Terre Haute, Indiana, on July 6, 1867. Joe's father, Joseph Z. Keaton, operated a grist mill on the Eel River, and young Joe served as his assistant for a time. Then, around 1880, Joseph Z. became proprietor of the Henderson House, a Terre Haute hotel to which he made a number of improvements, not the least of which was "a well-stocked bar-room" for overnight guests headed west along the National Road. By the time he was twenty-one, Joe and his parents had settled in Clay City, some twenty-five miles east of his birthplace. When the great land run of 1889 was announced under President Benjamin Harrison's new administration, Joe's father, by then a pensioner, gave Joe $100 and sent him to Edmond with a colony traveling from Terre Haute to secure homesteads.

"I was one of the fortunates," Joe said, "and held down 160 acres with a Winchester rifle for a while." Having nursed a lifelong fascination with circus life, he took the proceeds from the land sale and headed west. "I went to California with the intention of joining some show," he later wrote, "but no one seemed to appreciate my talent." The money eventually ran out, and Joe made his way back to Oklahoma, walking and riding the rails.

At nearly six feet, Joe Keaton towered over Myra, who was four feet eleven, making them an amusing sight when they were together onstage. Mostly, though, Joe worked alone, doing self-taught acrobatic stunts, principally a kind of backward handspring called a "flip-flap," a trick he perfected while working at a Clay City sawmill. Kinetic and charming, with a hair-trigger temper that could flare on a moment's notice, Joe Keaton was nothing if not brash. He quickly earned Frank Cutler's animosity by openly courting Myra, the company's soubrette, who would sing, dance, and play the organ.

"I learned the business fast," Joe reminisced in 1904, "and could soon do a blackface monologue, sing songs, and do a dancing act, which was the means of holding my position against the manager's wishes. I was a useful all-around performer, but the manager didn't like me paying attention to his daughter, and the result was that I was notified to quit. It seemed, however, that he could never get another performer to play the parts as I did and change acts as often; hence they sent for me again."

A full decade younger than Joe, Myra Edith Cutler was born in Modale, Iowa, on March 13, 1877. Her father, a local actor and playwright, was responsibly employed as a store clerk in the years leading up to her mother's death in 1887. Promptly, Frank Cutler abandoned shopkeeping for the lure of the stage, which made for rocky times over the next six years.

"Fail and back to Modale," as Myra put it. "Pa would earn twenty dollars and on the road again."

The Cutler troupe distinguished itself with the inventive one-acts and full-length plays Frank churned out and published through the A. D. Ames Company of Clyde, Ohio. One of Myra's earliest credits, at the age of twelve, was the role of a street urchin in the play *Rag and Tag,* in which she appeared with her brother Burt. Something of a prodigy, she had mastered the bull fiddle, the cornet, and the piano by age eleven, but cared little for show business—doubtless a source of tension between herself and her hardheaded father, who was a wandering minstrel when he married Myra's mother at the age of twenty-one. It may be that Myra saw in Joe's interest a means of escape from the grind of a traveling show that, as of 1892, had logged twelve hundred consecutive nights.

The Cutler Comedy Company traveled from Perry to Guthrie, but creditors caught up with them in Kansas and their brand-new tent was repossessed. Frank Cutler carried a letter of recommendation to the managers of the Eden Musee in Lincoln, Nebraska, and after a week's stand at Embleton Hall in Severy, Kansas, the company split, two members hopping a blind baggage west to San Francisco while the balance of the company headed north on the Santa Fe. To the end of her life, Myra would remember the trip to Lincoln that took two days over three different lines to cover something under three hundred miles. They had twenty-five cents left after paying for the tickets, and Joe, a survivalist at heart, took charge of laying in supplies.

"A five-cent sack of Bull Durham, two plugs of Horse Shoe Chewing Tobacco, and two ham sandwiches," Myra enumerated. "One sandwich for me and the other one for my father, my brother, and Joe. I got the Bull Durham."

At the Eden Musee, the Cutlers pulled out all the stops, putting on a four-act comedy-drama called *The Waifs of Sacramento.* The play was presented "in an acceptable manner," *The Nebraska State Journal* acknowledged. When it folded, Myra was sent to live with an aunt and grandmother in a town called Greenwood, twenty miles northeast of Lincoln. Joe, meanwhile, found work as a single at the musee and, for a while, with a locally based vaudeville act, the James Family of Swiss Bell Ringers.

"One day when I entered the hotel where I was staying, the clerk said to me: 'There is a young lady in the parlor waiting to see you.' And sure enough, there was the little girl who had kept her word and traveled all the way by herself to marry a fellow who hadn't even a chance in the show business at the time, and she was contented to be my wife and fight life's battles among strangers who, in those days, didn't have much use for the average showman."

They joined the Mohawk Indian Medicine Company, Myra on the roster as their pianist, Joe their acrobat, and on May 31, 1894, they were married during a stopover at Wilber, Nebraska, the Saline County seat.

"We became regular medicine show actors at seventeen dollars a week," Joe recalled. "We had to live on the lot, and I [had] to drive stakes, help put up the tent, pass and post up bills, fight rushes, put on three different acts each night, and help the doctor sell 'em six for five. Many a time I had to take a club along when I went to get my salary, and many a time I missed it by waiting a day too long."

A year into their marriage, Joe and Myra were camped at Longwood, Missouri, with a unit of the Umatilla Indian Medicine Company. Based in Detroit, Umatilla boasted of being the largest medicine company in the world, the leading imitator of the famous Kickapoo Indian Medicine Company that promised astounding cures based on herbal remedies and ancient tribal practices. Through more than a hundred traveling companies, Umatilla marketed a proprietary line of products that included Indian Cough Cure, Indian Relief ("a sovereign cure for rheumatism and all painful diseases"), Hair Restorer, Indian Hogah, and a mixture of beaver tallow and herbs, roots, and barks called Umatilla Indian Salve, "the most lulling and soothing dressing for old and indolent sores ever discovered."

The Keatons had no savings and a baby on the way. Myra, who was just starting to show, was the company's soubrette and pianist, Joe its all-around comedian. A month later, during a two-week stay at Aullville, Missouri, they were reported as having teamed for the first time, doing sketch comedy. A musical act, Billie and Allie Collins, shared the bill, and a requisite pair of Indians, Chief Rolling Thunder and squaw, lent authenticity to the spiel delivered by the company's frock-coated lecturer, one Dr. Middleton. A Umatilla ballyhoo was always free, the home office offering a varied enough line of panaceas to support a half hour or so of entertainment ahead of the inevitable pitch. The locals, in fact, were known to purchase the various Umatilla nostrums as an inducement for the show to stick around. Business at Aullville, where farmers lined the sidewalks and kids watched from the roofs of nearby buildings, was described as "splendid."

Given Myra's condition, it was destined that she and Joe would return to the bosom of her family, at least for the birth of their baby, who would be Frank Cutler's first grandchild. In the October 12 issue of *The New York Clipper*, the leading trade paper of the day, the Cutlers, traveling as a Mohawk unit, reported "quite a commotion." Burt M. Cutler, co-manager with his father, was married on October 3, "and a general good time was had after the show." Burt, the report went on, was made a Knight of Pythias two days later. "All is lively with us." And on October 4, 1895, Mrs. Myra Keaton presented her husband with a fine boy. "The mother and baby are getting along nicely." The dispatch didn't say exactly where these momentous events took place, but the Mohawks had been reported on their way to a tiny Kansas village at the junction of the Missouri-Kansas-Texas and the Missouri Pacific rail lines known as Piqua—the acknowledged birthplace of Joseph Frank Keaton.

Over the years, the story of the baby's birth got stretched and embellished to the point where the most widely accepted version was utter fiction, a whopper of Joe Keaton's invention that was embraced and retold by both Myra and her son. What Myra herself remembered most vividly was the knocking-around she took during the latter part of her pregnancy—a tumble from a buggy at six months, a tent blown down around her at eight months, a fall off a stage with just days to go. ("Thank God!" said Joe. "That's the third accident. Now we'll be all right.") What is known is this:

The Cutlers were up and running in Piqua on September 27, having settled in for a week's stay. Apart from Joe and Myra, the company consisted of Frank and Burt Cutler, baritone Frank Howard and his wife, minstrel Tommie Chase, and Dr. St. George, the lecturer, and his wife. By Joe's account, the night before his son was born, a heavy wind blew the company's tent down. "While we were trying to get the tent up again, a cyclonic blast lifted it out of our hands and it disappeared in the night." With no tent, the Cutlers were forced to move their performances to Piqua's Catholic Hall during a cold snap that, as the *Iola Register* put it, had "old Jack peeping through the cracks." Myra wasn't allowed onstage in her condition but was evidently present for rehearsals and performances. When she went into labor, she was taken across the street to the home of a German-born carpenter named Jacob Haen. A local midwife, Theresa Ullrich, was summoned to the Haen residence, and it was Mrs. Ullrich—not a horse doctor, as one of Joe's variations would have it—who delivered the boy.* Hardly pausing,

---

* Mrs. Barbara Haen (1851–1899) may have assisted at the birth, but Mrs. Ullrich (1863–1948) was generally acknowledged as the midwife.

the Cutlers announced plans to open in Galesburg, Kansas, for two weeks on October 7, and Myra and the new baby were left behind to recuperate.

Given their history of tensions, the Keatons and the Cutlers were bound to go their separate ways. By the end of the year, Joe and Myra were back with a Umatilla company, Joe working in partnership with an Irish comedian and jig dancer named Billy Farrell. Myra played the organ, and the baby, going on three months, was never far from the action. "His cradle was the till of our trunk," Joe remembered, "and his playground as a babe was the stage of wherever his father and mother were performing. The trunk was kept in the wings, and [he was] placed in the hat box of the till while we were doing our act." One night, somebody brushed against the lid of the trunk, knocking it shut and cutting off its occupant's air supply. A few weeks later, a hotel fire threatened to cremate the infant while under the supervision of a chambermaid. Prone to bumps and falls, he soon acquired himself a nickname.

The manager and lecturer of Umatilla No. 27 was the irrepressible George A. Pardey, once a well-known comedian on the legitimate stage who reinvented himself for the medicine circuits, initially with his own company, later for the Kickapoo and Umatilla organizations. Born in London, Pardey was a repository of colorful slang, a lot of which he inherited from his late father, actor-playwright H. O. Pardey. It was sometime in the spring of 1896 that Dr. Pardey observed the Keaton child as he bounced down a flight of stairs. "Gee whiz!" he exclaimed with characteristic zeal. "He's a regular buster!"

To an American like Joe Keaton, the word "buster" would have meant a small loaf ("Penny-worth of beeswax and a penny buster," i.e., cheese and bread). To an Englishman, however, the word would also have applied to the act of falling heavily or resoundingly, the common phrase being *to come a buster*. Or, similarly, *to come a cropper*. Had Pardey said "cropper," it might not have excited Joe Keaton's imagination, but "buster," used in this context, was an entirely new and interesting word. Joe, according to one account, told Pardey the name "Buster" Keaton would be known the world over before the boy was ten years old. And he set out to make good on the prognostication by giving the boy his first press exposure.

It followed an incident in which the baby had somehow gotten out of his trunk. On the floor, he had taken to "scuttling," as his mother put it, "like a crawdad on a creek bottom." On this occasion, which Myra placed in July 1896, the child made it onto the stage where his father was delivering

At the time of his son's birth, Joe Keaton was doing a blackface monologue that incorporated singing, dancing, tumbling, and high kicking. The infant would sometimes crawl onstage, bringing the act to a halt. Within a year, Joe had largely abandoned blackface for what was referred to at the time as a "rough Irish specialty."

a blackface monologue. His appearance got the crowd laughing in all the wrong spots, and the perplexed father pressed on until he felt a tug at his pants leg. Looking down, he observed his son seated on the floor, staring gravely at the audience. Breaking character, Joe gathered him up in his arms and held him out for inspection.

"This," he announced proudly, "is Buster."

It may not have been an isolated incident. Sensing a good thing, a surefire laugh, Joe might have arranged for the boy to make similar appearances at other performances, much like an adorable dog with impeccable timing.

"We'd be doing a melodrama," said Myra. "Joe would be rescuing me— the innocent maiden—from the villain's clutches and here would come Buster onstage. Toddle over to me piping 'Mama,' then to Joe piping 'Papa,' and that was it. Show over."

On September 12, 1896, the *Clipper* carried a lengthy report from Umatilla Concert Company No. 101, under canvas somewhere in the Midwest, in which the official nine-member roster included "Joe Keaton, black face Irish and all 'round comedy acrobatic song and dance and high kicker; Mrs. Joe Keaton, musical soubrette, song and dance and sketch act; Buster Keaton, low comedy."

He was eleven months old.

. . .

It was Joe Keaton's fervent hope to leave the tent shows behind and play vaudeville—the raucous, rib-nudging theatre of the people—but he and Myra had no act to sell, just a collection of random bits. Relying on the sketches and ethnic parodies he bought from suppliers like A. A. Shearer, Joe was using material available to anyone with thirty-five cents to spend. Tall and limber, with long legs that prompted his wife to describe him as "a pair of shears," Joe distinguished himself with physical business—high kicks, flip-flaps, contortions, and the like. (A pal named Johnny Stanley took to calling him "Leg-around-your-neck-Charlie.") A particular specialty was a hitch kick, for which he preceded one of his dazzling high kicks with a standing leap.

"Joe Keaton is a good impersonator of the Mississippi darky," judged a reviewer during a three-week stop at Weir, Kansas, "and put hieroglyphics on the floor with his feet that would hustle any song-and-dance artist to duplicate. His movements on the stage are zephyr-like and as mystifying as the 'Will o' the Wisp.' His tumbling and contortion, especially high kicking as he kicked seven feet, higher than anyone who has been in Weir for a long time, and, in fact, he is a brass band, a Dutch picnic, and a good-sized circus all by himself."

For a while they toured as Keaton & York's Pantomime Company—W. B. York being the learned professor extolling the remedies they sold—but the show ran aground in the spring of 1897, and the Keatons spent the balance of the summer with family in Perry. They finished off a difficult year in residence at the old Newmarket Opera House, a variety saloon in Kansas City where they managed to secure separate positions on the bill. Then Joe took on the added job of stage manager, a move that would keep them in the Paris of the Plains for nearly three months. The Newmarket was a shabby affair, dark and dingy and situated in the city's disreputable North End. Immediately, Joe placed an "At Liberty" ad in the *Clipper*, effectively summarizing the Keatons' selling points: "Comedy Sketch Team with good rough acrobatic and eccentric dancing. Both play parts. Small singing soubrette and knockabout comedians. A-1 wardrobe. Sober. Reliable Mgrs. only. For dates or combinations. Would like to hear from good knockabout acrobatic dancing and singing comedian to double with me."

The Keatons joined the California Concert Company for a brief spell in 1898, traveling through southeastern Kansas with Harry Houdini and his wife, Bessie. Houdini was performing an act called "Metamorphosis," a cabinet illusion to which he had added several novelties. Yet business was grim: "Our impresario's great problem then was to ameliorate the burden of salaries and hotel accommodations," the magician wrote. "A 'big week' was our only saving grace, and it was not forthcoming." Houdini was able to turn things around by passing himself off as a medium and conjuring a séance for the rubes. "Broke the record at Garnett for paid admissions," he recorded in his diary. "Spiritualism cause of it—Bad effect—1034 Paid Admission to see spiritualism."

Joe took on a partner that spring, an acrobatic dancer and character comic named Arthur Long. Together, Keaton and Long developed their own version of a much-copied specialty known as "Silence and Fun." Originated by a graceful dancer and singer known as Frank McNish, "Silence and Fun" took place on the set of a kitchen furnished with two barrels, a chair, a table, and a broom. McNish would deftly ascend to the tabletop, then move from the table to one of the barrels, then the other, then back to the table again, performing acrobatic rollovers, nip-ups, and splits as he went. The "Silence" part came from the fact that it was a dumb act, meaning that McNish did not speak but simply moved to musical accompaniment.

Keaton and Long called their innovation "Double Silence and Fun," but Joe was in the habit of talking onstage, and it was a struggle for him to keep quiet. The team offered "Acrobatic Double Songs and Dances" in a *Clipper* ad, as well as a "scientific and burlesque" boxing specialty that drew little interest. In July, Joe, Myra, and Arthur Long wound up with a stock and vaudeville company at a park near Pittsburg, Kansas.

"Joe did his big acrobatic act," recalled Guy O. Fritts, a local who was part of the stock company, "and his wife appeared in a saxophone specialty. Both played parts in the dramas we were putting on." Usually a feature of military bands, the sax was considered a novelty among wind instruments, and soloists—particularly female soloists—were rare. Joe spied the instrument in the window of a music store and thought it would look comical to have his diminutive wife play it onstage. Putting five dollars down on the thing, he took it back to Myra, who, with a little practice, was able to blow a respectable "Marching Through Georgia" while her husband did his human snake routine.

"When he gets to dancing," commented the *Pittsburg Daily Tribune*, "it appears as though his legs are boneless."

In August, the Keatons, once again a duo, joined Bert Christy's Vaudevilles at Hollis, Kansas, and remained with the company into November. The year ended on a high note, with Joe and Myra's first New York engagement, a spot on the bill at the newly remodeled Bon Ton Music Hall, the former Koster and Bial's, on the north side of Twenty-Third Street. A genuine two-a-day, the Bon Ton's announced policy was to present "programmes of a clean nature, wholly free from suggestiveness." The building smelled of fresh construction, a new stage and two promenades having been added, and the Keatons made enough of an impression to get invited back.

"Buster, at times, would join us in a sketch," Joe wrote of their young son, "and not having any particular part to play he would just 'butt in' any old time. In fact, he would howl and make so much noise that the stagehands would have to let him crawl out on the stage. He was always in the way of the stagehands, and after getting hurt several times the idea struck me to make him up in a counterpart of myself and just let him stand around. He made a hit, and by the time he was three years of age we found that he was capable of doing an act all by himself."

The earliest report of Buster having joined the act came in the March 18, 1899, issue of the *Clipper,* when the Keatons were traveling with J. T. R. Clark's German-American Vaudevilles and mistakenly identified as "Joe, Mira and Buster Keating." It was during their time with the Clark troupe that Buster suffered a pair of accidents that he liked to say "put me on the stage," Myra being concerned for his safety when left alone or with others. In Kinsley, Kansas, while in the care of Mrs. Altena Wolgamot (from whom the Keatons were renting a room), he poked his right index finger into the gears of a clothes wringer and ended up having the mangled tip amputated at the first joint. Later that same week, his throbbing finger duly bandaged, he pitched a brick into the air to loosen a peach he coveted and managed to open a gash in his scalp that took three stitches to close.

Buster continued to be billed alongside his parents when they joined the Oliver-Colby Company—Swiss bell ringers fresh from a world tour—and opened the summer park season in Topeka, Kansas, on May 23. (With admirable restraint, *The Topeka State Journal* praised their opening-day performance as "satisfactory.") Soon, he was dropped in favor of Joe and Myra as a duo, and apparently remained offstage when Joe took on a new partner and the billing became Keaton, Stevens & Keaton "in a new musical farce—a rollicking turn." W. O. Stevens, a pianist, quickly fell away, and the act was known as Mr. and Mrs. Joe Keaton while they played a string of theaters in Virginia.

They closed at Norfolk, Virginia, in late September and took off again for New York City—God's country to actors and entertainers. They had no bookings but quickly landed a week's work at Huber's Palace Museum, a towering edifice on Fourteenth Street that covered five city lots. The curio hall featured Enoch, a self-styled "man fish," an immersive exhibit known as Ah Sing's opium joint, an aerial rifle team called the D'Acos, and a fellow known as Captain Crittenden, who related his adventures in the Klondike to knots of wandering patrons. At street level, the star attractions in the museum's 850-seat theater were a family act known as the Five Olivers, comedians Coogan and Bacon, and the singing Allen Sisters. It was at Huber's that Joe returned to the development of a specialty based on Frank McNish's "Silence and Fun," in particular McNish's interactions with a sturdy table. In the finale of his act, McNish stood his two barrels on the table and steadied the chair on top of them. He then leaped from the stage into the seat of the chair, descended in two steps, did a rollover and a nip-up, and landed squarely in front of the footlights.

Myra, near the end of her life, recalled Joe attempting a similar feat, sans barrels, at the dime museum. "It ain't easy to jump over four feet straight up in the air," she said. "When he got tired he missed and his shins scraped on the chair rungs and the table edge." For the rest of Joe's life, she remembered, his legs were discolored from the knees down. "Six shows a day were almost more than he could stand. Our hours were from three p.m. to three a.m. But the crowd hollered for that jump, hoping he'd miss." The act still wasn't where it needed to be, but their week at Huber's paid big dividends. When the Keatons traveled to Massachusetts to appear with a comedy stock company at Fall River's Casto Theatre, an item in the *Clipper* announced that they had booked time at Tony Pastor's 14th Street playhouse as well as F. F. Proctor's three New York theaters.

The Keatons came to regard the Pastor engagement as a turning point, and Joe would credit Pastor's kindness with his and Myra's formal entry into vaudeville. This wasn't just an arbitrary declaration, for Tony Pastor was widely regarded as the Dean of Vaudeville, the man who stripped variety of its saloon-bred vulgarities and made it palatable for double audiences—meaning men and women.* In over thirty years of management, Pastor was responsible for introducing countless names to the New York stage, includ-

---

* An outgrowth of the British music hall tradition, variety performances were initially used to draw customers into American beer halls in the years immediately following the Civil War.

Tony Pastor.

ing Lillian Russell, comedienne May Irwin, actor Nat Goodwin, the comedy team of Weber and Fields, and George M. Cohan in the days when he was still one of the Four Cohans.

As the story goes, Joe had a chance encounter with Pastor on the sidewalk in front of the impresario's Tammany Hall showplace. It was a bitterly cold day, and it was Pastor's apparent concern for the well-being of four-year-old Buster that prompted him to invite them inside. Solo, Joe gave Pastor a sharp idea of what he and Myra could do as a team, and on the spot Pastor awarded him an engagement. Tony Pastor was a genial man, charitable and beloved by all, but there was also a brutal financial calculation at work: Pastor's theater east of Union Square was small for a vaudeville house—just 948 seats versus hundreds more at most competing venues. It was also in an area that had seen the residential mansions of the 1880s give way to small shops and boardinghouses. Where others could charge fifty cents for good seats and pay competitive rates, Pastor had fallen to charging twenty and thirty cents and paying considerably less than star salaries. By 1899, the biggest draw on a typically overstuffed bill at Pastor's was the proprietor himself—a former minstrel and circus ringmaster who graduated to singing comic songs and parodies in a husky voice.

Having essentially cracked the big time in just two weeks, Joe obsessively began fretting over the quality of the act. Other than their trip to Fall River, the Keatons remained at liberty, counting their pennies. They were back in New York in November, having landed a booking at the Bowery's Atlantic Garden, a colorful German taproom and concert hall that boasted the city's first ladies' orchestra. The act was bad, Joe conceded, and it didn't go over at all. ("The gong just saved it," Gus Elliott, of the Elliott Troupe of acrobatic jugglers, testified.) In Joe's words they "vamped out"—improvised and tinkered—over the next several weeks, playing the Bon Ton again, the Trilby Music Hall in Newark, New Jersey, and the 9th and Arch Dime Museum in Philadelphia. It was evidently at the Trilby and the 9th and Arch, both deliberately out of town so they could play "a joint on the quiet," that the act began to gel. The Keatons secured a return week at the Atlantic Garden to confirm it was working and were set to open the following Monday at Tony Pastor's.

Exactly what the Keatons did at Pastor's is lost to memory, other than it was described in the advance press as a "knockabout dancing and kicking act." It may also have had a courtship angle, for when it debuted on the afternoon of December 18, 1899, it had acquired a title: "The Eccentric Tad and Chic Soubrette." Billed ninth on a roster of fourteen acts, the Keatons opened the show and, by Joe's account, "broke seventeen chairs." Its earliest printed description, in the form of a display ad commissioned by Joe for *The New York Dramatic Mirror,* shows him and Myra taking turns with a chair that has been placed atop a table. In one vignette, Myra is standing on the chair, looming, for once, far above her husband and holding out a silk opera hat that Joe is expected to kick. In another, Joe is in midair, leaping onto the chair from the stage floor, intent upon landing on his knees. According to Joe, they were moved down on the bill at Pastor's while repairs were made, and it was a quarter to nine that first day before they could go on again. The house was jammed and they obviously got over, for Pastor assured them they had "nothing to fear."

Heralding their initial success, Joe took out a two-column ad in the December 23 issue of the *Clipper:*

Mr. and Mrs. JOE KEATON	Mgr's invited to look us over
The Eccentric Tad and	at Tony Pastor's this week and
Chic Soubrette.	the Proctor Circuit following.
	226 E. 21st St., N.Y. City.

Christmas Day was a particularly memorable one for the Keatons. Buster received a basketball as a gift, his father thinking, perhaps, that it might be of some use in the act. And Joe and Myra opened at Proctor's 1,550-seat theater on Twenty-Third Street, where they found themselves billed dead last on a program headlined by dwarf monologist Marshall P. Wilder. Closing night coincided with New Year's Eve, and from the wings Buster observed the celebratory commotion onstage.

"They were all talking about something," he said. "I didn't know what it was, but I knew it was good and thought it was mine—something to go

Joseph Frank Keaton, circa 1900.

with the basketball. They were calling it the twentieth century."

Nineteen hundred was the year Buster officially joined the act, although the actual event happened in fits and starts. The Keatons played out their time for F. F. Proctor, and worked Wilmington, Boston, and Providence, as well. Then Joe took an ad in the *Clipper* listing the dates they had open and offering "grotesque comedy, eccentric dancing, acrobatic jumping, high kicking, etc. Also the funniest routine of table comedy ever attempted." Working the mails, he secured return dates from Pastor and the Proctor circuit, but failed to attract any fresh offers. Consequently, he and Myra spent the entire month of March at liberty, and when they returned to Pastor's on April 2, they were no further up the bill than they had been the first time they were there.

Yet it was at Tony Pastor's that the act drew its first real press coverage apart from the trades. The occasion was a visit by the merciless Epes Sargent, veteran vaudeville critic for the New York *Morning Telegraph,* who wrote under the familiar byline CHICOT. "The Keatons do little that is funny," Sargent critiqued, "till at the close of the turn when Keaton does really good work on a table. For a finish they throw an orange and a stick of candy at the audience, following this up with a rag doll and the offer of a brickbat. The last half of the act is not bad. The opening is."

It wasn't a clothes wringer, a peach tree, or even a cyclone—as the story usually went—that put Buster Keaton back onstage but rather an ugly sprain that sidelined his father while working the 9th and Arch Dime Museum in Philadelphia. It was the week of April 9, 1900, and the Keatons were typically hugging the bottom of the bill. When Joe couldn't continue, Buster went on in his place and finished the week, presumably parroting a lot of the old man's patter, managing a few dance steps, and adding some wiseass embellishments of his own. Since manager C. A. Bradenburgh ran a relatively loose ship, devoted as he was to "the instruction of young minds," a four-year-old subbing for his ailing dad would not have been as incongruous as it might have appeared at a first-rank vaudeville theater like Keith's or the Grand Opera House. Buster showed he could hold an audience on his own that week, and his success in keeping the Keatons onstage may well have convinced his father it was time to bring him into the act. But it would take another six months for that to actually happen.

After appealing to Tony Pastor for yet another booking, their second in a month, Joe and Myra endured a long stretch of open time. Joe hustled work wherever he could find it—Ithaca, Boston, Patterson, Coney Island. "When we went into this business," he recounted in a 1903 interview, "we were what is called 'supper' actors. That is, we played three times a day—opened the show in the afternoon, closed it about supper time, and opened it again for the evening performance."

The summer season was looming when the Keatons again found themselves facing the judgment of Epes Sargent. As was his habit, Sargent took in the entire opening day's bill at Pastor's and had withering comments for the performers he found wanting. ("No woman over 140 pounds in weight should endeavor to appear kittenish," he said of Pastor's top draw of the week, comedienne Essie Clinton.) Eleven grafs in, Sargent revisited "The Eccentric Tad and Chic Soubrette."

"Mr. and Mrs. Joe Keaton talk less than they did and make more of a hit in proportion," he wrote approvingly. "The less they say the more effective they are, and some happy day when they do not talk at all, but work out the table part of the act, they will get much higher on the bill." A week later, when he similarly audited the bill at Keith's Union Square, Sargent once more found himself watching the Tad and Soubrette: "The Keatons did too much talking and singing to please, and should cut down to the acrobatic and table work again."

Over the next few months, the fifteen-minute act evolved a new identity. For a while, "The Eccentric Tad and Chic Soubrette" co-existed with another title that seemed to tacitly acknowledge Sargent's criticisms: "The Man with the Table."

"All sorts of original step-dancing and brisk knockabout work are introduced," said the *Dramatic Mirror* in September, "and the act winds up with an extraordinarily amusing series of tricks with a chair and a table, which serve as props for Mr. Keaton's agile antics." By mid-October, the Tad and the Soubrette had vanished entirely, and the table was now the focal point of both the title and the act itself. Buster turned five on October 4, 1900, and the Keatons took the stage as a threesome at Dockstader's Theatre, an old carriage works in Wilmington, Delaware, on October 15. The boy was made up as a miniature version of his father's character, complete with skull cap, red Galway whiskers, cutaway coat, and slapshoes, and told to simply lean back against the scenery and watch. His presence wasn't explained to the audience, and he was given no lines or business. The proprietor, William L. "Bill" Dockstader, who had presented Joe and Myra once before, took it all in but couldn't see the child as anything other than excess baggage.

"Dockstader booked the act supposing Buster was a performer," Joe said, "but when he found he was a mere babe, and that that was to be his first appearance, he said, 'All right, go ahead.' After the first appearance he said, 'Take him off, Joe. He's a handicap.' So Buster was closed without the regular two weeks' notice. Things ran along until Wednesday of that week, when Dockstader came back on the stage and said, 'Keaton, put Buster in the act for the matinee today, as there will be a lot of children present and he might make good with them.' So the kid again donned the eccentric makeup and took his position against a wing with his legs crossed and a wise look. He proved the laughing hit of the whole bill, and nothing I could do would amuse or entertain anybody. The audience couldn't see me at all, and Buster was one scream from start to finish. Dockstader came running back and said, 'Say, Keaton, you let that kid stay in the act. He's all right. I guess I must have overlooked something the first show.'"

Buster's take for the week was ten dollars—the equivalent to what his parents had been paid at Huber's museum just a year earlier. Eager to line up engagements for the 1901 season, Joe placed an ad in the *Dramatic Mirror* touting a successful week with J. K. Burke's traveling road company (again with Buster) and introducing "a genuine Comedy Act that we guarantee. Something doing for 18 minutes. A continuous revolution of one funny move to another. Eccentric acrobatic dancing, grotesque leg work and the funniest routine of table and chair in Vaudeville, or money refunded." The added inducement made it one of Joe's more effective ads, and when it brought the family a quick booking in Steubenville, Ohio, ahead of a standing date in Cincinnati, the formal billing was "Mr. and Mrs. Joe Keaton and Little Buster." A month later, Buster was being featured in his father's ads as "The Smallest Comedian."

Joe, Myra, and Buster spent the Christmas season with Joe's parents in Perry, where the elder Keatons had settled in 1894. It was from Perry that Joe tried drumming up business, inviting inquiries to 624 G Street via ads in the *Dramatic Mirror*. ("Talk about getting comedy out of a table! Why, we are simply full of splinters all the time.") With all time open after April 15, he offered to sign with "any reliable show for season 1901," but could put nothing together before hitting the Proctor circuit again in February.

Buster Keaton had been working consistently since October and had made a genuine hit with audiences in the Midwest. But now Joe was proposing to bring him into Manhattan, and in doing so there would be no getting around the fact that the Man with the Table would be breaking the law.

2

Keep Your Eye on the Kid

A T FIRST, ELBRIDGE T. GERRY would seem an unlikely adversary for Joe Keaton. The grandson of a vice president and one of the signers of the Declaration of Independence, Gerry was an esteemed member of the New York State Bar, a former commodore of the New York Yacht Club, and a prominent figure in civic and social circles. Famously brusque and more than a little self-righteous, Gerry was counsel for Henry Bergh, the founder of the American Society for the Prevention of Cruelty to Animals when, in 1874, he learned from Bergh of the plight of a child known as Mary Ellen McCormack, who was imprisoned by her stepmother, beaten regularly, and forced to live in rags in a cold-water flat. Police considered such complaints trivial and troublesome and refused to intervene. "No time is to be lost," Bergh wrote Gerry. "Instruct me how to proceed."

Within forty-eight hours, Gerry was able to establish legal standing, file a petition, and initiate a protective removal. In the aftermath of a successful criminal prosecution, he became convinced that an organization modeled on the SPCA was needed for the protection of children. There were, he reasoned, a number of charitable corporations, such as the Children's Aid Society and the Society for the Protection of Destitute Children, dedicated to the care of abused and abandoned kids, as well as religious and state-run institutions, but none, as far as he could tell, that assumed the task of seeking out such children or enforcing the protective laws already on the books.

At Gerry's instigation, the New York Society for the Prevention of Cruelty to Children was established in December 1874. Although he was joined by Bergh as a vice president in the new nonsectarian organization, and Quaker philanthropist John D. Wright became its first president, Gerry's not-so-subtle hand in the guidance of the NYSPCC prompted attorney Joseph Hodges Choate to dub it the "Gerry Society," a name that stuck with both the press and the public. Early on, Gerry turned his attentions to the state capitol in Albany, where laws advocated by the NYSPCC prohibiting child endangerment, and regulating certain kinds of child employment were enacted in 1876.

An ardent Anglo-Catholic, Gerry was obsessed with children who were employed

Elbridge T. Gerry.

on the stage and an absolutist in opposing the exhibition of "any child actually or apparently under the age of sixteen years." A particular target were so-called miniature opera and Pinafore troupes of fifteen or more children.

"One or two corrupt children will contaminate the entire troupe," he warned. "The result is as might be expected. Many of the girls become prostitutes at an early age, and finally end in low dance houses and concert saloons. . . . The boys usually become idlers, performers in the song-and-dance variety business, and ultimately end by being thieves or tramps."

Over time, Section 292 of the penal code evolved to where it explicitly forbade the employment of children as rope or wire walkers, gymnasts, wrestlers, contortionists, riders, acrobats, cyclists, singers, dancers, or in any "illegal, indecent, or immoral exhibition or practice." In 1879, Gerry, by then president of the NYSPCC, made headlines when society officers prevented a contortionist called Little Robert from appearing on the stage of Niblo's Garden and attempted unsuccessfully to take temporary custody of the boy.*

Throughout the 1880s, similar stories appeared in the press, characterized by jeering audiences, angry managers, and crying children forcibly

* Far less time and energy were expended on the exploitation of children in factories and sweatshops, Commodore Gerry apparently seeing less moral risk in compelling kids as young as four to work long hours, getting whatever schooling they could at night. In 1870, one of every eight children in the state held a full-time job. By 1900, the number had grown to one in six.

removed from the stage by agents of the Gerry Society, sometimes in mid-performance. The backlash against such tactics was so vociferous that in 1892 the state legislature passed the Stein Act to curb the NYSPCC's arbitrary use of the police power granted it under the penal code. It repealed the law prohibiting the employment of children under sixteen, and instead empowered the mayors of cities and the presidents of villages to license young performers upon payment of a nominal fee.

"The average child of the stage is better treated and more tenderly cared for, physically and morally, than the shop boy or girl, or the child who is obliged to work for a living in almost any branch of service," *The New York Times* editorialized. "No harm need come to a boy or girl from association with the members of such organizations as those of Mr. Daly, Mr. Palmer, the Messrs. Frohman, or any other reputable New York manager."

Elbridge Gerry, who naturally opposed any tinkering with Section 292, seized upon a technical error in the wording of the act to maintain that the amendment did not weaken the prohibition against underage singing, dancing, acrobatics, and the like. With his political muscle, Gerry got the mayor's office to effectively cede the granting of licenses to the NYSPCC, to where applicants were compelled to go to procure official blanks. The commodore's agents were still empowered to make trouble, and they still spent an inordinate amount of time haunting the wings of vaudeville houses and legitimate theaters.

Joe Keaton was used to tangling with characters like Terre Haute's "Nigger" Bob, a singing bootblack he brained with his box in a dispute over territory when he was fourteen. "I had fought every kid that ever looked like a fight," Joe said proudly, "and had carried more black eyes than all of them put together, which gave me the nickname of 'Dick Dead Eye.'" Gerry and his eponymous society weren't so easily dismissed, and Joe, strategizing from his holiday retreat in Perry, attempted a charm offensive abetted by some practical lies about his son and the act of which he was now a part.

Dec 27 [1900]
The Gerry Society

Dear Sir
    I have a Son age 7 years. That possesses great theatrical talent.
And in as much as he neither Sings nor performs any acrobatic feats.

Would like to arrange to introduce him on the Proctor circuit in Feb. I am contracted to open Feb. 1st. The boy is a <u>comedian</u>. And if you can encourage me in any way would call us soon as we get into New York. And complete the arrangements. Am willing to aid the Society in any way.

Resp Jos Keaton
624 G. St Perry Oklahoma

Gerry was in his final days as president of the NYSPCC, soon to take on the role of general counsel, when he dictated a curt response: "In reply to your letter of December 27th, 1900, application for permit to exhibit children in any theatrical performance in this city should be made at this office at least forty-eight hours before the date of the engagement. The proper blanks will be furnished thereat."

Gerry didn't seem to be catching Joe's drift. Buster wasn't one of those musical tots the commodore was known to lose sleep over. "I wish to state <u>again</u> that our little Son Does not in any way indulge in any dancing Singing nor any acrobatic feats whatever," Joe emphasized in a stringent response. "And that we have never exhibited him in N. York. But we have the opportunity now and should <u>he</u> be successful Am perfectly willing to aid your Society <u>in</u> <u>any</u> [way]. I received a letter from J. Austin Fynes [the Proctor circuit's general manager and former *Clipper* editor] Stating to communicate with you concerning our plans. So kindly send me proper blanks and will fill them out as you request." Aware that Section 292 made no mention of comedy, he added: "Our son's particular line of work is Comedy or talking or <u>Comedian</u>. On Mr. Duffy Sawtell[e] + Duffy <u>order</u>."*

A second reply from the NYSPCC was dated January 8: "In reply to yours of the 5th, referring to the employment of your son in theatrical exhibition, it will be necessary for you to sign the application blanks referred to at this office. They cannot be sent to you."

The Keatons were set to open at Proctor's Albany on February 25, but there would be no real scrutiny from the Gerry Society until they invaded New York City in March. Joe used their remaining time in Perry to shape

---

* James F. Duffy and Margaret Sawtelle were an Irish comedy team when they immigrated to the United States in 1891. In 1895, they added their three-year-old son Jimmy to the act, which became Duffy, Sawtelle & Duffy.

and rehearse the act, making five-year-old Buster an integral part of the action. He also attended to the sundry details of playing a string of seven theaters in as many weeks. Scene plots had to be sent to each location, the exact time of the act needed to be confirmed, as did billing for newspapers and programs, and clean lobby photos were required at least two weeks in advance. A plus was that the act could close "in one," meaning the final minutes could take place in front of the first drop—the one closest to the footlights—enabling the scenery for the next act to be set behind it. Joe also began taking two-column ads in the *Dramatic Mirror*, giving his son equal billing in "The Man with the Table" and heralding the busiest act in vaudeville. "Keep your eye on the cat," he urged in boldface type, "and Buster, the smallest comedian." The following week, just ahead of opening, the sign-off was simply: "Keep your eye on the KID."

The first performance in Albany clocked in at nineteen minutes, giving it weight on a bill awash with musical acts. That evening, the *Times-Union* reported the Keatons "convulsed the house" as the only comic relief in the entire show. Some of the performers on the bill in Albany were also with Joe, Myra, and Buster the following week in Montreal: the Willis Family of sibling instrumentalists and singer Zelma Rawlston, who worked exclusively in male drag and whose gimmick was a series of quick onstage costume changes, each more elaborate than the last. On March 7, while the Keatons were still in Canada, A. O. Butler, the resident manager of Proctor's 125th Street Theatre, appeared at NYSPCC headquarters on Fourth Avenue to sign an application for consent for Joseph F. Keaton, age seven, to appear in "speaking parts only" in a sketch at the management's Harlem location during the week of March 11, 1901—a total of six matinees and six evening performances.

Buster Keaton once told his elder son that Joe first rolled him across a floor at the age of three, teaching him how to curl up so that he wouldn't be injured when thrown the length of a stage like an outsize bowling ball. Although this would have been around the time the Keatons were appearing as a threesome with J. T. R. Clark's German-American Vaudevilles, and later with the Oliver-Colby Company, there are no contemporary accounts of the act that describe Buster as being part of any comedic violence. It appears likely that Joe began tossing him around only when the Keatons opened in Albany and were on what amounted to a make-or-break tour of the Proctor circuit.

"My father used to carry me on stage and drop me," Buster recalled.

"After explaining to the audience that I liked it, he would pick me up and throw me at a piece of scenery. Sometimes knocking the scenery down with me and sometimes not. He would often throw me as far as thirty feet."

Rehearsals for all Proctor houses took place on Mondays at 9:00 a.m. sharp, and having just made the four-hundred-mile jump from Montreal to New York City, Joe was ready with a version of "The Man with the Table" that had been picked clean of boyhood acrobatics. "The Keatons proved, as always, in high favor with their unique table act," the *Dramatic Mirror* reported, "in which they are now assisted by their promising little son, Buster." The act was in solid shape when a Gerry officer audited it that evening, putting down on paper the first detailed description of the act that would become known as The Three Keatons.

"The curtain rose on a country scene with a table in the center of stage. The Keatons, man and wife, appeared: the latter sang + danced and while so engaged, the man did acrobatic tricks on the table + while sitting on a chair on the table, the boy Joseph Keaton appears on the stage in the make up of an old man + with a broom pushed the chair from under his father, causing him to fall + then running off the stage. The boy came on stage numerous times + made funny commentaries on things his father was saying and doing."

Ever concerned with the word-of-mouth the act generated, Joe made a brief curtain speech explaining that the Gerry Society did not permit children like Buster to do acrobatic stunts, and that all interested parties should catch the unexpurgated version in another city. The next morning, he dutifully appeared at the NYSPCC offices to sign the application for Buster's appearance at Proctor's Fifth Avenue, their next stop on the circuit, and continued to do so every week thereafter. By the time they reached Proctor's Palace on Fifty-Eighth Street, the act had caught on and the *Dramatic Mirror* was calling it the laughing hit of the bill. "Buster is a diminutive five-year-old comedian who is unusually funny. He impresses one as a healthy, roguish child with a lively dash in him that is irresistible. Without appearing unnaturally precocious or impertinent, he manages to keep the audiences in roars from the time he is dragged on the stage by his father, sitting on a broom, until his exit, which he makes hanging on to his father's leg. The father does some remarkably clever acrobatic work in a loose-jointed lazy fashion, sorrowfully reprimanding his son for his pranks the while." The notice was accompanied by a group portrait of the Keatons—Buster, in full makeup, gamely aping his father's pose from the lower corner of the shot, his mother proudly resplendent in a dark floor-length dress and matching bonnet.

In April, Joe penned a jubilant letter to his friend Harry Houdini, who was in Germany as part of a European tour. "I am introducing my new (3) act at present," he wrote on fresh letterhead that illustrated Buster's role, "and I can truthfully say I <u>never</u> had an act before. This one is the <u>real thing</u>. I played Pastor's last week. And was reengaged for two shows per day. And I don't intend to play another (3) a day <u>engagement</u>. . . . You can't talk too much on the ability of my little comedian Buster and our Comedy Table work. There ain't another act like it. . . . The kid is 11 years old [*sic*]. And he hasn't growed hardly any since you saw him. He weighs 40 lbs. And he's a <u>corker</u>. The ushers quit work when he troupes. If possible get The <u>Mirror</u> of wk of March 25 and read the Pleasure Palace notes which gives an accurate description of the act. Also a two column photo."

While at Tony Pastor's, the Keatons once again came under the scrutiny of the *Morning Telegraph*'s Epes Sargent, who hadn't sampled the act in nine months. "The Keatons now number three persons," he reported, "the trio being completed by Master 'Buster' Keaton, a small boy with some infantile sense of humor. He is gotten up with a bald wig and Irish chin whiskers, and were his business on the stage cut in two it would be quite an addition to the act. As it is, with the evident purpose of pushing him rapidly to the front, he is permitted to interfere at times when the elder Keaton could more satisfactorily look after the comedy work. He is rather more clever than the average youngster and should not be encouraged to make a nuisance of himself at the outset. Aside from the too frequent appearances of the little chap, the act shows an improvement over its last appearance here. Keaton is working out his table specialty more intelligently and is bringing the turn to the front. Now that he has started in to work up the act he should not rest content until he has gotten it up as far as it will go."

If Joe Keaton took Sargent's critique to heart and made an effort to limit his son's time onstage, it isn't evident in subsequent reviews. Having inherited his father's rough-hewn gift for personal mayhem, the boy typically commanded more ink than both parents combined—which was seemingly fine with Joe, who knew a genuine meal ticket when he had one. In May, Buster briefly made news when the Keatons were set to play Coney Island's Steeplechase Park, and Superintendent R. J. Wilkins of the Brooklyn Society for the Prevention of Cruelty to Children—not Elbridge Gerry's New York Society, whose authority existed only within the borough of Manhattan—

objected to the engagement. In a hearing before New York mayor Robert Van Wyck, Wilkins maintained that Buster participated in acrobatic stunts and that in any event it would be a shame to exhibit him before "the low crowds frequenting the island." This set off the mayor, a scandal-plagued Tammany man, who informed Wilkins that he had been to Coney Island frequently and the crowds had always been orderly in his experience.

"I think that the people are entitled to their enjoyment as much as any other," he said in approving the application.

Myra attempted to weigh in, vowing that Buster would never be exposed to evil influences, but Van Wyck cut her off.

"When you have won a case," the mayor advised her, "never say a word."

The following day, Joe, in high spirits, dispatched another long, effusive letter to Houdini: "Tell little Bessie that Buster when grown won't be much larger than she is. He has developed into a real comedian and is only about a foot high. Very small for his age. But excruciatingly funny in his line. He would make a hit with you to see him work which consists of funny imitations. And [he] burlesques all my work. He has easily been the laughing hit in every bill we have played. And I can make good if no one is in but the ushers. . . . We have just finished Proctor's 6 houses and closed the show at four of them."

Booked into October, the Keatons were playing the summer parks when they were offered time on impresario Martin Beck's coveted Orpheum circuit, a trail that stretched from Chicago to San Francisco and down the coast to Los Angeles. Eager to get out of New York and beyond the reach of the Gerries, Joe leaped at the chance even though his relationship with Beck, a hard-nosed German, was strained from the outset. It was Beck who helped organize the theaters between California and Chicago under the Orpheum banner and made it economically feasible for the best acts in vaudeville to travel west.

"It was the non plus ultra of vaudeville booking," said Epes Sargent, "and it fell only to the better class of acts."

Following a week in Kansas City, the Keatons advanced to Omaha, where Beck and his management had renovated the 2,200-seat Orpheum (formerly the Creighton) in shades of white and gold, hoping to cater, in the words of the new resident manager, to "the better class of theatergoers at all times." The circuit had more than doubled in size in the previous year, enabling it to offer up to twenty weeks of employment to New York–based acts willing to play the West Coast (although Joe, owing to solid bookings into February

1902, could clear only enough time for six). The Three Keatons were billed dead last for the season opener in Omaha, but proved so popular they were bumped up to third on the bill when they opened in San Francisco on October 6. Traveling with them to the coast were Laura and Johanna O'Meers, sibling tightwire walkers who were touring the country after making a hit at the London Hippodrome. What they found at the end of the Orpheum trail was a rattletrap barn of a theater, an old beer hall sadly in need of repair but too popular to be closed for even a brief period of time. (Many of the better seats, at a top price of fifty cents, were held on a subscription basis.) San Francisco was full of attractions for visiting easterners—the famous Cliff House, the adjacent Sutro Baths (the largest natatorium in the country), the city's legendary Chinatown—and there was an inexhaustible supply of good restaurants.

The first matinee performance filled every seat, and according to the *San Francisco Chronicle,* Joe, Myra, and Buster made a solid hit with an evening crowd that was packed to the doors—even standing room was sold out.

"Buster is full of sarcastic sayings," wrote the man from the *Examiner,* "and the way he 'joshes' Keaton would make people feel like spanking him if his remarks were not so funny."

Declared *The San Francisco Call,* in what was to become a familiar refrain, "Buster is easily the star of the Keaton family, and he succeeds in keeping the house in roars of laughter while he is on the stage."

The act was extended a third week, cutting into time originally allotted to Los Angeles. When they finally reached L.A. (where the Sisters O'Meers preceded them), the climate was arid but the reception chilly.

The eight acts on the bill at the 1,500-seat Orpheum included farceurs Monroe, Mack, and Lawrence (performing their famous sketch "How to Get Rid of Your Mother-in-Law"), a trio of acrobats known as the De Courcy Brothers, and a singing comedian named Tommy Baker. The Keatons opened the show while many patrons were still taking their seats, leaving better spots on the bill to the O'Meers and the De Courcys.

"They say, 'Open the show,' we open it," Buster said. "It's going to hurt the other acts a lot more than us. A wild laughing act, and the next four turns look lousy. The big boys didn't give a damn—let 'em look lousy, let 'em quit. The word went down the line: 'Make it tough on all those babies.'"

In Los Angeles, the *Times* lumped the O'Meers, the De Courcys, and the Keatons together in its notice, approving of the former two while dismissing the latter—who were advertised as "grotesque comedy acrobats-dancers"—as merely living up to their billing. The reviewer for the rival *Los Angeles Herald* thought the entire program, with the exception of the O'Meers and the De Courcys, "barely up to the standard." Monroe, Mack, and Lawrence, he judged, overworked the mother-in-law "monstrosity" terribly. "Tommy Baker, billed as an original monologist and parody singer, forgot to unpack his originality last night and his voice takes a circuitous route via his nose." Even Buster, who had truly come into his own on the Orpheum tour, failed to impress. "The smallest Keaton's precocity would be interesting if it were not so iterative," the man sniffed, echoing Epes Sargent's judgment of six months earlier. But if anything, Buster's place in the act had actually grown in the interim.

Beginning in Omaha and continuing down through California, the Keatons were paid weekly in gold, which, after expenses, went into the family grouch bag, a purse made of chamois that Myra dangled from a string around her neck and kept hidden under her dress. As it filled with ten- and twenty-dollar gold pieces—the Keatons were getting $225 a week—the bag grew so heavy she was forced to buy a money belt.*

"The best American plan hotels, where we stopped, charged only $1.25 per day per person for room and board," Buster detailed, "which came to $26.25 a week for all three of us. All of our other living expenses, including tips, Pop's beer, and other modest luxuries ran no more than fifty dollars a week, and traveling expenses averaged thirty dollars a week. So Mom was stashing away almost $120 a week." By the end of the Keatons' abbreviated Orpheum tour, he estimated she was carrying about $1,600 in gold on her ninety-pound frame.

In its earliest days, the act known as The Three Keatons was broadly acrobatic, "eccentric" in the sense that Joe Keaton lacked formal training and formulated the bizarre things he did onstage through trial and error. Buster's role was to ape the old man's actions, a pint-size doppelgänger bent on heckling and bedeviling him.

"I just watched what he did," Buster once said, "and then did the same thing."

---

* Acts working west of Chicago were typically paid a 25 percent premium over and above their weekly salaries. Closer to home, the Keatons were in the $150 to $175 range.

This early photo expertly encapsulates what audiences could expect from "The Man with the Table," Buster gleefully laying waste to his father's acrobatic turn while Myra looks on in horror. "What makes you so small?" Joe demanded. "I was raised on condensed milk," came the boy's reply.

In May 1901, when he had been with the act eight months, the youngest Keaton was described in one of Joe's trade ads as "absolutely the funniest imitating and talking comedian of modern times," suggesting the acrobatics the boy engaged in were a small part of the total package.

"You'd call it pantomime," Buster acknowledged, "although my father kept talkin' all the time. He never said the same thing twice. He just tried to convince the audience that there was only one way to bring up children and that was to make 'em mind. Be gentle and kind to them, but make them mind. By that time I'd knocked both of his feet out from under him with a broom or something—the chase was on again."

Myra would sing "Tobie, I Kind o' Likes You" and Joe would verbally admonish the boy, but physical action between the two was likely limited to a roll across the stage as a climactic stunt, the boy obviously skilled and unhurt as he made his exit.

"All little boys like to be rough-housed by their fathers," Buster said in his autobiography. "They are also natural tumblers and acrobats. Because I was also a born hambone, I ignored any bumps or bruises I may have got at first on hearing audiences gasp, laugh, and applaud."

Over the fall of 1901, as the mocks and insults grew more pointed, the comic violence, particularly along the Orpheum trail, appears to have become more pronounced. "On the stage during his father's vaudeville turn, Buster struts around, cutting up all sorts of fascinating pranks and keeping the house in roars of laughter." In November, Joe described the act as "all action and laughs" and the press began to take notice. At first came the observations that were Buster's lines not so good he'd be in for a spanking. Then at the end of the year at the Hopkins Theatre in Chicago: "Of the children in this week's bill, 'Buster' Keaton is the cleverest. He wears exaggerated shoes, red whiskers and other 'accessories' in the makeup that the Ancient Order of Hibernians egged in New York, but this boy is a born comedian, and if his father does not kill him some day while tossing him about the stage he will be another Jeff De Angelis.* 'You are very short,' his father says to him. 'Yes, and if I were not, *you* would be when payday comes,' he answers, which is doubtless true."

To facilitate the grace with which Joe threw Buster around, he had a suitcase handle sewn into the back of the boy's costume, an innovation he once said came from the act's first appearance as a threesome at Tony Pastor's.

"I could take crazy falls without hurting myself," Buster said, "simply because I had learned the trick so early in life that body control became pure instinct with me. If I never broke a bone on the stage, it is because I always avoided taking the impact of a fall on the back of my head, the base of my spine, on my elbows or my knees. That's how bones are broken. You also bruise only if you do not know as I do which muscles to tighten, which ones to relax."

He had the added advantage of a costume shrewdly designed to absorb the shock of a hard landing. "You see this pad in my trousers?" he asked a skeptical reporter from the *Cleveland Plain Dealer*. "Well, that's usually where I land. Now lift that coat. Pretty hard to get a bruise through that, don't you think?"

Although Buster enjoyed mixing it up with his father, he soon noticed that when he flashed a big smile the audience didn't laugh as much. "Some other comedians can get away with laughing at their own gags," he said. "Not me."

He adopted expressions of sadness and bewilderment, even deadpan, but tried never to let on that his twice-daily forays onstage were actually a form

* Jefferson De Angelis (1859–1933) was an acrobatic comedian who achieved fame in vaudeville and advanced to Broadway and occasional film work.

of play. "If something tickled me and I started to grin," he said, "the old man would hiss, 'Face! Face!' That meant freeze the puss. The longer I held it, why, if we got a laugh, the blank pan or the puzzled puss would double it." The Keatons were such a riveting act that when the old theater adjoining the Hopkins caught fire on the night of December 28, pouring smoke into the auditorium, the audience of nearly two thousand remained seated as Joe, Myra, and Buster continued onstage, filing out in an orderly manner only when prompted to do so.

The Keatons entered the year 1902 with bookings in Tennessee and Kentucky, Joe deliberately limiting their time in New York to the friendly management of Tony Pastor, whose longtime business manager, Henry Sanderson, ran interference with the Gerry Society. Joe retired "The Man with the Table" as the formal title of the act, opting instead for the more inclusive "Fun and Nonsense." The Keatons played Wilmington, New Haven, Rochester, Syracuse. They laid off the month of May in Perry, then worked the summer parks—St. Joseph, Grand Rapids, Toledo, Columbus.*

It was a year spent almost entirely out from under the authority of the Gerry Society, and when they returned to New York in September, it was again to Pastor's, and again with a wary eye cast for officers of the NYSPCC.

"Most of the Gerry Society agents were known by the theater managers, which made it fairly simple to delete my act when one of them came snooping," said actress-comedienne Elsie Janis, who, as Little Elsie, a gifted mimic, made her New York debut at the age of eight. "At the Monday matinee, they were usually in evidence. I would do the 'Gerry' version of my act [which included no singing or dancing]. They would approve and go away. Then, at every performance I would step a little further across the line of restrictions."

With his father's relentless promotion, Buster began to get a taste of what stardom was like. While the Keatons were touring with the Jessie Harcourt Comedy Company, Joe hit on the idea of hosting a matinee reception at every stop, with Buster inviting the children in the audience onstage after the performance and offering each one a handshake and a candy bar.

These were dutifully covered in the local press, and Joe sent accounts to the *Clipper* and the *Dramatic Mirror* in which Buster invariably "took the town by storm" and "carried off the honors." The result on a practical

---

* Uncooled vaudeville houses tended to close in late May for the summer, ceding audiences to parks, outdoor amphitheaters, and lakeside resorts. Acts that didn't play the parks used the free time to develop new material.

level was that the Harcourts broke three matinee house records in as many weeks.

When the Keatons finished with the Harcourt Company in December 1902, they embarked on a tour of the B. F. Keith circuit, commencing with Keith's Union Square on December 15. It was, for all practical purposes, the same act the Keatons had been playing out of town in direct defiance of the Gerry Society. "A man, a woman, and a little boy (Buster) who is pretty near the whole act, and does some very fair acrobatic comedy work," house manager E. F. Rogers wrote in his opening-day assessment, "the laughs coming almost entirely from the little fellow, who is really very clever. . . . They have eliminated much of the talking that they used to do and the act is now very good." The act, according to the *Dramatic Mirror*, "went with a rush, and the Keatons began their tour of the Keith circuit in the 'two-a-day class' with a decided boom."

To underscore Buster's place as a singular attraction—and help put him out of reach of the Gerries—Joe splurged on a quarter-page display ad in the December 20 issue of the *Clipper*, laying the words "comedy" and "comedian" on thick: "BUSTER is not a midget performer [as some managements liked to advertise him], but a revelation in eccentric juvenile talent properly directed to produce the lasting comedy effects. The most unique character in vaudeville. A miniature comedian who presents irresistible comedy, with gigantic effects, making the ladies hold their sides, and the men, too." He signed off by listing all the bookings they had through the end of April, showing March as open but soon to be filled by time on the Proctor circuit.

The Keatons eluded any enforcement action on the part of the Gerries and completed the week at Union Square, only to get caught when they slipped back into town in January for another stand at Tony Pastor's. Auditing an evening performance, a Gerry officer yanked Buster from the bill, forcing Joe and Myra to cobble something together without him.

"The Three Keatons are only two this week, for Buster is out of the turn," Epes Sargent noted in the Thursday edition of the *Telegraph*. "They do not do very well, for the youngster's absence appears to disarrange their plans and they seem to be somewhat at sea. They have done better than this in a double act, and have played with more apparent humor than they now display. An act of this sort is largely dependent upon the amount of spirit with which the work is done, and the fact that Buster is temporarily out of the turn should not be permitted to deaden the act."

"Well," said Joe, recalling the matter in a 1904 interview with the *Portland Daily Advertiser*, "Buster was sore. He wanted to be with us, and kicked like a good one because he couldn't. He came up to me and said: 'Daddy, I want to go out and sell papers, do something. Give me some old clothes and some papers and I will get out in the cold like the other newsboys. When night comes I will curl up on some doorstep and let a policeman find me. He will take me before the judge who will ask me who I am. I will tell him I am Buster Keaton and was kicked out of Pastor's because I was earning a living and helping my parents. Then they'll send me back.' I didn't let Buster do this because the weather was too cold, but if it had been warmer I would have just for the fun of it."

The Three Keatons moved on to Washington, where at Chase's (the home of "polite" vaudeville in the nation's capital) they shared the bill with family friends Jack Norworth and contralto Louise Dresser, as well as a renowned European act called Lockhart's Performing Elephants. Freed from the oversight of the Gerry Society, Buster arranged to borrow one of Sam Lockhart's animals, which, when closing in one, was positioned directly behind the first drop. As Buster announced, "My next impression, that of an elephant turning around," Lockhart would give the cue, bringing forth an earsplitting roar that had the folks in the fifty-cent seats jumping out of their skins. As they left town, Joe filed copy for a defiant ad in the January 31 issue of the *Clipper*:

> LOST—One week in three years, so let us feel gay.
> FOUND—This week at Buffalo with a man named Shea.

The charismatic Mike Shea had opened Shea's Garden Theatre, Buffalo's first vaudeville house, in 1898 and added Shea's Toronto to his holdings the following year. In September 1902, he wrote Joe Keaton offering two weeks' work at $150 per, a simple hundred-mile jump connecting the two venues. Joe was eager for earlier time and pressed for it, but Shea, one of vaudeville's most respected impresarios, coordinated and booked his showplaces well in advance and held firm to the weeks of January 26 and February 2, 1903. The footlights in Buffalo were still gas jets, Buster would remember, and the place in Toronto, formerly a dime museum, was an upstairs affair.

The Keatons arranged stops in Cleveland, Rochester, Detroit, and Pittsburgh as Joe made plans to fulfill a March booking at Proctor's 23rd Street. On March 20, he appeared at the NYSPCC offices to complete the application for consent, with Superintendent E. Charles Hoffmeister witnessing his signature after Superintendent E. Fellows Jenkins refused. Jenkins, in fact, told Joe that he would object to the child's appearance. "They filed a complaint that he was made black and blue by being thrown around," Joe said. "He was taken off. The members of the Gerry Society said if the mayor would examine him he would find the boy covered with bruises."

No application was made for the Keatons' subsequent booking at Proctor's 125th Street, where they were advertised for the week of March 30, 1903. That evening, a Gerry officer attended the performance and saw no minors at any time during the performance. "The child Joseph (Buster) Keaton, 9 yrs. of age, did not appear." The next day, March 31, Joe Keaton left notice with the NYSPCC that application would be made directly to Mayor Seth Low's office on Thursday, April 2, at noon. "Buster," said Joe, "went before the mayor and the mayor looked him over. 'Why he is just as free from hurts as one of my own boys,' was the way he put it.* 'I will have to give you a special license.'"

In the mayor's presence, Joe solemnly pledged that Buster would do only verbal comedy—no singing, dancing, or acrobatics. He was doubtless sincere when it came to the singing and dancing part, since such musical interludes could easily be cut. As for acrobatics, Joe maintained that what Buster did onstage was the work of a skilled comedian—and that comedy, of course, went entirely unmentioned in the penal code. "The law," Buster commented, "didn't say a word about taking me by the nape of the neck and throwing me through a piece of scenery."

The records of the NYSPCC show that Buster was approved for the three remaining days of the Keatons' stand at Proctor's, a total of six performances. On the last day of the engagement, Joe permitted himself a bit of gloating at the expense of the Gerries. "Have you seen Buster, the most talked of Comedian in Vaudeville, at Proctor's 125th St., NY, this week?" his ad in the *Clipper* inquired. "O, fudge, daddy fixed it with the judge." They left town immediately thereafter to rejoin the Harcourt Comedy Company, spending the month of April in places like Lewiston and Bangor. ("Buster is the kid that makes the people LAUF. Like Quaker Oats, leaves a smile that won't come off.") But ahead lay another tour of the Keith circuit that

---

* This was either an invention on Joe's part, or Mayor Low was stretching the truth for effect. Although two nieces and a nephew lived with the mayor and his wife, he had no children of his own.

would pull them back to New York City and the jurisdiction of the Gerry Society. Seeking a truce with Superintendent Jenkins, Joe uncharacteristically humbled himself.

"We wish to thank you for the kind considerations for the last two New York engagements," he wrote. "And I trust I have kept with in the boundary lines of the conditions of the permit. which was issued to us. This engagement ment a great deal to us. As the little fellow was the life and foundation of our performance. and with out him. The act was weakened materially and as the Manager of the Proctor Circuit said in a recent letter to me, I don't care to play the act, unless Buster is working in it. Again I wish to thank you for the extreme kindness on your part. We have one more New York engagement to fill at Keiths Union Sq. N.Y. Can I apply to you for application in the usual way? Or shall I proceed to the justice of the piece. I merely ask this. as we will be out of town the week previous and will haft to trust this matter entirely with the resident Manager of the Keith Theatre. Any information you can give me will be thankfully received."

Jenkins was unmoved: "In reply to yours of the 8th, it is not the duty of the Society to make out applications for persons desiring consents to perform children. It has done so as an act of favor to the theatrical proprietors and managers of performances. When this favor has been abused it withdraws this courtesy. This was your case. You deliberately violated the law as well as the Mayor's consent given you for a performance, which did not permit your child to do the acts that he did upon the stage. This Society would respectfully state to those who apply to it that it would be necessary hereafter for you to make your own applications conforming to the law, and the Society will act thereupon hereafter as it deems just and wise. It does not at the present time intend to recede from that position."

Undeterred, the Keatons, Buster included, opened at Keith's on May 18. "He is a very clever 'kid,'" the house manager wrote in a candid assessment, "and while it was necessary to modify some of the rougher parts of the act through instructions from the Gerry Society, he still made good to the fullest extent. The father and mother do not amount to very much, but still do nothing to offend." Even in its bowdlerized state, the act registered well enough for *The New York Times* to feature it in its vaudeville column of May 21, 1903, giving the act known as The Three Keatons its most detailed description yet.

"Keaton *père* comes on the stage in the full glory of red galways, a comic makeup consisting of face white-plastered to the cheek bones, where a rosy flush forms a sharp angle, coming to a point just beneath the eyes. He wears loose, baggy trousers, no coat, and white spats. Baby Buster is made up and dressed exactly like his father, but diminutive face and figure increase the ludicrous effect in his case. The elder Keaton is an acrobat of considerable ability, and he indulges in some grotesque acrobatics. The boy imitates him, but he is funniest in the occasional exchanges of conversation which punctuate the act." Buster tells the audience that on trains he is four years old, but in New York he is ten. As constant commands of silence issue forth from his father, he goes on to explain himself.

"When we travel, Daddy puts a short skirt on Mama. He buys a full-fare ticket for himself, a half-fare for Mama, and as for me—well, it's into the dog basket. While they are eating the chicken sandwiches, I get a dog biscuit. Once, the conductor asked for tickets, and I thought he was speaking to me. So I said, 'My papa has the tickets.' That time I didn't get a dog biscuit for a week. Generally, though, all I have to do is stay in the basket and growl when the conductor comes through. But if I don't growl, I don't get a biscuit."

"You're a blockhead," remarks Joe.

"Well," Buster retorts, "I'm a chip off the old block." He runs several circles around his father.

"What are you doing?" Joe demands.

"Just running 'round the block."

Buster comes down to the footlights and, after clearing his throat, announces: "Ladies and gentlemen, I will now sing that pathetic little ballad entitled, 'What Right Has a Man to Buy a Collar Button When He Has a Wart on the Back of His Neck.'"

After the song, Joe steps forward. "Can you read your A-B-Cs?"

"I have never read them," Buster admits.

"What have you read?"

"I have red hair."

The boy indulges in some winning imitations, and as the act ends, Joe kisses him "with an affection that is amusing by reason of their previous exchanges of good-natured raillery." For an encore, Joe says, "I will now give an imitation of a bad singer singing a coon song." And as he begins to sing, Buster pipes up: "That's no imitation!" It all ends with his father chasing him offstage.

Escaping to Boston, where a rougher version of the act was presumably on display, the Keatons made good in a difficult place on the bill, up next to the moving pictures known as the Vitagraph. ("Mrs. Keaton's playing of 'On a Moonlight Winter Night' was capital," noted the *Globe*.) They hit Philadelphia, then transitioned to the western parks circuit for the balance of the summer. "What do you think?" Joe wondered in a late August ad. "On our way to Oklahoma, Buster refused to ride in a dog basket and we had to pay car fare for him. Then some cuss swiped his dog biscuits and the poor little heel didn't get anything to eat all day." Laying off in Perry, Joe assembled a fall route that would keep them in the Midwest or at liberty into the new year. He would, in fact, not be in direct communication with the Gerry Society again until 1905.

3

Big Frog in a Little Puddle

T HE OLD MAN would never let us out of work," Buster Keaton once lamented. "I wanted to go to school, and he wouldn't let me." It is a fact of Keaton's early life that his exposure to other kids was limited to professional children, many of whom, like Elsie Janis, were older by several years. A 1903 account in *The Indianapolis Morning Star* has him gleefully mixing with boys his own age during a stop at that city's Imperial Hotel, turning handsprings on the statehouse lawn and racing others around the square until a collision with a large dog sends him headlong to the pavement. "In his spic-and-span clothes he impressed them when his mother allowed him to run and play in the street, but Buster soon made himself one of the boys."

Joe's decision to put Buster in a public school, according to one version of the story, was inspired by the backstage challenge of a fellow performer, almost in the form of a dare. The more likely version has Joe's mother, Lydia, raising the subject during a monthlong retreat to Perry in May 1902. Buster was six at the time, the age at which most children entered kindergarten, but Myra had to admit there were no immediate plans for the boy's education. Mortified, she bought some basic textbooks and supplies, and once they had cleared September engagements at Pastor's and Proctor's 23rd Street, the Keatons settled in for a week's stand at the Bon Ton Theatre, across the Hudson River in New Jersey. Buster had just passed his seventh birthday, and the plan was for him, armed with a letter from the New York Department of Education, to enter the first grade.

"One morning, I tried it in Jersey City. They sez I can go to school there and, every town that we played, attend school in the morning and leave around two o'clock to go to the matinee. My first morning in school, well, I played with a lot of school acts and I knew all of the comedy lines. And from the minute I recognized something that the teacher said, like, 'What's an island?' Hand up: 'It's a wart on the ocean.' And they asked for silly things like, 'Give me a sentence with the word DELIGHT.' I sez, 'The wind blew in de window and blew out de light.' So I had an answer for darn near everything she asked and the kids go into hysterics. Then I got a note: 'Don't send this boy back here again.' So I got kicked out of school the first morning." It then fell to Myra, who'd only completed the eighth grade herself, to give Buster his lessons. "Later, we hired a governess from Massachusetts, a nice old maid who wanted to travel and see the country. She saw it, all right."

Keaton was asked by a TV interviewer if he enjoyed working all through his childhood, day after day. "Oh sure," he responded. "Every show's a different show with us." Once he was fully integrated into an act that had originally been a two-hander, he developed an easy onstage rapport with his father that naturally led to improvisation and a boisterous kind of one-upmanship. "He frequently surprises his father by springing new gags and bits of business on him without previous warning or rehearsal," a cover story in the *Dramatic Mirror* revealed, "and manifests an interest in his work that is really remarkable in one so young." A review in the same publication of a January 1904 performance at Keith's Union Square judged Joe, Myra, and Buster Keaton the laughing hit of the program. "It is seldom that such hearty laughter is heard in a theater as that which greeted the efforts of Buster, who is an exceptionally clever lad. Every word and action set the house in a roar, and his imitations of [English-born actor] Dan Daly, [Irish serving girl impersonator] James Russell, and [sketch comedian] Sager Midgley brought him so much applause that it is a wonder his little head is not turned completely around."

Mayor Seth Low left office at the end of 1903, but the "special license" he gave Buster continued to provide cover well into the George McClellan administration. Joe took care not to antagonize the Gerry Society, but the act onstage at Keith's was now more or less the same as what municipalities outside of New York got to see. "After I was seven," Buster recalled in his autobiography, "Pop would punish me for misbehaving while we were working on stage. He knew I was too proud of being able to take it to yell or cry. I don't think my father had an ounce of cruelty in him. He just didn't think it was good for a boy as full of beans as I was to get away with too much."

Joe would tell the audience, "It just breaks a father's heart to be rough." Then he'd blithely send Buster sailing across the stage or through a flat in a manner that would have any ordinary kid screaming bloody murder. Once, during a matinee performance, he innocently slammed the boy into scenery that had a brick wall directly behind it. Given his druthers, Joe seemed more inclined to kick his son in the pants—"a hell of a wallop"—with a number twelve slapshoe. "[Buster] had a persistent habit of getting in his father's way," noted the reviewer of a Brooklyn performance, "and each time his irate parent would gently push him aside, sometimes pushing him the entire length of the stage. Each time the human rubber ball would arise, and approaching his athletic pater would meekly say 'I'm so sorry I fell down' in a manner that would get upon the risibilities of an incurable dyspeptic."

"I rode the punches or got hurt," Buster said. "Now a strange thing developed. If I yelled ouch—no laughs. If I deadpanned it and didn't yell—no laughs. 'What goes?' I asked. 'Isn't a kick funny?' 'Not by itself it ain't,' said Joe. So he gives me a little lesson: I wait five seconds—count up to ten slow—grab the seat of my pants, holler bloody murder, and the audience is rolling in the aisles. I don't know what the thunder they figured. Maybe that it took five seconds for a kick to travel from my fanny to my brain. Actually, I guess, it was The Slow Thinker. Audiences love The Slow Thinker."

In Portland, Maine, as Joe told a reporter for the *Daily Advertiser* the story of how Buster got into the act, the object of discussion was tumbling around the hotel room "much as all children play." At first, Joe explained, Buster didn't have much to say onstage, but his part got bigger as he grew older. "Yes, and I am still learning jokes," the boy interjected, having by then mastered impressions of the Russell Brothers, Daly, Midgley, monologist Press Eldridge, and comic Jim Morton (who did what was politely referred to at the time as a "nut" act).

"I was just a harebrained kid that was raised backstage," Buster explained in a 1958 interview. "He tries everything as he grows up. If there is a wirewalker this week, well he tries walking a wire when nobody's looking. If there's a juggler, he tries to juggle—he tries to do acrobatics—there's nothing he don't try. He tries to be a ventriloquist—he tries to be a juggling fool, a magician—Harry Houdini. I tried to get out of handcuffs and straitjackets."

For Christmas 1901, "Santa Clause" brought Buster an autograph book, and he eagerly began filling it with inscriptions from the actors and managers he encountered on the road. Of the scores of signatures he collected, which included those of Louise Dresser, monologist Fred Niblo, and Tony Pastor, he was proudest of a bit of doggerel composed by W. L. Dockstader, the first man to put him on a vaudeville stage:

> Buster, you're a dandy,
> Buster, you're a brick,
> Buster, you can make
> all juveniles look sick.
> Someday you'll be a great one,
> me captain of the crew.
> But don't forget old Wilmington
> the place of your debut.

Joe was so taken with the inscriptions, many in carefully wrought verse like Dockstader's, that he began quoting them in his ads. He proudly positioned his son as the star of the act, often having his name set in larger type. The Keatons worked the summer parks in June and July, then laid off for the balance of the summer at New York's Ehrich House, a professional boardinghouse on Thirty-Eighth Street that Joe and Myra considered their permanent address.

"The food was good," said Buster, "the atmosphere was friendly, the rooms were large and comfortable with lots of storage space in case you wanted to leave a couple of trunks behind while you went on the road." He got to know the whole neighborhood, and all the kids especially. "So I was in ball teams and everything else. And I joined the YMCA and got into basketball teams and everything else that there was."

The Three Keatons were reported to be on a "long rest" that summer, but the fact of the matter, carefully hidden from crowds in places like Lowell and Newport, was that Myra was pregnant with her second child, the first of what Buster came to refer to as the Pullman babies.

Family acts were a staple of vaudeville, and Joe had visions of expanding the original threesome to four, five, six, or more, a sort of comic version of the Cohans. "I am proud to inform you of a new arrival," he grandly announced in a letter to the *Clipper,* "born to us night of Aug. 25. Another Buster. Mother and boy doing finely." The baby, who, after Houdini, was named Harry Stanley Keaton, kept Myra out of the act when commitments to the Keith circuit came due toward the end of September. Yet she was hardly missed when Joe and his elder son opened a stripped-down version of the act in Boston on September 26. All the same, Myra was soon back onstage, costumed in a bandmaster's uniform that somehow seemed to go with the saxophone, occasionally even appearing—in quick change fashion—as a carbon copy of her husband and son. Ever an eye on the future, Joe ended the year with a new signature line for his ads: "Keep your eye on H. Stanley Keaton."

Joe, by now, was refusing to make application to the Gerry Society for any of Buster's New York appearances, leaving it to the resident managers of the individual theaters to do so if they saw fit. E. Charles Hoffmeister, the superintendent of Proctor's 23rd Street, did so for a late January engagement that came off without incident, as did manager Howard Graham, who made application to the mayor's office ahead of a booking in Albany at Proctor's Pearl Street theater. The Keatons, who hadn't played the state capital since 1901, opened to standing-room-only business on February 13, 1905. The following morning, possibly alerted by a news item that referred to Buster as "the human rubber ball," the superintendent of the Mohawk & Hudson River Humane Society, which saw after the welfare of children as well as animals, called on Graham to accuse him of violating the child labor laws by permitting Buster to perform "acrobatic stunts." Graham told the man he was doing nothing of the kind: the father playfully tossed the boy about the stage. The father also jumped over a table several times, and the child mimicked him on a chair. He did not regard these crude tricks as "acrobatic."

Three days later, Graham found himself hauled before a judge who, like the mayor, was unfamiliar with the Keaton act. Graham's counsel said it was Mr. Proctor's intention to carry the matter to the highest court so that a final decision on child performers might be secured. Still, the humane society wanted the boy produced so that the court could determine his age, and the case was sent over until Saturday morning, when both Buster and Joe could appear. The "argus-eyed" agents of the humane society, snarked a local paper, "undoubtedly thought the father and mother had so little regard for this youngster that they would kill him in their act. Of course, the boy was bound to be injured by being in company with his mother and father. He should be on the street selling papers."

The following morning, father and son were duly in court, and the alleged victim at the center of it all proved himself "a little man and a wonder." Dapper in a sack coat, vest, white shirt, and stand-up collar, Buster had topped himself off with a black derby and was sporting a gold watch chain from which hung a diamond locket. "He told the court he was eleven years old and laughed over the proceedings. When he looked at the usual crowd of

spectators in Police Court, he said, 'Gee, that crowd looks like the gallery.'"
The judge asked if the society's superintendent had actually witnessed the
act, and the man had to admit that he hadn't but "had a representative
there." Buster, the defense pointed out, worked just thirty minutes a day—
fifteen at the matinee and fifteen at the evening performance. Manager Graham effectively prevailed when the matter was adjourned until the following
Thursday, by which time the Keatons were 150 miles away in New Haven.

The experience left Joe seething, and he impulsively announced the family would leave for England as soon as he had cleared sufficient time. In
April, Buster, sans makeup, appeared on the cover of the *Clipper*, serene
and heavy-lidded, a true prince of the vaudeville stage, the accompanying
copy, in a rebuke to the Gerries, going on about how happy and healthy
he was. "He enjoys his work on the stage thoroughly, and is such an expert
little gymnast that no matter how his father throws him he lands in a safe
position." Officially, Buster was now eleven and boldly singing two popular
songs in the act, "Listen to the Big Brass Band" and "I'll Be Your Dewdrop,
Rosey." The Keatons returned to Dockstader's in May, played the summer
parks in June, then disappeared off the grid in July, not to Perry, where temperatures were pushing 100 degrees, but rather to an idyllic summer retreat
they first sampled in 1902.

At the turn of the century, Muskegon, on the eastern shore of Lake Michigan, was a city in transition. Coming off the heady days of the great timber
harvest of the 1870s and '80s, when it supplied the wood that earned Grand
Rapids, forty miles southeast, the nickname Furniture City, it was now in a
push toward industrialization that would make it the home of Continental
Motors, Shaw-Walker office filing equipment, the Amazon Knitting Company, Brunswick Bowling Products, Chase Brothers pianos, and dozens of
others. Given its location, it was also a prime distribution point for the western coast of Michigan, one of the top fruit growing regions in the nation.
It wasn't the plentiful work that attracted summer visitors from Milwaukee
and Chicago, who made their way across the Great Lake on the majestic
Goodrich ferries, but one of the country's few clearwater beaches that abut-
ted the neighborhood of Bluffton, some four miles south of downtown.
Temperatures rarely climbed into the eighties, recreation was plentiful, and
refined vaudeville could be enjoyed twice daily at the Lake Michigan Park
Theatre.

The Three Keatons had made their way to Muskegon during a tour of the
summer parks, opening at the spacious wooden pavilion on June 29, 1902.

Streetcars delivered crowds from the city center, following a route along the lakeshore and trundling through a residential area wedged between Lake Michigan and Muskegon Lake known as Pinchtown. The bill that first day consisted of five acts, the headliner comedienne Wenona Winter starring in a sketch with her father, an old-time minstrel favorite named Banks Winter. After turns by a trombone soloist named Katie Roth, a pair of talking comedians, and a "tramp equilibrist" who called himself Spaulding, the Keatons closed the show in high style, earning praise from *The Muskegon Morning News* as "one of the brightest and funniest comedy acts."

Joe loved the relaxed atmosphere of the place, a complete departure from life on the road, and regretted not having more time to enjoy it. Three years later, after carving out a break in the schedule that left the entire month of July free, he returned with the family that now numbered four, determined to take a well-earned rest. They sunned, swam, hiked, went boating, and fished, cooking up the mounds of perch they caught in an open skillet. The last week of their stay, before hitting the road for Ohio, they again played the Park Theatre, this time as the undisputed headliners. Although billed as The Three Keatons, little Harry (under the nickname "Jingles") was brought onstage in a go-cart and did a take-um of sorts, ogling the family's antics just as his older brother had when he was just starting out.* "At that time we had to have a lantern to get to the theater from Verette's Boarding House," Buster said, fondly recalling the undeveloped nature of the place, "and Frank Pascoe was called 'The Man in the Woods.' "[†]

With Jingles expected to turn the act into The Four Keatons, Joe ratcheted up his public contempt for the Gerries. "What most burned up Pop," said Buster, "was that there were thousands of homeless and hungry abandoned children of my age wandering around the streets of New York, selling newspapers, shining shoes, playing the fiddle on the Hudson River ferryboats, and thousands of other small children working with the parents in the tenement sweatshops on the Lower East Side. Pop couldn't understand why the SPCC people didn't devote all their time, energy, and money to helping them."

To Joe Keaton, the situation must have been mystifying. Why in the

---

* The origin of the name "Jingles," reflecting the child's noisy handling of his toys, was laid to Houdini, although he was likely no more responsible for it than he was for the name "Buster."

[†] Frank P. Simpson (1873–1949), the proprietor of a tavern on the main road to Lake Michigan Park, was widely known as Frank Pascoe and sometimes by the nickname "Bullhead."

world would he do anything to injure the boy? Buster was the star of the act, rightly so, and if he couldn't work, The Three Keatons couldn't work. Besides, the entire act was a travesty of modern child rearing, corporal punishment carried to a ridiculous extreme. Audiences could relate, because in the early 1900s the vast majority of parents whacked their kids when they got out of line and saw nothing wrong with it.

"Neither Mom nor Pop was demonstrative," Buster said, "but not many children expected that of their parents in those days. You were supposed to please them. When I disobeyed orders I got a good clout over the backside. Nobody expected me to like it, or cared whether I did or not. The clout told me, in the one way a normal and mischievous boy understands, to behave himself. When I failed to get the point, I got another clout."

The Keatons slipped into New York to play Proctor's 58th Street location in March 1906, and Joe once again balked at obtaining a permission slip, maintaining that he was in full compliance with state law. Epes Sargent, now with the newly established trade paper *Variety*, took notice, assessing the Keaton act alongside that of the week's headliner, former heavyweight boxing champion James J. Corbett. "Another strong hit is the Three Keatons, including 'Buster,' the human mop. The way the youngster is thrown about the stage without damage to else than his clothes is a thrilling sight, and yet Keaton declares that he has to moderate the act here in town on account of the Gerry Society."

Apart from that single week at Proctor's, the Keatons stayed out of Manhattan. Exile seemed to sharpen Joe's appetite for publicity, and in Maine he and the press agent for Portland Theatre manager Jim Moore hatched a plot to have Jingles kidnapped off a city street in broad daylight. The idea was to run up an hour or two of anguished suspense, get the local papers involved, then have the boy discovered happily parked on a bench at Union Station, gnawing on candy. The plan went sideways when the prearranged snatch took place in plain sight of a crew of workmen excavating a foundation for the new Keith's theater on Preble Street. A score of men and boys, Joe among them, gave chase, and the hapless prop man recruited to play the bad guy hailed a cab to make his escape. At the station, Jingles was placed where an officer could easily find him, and the man beat a frantic exit through the smoking room, never to be seen or heard from again. Relying on a detailed description of the perpetrator, Joe told the *Advertiser* he was obviously the same guy who had been following them from city to city, adding for good measure that Buster himself had been abducted five years earlier. Coverage of the event reached as far as New York, where the *Morning Telegraph* ran with it as a special dispatch.

In Cleveland, Buster gave an interview to the *Plain Dealer* denying he ever got hurt onstage and claiming he endured more pain in a Philadelphia barbershop than he ever felt at the hands of his old man. "The barber put the snippers, or whatever you call 'em, on the back of my neck an' gee! they pulled. I yelled as loud as I could, an' that's pretty loud." The article, headlined "BUSTER LAUGHS AT HIS BUMPS," served as an announcement of sorts: "In a couple of weeks, Papa an' me are goin' to go out in a stock company for a short time. He thinks it would be good trainin' for me. Mama says probably in some plays they'll want to put curls on me an' make me play little girl parts, but just let 'em try it! Not for Buster! Not for Buster!"

The real reason Joe Keaton sought the ease and security of a stock tour at a time when the family would normally be working the summer parks was that Myra was seven months pregnant with their third child. After much dickering Joe reached an understanding with George M. Fenberg, who had eastern, western, and northern companies under his management and promised his audiences "a change of play at each performance." The understanding was that Myra could appear as health permitted, and that Buster would be available for children's parts as well as the olio. Fenberg had a vast repertoire of plays at his disposal, melodramas and broad comedies aimed at working-class audiences with titles like *In a Woman's Power, Dangers of New York, Beware of Men,* and *Sporty Mr. Davis.* Engaged as leading man for the company of twenty was Charles H. Stevens, who had recently toured the Northeast in *Monte Cristo* with James O'Neill. The specialties on the tour included cornetist Marie McNeil, singer-dancer Tommy Schearer, and comedian Harry Jenkins.

With the Keatons headlining, Fenberg's eastern company began its preliminary season in mid-August with stops in Rhode Island and Connecticut. At New London, Connecticut, Myra was unable to appear opening night, and Joe and Buster managed to hold the stage—and a standing-room audience—for nearly half an hour. After three weeks, the company opened its regular season in Worcester, Massachusetts, drawing well despite competition from three other shows and the heat hovering around 100 degrees each day. And as he had done during the Keatons' 1902 tour with the Harcourt Comedy Company, Buster hosted a candy matinee, giving the kids in the audience a chance to meet both him and Jingles, now two years of age.

Buster in costume for Little Lord Fauntleroy. He once described the part as "the longest role, except Hamlet, in the English-speaking theatre."

Before long, he was pressed into service for the first time as an actor, nearly fulfilling his mother's prophecy of having to play "little girl parts." The play was *Little Lord Fauntleroy,* and he did indeed portray the title character in shoulder-length curls, red velveteen, and lace. "My part alone was seventy-five solid typed pages," he said. "In between, when I wasn't Little Lord Fauntleroy, I was little Willie in *East Lynne. East Lynne* was four acts long, like most of the tear-jerkers in those days. Little Willie died in the third act. As the curtain went down, I'd rush backstage, slap on a Johnny Ray wig—that's a bald-headed wig and some galways—and run back on stage again to do a rough and tumble with my father." Despite the Herculean effort it took to learn his lines, Buster got bored with the role of Lord Fauntleroy and began injecting slapstick into what was otherwise a charming period drama, much to the fury of manager Fenberg.

It was during a stop in Lewiston, Maine, on October 30, 1906, that Myra presented Joe with a daughter, who was named after family friend Louise

Dresser. Predictably, Louise Josephine Keaton was welcomed in the press as the fifth Keaton, and by year's end, at the tender age of two months, she was already being included by name in her father's trade ads, where the act was being touted as "The Man with a Wife, Three Kids, and a Table."

The Keatons closed with the Fenberg company on December 23. Back in New York, Joe told *Variety*'s Burt Green he was tired of being a big frog in a little puddle, and that henceforth the act would work only the larger cities, giving the smaller ones suitable to the Fenbergs of the world "a good long rest." The new year was to have started out at Proctor's Fifth Avenue, a house the Keatons had played numerous times, but Mayor McClellan's office denied permission for Buster to appear because the theater was now permitting smoking. Other Keith-Proctor houses with smoking balconies were similarly canceled, and Joe began incorporating the following statement in his ads: "Important to Managers—Buster will be 16 years of age October 4, 1909."

In Boston, the Keatons appeared on a bill with Harry Houdini for the first time in a decade, and Buster tagged along one morning after the mail. "A big xylophone was standing in the wings," he remembered, "with a leather cover strapped over it and cinched with a heavy Yale padlock. [Houdini] says, 'Now look at that.' (He's only got an audience of one—me, a kid.) 'They think that's safe and nobody can touch it.' He grabs the padlock with one quick movement and *instantly* hands it to me open. I looked at it and felt dizzy for a minute." When the Handcuff King was late to the stage one night, Buster was sent out to hold the audience with some impressions. "Mr. Houdini may not be able to appear tonight," he announced. "He lost the key to his dressing room."

In Newark, Jingles managed to impress audiences as well as a reviewer for the *Evening News,* who described a reception "that must have intensified the family pride in him." In Buffalo, Joe exhibited seven-month-old Louise as well as Jingles, and the *Courier* had them both doing "some Keatonesque stunts" on the stage at Shea's. "It is a treat to witness the 'art' of Mr. Keaton's two and one-half-year-old child. For knockabout acrobatic comedy work the Keatons are unequaled."

Still, neither child rivaled their older brother as the principal attraction. In St. Louis, Joe reported a big hit, Buster stopping the show. "His act runs from twelve to fifteen minutes overtime each night."

. . .

In his six years on the two-a-day, Joe Keaton had deftly avoided getting caught in the skirmishes that frequently erupted between players, managements, and the various circuits, beginning with the debacle of the White Rats strike of 1901. Contrary to Buster's assertion in his autobiography (which may have been an assumption on the part of co-author Charles Samuels), Joe wasn't a member of the Rats ("star" spelled backward) and openly disparaged the union's tactics in a letter to Harry Houdini. "Vaudeville is very rotten here[,] nothing doing. The Rats has put it on the <u>Burn</u> for <u>fair</u>[.] Proctor has put in stock company in all his houses. Jake Wells two houses puts in <u>stock</u>. So has Chases two house[s, and] Keiths Providence. So you see Vaudeville has had its day <u>unless</u> there's a change <u>soon</u>. I send you under separate cover a copy of the White Rats damable sheet as the actors call it. As I thought it would be interesting to you."

But in fulfilling his pledge to work only the larger cities, Joe fell into the middle of one of vaudeville's ugliest episodes, in which the Klaw and Erlanger legitimate theatre trust joined forces with the Shuberts to go up against vaudeville's Keith-Albee, a practical monopoly, in a big way. Klaw and Erlanger would supply the talent, the Shuberts would furnish the theaters, and agent William Morris would book the circuit. Scores of acts signed on, in part because Morris was so well liked, but also because E. F. Albee, the general manager of the Keith organization, was so widely despised. Among the acts gathered under the new "Advanced Vaudeville" banner were George Fuller Golden, founder of the White Rats; comedian Joe Welch; emcee James J. Morton; tramp juggler W. C. Fields; and The Three Keatons. In fact, so many top-line acts signed with the new concern that Keith-Albee and the affiliated United Booking Office forced a circuit-wide boycott of any act that aligned with Morris.

On Labor Day 1907, Advanced Vaudeville was offered at seventeen theaters stretching from Boston to Kansas City. Now blacklisted at the Keith and Proctor houses they had played since 1900, the Keatons found themselves at the Garrick in St. Louis, playing the K&E time in the company of some 140 other acts. They jumped to Louisville, Pittsburgh, and Philadelphia, where the headliners were Mr. and Mrs. Jerry Cohan, parents of the great George M., in a tab version of their son's *Running for Office*. Up in Boston they shared the bill at the Tremont with headliner Joe Welch, a gentile who made a career of portraying mournful Jews, W. C. Fields, and an all-animal sketch aimed at kids titled "Dogville."

"Buster Keaton is growing to be a sizable sort of boy," the *Post* observed, "and his energetic father has to work hard nowadays in flinging his young hopeful around the stage. . . . In a couple of years he will be able to lick the old man."

Louise Keaton passed her first birthday during a stand at Montreal's Academy of Music, but the new circuit was rapidly unraveling. Klaw and Erlanger weren't really interested in challenging the dominance of Keith-Albee in vaudeville, but rather in forcing Albee to buy them out using Morris and the acts he booked as pawns in a high-stakes game of chicken. The gambit paid off, and in November 1907, Albee's United Booking Office began honoring all outstanding contracts held by Klaw and Erlanger, part of a settlement that called for K&E to abandon vaudeville, netting them a profit of between $1 million and $2 million. And while the fallout for the Keatons was minimal, it was Louise's simultaneous appearance at a New York theater that gave the Gerry Society everything they needed to finally close in on her father.

New York's blue laws, which prohibited everything from Sunday liquor sales to baseball games, dated to the seventeenth century. (A colonial version from 1695 legislated "no traveling, servile laboring and working, shooting, fishing, sporting, playing, horseracing, hunting, or frequenting of tippling houses" on the Lord's day.) Over time, workarounds came into play, and for vaudeville these assumed the form of "sacred concerts" that took the place of regular weekday performances. By 1907, there were nineteen theaters in New York City, including all the Keith and Proctor houses, giving afternoon and evening shows that varied little from what they offered the rest of the week. In a nod toward piety, some dispensed with scenery and went easy on costuming, but in general a Sunday concert was as sacred as a circus.

One of the venues that gave regular Sunday performances was Chelsea's Grand Opera House, a sturdy neighborhood institution at the corner of Eighth Avenue and Twenty-Third Street. Having just returned to Ehrich House for a brief layover, the Keatons were at liberty when the Grand's manager, John Springer, invited them onto his bill for Sunday, November 17. It was being framed as a benefit, Buster remembered, and that Springer asked for all five of the Keatons. Joe warily consented after Springer gave his assurances there would be no trouble from the Gerry Society, and the matinee went without incident. The Keatons were set to go on last at the evening performance, but in the audience were Officers Robert Cosgrove and Obadiah Cunningham of the NYSPCC. Cunningham, in his report, noted that the Keatons went on at about 10:45 p.m., and that Myra played the trombone and did "lightning change acts" but no acrobatic stunts. Buster, he reckoned, was about fifteen years old.

"The older of the three Keaton children wheels a baby carriage on stage; the carriage contained a child about three years old. After some horseplay indulged in by the father and the son, the latter wheeling the baby carriage in front of him to prevent the father from catching him, they return to the wings and immediately the three-year-old child appears alone and runs across the stage. Keaton follows and catches its clothes and the dress of the child falls off, leaving him in a gymnastic suit. The father then seizes the child and holds the child's head between his legs while he attempts to put the dress on. The fifteen-year-old boy returns to the stage and then kicks the three-year-old child gently in the buttocks. The father finally succeeds in getting the dress on [the] child. The father and the older boy then go through a series of acrobatic and comic feats, turning flip-flaps and somersaults. The three-year-old child imitates the father and the older son. They are on about three minutes this time. All three then leave the stage, and in answer to an encore the father returns with an infant about one year old in his arms and he places this child on the floor of [the] stage giving the impression it is about to dance, but the child is unable to stand alone and fell down. The father then said, 'I guess it is too slippery.' Father and child then leave the stage, and in answer to applause the whole family appears and bows to the audience."

The next morning, court warrants were issued for the arrest of Joe Keaton and John Springer. A Gerry officer found Joe at home "in one large furnished room" at Ehrich House and took him into custody. "Keaton admitted that he had placed his three children on [stage] at the Grand Opera House last night, that he knew it was a violation of the law for him to do so, but that the Dramatic Mirror representative was anxious to write up the whole family and Keaton put them all on to oblige him." Joe also showed the arresting officer a postcard from Springer telling him not to fail to put Jingles on during their Sunday performances. Later that same morning, Springer himself was arrested and admitted to bail at the Seventeenth Precinct Station House. He did not say anything to the Gerry officer.

On Monday afternoon, the two men appeared before Magistrate Peter T. Barlow. Springer promptly asked for an adjournment, but Keaton wanted to plead guilty so as not to conflict with a booking the following week in Mobile, Alabama. Magistrate Barlow set bail for the two men at $500 each and scheduled an examination for the following day. On Tuesday, Springer, who had a history of violations stretching back to 1900, denied knowing anything about the appearance of the Keaton children at his theater, claiming the postcard regarding Jingles had been written by his son, John H. Springer. This didn't wash with Barlow, who told him that as the manager and proprietor of the theater, he was responsible regardless of what he did or didn't know. With Myra and the kids looking on, Joe was uncharacteristically quiet, eager to put the whole matter behind him and not jeopardize the family's upcoming tour of the South. Both defendants waived further examination and were admitted to bail at $300 each for trial the following week at the Court of Special Sessions. With his bail covered by William Morris, Joe skipped town to make his date in Mobile, forfeiting the money and causing a bench warrant to be issued for his arrest. Springer, who pleaded the fifth, was found guilty of exhibiting the children and fined $150. Keaton, found guilty in absentia for consenting to the same, was fined $75.

Taking his leave, Joe vowed to keep the act—and Buster specifically—out of New York until the boy was officially sixteen, some two years hence. It meant playing a lot of the smaller cities he had intended to eschew, as well as the so-called Death Trail of two- and three-night stands between New York and Chicago. The risk of more fines and possible jail time made it the only real course of action. Then, on October 4, 1909, there would be a triumphant return to Gotham for Buster Keaton and his family—and a round of collective nose-thumbing at the dreaded Gerry Society.

4

Not Like the Old Man Anymore

ACED WITH AN ABSENCE of nearly two years from the stages of New York City, the Keatons played the Orpheum time and found bookings wherever they could. "If nothing takes place will leave here quick," Joe wrote a cousin from Chicago. "Must have work." Things picked up again, and the family contemplated a long summer's rest in Muskegon. Then, as if to prove her mettle as a Keaton, little Louise marched out of a French window on the second floor of Ehrich House and managed to survive the fall with severe facial lacerations and a dislocated jaw. Gathering her up in her arms, Myra commandeered a horse and buggy and rushed her to the hospital. "The doctors massaged her jawbones back into their sockets," Buster remembered, "and sewed up her tongue which had been all but cut in two." Two weeks later, *Billboard* reported her as having fully recovered from her injuries, and that she could "talk as well as ever."

Any calamity, real or imagined, was grist for Joe Keaton's publicity mill. Chastened by the debacle of the Jingles kidnapping plot, he stuck with fanciful tales of life on the road. One evergreen, which he fed to local newspapers on countless occasions, concerned the saving of his family from a terrible death. En route to New York, the story went, the Keatons' train stopped at Elizabeth, New Jersey, where the brakeman announced a twenty-minute delay. The family repaired to the lunchroom, and Joe, who finished first, stepped outside to wait. Attracted by a sign that read SALOON, he hastened to wash down his lunch with a mug of beer. While inside, he heard the conductor call "All aboard!" and made it to the platform just as the train was pulling away. Surrounded by Myra and the kids, he soon received word that the train had run into a ditch. "Thus," the item concluded, "did father save his family through the kindly offices of a glass of beer."

Another had Joe pawning his wife and infant child in Missouri when the show went broke and he couldn't cover a hotel bill. Leaving Myra and Buster as collateral, he set off by himself to earn their ransom, failing miserably. In his absence, Myra fell ill and was methodically picked clean of her jewelry by the landlady, who also took the baby's necklace. Eventually Joe was able to make good and come up with the cash, and the family was reunited at some remote locale. "The door receipts for that night were just an even $7, lucky number. Now nothing can separate the family and two more little Keatons have been added on the register of the hotel to have their bill settled."

Still another concerned the very real threat of hotel fires, with Joe claiming that he and the family had survived three inside of fourteen months. He always managed to get his loved ones out safely, the story went, and had always been able to save something—and that something was always the same. "When they had all got down the fire escapes, and had reached a place of safety, Joe would find clutched tightly in his hand—a cake of soap."

When the Keatons returned to Muskegon in July 1908, big things were happening. Plans were under way for a hotel that would, in the judgment of *The Muskegon Daily Chronicle,* give "the finishing touch" to the shoreline as a summer resort. Meanwhile, a strip of land along the western shore of Muskegon Lake was being platted to create forty-four lots. "This property seems to be an ideal site for summer homes for those who want to be in close touch with the city and still enjoy the benefits of lake breezes and a location near a lake; who are looking for all the pleasures of a summer without being more than a few steps away from a street car line." According to the *Chronicle,* more than half the lots had already been disposed of to buyers who planned to build.

Joe Keaton, along with fellow vaudevillian Paul Lucier, was in the market for plots in what he hoped would become a genuine actors' colony. "There were about eighteen or twenty vaudeville actors living there with their families," Buster said. "That meant Mom could play all the pinochle her heart craved and Pop would not run out of fellow performers to swap yarns with." Having initially committed to four lots in the new development known as Edgewater, Joe worked a deal with real estate agent C. S. Ford to sell the remaining inventory on a commission basis during the upcoming season.

"The result," the *Chronicle* reported on October 10, "has been that the agent has heard from Mr. Keaton every week, and every week has brought another sale or two. This week the Keatons were at Union Hill, N.J., having been booked in for a number of weeks playing eastern time. While playing at Union Hill, Mr. Keaton sold two lots to T. Kay Smith, a monologist, who plays next week at Johnstown, Pa. Last week he sold four lots to Frank Rae of Rae & Broche. Mr. Rae will have his cottage erected next spring and early in the summer will bring his $1,500 launch around from New York City via Buffalo and the lakes."

By the end of October, all but two of the original forty-four lots had been taken, the latest purchasers being Tudor Cameron of the song-and-dance team of Cameron and Flannagan; Bonnie Gaylord, Cameron's wife; and a British comedian named Harry Piquo, who bought four lots. When Joe finally took full account of his commissions, all carefully tallied by Myra, he was able to claim six prime lots he had set aside for himself, the titles for which were recorded on December 11, 1908. The following day, an uncommonly carefree verse occupied Joe's usual ad space in the *Clipper:*

> Next year, in October, there'll be a fluster,
> Because of the sixteen Summers of Buster.
> Till then us for the leafy bowers!
> Gerry Society please send flowers.

The Keatons laid off for the Christmas season, hitting the road again on December 28 and playing stands within short jumps of New York City— Reading, Wilmington, Union Hill, Harrisburg. Then they headed south to Alabama, Arkansas, Texas, and Georgia, Buster booking all the travel himself and keeping track of the family's room-and-board expenses in a special pocket-size datebook. At age twelve, he loved being treated as fully grown and the equal of all the other performers on the bill. "Isn't that what most children want: to be accepted, to be allowed to share in their parents' concerns and problems?"

Advance press included a photo of the four eldest Keatons, each costumed exactly alike, stairstepping downward from Joe to Jingles, the billing "The Four Keatons and Buster" justified by two-year-old Louise's appearances at matinee performances. Eager to commemorate Buster's elevation to theatrical adulthood, Joe announced in the trade press that the Keatons would return to the New York stage on the very day of the boy's emancipation, October 4, 1909, at Keith & Proctor's Fifth Avenue. In May, the family traveled to Muskegon, where a six-room Keaton bungalow would soon rise on a prime lot at the base of a giant sand dune known as Pigeon Hill. It was while the Keatons were in residence at Muskegon that a letter arrived from England, addressed to Joe in care of Frank "Bullhead" Pascoe, whose saloon served as a sort of branch post office for many of the seasonal residents. As Joe later recounted it, the letter was from Alfred Butt, the manager of the Palace Theatre of Varieties in London's Cambridge Circus, offering the Keatons a week's engagement at £40 (roughly $200 and below the act's usual figure). It also said that if they were willing to make the jump, they could stay there indefinitely "if there was any merit" to their act.

Joe, of course, had been keen on playing abroad for years. "I am getting the European fever my self," he wrote Harry Houdini in April 1901, "and should I be lucky enough to land about a 12 weeks run, I am the lad to take a chance. . . . In fact I am very anxious to get over there in Oct[ober] or later. And I want you to be my assistant <u>Manager</u>. You can't talk to[o] much on the ability of my little comedian Buster and our Comedy Table work. There ain't another act like it. And my Sal[ary] is 225 for 12 weeks or more."

In 1905, Joe announced the family would spend much of the following year playing "the leading music halls through the English provinces, Ireland and Scotland," but scuttled the plan when work at home proved so plentiful and Myra's pregnancy intervened. In subsequent years, his wanderlust subsided as he grew to like the occasional holidays they took. Still, it was a temptation to finally see the British Isles. "I had $1,400 in cash at the time I received that letter," Joe recalled. "So the journey commenced." Back in New York, he went to a steamship agent on Fourteenth Street to purchase tickets, and ran into actor Hal Godfrey, who was there changing money.

"What are you doing here?" Godfrey asked.

"Going to London," Joe replied.

"Oh! Mercy on you, Joe. I've just got away." And Godfrey made his exit with a look of pity on his face.

Deflated, Joe asked if he could get his money back, only to be told that the deal had been made. "That night, one friend would sympathize; another would say: 'Go to it, old man; it's opening up a new field. You'll be a riot,' but what Hal said was most prominent. I went home and told the family London was all off. That started something. Tears streamed down little

Buster's face; Mother's too. Visiting friends said: 'Don't disappoint Mr. Butt, manager of the greatest music hall in the world.' So they persuaded me to go."

They made the crossing on the SS *George Washington,* a new luxury liner built by the Germans on a grand scale. Fussing all the way, Joe later claimed he did everything he could to get thrown off the ship, even making an attempt to sell Louise off as an "orphan child," a gambit that came close to causing a scrap. "But they wouldn't put me off the boat. Instead they told me that if I tried to auction off any more babies they would put me in irons." He resigned himself to the trip, and celebrated his July 6 birthday at the captain's table. Exiting the boat train at Paddington, they were met by Walter C. Kelly, vaudeville's famed Virginia Judge, who had arranged for lodgings. (It was Kelly who induced Butt to offer the Keatons an engagement in the first place.) After a chaotic four-mile cab ride and a generous round of American-style tipping, all passengers and luggage were delivered to what Joe sourly deemed "a questionable place." The next morning, they called on Mr. Butt at the elegant Palace Theatre, originally commissioned by Richard D'Oyly Carte as a home for English grand opera. The Keatons, Joe noted, were completely unbilled. ("Not even a photo out.") When he asked the stage manager for an explanation, the man simply said he had no time to argue.

At rehearsal, Joe presented the house conductor with "a nice set of orchestrations" from the American music publisher Fred Helf, particularly a beautiful overture. The first number went well.

"But when mother pulled the saxophone [out] you could hear them all through the pit. 'What the blooming hell?' said one. 'Are they going to play that?' 'I never saw one in tune in my life,' said another. By that time, mother had broken down. I was trembling and all I could think of was Hal Godfrey. Rehearsal over and no 'props.' We need brooms, a chair, pistol, gong; any old Mammy has them in her log cabin. They couldn't get them."

The stage was full of traps and splinters, forcing Joe to dial back some of the physical business for the sake of his son's hide. "Pop couldn't use me as a human mop," Buster said, "but he had his usual fun throwing me into the scenery and out through the wings." It was only a minute or so before they had the crowd laughing. "Nine-tenths of the time I was in the air and the rest of it, on my neck. Joe gave me the works."

"They went very well with the gallery," said William "Billy" Gould, the London correspondent for *Variety.* "In fact, I never heard before [a] gallery so insistent for an encore. They applauded and hollered 'Encore!' for fully three minutes, but the stalls were quite reserved. . . . I predict that the Three Keatons will be a riot in the provinces or in any of the London halls, barring the Empire, Alhambra and Palace." Gould was standing alongside Butt at the rear of the house.

"Fine applause," he remarked. "Why don't they allow them a bow?"

Butt wouldn't permit it. "It isn't on the level," he said.

The following night, the manager moved them up so early on the program there was virtually nobody on the lower floor or in the stalls. It took their friend Kelly to explain the problem with the people who frequented the higher-priced seats. "You actually scared the audience," he told Joe. "They think you are hurting Buster. The act is too brutal for them."

The next morning, Butt called Joe into his office. "I shall ask you," he said. "Is that your own son or an adopted one?"

Joe told him that Buster was his own son.

"My word!" Butt exclaimed. "I imagined he was an adopted boy and you didn't give a damn what you did to him."

That same day, Joe furiously booked return passage, abandoning all hope of spending more time in Great Britain. "We could book up three years if we wanted to stay," he fumed, "but the boat would sail Tuesday rather than Wednesday if I had my way."

Buster was just as adamant: "Coming back in a hurry," he wrote a friend in Muskegon. Upon arriving in New York on July 28, Joe promptly vented his disgust to *Variety* and the *Dramatic Mirror*, saying he hated the food and the warm beer, while taking care to acknowledge the hospitality of the American players who were "bully and did everything in their power" to make their short stay a pleasant one. "The day we sailed from God's country," he added, "my father died and I never knew of it until I came down the gangplank again, once more back home—and believe me I am a better Yankee than ever I was before."

Back in Michigan, the Keatons took possession of their new Edgewater cottage, the first home they had ever truly had, which, Buster estimated, "couldn't have cost more than $500.00 to build." Joe christened the place "Jingles Jungle" and nailed up a sign to that effect. More vaudeville stars had joined the actors' colony, the latest being the Four Floods, an acrobatic troupe looking to retire on twenty acres of land on the north shore of Mus-

The Keaton family at their summer cottage in Bluffton. From left: Louise, Harry, Buster, Myra, and Joe, who christened the place "Jingles Jungle."

kegon Lake. (By now, Joe was such a booster that *Variety* began spelling the city's name "Muskeaton.") The August exodus of resorters had already begun when Joe caught a string of forty white bass in the lake, one of the best hauls of the season. Proudly posing for photos, he vowed to use some of the shots in his trade ads, further burnishing the allure of the place as a summer destination.

Newly energized, the Keatons opened their 1909–10 season on August 23 in Philadelphia, where they bested headliner Pat Rooney, who was appearing in a farce comedy titled *Hotel Laughland*. "Joe Keaton and his whole family certainly never went better than they did today," manager C. H. Barns reported. "He is not handling the boy as roughly as he used to, and there is no end of fun right from the first. Little 'Jingles' caught the crowd very strong, and in fact, the act was a scream all the way through. [It is] now one of the best knockabout acts in vaudeville, and appeals to the women and children particularly."

Leading up to Buster's grand reemergence in Manhattan on October 4, Joe composed an autobiography in rhyme and began serializing it in *Variety*. Under the title "The Origin of the Three Keatons," the first entry was published on September 26:

A fellow there was who hailed from the west,
Who once drove an old prairie schooner,
Who has the right dope but hit the wrong trail—
This thin Oklahoma boomer.
He sit one day in front of his shack,
With an old faded circus poster,
And grinned as he looked at the comical clown,
And wished he, too, was a joker.

The series stretched into November, by which time Buster's birthday had passed but not without incident. Having intended for half a year to reintroduce the act at Keith & Proctor's Fifth Avenue Theatre, Joe learned that house manager G. E. McCune was planning to have them on first. Angrily, Joe canceled the booking, berating agent Eddie Keller for abetting such an insult. On short notice, he picked up two weeks with Mike Shea and directed Keller to find them another house in New York City, the result of which was that Buster actually turned fourteen on a stage in Toronto.

Meanwhile, the new booking Keller secured was a happy outcome, for Hammerstein's Victoria, which billed itself as "America's Most Famous Variety Theatre," constituted the absolute pinnacle of vaudeville in the days before the Palace eclipsed it. The young man who took the Victoria's stage on October 18, 1909, was not much different from the five-year-old who made his New York debut at Proctor's 125th Street in 1901. Time had increased his size, but he was still shorter than his mother, who at four feet eleven had several inches on him. In terms of makeup and costuming he remained the mirror image of his father, but the face under the greasepaint now displayed the high cheekbones and chiseled good looks of a cigar store Indian. And where in earlier years he could sing pleasingly, he was now prone to recitation with musical accompaniment, a result of his voice changing and "rasping like a phonograph when the needle is not working well."

Finally freed of the threat of arrest, Joe, Myra, and Buster Keaton were seen with greater frequency in New York City, playing a total of six week-long stands in Manhattan and Brooklyn during the first four months of 1910 alone. On April 20, while the family was appearing at the Star, the first of two back-to-back engagements in Brooklyn, the local Elks lodge tendered Joe a testimonial dinner, a kind of commemorative celebration of The Three Keatons over the previous decade, during which they had climbed from obscurity to become one of the standard acts in vaudeville. Joe took

The Keatons on the road, circa 1910.

the opportunity to spin tales of the boom days in Oklahoma, leading to a loosely truthful account of the time he met his wife and got up a sketch that became the framework of the present act. It was an evening in which Buster was on prominent display, pledging to join the Elks as soon as he was of age but, given the timing, also effectively signaling an end to the act as the public had come to know it.

The transformation began with the abortive trip to England and the reaction in the stalls to the act's apparent brutality. As the week progressed, Joe and Buster backed off on the freewheeling violence and managed to strike a more pleasing balance between mayhem and entertainment. Once home, they stuck with the new formula and found it worked even better than the old, the governing theme the same as always, that Buster "must behave." Then, in making a jump between Pennsylvania's Union Hill and Harrisburg in February 1910, both Joe and Buster were reportedly injured when a freight engine of the Pennsylvania Railroad jammed into the rear of their sleeping car. Press accounts had Joe, who was shaving at the time, losing three teeth in the jolt, while Buster suffered a concussion and an unspecified fracture. Years later, Buster said they hadn't been hurt at all, and the record shows the Keatons opened as scheduled at the Harrisburg Orpheum that same day.

What actually came of the pileup of passengers, grips, Myra's saxophone, Joe's old Blickensderfer typewriter, and the like was a new bit based on the premise of Joe staring into a little travel mirror, his face generously lathered, shaving himself with a wooden straight razor. As Myra plays the saxophone, oblivious to the action around her, Buster ties a long rubber rope to a hook above the mirror. With his basketball tethered to the other end, he walks the full length of the stage, the line getting unbearably taut, the crowd's laughter building with every step. "I let him have the basketball in the neck and—*bop!*—he gets his face slammed into the mirror and looks like a custard pie had hit him. Always had to remind him to go into the routine—he hated the taste of soap. So I'd remind him out loud, and he'd crack, 'Are you trying to tell the author what to do?' "

Another new piece of business had Buster fighting off an attacker, only to reveal the struggle was actually with himself. "I used to do a thing comin' out of a set house door of the stage," he said during an interview for Canadian TV, acting it out, "and we'd grab the piece of scenery here comin' out or hold the door here and my own hand on my neck. And from the front, it looks like somebody has got me by the neck. And I'd yell blue murder and shake the scenery and everything—and with my feet going in all directions. And my old man comes up there to free me. And he used to kick over my head, and his foot would come down there and knock me loose from there. And as I'd slid back across the stage this way, he saw that it was me who had a hold of myself, and he'd chase me right out of the theater, see."

It was soon decided that Jingles, who did a little dance in the act and stood on his head, would leave the stage at age six to begin school, and that Louise, whose stage name was Joy, would vanish behind the scenes completely until she too was ready for classes. "The next five years—what years!" Buster exclaimed. "Sending the kids off to school one by one, Jingles to that Kalamazoo military academy and, later on, Louise to a Muskegon school. That brought the three of us back together again—the original three who went through all the hard times together. Success, sure. Money, sure. But this was the *old* times."

Something else was happening. Joe Keaton, at age forty-three, was beginning to feel his years after a lifetime of hitch kicks, jumps, tumbles, and the hard physical labor of touring the circuits with one of the most rigorous of all knockabout turns. "In his efforts not to be violent with [his] son," went a contemporary press account, "Papa Joe steps into Buster's face from a chair on top of a table and leads him around by the lip. Papa Joe and Buster open with a soft-shoe dance while singing 'I'm the Father of a Little Pickaninny' except that they substitute 'Acrobat' for 'Pickaninny.'" As the onstage action stretched to thirty minutes or more, Myra's saxophone specialty became a necessary rest period for Joe, a few minutes when he could collapse backstage and marshal his strength for the second half. And where before he was principally a beer drinker, Joe had more recently taken to whiskey, relegating the lagers he formerly favored to supporting roles as chasers to the hard stuff.

Tired of traveling, Joe kept the act in the vicinity of New York City, where he could return home at night to the familiar comforts of Ehrich House and hang out with his pals at the Vaudeville Comedy Club, a group of kindred souls that limited its membership to comedians, monologists, pantomimists, and comedy acrobats. For 1910, the family's summer sojourn to Muskegon began May 5 and stretched into August.

"By golly, we got here after passing through some awful weather," Joe reported in a letter dated June 7. "And I brought with me the season's first sunshine. Found my case of Green River waiting here for me." Green River was a connoisseur's drink, the "whiskey without a headache" that "blots out all your troubles." Wrote Joe: "I have the finest location on this lake and every comfort for the weary and inner man."

When the Keatons opened their season in New York at Hammerstein's, a leaner, more varied act was on display, one that depended less on Myra than ever before.* "Buster and Joe whooped it up some for twenty minutes or more," *Variety*'s Dash Freeman recounted. "Buster is becoming a big boy, but Joe is still able to throw him about, and the kid is fast developing into a first-rate tumbler. A bit of new business with the brooms is extremely funny. Father and son have lots of fun with it." Brooms had always been part of the act—Buster made handy weapons of them—but the new business put them in the hands of both combatants. As they squared off, mercilessly trading whacks with rhythmic zeal, the orchestra picked up on the cue and flew into Verdi's "Anvil Chorus." Buster credited the innovation to Joe's penchant for punishing him onstage, in this case because the old man discovered a pipe in his jacket and considered him too young to be smoking. "And they

---

* That summer in Muskegon, Myra had sat out their traditional week at Lake Michigan Park, leaving Joe and Buster to take the stage as The Two Keatons, part of an all-headliners bill assembled by the actors' colony to raise funds for a clubhouse.

Buster in his more mature stage persona at the approximate age of sixteen.

always told me that my own mother began rolling her own at fifteen," he said. "And when he [later] found the cigarettes, the tune was 'a man smokes a pipe.' Well, we gave the comics a new routine that day of the pipe, and they've used it ever since."

Buster was hurtling toward adulthood. He bought his first automobile at the age of thirteen, a lightweight contraption with a one-cylinder engine called a Browniekar, and upgraded to a secondhand Peerless Phaeton—a seven-seater—the year he turned fifteen. He also began to grow, and was taller than his mother by the time he legitimately turned sixteen in October 1911. Sixteen or not, he was still a missile as far as Joe was concerned, although hefting him was becoming more of a strain. Just after Buster's birthday, Joe famously pitched him for just about the last time. The scene was Poli's in New Haven, a theater the Keatons knew well. New Haven was notorious in vaudeville for the rowdy Yale students who made great sport of heckling performers, but the place couldn't be avoided if acts expected to play the lucrative Poli time in the states of Connecticut, Massachusetts, and New Jersey.

At the performance in question, some undergraduates had positioned themselves in the front row so that whatever comments they made were within easy earshot of the stage. As the headliners, the Keatons went on next to last, having stopped the show the previous week at the Poli house in Hartford. The first segment of the act got over beautifully.

"Three in the front row begin ribbing us," Buster remembered. "The old man stops and says, 'If you want to be the comics, come on up here and we'll be glad to sit down there.'

" 'Go ahead,' they say. 'You stink anyway.'

"Joe begins to come to a boil. 'One more crack,' he says, 'and I'm coming over.' "

Myra emerged to play her solo, and the vigorous response was, in Buster's memory, enough to rock the theater. As she took her bows, Joe stepped to the footlights and, giving the crowd a big wink, said, "Don't spoil her, boys. She's hard enough to handle now."

"She stinks, too!"

That did it. Impulsively, Joe reached for the nearest weapon—which just happened to be his boy. Grabbing him by the nape of the neck, he said under his breath, "Tighten up your ass." The next thing Buster knew he was airborne, hurtling toward the front row.

"He has to clear the orchestra pit," Buster emphasized, marveling at the velocity of Joe's throw. "The orchestra pit is six feet wide. Gotta clear that."

In all, he traveled three, maybe four yards prior to impact. "[Hit 'em] broadside," he said proudly. "Three of 'em." The damage, he added, was considerable. "My slapshoes break the nose of one; my hips crack another's ribs. I'm back up and on with the act before the ushers and cops get down the aisle. One guy had to be carried out."

Joe's confidence in Buster's ability to safely land was once again justified. "The thought never entered his mind that *I'd* get hurt," Buster said of the event. "He *knows* I'm all right."

Joe Keaton was already looking to the day when Buster would go out on his own, effectively bringing the act known as The Three Keatons to an end.

They had worked thirty-nine weeks over the 1909–10 season but cut back to just twenty-nine weeks for 1911–12. Nineteen eleven was also the year Joe announced he had purchased eleven lots on Muskegon Lake and planned to erect a summer hotel for actors on the site. ("Joe," commented *Variety's* Billy Gould, "will never be satisfied until he can play New York and sleep in 'Muskeaton,' Mich., nightly.") Apart from fishing and piloting a twenty-five-foot launch dubbed *The Battleship*, Joe's daily routine at Bluffton was hinted at in the lyrics of the "Actors' Colony Clubhouse Song," which he presumably had a hand in writing:

> Meeting with the boys at Pascoe's
> at the closing of the day—
> Syl and Bub and Clark and Keaton;
> after all the fish were eaten,
> we would go on our merry way—
> Then when we would reach the clubhouse
> we'd sing another song or two—
> Then we'd drink 'til early dawn,
> until all the beer was gone—
> and go home to sleep at cock-a-doodle doo.

Buster's affection for his adopted home was on full display in a datebook he kept, where a retreat to Muskegon was celebrated as "HOME" and frequently decorated with little sprite-like figures labeled "JOY." Conversely, the late-summer return to work was accompanied by banners and figures sporting the word "GLOOM."* In between, he passed his days swimming and playing baseball, having formed a sandlot team initially called the Juniors, later the Colts.

"There was a bar in Pascoe's Tavern, and a club to which all the actors belonged. As for me and the younger children, we just got into bathing suits each morning on getting up and never took them off until we went to bed." Occasionally, he got stuck babysitting his sister when all he wanted to do was play baseball. "I used to fill her clothes with sand so she couldn't crawl away. She'd sit there happily, scooping handfuls of sand out of her little skirt."

---

* These were accurate renditions of the Joy and Gloom comic strip characters created by Hearst editorial cartoonist T. E. Powers.

An artist rendered highlights of the Keaton act once Buster had grown too big to blithely toss around. "The funny thing about our act," Buster commented, "is that Dad gets the worst of it, although I'm the one who apparently receives the bruises. Dad has had a sprained wrist for years from throwing me. I've only been hurt a few times."

At Bluffton, the Keatons gave little thought to the act, which remained a certified crowd-pleaser, even on the occasions when it stretched to thirty minutes or more. "This well-known family was a genuine hit," reported W. W. Prosser, manager of the Keith's Gay Street theater in Columbus, Ohio, "going bigger than at any time they have ever played this house. The audience howled with delight and, notwithstanding the unusual amount of time consumed, the act at no time became tiresome."

The matter of Buster's size was raised frequently as his seventeenth birthday loomed. "The same hit," wrote Prosser's counterpart in Cleveland, "but Buster is growing larger all the while, and it won't be too many seasons before he'll be throwing the old man around."

Joe could still kick, but sometimes his aim was off. "He missed my hat once in New Haven [doing the self-struggle bit]," said Buster, "and got me in the back of the neck." The boy fell backward and bounced his head on the floor. "I was out for twenty-two hours, Myra by the bed all the time. Concussion. Since he couldn't throw me anymore, he began sliding me around on the floor. Like a human toboggan. That's when I told a reporter that I'd given polish to the American stage."

A manager's report from Philadelphia in February 1913 assessed a new, leaner version of the act: "Although Buster Keaton is pretty nearly a full-grown man, nevertheless he keeps up the kid illusion very well, and the new material introduced in a measure takes the place of the former act when Joe could more easily throw the kid across the stage. It is really a very amusing act. Got plenty of laughter and applause and closed strong."

It wasn't so much getting even as a necessary shift in dynamics. From the beginning, it had been little Buster versus big Joe, David and Goliath. Then Buster turned eighteen and grew three inches in the space of a year. Suddenly the act was two adults giving each other comedic hell and showing no mercy. Buster remembered a particular matinee at Hammerstein's when Joe lingered too long at a taproom down the street. "In his hurry he forgot to put on the felt pad he had been wearing under his trousers ever since I got strong enough to hurt him when we did our 'Anvil Chorus' work on each other with the brooms." Buster gave him a good whack, and Joe turned green with pain.

"Christ!" he yelled. "I left the pad off!" And the audience roared at the language.

"Are you going through with it?" Joe asked him.

"Sure," answered Buster. "It's part of the play." Whereupon he let him have it again.

"Going through with it?" Joe repeated.

"Yes," said Buster firmly.

"But remember," he appealed. "I'm your father."

It made no difference. Buster laid into him, and Joe laid back. The orchestra launched into "Anvil Chorus," and by the end of the bit Joe was black and blue. Staggering toward the audience, he delivered one of his most memorable ad libs.

"This is the last time," he vowed in a stage whisper, "I let George M. Cohan write anything for me."

In 1914, Buster purchased his own modest cottage at Bluffton, a half mile from Jingles Jungle, in the heart of the neighborhood. The place afforded him a measure of privacy while abetting an intense interest in the opposite sex. Joe had warned him to stay away from local girls lest someone's father came around with a shotgun, but the one time he frequented a local bordello, he came away with an apparent dose of the clap that kept him out of commission most of one summer. (The problem was ultimately determined to be a pulled groin muscle, exacerbated by the home remedies and patent medicines he was given.) A neighbor girl, Mildred Millard (of the family act The Three Millards), could remember Buster sitting out the Friday-night dances at the park pavilion "in his old red sweater and khaki pants," mixing with the other actors and keenly aware of Mildred's father, sixty-four-year-old Leroy "Pop" Millard, who kept an eagle eye on him. Still, it was Muskegon that presented Buster with his first serious infatuation, an attractive girl from Chicago named Marie Boone. Myra felt sure the relationship would end in marriage, but the two eventually went their separate ways. "She wasn't an actress," was all Buster would say.

The season began late that fall, with Buster observing his nineteenth birthday in Davenport, Iowa, the first of a series of split weeks the Keatons played in Cedar Rapids, Springfield, Decatur, and Waterloo before heading on into New York. They laid off the entire month of December, and when they went back to work in January, it was with the knowledge that they would be spending the month of April in Muskegon so that Myra could undergo an operation.

It was too cold to swim, and there weren't enough players to get up a game of baseball, so Buster applied himself to an engineering project so outlandish it would become something of a tourist attraction. The previous summer, he and a longtime neighbor, monologist Edward Gray, got up an act for the Elks benefit, calling themselves Butt and Bogany, the lunatic jugglers. It was a riot of sharpshooting and broken dishes, and it opened the show with earsplitting bravado. (The two later emerged in their regular personas, Gray appearing as the droll Tall Tale Teller in the seventh position with The Three Keatons closing.) The much older Gray astonished the audience with a burst of energy few had ever witnessed, since he was regarded as the colony's laziest resident. So when Ed complained one day of being unable to find an alarm clock that could get him up at a decent hour, Buster saw a chance to create the automated house of the future.

First came the clock, which was augmented by what Buster called the Awakener. When the alarm went off, Gray would have thirty seconds to leap out of bed and silence it before a form of Armageddon would erupt. A series of weights and counterweights controlled by the clock simultaneously turned the gas on and ignited the burner under the coffeepot. Meanwhile, a mechanical arm plucked off the sheet and blanket, while the bed itself was made to rock as if an earthquake had hit. Other improvements followed. "Gray avenue is still one of the famous thoroughfares," *Billboard* reported in July 1915, "and the Gray cottage is noted as the only house in the world in which everything is run on the automatic order. It is a center of attraction. Ed Gray, [theater manager] Tommy Burchell, and Buster Keaton have contrived to fix the house so the clock can be wound up simply by pressing a button. The house is known as the lazy man's paradise, and even the flies are kept out by automatic device."

Buster's masterpiece was widely acknowledged to be Gray's outhouse, which sat on a rise favored by picnickers and was commonly treated as if it were a public facility. He took the little building apart, anchoring its four walls at the base with spring hinges and sawing the roof in two. "I put a long pipe under the outhouse and attached a bolt. From the bolt I ran a line to Ed's kitchen window, hanging on it some red flannel underwear and old shirts to make it look like a clothesline." If Gray observed an unauthorized user from his window, he could yank the line at a well-timed moment and cause all four walls and the roof to fall away. Buster was so pleased with the result he eventually equipped the outhouse at Jingles Jungle to erupt in gunshots and fire bells whenever the chains dangling from a mock pair of tanks were pulled. This time, it was unnecessary to make the walls fall away; the victim would usually sprint through the door like a jackrabbit, achieving roughly the same effect.

Joe Keaton turned forty-eight on July 6, 1915, and the Actors' Colony celebrated as if it were the biggest holiday of the year. Following a morning of baseball, during which the old actors' team, the Muckets, trimmed the Colts 3–1, a parade of more than three hundred began a noontime march through the crooked streets of Bluffton, Joe and Myra leading it atop an elephant called Minnie from neighbor Max Gruber's menagerie.* They were followed by a fourteen-piece version of Wallace Ewing's Zouave band, a Chautauqua favorite imported from Champaign for the day at fabulous expense. Then came a horse and Shetland pony, several trained dogs, and a host of

---

* Minnie, formerly of the New York Hippodrome, was a familiar visitor to Jingles Jungle, where, according to *The Muskegon Daily Times,* she "walks around through Joe's house and helps herself to good things to eat, and makes herself quite at home all over the place."

other four-legged performers, all preceding the professional residents of the colony itself, actors of all stripes, including Buster and his pal Lex Neal, who meandered up into the grove at Lake Michigan Park and then down to the shore of Muskegon Lake, where they broke ranks and set off for Bay Mill, where an elaborate picnic spread awaited.

"Never in the history of the colony," proclaimed an item in the *Chronicle,* "have so many actors been gathered together on the Muskegon lake shore."

The birthday gala was one of the highlights of Joe Keaton's life, an event where, as the paper put it, "every actor, no matter how big he is on Broadway, or any other way, nor how bold his name stood out in newspaper ads during the winter season, was a just plain actor . . . while Joe Keaton and Ma Keaton were the whole show." But Joe's time in the limelight was rapidly drawing to a close, and the 1915–16 vaudeville season would be the last full season for him and the family. Now approaching twenty, Buster had reached his full adult height of five six, but with his weight hovering around 130 pounds, he could still project the illusion of the underdog onstage. In movement he was angular and economical, as far removed from the average vaudeville comic as one could be. When thrown, he didn't just hurtle through the air, he took flight.

"Any time that you leave the ground," he liked to say, "it's your head that will steer you." And where Joe was all fury and instinct, Buster was a born actor, graceful and natural. Over the fifteen years he was part of the act, he never ceased perfecting the art of getting thrown around.

They spent the holidays in Muskegon, where Louise, age nine, was enrolled at the Ursuline Academy, a local boarding school for girls, and Harry, age eleven, was a cadet at Barbour Hall Junior Military, a Catholic boys' school at Nazareth, some eighty miles southeast.

"The act had to change," said Buster, "but Joe was changing too. Not like the old man anymore. Mad most of the time, and could look at you as if he didn't know you."

Myra urged her elder son not to take it personally. "It's old Father Time he'd like to get his hands on," she told him. "Man or woman, some can take getting old, some can't."

"It made it more understandable," Buster conceded, "[but] no more standable. Anyway, like the Indian said, it went on like that for a while, then it got worse. When I smelled whiskey across the stage, I got braced." To the outside world, and the trades in particular, the act was, in the assessment of *Billboard,* "better than ever." Rolling into New York ahead of a stop at Keith's Royal, they played a Sunday concert at the Columbia to a grand reception. The booking at the Royal, the new Keith venue in the Bronx, was prelude to the Keatons' only appearance at the famed Palace, Martin Beck's Times Square landmark that had become America's premier vaudeville house in just three short years. Though formally known as B. F. Keith's Palace, Beck, having initially built the place to anchor his eastern chain of Orpheum theaters, took a proprietary interest in the place and oversaw all aspects of its programming. Loud and gruff, Beck was never a particular favorite of Joe Keaton's, but a Keith-Orpheum route had grown to mean forty to eighty weeks of straight time, a virtual bonanza for an act that could meet his exacting standards.

The matinee of April 24, 1916, played to an overflow audience, with the Keatons in the number three spot, following the Mutual Weekly newsreel and a colored musical act called the Royal Poinciana Sextet. Joe was already on edge over the billing, which placed them dead last in the print ads—if they were mentioned at all—and he blamed Beck for the slight. Still, they got over well with the Palace's elite audience, at twenty-three minutes holding the stage longer than any other act on the program. It was the shuffling Beck did between the afternoon and evening performances that compounded the insult. Moving the headliner, actress Helen Ware, up with the early entries, Beck decreed the Keatons would now open the show, putting them on when the people out front were still finding their seats. "The Keatons were popular favorites with the few present at the early hour," *Variety*'s Winn O'Connor reported. "Some corking good bits have been added to the comedy routine, particularly those utilized to cover the encore. The real value is lost, however, in such an early position, and a spot lower down would have doubly benefitted the act and the show."

Joe stewed the rest of the week, gracefully accepting the handicap of the initial position while privately cursing Martin Beck for the disrespect he had shown. "Pop could not stop talking about this outrage," Buster said. "He called Beck every name in the book."

He finally boiled over one afternoon when, while onstage, he spied Beck standing in the wings, arms folded, glaring at him.

"Okay, Keaton," Beck said in a harsh whisper, "make *me* laugh!"

Joe's face turned purple with rage. "I'll make you laugh, Martin Beck, you low-down, no-good bastard!"

The next thing Buster knew, Joe was racing toward Beck like an angry bull. "Beck ran, Joe right behind, out of the theater and up Forty-seventh

Street. The stagehands tried to grab him and slowed him down a few seconds, and he lost Beck in the crowd. It was a good thing. He'd have killed him for sure."

Left on the stage alone, Buster didn't know what to do. He sang a song, did a jig, and offered a recitation until his father returned and the act could go on. Instinctively, though, he knew The Three Keatons were done for. The next day, Beck ordered the act shortened to twelve minutes, effectively destroying the momentum it built. Joe retaliated by elaborately winding a dollar alarm clock and, explaining the situation, setting it down on the Palace stage in front of the footlights. They began their turn, and when the clock went off, exactly twelve minutes in, they stopped whatever they were doing, no matter how riotous, and calmly walked offstage. And in doing so, the Keatons bid their farewell to the big time.

Effectively barred from the Keith-Orpheum circuit and the attendant services of the UBO, all the Keatons had left were the smaller independent circuits, regional in nature and considerably less prestigious. Within two weeks, Joe had signed with Joseph M. Schenck, general booking manager for Marcus Loew Enterprises, to open at Loew's American Roof on Forty-First Street. Eager to bring major acts into the fold, Schenck paid them $300 a week, the same money they had been getting from Keith, and the Keatons delivered—the *Clipper,* for one, pronouncing them the hit of the show. ("Took five bows.") Marcus Loew himself was considered the Keith of the small time, a square guy whose word was his bond, but outside of New York, Loew controlled only eight vaudeville houses, hardly more than a couple of months' worth in terms of a route. And playing the small time meant giving three shows a day instead of two, something the Keatons hadn't done in fifteen years. "The entire profession assumed you were on your way down—and maybe out—if you accepted small time booking," Buster said.

Calling it a day, the Keatons fled to Muskegon for a long summer's rest, Joe observing a twice-weekly route to the post office that included stops at the Occidental Hotel bar, the Elks lodge, and various businesses along Western Avenue. Accompanied by a reluctant Buster piloting either *The Battleship* or the Peerless, Joe would "pick up a letter or so, buy a two-cent stamp, and then [make] all the same stops over again working our way home." There was a gala gathering at Edgewater on July 17 to say farewell to the ramshackle houseboat known as the Cobwebs and Rafters, Joe having donated the land for a new club headquarters to be called the Theatrical Colony Yacht Club (TCYC). The building, in the form of a commodious bungalow, was dedicated in early August, with the mayor, police chief, and a couple of aldermen officiating, and with Myra serving as president of the woman's auxiliary. Joe, the steward for the TCYC, was also pitcher for the colony's baseball team, while Buster served as catcher, shortstop, or utility man.

Come fall, their options limited, the Keatons signed with Alexander Pantages, a Greek immigrant in the process of building one of the most important independent vaudeville circuits in the nation. Working the West Coast and Canada from his base in Seattle, Pantages was in direct competition with Orpheum in a number of cities, and their rivalry had gotten so heated that Martin Beck issued an order that any act working the Pantages time was automatically barred from the Orpheum circuit. So, naturally, it appealed to Joe to lock arms with Pantages and blow a loud raspberry at Beck, their mutual enemy.

Pantages liked to roadshow his companies, meaning the program would remain fixed as it moved from theater to theater. Paired with the Keatons as the lead attraction would be a one-act musical-comedy titled *Mr. Inquisitive* featuring the husband-and-wife team of Earle Cavanaugh and Ruth Tompkins. Rounding out the program would be the ethnic comedy team of Rucker and Winfred, a pair of dancers known as Burke and Broderick, and Izetta, a lively ragtime singer who billed herself as the Eva Tanguay of the accordion. The company opened in Winnipeg on October 2, 1916, just two days prior to Buster's twenty-first birthday, playing three shows a day—at two thirty, seven thirty, and nine o'clock. "Three-a-day with such a tough act wore Joe and Myra out, and got me down too—the bruises never got a chance to heal," said Buster. "And now Joe was so sore that it was eating him up. 'You think I've been drinking? Watch me now.'"

The Keatons made their usual hit. ("The intensely dramatic plot of one member trying to annihilate the other is well staged and nerve-wracking in its suspense," commented a reviewer for the *Free Press*.) They were three weeks in Canada, making their way west to Calgary and Lethbridge, then down into Montana, where they spent five days working the Pantages house in Butte. It was a grueling route that incorporated a week of one-night stands, and Joe, now in his fiftieth year, was struggling to keep up.

"You have to say, 'Poor son-of-a-bitch, fighting something he'd never catch up with,'" Buster reflected. "But, sweet Jesus, our act! What a beautiful thing it had been. That beautiful timing we had—beautiful to see, beautiful to do. The sound of the laughs, solid, right where you knew they would be . . . But look at what happened—standing up and bopping each

other like a cheap film. It couldn't last that way. Every time he got a snoot-
ful he'd sound off about Martin Beck. No matter who—agents, theatrical
managers, anybody—tell 'em what he's going to do to Beck. With his mind
on Beck he'd come on the stage wild. That's when I had to fasten a rubber
rope onto that old basketball of mine and keep swinging it around like a
hammer thrower to keep him off me. Get him running, let out the rope a
little, and bop him on the fanny. There were times it was him or me, but we
had to keep it funny—me on the old table like a ringmaster: 'Hup, Prince!
Hup, Prancer!' Audience laughing like hell and my dad falling on his face."

The tour continued into the holiday season, playing a beefed-up version
of the bill in Tacoma, Portland, and San Francisco over Christmas week. The
act, now reduced to sixteen minutes with Myra's solo, was still the big noise
in the closing position, but a shambles to anyone who knew the difference.
It was that week in San Francisco that Buster told his mother, "I'm going to
break up the act." She made no objection. But how to tell Joe? "He would
break down and cry like a baby, plead for another chance," Buster said. "I
was not prepared to watch my father go to pieces. I was not sure I could go
through with it. Not that I wasn't damn mad at him."

The solution was not to tell him at all. As scheduled, they played Oakland the first week in January, then made the journey south to Los Angeles,
where they were set to open at the Pantages theater on January 8, 1917. As
Buster told it, he and Myra swiped their trunks from the alley out back of
the theater, gave the manager some money for Joe, and ran. "As we say in
the theatre, we left Joe with egg on his face. Left him with his trunk and the
old beat-up table he had started with."

Five days later, Buster and Myra Keaton were in Detroit, where she would
be staying with friends. A few days after that, Buster left for New York,
where he would seek out a new career for himself as a single in vaudeville.

5

I Cast My Lot with the Pictures

ONCE HE REALIZED what had happened, Joe Keaton made his way back to Muskegon, where, as Buster figured it, he had pals, money, and two of his three children at hand. ("Pop wasn't going to die in Muskegon of either hunger or loneliness.") Meanwhile, the eldest scion of "fun's funniest family" traveled on to New York and Ehrich House, where he arrived, according to his datebook, on January 18, 1917.

When settled, Buster called at the offices of Max Hart, the top vaudeville agent of the day, who was in the process of transforming a $300-a-week single named Eddie Cantor into the $3,500-a-week star he would become for Flo Ziegfeld. Hart, forty-two, had a legendary nose for talent, and could see past the trappings of a bad act in mining what was good and valuable in a performer. So he was not bothered in the least when Buster told him he had broken up The Three Keatons and wanted, for the first time in his life, to work on his own. "I'll get you all the work you want," Hart told him, and he marched him over to the Forty-Fourth Street office of J. J. Shubert, who was assembling his annual summer revue, *The Passing Show.*

"This is Buster Keaton," Hart said to Shubert. "Put him in your show."

Shubert looked him over and said, "Can you sing?"

"Sure I can sing," said Buster, somewhat amused at the question since he was infinitely more valuable as a comedian than as a singer. Shubert, fortunately, engaged him without asking him to croon.

Starring DeWolf "Casey at the Bat" Hopper, comedic acrobat Jefferson De Angelis (to whom Buster was sometimes compared), singer Irene Franklin, and actor-comedian Chic Sale, *The Passing Show of 1917* was set to open

Joseph M. Schenck.

at the Winter Garden on April 26 following a week's shakedown in Pittsburgh. Rehearsals hadn't yet begun, and Buster was to have a voice in determining what he was to do in the show. Still, with time on his hands and a wait of nearly three months until the first performances, he was fidgety and nervous, unsure of what to do with himself. After ten days in New York, which he filled mostly by seeing shows, Keaton returned to Detroit to visit his mother, who, on his twenty-first birthday, had given him a membership in the Benevolent and Protective Order of Elks. From there he traveled to Muskegon, where, on February 2, he was inducted into Elks Lodge #274 with his proud father at his side.

The Keatons briefly regrouped in New York City, where Joe told the *Telegraph* he was lonesome for his family. According to the *Clipper,* he tried to persuade Myra and Buster to go back out on the road with him, but it was no good. Myra never had any particular love for the stage, and Buster felt the old act had run its course. However, Myra took pity on her husband of twenty-four years and rejoined him in Bluffton, even though the Keatons' summer cottage had no plumbing, heating, or insulation.

It was sometime in March, just prior to the start of rehearsals for *The Passing Show,* that Buster encountered someone he knew on the streets of Manhattan. In the early 1950s he told biographer Rudi Blesh it was an old vaudevillian named Lou Anger, and he repeated the claim in his 1960 autobiography. But in 1928, and again in 1930, he said it was Joseph Schenck, the booking manager for Marcus Loew and the man who introduced The Three Keatons to small-time vaudeville. Schenck, who had started producing his own movies, told Buster he was making some two-reel comedies. "He wanted to know," said Buster, "if I wanted to try the movies."

Moving pictures, or "flickers," as Joe Keaton dismissively called them, had been on the bills of vaudeville houses since the very beginning of Buster's career. At Dockstader's it was Siegmund Lubin's Cineograph; Keith's had the large-format Biograph; Tony Pastor's longtime choice was the Vitagraph (which made its public debut there in 1896); and George K. Spoor's Kinodrome was an attraction along the Orpheum trail. Other brands proliferated—Lifeograph, Kinetograph, Casinograph, Cineomatograph— most offering thrilling scenes of fires, races, demolitions, beauty pageants, and occasional story pictures like *The Great Train Robbery*. Gradually, movies gained in importance, and in 1916 the *Telegraph* suggested the record business at Loew's American Roof wasn't due to the Keatons or the other live acts on the bill, but rather Charlie Chaplin's *The Floorwalker,* which was shown at the conclusion of the program.

"I had no more idea than anyone else at the time what the growth of pictures was to be," Buster said. "One feature of the films did appeal to me, and that was that it would mean staying in one place for a while. I had been traveling on the road for over twenty years. I took my gamble and cast my lot with the pictures."

Schenck was new to the movie business, having produced his first film, a feature titled *Lost Souls,* the previous year. He had the instincts of a gambler, though, and lured actress Norma Talmadge away from Triangle with the lavish promise of $1,000 a week, her own production company, and 25 percent of the profits. The result was his second picture, *Panthea,* which opened on Broadway at advanced prices and began Talmadge's impressive climb to stardom. By then, Schenck had married her and contracted with comedian Roscoe "Fatty" Arbuckle to make a series of comedy shorts. Contemplating a production slate that called for six features a year from his wife and eight to twelve shorts from Arbuckle, Schenck secured a four-story plant on East Forty-Eighth Street, the former home of the Paper Novelty Manufacturing Company, and poured $100,000 into equipping it for moviemaking. The result was two vast stages, each 100 by 125 feet, reputedly making it the largest such facility in the East. The cost of lighting gear alone was said to have run $35,000. Nevertheless, to writer Anita Loos it was "ramshackle to a degree," a place seemingly thrown together on the fly.

Keaton had seen some of Arbuckle's comedies for Mack Sennett and told him that he greatly admired them. Arbuckle, in turn, had seen the Keaton act onstage and returned the compliment, allowing as how he had "always liked it." He had full creative control of his pictures and could easily have nixed Keaton's addition, but instead he embraced the younger man as a

A tax assessment photo, circa 1940, of the 20th Century Garage at 320 East Forty-Eighth Street in New York City. In 1917, this building housed the Norma Talmadge Studio where the Comique comedies The Butcher Boy *and* The Rough House *were produced.*

kindred spirit, an apprentice of sorts in the relatively new trade of making films that were funny.

"Roscoe—none of us who knew him personally ever called him Fatty—took the camera apart for me so I would understand how it worked and what it could do. He showed me how film was developed, cut, and then spliced together." A supremely inventive man with a grace and dexterity that belied his great weight, Arbuckle didn't so much write his films as work them out laugh by laugh.

"Not a scrap of scenario paper in my studio," Arbuckle said. "I wouldn't know what to do with a manuscript in my hand. I plan out the pictures, and we rehearse them—that's all."

When they began shooting *The Butcher Boy* on the morning of March 19, 1917, Buster had already worked out business for the first half of the film, which was to take place in the bustling interior of a general store. "You only had to turn me loose on the set and I'd have material in two minutes, because I'd been doing it all my life." Dressed in overalls and a pair of slapshoes, he makes his entrance sporting a pork pie hat with an impossibly flat crown and similarly abbreviated brim. "In those days, almost every comedian you saw affected a derby hat," he explained. "Even Harold Lloyd, when he was playing his Lonesome Luke character in 1917, wore a derby—which he later deserted for his signature straw hat and horn-rimmed glasses. So I decided to get a hat that was my very own. I knew straw was too fragile for my kind of antics, so I chose felt and designed this particular pork pie. I took a good Stetson and cut it down, then I stiffened the brim with sugar water."

In a nod to his earliest days onstage, Buster is immediately attracted to a display of brooms stuffed into a couple of barrels. He selects one, hefts it, yanks off a few straws, casts it aside. A second leaves him similarly unimpressed, and after returning it to the barrel, he uses a foot to retrieve the first off the floor and return it as well. With Arbuckle, whose dexterity with small props—particularly a butcher knife—is on full display, Keaton explores the comedic possibilities in a pail of molasses, virtually cementing himself to the floor with it. The slapstick highlight of the sequence is a rowdy fight with bags of flour primed to explode on impact, Keaton taking a direct hit from Arbuckle that literally knocks him off his feet.

"Roscoe explained the technique in pictures was different from the stage," he said, "particularly in taking a pie or a pot of molasses in the face, because

A still posed on the set of The Butcher Boy *(1917). Al St. John wields the pitchfork while his uncle, Roscoe "Fatty" Arbuckle, reacts at the prospect of being impaled. Josephine Stevens looks on, as does Arthur Earle, who plays her father, the store proprietor. Keaton, in his motion picture debut, attempts to pull Arbuckle to safety.*

the toughest thing is to keep from flinching when you see it come. We're doing a scene in a bakery and there are a lot of three-pound sacks of flour lying about. Fatty picks one up and throws it at the baker who ducks, and I get it. So he explains: 'Now, Buster, you just keep looking over in that direction until I say *turn*. When you turn, it'll be there.' So I do just like he says and look away until he says turn. Bowf! I get it. I thought my neck was broken. It exploded just like a bomb. That Arbuckle was a dead shot, and that sack came with all his three-hundred pounds behind it. My eyes, nose, and ears were filled with flour—but it got the laugh."

In the film's second half, set in a girl's boarding school where Josephine Stevens, playing the shopkeeper's daughter, has been sent to keep her and Fatty apart, Keaton enlivens the action with a display of acrobatics he perfected over a lifetime in vaudeville. He takes a variety of spills, tumbles roughly down the front steps of the store, and in one spectacular shot is sent hurtling through the doorway of a bedroom, where he pulls a backward somersault, spinning on his head so as to land facing the opposite direction.

"From the first day on I hadn't a doubt that I was going to love working in the movies. I did not even ask what I'd be paid to work in Arbuckle's slapstick comedies. I didn't much care." Buster's usual share of the Keatons' weekly take in vaudeville was $300, and the Shuberts had agreed to pay him $250 for *The Passing Show*. Yet on his first day of filming for the Comique Film Corporation (pronounced, according to Arbuckle, *Co-meek-ee*) Keaton's datebook shows that he was being paid $40 for the week. And, as he said, he didn't much care. "I'd fallen in love with the movies—with the cameras, with the rushes, the action, the slam-bang—with all of it."

The Butcher Boy took three weeks to work out and shoot. Then Arbuckle invited Keaton into the cutting room to observe the editing process. "By the time I'm through," Arbuckle said in an interview, "I have about 15,000 feet of film—and all I need is 2,000 feet. I've got to skim the cream off that milk. I go over all the films and pick out the best scenes. Then is the time I write the story. I make out the scenario from the scenes I intend to use. In this scenario every scene is numbered. When I have it finished, I take the reels, find the scenes I want, cut them out, and put them in numbered pigeon-holes. I write the titles that connect up these scenes and then everything is in shipshape order for making up the necessary two reels."

Schenck arranged to distribute the new Arbuckle comedies through Paramount, which was asking $35 a day in first run—top dollar for a two-reeler that didn't star Charlie Chaplin. Released on April 23, *The Butcher Boy* was an immediate critical and commercial hit, playing more than three hundred theaters in its first week alone. Ben Grimm, in a notice for *Moving Picture World,* praised the film's free-for-all as "one of the best comedy battles" yet staged. "The main ammunition is flour, and what don't happen in that store when the flour bombs begin to fly is hardly worth mentioning. . . . Buster Keaton does some excellent comedy falls." With a new picture set to start, Keaton's salary was bumped to $75 a week, a measure of the added value he brought to the movie.

To help fill the pipeline, Schenck acquired an Arbuckle short made for Keystone that went unreleased when its star left the company. Filmed the previous summer, *A Reckless Romeo* was passed off as the second entry in the current series, though reviewers instinctively saw it as a throwback to Arbuckle's Sennett days. Released just a month after *Butcher Boy, A Reckless Romeo* bought Arbuckle and his company some badly needed time and put Paramount on course to releasing eleven Arbuckle comedies for the 1917–18 season. So great was the anticipation for a second picture that contracts to show it reportedly outpaced those for the first by some 35 percent.

Keaton's second movie with Arbuckle was titled *The Rough House,* and it took no less time to make than the first—about twenty camera days for an eighteen-minute subject. Advance publicity hinted at a troubled shoot, with opening scenes set at Churchill's famous Broadway cabaret abandoned at a cost of $10,000, along with almost any hint of a story concerning Mr. and Mrs. Rough, whose house by the sea is invaded by Fatty's mother-in-law. What remained was a relentless slapstick assault on the senses, substituting frenetic action for what the film lacked in inventiveness. Making his entrance on a bicycle and catching his neck on a clothesline, Keaton was called upon to execute no fewer than twenty falls during the course of the action, conclusively demonstrating that he could handle without injury practically anything in the line of physical comedy. At the completion of *Rough House,* he was raised to $100 a week.

By the time of his third Arbuckle, *His Wedding Night,* the company had relocated to the former Biograph studio in the Bronx. Keaton liked to say the move was due to all the noise they made on Forty-Eighth Street, which interfered with the shooting of the Norma Talmadge pictures, but it was more likely Schenck's need to improve the bottom line. Producer-distributor Pathé took a six-month lease on the space Arbuckle vacated, while George Backer, president of Foursquare Productions, rented another portion of the building. And Talmadge herself would soon begin shooting *The Moth,* her fourth feature under Schenck's management. The Biograph, on the other hand, was a spacious and well-appointed facility built expressly for the making of motion pictures—four floors of offices, dressing rooms, a kitchen and dining room, even an on-site power plant and film-processing lab. And atop the building a large glass-roofed studio that could be seen for blocks around.

"Everyone there was doing drawing-room pix," Buster remembered. "Tails and evening gowns were all over the place. If you spoke American out loud, monocles dropped by the dozen."

The Arbuckle company settled into a comfortable production routine. Schenck, focused on his wife's films, was a hands-off producer, leaving the day-to-day of running the studio to Lou Anger, the former Dutch dialect comic who served as his general manager. It was the affable Anger who persuaded Arbuckle to leave Sennett to make pictures for Schenck in the East, and who was subsequently charged with keeping the operation running smoothly and within budget. Al St. John, Arbuckle's lanky nephew, lacked Keaton's hard-earned skills as an acrobat but was seemingly fearless in the stunts he'd attempt for the camera. And Roscoe acquired a lively new comedienne in the person of Alice Lake, who had appeared in *A Reckless Romeo* and lent some continuity to the series after the departure of Josephine Stevens. William Jefferson, son of actor Joseph Jefferson, was one of the company's supporting players. Herbert Warren, longtime leading man for French-born actress Valerie Bergere, was the company's chief scenario writer, and Frank Williams, Arbuckle's cameraman at Sennett, had come east to continue working with him.

"He was one of the greatest friends I ever had," Keaton said of Arbuckle. "I was only with Arbuckle about three pictures when I became his assistant director. It wasn't a case where he came up and said: 'From now on, you're assistant director.' You fall into those jobs. He never referred to me as the assistant director, but I was the guy who sat alongside of the camera and watched scenes that he was in. I ended up practically co-directing with him because he was considered one of the best comedy directors in the business."

Keaton may have been moved behind the camera for *His Wedding Night* because he was needed less on-screen than in either of his previous films. The result was a more inventive, less frantic comedy than its predecessors. When Buster sidles up to the soda fountain and hints at wanting an illicit beer, Arbuckle obliges, adding a small footrail, a spittoon, and sawdust on the floor. Later, an effeminate man enthuses over a perfume display, and Fatty hauls out a sponge, a long-handled brush, and a small tub so the customer can literally bathe in the stuff while being drenched with seltzer water. Then Buster, having delivered a wedding gown to the proprietor's daughter, puts the dress on to model it, and the screen in her bedroom drops for a dramatic reveal, complete with spotlight, then magically rises up again as he steps forward and strikes a pose. "I didn't know it at the time," said Keaton, "but I turned out to be Arbuckle's whole writing staff for gags."

His Wedding Night was made during some of the hottest days of summer, forcing Arbuckle to limit shooting under the Biograph's glass canopy to just thirty minutes at a stretch. He turned out two more shorts in as many months, a further step forward titled *Oh! Doctor* in which he abandoned his usual costume of ill-fitting trousers and an undersize derby for street clothes and a comparatively adult persona, playing a henpecked husband with Buster filling the role of his bratty child, and *Fatty in Coney Island,* in which the Arbuckle unit invaded Brooklyn's Luna Park for a tour of the attractions that would serve in future years as a sort of time capsule of the famed amusement resort in its prime. *Coney Island,* in particular, was made quickly for an Arbuckle comedy, as if a measure of fatigue had crept into the process. ("We just went down there, went on the concessions at Luna Park, and got in trouble," Keaton said dismissively. "That was all there was to that.") The critical reaction was somewhat muted, with the *Exhibitors Herald* going so far as to accuse Arbuckle of vulgarity. "There are many comedy points in *Fatty at Coney Island* [*sic*] which are clever, original, and funny, and some that do not reach the objectionable, but for the exhibitor catering to the high-class audience, this production should be taboo."

Seeking new territory and a fresh jolt of inspiration, Arbuckle petitioned Schenck for a move back to California, where he preferred the climate and could more easily shoot outdoors in winter. "We made about six pictures in New York," Buster said, "and then moved . . . to the [West] Coast because we were too crippled and too handicapped in the East trying to do exteriors. Those type of pictures, at least seventy-five percent of all our pictures, would be exteriors."

Veteran director Allan Dwan would vividly recall the experience of shooting *Panthea* with twenty-two-year-old Norma Talmadge. Dwan had already made a picture with her at Triangle and knew what to expect. "She was a very good worker, never late," he said, "but one morning she didn't show up at 9:00 when we were supposed to start. At 10:00 she finally came in, and I was a bit concerned—thought maybe she'd been ill or something. I went to her dressing room and she was crying. 'What's the matter?' I said. 'What's happened to you?' She said, 'I'm married to Joe Schenck.' I said, 'That's fine. When?' She said, 'This morning.'"

In the opinion of some, the eldest of the three Talmadge sisters had made a calculated move to secure both her career and her financial future by marrying a man old enough to be her father. "During the few weeks of their courtship," Norma's watchful mother, Margaret L. "Peg" Talmadge, wrote in her 1924 book *The Talmadge Sisters,* "Mr. Schenck had come to be a sort of big father to all of us, and to this day, Norma always calls him 'Daddy.'" Mrs. Talmadge, who lived with her daughters and prized a close-knit family, was against any of them marrying anyone at the time and was skilled at getting rid of the suitors who invariably came around. Norma, it's been suggested, had a low boredom threshold when it came to men, and her mother had subtle ways of making them seem dull and—occasionally—ridiculous. The Russian-born Joe, with his slight accent and his immigrant's fondness for an unflattering derby, was an easy target, but in his case Peg was mindful that he was the gifted Norma's most convenient ticket to fame and great fortune.

"Joe was no Rudolph Valentino," said Anita Loos. "His hearty appreciation of Jewish dishes was a constant hazard to his waistline. I think of Joe with the fondest memories, but they also bring forth the aroma of a special sort of smoked sturgeon that came from Barney Greengrass's delicatessen on West End Avenue." An industrious man with a knack for math, Schenck was still in his teens when he landed a job in a New Jersey wire factory paying $4 a week. He took night courses, and was a licensed pharmacist at the age of nineteen. In 1899, he went to work at Hornick's at 111th and Third and persuaded the druggist to put his brother Nicholas, two years younger, on the payroll. In 1901, they bought out the store with a down payment of $1,500 and went looking for other enterprises. On a summer Sunday, the Schenck brothers took the Amsterdam Avenue trolley to the Harlem River to beat the heat and saw crowds swarming with little to keep them amused. Before returning home that day, they deposited $150 on the rental of a modest beer concession called the Old Barrel and turned a $1,200 profit in just three months. The following year they added free entertainment to the bill of fare and cleared $16,000 for the season.

In 1905, Joe and Nick, in league with a partner named William Mundt, incorporated the Fort George Amusement Company and began construction at the trolley terminus in Washington Heights. The result was Paradise Park, an attraction that charged no entry fee and boasted a roller coaster at ten cents a ride, a Ferris wheel of Nick's own design, and a music hall offering nine acts of vaudeville. Along about this time, they made the acquaintance of Marcus Loew, who already owned a small collection of theaters and nickelodeons and who would take the brothers to the Harlem Casino after hours and quiz them on their prospects. In time, Joe took charge of the People's Vaudeville Company, which Loew had established in 1904 with a capitalization of $500, and installed his brother Nick as manager of the company's theater in New Rochelle. By 1909, People's controlled twelve houses and would eventually morph into Marcus Loew's Enterprises, with Joe as general booking manager and Nick overseeing its real estate interests. When the vogue for Paradise faded, the Schencks took over Palisades Park on the New Jersey side of the Hudson River and poured some $500,000 into making it the biggest amusement park in or around greater New York City.

The wedding of Joe Schenck and Norma Talmadge was a low-key affair but hardly a secret, as legend would have it. *Variety* carried news of the marriage license in its issue of October 20, 1916, and the following week reported October 27 as the date set for the civil ceremony in Stamford. Then, so that Peg Talmadge could attend, they pushed it back to the morning of October 31, Joe letting it be known that presents were unnecessary and that a dinner would likely take place at a later date. The honeymoon was put off until the completion of *Panthea,* and Joe was back in his Times Square office by noon.

"He was nineteen years older than his bride," wrote Loos, "but it seemed possible that she was in love with him—many a Broadway baby had been. I could understand being in love with Joe, because I've always been a pushover for power that's governed by gentleness. I hoped that Norma would appreciate that rare combination and I waited with curiosity to find out."

Panthea, which was to be released through Lewis J. Selznick's Select Pictures, was filmed at the Biograph. It was well known around town that Joe Schenck was overextended, and he later said he never worked so hard on another production in his life, going so far as to sleep on a cot at the studio in order to keep the picture on track. "I knew very well that I could borrow enough money to make a picture with Norma," he said, "and that the picture was bound to make money." Once *Panthea* was in the can and Arbuckle under contract, Schenck purchased the building on Forty-Eighth Street and set about assembling his own organization, commencing with Lou Anger, who in turn hired Norma's younger sister Natalie as his assistant.

Unlike her two sisters—the youngest of the three being Constance—
Natalie Talmadge had little interest in being an actress. "She was the serious
type, of studious bent," wrote her mother, "with contemplative eyes and soft
voice." When she graduated from Brooklyn's Erasmus Hall, rather than go
on to college or embrace the drama, Natalie enrolled in a business course,
polishing her typing skills and mastering the basics of bookkeeping and
stenography. Then she pitched in helping her mother with her sisters' fan
mail, bringing a level of organization to the task that soon made her indispensable. She became their financial and executive secretary, a salaried post
she held until Anger lured her away.

Buster Keaton met Natalie Talmadge, whom everyone seemed to call
"Nate," the first day he was on the set of *The Butcher Boy*. At age twenty,
she was six months younger than he, reserved and competent and a bit grim
at times. A brunette, she lacked Norma's distinctive profile, nor was she
as cheerfully sexy as her younger sister, Constance, a blonde whom their
mother nicknamed "Dutch" because of her childhood chubbiness. Still,
Natalie had the Talmadge genes and was in the process of growing into her
looks, which would prove somewhat more durable than Norma's. "I was
attracted to her at once," Keaton wrote. "She seemed a meek, mild girl who
had much warmth and great feminine sweetness." A relationship developed,
and according to Minta Arbuckle, Roscoe's wife, they took to spending
weekends at a beach house on Sheepshead Bay, where Minta's husband was
having an affair with Alice Lake. Nate and Alice, with their shared roots in
Brooklyn, became the closest of friends, and when Comique decamped for
California, she went along in her capacity as Lou Anger's assistant and the
company's financial manager. And so, as it turned out, did Joe and Myra
Keaton.

From a humble beginning in 1913, Herbert M. Horkheimer took a $7,000
inheritance and created the Balboa Studio complex out of a single building once occupied by the California Motion Picture Company and, for a
brief spell, Edison. Four and a half years later, when Roscoe Arbuckle and
Comique arrived to claim space at the facility, Balboa had grown into the
largest single employer in the city of Long Beach, some thirty miles south
of Hollywood. Horkheimer, who partnered with his brother, Elwood, was
a showman of the old school who considered his compact studio complex
as much a product as the films that emerged from it. The score of build-

ings that housed its various departments were uniformly painted green with white trim, and the grounds were fully landscaped to give the campus a cohesive look, even as it occupied all four corners of a major intersection. A new enclosed stage had doubled the studio's production capacity, while the largest glassed-in stage in the industry was nearing completion. "There are larger studios in Southern California than Balboa when it comes to the ground space utilized by several," commented a midyear article in *Motography*, "but none of them begin to own the amount of equipment that the Horkheimer Brothers have assembled."

The Horkheimers churned out serials for Paramount and Pathé, Jackie Saunders comedies for Mutual, dramas starring Anita King "The Joyous Outdoor Girl," Knickerbocker Star Features, Fortune Photoplays, and a series of movies featuring Gloria Joy, vaudeville's reigning "Child Wonder." Baby Marie Osborne was probably the biggest star the Horkheimers brought forth, but none compared in stature to Fatty Arbuckle, who was widely considered second only to Charlie Chaplin in popularity. Arbuckle's arrival at the bustling studio at Sixth and Alamitos was a big deal, a cause for celebration and a shot of prestige for the perpetually struggling Horkheimers. The

On the grounds of the Balboa Studio complex at Long Beach, California. From left: General manager Lou Anger, scenario editor Herbert Warren, Roscoe Arbuckle, Alice Lake, Luke (the star's dog), Keaton, and Al St. John.

fact that Buster Keaton, Al St. John, and Alice Lake accompanied him was nearly lost amid all the ballyhoo.

Buster actually arrived a few days ahead of the others and immediately sent for his parents with the notion of putting Joe in the movies. The Man with the Table never thought much of the idea, and had summarily rejected a proposal from William Randolph Hearst to make a series of two-reelers based on the popular comic strip *Bringing Up Father*. ("You want to show The Three Keatons on a bedsheet for ten cents?" he erupted.) But now he was retired, itchy and restless, and Buster thought he'd do well in pictures if he'd give it a try. The first Arbuckle to be made in California, *A Country Hero*, would be rich in location work, and if Joe got over and stuck around he and Myra would spare themselves the torments of another Muskegon winter. There was also the likelihood that Buster actually missed his parents, the old man in particular. "I never had that thing: At what age did I hate my father?" he said in a 1963 TV interview. "Oh, no. We were the best of friends."

Arbuckle conceived *A Country Hero* as taking place in a small rural village, and spent his first days in California scouting locations. Unable to find anything suitable, he decided to build the burg he called Jazzville on the Balboa lot, utilizing a patch of ground set aside for exterior sets. Just a mile from the seashore, the studio was cooled by ocean breezes, and the pleasant smell of salt air was ubiquitous. Scenes at the beach could be made with a three-minute trip by automobile. Other handy locations included the Pike amusement arcade, the canals in the neighborhood of Naples, and a large field near Orange and Alamitos Avenues. "In Long Beach I have discovered through observations there is a greater percentage of sunshine," Arbuckle said in an interview, "and this is a big factor in making pictures."

Filming began on October 17, an open call bringing 250 respondents to fill 150 spots as "country village inhabitants." About fifty were promptly put to work, populating the street built out behind the new Balboa stage, Arbuckle playing the village blacksmith and Joe Keaton essaying the role of Cy Klone, the garage owner and Fatty's rival for the affections of schoolteacher Alice Lake. Joe didn't adapt to filming easily and immediately disliked the common practice of shooting out of sequence, complaining that he didn't know what he was doing half the time. Then in one scene he was instructed to kick Buster, which would normally have come as easily to him as breathing, but the shot was composed so that Joe was at the right of the frame, and for the gag to read properly he'd have to use his left foot instead of his right. "No, sir," he declared. "I've been making a living for twenty

A raucous moment from A Country Hero, *the first Comique short to be produced in California. Joe Keaton, as Cy Klone, is dunking Arbuckle, Buster, and Alice Lake in the water trough outside Fatty's blacksmith shop.*

years kicking my son around, and I'll be damned if any cheap movie stage manager is going to start in now to teach me to do it."

Al St. John, a city dude, comes motoring into Jazzville at the wheel of a Ford Model T, up to no good. He soon finds himself dunked in a water trough out front of Fatty's place, a fate awaiting multiple cast members as the story unfolds. Al joins in at the annual village ball, where Fatty, in drag, impersonates a Spanish dancer, and Buster, in a veiled send-up of dancer Fatima Djamile, wriggles his way through a Coochee-Coochee number in which a long black stocking produced from a cigar box stands in for a venomous snake. Al, intent on luring Alice to the big city, is thwarted when his car stalls in the path of an oncoming locomotive.

"Look!" Fatty says proudly amid the wreckage of Al's vehicle. "I saved the crank!"

Along with the cost of hiring the Southern Pacific, whose tracks ran alongside the studio grounds, Arbuckle acknowledged wrecking two identical automobiles in getting the shot.

"What we did to Fords!" exclaimed Buster. "Whatever kept Henry from suing us all for libel?"

The finale was a boisterous free-for-all in a crowded restaurant in which Fatty fights off five adversaries with dinnerware, breakaway chairs, and an upright piano he uses as one might a cudgel. (Two of the chairs aimed at Arbuckle failed to break properly, landing him in the studio infirmary with a concussion.) Alice Lake gets flung clear across the room, Three Keatons–style, once Al's slicker character has been vanquished, leaving Fatty with both the girl and the money at the fade-out.

A Country Hero was released on December 17, 1917, making it the seventh Arbuckle comedy in eight months—a prodigious output for a major comedian. Joe decided he liked picture work well enough as long as Buster was involved, and settled into a rented house near the studio with his bull pup, some Black Minorca chickens, and Myra.

"No more tips to stagehands," he vowed. "No more to porters, bellhops, hall boys, hat boys, or the like. I've finished bribing myself through life. A barber in Long Beach shaved me the other day and through sheer force of habit I tipped him, and so far was he from expecting a tip that he wanted to shave me all over again."

By Buster's own account, he was responsible for co-directing *Fatty in Coney Island,* and doubtless served in the same capacity on *A Country Hero.* It is possible, in fact, to see an artistic progression in the Arbuckle comedies as Keaton began stationing himself alongside the camera, moving them away from what Harold Lloyd once called "the hodgepodge of slapstick." He had a natural sense of where the action needed to go, although he was slow to question the older man's instincts.

"You must never forget," Arbuckle had told him, "that the average mentality of our movie audience is twelve years."

Such advice didn't sit well with Buster, who started taking films seriously after seeing *Tillie's Punctured Romance,* Sennett's pioneering 1914 feature, then thrilling to D. W. Griffith's *Birth of a Nation,* which he considered a masterpiece.

"I thought that over for a long time," he said of Arbuckle's pronouncement, "for three months in fact. Then I said to Roscoe, 'I think you'd better forget the idea that the movie audience has a twelve-year-old mind. Anyone who believes that won't be in pictures very long, in my opinion.' I pointed out how rapidly pictures were improving technically. The studios were also offering better stories all the time, using superior equipment, getting more intelligent directors . . . 'Every time anyone makes another good picture,' I said, 'people with adult minds will come to see it.'"

In time, Arbuckle came around to Keaton's way of seeing things, and the epiphany may have occasioned their first true collaboration. *Oh! Doctor,* their fourth film together, broke the formula Roscoe had seemingly established for his Schenck productions. *Coney Island* moved the series outdoors, where the unusual surroundings took the menu of gags in a new direction. The move to Long Beach brought them the scenic features of Southern California and gave them the world of Jazzville in which to work, but all these films were episodic affairs—in "two parts" as it was commonly stated. That changed with their next picture, a deft parody of cowboy dramas titled *Out West.*

The film's opening sequence was to take place aboard a freight train, Fatty a stowaway avoiding capture by the conductor and his henchmen. Since Buster wasn't required on camera for any of this, it's likely Arbuckle left it to him to visualize and direct the chase, a monumental task given that the action would be staged on the Salt Lake Route through the Mojave Desert south of Las Vegas. Joe Keaton would play the conductor, and there would be a limited amount of time to capture the footage they needed. (Joe would ruefully count three days away from the "Anheuser-Busch pond.") The sequence would have to be thoroughly worked out in advance, and the process would yield what arguably is the first great Keaton gag devised for the screen.

Fatty is hiding inside the engine's near-empty tank, which conceals him until the train stops to take on water. (The introductory title card: "Fatty, a drifter drifting from prairie to town . . .") Having saved himself from near drowning, he makes his way to the caboose, where Joe and his two cohorts are eating lunch. Spying from above, Fatty uses his necktie and a safety pin to fish meat, a coffeepot, and bread from under their noses, but when the pot comes splashing down, they scramble and the pursuit is on. With the four men racing atop the train, Keaton artfully undercranks the action. Losing his grip, Arbuckle tumbles to the desert floor, where, collecting himself, he pauses to have a quick smoke. Here is where Keaton frames a gag on a scale that would become familiar in his later films as a director: With the train racing along in the background, Fatty rolls himself a cigarette, casually striking a match on a passing car. He takes a couple of drags, tosses the butt aside, then gracefully reboards the train as the caboose whizzes by.

Unlike the intimate bits of business Arbuckle often embraced—things he could easily have done in vaudeville—here was a gag that could have been contrived only for the screen. "On the stage, even one as immense as the New York Hippodrome stage, one could show only so much," said Keaton, explaining the very real excitement he felt. "The camera had no such limitations. The whole world was its stage. If you wanted cities, deserts, the Atlantic Ocean, Persia, or the Rocky Mountains for your scenery and background, you merely took your camera to them. In the theatre you had to create an illusion of being on a ship, a railroad train, or an airplane. The camera allowed you to show your audience the real thing: real trains, horses and wagons, snowstorms, floods. Nothing you could stand on, feel, or see was beyond the range of the camera."

As Fatty is pushed off the train, Joe and the others waving a cheerful good-bye, the scene switches to Mad Dog Gulch, the nearest settlement, where Buster is Bill Bullhorn, the cigar-smoking, brandy-guzzling proprietor of the Last Chance Saloon. Steely-eyed—after a little 80-proof eyewash—Bullhorn shoots down a man cheating at poker, examines both hands, and informs the deceased's opponent, "You would've lost anyway." He opens a cellar door, neatly kicks the body through it, dropping a flower from his lapel in after it and doffing his hat respectfully, then pulls the door closed with a lithe foot. As a caricature of the villainous Jack Rance from Belasco's *The Girl of the Golden West*, Keaton instantly takes command of the picture, establishing himself as a star in the making, an eventual challenger to Arbuckle's preeminence and perhaps even Chaplin's.

"[Arbuckle] would turn you loose," he said. "Because he didn't care who got the laughs in his pictures. He wanted 'em in there."

Roscoe made the point himself in a contemporary interview: "I am interested in making good pictures, not pictures good only for self-exploitation."

Wandering the desert, his mouth as dry as cotton, Fatty is spotted by Indians.

"Look! Big fat Paleface!" says one.

"Catch him," orders another. "Plenty food for winter!"

In a hail of arrows, he rolls into the Last Chance, where, guns blazing, he foils a raid by the villainous Al St. John. Fatty, it turns out, is quite the shot in a frenzied sort of way, keeping Bill's top hat aloft with his six guns. ("It has to be an old hat," Keaton said of the bit. "You couldn't use a new hat. Otherwise, you don't get your laugh. Audiences don't like to see things getting spoiled.") Fatty applies for the late bartender's job, quickly developing an attraction to Sue, the Salvation Army girl played by Alice Lake.

Al returns with some local rabble-rousers and drunkenly attempts to take

As the deadly Bill Bullhorn, proprietor of the Last Chance Saloon, Keaton stole the show from Arbuckle and Al St. John in Out West *(1918), a picture he also co-directed.*

advantage of Sue, prompting Bill to order him out. When he is not so easily dissuaded, Fatty suggests they send him on "a visit to the cellar." Bill opens the cellar door welcomingly as Fatty proceeds to smash at least twenty bottles over Al's head. Then he tries shooting him half a dozen times, all to no effect. Desperate, Fatty discovers Al's Achilles' heel—he's ticklish. Finally ejected, Al angrily declares, "They'll pay for this!" Presently, he and his gang are back, and Sue is abducted as Fatty and the others give chase. A chaotic gun battle ensues. Al drags his captive to his hilltop hideout, with Fatty, on horseback, in hot pursuit. Having once again subdued Al by tickling, Fatty finishes the job by shoving the entire cabin down an incline and into the ravine below, leaving the building utterly destroyed and Al in a heap. Back at the summit, Fatty and Alice embrace for the fade.

Not only was *Out West* a wonderfully cohesive film, it was also unlike anything Arbuckle had ever done. As with *Oh! Doctor*, he completely abandoned his default character of an overgrown child, coy and calculating, and Keaton commendably kept him out of a dress, a device that followed him from vaudeville. "Once you've got your realistic character, you've classed yourself," Buster once remarked. "Anytime you put a man in a woman's outfit, you're out of the realism class and you're in *Charley's Aunt*."

The shoot wasn't without its mishaps. The chase Buster staged atop the moving train ended abruptly when Al St. John lost his footing and was thrown fifteen feet to the ground—a fall that could have killed a less durable man. (The *Los Angeles Times* considered his survival "miraculous.") "He was hard as a brick wall and fast on his feet," said Buster admiringly. "No man that size ever took such falls." Alice Lake fell from a horse, Roscoe was injured when a gun fired at close range sent a piece of wadding into his hand, and Keaton himself muffed a jump off a cliff that earned him three days' bed rest.

In a letter to a pal back in Bluffton, Joe Keaton admitted he liked the climate and his new work but bemoaned the fishing to be had in California. "Our latest picture is 'Fatty Out West.' I haven't any part to speak of, but Buster has—it's a scream. I am the conductor on a railroad train. I am glad you liked my first picture, 'The Country Hero,' where they say I handled my daughter pretty rough when I took her out of the water trough. When they told me I was too strenuous, I told 'em that was what they got for sending to Pigeon Hill for a man to play the part who had been fed upon Muskegon Lake walleye, Frank Pascoe's fried perch and with 'Best' to wash it all down. Muskegon climate makes a man feel his powers and stays by him in far countries, and when I rescued the child from the depths of the trough I may have forgotten myself for the moment."

Released nationwide on January 21, 1918, *Out West* enjoyed the best reception of any Arbuckle picture since *The Butcher Boy*. The film, said *Variety,* "hits a better comedy tempo than any of his recent productions."

Billboard: "Nothing of the usual stuff of which comedies are made is to be found in Fatty Arbuckle's new western film. *Out West* is new. And from the moment when Fatty is first shown, hiding in a locomotive tank, to the final fade-out it sparkles with fun and action and originality."

Motography: "This is bound to be a sure fire hit. It is a departure from what the big comedian has done in the past, and its burlesque on the familiar western dance hall with its two-gun man made even the sometimes hard-hearted and unrelenting reviewers and critics laugh."

Exhibitors, normally the toughest of audiences, were equally enthusiastic.

"The star's best yet," reported a manager from Payson, Utah. "Fatty takes the first seat for this. Brought more laughs than any other picture I've run."

Another from Viroqua, Wisconsin: "About the best Arbuckle comedy to date. Business big. Many stayed for the second show."

Arbuckle was contemplating the start of his next picture when Charlie Chaplin, accompanied by his manager Alf Reeves, stopped by the Balboa

Charles Chaplin tours the Balboa Studio on January 5, 1918. From left: Keaton; Alf Reeves, general manager of the Chaplin Film Corporation; Chaplin; studio executive H. O. Stechan; H. M. Horkheimer; Al Gilmore (later to become Keaton's assistant director); and Lou Anger.

lot for a visit with his Sennett colleague, whose old trousers he supposedly used in building his famous tramp's outfit. Roscoe was vacationing in San Francisco, however, and it fell to the rest of the company to welcome the world's most popular comedian.

Chaplin, whom Keaton loved but had never met, was riding high: Having built a new studio complex in Hollywood, a quaint affair designed to look from the street like a row of English cottages, he had just completed his first production, *A Dog's Life,* under a million-dollar contract with First National. The contrasts between the two men were stark: Arbuckle, a salaried employee of Comique, was turning out ten comedies a year in rented space at an annual cost of $300,000. Chaplin, as his own producer, was committed to eight pictures a year for First National, each bringing an advance of $125,000 and a 50 percent share of the net profits. Keaton, who lacked Chaplin's business acumen, could admire the independence he achieved without envying the money. All that mattered to Buster was having the wherewithal to put his increasingly elaborate ideas on-screen. As Arbuckle once observed, he "lived in the camera."

Normally, the Arbuckle comedies were budgeted at $30,000 apiece, but costs for both *Country Hero* and *Out West* approached $35,000. According to Arbuckle, it took $1,000 just to hire a train, extras cost $5 a head (plus costuming), and then there were the exterior sets for Jazzville and, for *Out West*, Mad Dog Gulch, which was built at nearby Signal Hill, where the Horkheimers controlled eleven rustic acres. In an apparent effort to offset cost overruns, the next Comique short, *The Bell Boy*, was conceived as an interior job, the action taking place largely inside the Elk's Head Hotel in the village of Ouch Gosh, Pennsyltucky. A redressed Jazzville would serve as the background for incidental exteriors and, in place of a train, an old horsecar would trundle along a makeshift track. In such a contained environment, Arbuckle was truly in his element.

The Bell Boy was packed with inventive miniatures. Doubling as the hotel barber, Fatty trims "Jassrutin the Mad Monkey" (a grotesquely bearded customer) in stages, turning him into a succession of historic figures—General Grant, complete with cigar, Abe Lincoln, and finally the Kaiser, who gets finished off with a quartet of custard pies. The hotel elevator is powered by desk clerk Al St. John's old horse, who stands at the ready in the street outside. Joe Keaton, playing a top-hatted banker, engages in an energetic kicking routine with his son that is probably as close as they ever came to committing a flash of their vaudeville act to film. As Fatty's sidekick, Buster gets his head caught between floors when the elevator stalls, and his pal tries dislodging it with a wooden plank. In the confusion, Miss Cutie Cuticle, the inn's new manicurist, seesaws twelve feet into the air, landing on the elk's head overlooking the hotel lobby, and Buster gets himself caught on the antlers trying to rescue her. All the while, he and Fatty compete for her attention.

"The funniest-looking accident we ever had was when [we were] making *The Bell Boy*," said Alice Lake. "A crazy old elevator we were using fell to pieces and I was dangling in mid-air on the end of a rope. One of the boys was inside of what was left of the elevator and I was left whirling around in space while he was being rescued from the debris."

She added: "I've noticed this about comedies: The gags that seem funniest at the studio will often look dead on the screen, while something that hasn't made you smile on the set will make you shriek with laughter when you see it in the picture."

If indeed *The Bell Boy* was conceived as a budget job, the plan went awry when the picture's scope predictably expanded for the second half. Fatty hatches a plot to gain Miss Cuticle's notice by having Al and Buster stage a bank robbery he can foil, but he doesn't count on a crew of real crooks knocking over the Last National at the very same time. The furious clash between the pretend bad guys and the real ones has Keaton bounding over walls and partitions while Al tries clobbering the various perps with anything at hand, frequently missing his targets completely and scoring direct hits on Fatty. The spectacular climax comes when the crooks commandeer the horsecar and make their escape, running it up a steep ridge on Signal Hill.

"The big moment was supposed to come near the top of the hill when the traces broke, jerking the driver through the air so that he landed squarely on the horse's back," Buster related. "Meanwhile, the horsecar with the bandits still aboard rolled downhill right into the bank they'd just held up. But the driver missed the horse's back the first time he tried it. When the driver proved a bit shy about repeating the jump, I offered to double for him. It was a tough jump to make because the horse had to be kept four and a half feet ahead of the car. This prevented his kicking the front of it with his hind hoofs. I had the prop man put a box in the car for me to stand on. This enabled me to make a better take-off. I also wound the reins tightly around my wrists so they couldn't slip."

Without blinders, the horse could see Buster coming, and the moment he jumped, the animal bolted, dragging him nearly the length of a city block before anyone could stop them. Unhurt, Buster accomplished the impressive stunt on the second try, sending the car hurtling backward down the hill toward the bank and the hotel beyond it. Moments later, it smashes through the wall of the Elk's Head and rolls to a stop in the middle of the lobby, sending guests scattering amid all the dust and the wreckage as Fatty and the others descend upon the criminals. Amply rewarded for his bravery, he claims the girl and a tidy reward at the climax.

Also in *The Bell Boy* was Natalie Talmadge, who had transitioned to the role of Roscoe Arbuckle's private secretary. Nate had appeared briefly in *His Wedding Night, Fatty in Coney Island,* and *A Country Hero* and was, with her rainbow-colored knitting bag, a constant presence on the Balboa lot. Released on March 11, *The Bell Boy* was greeted with a level of excitement normally reserved for the Chaplin comedies. *Variety* praised it as "excruciatingly funny" and went on to report the "rapid, acrobatic comedy of these three slapstick comedians had the audience in hysterics at the [New York] Rialto Sunday afternoon."

A hardened exhibitor in Michigan pronounced it "the best comedy Arbuckle has ever made," while another in Omaha went even further: "I never saw a better comedy in my life than *The Bell Boy* with Fatty Arbuckle, yet it's clean, full of action, and MAKES YOU LAUGH."

As Peter Milne in *Motion Picture News* concluded, "A better comedy than *The Bell Boy* would be hard to find, and this statement may be taken to include the Chaplins and the Sennetts."

If *The Bell Boy* wasn't quite the exercise in cut-rate filmmaking it was originally intended to be, Arbuckle's next, *Moonshine,* was bargain basement, a minimalist goof on movie melodramas that drew its scenery not from the carpentry shop but from the natural splendor of the San Gabriel Canyon forty miles northeast of Long Beach. Spring rains complicated the shoot, but the result was another unusual comedy, one in which the conventions of screen drama were held up to ridicule, an insider's take that threatened at times to fly completely over the heads of Arbuckle's devoted audience.

The film opens with a "rehearsal" of a scene with two bootleggers, the mechanized entrance to their hideout "the director's idea." An actor's dive into a river is celebrated in an intertitle as a great stunt. "His paycheck is well earned." Fatty is the captain of the revenuers and Buster his faithful lieutenant. The call for reinforcements triggers a memorable sight gag—the emergence of fifty deputy agents from the same car in which Fatty and Buster arrived, a basic split-screen effect for which the car was stabilized with jacks and a portion of the image blocked off. Al St. John appears as Alice's persistent suitor and mugs ferociously into the camera. She fights him off, gets the better of him, then her father (Charles Dudley) comes on the scene.

"Calm yourself, my child," he says. "Wait until you're married to hit him as much as you wish."

Alice gets spanked, choked, and tossed into the river and endures it all in high style, declaring her love for Fatty.

"This is absurd," complains Dudley. "You abuse my daughter and she embraces you."

Fatty explains, "This is only a two-reel short. No time for preliminary love scenes."

Dudley responds: "In that case, go on . . . I don't care. I don't want to ruin your masterpiece."

Too clever for its own good, *Moonshine* proved a disappointment to some exhibitors after the high-water marks of *Out West* and *The Bell Boy.* Yet all reported big business, with some theaters billing the Comique two-reelers over the feature films they accompanied. With *Moonshine* in distribution, the last Arbuckle of the season became *Good Night Nurse,* another location job filmed at the Arrowhead Hot Springs resort at the foot of the San Bernardino Mountains. After opening with an imaginative drunk sequence, the picture reverts to the old Sennett mainstays of slapstick and drag as Fatty's wife ships him off to a drying-out clinic to kick the habit. Unduly impressed, *Variety*'s Josh Lowe pronounced it "the best of Arbuckle's current Paramount series" after viewing it alone in a New York projection room. "The doctor who operates is Buster Keaton and the intern is Al St. John. No one say more?"

In late April, while *Moonshine* was being readied for release, Joe and Myra Keaton motored up to Los Angeles to replenish the home bar, the one critical disadvantage to living in Long Beach being that it was a dry city. Joseph Furness, their host at the Continental Hotel, knowing that Joe was a devoted Elk, subjected him to a Red Cross benefit performance that sent him fleeing the scene at half past nine, insisting that Furness at least find him somewhere he could get his feet wet. Patsy Smith of *Variety* caught up with Joe long enough to ask how he liked working in pictures.

"Oh, it's all right," he conceded, "if Arbuckle wouldn't try and tell me how to kick my boy. Hell, ain't I been kicking him all his life?"

The great days of making comedy shorts in Long Beach couldn't last. The United States declared war on Germany the same month Buster Keaton first stepped before a camera, and he registered for the draft in June 1917. Now, with the Selective Service Act supplying American soldiers at the rate of more than six thousand a day, the war in Europe was threatening the smooth-running Comique assembly line. Roscoe Arbuckle himself was safe, his draft board having determined that he was "a little overweight to do private duty." Buster, however, was classified 1-A in April 1918 and called to duty in June. Transferred from New York to the local draft board in Long Beach, he sought, and was granted, a two-week delay on induction so that he could complete the first picture of the 1918–19 season, a brilliant return to form for Arbuckle and company titled *The Cook.*

In late May, Patsy Smith had a gloomy letter from Joe Keaton, who let her know he was giving up on the movies. "Buster has joined the submarine service at San Pedro," she reported in her "Among the Women" column, "and Joe's 'War Garden' at Long Beach is all shot to pieces. He can't even laugh at the practical joker who planted garlic among his sweet-smelling vegetables and flowers. Joe's mother died in Sacramento a few weeks ago and his heart is pretty full of sorrow just now. Back to Muskegon for Joe and Myra to join Jingles and Louise."

6

Getting Restless

ROSCOE ARBUCKLE'S *The Cook,* a slick reworking of his late Sennett comedy *The Waiters' Ball,* was destined to be the last Comique short made at the Balboa studio. Financially, the Horkheimers were unable to weather the drop in cash flow that accompanied America's entry into the war. Suddenly, they found themselves with more product on hand than they could possibly place. Finally, on March 25, 1918, while *Moonshine* was being filmed out on location, the sole owners of the Balboa Amusement Producing Company—the two Horkheimer brothers and their sister, Florence—surrendered to voluntary bankruptcy, and control of the studio passed to the Los Angeles Wholesalers Board of Trade. Besides Comique, the production companies of actresses Kathleen Clifford and Anita King were still in residence, as was an obscure outfit called the Mona Lisa Company. Essential purchases had to be made on a cash-only basis, and things got so bad that Arbuckle was forced to issue a statement in mid-April emphasizing he had no ownership stake in the company but was merely a tenant renting space— sometimes for as much as $4,500 a week.

In February, while Arbuckle was shooting *The Bell Boy,* the chamber of commerce of the city of Santa Ana, where both Roscoe and Al St. John spent their boyhoods, made a formal proposal to lure the Comique production team eastward. There was also interest from Glendale and Culver City, but Arbuckle, who was married in Long Beach in 1908, had a sentimental attachment to the place, owned a house there, and liked having the ocean nearby. Despite the undeniable quality of *The Cook,* a malaise settled over the company, in large part because they were about to lose Buster Keaton just as he and Arbuckle had settled into working as a precision comedy team, not simply as star and support.

With the first part of *The Cook* set in the kitchen and dining room of an upscale restaurant, Fatty the cook and Buster the waiter toss around cups of coffee, bowls of soup, plates of stew, and glasses of milk as gracefully as if they were handling billiard balls. Keaton adroitly trades steps with the dancer in the floor show, Arbuckle picking up the rhythms of the band in the kitchen and fashioning a risqué costume, something other than plain drag, from the cookware at hand. It's all jazzy and joyous, the sort of action that comes from a pair of comics in perfect sync with each other, something wondrous that only happens organically. Seamlessly, Arbuckle slips into a parody of his Long Beach neighbor Theda Bara, melding her Cleopatra from the previous year with the Salome she was then filming, the head of St. John the Baptist delivered to her in the form of an enormous cabbage, the asp that takes her life a handy string of sausages.

The story in its final minutes shifts to the seashore and the Long Beach Pike, with its concessions, its goat carts, and its landmark roller coaster, the Jackrabbit Racer. When these scenes were made, Keaton was literally on borrowed time and the company was working feverishly to get the film in the can. A woman journalist visiting the location observed an Arbuckle "like an island entirely surrounded by children," a sprinkling of adults visible only upon closer examination. Roscoe, seated in a lifeboat with his pit bull terrier Luke at his side, is stressed, describing himself as "in the midst of a sea of troubles." When pressed, he is vague: "Oh, one thing or another. Some props have to be fixed up—some spoiled film—just the usual lot of a film actor." He soon takes her off to a boat shelter where there is little escape from the crowd, which surges and ebbs, and where Keaton and Al St. John are solemnly clustered with Lou Anger. "In a corner sat little Alice Lake, peach-like, diminutive, blissfully negotiating a Liberty steak sandwich as big as her hand."

The Cook was completed on Saturday, July 6, 1918, and the night was devoted to a farewell party thrown in Buster's honor at Gus Mann's Jewel City Cafe, a swank waterfront nightspot in neighboring Seal Beach. The entire Arbuckle company was there, as were spouses, girlfriends, and business associates from Los Angeles. The highlight of the event was an impromptu minstrel show in which Roscoe served as interlocutor. The end men, in addition to Buster, were Al St. John, Lou Anger, and Sennett director Eddie Cline, whose Keystone comedies were also distributed by

Arbuckle, Al St. John, Keaton, and Luke pose on the sand at Long Beach during the filming of The Cook *(1918).*

Paramount. Keaton, clad in a tablecloth, a napkin hanging from each ear, performed his snake dance from *A Country Hero* while wielding a string of hot dogs. At the end of the evening, Roscoe presented him with a new wallet containing $100 to defray camp expenses. Keaton reported to the draft board in Long Beach the following day.

. . .

Natalie Talmadge lived in Joe and Myra Keaton's extra bedroom while work-ing for Roscoe Arbuckle, but once the Keatons returned to Muskegon and Buster's induction was imminent, there was little to keep her in California. Spring visits from her sisters convinced her she might have a future in pic-tures after all, and so when Dutch traveled east in early July, just days prior to the completion of *The Cook,* Nate went with her. In Chicago, she made time to visit Jingles Jungle, where she showed Myra Keaton a signet ring she was sending Buster for good luck. Decades later, Myra would remember thinking: *A ring will soon be going the other way, looks like to me.*

Camp Kearny, a massive tent city on a mesa north of San Diego, was where Joseph Frank Keaton formally entered the U.S. Army on July 8, 1918. After a few days in quarantine, he was vaccinated in double doses and subjected to ten days of rudimentary drills with the aim of shipping him and the rest of the Fortieth Division off to France as quickly as possible. A new German offensive was under way, and the Allied response was to be overwhelming manpower. On July 24, he was assigned to the 159th Infantry, Company C, the company Roscoe Arbuckle had adopted as "little brothers" just two months earlier. The Fortieth Division was famously known as the Sunshine Division because it was assembled from the California National Guard and those of other western states.

Keaton, who took the responsibility of soldiering as seriously as he did his comedy, felt ridiculous in the oversize uniform he was issued. "My pants were too long, my coat looked like a sack, and wrapping army put-tees around my legs was a trick I never mastered." He studied Morse code, map reading, and semaphore signaling when no one else seemed to care about such things. "On mastering these subjects I discovered I was the best-informed private in my outfit. I never met an enlisted man, including some who had joined up during the Spanish-American War, who had more than glanced occasionally at an Army training manual."

They left Camp Kearny by rail on July 28, arriving at Camp Mills, Long Island, a week later. There they were subjected to more inoculations and equipped for overseas duty. Natalie, it turned out, was only ten miles away, staying at her sister Norma's place in Bayside. Buster finagled a phone call to the Schenck estate, and she grandly arrived at the camp's Hostess

House in the family's chauffeured Packard as might a visiting dignitary. Confined to base, her entrance gave Buster an idea. Due to the summer heat, officers weren't wearing their jackets, and their khaki shirts and black knit ties looked the same as everyone else's. "If I rolled out of camp with my girl in that eye-popping car I might easily get by the sentries, it seemed to me. I would not, after all, be wearing my private's overseas cap or my oversize jacket. Unless one of the sentries looked over the side of the car, he would never see my baggy pants and clodhopper hobnailed boots."

In what could have been a scene from one of his later movies, Keaton got into the car and, languidly saluting as officers did, passed through both the inner- and outer-sentry stations completely undetected. Having successfully cleared the perimeter of the camp, he and Natalie headed south to Long Beach, where a restaurant and dance hall called Castles by the Sea awaited. "We had a wonderful eight or ten hours together that day. My girl paid the check as I didn't have enough money on me." Then they drove back to Camp Mills, where the sentries saluted him smartly.

Keaton shipped out a day or two later on the HMS *Otranto,* a Royal Navy troopship that had earlier seen passenger service. The wartime sleeping arrangements were spare: hammocks strung three across and stacked in four claustrophobic tiers. ("The cooties we were to know so intimately later were already on board.") At Liverpool, they were walked to a rest camp, where they were served yellow cheese, hardtack biscuits, and unsweetened tea, then sent via rail to Southampton, where they were staged for transport across the English Channel into France. The boat was packed so tightly, he remembered, they had to endure the cross standing up. When they reached Le Havre, they were marched eight miles to another camp, where Keaton got his first taste of sleeping in the Gallic elements and, later, on the chilly floors of old mills, barns, and stables. "There is always a draft close to the floor of such farm buildings, and I soon developed a cold which imperiled my hearing. In that war we saw little but rain and mud."

Moved by rail in the French boxcars known as forty-and-eights (because they were designed to carry either forty men or eight horses), they spent the next two months in and around the French village of Nérondes. "Because of my size," said Keaton, "I was the last man in the last squad. When we were marching down French roads there would be a crowd of kids watching us. I'd stump my toe and fall down . . . make it look like an accident, you know. Then I'd run to catch up with the file and fall down again. After a while there would be another regiment of kids following us." He proved himself as a team leader, his mime skills enabling him to communicate effectively with the locals, and was eventually promoted to the rank of corporal. The regiment, now part of the Sixth Depot Division, sent four-fifths of its personnel to the front line as replacements, many of whom were subsequently killed or wounded. Miraculously, Keaton never saw any actual fighting: "[I got] just close enough to hear it, but by the time I hit the front, the Germans were in retreat, which was a great thing. I was tickled to death at that."

With the war winding down, they were moved at the end of October to Saleux, near Amiens, where the regiment became part of the Second Corps, which had suffered heavy losses in the pivotal Battle of St. Quentin Canal. The armistice with Germany was signed at Compiègne eleven days later.

Joe Keaton's retirement from the picture business was the subject of a June article in the *Muskegon Daily Times*. "Buster is fast winning his way to a stellar position," the paper reported. "He and 'Fatty' Arbuckle have done their best to make a movie actor of Joe, but Joe quit. You could never make Joe believe in a hundred years that there is any sense in that movie game." Now referring to himself as "Captain Joe Keaton, campaign manager of William Flemen for commodore of the T.C.Y.C.," he was eager to get home to Bluffton in time for the start of the summer season. "If you see anyone on the stern of the Goodrich boat on the morn of June 7 trolling, it will be me."

It wasn't long after Joe's reappearance at Edgewater that his pal Flemen got him a job at the Linderman Machine Company, where some year-round residents of the theatrical colony, such as Pop Millard and his daughter, Mildred, were contributing to the war effort. Put to work in munitions, Joe personally signed every shell he produced with the chalk inscription "GIVE 'EM HELL BUSTER!" According to Joe, it was while he was working at Linderman that a telegram came from Will Rogers:

I HEAR YOU ARE WORKING IN A FOUNDRY STOP
WHAT WAGES DO YOU GET

                                                            BILL

The Keatons had known Rogers since 1905, when he was doing a fancy roping act on a bill they shared in Pittsburgh. Joe, in fact, claimed he was present when Rogers uttered his first words on a vaudeville stage: "A feller up here doesn't have such an easy time. If he misses a trick, he can't cuss."

Rogers was on his way to New York, and Joe referred him to Carl Ehrich on Thirty-Eighth Street, scribbling an endorsement on a 3 Keatons business card. Years later, when Rogers' wire arrived, he responded:

THIRTY FIVE CENTS AN HOUR STOP FAMILY ALL
RIGHT STOP BUSTER IS IN THE TRENCHES AND I AM
MAKING THE CANNONS FOR HIM

JOE

Rogers' reply:

I WILL PAY YOU FIFTY CENTS AN HOUR TO QUIT
COME ON TO NEW YORK

BILL

Rogers went so far as to scratch out an employment contract, but Joe didn't need the money so much as a way to do his patriotic duty. He and Myra still owned a number of properties, and Joe Schenck was sending them twenty-five dollars a week while Buster was away in the service. When Rogers was next in Chicago with the *Ziegfeld Follies,* he threw a party at a place known as Madame Gaufanti's, and Joe made his entrance just as things were getting started. "Joe hooks his foot around Bill's neck," *Billboard* columnist W. H. "Bill" Rice recounted, "much to the horror of Mrs. Rogers. Joe said: 'Mother and I are over at Muskegon making bullets and the boys are in France shooting them.' Will had sent him $50 for a Christmas present and he came over on the boat to thank him. I had the pleasure of taking him back to the boat in a snowstorm and locked him in his cabin."

All that remained for Joe's elder son was the part about getting home. The war ended sooner and more abruptly than anyone thought possible, and planning for such an unprecedented demobilization was far from complete. Overcrowding, bad weather, and the threat of influenza were common to all the camps. Abruptly, priorities shifted to education and entertainment for thousands of restless troops eager to leave. "Our division did a lot," Buster said, "same as the other divisions. Headquarters troop sent out to find what talents you've got throughout the division, assembled them all at headquarters, put them under command of a chaplain, gave them a regimental band to travel with them in trucks, and tried to produce a show—just to entertain the different places around your section—while we're all waiting for boats

Corporal Joseph F. Keaton (center) in France as a member of the Sunshine Players.

to go home. There was no money donated, no scenery, no props, no nothing. And a division in the first World War ran around thirty-eight thousand men, almost double what it was in the second one. So out of that they managed to find around twenty-two men that could sing or dance or do something. We organized a minstrel show. Oh, we'd probably play about three camps a week and always get back to our own base."

They called the troupe the Sunshine Players and titled the loosely organized show they gave *AWOL To-night*. Arthur Penney of the 115th Train Headquarters wrote and produced the minstrel sketch and sang bass solos. Otto Pincher, also of Los Angeles, did a monologue. Keaton told jokes and perfected a version of his snake dance, which came to be known in the Fortieth Division as "Princess Rajah." Draped in dog tags and mess kits, he made the bit so popular he was asked to perform it at private functions, including at least one dinner given for a brigadier general. After having made a hit with the brass that night, he was offered a ride back to camp in the general's official car. Once on the road, he induced the orderly driving to make a detour to the town square in Bordeaux and the Hotel Grand. "None of the carousing privates, corporals, sergeants, and young officers there had seen a general for six months, and they all jumped to their feet as the car stopped before the hotel." The crowd fell silent as the orderly, with considerable fanfare, got out, hurried around, opened the door, and stood at attention. After a pause, Keaton, bedraggled in his sagging trousers, knotted puttees, shrunken cap, and outsize boots, stepped into view and airily said, "I won't need you anymore this evening." He got about fifteen feet toward the entrance to the hotel before he was recognized and showered with bottles, eggs, apples, and curses.

In December, he was assigned to a train carrying some nine hundred wounded men to a redistribution center at Le Mans. As the only noncommissioned man on the trip, he was supposed to make the return connection to Amiens at Paris—a connection he conspired to miss. Paris was out of bounds, making him technically AWOL, but having just been paid, he was able to treat himself and some buddies to a good meal and a room at the elegant old Hotel Brighton. It was a welcome respite from months of sleeping on hard, chilly surfaces, and it underscored just how bad his hearing had gotten. "Before I was overseas a month my superiors had to shout orders at me." Now he was almost stone-deaf, the result of a lingering low-grade infection, and the fear of remaining so was driving him crazy. "The army doctors said they had never seen a case like mine, and I guess they were telling the truth, for none of them were able to do anything for me."

On December 27, the regiment was moved from Amiens to Cadillac, south of Bordeaux, to await transport back to the United States, and on February 20, 1919, Keaton was transferred to an embarkation camp. A month later, on March 22, he finally sailed for home aboard the USS *Edgar F. Luckenbach,* a commercial cargo ship that had been chartered by the army as a troop transport. Loaded down with nearly 2,300 troops, 2,036 of whom were the officers and men of the 159th Infantry, the *Luckenbach* took two full weeks to make the crossing to New York.*

Upon landing in Brooklyn, Keaton was sent to a debarkation hospital on Sixth Avenue in what had formerly been the Siegel-Cooper building. Specialists told him he would have to remain under observation for a while, but that with proper treatment his hearing would be restored. As soon as he could, he called Natalie on Long Island. Joe Schenck's Times Square office was closer, so she asked him to hurry over.

"You look terribly peaked, Buster," Schenck said sadly. "You've lost so much weight. I never saw you look so sick and miserable."

"Why shouldn't I look miserable—with my beauty gone forever?"

Schenck ignored the wisecrack. "Of course you haven't any money," he said, handing over all the bills in his wallet.

---

* Of the 2,036 men of the 159th Infantry aboard the ship, only 561 were native sons. The rest were replacements for those killed or wounded in action.

The first thing Keaton bought with the money was a new uniform and shoes that fit. He wore them the night he had dinner with Nat (as he always called her) and Peg Talmadge in their apartment at the Hotel Savoy. ("He used to come home with her for dinner now and then, and all three of the girls were quite devoted to him," Peg commented, "but I cannot remember that I ever thought of his comings and goings as of any special import.") After ten days in New York, he was transferred to the three-thousand-bed receiving hospital at Fort McHenry, Maryland, where his hearing and general health were judged to be much improved. One day, the doctors at the hospital okayed a walk, and Buster headed for the Maryland Theatre on Franklin Street, the house the Keatons always played in Baltimore. "I walked through that stage door and the house manager, the crew, the orchestra boys, and the acts greeted me like a long lost pal." To his delight, tenor Artie Mehlinger, an old friend, was on the bill with his partner George Meyer, and he watched their act, a "musical mélange," from the wings.

After a few days, Keaton was returned to New York. He should have been mustered out with the rest of the Fortieth Division at Camp Kearny, but on some paperwork he had given Muskegon as his home, so he was instead sent to Camp Custer at Battle Creek, Michigan, about a hundred miles southeast of Bluffton. At Custer he was processed, discharged, and issued a cash payment of $220.75 that included a $60 travel bonus. "The mistake enabled me to see my folks and our old neighbors, but I was so eager to get back to work that I stayed in Muskegon only three days." He boarded the California Limited in Chicago on May 2, 1919, and arrived back home in Los Angeles on the sixth. He had been gone almost exactly ten months.

A lot had changed for Roscoe Arbuckle in the interim. By the time he bid farewell to Buster Keaton, he had already lost Joe Keaton, Natalie Talmadge, and scenario editor Herbert Warren, and would soon lose publicist Paul "Scoop" Conlin as well as Alice Lake. The pleasant Balboa studio was no longer tenable as a base of operations, and it's significant that while neither of the Horkheimer brothers was present for Buster's party at the Jewel City Cafe, W. A. S. Douglas, president of the Diando Film Corporation, was. Diando was where Baby Marie Osborne landed when she left Balboa, her father, Leon T. Osborne, being vice president and co-owner of the new concern. Douglas and Osborne took over the former Kalem studio in Glendale, thirty miles north of Long Beach, and when Arbuckle announced on

July 17, 1918, that he was leaving Long Beach "for purely business reasons," he indicated that he and his staff would be moving "temporarily" to Diando.

The arrangement lasted all of one picture, a western titled *The Sheriff*, in which a Black child called Snowball and Arbuckle's dog, Luke, did their best to compensate for Buster's absence. The next one, *Camping Out,* was shot on Catalina Island and served as Alice Lake's swan song before moving into features. By the time of *Love,* Arbuckle's third as a transient filmmaker, the company had set up shop at the old Bison Pacific Coast Studios on a stretch of Allesandro Street that was home to a number of early studios, including Selig Polyscope, where Roscoe appeared in some of his earliest comedies, and the Mack Sennett lot where he gained fame as Mabel Normand's frequent co-star.

Following the completion of *Love,* Arbuckle, bound for New York, converged with Joe Schenck and Adolph Zukor in Kansas City to sign contracts that had been in the works for eight weeks. The new agreement was valued at $3 million over thirty-six months, a figure Zukor confirmed in a wire to Famous Players-Lasky, which would continue to distribute the Fatty Arbuckle comedies under the Paramount name. Two months later, with some of that money burning a hole in his pocket, Arbuckle closed a deal to buy the Vernon Tigers of the Pacific Coast League, something he admitted he did just to please Lou Anger, a baseball bug who would act as the team's general manager. When Buster reappeared in May, having turned down offers from both William Fox and Warner Bros., he was put to work clowning with Roscoe and Al St. John at the season opener, suiting up in team colors and wielding a bat and ball made of plaster. Arbuckle's replacement for Alice Lake, an actress named Molly Malone, served as the team's mascot, and those in the stands included stage and screen star Bessie Barriscale, actors Jack Pickford and Lew Cody, and Fox cowboy hero Tom Mix.

Keaton later said he was offered $1,000 a week to jump ship, but his loyalty to Schenck and Arbuckle trumped money, and he stuck with the $150 a week he was getting when he left for Camp Kearny. He knew that big changes were afoot, because Arbuckle was keen to move into features and play more sophisticated roles. Al St. John was also getting restless, and it would be only a matter of time before he went out on his own.

In June, work commenced at Pacific Coast on *Back Stage,* the second comedy owed under Arbuckle's new agreement with Zukor and Famous Players. Fatty is stage manager of the Hickville Bijou, where Buster and Al St. John are stagehands contending with the week's arrivals: Julius Hamlet

Omelette, a pompous actor; Clarence Marmalade, an eccentric dancer and high kicker in the tradition of Joe Keaton; and a malevolent strongman, Professor Onion, who lords it over his diminutive assistant (Molly Malone). Given the simplicity of the setup, the picture didn't come together easily. Roscoe fell ill with what was feared to be appendicitis, and filming extended into August, something of a record for an Arbuckle two-reeler. The second half of the picture became a performance executed by Fatty and his stage crew when the real actors walk out, Keaton again falling back on a drag dance routine, this time acting Fatima to Arbuckle's King Murad.

A troubled production redeemed by its acrobatics, *Back Stage* drew a mixed reception from audiences and exhibitors, due in part, no doubt, to the shooting of Molly Malone by an enraged Professor Onion. Left for dead amid the climactic slapstick, she is visited in the hospital by Fatty at the fade-out, but the cold-blooded attack made for a dark, unsettling turn to an otherwise lighthearted story. *Back Stage* was the last film Arbuckle would make on Allesandro Street, a new plant having been secured in Culver City. The move to the Henry Lehrman studio* on Washington Boulevard, with its commodious stage and modern amenities, was announced in July while *Back Stage* was still in production, and came just a day after the news that Al St. John had been signed to a five-year contract by Warner Bros.

When they were working at Balboa, Keaton lived for a while with Arbuckle in an ocean-view home he owned near the studio. Roscoe hated being alone, and always wanted people and a certain level of commotion around him. (When he first hit town, he had scenario editor Herbert Warren and his wife, Valerie Bergere, sharing quarters with him, while Buster took an apartment on Third Street.) The two men were inseparable. They socialized together, traveled together, worked together.

"Arbuckle was that rarity," said Keaton, "a truly jolly fat man. He had no meanness, malice, or jealousy in him. Everything seemed to amuse and delight him. He was free with his advice and too free in spending and lending money. I could not have found a better-natured man to teach me the movie business, or a more knowledgeable one. We never had an argument."

Back from the war, Keaton saw that Arbuckle was in a state of flux,

---

* Henry Lehrman (1886–1946) was regarded by Arbuckle as a mentor when the two men were together at Keystone. "All my mechanical knowledge of pictures I learned under the direction of Lehrman, who directed all but about two of my pictures," he said. When Arbuckle rented the Lehrman studio, he suggested it wasn't just loyalty that influenced the decision: "It was the only way I could get back money he owed me."

unsettled at work and in search of a new place to live. At the Hollywood Hotel, Buster shared a room with an actor named Ward Crane, who was a protégé of Allan Dwan's, but he was just as liable to end up on someone's couch for the night.

"Buster was probably the original man who came to dinner," said actress Viola Dana, who had a house she called Heartsease in Hollywood Heights. "My brother-in-law [director Bernard Durning] brought him home for dinner one night and he stayed for [months]. And, of course, Buster became one of the family. My mother was crazy about him—he was like a son to her—and wherever we moved, we figured on Buster. I think the extent of his wardrobe was a toothbrush, which he carried in his pocket."

Viola Dana, née Flugrath, was two years younger than Buster but entered show business at around the same age, dancing at Coney Island for tossed coins at the age of three. She was in "The Littlest Rebel" when it was a vaudeville sketch and, with her younger sister, Leonie (later the actress Shirley Mason), in a 1905 revival of *Rip Van Winkle*. She acted in road companies with such stars as Dustin Farnum and William Faversham, and made her screen debut in 1910 in a four-scene version of *A Christmas Carol* for the Edison Company. She alternated between the stage and screen, and at fifteen was cast by producer Arthur Hopkins and playwright Eleanor Gates in *The Poor Little Rich Girl,* a role that followed her well into adulthood. It was at the Edison studio that she met her future husband, the casting office's John Collins, who would go on to direct a number of her films. Collins died in the influenza pandemic of 1918, leaving her a widow at the age of twenty-one.

Actress Viola Dana and Keaton shared a great affection for each other. Into her late eighties she was still speaking fondly of him.

"Vi" Dana was a striking screen beauty, a vivacious four-eleven with big green eyes, thick brown hair, and a ribald sense of humor. Principally a tragedian, she was making a move into comedies when she met Buster Keaton, and the two of them hit it off instantly. "I like you," she said to him. "We like us," he responded. Buster thought her funny and game in the same way Alice Lake was, willing to try practically anything. She pitched for the Metro ball team in high heels, bobbed her hair before it was fashionable, and could do backflips and cartwheels, and walk on her hands.

"The four of us," she said, "used to go out together: Buster and myself, Roscoe and Alice. Buster and I were what the fan magazines used to call an *item*. It was all harmless fun, really."

Natalie Talmadge was still on the East Coast, playing supporting roles in her sisters' movies—*The Isle of Conquest* with Norma, *A Temperamental Wife* and *The Love Expert* with Dutch. She and Buster kept in touch with letters and postcards, but except for the few days they shared in New York, they hadn't seen each other in more than a year. Meanwhile, Baron Long's Ship Cafe in the seaside resort town of Venice became a second home for Keaton, Dana, Arbuckle, and their circle of friends.

"Venice was what we called a 'wet' town," Vi said, recalling it as the west side's answer to Seal Beach. "You could drink there, and many of us got drunk there. A lot of cash flowed across the counter. . . . Roscoe loved to play the host, to circulate amongst the tables, have a few laughs, and pour a few drinks. By the third trip around, we saw that he was beginning to get a little tipsy. He would start to complain about the sea breeze, and how it was making him dizzy."

A new picture began in Culver City, but now there was just Arbuckle and Keaton to do the heavy lifting, with rubbery Jack Coogan brought into the fold to play Al St. John's parts, Coogan having essayed the role of the eccentric dancer—a "sis" in contemporary parlance—in *Back Stage*. The film was called *The Hayseed*, yet another story set in the rural equivalent of Jazzville, where Fatty works out of the general store and delivers the mail with Buster's assistance. Coogan is the heavy, a crooked sheriff after the hand of Molly Malone, while Arbuckle's dog, Luke, saves the day, drawing nearly as much screen time as Keaton himself. The result was well received, as thorough an Arbuckle subject as any produced under the Comique label. Buster brought the knockabout and some clever broom work, but the picture emerged as Fatty's from start to finish, reflecting Arbuckle's determination to play a more rounded character, even when shading took precious screen time away from the usual horseplay. Paramount headlined an ad aimed at exhibitors with the words "He's Human" and accompanied it with a shot of the star giving Luke a big, fervent hug. "That's one reason millions crowd to see any Fatty Arbuckle picture. And he's funny!" Mentioning the comedy in *The Hayseed* came almost as an afterthought, yet *Variety*, in catching a showing at New York's Rivoli Theatre, calculated a laugh every forty-five seconds.

"You only star in movies from picture to picture," Arbuckle said. "If two or three pictures are bad, you're not a star anymore. It's a constant worry. That's why movie people are temperamental. It's a terrible strain!"

In August, he and Keaton traveled north to entertain ahead of a match between the Tigers and the San Francisco Seals, but even the recreational game of baseball had begun to wear on him. "It makes me too darn nervous," Arbuckle complained. "After two and a half hours of that, I can't do anything else I want to. The excitement makes my stomach feel bad."

Buster could sense the weariness in the man and knew the great days of the Comique two-reelers were drawing to a close.

A new picture called *The Garage* was a kind of summing up of the brand and how it had blossomed over the course of the series. Once more, Keaton was a full partner in the action, not merely an accessory as he had been in *The Hayseed*. Molly Malone was again the love interest, Jack Coogan a supporting player, and Luke dependably gave chase to Molly's unwanted suitor

Keaton and Arbuckle appropriate a gag from The Garage *for this publicity shot, marking the end of their historic collaboration.*

and, ultimately, to Buster himself. The opening moments even offered a reprise of the first scene Keaton ever played before a camera, Fatty letting fly with a missile—in this case a wet sponge—that knocks Buster off his feet. And, as he does in *The Butcher Boy*, Buster responds by hurling a pie.

Reed Heustis, a features writer for the *Los Angeles Herald*, visited the set in late October as those early shots were being made. Arriving at the Lehrman studio, Heustis first comes upon Lou Anger, then discovers Roscoe in his upstairs dressing suite, which, Heustis notes, "reminds one strongly of Atlantic City and the bathhouses there." He watches as Arbuckle prepares a shot in which he is knocked into a tub of water on top of actor Dan Crimmins, who is playing the boss. "No entrances nor exits to these pants," Heustis observes of Arbuckle's costume. "When Roscoe's in, he's in. Sewed up for the day, so to speak. With Roscoe will be Buster Keaton, also sewed up. Buster is the pleasant-faced young acrobat who will rise to stardom some time in April, and who truly, beyond the mere laudations which are so easy to write and which so seldom ring true, is of big league timber." And it is with this last line that Heustis became the first to announce to the world that Buster Keaton would soon be the star of his own line of comedies.

"It is a chill October morn, but never mind that. The three boys must be wet, and wet they get. Each in turn dives into a big vat of water standing on the stage and then go into their 'gag,' which consists largely of resuscitating Dan, nearly drowned, by a means of a garden hose and a flow of ice water. Earn their salaries! Thrice over. Then Buster and Roscoe warm up, go through a sort of clog dance—not for the camera, but for the corpuscles—which ends in the familiar thunk, de thunk, thunk, thunk, the last two thunks when Roscoe and Buster do a fall which shakes even the stage and many a stout heart."

Production on *The Garage* continued through most of November, the action moving out into the streets of Culver City, where the building catches fire, trapping Molly on the upper floor, smoke billowing through the window as the townspeople scramble to save her.

"Arbuckle was one of the worst rough-houses in films," Keaton said. "We were doing a fireman scene in *Garage*. I made a flying leap for the brass pole and started down head first, did a turn, and continued on down with my head up. I saw Arbuckle, two hundred pounds, coming down toward me. He looked down, gripping the pole, then landed square on my head!"

Molly leaps into a life net, only to bounce up and land on a set of utility wires stretched high over the street. Then the noontime whistle blows and everyone walks off to lunch, leaving her stranded with just Fatty and Buster left to rescue her. They climb the telephone pole and work their way out to her, forming a human chain, Fatty dangling by his feet and handing her down into the waiting arms of her father. Then, just as Buster loses his grip on his partner, Molly rolls around the corner in an open car, affording them a safe landing in its cushioned seats. Fatty pulls her into the back alongside him and calls "Home, James!" as Buster assumes the wheel. And the three of them drive happily off together, drawing the Arbuckle series to a satisfying close with what, in Keaton's estimation, was the best picture of the lot.

"It was a honey," he said, relishing the memory. "It was a pip."

Jasper, Alberta

OCTOBER 2, 1964

A N IMPROMPTU STORY CONFERENCE in his private railcar, and Buster Keaton is in the process of improving on an idea.

"There's only one thing that sells the gag," he says, rising, his ever-present cigarette holder clenched between his teeth. "The duck hunter was lining up on a duck. He's gonna shoot come hell or high water. So, that camera"—pointing off to his left—"just missing the tunnel by three feet. He's just missing it. He pans maybe a little bit with me, but as I come into his shot, I bring my gun up to follow a flight"—miming a hunting rifle as he pivots—"and when I get here, I shoot—and my gun is only about five feet from the tunnel when I shoot. So I've shot right into it."

Gerald Potterton conceived the idea when he first met Keaton in New York, intent upon selling him on *The Railrodder*. After listening to a bare-bones summary of the plot, Keaton was dubious.

"Well, it's a crazy idea," he concluded, "but if you write a wild duck [dinner] into my contract, I'll do it."

Now Potterton picks up on what Keaton is saying. "The whole gag is in panning," he says, framing the shot with his hands as he turns. "Panning . . . panning . . . tunnel . . . bang. He goes in it—BOOM—like that."

"All you can see probably is the top of my hat," agrees Keaton, "and the gun barrel." He indicates eight or nine inches with his fingers. "About that far." He mimes the rifle again. "Slowly get that gun into position and get it just once. Now to this shot—" Swiftly, he rotates on his feet. "Bang. And we got it." Capturing the exchange on film, documentarian John Spotton marveled at Keaton's professionalism: "He's got such vitality, such enthusiasm.

And he's game to try anything at all. Buster can see whole sequences in his head—and his memory for continuity is unbelievable."

Said Potterton, "There were certain gags which I wanted to do, like he shoots into the tunnel, certain little things like that I'd done little storyboard drawings for, which Buster didn't mind. I wasn't trying to out-direct him or anything. We had a sort of rough idea of some of those things, and it was actually the duck blind—that was his thing, and it was gorgeous. It's a fabulous bit. I was just going to have him hiding behind the little box, but no." He laughs. "He thought he could definitely do better than that. He said, 'No, it's too simple what you've got there, too simple.' And he went to a lot of trouble to prepare the little cart and go out and get an axe and chop down things, so that he made himself a duck blind, a place to hide."

Decking out the speeder with chicken wire and tree branches, as Keaton envisioned, was going to take some time. "Of course, I was a bit impatient," Potterton admitted. "We were on that single-line track through the Rockies at that point, and we were always worried about oncoming trains, so we'd have to get everything off the line quickly. I must say I thought: 'Boy, that's going to take forever.' And the crew hung around and said, 'Oh God, it's just going to take us forever to go and cut all that stuff.' But that made the gag, you know? That made the difference. It just made the whole thing work. Just before he goes in the tunnel you see those little baggy eyes looking around before he shoots the gun. That's a great thing, and that was him. I mean, he *was* the film. The film wouldn't have worked without him."

The payoff to the gag is at the other end of the tunnel. There are workers inside, and when the gun goes off, they come racing out in all directions, Buster and the speeder hot on their tails. Making the first shot, the Italian work gang in their hard hats run quickly out of camera range. "But they've got to be there," Potterton says, running into the scene and pointing. "We can't see anybody." He has trouble explaining to them that they've run too far. "*Bueno, bueno,*" he tells them, gesturing, "but you gotta run up to here, see? No further."

Now Keaton the director steps in. "Boys, come down towards me," he tells them, expertly bringing order to a measure of chaos. "You come to this spot," he says to one of them, pointing. "You come down here," he says to another, taking his arm, "to about . . . here." Then he begins to take roll. "One, two, three, four, five, six, seven," he counts, assessing just how many will read in the shot. "One more," he calls. "Right in here and . . . you on this side. Yes, you." Now he steps back. "You see about where you are?"

He walks to where Potterton and the crew are standing by the camera.

"I don't think you should pose them like that," Potterton says, but Keaton is ahead of him.

"I don't mean to pose them," Keaton says. "I'm just giving 'em a general spot to run to."

"But they'll all run there and stand there like soldiers."

"Well, you're never going to do it any other way with them," returns Keaton, peering through the camera. "If they come runnin' out there, they'll bunch up on you if you just told them to run out. But if they hit *approximately* those spots . . .'"

To the workers he calls, "Want to try it once?" And to Potterton he says, "I'll be the scooter, on foot." Keaton positions himself on the track inside the tunnel and hollers, "Go, everybody! Go!" Out come the workmen, all spread out, some poised to throw rocks, followed by Keaton, furiously racing after them. But some of them have stopped on the track in the path of the speeder, while others have again run too far. Keaton points out the places they should stop, and Potterton joins in, showing them how to run, stop, turn around, and throw. "What'd you say they did?" Keaton asks.

"They should come out running like this. Fast."

"Oh yes, as fast as you can run."

"And no smiling."

Keaton, always wary of over-rehearsing something, is ready. "Okay," he says. "Start the scooter."

Says Potterton, "We're going to run it, okay?"

Keaton climbs into the speeder, still festooned with tree branches, and pilots it back into the tunnel. Potterton is still a bit unsure of how it will go. "Well, let's try it once this way anyway," he says with a certain resignation in his voice, and the workmen follow Keaton into the darkness of the tunnel. "Start rolling!" Potterton yells, running out of the shot as he hears Keaton gunning the engine. What follows comes off beautifully, the product of forty-four years of filmmaking experience, and Potterton's face, apprehensive at first, blossoms into an expression of utter delight.

"There was a time when he really got into a sequence that we were doing," he said of Keaton, "and [he was] looking through the camera and standing on the track and looking around. There were, for me, those fantastic flashes of the twenty-two-year-old Keaton way back there, his great face and the way he moved, and you'd just forget that he was getting on in years. He was really quite sick when we were doing that film, but occasionally there was that wonderful spirit of youth and fabulous vitality that was in his films."

• Part Two •

THAT WONDERFUL
SPIRIT OF YOUTH

7

The Comedy Sensation
of the Screen World

THE END OF THE COMIQUE SERIES, just four entries into a twenty-two-picture commitment, was not yet official. In December 1919, Roscoe Arbuckle traveled to New York to scout material for the new year.

"I have all the money I want," he told *Variety*, "and at the conclusion of my present contract, I will stop making pictures myself, but may be interested in having others appear before the camera just to keep them occupied. While I am east, I am having Buster Keaton make a picture on his own. Let 'em all have a chance. I don't want to be hoggish."

A week later, the paper reported in front-page news that Arbuckle had acquired the screen rights to Edmund Day's 1907 melodrama *The Round-up* with an eye toward playing Sheriff "Slim" Hoover, a role popularized on Broadway by Maclyn Arbuckle, a rotund actor who was of no relation. The significance of the development was that the play wasn't a comedy, and that any film version would by necessity be a feature, not a short. "Arbuckle is ambitious to do more legitimate things before the camera. He has grown tired of confining his acting to slapstick and firmly believes he is capable of finer work."

Meanwhile, the picture Arbuckle was having Keaton make "on his own" was slowly taking shape. The loosely worked-out story was of Buster's own devising, and the crew would be Roscoe's own, otherwise on hiatus while the star was out of town. But Keaton wasn't ready to start just yet, and he waited until Arbuckle's return to select a leading lady. One of the girls they jointly interviewed was Bartine Burkett, a twenty-one-year-old actress working for Eddie Cline as one of the Fox Sunshine Comedy Girls. A native of Robeline,

Louisiana, she had been in pictures since 1916 and met Lou Anger's principal qualification for the job in that she came cheap.

"The first thing Roscoe said was, 'We're going to lunch before we interview you. Wanna go with us?' Without hesitation, I said, 'I'd *love* to.' Hollywood actresses were known then, as now, to be the hungriest women in the world. I remember having lots of fun with those two at lunch, and when we were through and walked back to the studio, Mr. Arbuckle casually said, 'Goodbye—I guess you'll do as Buster's first leading lady.' Buster said nothing, but took me by the arm and piloted me to their studio office, had me go in first, then he came in and carefully closed and *locked* the door. I was puzzled and surprised by this, but, strangely, not in the least disturbed or frightened. It seemed the longer I knew Buster, the more I understood that no one could ever have, for a moment, been frightened by him in any way. He looked at me and asked, 'Do you like juggling?' I said, 'Uh huh,' and he took some balls out of a drawer and entertained me with the best juggling act I've ever seen."

Over the holidays, Arbuckle played host to Adolph Zukor, who was paying one of his occasional visits to the Famous Players studio in Hollywood. Since their earliest days on Forty-Eighth Street, Keaton and Arbuckle had relieved the stress of grinding out gags by resorting to the time-honored device of the practical joke. A whopping good prank engaged the mind, made enemies, imperiled life and limb. Yet the cruelest of these tended to be the most banal, such as the withdrawn chair or the hot foot. The main requirement for a joke around the Comique studio was that it had to be funny and that, ideally, it rose to the level of artistry. "Our practical jokes were of the sort the victims could laugh at with us later on," Buster said proudly. "They were quite ingenious."

A good example of the black art as practiced by Keaton and Arbuckle was the treatment accorded the visiting Zukor, who, while not exactly Arbuckle's employer, was nevertheless his customer. Zukor, they reasoned, must have a pretty good sense of humor if he distributed their pictures, so they created an elaborate scenario. Roscoe had leased a Tudor-style mansion in the West Adams district, a $100,000 showplace known as the Randolph Huntington Miner residence, and there he decided to throw a formal dinner party in the guest's honor. And since Zukor had never personally met Buster, it was he who would serve that night as Roscoe's butler. ("We relied," said Keaton, "on the theory that no one looks at the butler.") A guest list was assembled: Sid Grauman, a well-known practical joker whose new Million Dollar Theatre played the Paramount and Artcraft pictures produced by Famous-Lasky, Viola Dana, Alice Lake, Bebe Daniels, and Anna Q. Nilsson. All were in on the joke, and the women were coached ahead of time so as to avoid giving it away.

Keaton began by serving the shrimp cocktail to the men, boorishly ignoring the ladies and earning a loud and vulgar rebuke from the master. Back in the kitchen, he made an ungodly racket preparing to serve the first course while Roscoe was left to explain to his guests at the dining table all about the "servant problem." What happened next appeared in *Variety:* "Buster made his first entrance with a huge soup tureen, the contents of which he promptly upset. Then he dropped a huge turkey on the floor, leaned over to pick it up when the door leading to the kitchen struck him in the rear and projected him on top of the fowl. At this juncture, Arbuckle seized a bottle of wine and whammed Keaton over the bean, knocking him unconscious."

Dragged into the kitchen, Keaton snuck up the back stairs, changed his clothes, and presented himself at the front door as a late arrival. Seated next to Kansas City exhibitor Frank Newman, it dawned on them what had happened, and Grauman was the first to lose his composure. Zukor didn't smile but said evenly, "Very clever boys, *very* clever!"

It is significant that in the three years Joseph Schenck produced the Norma Talmadge and Fatty Arbuckle pictures, he kept his day job as general booking manager for the Loew vaudeville circuit, a position he had held since its inception. Over time, his portfolio grew to include his sister-in-law Constance Talmadge's movies, a string of *Mutt and Jeff* cartoons, and Special Films, Inc., a kind of repository for projects that didn't fit into any of the other categories. Schenck, in partnership with his brother, also retained his interest in Palisades Park. Combined, his personal earnings for the year 1919 were estimated at between $1.5 million and $2 million. All this, of course, took a toll on his involvement with the Loew organization, and most of his responsibilities had fallen to his lieutenant, a man named Jake Lubin. It was at Loew's advice—and out of fairness to Lubin—that Schenck finally announced his retirement from the Loew circuit in order to give more and better attention to his picture interests. He would, he said, locate an office of his own around Times Square.

Marcus Loew was moving into production as well, and while he was still amassing theaters, he purchased Metro Pictures Corporation, now the home studio of Alice Lake, Viola Dana, Bert Lytell, and Nazimova, for a price in the range of $3 million. Metro had no comedy stars, so when Schenck told Loew that Roscoe Arbuckle was moving into features and that he was going to start making two-reelers with Buster Keaton, Loew instantly said, "We'll contract for him." And suddenly, the first film Keaton was to make on his own took on an unexpected urgency. Filming of *The High Sign* got under way the week of January 12, 1920, but since two other companies were already sharing the Lehrman studio in Arbuckle's absence, Keaton and his crew were forced out onto location, principally along the Venice oceanfront and, to make his entrance, Redondo Beach, where, appropriately, he was thrown off a passing train. The intertitle:

Our Hero came from <u>Nowhere</u>—
he wasn't going <u>Anywhere</u>
and got kicked off
<u>Somewhere</u>.

Buster helps himself to a paper, opening it to find it is one increasingly larger sheet of unruly newsprint. But in it he sees a want ad for a boy to run a shooting gallery. ("Must be expert shot to attract crowd.") To sharpen his aim, he lifts a gun from a distracted cop, replacing it with a banana, and wanders off to the beach for some target practice. There, in a good-luck cameo, he encounters Al St. John, who witnesses some fancy shooting before predictably becoming a target himself. Satisfied, Buster applies for the job, but the business is really a front for a gang of Black Handers called the Blinking Buzzards. And, presently, he finds himself recruited as both bodyguard and assassin of their current extortion target, the town miser August Nickelnurser. Throughout

Ingram B. "Cupid" Pickett, Keaton, and Bartine Burkett in The High Sign, *Buster's first film as star as well as director.*

it all, the gang members give each other the high sign—hands crossed at the nose, fingers outstretched to symbolize the wingspread of a bird.

Keaton seemed to enjoy the intricate process of making the movie, ensuring that each gag, no matter how outlandish, served the logical development of the story. "Even at this time," he later explained, "the moving picture comedy was getting to be more legitimate, logical, and consistent, and the people were more human and less like the heroes of the comic strips. They were beginning to put things on the screen because they arose from the situation, as in stage plays, and not because they were supposed to be independently funny or because certain properties that could be used happened to be at hand."

Bartine Burkett would remember a man clearly tickled by what he was capturing. "I've never known anyone to laugh more than he," she wrote. "In fact, when we were shooting, he spoiled many a scene by cracking up with laughter."

Keaton assumed a brotherly air with her, collecting her each morning at her family home, and taking her to the weekly dances at the Hollywood Hotel, where he would diligently fill her dance card, cajoling the reluctant, and then disappear.

"He was always expected up in Viola Dana's apartment. . . . I'm sure they did a bit of drinking, and I would not see Buster again until right on the dot of eleven thirty—he would appear and announce that it was time for me to go home—my family having told him in no uncertain terms that I must be home before midnight. . . . I could always smell liquor on his breath, but this never posed a problem, for he seemed to always have himself well in hand."

The infatuation between Vi Dana and Buster had run its course, and she was by then seriously involved with daredevil stunt pilot Ormer Locklear— so much so that Locklear had to deny rumors in the press that the actress and he were secretly married. Bartine remembered "long lapses between working dates" reflecting the casual way in which the company worked. Once, while trapped shooting *The Round-up* on location at Lone Pine, Arbuckle sent for prints of his Comique comedies, and Keaton, Lou Anger, Jean Havez, and cameraman Elgin Lessley decided to take the week off and deliver them personally.

"They had a shot," Buster remembered, "and Arbuckle says, 'Put an Indian makeup on Keaton and let me shoot him.' George Melford, the director, says 'All right.'"

Keaton did the shot expertly, and collected a $5 stunt check for his trouble. Then he and the others went quail hunting for the balance of the week.

On the days Bartine did work, Keaton would chauffeur her between Hollywood and Culver City, tossing off greetings to the cars and pedestrians headed in the opposite direction.

"His timing was fantastic!" she recalled. "We would be deep in conversation, but when someone approached and passed us, either on foot or in some vehicle, he would interrupt, bow ceremoniously, and inquire of this person the state of his health. Where was his wife today? How many children did he now have in school? Whatever happened to that one who was expelled? All that kind of thing, without ever repeating himself. I would sit there literally doubled up with laughter."

But as work progressed on *The High Sign*, Keaton grew increasingly convinced the film was no good. Never before had he directed without Arbuckle present. There were, of course, others to bounce ideas off, but there wasn't the deep well of experience that came from having worked both sides of the camera as Roscoe had. It was he, after all, who had taught Buster picture technique, and Keaton, at one point, may have asked him to step in, for Bartine could remember shooting a scene in a flooded basement that was actually directed by Arbuckle. It was, however, Keaton's hand as a director that stayed with her. He was, she said, "very good because he had a sense of comedy. He knew what he was doing about it, and . . . just by telling me what to do and how to do it in his own way, he was always sort of different. His direction was not anything like any I had had."

When the picture was finished, Keaton wanted it shelved. Lou Anger, who had $12,000 of the company's money tied up in it, at least wanted to see how it would play in front of an audience. They took it out, but Keaton already knew he needed a stronger debut to put the new series over. One problem was particularly vexing. Throughout the picture, the Buzzards' high sign had been used to punctuate gags and goose the laughs. So Keaton pulled one on the audience: The banana he plants on the cop finds its way into the hands of a Buzzard, who eats it and drops the peel on the sidewalk. Buster rounds the corner, giving every indication he's going to slip on it, but then he steps right past it instead and gives the high sign as he disappears from the frame. In preview, the gag fell flat. "Not a titter," he said in a 1954 talk with author Paul Gallico, "and nobody can figure out why. Finally, I get the idea and we go back and shoot the scene over again. We do it the same, only this time, after I walk over the peel and into the camera, giving the high sign, the camera follows me and I slip on another banana peel that I haven't seen and down I go. Yaks! The audience wants his comic to be human, not clever."

The first motion picture to star Buster Keaton reached the screen as a feature, not a short, and brought with it a complicated history. When Bronson Howard's *The Henrietta* first appeared in 1887, it was widely hailed as the playwright's masterpiece, a timely satire about "the American passion for speculation, the money madness that was dividing families." It proved so popular it was retooled for modern tastes in 1913 by Winchell Smith, author of *Brewster's Millions,* and Victor Mapes. Inelegantly titled *The New Henrietta,* the play featured Howard's original star, William H. Crane, once more in the role of Wall Street banker Nicholas Van Alstyne, and Douglas Fairbanks as his feckless son, Bertie. Two years later, Fairbanks starred in a film adaptation called *The Lamb,* but it bore only a passing resemblance to the play, and Fairbanks embraced the idea of faithfully remaking it with the original stage cast in 1919. Now in charge of his own studio, Fairbanks brought Winchell Smith out from New York to oversee the film and engaged scenarist June Mathis to write the screenplay. Pulling the *Henrietta* cast together took longer than expected, and the actor's interest began to wane. He moved on to *The Mollycoddle,* an action picture more in keeping with his emerging screen image, and in March 1920, Marcus Loew snapped up Smith, Mathis, Crane, and *The New Henrietta* as a package. And with Doug Fairbanks out of the picture, it made perfect sense to drop the studio's new comedy star into the plum role of Bertie the Lamb.

According to one report, Buster Keaton was still tinkering with *The High Sign* in Culver City when *The New Henrietta* began filming on March 23 at the Metro studios in Hollywood. At around the same time, word leaked out that Roscoe Arbuckle had renegotiated his deals with Joe Schenck and Adolph Zukor and would be limiting his future output to five-reel features.

"I'll do *Brewster's Millions* and *The Traveling Salesman,*" Arbuckle said, "instead of the two-reelers which take me twenty-four hours a day to make—and I can't sleep nights when I'm making one."

Over the next month, the elements of Keaton's production team were put into place. Eddie Cline was hired away from Fox to direct (or, more accurately, co-direct), Jean Havez was retained to write the scripts (such as they were), and Metro was getting the old Lone Star studio at Cahuenga and

Keaton, as Bertie Van Alstyne, unwittingly heads off a raid on the slumping Henrietta Mine stock in The Saphead *(1920).*

Romaine Streets into shape for Keaton's exclusive use, clearing it of old sets. In charge of the operation would again be Lou Anger.

Across the street, Keaton had the run of the Metro lot, where his pal Viola Dana was making a picture called *The Chorus Girl's Romance*. They posed for stills together, clowning, she down on the ground, an alarmed look on her face, Buster casually "applying cave man tactics" with his right foot squarely on her neck. They were both Metro stars now, in the social swim that stretched from Venice to downtown Los Angeles, Vi with Lieutenant Locklear, Buster living on West Adams with Roscoe and Minta Arbuckle and occasionally escorting Alice Lake. A typical night at the Palm Court of the Alexandria Hotel placed them among the young royals of Hollywood—Charlie Chaplin with actress Florence Deshon, Lew Cody with Bebe Daniels, Blanche Sweet with director Marshall Neilan, Dagmar Godowsky with actor Frank Mayo.

"The evening would begin generally in the ballroom of the Alexandria with two reprobates falling down the main staircase: Buster Keaton and Lew Cody, both acrobats," said cameraman Byron Haskin. "They'd do 108s down this stairway—KA-RA-LA-BOOM!—into the middle of the dance floor. You knew the evening had begun! The dance floor was so solidly packed every night that you could lift your feet and still stay up."

Katherine Albert, who had a small but important role in *The New Hen-*

rietta, remembered Keaton as "an earnest young man in those days, trying very hard to make a go of what he thought his one big chance." In playing a relatively straight part in an important feature, Keaton was doing what Arbuckle had just done in *The Round-up* but with far less name recognition. Given the challenge, his measured performance as young Van Alstyne was a quiet triumph, his first dramatic turn since his days with the Fenberg company in 1906. To the *Los Angeles Times* he gave an interview in which he groused over the "kippy clothes" he was required to wear and joshed about joking up the role the way he had *Little Lord Fauntleroy.* "Don't know why they chose me for the part anyhow," he said, "only I've got a blank pan. Saw a nice, fluffy pie on the set the other day that would've looked good on the hero's face, but he got away just in time. Winchell Smith watches me all the time. He's the author and he's afraid I'll do something all wrong. I had to be shaved in a scene the other day, and Mr. Smith was scared to death. He thought I might try to get funny and eat the soap! Mr. Smith certainly does worry about me."

Smith indeed helped shape Keaton's performance, shrewdly guarding the integrity of the play and drawing out his natural gifts as an actor while the credited director, Englishman Herbert Blaché, saw to the camerawork. ("I didn't pay enough attention to him," Keaton, who could scarcely remember him, admitted.) Most of the publicity went to the seventy-five-year-old Crane, whose history with the material went back more than thirty years. But the new screenplay had thrown the weight of the story to Bertie's character, so much so that a month into filming the title was officially changed to *The Saphead,* the Henrietta in the original having been, among other things, a racehorse and a mining conglomerate. "William H. Crane was really the star of *The Saphead,*" said Albert, "but before it was finished deadpan Keaton had tucked it under his arm and walked away with it."

Production on *The Saphead* wrapped on May 16, 1920, and the Metro annex, which, as the Lone Star, had housed Charlie Chaplin and company back when Chaplin made a dozen two-reel comedies for Mutual, was ready for occupancy. Built in 1914, it had office space, dressing rooms, an on-site laboratory, and an open stage that measured 100 by 150 feet and rose four feet above the yard.

"So I had a city lot there," said Keaton, "a good-size block for a studio. We had all the room in the world for one company—plenty of room."

Joe Schenck, he recalled, presented him with a new contract, paying him $1,000 a week and 25 percent of the profits.

"I suggested that I make only features in the future, but he wouldn't agree. Schenck insisted that I return to the two-reel field. I couldn't convince him that comedy features were the coming thing. If I'd won that argument it could have made a big difference in my career. Neither Chaplin nor [Harold] Lloyd were making features at that time* and I would have had a head start on both of them."

The deal with Metro, which was finalized on June 1, 1920, committed the ten stockholders of the Comique Film Company—a group which included Joe and Nicholas Schenck, Lou Anger, and songwriter Irving Berlin—to delivering eight two-reel comedies "with Buster Keaton as the star or feature player" within one year. In return, the distributor agreed to reimburse Comique the documented cost of each film (not to exceed $45,000) as an advance against 70 percent of the gross receipts. Production on the first picture under the agreement was to commence within thirty days.

In Hollywood, Anger gave Keaton and Eddie Cline a budget of $30,000—the same as for an Arbuckle comedy. The story, developed in collaboration with Jean Havez and gagman Joe Mitchell, was based on a simple premise: A newly married couple is given a kit home from the Portable House Co. to build themselves. More than twenty-five thousand American families had assembled dwellings such as these since the creation of the Sears Modern Homes Department in 1908, their houses shipped to city lots and farms direct from one of the company's dedicated mills. But what would happen if the numbers on the boxes got mixed, making it impossible to assemble it correctly? What would the thing look like? And what problems would it present to a newly married couple? As a premise, it was, as *Picture-Play's* Malcolm Oettinger later put it, "mechanically perfect."

Shooting began the week of May 24. Since Bartine Burkett was starring in her own series of one-reel comedies for Universal, her place as Buster's leading woman was taken by twenty-year-old Sennett starlet Sibye Trevilla, who had worked with the likes of Charlie Murray, Ben Turpin, and Raymond Griffith, and who would assume the name Sybil Seely for the Keaton pictures. And from back in Muskegon, where Buster's appearances in the Arbuckles were closely followed, Joe Roberts, vaudeville veteran and the Keaton family's enormous Edgewater neighbor, was recruited to play a cameo as a surly deliveryman with an upright piano slung over his shoulder.

* This isn't quite accurate. Chaplin was already at work on his first feature, *The Kid,* but it wouldn't go into release until February 1921. Lloyd followed in 1922 with his first five-reel subject, *Grandma's Boy.* Had Keaton gone straight into features in May 1920, he conceivably could have beaten both men to market with a fall release.

As with *The High Sign,* Keaton and his team went for gags that logically arose from the situation, but the new story was simpler and more consistent in its point of view than with the earlier picture, an exercise in what Orson Welles called "the comedy of futility." Gags, Keaton once said, were either natural or mechanical. "Both get laughs, but the natural gag is the one we lay awake nights trying to dream of." And he had in Eddie Cline, a true veteran of screen comedy, someone who had fallen into picture work as a jack-of-all-trades and could see a scene from every conceivable angle.

Born in Kenosha in 1891 and reared on Chicago's East Side, Edward Francis Cline was brought to Los Angeles at the age of twelve. He played baseball in high school, pitching for Polytechnic, and was good enough to be offered a professional contract. (This alone would have qualified him for a job at the Keaton studio.) He joined Sennett as an extra in the fall of 1914, and was soon one of the Keystone Cops. Sennett, he found, took a lot of his ideas from French farces, and employed a full-time translator to write synopses. But the self-styled King of Comedy's instincts were loud and crude, as befit the times. "I had my idea of comedy—rough, slapstick, and funny," Sennett said. "I'd make that or nothing."

Keystone's brand of comic mayhem required less talent than fortitude, and it was easy for someone with no particular training to get a job. There was, though, the chance to learn from some of the true giants of the art form, men like Chaplin, Ford Sterling, Charlie Murray, and Mack Swain. "We used to meet in an old barn," said Cline, "and under the tutelage of these fine masters we were taught the fundamentals of broad pantomime."

Cline himself became a director in 1916 and was instrumental in developing the Sennett Bathing Beauties, who supplanted the Keystone Cops. "Some of the Cop pictures earned Sennett as much as $50,000 net. But they had run their course, not so much through the repetition of the gags which motivated them, but rather because the American public had changed its views on acting. The Keystone Cops and the central figures who played around them were pantomimists, pure and simple. When pictures became more articulate through improvement in the camera as well as in the technique of acting itself, the Keystoners were out of place."

By the time Cline signed on with Comique, he was a firm believer in Keaton's mantra of logic and consistency, a thoroughly modern approach to the job of making people laugh. And at the core of the new picture would be a pair of well-rounded characters, a believable young couple who clearly love each other and are cheerfully assuming the arduous task of building a house for themselves. Sybil Seely wasn't necessarily hired for her acting chops, but she turned out to be an ideal match for Buster, energetic and expressive and, like Alice Lake, willing to do her fair share of the hard and sometimes dangerous work. Their chemistry was unmistakable, warm and natural. Then someone came up with a framing device in which the action progresses over seven days, with the passage of each day delineated by a leaf from the calendar. Yet, the resulting title, *One Week,* suggested a lampoon of the old Elinor Glyn potboiler *Three Weeks.*

Utilizing the new studio and its surrounding neighborhood, the marriage of Buster and Sybil is staged, establishing the animosity of Handy Hank, "the fellow she turned down." Hank, it turns out, is sourly driving their honeymoon car, an uncomfortable circumstance that leads to their abandoning it for another while still in motion, Sybil managing the jump effortlessly while Buster is caught between the two cars until a motorcycle catches him, roughly carrying him off in the opposite direction. In the distance, he sees Hank abandon the first car for the second and gives chase, halting them with the unwitting help of a traffic officer. Regaining control of the driverless first car, they arrive at the lot Buster's Uncle Mike has given them to greet the arrival of their new house. Buster opens the directions:

1. To give this house a snappy appearance put it up according
   to the numbers on the boxes.

The next day, Tuesday, they are already well along, Buster sawing away as Sybil prepares breakfast on a camping stove. Hank comes upon the scene, notices the numbers marking the boxes, and, unseen, gleefully alters them with black paint. The funhouse effects begin almost immediately as an entire wall rotates on its axis, carrying Sybil skyward while Buster is dropped to the ground. Unsure of where she has gone, he wanders away, only to have the wall come crashing down around him, a window opening saving him from certain injury. It's a gag he had used previously in *Back Stage,* where the device was merely a featherweight scenery flat, and it's a gag he'd revisit again to even greater effect.

On Wednesday, the completed house is revealed to be a cubist nightmare of a structure, its windows at odd yawning angles, its doors leading nowhere, its roof wholly inadequate to the necessity of keeping the elements out. It's architecture as if by Caligari, bold and senseless, and Buster stands puzzled before it, scratching his head. Sybil is unfazed. Good-naturedly she beckons him, draws him to the side, where she has painted two hearts and an arrow

Buster regards his handiwork in One Week *(1920). Built on the Metro Pictures lot, this kit house was as much a character in the picture as any of the human participants.*

on the wall, and he cannot resist but to give her a kiss. There's nothing artificial here, an elaborate sight gag followed by a warm, human interlude, a genuine rapport between two characters affirmed and then reaffirmed.

Walls rotate. Floors sag as if made of rubber. Nerves fray. Buster tacks down a rug, then carves a hole in the center of it to retrieve his jacket. Sybil, taking a bath, drops the soap and asks the cameraman to cover the lens while she reaches for it. Then Buster walks through a door in the bathroom and drops twelve feet to the ground below. It was, he recalled, "a sensational fall," but the aftermath gave him a bad scare—his first in three years of making movies.

"To lessen the impact, we dug a deep, very wide hole in the garden, filled this with straw, and replaced the squares of sod on top of the straw. The lawn looked solid but collapsed like paper when I fell on it. I only felt a jar at the time. It was about two hours before quitting and I finished out the day. But as I was getting dressed I discovered that my left elbow had swelled to double its normal size. I could not even get my jacket on. My other elbow, my back, and both arms were also swelling up fast. Al Gilmore, my unit's physical trainer, put me under a shower with the water as hot as I could stand. He kept me there for fifteen minutes, then got me under an ice-cold shower for almost as long. When I was dry he rubbed me down with olive oil. That was to prevent the horse liniment, which he applied next, from taking my skin off. Under this treatment the swelling went down little by little."

Friday the thirteenth brings the housewarming and a violent storm, which causes the structure to shift on its foundation and then spin like a merry-go-round. The guests indoors are thrown around the room, while outside Buster tries hurling himself through the one ground-level door but keeps missing and bouncing off the clapboard. When he is finally successful, he's thrown around the interior in one continuous shot and back out the same door. Eventually Sybil and the guests are thrown clear of the house and into the chaos of the mud and the wind and the driving rain. When Kevin Brownlow marveled at the combined effect during a 1964 interview, Keaton emphasized the simplicity of it all. "We built it on a turntable," he said, "and buried the control belt. . . . You just dig a ditch down about that far and lay your stuff in there and then put boards over it and then shovel dirt and grass on top of it. And that's it." Setting up such a gag, he estimated, took about three days out of the schedule.

On Saturday, with the storm now past, the house is a shambles, a decrepit shadow of its former self. "Now look at the darned thing!" Sybil cries.

"I guess it's not used to the climate," Buster suggests, kissing her gently.

Just then a man walks up and shows them that they've built on the wrong lot. "Yours is across the railroad track," he says, pointing. Sybil considers having a meltdown, while Buster starts fashioning a way of moving the house by rolling it along on barrels.

Sunday finds them carefully towing it behind their car, but the chain breaks as the house is trundling over the track, and no amount of effort can budge it. Around the bend, a train is approaching, and Buster pulls Sybil to safety. The two cover their eyes, expecting the worst.

Then the near miss: The train is actually on an adjacent track, and it harmlessly roars past, leaving the misshapen house intact. Buster and Sybil look, can't believe it, and heave a collective sigh of relief. But it's the banana peel gag writ large, and a train coming from the opposite direction races into the shot, smashing into the house and reducing it to kindling. ("I always wanted an audience to outguess me," Keaton said, "and then I'd double-cross them sometimes.") Collecting themselves, Buster takes Sybil's

Keaton poses with Sybil Seely, the former Sennett Bathing Beauty who was his leading lady in his first three comedy releases. Their chemistry was unmistakable, but their teaming was interrupted by Sybil's pregnancy. Replaced by Virginia Fox, she returned for one of Keaton's strongest two-reelers, The Boat (1921).

hand and places a FOR SALE sign on the rubble, thoughtfully attaching the assembly directions as well. Then, hand in hand, the two walk off into the distance, having just completed the best and most important two-reel comedy of the season.

With *One Week* in the can, Keaton permitted himself a short vacation before embarking on the second of the eight films he owed the distributor. Having lured Joe Roberts west, he now sent for his mother and father, taking a lease on a four-bedroom house on Ingraham Street in the Wilshire Park district with the aim of putting Joe Keaton back into pictures. The new short was shaping up to be a prison yarn, with the two Joes as malevolent inmates, Sybil as a cute society girl (and warden's daughter), Eddie Cline as the jail's amiable hangman, and Buster as an innocent victim of mistaken identity. Filmed over the month of July, *Convict 13* lacked the Big Idea that so beautifully animated *One Week,* and may have been conceived as little more than a showcase for Roberts and Keaton *père.* Starting off on a golf course, Keaton mined material explored previously by Chaplin, with the action only catching fire in the final third, when Joe Keaton initiates a breakout with a couple of well-placed kicks and Buster saves the day by reprising a gag from the later days of The Three Keatons where he subdues the old man—and about a dozen others—by taking a speed bag from the prison gym and swinging it from a length of rope. In the end, Sybil wakes him from a bad dream, trivializing all that's come before.

Understandably, Keaton never talked much about *Convict 13,* but now he was working at a fever pitch, building a backlog of pictures ahead of the September 1 release of *One Week.* In August he began work on what was referred to as a "rural comedy," Sybil Seely and Joe Keaton its only announced players.

"Two or three writers and I would start with an idea," Buster said of the development process, "and then we'd work out a strong finish and let the middle take care of itself, as it always does. Sometimes we'd work out a gag in advance; other times it would work itself out as we went along."

For what came to be known as *The Scarecrow,* the idea was the matter of courtship and marriage in the American heartland, and the strong finish would be the marriage part, which would take place aboard a speeding motorcycle, Buster at the handlebars, Sybil in the sidecar, and the minister perched somewhere in between.

To open the picture on a scene of domestic harmony, Keaton created the cinematic equivalent of Ed Gray's house in Bluffton, a one-room bachelor pad that Buster and Joe Roberts have tricked out with space-saving conveniences. The console phonograph converts into a gas-burning stove and oven. The bookcase has an icebox built into it. Condiments hover over the dining table like a culinary mobile, each item dangling from its own dedicated string. The bread basket is on wheels, the communal dinner napkin retractable. The bathtub automatically empties as it collapses into a settee. The bed folds into the wall and reveals in its place an upright organ.

Both men are friendly rivals for Sybil's hand in marriage. Joe Keaton is her father, and Luke, on loan from Arbuckle, is her dog. She makes her pop a cream pie, but when she sets it out to cool, Luke devours it, making it look as if he's foaming at the mouth. "Mad dog!" Buster shouts as he takes off in a run, and Luke, as he always so expertly does, gives chase. The pursuit is long and furious, through the ruins of an old building, in and out of windows, up and down ladders. Watching from a safe distance, Big Joe ducks into a drugstore and emerges with crutches, iodine, arnica, dog bite, cotton, and gauze, all of which Buster will likely need if the chase doesn't end well. Keaton dives into an enormous haystack, momentarily throwing Luke off the scent until he sees the hay and his quarry loaded onto a conveyor belt and fed into a grinder. Fascinated, the dog sits and watches with rapt attention, patiently waiting for Buster's remains to shoot out the other end of the machine. When he miraculously surfaces intact, Luke happily rushes to him and offers to shake. "Friends?" says Buster, taking his paw.

By now, Keaton's screen persona was coming into sharp focus. From vaudeville he brought the integrity and deportment that had become so familiar to live audiences, while the screen permitted a level of inventiveness he could never fully explore onstage. He was also unafraid of suggesting complex relationships with other characters, whether it was marriage with Sybil, friendship with Big Joe, or pals with Luke, all of which were grounded in the realities of everyday life, a seriousness rarely invoked in other two-reel comedies. Lastly there was the Keaton visage, unusual if not unique in the world of film, unsmiling but certainly not without expression or feeling. There were those who would fail to see the humanity in him, who preferred the emoting that Chaplin brought fully featured to his pictures, but for audiences that considered the viewing experience a collaborative effort, he instinctively invited them into the action, and what they saw in return was a reflected humanity, a bit of themselves in what was superficially regarded as a blank pan.

The Scarecrow was emerging as a rollicking windup toy of a movie when the first trade review of *One Week* appeared in August. "Put all your money on this Keaton comedy," Joseph L. Kelley urged exhibitors in *Motion Picture News,* "it's a feature in itself. Unfortunately it is only two reels, but into this two reels Buster Keaton, guided by the experienced hands and fun-making skill of director Eddie Cline, has crowded more good, clean, wholesome comedy than has been seen in similar reelage in a long time. Not only is the comedy of the real hilarious brand, but without an exception every incident, every situation are original and present a front new to the comedy-loving public. . . . Buster is a show in himself and is one of the few eccentric comedians working before the camera who appreciates that the day of the pie-throwing comedy has passed."

A cause for celebration, the *News* review was followed the next day by a similar rave for *Convict 13* in *Wid's Daily:* "*Convict 13* gives ample proof that Buster Keaton's first two-reel comedy, *One Week,* was more than a flash in the pan. It's another winner. This comedy organization seems on the high road to big success. The two pictures shown so far reveal the hand of an expert in every department. This 'hand' is undoubtedly the result of the combined heads of Keaton and Eddie Cline, who is sharing in the directing. They have included in this a number of new gags, and the comedy sequences are working out with such an easy rapidity that their effect is tremendously funny."

Added Edward Weitzel in *Moving Picture World:* "The combination of comic gifts possessed by this young man who has known the smell of greasepaint since he was five years of age has put him into the front rank of screen comedians. Attracting attention by his remarkable acrobatic stunts, he has developed into an actor of rare skill along certain lines. His work is as clean-cut and legitimate as that of the best actors of serious parts and he is in a class by himself."

Metro supported the release of *One Week* with full-page advertising in the trades ("ENTER BUSTER KEATON" was the headline) and a publicity guide for exhibitors that offered exploitation tips, sample ad designs, and editorial content that could be fed to the papers. "*One Week* starts Buster Keaton on his larger career for the screen," it trumpeted. "He has begun where other comedians have left off. He has packed his first two-reel subject with a bundle of brand new gags that will set your patrons laughing until (if they wear 'em) their false teeth will drop out and their waist-bands will shimmy."

The company reported "a great wave of interest" in the forthcoming series and that prints of *One Week* were in stock at all twenty-five Metro exchanges. The rollout, however, was slow in coming. The first places to see the picture were towns like Denton, Texas, and Sandusky, Ohio. Thanks to Sid Grauman, the film opened in Los Angeles at the Million Dollar on September 15, but it wasn't until the end of the month that the Jacob Lourie group followed Grauman's example and took the film for its two Boston houses, the Beacon and the Franklin Park. More notice came Keaton's way with the release of *The Saphead* on October 18, features naturally commanding more press attention than shorts, and when the selection of Buster's new leading lady was announced, it made papers nationwide.

It was a couple of weeks ahead of the release of *One Week* that Sybil Seely learned she was pregnant and would have to sit out the balance of the season. Earlier in the year she had married writer Jules Furthman, and it may have been at his urging that she stepped away from the rigorous Keaton series when she was scarcely two months along. Sybil's replacement, Virginia Fox, also came from Sennett, where she had appeared alongside Sybil as one of the Bathing Beauties under Eddie Cline's direction. The official word (which may not have been far from the truth) was that she was picked because, at five feet, she was small enough to stand under Buster's outstretched arm.

The Scarecrow wrapped with another chase, the two Joes scrambling, Buster and Sybil making their escape on a purloined motorbike, inadvertently scooping up a man of the cloth along the way. Buster loosens an oversize nut and slips it on Sybil's finger for the impromptu ceremony, and all three ride headlong into a river for the rousing finale, splashing to a soggy iris just as the couple is pronounced man and wife. As with *Convict 13,* the picture was shot in a breezy four weeks, expertly assembled by Keaton himself, and was ready for trade reviewers in early October. By then, work had already commenced on the fourth Keaton comedy, which carried the working title *Back Yard.*

Gradually, *One Week* made its way into larger markets, placements fueled by strong word of mouth. "It is certainly great," wrote George Mayne of the Swanson Theatre Circuit in Salt Lake City. "I expected good work from [Keaton], but he more than surprised me. Our audience simply went wild over his work, it was so different and original. I look for him to rank as the leading funmaker of America."

Arbuckle, meanwhile, worked the spectators, generously dictating a letter to go to some twenty-five thousand fans. "I did not desert the two-reelers," he wrote, "until I felt perfectly sure I had found a worthy successor—one that could make you laugh more than I did. That man is Buster Keaton."

When the picture finally opened in New York the week of October 24, it debuted simultaneously at two Broadway houses, the Rivoli and the Strand.

"This is a refreshing, entertaining, and altogether novel two-reeler," judged *Variety,* "well able to arouse and keep an audience in good humor." In time, Keaton's shambolic solo debut would amass worldwide rentals of $114,798, returning a handsome profit.

In *Back Yard,* which came to be known as *Neighbors,* Keaton explored the same themes of courtship and marriage as in *The Scarecrow* but this time in an urban setting. In contrast to the vast country landscapes in the former picture, the scene of Buster and Virginia's burgeoning romance became the constricted space between two tenement houses, clotheslines connecting them overhead and a gated fence dividing the common yard. The set gave Keaton three levels of elevation and a span of some thirty feet in which to execute some truly original gags, particularly one in which he leaps from

The cast of Neighbors *admires the signage on the new Keaton studio in Hollywood. Built in 1914 as the Climax Studio, it went through multiple occupants until Charles Chaplin arrived in 1916 to produce a dozen two-reel comedies for Mutual—a series that included such highspots as* One A.M., The Pawnshop, *and* Easy Street.

Virginia's third-floor window, rides a clothesline back to his own building, slides down and around a banister and back out a second-floor window, riding another clothesline back into Virginia's building, where he crashes into Joe Roberts, her hostile father. At six three and nearly three hundred pounds, Roberts made an ideal screen heavy opposite Buster, who was a full nine inches shorter and about half his weight.

Big Joe sends him back on the same clothesline dangling by his feet, causing Buster to helplessly shift positions with a rug his father (Joe Keaton, in a nod to typecasting) is in the process of beating. A mighty whack sends Buster swinging, and he knocks Joe a good six feet onto the dirt. Rousing himself, Joe unclips Buster's feet, dropping him headfirst into a barrel of rainwater. But the barrel has no bottom, and Buster's head is stuck in mud, his struggling legs splayed above him.

"Are you comfortable?" Joe inquires. The old man tries unscrewing him as Big Joe offers encouragement from the opposite window.

"I know a better way than that to break his neck," he shouts.

"He's my son," returns Joe, "and I'll break his neck any way I please."

Buster became so consumed with choreographing the final scenes in the picture, which included a walking three-high shoulder stand worthy of any circus act, he completely forgot it was the day of his twenty-fifth birthday. That night, with the picture wrapped, Joe and Myra hosted a gala party on Ingraham Street, and all of Buster's studio personnel, from Lou Anger down to office boy Luke McGluke, were present. Also on hand were Alice Lake, Roscoe Arbuckle, Viola Dana, Vi's sister Shirley Mason, her husband Bernard Durning, and Buster's pal Lew Cody. It was October 4, 1920, and for a newly minted screen star named Buster Keaton, life couldn't get much better.

Convict 13 was released on October 27 and found a ready market for more pictures from the man responsible for *One Week*. In New York, the managing directors for the Strand and the Rivoli confirmed bookings for more Keaton shorts, and small-town managers reporting in to the "What the Picture Did for Me" department of *Exhibitors Herald* registered their collective enthusiasm.

"Book the series and start advertising," urged Joe Yaeger of the Shuler Auditorium in Raton, New Mexico. "His work with William H. Crane in Metro's coming big feature will undoubtedly help to put him into a distinctive class by himself. Original high-class slapstick comedies with a plot and punch fit for any audience."

Metro supported with another round of full-page ads, this time selling the entire series with *One Week, Convict 13,* and *The Scarecrow* highlighted as the first titles ready. "Book 'em and prepare for an avalanche of business!" the headlines screamed. "Crowds are fighting to see his comedies!"

Keaton was also starting to gain notice in the commercial press, reflecting a growing awareness that screen comedy was acquiring a fresh new vocabulary, one not rooted in personality so much as technique.

Just as *Convict 13* was playing its first engagements, Keaton embarked on his fifth picture for Metro, *The Haunted House*. He was now halfway through his first year's commitment and benefiting from a regular routine of production that had him filming four weeks out of six and writing and editing in between, his only leisure the impromptu baseball games that broke out nearly every day. But where the grind of making short comedies wore on Roscoe Arbuckle, Keaton was invigorated by the challenge. "Sometimes we'd do nothing all day," he said. "Then the next day twenty minutes of film."

Most of Keaton's waking hours were given over to the development of gags, the logic of gags, the mechanics of gags. "Shaving was a great time to round out a routine," he noted, adding that the bathtub was another good place to think. "We always carried three men on our scenario staff and worked with them, and by the time . . . we were ready to start a picture, my head technical man that builds my sets, my head prop man, my head electrician, assistant director—everybody knows what we've been talking about for weeks." This also effectively made everyone on the staff a gagman. By carrying the entire picture around in his head, Keaton had the flexibility to try new things as he went. "I would shoot material for five or six two-reel films in order to make a successful single film, because in assembling the film I would cut out four-fifths of the scenes in order to keep only the best."

In a 1962 interview, Keaton described himself as producer, player, principal scene planner, chief gag writer, and director in collaboration with Eddie Cline, who lacked the eye and temperament to really excel at the job. "Eddie was too kind-hearted to be a great man," said Sennett actor A. Edward "Eddie" Sutherland, who worked for Cline and would become a director himself. "He wouldn't fight with people, he'd agree with them, and you can't be a comedy director, or really be a director, without a little ferocity. Aggressiveness—whatever the word may be—at least you have to get your own way once in a while. And you have to have a conception of the whole thing, because an actor's point of view is certainly biased. The writer only sees what he wrote. But a director has to see the whole picture as a completed entity."

Keaton, with all the energy of an athletic man in his twenties, had a zeal for the job that Cline seemed to lack. When shooting, it fell to him to visualize a shot and rehearse the players, while relying on Cline to watch and make suggestions. "He'd be out there looking through the camera, and I'd ask him what he thought. He would maybe say, 'That scene looks a little slow.' And then I'd do it again and speed it up." And Keaton knew that in comedy, clarity was important: if the audience was busy trying to figure out what was happening, they weren't going to laugh. "I like long takes, in long shot," he said. "Close-ups hurt comedy. I like to work full figure. All comedians want their feet in."

Keaton was also superior to Cline in directing his actors. "We used to say one of the hardest things to do in pictures is to *un*rehearse a scene. In other words, you get so mechanical that nothing seems to flow in a natural way. Cues are picked up too sharp and people's actions are just mechanical. Well now, to get that feeling out of it is to unrehearse the scene, and we generally did that by going out and playing a coupla innings of baseball or somethin'. Come back in and someone'd say, 'Now what did I do then?' I'd say, 'I don't know. Do what you think best and then go ahead and shoot.' That's unrehearsing a scene. Coffee break or somethin'."

It was Keaton who selected the takes and did the editing, having learned the art of cutting comedy at Roscoe Arbuckle's elbow. He moved rapidly, working with an assistant he referred to as his cutter. "He's the fellow that broke your film down and put it all in the racks there and had them all there. I'd say, 'Give me that long shot of the ballroom.' Or whatever, and he'd hand it to you . . . you'd start off with this. 'Give me the close-up now of the butler announcing the arrival of his lordship.' All right . . . As I cut them, he splices them together, running them onto the reel as fast as I hand them to him." It was, Keaton contended, more complicated to make a good two-reel comedy than a five- or six-reel drama. "We used to study frames of pictures, for the love of Mike."

Keaton was now working at such a breakneck pace that he finished *The Haunted House* on Friday, November 26, and began shooting *Hard Luck,* his sixth picture for Metro, the following Monday. That same week, his baseball team, the Keaton Komics, found time to defeat the Brunton Studio 19–12 and claim the Southern California championship, a point of pride nearly equal in importance to the business their movies did. (Buster himself was responsible for five hits in as many trips to the plate.) The rest of the year was something of a blur, with Keaton working seven days a week, determined to finish *Hard Luck* by Christmas.

In early December, Metro Pictures president Richard A. Rowland issued a lengthy statement lauding the company's progress during the year 1920. It had started with Marcus Loew's acquisition, which led to a $250,000 expansion to seventeen acres, with five new buildings and additional stages. Then Alice Lake was signed to a Metro contract, as were America's "big three" dramatists, Bayard Veiller, Eugene Walter, and Winchell Smith. Veiller went on to become Metro's executive in charge of production and was instrumental in bringing other noted writers into the fold, most prominently Irvin S. Cobb, Hulbert Footner, and George Kibbe Turner. More stars were added: Ina Claire, Emma Dunn, the celebrated dancer Doraldina. Alice had a breakout hit with William Hurlbut's *Body and Soul* and was elevated to full stardom late in the year. Metro also had Rex Ingram's production of *The Four Horsemen of the Apocalypse,* which would be released in early 1921 as an "extra special deluxe" and make a star of Rudolph Valentino, but the most attention-grabbing passages in Rowland's statement were reserved for Buster Keaton—remarkable in that Keaton was not even one of the company's contract players.

"Buster Keaton in the not far distant future will wear undisputed the crown of comedy king of the season," he wrote. "Even now he is the greatest comedy sensation since the heyday of Charlie Chaplin and Roscoe Arbuckle in two-reelers. Buster Keaton is equipped by nature and his long experience in the theatre with everything that a comedian needs. He has a sense of comedy values that is extraordinary, and knows every 'gag' or device that can be relied upon to provoke laughter."

Bookings for the Keaton comedies, Rowland continued, had surpassed the company's greatest expectations. Grauman's Rialto and the Alhambra theater in Los Angeles, for example, broke long-standing policies by holding Keaton shorts for three weeks and longer. "We have the highest opinion of Buster Keaton as a drawing card," he concluded. "In our belief he is the comedy sensation of the screen world."

On the heels of Rowland's endorsement came the Los Angeles premiere of *The Saphead,* an event heralded by Grace Kingsley in the *Times* with the headline "BUSTER KEATON WINS." "Let's end the suspense right now," she wrote. "As Bertie the Lamb in Winchell Smith's delicious comedy at Tally's Broadway, Buster Keaton makes the most of his fine opportunities. In fact, he realizes a really high standard of mimetic art by investing the role of Bertie with scores of really fine touches of kindly satire and pathos, as well as of nicely balanced comedy. What is more, perhaps, he keeps the characterization always in the realm of the thoroughbred, even as the author conceived it. Even in the scenes in the stock exchange, when he tumbles about on the floor in the pursuit of everybody who is yelling 'Henrietta!' responding thereto, 'I take it!' he's the man of gentle birth, merely overtaken by unhappy circumstances. . . . In short, Buster Keaton is about five-sixths of the picture, with [a] fine and masterly characterization, that of William H. Crane, as the testy old dad of the family. By all means don't miss *The Saphead.* It's the best thing Broadway has seen in a long, long time."

Buster, meanwhile, was focused on finishing *Hard Luck,* which he would come to regard as a personal favorite. "It was the biggest laughing two-reeler I ever made," he said. It was also the film that veered closest to Chaplin in that he played a tramp, a character completely bereft of means. Yet he always deflected comparisons between his character and Chaplin's, considering them irrelevant.

"Chaplin's just an automatic bum," he'd say. "He'd do anything in the world to keep from workin'. The only time when he'd wash somebody's car was just to get some eatin' money, where I used to try to work and try to earn a living. Just had a little trouble doin' it." Unlike Chaplin, he refused to sue for the audience's sympathies, to "get sorry for himself," as he put it. "In our early successes, we had to get sympathy to make any story stand up. But the one thing that I made sure—that I didn't ask for it. If the audience wanted to feel sorry for me, that was up to them. I didn't ask for it in action."

Since Keaton grew up deflecting the audience's sympathies, it seemed only natural for him to do the same on-screen. And by draining any hint of sentiment from the action, he gave *Hard Luck* an astringent quality rare among comedies of the day. "I started out in that picture—because I was down in spirit and heart and everything—to do away with myself. So I set out to commit suicide. There were about six gags in there that were pips. Number one is that I got a rope and got out on a sawed off log, which put me three or four feet above the ground, and I could throw a rope up over a limb of this tree, tied myself off to it, bid goodbye to the world, stepped off the stump, but the limb I'd tied off to was so limber that it just let me go down to the ground with just a light strain on the rope. I ended up lying flat on my back on the ground, trying to get up. Of course it didn't work. By that time, somebody over there says, 'Hey! Will you catch that dog or cat or something?' And I got up to run, forgetting I was tied off, and nearly killed myself. I got that rope off my neck in a hurry then. Then the next thing I did was go to Westlake Park and dove off the bridge. I didn't know there was only two feet of water there. I nearly broke my neck with that dive."

Buster's luck changes when he's embraced by the members of a country club who think he's a daring explorer on a hunt to collect armadillos for a museum. Virginia tells him to take a horse from the stable, and the middle of the story, with the fox trailing along behind him and Joe Roberts as a bandit called Lizard Lip Luke, took care of itself. The strong finish for *Hard Luck,* the brainchild of Eddie Cline, was also the most improbable one Keaton ever put on-screen, the sort of absurdist conceit he'd later shun as untenable in features. "I got out by a country club, in an open-air swimming pool, and there was a very high diving platform there for some professionals. So just to show off in front of the girls lounging around the pool, I climbed

Keaton's fondness for Hard Luck *(1921) was in no small part due to the surreal ending in which he plummets off a high dive, misses the pool, and emerges from the resulting hole with a Chinese family in tow. "That was a fade-out of a two-reeler," he later stressed. "We wouldn't have dared use that in a feature picture."*

up to the top of it, and posed, and did a beautiful swan dive off the top of that thing. And I missed the pool. I made a hole in the ground, disappeared. People came up and looked down in the hole, shrugged their shoulders, and the scene faded out."

Figuring out how to film such a scene without cheating it took time and ingenuity, while the actual shooting of it was, by Keaton's reckoning, the greatest thrill of his life. "We constructed a tank so that a portion of the pool was covered with thin wax, the wax in turn being covered with a paper imitation of tiles, so that when my hands hit the wax it would give way and I would go into the water. It was a perfect imitation, so perfect in fact that from the top of that diving platform I couldn't tell which was paper and wax and which was tile. I was so scared that if I hadn't lost my balance due to a sudden wind, I would never have left that platform. Down I went and then bang! I broke through the wax, but it cut my head and shoulders. That got a laugh, but not as big a laugh as the last few feet of the picture. In that shot the pool was deserted and overgrown with trees and shrubs. The hole I made in the tiling was still there. The screen flashed one of those 'Years

Later' captions, and I emerged from the hole with a Chinese wife and [two] half-breed children."

All the time and trouble paid off when they put the picture in front of a preview audience. "There was something like four outstanding [laughs in the picture]—what we called 'belly' laughs," Keaton said in a 1958 interview. "Today they call just a substantial, hearty laugh a belly laugh. We didn't— that was just a laugh. [By belly laugh] I mean a rock-the-[building laugh]. I mean that the theater didn't forget for a while. . . . That [diving scene] was the fade out of the picture, and that audience would be laughing getting into their cars out in the parking lots. It was so darned ridiculous that there was no way to time the laugh, because if the audience stayed in there and watched the feature picture coming on now, they'd *still* be laughing at the middle of the next reel of the feature!"

Symbolically, Keaton ended the year 1920 with a full-page ad in the Christmas number of *Motion Picture News*. Under the headline "BUSTER KEATON AND HIS DIRECTOR" was a photo of Keaton and Eddie Cline, whom he had taken to calling "E. Francis." Seated side by side, Buster has blankly removed his pork pie hat and is holding it in front of Cline's face.

8

The Most Unique and Original Comedian

B USTER KEATON'S POPULARITY with audiences built so rapidly that by the end of the year 1920, just four months after the release of *One Week*, exhibitors across the nation were pairing *The Saphead* with *The Scarecrow* for an all-Keaton program, and Metro exchanges were supporting the trend by accepting bookings for the latter film long before its official release date of December 22. In New York, where the feature played the 5,200-seat Capitol Theatre, director Herbert Blaché's habit of staging the action in long shots made, in *Variety*'s judgment, "the scenes look like miniatures and the characters like pygmies." Notices were mixed, most finding the film an unsteady blend of drama and burlesque, with Buster being the only reason for sticking with it.

"*The Saphead* is a badly constructed photoplay, of course, with its jumping back-and-forth between self-styled serious comedy and extravagant farce," offered the unsigned review in *The New York Times*. "And for this reason it is annoying to some, and would be to the writer if its farce were not so good. When he saw the picture he simply ignored its every pretension to verisimilitude, and sat back and laughed at Buster Keaton's finished clowning. Leave only this clowning in the picture, with just enough of the stupid old plot to give it coherence, and you'd have one of the best broad comedies the screen could show."

Keaton, having long since washed his hands of *The Saphead*, described its making in an interview as "a bore." Instead, he indulged his gift for slapstick suited to the demands of the modern screen. *The Goat*, a slick tale of mistaken identity filmed largely on the streets of Los Angeles, was completed in January 1921. For it, Keaton brought a second director into the fold, Sennett veteran Malcolm St. Clair, whose résumé was similar to Eddie Cline's and who would alternate with Cline for the foreseeable future. Tall and energetic, St. Clair had been the sports cartoonist for the *Los Angeles Express* before joining Keystone, where it was, he once said, "all gags and no sense." Wielding a lighter touch than Cline, he might well have urged Keaton in a new direction had the two men been better suited to each other. Cline agreeably played a cop in *The Goat* while St. Clair enacted Dead Shot Dan, "a highly intelligent and kindly-faced murderer." The finish sent an elevator containing Joe Roberts clear through the roof of an apartment building, Buster having established that he could control the speed and direction of the thing by simply moving the arrow on the dial above the door.

With *The Goat* finished, Keaton started on the eighth and final picture he owed Metro for the season, an untitled affair that advanced the automated house of *The Scarecrow* even further, using electricity to power the labor-saving features instead of pulleys and counterweights. He was shooting with Cline one day in late January when, while riding a mechanized staircase to the second floor of the interior set, the sole of one of his slapshoes got caught in the webbing that held the steps together. Thrown clear at the top, he fell twelve feet to the floor, breaking his right leg at the ankle. Rushed to Good Samaritan Hospital, it was estimated he'd be laid up for at least six weeks. In reality, it would be five months before he would be back at work again.

The immediate problem, that of delivering Metro's eighth picture, was solved by taking *The High Sign* off the shelf. Not an ideal solution as far as Keaton was concerned, but Lou Anger never thought it as bad as its director made it out to be. It was imperative, though, to make it look like a new two-reeler, not some leftover or a trunk item. News of Buster's injury was kept quiet, while word was put out to the press that his seventh comedy, *The High Sign,* had been completed and shipped to New York. As a further diversion, *Variety* reported that the entire Keaton company would be heading east in April, and that at least two pictures would be shot in New York City. Finally, on February 19, *Camera!* carried an item that Keaton would be unable to work for several weeks as a result of torn ligaments sustained in a scene. Two days later, *The Haunted House* was released nationwide.

Confined to bed and unable to work, Keaton was forced to confront the fact that his private life didn't amount to a whole lot. Myra visited him every day, and he had pals like Viola Dana and Lew Cody stopping by, but up to the point of taking the house on Ingraham Street, he had led a transient lifestyle, content to sleep on someone's couch rather than taking a place of his own. It was Bluffton where he spent his happiest days, and when a woman from *Picture-Play* came by for an interview, he showed her an ad for *The Saphead* from the *Muskegon Chronicle*, his name set in larger type than the film's title:

Starring Muskegon's Own
BUSTER KEATON
in his first big feature production
(Direct from the Capitol Theatre, New York,
where it played to Record-breaking houses.)

"Muskegon's own!" he exclaimed. "Sounds like a bottle of catsup." She naturally wanted to know if he had been born there.

"No," he said, "but I lived there between seasons on the road and went to school—oh, it's the old home town all right. I get an awful kick out of that ad."

When news of the accident reached Natalie Talmadge in Palm Beach, where she was wintering with her mother and her sister Norma, she wrote Buster a letter: "I am alone now, the only one left living with Mother. If you still care, all you have to do is send for me." His reply wasn't immediate; he hadn't seen her in nearly two years. After a few days of enforced solitude, he wired her that his leg wasn't strong enough to go to New York, but that he'd be there when it was. Grace Kingsley broke the news on February 2 in the *Los Angeles Times*. "Some people seem to think the only way to capture those lovely Talmadge sisters is to strong-arm 'em," Buster was quoted as saying, "and I don't know but I may do that if necessary. That is, if nobody beats me to it with Miss Talmadge. New York, you know, is full of enterprising Greeks* and Miss Talmadge is the loveliest girl in the world."

Not to be outdone, the *Herald* tracked down Natalie, who just laughed and said, "There isn't anything to tell." Norma took the phone and explained that most of the courtship had been "conducted by telegraph." In Muskegon, the *Chronicle* mistakenly characterized the relationship as a "war

---

* He was referring to a brother of Constance Talmadge's husband, tobacco importer John Pialaglou, who was Natalie's frequent escort.

romance." And in *Variety,* the deception continued with Buster supposedly "working a double production schedule out at the Metro" so that he would have time to fly east for the wedding. It soon became evident that Keaton wasn't working, and that his salaried personnel were being loaned to other studios. Jean Havez was seen on the Lasky lot supplying bits for an Arbuckle feature, Joe Mitchell was loaned to Harry and Jack Cohn for work on their Hall Room Boys series, and Mal St. Clair was working at Fox after Lou Anger put out word that *The Goat* had been completed as Metro's eighth and final release.

The *Picture-Play* interviewer, Emma-Lindsay Squier, asked Buster when he and Natalie were going to be married. "I don't just exactly know," he replied. "That's up to my better nine-tenths—meaning Natalie—and, of course, the condition of my leg has something to do with it. I've been in bed now for five weeks, and the doctors think that I'm in for three more. Then I'll have to dash around on crutches for a while—and after that— New York!" On March 23, it was reported the engagement was suddenly off. Natalie had broken it but refused to say why. One possible reason had appeared in the *Los Angeles Times* in late February, when the paper published a publicity photo of Keaton and Vi Dana on the Metro lot, demonstrating how a screen kiss was filmed for a group of visitors. The headline didn't help: "HERE'S A REAL ROMANCE." Neither did the subhead: "You Didn't Know About It, Either."

Two weeks later, sprung from the hospital and hobbling around on crutches, Keaton announced he was off to New York to collect his bride. He added that the wedding would occur almost immediately upon his arrival so that Natalie wouldn't have any time to change her mind. Accompanying him would be Lou Anger, who would serve as best man at said wedding. In Manhattan, *Billboard*'s Marcie Paul went to the Forty-Eighth Street studio to get a look at Buster's intended and found "a slim little dark person, wholly adorable, and unmistakably a Talmadge." There was, she noted, no engagement ring. "Natalie doesn't know when they are going to be married, because she doesn't know when they are going to see each other again, and she doesn't like to talk about things before they happen."

Buster's arrival came at a time when both Norma and Dutch were ill— Norma slightly, Dutch somewhat more seriously—and Nat was understandably distracted. "She had only one objection to marrying me," he said. "She hated to leave New York, something that was not hard to understand." The cloud of indecision lingered more than a month, during which time *The*

High Sign was released to a better reception from audiences and exhibitors than its maker ever expected. (*The New York Times* found it "ingenious and irresistibly funny.") To continue the ruse that it was newly made, Eddie Cline's name was added to the credits, and a press statement explained away the absences of Virginia Fox and Joe Roberts by noting that even actors and actresses were entitled to vacations. "Such is the belief of Buster Keaton, Metro comedy star. As a result, *The High Sign,* the latest Keaton comedy, will make its appearance with an entire new cast supporting the sad-faced comedian."

Six releases in, Keaton's stoic countenance had become his trademark, a meme now perpetuated in studio publicity.

"Why don't you ever smile in your comedies?" asked Squier.

"Oh, I don't know," he answered. "It's just my way of working, I guess. I have found—especially on the stage—that when I finish a stunt, I can get a laugh just by standing still and looking at the audience as if I was surprised and slightly hurt to think that they would laugh at me. It always brings a bigger laugh. Fatty Arbuckle gets his humor differently. The people laugh *with* him. They laugh *at* me."

Back in his Arbuckle days, Buster's expression wasn't quite so regimented, and he was known to occasionally smile and even laugh. But for Metro he was variously the "frozen-faced comedian," the "boy with the funeral expression," and most often simply "sad-faced." It was an image in the press that perfectly underscored his predicament with Natalie, haplessly hanging around New York, biding his time.

"Peg was still searching the horizon to find a better mate for Natalie," Anita Loos, who was co-writing Dutch Talmadge's features, deduced, "but there weren't even any gigolos around to take up the slack."

In April, a wire photo circulated in which the couple was seen shopping in New York, Keaton grimly dapper in a three-piece suit, bag in hand. A week later, an item appeared in the "Among the Movies" column of the *Nebraska State Journal:* "If Buster Keaton did make his trip to New York for the express purpose of marrying Natalie Talmadge he was rather defeated in it, because Natalie now says that she hasn't enough clothes for a trousseau and he will have to wait until she gets a few more. Latest reports are, then, that Mr. Keaton will stay in New York a while until his lame knee [*sic*] heals, and then go back to California for a season, returning a few months later to claim his bride. This little misunderstanding as to time and clothes, if such it was, might have been avoided if Buster and Natalie had been carrying on a regular courtship with letters instead of the wordless, letterless, wireless sort."

By the middle of May, Natalie was promising the press that the marriage would take place within a month and that there would be no elopement. Finally, Keaton could stand it no longer. "We gotta bring this thing to a head," he insisted.

"Oh, Buster, you know where I'm going."

"Okay, where and when will we be married?"

"Let's make it a week from Saturday at my sister's home."

But when Buster, still walking with a cane, appeared at the municipal building with Nat, Dutch, and their mother to take out a license, the date had been slipped three days to May 31—which also happened to be the twenty-seventh wedding anniversary of Joe and Myra Keaton. It was a symbolic gesture, likely in consolation since none of the family would be able to attend. The venue was indeed the Bayside home of Norma Talmadge and Joe Schenck, a colonial with six bedrooms and a spectacular view of Little Neck Bay. Playing up the subdued atmosphere of a country wedding, the

The wedding of Natalie Talmadge and Buster Keaton at the Joseph Schenck estate on Long Island. From left: Ward Crane, Buster, Natalie, Margaret "Peg" Talmadge, Constance Talmadge, Norma Talmadge (obscured), and City Court Justice Louis A. Valente.

piazza that afternoon was laden with flowers—snowballs and other late-spring varieties—and the guest list was minimal, just family and a few close friends and co-workers. Dutch Talmadge, who persisted in characterizing the courtship as a "mail-order romance," was matron of honor for her sister, while Buster's pal Ward Crane served as best man. In keeping with the easy formality of the occasion, the bride wore a frock of pale gray designed by her sisters, the groom a double-breasted suit and bow tie. Justice Louis A. Valente of the city court officiated.

Peg Talmadge, who considered Natalie the "home girl" of the three, made little effort to suppress her melancholy at losing her middle daughter to the West Coast. "It was difficult for me to share Natalie's assurance that 'all would be as it had been before,'" she wrote in her memoir. "I knew separations were bound to come, though I did not dim her happiness by any such prophecies."

Apart from empty-nest syndrome, Anita Loos, who attended with husband John Emerson, sensed an element of buyer's remorse: "Peg's smile was forced; she considered Natalie's marriage as a mere substitute for movie stardom. I disagreed. I used to think that looking across a pillow into the fabulous face of Buster Keaton would be a more thrilling destiny than any screen career."

The Keatons spent their honeymoon en route to Los Angeles, where Buster could mercifully get back to making pictures. He had been away nine weeks, an intolerably long stretch for a man so thoroughly engaged in his work. They stayed with Lou Anger and his wife, singer-actress Sophye Barnard, while Buster searched for a suitable place for them to live. They settled on a relatively modest five-bedroom rental on Westchester Place, less than half a mile from Joe and Myra's house on Ingraham Street, and stocked their new home with wedding gifts, among them a diamond solitaire Buster gave Natalie, a $2,000 Belgian police dog (Dutch's contribution), and a fully equipped Rolls-Royce limousine that came from Norma and Joe. Still, the surroundings were considerably less grand than what Natalie had grown used to.

A certain tension between the two was evident from the start. On June 13, the couple attended a benefit baseball game sponsored by the *Los Angeles Herald*. Shirley Mason, Vi Dana's sister, had just relinquished her position as guest umpire of the Vernon-Oakland matchup and was looking for a seat. When she saw one and hopped into it, she didn't realize at first that she was occupying the box immediately next to the Keatons.

"Hello, Buster!" she called. "When did you get back from the wedding trip?"

"Hello, Shirley!" Keaton responded. "Wedding trips mean nothing between friends." And with that he leaned across the railing and gave her a kiss.

"Bride Natalie was there, looking on at it all," an eyewitness reported. "She never said a word. But it's a safe bet that by now Buster knows just what she thought." The next day, the paper reported that Keaton had returned to the studio on Lillian Way and was once again engaged in the task of making movies.

The time waiting on Natalie Talmadge in New York wasn't entirely wasted. With Metro's distribution agreement at an end, Joe Schenck was seeking better terms. And Keaton, like Arbuckle before him, was looking at a case of burnout. "I made eight comedies in the last year," he had said from his hospital bed. "I intend to make that many next year. And each one has almost a hundred gags in it—just figure that out and see what happens to your imagination at the end of three years. That's why practically all comedians go sooner or later into five-reel stories with a comedy angle. It's easier to let someone else worry about the laughs."

He loved the process of making films, the mechanics and the problem-solving. What he didn't like was the constant pressure of coming up with fresh, funny ideas. "I string all my stuff together—no, not alone, because everyone in the company helps. But I mean that I've never yet bought a scenario, and I've had thousands of them offered me. I can't find funny scenarios. If I could, I'd pay a wonderful price for them." His solution, at least in the short term, was to make fewer films and use the extra money to properly stage the increasingly intricate gags he envisioned.

Schenck had been in business with Associated First National since 1919, the year they began distributing the Norma Talmadge dramas and her sister Dutch's feature comedies. They also had a six-picture deal with Charlie Chaplin that was due to expire with the delivery of *The Pilgrim* in 1922. Originally a circuit of independent exhibitors, First National was in the market for a new series of two-reel comedies, while Schenck was looking to consolidate all his picture interests under a single banner. On May 24, 1921, a week before the marriage that made Buster Keaton his brother-in-law, Schenck entered into a contract with First National for the distribution of six Keaton comedies with an option for another six. Where Metro had reimbursed Comique up to $45,000 per film, First National now guaranteed a flat $70,000 advance, regardless of cost. In return, they would retain all revenues up to $120,000, then split the gross income beyond that figure on a fifty-fifty basis.

The hiatus at the Keaton studio had taken a toll. Jean Havez left to work for Harold Lloyd, leaving Comique with Joe Mitchell as its sole writer. Mitchell, fifty-five, was a good man whose motion picture experience dated back to the Lubin company, where, as an actor, he was reputedly involved in the making of the first film comedy in 1898. As a writer, Mitchell had fashioned a touring vaudeville act for himself and partner Paul Quinn, and co-authored a German soldier sketch for Lou Anger in 1909. Anger elevated him to head writer and went looking to beef up the scenario staff. About the same time, publicist Harry Brand returned to Comique, where he had earlier served as Al St. John's press agent. Short of staff, Keaton fell back on one of his surest creative instincts, the show business parody.

"During my vaudeville years I never enjoyed anything more than doing burlesques of the other acts on the bill," he said. "The first I ever tried was one of Houdini getting out of the strait jacket. I was then about six."

Now that he was making movies, Keaton took aim at one of the industry's best-known producers, Thomas H. Ince. "Ince," he said, "started takin' himself very seriously and his pictures come out saying, 'Thomas H. Ince presents Dorothy Dalton in *Fur Trapping on the Canadian Border*. Written by Thomas H. Ince. Directed by Thomas H. Ince. Supervised by Thomas H. Ince, and this is a Thomas H. Ince Production.' Well, [we'd start] the picture with that, saying 'This is a Keaton picture. Keaton presents Keaton. Supervised by Keaton. . . .'"

It was a wonderful inspiration, but going back to work while his ankle was still mending meant keeping the slapstick to a minimum. "If we can't have falls and chases, what's left?" said Jean Havez, presumably as he was walking out the door.

In time, Keaton decided a movie send-up on the order of *Moonshine* wasn't viable. "In comedy, like any other kind of picture, you have to do stuff that will be appreciated outside of New York and Chicago. In big cities the people are sophisticated enough to understand travesty and the more subtle bits of humor, but they don't get over elsewhere."

Instead, he opted for containing the comedy within the setting of a legitimate theater, effectively minimizing the action while giving himself more opportunities for like-minded gags. "We don't need falls or chases," he concluded, envisioning instead a world where every part, every job, every seat was filled by a variation of Buster Keaton. "The whole picture is a visual gag. I hardly have to do anything."

The development of the untitled picture was augmented by the arrival of a new scenarist, a local newspaperman and magazine writer named Clyde Bruckman. A sportswriter for the *Los Angeles Times* and later the *Examiner,* Bruckman had been working for the studios, primarily as a title writer, since 1919. He had also published in *The Saturday Evening Post* and fancied himself a minor-league Ring Lardner. Bruckman was with Warner Bros., writing for comedian Monty Banks, when he ran into Harry Brand, an old friend from his newspaper days.

"Why don't you come over with Keaton?" Brand asked.

"How do I know Keaton wants me?" Bruckman responded.

Brand knew; both he and Bruckman had played on an amateur baseball team called the Scribes, and "Bruck" was a terrific pitcher. The next day, Bruckman had a call from Brand inviting him to lunch at the Keaton studio. He went, hit it off with the boss, and was hired on the spot.

The centerpiece of the new picture was to be a minstrel performance on the stage of an opera house, Keaton figuring he could fit nine images of himself onstage in a single shot. Buster the Interlocutor would occupy the center of the frame, while Buster in blackface would hold down the right and left ends, one as Brother Tambo, whacking the tambourine, the other as Brother Bones, rattling a pair of clappers. Three other Busters would flank Mr. Interlocutor on either side, strutting and playing until the line: "Gentlemen! Be seated." Envisioning such an ambitious shot was one thing; actually getting it on film was another.

The technique of multiple exposures had been used before, but generally only to show the same actor side by side, playing, for instance, identical twins. At its simplest, this involved masking off half the image, leaving half the frame of film unexposed, then winding it back in the camera and masking off the other half of the image. What Keaton was proposing was to do this nine times over. "Every move, song, and dance exactly in unison," said Clyde Bruckman, who was present for the filming. "That meant taping off the lens into nine equal segments accurate to the ten-thousandth of an inch."

Well, not exactly. Shortly before his death in 1955, Bruckman described how Keaton pulled off the effect, building a lightproof box that fitted over the camera, its front comprised of nine equally spaced shutters that could be opened and closed independently of one another, allowing for the exposure of nine different vertical slivers of the frame, rolling the film back in the camera each time. While Bruckman's description clearly explains the idea behind the effect, silent era camera expert Sam Dodge said it couldn't have been achieved with a box mounted in front of the lens:

"The camera used to shoot these scenes was a Bell & Howell 2709. They started in 1912 and were the top of the market, the Rolls-Royce camera of their day. The multiple Buster Keaton characters were all done with mattes *behind* the lens. They could be custom-cut for these scenes, but Bell & Howell made such a huge variety of mattes that there easily could have been mattes that would work for each scene. They required a sharp, hard-edged vignette. Keaton put a lot of pressure on the cameraman to get the mattes positioned just right every time. There were also in-front-of-the-lens mattes in the matte boxes of the time, but they gave a softer edge to the blocked image."

Making these shots was a tedious process, Buster the sole presence on a crowded stage, working in perfect synchronization with the other exposures. "Actually," said Keaton, "it was hardest for Elgin Lessley at the camera. He had to roll the film back eight times, then run it through again. He had to *hand crank* at *exactly* the same speed, *both* ways, *each* time.* Try it sometime. If he were off the slightest fraction, no matter how carefully I timed my movements, the composite action could not have been synchronized. But Elgin was outstanding among all the studios. He was a human metronome."

An accomplished still picture photographer, Lessley, thirty-eight, had been shooting movies since 1911, initially with the Méliès Star Film Company of Santa Paula, California, later with Keystone, where he brought clarity and depth to a category that didn't always value such things. He first photographed Roscoe Arbuckle in 1915, and later followed him to Comique. When Arbuckle moved into features, Lessley remained with Keaton, forming a perfect union of technical expertise and comic ambition. Keaton always dictated the setups on important scenes, but gave Lessley his head on incidentals.

* A hand-cranked camera exposed sixteen frames of film with two complete turns of the crank made in one second's time. This equaled sixty feet of film a minute, the standard established in 1917 by the Society of Motion Picture Engineers (SMPE). By 1921, filming speeds tended to be faster, commonly twenty to twenty-four frames per second, but a lot depended on the individual cameraman and the effects desired by the director.

The all-Keaton minstrel line from The Play House *(1921).*

"He would go by the sun," Keaton said. "He'd say, 'I like that back cross-light coming in through the trees. There are clouds over there right now, so if we hurry up we can still get them before they disappear.' So I would say 'Swell' and go and direct the scene in front of the cameraman's setup. We took pains to get good-looking scenery whenever we possibly could, no matter what we were shooting."

In filming the minstrel show, Keaton left the technical mastery to Lessley while concentrating on the precision of his own movements, which had to be keyed to all the other exposures. There were no retakes—a mistake meant the whole process had to start over from the beginning.

"My synchronizing was gotten by doing the routines to banjo music. Again, I got a human metronome. I memorized the routines very much as they lay out dance steps—each certain action at a certain beat in a certain measure of 'Darktown Strutters' Ball.' Metronome Lessley set the beat, metronome banjo man started tapping his foot, and Lessley started each time with ten feet of blank film as a leader, counting down. 'Ten, nine, eight,' and so on. At 'zero'—we hadn't thought up 'blast off' in those days—banjo went into chorus and I into routine."

It is a bravura sequence, Buster as ticket buyer, Buster as bandleader,

Keaton also portrayed various members of the audience in The Play House. *"The film has a peculiar aura, not quite like anything else he made," wrote Penelope Gilliatt. "It is dreamlike and touching, with roots in a singular infancy that he takes for granted."*

Buster as all six musicians in the pit, Buster as stagehand, Buster as the minstrel line, Buster as the spectators in three different boxes, Buster onstage doing an expertly coordinated dance number with himself—twenty-six individual Busters in all. As technically perfect as it all turned out to be, its effectiveness ultimately rests on Keaton's extraordinary gifts as an actor. In using posture and attitude to convey character, he is always wry and understated, keeping them all human and never reaching for laughs. First he is a man and his wife, a banker type, stiff and credulous, she impassively fanning herself, slightly bored with it all. He consults his program, which heralds Buster Keaton's Minstrels—ten cast members and fourteen staff, all Keaton. Scratching his head, he comments to his wife, "This fellow Keaton seems to be the whole show." In another box, a lollipop-licking boy and his dowdy mother rain candy and soda pop down on the elderly couple beneath them. The old man snores loudly as his haughty wife berates him, mistaking the sticky sucker in her lap for her eyepiece. In what must have been a relief to Lessley, these are all simple two-shots accomplished with a standard matte behind the lens.

In all, it's six and a half minutes of pure comic genius, beautifully mined for all its satiric potential. Keaton later said he regretted not extending the idea into the rest of the film, saying he made "one very bad mistake" by not doing so. "I could have made the whole two-reeler just by myself, without any trouble. But we were a little scared to do it, because it might have looked as though we were trying to show how versatile I was—that I could make a whole half-hour picture all alone, without another soul in the cast. That's the reason why we brought other people into the second reel, and that was a mistake."

At the time, Keaton saw an opportunity to turn the film into a rumination of sorts on the notion of perceived reality, almost as the cinema's master magician Georges Méliès might have done with the luxury of two reels at his disposal. Awakened from his dream by Joe Roberts as his apparent landlord, Buster's room is stripped of its furniture and he is ordered out. As he exits, they dismantle the walls to reveal it's all another stage set, and Buster the stagehand had merely been loafing on the job. Identical twins appear, each seeking a dressing room, Buster just missing the fact that there are two girls and increasingly perplexed by their comings and goings. In the property room, he glances at himself in an old shaving mirror and is startled to see himself multiplied by three. He emerges to find the twins in front of standing mirrors, now suddenly a quartet.

Told to "dress the monkey" ahead of an animal act, he opens the door to the chimp's cage and unwittingly lets him escape. Seeing no alternative, he blackens himself up with cork, dons evening clothes, and proceeds to channel Peter, the famous "educated chimpanzee" who shared the bill with the Keatons during their ill-fated week at London's Palace. ("A chimp as a headliner!" Buster exclaimed. "Ever hear of such a thing?") Peter's act consisted of taking a formal meal, puffing on a cigarette, doing stunts on roller skates, and driving his own automobile. Keaton mimes the creature with uncanny fidelity, turning on his trainer and climbing the scenery, leaping about the stage in a way that must have made his doctors wince.

A flat comes crashing down, bringing the startled audience to its feet. Buster pilots a bicycle in a figure-eight pattern, then hops through a hole in the backdrop. In the resulting confusion, the Zouave Guards resign and he is left to recruit a crew of ditch diggers to replace them. Under Buster's command the act is a kaleidoscopic shambles in which the collapse of a scenic wall sends him sliding down the aisle and out the doors of the theater where, in a momentary daze, he purchases a ticket before wobbling back inside.

Having invested the first act with truly extraordinary material, Keaton was faced with the problem of devising a third act strong enough to balance it. While not as visually arresting, the solution was to introduce a young lady, one of the twins, who can "stay underwater longer than the bottom of a river." Onstage, she dives into a tank of water to demonstrate, only to get her foot caught at the four-minute mark. Buster heroically comes to her rescue, ineffectually at first, then decisively when he retrieves a heavy mallet and shatters the glass. The massive rush of water engulfs the house, sends the spectators fleeing, and blows the theater's doors off their hinges. Having turned the orchestra pit into a swimming pool, Buster dives in and retrieves the waterlogged girl, then commandeers a bass drum as a vessel and paddles himself off using a violin as an oar.

As a dazzling fantasia of film technique, *The Play House,* as it came to be known, had no equal in the realm of two-reel comedies. When it played L.A.'s Kinema Theatre in late September, it shared the bill with sister-in-law Constance's *Wedding Bells,* and the Keatons were on hand, the house packed. Seated in the club loges, Buster was rigid during the unspooling of his own picture, grim and judgmental amid the gales of laughter. It was only when Dutch's feature, a clever reworking of a popular stage comedy, came on that he relaxed and permitted himself to enjoy the show. At one point, he laughed out loud and found the people surrounding him were watching him rather than the screen, wondering if such a thing were even possible.

Keaton had fretted that the opening of *The Play House* left the picture top heavy, and he was right to some degree—nothing could beat that first act. While the *Los Angeles Herald* unreservedly pronounced it a riot, the verdict in the *Times* was more measured: "Buster Keaton starts off three laps ahead of everybody in his comedy *The Play House,* which is billed high, wide, and handsome along with the Talmadge story. Buster tricks you all over the place. You see so many Busters in so many different disguises that you would hardly recognize yourself in the mirror, you feel so dizzy. Finally, however, the star's little variety show expands into routine comedy—very much routine, and less comedy than usual. *The Play House* is really somewhat of a comedown for a man who has been climbing steadily."

In the coverage surrounding the marriage of Natalie Talmadge and Buster Keaton, it was widely reported that the bride would appear with the bridegroom in his next picture. A few weeks later, Nat was embracing the role of homemaker, and Buster had no comment on married life when visited at the studio by a writer from *Motion Picture* magazine. "It's too soon yet to say anything," he told the guy. "I've only been married three weeks." Enigmatically he added: "Marriage is fine as an institution, but bad as a habit."

Then a July 1 item in the *Toledo Blade* confirmed by way of night letter the fact that Natalie had "temporally" retired from the screen, having told her mother she was merely giving up a job, not a career. "She is completely wrapped up in her husband and her home, they tell us, and is not spending much time at the studio at present. Maybe later we'll hear from the youngest [*sic*] Talmadge sister via the silver sheet—but not now says she."

A fuller statement of her intentions made the August 1, 1921, edition of the *Los Angeles Evening Herald*, where it appeared under the byline of Natalie Keaton herself. "I have taken up an experiment costing me $104,000 to determine whether I can become a successful housewife," she wrote. "In other words, I am turning down an offer of $2,000 weekly in real, honest-to-goodness money which would be paid to me if I appeared in the movies because I want to star in a kitchen role." She went on to say that when she made up her mind to marry Buster Keaton, she also made up her mind to be the manager of their home. "At present I am looking over Los Angeles and vicinity for a site for that home. I prefer that it be on a high hill. It will be big and roomy. There will be a vegetable garden, a flower garden, a bridle path for horseback riding, and a swimming pool. For years I have been building a 'castle of dreams' and this is to be my castle. I will be just an old-fashioned housewife, and plan to make the hours spent in my home the golden hours of my life."

When Grace Kingsley profiled the couple for the *Los Angeles Times,* Buster kept quiet and let Nat do most of the talking. She revealed that producer John Golden, a Bayside neighbor, had offered her a part in a Broadway play, but that she chose Buster instead. "I never cared a cent about public life. I always wanted to stay at home." And she dismissed rumors of other beaux: "Nobody else ever really had a chance for a minute. But I thought I'd keep everybody guessing a bit." Kingsley described her as sweet-faced, looking "like a little Quaker" with clear brown eyes and a disarming sense of mischief. "Let's go for a race in my new Mercer!" Nat urged. "I certainly can make that old bus hum!"

In October, Constance Talmadge arrived from New York and invaded the Keaton household on Westchester Place, dragging nine trunks and seven bags of clothing along with her. As the vanguard of a small army of relatives relocating to the West Coast, she entertained questions from the press as Buster showed her around. "Los Angeles is the greatest motion picture center in the world today—always has been and always will be," she declared, having first come to prominence in D. W. Griffith's *Intolerance,* filmed in

Hollywood in 1916. "And now we're all going to be together again in good old Los Angeles, for Norma is coming within six weeks with Joe." Has Hollywood changed? she was asked. "Yes, I find Hollywood changed. The cellars are now all upstairs."

Joe Schenck ("the big brother-in-law" as Dutch and Nat referred to him) was moving all his picture operations westward, having leased out the New York studio to Lewis J. Selznick and taken a part interest in the Robert Brunton Studios—soon to be renamed the United Studios—where the Talmadge features were to be made in the future. In April, the *Times* had reported that Keaton was looking to purchase a studio of his own, but nothing, it appeared, suited him nearly as well as the stage he was already using. The move from Metro to First National, announced in June, forced the issue, and *Moving Picture World* confirmed Comique's purchase of the lot—which would officially become known as the Buster Keaton Studio—the following month.

By alternating between two directors, Buster Keaton was able to pass from one film to the next with a minimum of delay. Upon completion of *The Play House,* he reportedly put Eddie Cline in charge of cutting the picture and began shooting *The Village Blacksmith* with Mal St. Clair the next day. The new comedy was conceived as a parody of the Longfellow poem, which Buster used to recite onstage. The illustrated title card quoted the first two lines:

> "Under a spreading chestnut tree
> The village smithy stands;"

Cut to Buster at the base of a California palm tree so tall it takes an extreme long shot to take it all in.

> "And the muscles of
> his brawny arms
> Are strong as
> iron bands."

Buster flexes his arm and a great muscle erupts under the sleeve of his shirt. When it fails to retreat, he jabs it with his tie tack and it bursts like a balloon.

"And children coming
home from school
Look in at the
open door;"

As he works away at the forge and anvil, two schoolboys stop and watch from the street. Joe Roberts, the shop's owner, comes ambling along, lunch pail in hand, and roughly shoves them aside. Meanwhile, a closer shot reveals that Buster, instead of hammering out horseshoes, is cooking himself breakfast.

The Village Blacksmith was a troubled collaboration, St. Clair preferring a slower tempo than Keaton, and while the film had some clever intervals, such as when Buster acts as shoe salesman to a persnickety horse, there were none of the big ideas audiences had come to expect of him, nor any particularly cinematic ones. "Mal was a great director and eventually became the darling of the New York critics," said his writing partner Darryl Zanuck, "but he was inarticulate." When they completed the film in August, Keaton and St. Clair came to an amicable parting of the ways. With a sure sense of visual storytelling, St. Clair would go on to distinguish himself with romantic comedies populated by the likes of Adolphe Menjou, Florence Vidor, and Pola Negri, as well as with the initial film versions of *The Show-Off* and *Gentlemen Prefer Blondes*.

Playing it safe, Keaton returned to familiar territory for his next picture, picking up with his lovestruck couple from *One Week,* last seen walking off in the distance, the abject ruins of their do-it-yourself house in the foreground. Why not take these two characters, advance the calendar several years, and give them another project to tackle? Sybil Seely had given birth to a son, Jules Furthman, Jr., in March and was available, so Buster gave Virginia Fox the month off, welcomed Sybil back into the fold, and proceeded to create one of his strongest comedies, a fitting companion to the picture that first put him on the map.

The premise for the new two-reeler was even simpler than for *One Week.* Buster has built a boat in the basement of their house and is intent upon launching it. What follows is a panoply of comic destruction, a celebration of defective reasoning and, as the critic Gilbert Seldes would put it, "intense preoccupation." In the film's opening moments, Buster discovers his newly completed craft is too big to fit through a rolling door, so he gets busy with a crowbar and chips away at the brick wall surrounding it. (This gag, he recounted, was inspired by the memory of an actual incident. "The manager of a theater on the old canal at Utica built himself a swell cruiser in the cellar of the theater and had to knock out a side of the theater to get it into the water.") Deciding he's done enough, Buster marches over to the Model T, where Sybil and their two sons are waiting, and starts the engine, gingerly dragging the boat by a towline through the still-inadequate opening and making it considerably larger as he does so. And when it finally clears the gaping hole, the entire house, after a splendidly timed beat, collapses in its wake. "The main thing that makes an audience laugh," he said, "is that something happens to me that could have happened to them. But it didn't—and they're glad."

Perplexed but undeterred, Buster salvages a bathtub and a couple of oars from the rubble and soldiers on. After managing to drive his car off the dock, sending it bubbling to a watery grave, he is ready for a christening. The name on the ill-fated boat is *DAMFINO,* and like so many things in Keaton's work, it too can trace its lineage back to his early years, in this case to Muskegon. In 1914, a Chicago-based agent named Eddie Sawyer eased his boat in alongside Joe Roberts' dock, and the name painted on the bow was *DAMFINO* (as in answer to the question "Where are we?"). Keaton always relished the name, and may have settled on the idea of a boat picture in order to use it.

Sybil attempts to smash a Coke across the bow, but the bottle holds and all she manages to do is chip the paint. Hanging down from above, her husband produces a hammer and finishes it off. Then, standing aloft, his back to the camera, he gives the signal. Sybil releases the rope tethering the vessel, sending it gracefully sliding stern first down the slipway and into the water, where it smoothly and thoroughly proceeds to disappear below the surface. This simple shot, one of the most surefire laughs in Keaton's entire body of work, took three days of location time to work out all the bugs. "She simply would not go straight down to the bottom," he said. And the laugh, he knew, depended on the absolute lack of hesitancy in the *DAMFINO*'s voyage to the ocean floor.

"We got that boat to slide down the waves. Now, we got something like sixteen hundred pounds of pig iron and T-rails to give it weight. We cut it loose and she slows up, slows up so slow that we can't use it. Well, you don't like to undercrank when you're around water. If you undercrank water, immediately you see it shows, that it's jumpy. Well, first thing we do is build a breakaway stern to the boat. So when it hits the water it would collapse and act as a scoop, to scoop water. That worked fine, except the nose stayed

Buster is ready to launch The Boat.

in the air. We've got an air pocket in the nose. We get it back up and bore holes all through the nose and everyplace else that might form an air pocket. Try her again. And there is a certain amount of buoyancy to wood no matter how much you weigh it down. She hesitated before she'd slowly sink. And our gag's not worth a tinker's damn if she don't go straight right down to the bottom. So for a finish, we go out in the bay at Balboa and drop a sea anchor with a cable to the stern, a cable out of a pulley over to a tug out of the shot. We've got all of the air holes out of it and the rear end to scoop water—I actually *pulled* that boat down. That's the way we got that scene."

Never was there a thought of abandoning a stubborn gag; good ideas were too precious to waste. "Material was always the number one item for all comics," Keaton said. "Digging up new gags. We just slept and ate 'em, tryin' to dig 'em up. The next thing is when you got your gag, photograph it right and do it right. Don't be careless with it. The other comics around generally were workin' for somebody on a low budget and if they got the scene halfway they said, 'That's it.' Okay it, and it's the next setup. It didn't work with us that way. We spent three days making that gag photograph. Maybe we could afford to—that's why. But it made a big difference."

Having handily destroyed both his house and his car, Buster settles into a life of domestic tranquility on the now seaworthy craft, Sybil doing the cooking and cleaning and seeing to the children while he tends to navigation and maintenance. They sail out into open waters, where a storm at sea threatens to scuttle the craft. Buster secures the family belowdecks and radios for help. At the other end of his SOS is Eddie Cline, their sole chance at rescue.

"Who is it?" he wants to know.

"*DAMFINO*," comes the reply.

Cline reacts with disgust, as if he's just been asked if he has Prince Albert in a can. "Neither do I," he responds, terminating the exchange.

Buster's backward ingenuity has left two holes in the hull, and now it's taking on water. He gathers the family up on deck and, using the bathtub as a lifeboat, sets them adrift. Sybil and the boys watch helplessly as he goes down with the ship, where all that's left of him is his hat floating on the surface of the water. It's as bleak an ending as a comedy ever had, and Keaton the director lingers on the image before he buoyantly resurfaces and joins the others in the impossibly crowded little tub. Soon, it is taking on water too, and they prepare to drown as a family unit when they discover they're actually sitting in just two feet of water. Relieved, they stand and slog toward the shore as Sybil asks, "Where are we?" Buster mouths the answer, but an intertitle is unnecessary. And they all walk off into the distance, just as they did the previous year in *One Week*.

The Boat wrapped in late September with tank work at the Brunton studio. But an event that month cast a cloud over the picture and, at one point, filming was briefly suspended. On September 5, 1921, a party had taken place in a twelfth-floor suite occupied by Roscoe Arbuckle at San Francisco's St. Francis Hotel. Arbuckle wasn't the host—he was sharing the rooms with director Fred Fishback and actor Lowell Sherman—and people came and went over the course of the afternoon. There was plenty of drinking, and one of the guests, an actress and model named Virginia Rappe, fell ill. The hotel manager and, eventually, the house physician were summoned. Arbuckle described her as hysterical.

"We carried her into another room and put her to bed," he said. "The doctor and all of us thought it was no more serious than a case of indigestion, and he said a little bicarbonate of soda would probably relieve her."

Arbuckle returned to Los Angeles the following day.

It was on September 9 that Arbuckle learned that Rappe had died in a private sanitarium. "I was making a picture," said Viola Dana, "doing night shots and using Roscoe Arbuckle's garage and bedroom. At eleven o'clock, Roscoe came in with Sid Grauman and Joe Schenck. Roscoe said, 'How much longer are you going to be, Vi?' I said, 'Not much longer.' His secretary [Katherine Fitzgerald] was there, and he said, 'Vi, can you spend the night here with Katherine?' I said, 'Yes, I don't have to work very early tomorrow.'

Roscoe Arbuckle with attorney Frank Dominguez.

'Fine,' he said. 'Now listen, kids. I have to go up to San Francisco. I can't tell you why. But for God's sake don't die on me.' We thought that was very strange, but we thought no more about it until the next day when we saw the papers. Then, of course, we knew exactly what he meant."

Upon arriving back in San Francisco in the company of Lou Anger and attorney Frank Dominguez, Arbuckle was arrested and charged with first-degree murder. Details to be placed before a grand jury emerged in the press. Arbuckle, according to a witness, took hold of Rappe, who was Henry Lehrman's girlfriend, and said, "I have been trying to get you for five years." He pulled her into an adjacent bedroom and locked the door, and when it was opened sometime later—in answer to repeated pounding by other partygoers and an attempt at breaking it down—Rappe was unconscious on the bed in a disheveled state, her clothing torn, her body bruised. When she came to, and later on her deathbed, she blamed Arbuckle for her injuries, particularly a ruptured bladder, which led to her death from peritonitis. She was thirty years old.

The Arbuckle case immediately became the principal topic of conversation in show business circles. "Nobody is too busy apparently to discuss or listen to the 'most sensational story ever involving the fourth greatest industry,'" Guy Price observed in the *Los Angeles Herald*. "Not even the divorce and remarriage of Mary Pickford attracted so much general comment. And Charlie Chaplin's marital *faux pas,* in comparison, becomes completely obliterated." In an ominous move, Roscoe's old friend Sid Grauman ended the world premiere engagement of *Gasoline Gus,* his latest feature comedy, early on its last day at the Million Dollar, setting off a chain reaction that spread across the country. But even before Arbuckle pictures were being pulled from bills nationwide, attendance figures showed a steep and immediate decline—in some locales by as much as 50 percent.

At the center of the allegations against Arbuckle was a woman called Bambina Maude Delmont, who, as Mme. Delmont, was run off the island of Santa Catalina in 1919 for operating a "beauty parlor" (a slang term for a brothel) at the Avalon dance pavilion. She was also rumored to be a serial extortionist. "She would provide girls for parties," said stuntman Bob Rose, "and she ran a badger game. She'd get one of these young girls in on a party and have her claim that a producer or director had tried to rape her. Because in those days, they had open house almost. Even tourists would come in on the big Saturday-night parties. So she'd break in on these parties with these girls and try to frame someone."

Virginia Rappe wasn't a prostitute, nor had she known Maude Delmont for more than a few days. The connection between them was Al Semnacher, who said he was Rappe's manager and the man who invited her to join them on a drive north from Los Angeles over the Labor Day weekend. Maude Delmont was soon discredited as an unreliable witness, her testimony blown full of holes at the coroner's inquest. Yet it was her lurid account the reading public saw first, and it established a widespread impression of the private Arbuckle that proved impossible to dispel. Lacking evidence to support the murder charge, the coroner's jury found that Rappe nonetheless died from injuries inflicted by Arbuckle and charged him with manslaughter. So while Buster Keaton was busy filming *The Boat,* Roscoe, held without bail, was languishing in a jail cell some four hundred miles away.

Visibly upset, Keaton called a halt to production the day Arbuckle was arrested, and declined to shoot the following day as well. "We just couldn't work," he told Grace Kingsley, fighting back tears. "San Francisco people are doing the whole thing. What right has anybody to condemn a man before he is heard?" Kingsley asked if he was going north to see his old friend. "You bet we are, just as soon as we can find time. We laid off work so long that we've got to get busy!" When Frank Dominguez returned to Los Angeles with the express purpose of looking into Delmont's background, Keaton offered to testify as a character witness, as did other friends of the defendant.

"Mr. Dominguez talked us out of going to the trial. He said that there was bitter feeling in San Francisco even against him for taking a case that local people felt should have gone to one of their own lawyers. 'They would resent you fellows even more,' he said, 'and discount your evidence, feeling you were merely Arbuckle's front men.'"

On Sunday, September 18, nearly six thousand people filed past Virginia Rappe's body at a small funeral parlor on Hollywood Boulevard. A private Episcopalian service held the next day was limited to those who knew the deceased, while a thousand onlookers crowded the street outside. Among the pallbearers that day were director Norman Taurog and the comedians Larry Semon and Oliver "Babe" Hardy. Henry Lehrman, stuck directing a picture in Great Neck, Long Island, sent an elaborate display of lilies dedicated to his "brave sweetheart."

Dominguez's investigation led him to believe that Delmont and Semnacher had conspired to blackmail his client, an assertion he put before the court. The following day, the charge of rape was dismissed, leaving involuntary manslaughter as the only count against Arbuckle, enabling him to post bail after nineteen days in stir. To his surprise, the Southern Pacific Depot at Third and Townsend was jammed with well-wishers, mostly women, some bearing flowers. "Arbuckle was not particularly glad to see them," a man from *The New York Times* reported. "He smiled and shook hands with them, and thanked them all, accepted the flowers and rolled a brown paper cigarette deftly with his left hand, his right busy shaking hands. There was nothing of the comedian in Arbuckle tonight. The experience he had undergone in San Francisco has chastened him."

Accompanied by his wife, Minta, and her mother, Arbuckle passed the twelve-hour trip to Los Angeles in seclusion, but was all smiles when he detrained at L.A.'s Central Station sporting a green cap and clad in a dark gray business suit. Fifteen hundred people had turned out to meet him, a repeat of the scene at the San Francisco depot on a larger, more impressive scale. Among those on hand were Eddie Cline, comedian Hank Mann, and exhibitor Mike Gore. Actor Bull Montana broke through the crowd and was the first to offer a hearty greeting. "Thank you, Bull," Arbuckle was heard to respond as cameras flashed.

Then Keaton extended a hand: "Glad to see you again, Roscoe. You're looking good. Welcome home."

He and Lou Anger stayed protectively close as the passengers slowly made their way to a fleet of waiting cars, Roscoe responding to shouted questions from the press with, "Nothing to say," Frank Dominguez backing him up.

Said Minta, "We're all going right out home—to Roscoe's house, you know. It's to be a real homecoming for us all in more ways than one."

Back at the mansion on West Adams, a party was already in full swing, although Arbuckle, known for one of the best cellars in Hollywood, had taken the pledge. As night fell, the place was ablaze with lights and a steady stream of limousines delivered the famous and the merely wealthy to offer their congratulations. Roscoe smiled his old familiar smile, humbly and sincerely thanked each of them, and rolled countless brown paper cigarettes. Buster, accompanied by Natalie, surveyed the scene: "What could you say to the poor bastard? He was getting the works. A funeral would have been more cheerful. Half the people there whispered and tiptoed around, and the others laughed too loud."

With Arbuckle safely home for the moment, Keaton launched into preparations for his next First National release, *The Paleface*. Yet Arbuckle was still being hectored by the authorities. In a lather, Adolph Zukor ordered Frank Dominguez off the case, replacing him with Gavin McNab, probably San Francisco's best-known attorney. On October 8, Arbuckle was compelled to return to the city, where he was summarily arrested on federal Prohibition charges. Five days after that, he was required yet again, this time for his October 13 arraignment, at which he entered a plea of not guilty. His manslaughter trial was set for November 7, 1921.

Keaton may have settled on an outdoor story like *The Paleface* because his newly acquired studio was under construction. With only an outdoor stage at his disposal, he was too often at the mercy of the weather, leading to marathon card games in his dressing room when he should have been shooting. Enclosed studios were the norm back in New York, but California had been slow to adapt. When the Brunton lot was designed and built as the Paralta Studios in 1918, five steel-and-glass stages, each large enough to hold five or six sets, were at the center of the layout. As with their open-air counterparts, these indoor stages were intricately rigged with muslin curtains to soften and diffuse the sunlight. But the coming thing on the West Coast were so-called dark stages that blocked out the sun entirely and depended on banks of sizzling arc lights and Cooper Hewitt mercury-vapor tubes for illumination. These did away with the muslin draperies, and to a man like Elgin Lessley, a dark stage held the promise of more creative indoor filming, free of the vicissitudes of natural light. So when applications were made in

October 1921 to move the dressing rooms and wardrobe shed to one side of the lot and make room for a new open stage, nearly 150 feet square, allowance was also made for the construction of a dark stage at a projected cost of $50,000.

Shot mostly at the rugged Iverson Ranch in Chatsworth, twenty-five miles northwest of the studio, *The Paleface* became a watershed for Keaton in that it established a storytelling convention that he would return to frequently. The setup to the film portrayed an Indian land swindle and a murder—heavy stuff for a two-reel comedy. It wouldn't have worked with most comedians of the day, but Keaton's natural reserve enabled him to put a stark dramatic opening across that was completely devoid of gags. After ten starring comedies, his pact with the audience was such that they would stay with him as he served up three completely laughless minutes anticipating his entrance.

The opening title:

> In the heart of the West,
> the Indian of today dwells in
> simple peace.

Cut to Joe Roberts as the tribal chief, sitting placidly outside his teepee, puffing on a long calumet.

> But there came then a group
> of oil sharks to steal their land.

What follows is an executive meeting at the office of the Great Western Oil Company. The president is called away by a ruffian who produces a document. He recounts how he lay in wait outside a government land office for an Indian messenger bearing the lease to their tribal land. The thug creeps up on him and brutally cracks him over the skull, killing him instantly. He steals the coveted paper and presses a coin into the victim's hand.

> "And that's how I persuaded
> him to sell the lease for a dollar!"

The company president returns to his meeting with the paper, and as the others gather around, he begins composing a letter of demand to the chief.

"We'll give him twenty-four
hours to get off the land."

When the chief receives Great Western's notice to vacate, he is outraged and calls a tribal council. "White man kill my messenger," he announces, gesturing to the fence that marks the boundary of the reservation. "Kill first white man that comes in that gate." And so a deadly vow of revenge does double duty as the picture's first surefire laugh. The camera holds on the gate until Buster tentatively peers through, an intrepid lepidopterist with butterfly net in hand.

The Iverson property at the base of the Santa Susana Mountains, with its distinctive sandstone formations suggesting scenes of China, India, Australia, the South Seas, and practically every state of the union, had been serving as a handy filming location since 1912. Keaton seemed to regard it as a wonderland of possibilities for staging memorable stunts and effects, the more spectacular the better. In the ensuing chase, he races down a steep grade, tumbling head over heels to elude the tribe, then is propelled chute-like into a tall tree that abruptly breaks his flight. Collecting himself, he leaps directly into the cluster of Indian braves below, bouncing off them as if by a trampoline and landing safely onto the cliff opposite.

Even more breathtaking is his escape over a steep gully, a rickety suspension bridge offering only a dozen staves and a pair of wires to support him. He manages to cross anyway by placing the loose boards one after another in front of him, only to be met by more Indians on the other side.

"Below the camera line, men were stationed underneath to catch him in case he fell," observed Ethel Sands, a visitor from *Picture-Play*, "as there were several sharp rocks which wouldn't have been particularly soft for even a comedian to fall on. His director [Eddie Cline] enjoyed it immensely—he just roared laughing at Buster, which rather surprised me, as I didn't think a comedian's company could get so much fun out of it, but they do apparently."

Trapped between the two bands of Indians, Buster leaps into the chasm, a climactic stunt that gave even the normally fearless Keaton pause.

"Personally," he said in a 1930 interview, "I've never had the slightest fear of jumping off into a net from a great height, or doing a dive into water, and the only kick I got out of a net jump was during the filming of *The Paleface* when I had to drop eighty-five feet from a suspension bridge into a net. The day before we shot the scene, the technician who set up the net—and who claimed to be a former fireman—offered to prove the net was safe by making the jump himself. I told him to go ahead. He jumped and, failing to hit

the net properly, broke a leg and a shoulder. When I stood in the same spot the next day with the cameras grinding, I couldn't think of a thing save that man who was in the hospital. I came darn near not doing that scene, but because I didn't want to show yellow before my own gang, I did the jump and it was successful."

Returning to Comique after a six-week vacation that took her to Pittsburgh, New York, and Atlantic City, Virginia Fox was assigned the nominal role of the "Indian squab" in *The Paleface,* making her the only female in the cast. After Buster saves the day for the chief and his tribe, he claims Virginia as his reward, and they end the picture on a dip kiss that, with the aid of one of Clyde Bruckman's distinctive intertitles, lasts two entire years.

Unusual in depth and scale for a two-reeler, *The Paleface* would cause Robert Emmet Sherwood, the future Pulitzer Prize–winning author of *Idiot's Delight* and *Abe Lincoln in Illinois,* to hail it as "a veritable epic" in the pages of *Life* magazine: "It is strange that the silent drama should have reached its highest level in the comic field. Here, and here alone, it is preeminent. Nothing that is being produced in literature or in the drama is as funny as a good Chaplin or Keaton comedy. The efforts of these young men approximate art more closely than anything else that the movies have offered. They are slapstick, they are crude, they are indelicate to be sure, but so was Aristophanes, so was Rabelais, so was Shakespeare. How many humorists who have outlived their own generations have been otherwise?"

. . .

With the release of *The Play House* on September 19, 1921, First National took ownership in a big way. "Keaton Is Ours!" crowed a display ad in *Variety*. "No longer a prospect—<u>Now</u> a gold mine!" Mindful of exhibitors who had loyally booked the Keaton comedies when Metro had them, the new distributor announced it was making its two-reelers available to theaters on the open market, not just to First National franchisees. "They will be in two groups of three each. You can contract for the first three as a series or each release separately. Nothing funnier made! Get busy!" A three-page display touting the entire fall lineup followed in *Exhibitors Herald*. Featured up front alongside *The Play House* was Chaplin's *The Idle Class*, set for an October release. Also from First National: Pola Negri in *One Arabian Night*, Richard Barthelmess in *Tol'ble David*, Norma Talmadge in *The Sign on the Door*, Constance Talmadge in *Woman's Place*, new releases from directors Raoul Walsh and John M. Stahl, and Marshall Neilan's *Bits of Life*.

First National's superior reach was apparent from the outset. Metro released *The Goat*, its eighth and final Keaton subject, on October 15 and achieved worldwide rentals of $101,041, a figure on par with its other Keaton pictures, while the corresponding "played and paid" number for *The Play House*, put out by First National a month earlier, was $155,286—a jump of more than 50 percent. *The Boat*, at a cost of $22,000, posted similar results when it was released on November 28. With the first series of three completed, Keaton embarked on the second series of releases with what was to become the best known and most celebrated of all his short comedies, *Cops*.

As with *The Paleface*, the making of *Cops* coincided with the construction of the dark stage on the Keaton lot, encouraging a story line that required no interiors. And, as was always the case with Keaton, the simplest concept yielded the best results. "You could write the whole plot on a postcard," he said. "We do the rest." What he envisioned was a pursuit through the streets of Los Angeles "just ducking cops in all directions. Just a common ordinary chase sequence." But it would all lead up to a powerful finish in which Buster was chased en masse by the city's entire police force. "Three hundred and fifty [cops]," he said in a 1963 interview. "And it was because we could only find three hundred and fifty cop uniforms."

The logistics of such a shoot required pre-planning on a scale Keaton and his production team had never before attempted. Every gambit, every evasion had to be thought through in advance. Locations had to be selected, extras scheduled and costumed. No picking up a quick shot a block from the studio—too many moving parts to coordinate. He was always proud of the fact that he never worked from a script, but the paperwork needed to make

Cops must have come awfully close to one. Even so, his organic method of working gave him plenty of leeway.

"The director, a couple of scenario writers, and I sit around and discuss a scene. That is how the gags are made. Then we shoot the scene. Lots of things develop during the actual taking of the picture which we hadn't thought out at all." The matter of rehearsal was anathema to him. "For any of our big rough-house scenes where there is a lot of falls and people hitting each other, we never rehearsed those. We only just sat down and talked about it. [I'd say], 'Now he drops that chair, you come through the door and come through fast, and this person here sees you come and throws up their hands and from the center door you can see it. Now you come through and just about hit him. If you miss, get her.'" Then they'd walk through it to get the timing. "If you had to do it a second time, invariably somebody skinned up an elbow or bumped a knee or something like that, and now they will shy away from it the next take, or they will favor it. See, you seldom got a scene like that as good the second time. You generally got them that first one, and anybody in that scene is free to do as he pleases as long as he keeps that action going. So, even your extras can use their imagination."

In *Cops*, the action is set in motion by Virginia's rejection of him as a suitor. "I won't marry you," she tells him, "until you become a big business man." Thus motivated, Buster resolves to prove himself a wheeler-dealer. He is tricked into buying a wagonload of furniture drawn by a downtrodden horse named Onyx. (Clyde Bruckman bestowed the name because the animal purchased for the role was a bedraggled white in color.) Onyx is singularly lacking in energy, and Buster's efforts to urge the horse along have no discernible effect. Finally, he takes the bit in his mouth—literally—and starts pulling the wagon alongside the horse.

"We planned it to lead into another gag," Buster remembered. "We wanted to pan the angle shot slowly from me and on to show Onyx riding in the wagon and then to the furniture all unloaded and piled in the street. For two days we tried to get Onyx up into the wagon but he wanted no part of it. He wouldn't walk up a ramp, refused to be hoisted in a veterinary's belly band, kicked whenever we came near. Saturday we passed up the baseball game to work on the problem. But no soap. That night we quit, tired and disgusted. Monday morning we saw the reason for it all—a brand new colt standing wobbly alongside of her. *Her* I said. What a bunch of dopes we were."*

---

* Keaton, it should be noted, named the colt "Onyxpected."

It's the day of the city's annual police parade. Bruckman's title:

Once a year, the
citizens of every city
know where they can
find a policeman.

Coming upon the vast sea of marching blue uniforms are Buster, Onyx, and the loaded wagon of furniture. All that was left to do was to spark a pursuit. "I tried to cut through the parade and I couldn't do it, so I just joined it. And before anybody could stop me, some anarchist up on top of a building threw a bomb down on the police parade, but it lit in my wagon. So when it went off, the whole police force was after me."

Instantly, Buster has hundreds of cops on his tail. Onyx breaks into a gallop, the viewing stands clear out, and a hydrant is sheared off, sending a geyser of water skyward. The old wagon collapses, and they're all upon it, but the suspect is nowhere to be found. When he appears under an open umbrella, the cops give chase, swarming everywhere. Charging bands converge on a street corner, smoothly snaking past each other while Buster hides inches away. Everywhere they go, he outruns them. Emerging from a Hollywood alleyway and onto a busy street, he grabs on to a passing car and neatly whisks himself away. Was the car going that fast? Keaton was asked during a TV interview. "No," he replied, "that's undercranked a little bit—but not much. The actual speed, I guess you could say . . . Well, when a man runs one hundred yards in ten flat, you know what his actual speed is? Nineteen miles an hour. That car's only going about fourteen 'cause you couldn't take it that fast. Take your arm right out of your socket. Couldn't take it."

Two cops approach from opposite directions, their batons raised. Buster dashes between them, and they knock each other out cold. At a construction site, he climbs a ladder that teeters on the top of a fence, a cop at one end, he at the other. Soon reinforcements arrive and converge in full force. Buster ducks into the Fifth Precinct Police Station and they follow him in, packing the building until the walls nearly bulge. He emerges in uniform, completely unnoticed, and closes and locks the doors. Just then Virginia, the mayor's daughter, comes along and rejects him for the spectacle he's made of himself. As she walks away, he unlocks the doors and allows himself to be pulled inside. To suggest the darkest of outcomes, the THE END card is illustrated on a tombstone, Buster's pork pie hat, cocked at a saucy angle, resting atop it.

An entire municipal police force gives chase in Cops *(1922). "This chase sequence—how much of it was planned way in the beginning and how much came out in the actual doing?" Studs Terkel asked. "Well," said Keaton, "as a rule, oh about fifty percent you have in your mind before you start the picture, and the rest you develop as you're making it."*

The filming of *Cops* stretched over a large swath of the city, adroitly taking advantage of actual streetscapes as well as the standing sets at several different studios. "That poor horse filmed at nine different spots all around L.A. and Hollywood," said renowned location historian John Bengtson, who has identified every scene in the picture, "and at the Goldwyn, Metro, and United backlots." That the completed film is so seamless in its jumps from setting to setting is a testament to Buster Keaton and the expert team he and Lou Anger had assembled at the Keaton studio.

There was now a general feeling among critics that Buster Keaton, with his new series of comedies for First National, had risen to the same level of artistry as Charlie Chaplin, creating a body of work unparalleled in the world of film. "Keaton," declared *The New York Times,* "is one of the few really accomplished clowns of the screen, constitutionally comic, it seems, and never more so than in *The Play House*." Notices celebrated his magical use of the camera, and the word "unique" popped up with striking frequency.

"The most unique and original comedian," said *The Milwaukee Journal*. "An amazing bit of double photography seen in this picture. There's a whiff of love interest and plenty of comedy. You ought to see this picture. It's so unique it's uncanny." *The Atlanta Journal* also invoked the word, calling *The Play House* photographically unique: "Keaton has never made a comedy with more ingenious contrivances to amaze the audience. Neither has any other film comedian."

In New York, *The Boat* was similarly praised by the *World*'s Heywood Broun, who singled it out on a bill at the Rivoli, where the main attraction, UFA's *Mistress of the World: The Dragon's Claw*, was given relatively short shrift. "The feature film is magnificent," Broun said of the epic German production, "but it has neither the ingenuity nor the imagination of the Keaton comedy. Peculiarly enough, few so-called serious pictures of home manufacture employ processes of thought to any extent. It is only the business of being funny which sets producers and actors to thinking. Keaton is an exceedingly agreeable performer, and the material that has been devised for his talents in *The Boat* is altogether exceptional.

"Much has been done already on the screen in the development of trick automobiles which explode at convenient moments, and farcical aeroplanes and disorderly submarines, but nothing within our experience has equaled the antics of Keaton's yawl. From the moment of its launching, when it slides down the ways to sink nose first with a preliminary gurgle and a few bubbles, the little yacht achieves an altogether fascinating irrationality. Through this comedy we move like merry dream people, as Keaton's yacht cruises its sharp course in spite of bridges, docks, and all respectable inanity which is reared against it. Our own feeling of self-sufficiency was vastly stimulated by the scene in which Keaton and his crew sank in the middle of the Pacific only to step out and find that the water came no higher than their knees. The catastrophe occurs at night, and the picture leaves the characters standing wandering upon some dark and dry land set at an unknown spot in an elemental wilderness.

"In this," Broun concluded, "there is poetry."

9

Spooling Comedy

THE MANSLAUGHTER TRIAL of Roscoe Arbuckle commenced on the afternoon of November 18, 1921. Two days of medical testimony outlined the deceased's physical condition at the time of her death, and constituted, in the assessment of Otis Wiles, staff correspondent for the *Los Angeles Times,* a sort of Cook's tour through all the organs of the human anatomy. Arbuckle, Wiles noted, sat restlessly, seemingly perplexed by all the terminology. "His position was that of the bad boy in school, a sort of a painful expression emphasized with a wrinkled brow whose thoughts were of the old swimmin' hole or the fish that awaited the dip of his hook and sinker in the spring creek."

Maude Delmont was not called as a prosecution witness, leaving the dirty work to a pair of uninvited showgirls who attended the party at the St. Francis. Yet the resulting testimony seemed in the main to favor the defense. Arbuckle appeared downright cheerful as the day drew to an end. As the court adjourned for the Thanksgiving holiday, *Variety*'s San Francisco correspondent said the case was expected to be in the hands of the jury no later than the Monday of the following week. "It is the consensus of opinion here Arbuckle will be acquitted of the charges against him."

On November 28, Arbuckle himself took the stand as the defense's last witness. His testimony, which brought mobs of the curious to the hall of justice, was characterized as sober and consistent, and he proved to be his own best witness.

"What was the first thing you did in room 1219?" he was asked under cross-examination.

"I closed the door and locked it. I wanted to dress."

"Was there no other reason?"

"No. No other reason. I went straight to the bathroom and opened the door. The door struck Miss Rappe, as she was lying on the floor. She was holding her stomach and moaning. She looked sick, as if she was short of breath."

The case went to the jury of five women and seven men on the afternoon of December 2, and thirty-one hours later there was still no verdict. The first ballot had shown nine for acquittal, and after twenty-two ballots the count stood at ten for acquittal and two to convict. The judge in the case polled the jurors individually and then excused them as hopelessly deadlocked on December 4.

"Arbuckle appeared greatly disheartened," the *Times* reported. "His wife broke down and wept." A new trial was set for January 9.

"This case has put quite a crimp in my pocketbook," Arbuckle admitted upon his return to Los Angeles. "I resent the damage it has done me because I know I am a victim of circumstances. If I had had any connection with the death of Virginia Rappe I would have said so. That is the kind of man I am. All of the dirt in this case was brought in by Mr. [District Attorney Matthew] Brady. The evidence consisted of what certain persons thought they knew—not what they were sure they knew. I have always tried to be a good scout and to treat people in the right way.

"I do not know whether I will ever appear in pictures again. Of course, I want to. If the public wants to see me then I will go back to my work. If they don't I'll do something else. I won't act again unless the public shows that I will be well received. At present I have no position, no contract, and am not financially interested in any of my pictures, released or awaiting release. I have spent some very unhappy days, but my conscience is clear and my heart is clean. I have nothing to apologize for."

In the run-up to the second Arbuckle trial, Buster Keaton was dealing with a crisis of his own. *The Village Blacksmith*, retitled simply *The Blacksmith*, had been previewed for James Quirk, the influential editor of *Photoplay*, and Quirk had excoriated the picture in the magazine's January issue. "It's a sad day when one of our comedians fails us," he wrote. "Buster Keaton is guilty this month. There is hardly a smile in his latest comedy, if such it can be called. The situations are forced and his work laborious. His scenario writer should consult Webster and discover that the words silly and funny are not synonymous."

It was by far the worst notice a Keaton comedy had ever received—and *Photoplay* was the top movie magazine of the day, boasting a circulation of two million. The people at First National were alarmed, and Keaton knew he had to do something to salvage the picture. *The Boat* was hastily advanced to fill the hole in the release schedule, and as soon as *Cops* was finished Keaton set about fixing *The Blacksmith*. Judging from the changes he made, he decided there wasn't enough slapstick in the thing, and that too much of it played out within the confines of the blacksmith shop. He removed a tedious scene in which he got oily handprints all over Virginia's white horse, business that made the later trashing of a white Rolls-Royce seem repetitious. He also moved the film outdoors with an inventive chase sequence in which Big Joe takes off after Buster when he is inadvertently hit by his car. The result was a livelier, faster-paced comedy—no masterpiece but certainly an improvement over the first version.

"It's heartbreaking work, that's all I have to say," Keaton, in a black mood, said as he rested between shots. "We gave up trying to follow a script months ago, because the gags that looked funniest on paper flopped cold on the screen. Now we make up our laughs as we go along, and the going is tough!" He shook his head dolefully. "Look at me—I'm getting gray-haired."

Eddie Cline tried stirring him up, but Buster was having none of it.

"The future?" he echoed when asked about his plans. "Who knows? I don't. I'll keep on spooling comedy until the fans get fed up on my stuff, then I'll go back to vaudeville."

When finally released in July 1922—an entire year after the first scenes were made—many exhibitors billed *The Blacksmith* ahead of the five-reel feature, an increasingly common practice as Keaton was often considered the bigger draw. "Buster Keaton, of the lugubrious countenance, has some of the funniest tricks of his career in this conglomeration of incidents," raved Stuart Gibson in *Motion Picture News*. The notice in *Exhibitors Herald* similarly proclaimed it "one of his funniest." And although it turned a respectable profit, Keaton regarded *The Blacksmith* as "a dud," an attitude he maintained for the rest of his life.

Ahead of the second trial of Roscoe Arbuckle, Joe Schenck addressed a gathering of the First National Exhibitors' Circuit of Northern California, deploring the treatment accorded the defendant. "Wild rumors that thousands and thousands of dollars are being spent in defense of Arbuckle are without foundation," he said. "As a matter of fact, the cost of the first trial was only $35,000, and this includes the amount paid attorney Gavin McNab.* I ought to know something about this matter, as I put up the money to foot the bills."

The new trial got under way on January 11, 1922, with a notable decline in interest on the part of the public. Maude Delmont, who had been arrested and convicted on bigamy charges the previous month, was again not called upon to testify, leaving the two showgirls from the first trial to continue to act as the key witnesses for the prosecution. Fred Fishback returned as a defense witness, and Arbuckle's full testimony from the earlier trial was read into the record. The case dragged on until February 1, when it was finally sent to the jury. Fourteen ballots later, the judge again declared a hung jury. Surprisingly, the split this time was ten to two in favor of conviction. Minta Arbuckle once again broke into tears, while the defendant and attorneys on both sides reacted in stunned silence. Jurors who spoke out afterward said the case for the defense was weak.

While the jury was deliberating, Hollywood was rattled by another scandal, the murder of Paramount director William Desmond Taylor. Arbuckle began to tear up in court when he got the news. "Taylor was the best fellow on the lot," he said. "He was beloved by everybody and his loss is a shock." As the lurid details of the Taylor case emerged in the press, they added another layer of debauchery to American perceptions of how those of the film colony conducted themselves. Ten days after Taylor's body was discovered in a Westlake bungalow, thirty members of the Independent Screen Artists Guild met in Los Angeles to issue a statement asking for fair play from the moviegoing public.

"We are not rampant with vice. . . . We are law-abiding citizens, and we rear families," it said in part. "And yet William Taylor's death has resulted in aspersions being cast upon this industry and upon us, for we are striving to make the world a better place to live in through the screen. And we, who have accepted that responsibility placed upon us by the public through their patronage, feel it a personal affront to assume through innuendo that we are not worthy of that honor." Among those authorizing the statement,

---

* Schenck was a straight shooter, and the $35,000 figure for Arbuckle's first trial—which would equate to $500,000 in today's money—was likely accurate.

which ran in full in most major American newspapers, were Joseph M. Schenck, Charles Chaplin, Thomas Ince, Mack Sennett, Louis B. Mayer, Norma Talmadge, Constance Talmadge, Ben Turpin, director King Vidor, and Buster Keaton.

Coming up with fresh ideas was always the hardest part of moviemaking for Keaton. "Each day I put in a certain number of minutes on the story," he said. "Ideas are given and either accepted or rejected. Old ideas are worked over in the hope of finding a new angle. New ideas are considered and built up. Everyone at the studio suggests and everybody's suggestion gets consideration." It was a hectic way of working, and not all writers fit into the process. Clyde Bruckman adapted and seemed to have a natural talent for it. Others over the years couldn't abide the egalitarian nature of the process and quickly moved on.

The next two comedies from the Keaton studio were considerably different from those that came before, doubtless reflecting the influence of Broadway humorist and *Variety* columnist Thomas J. Gray, who arrived in December 1921 and, working with Joe Mitchell and Clyde Bruckman, brought the writing team to three in number. The author of the *Greenwich Village Follies* and two Music Box Revues, Gray had a background similar to Mitchell's in that he specialized in funny vaudeville and revue sketches, but he was also an accomplished playwright and song lyricist. In New York, Gray had written briefly for Roscoe Arbuckle but played the fish-out-of-water card in Los Angeles, where he denied having come west just to avoid the benefit season.

The first film reflecting Gray's participation, *My Wife's Relations,* was firmly set in "the foreign section of a big city," possibly Greenpoint, the portion of Brooklyn known as Little Poland. Said Keaton, "*My Wife's Relations*—that is, the hazy idea of it—was born when Eddie Cline and I saw a postman in the East, unable to read the inscription on a letter in a foreign settlement, compare it to the lettering on a sign board." With Buster, for once, was no ingénue but a substantial character actress named Kate Price, who was twenty-three years his senior and nothing at all like the wispy Virginia Fox. In the film's opening, he gets framed for breaking a window, then, due to the language barrier—the judge doesn't speak a word of English—finds himself married to the daughter of a family of Irish roughnecks. Buster has a hard time fitting in until they mistakenly think he's due for a big inheritance and

An aerial view of the Keaton lot showing the dark stage added in 1921. Exterior sets constructed for My Wife's Relations *and* The Frozen North *are visible at the right.*

decide to put on the dog. His escape from the liveried digs they've all moved to has him climbing out a top-floor window and descending four flights by swinging from awning to awning, a breathtaking stunt he performs in a single shot, typically refusing to cut or cheat the effect in any way.

Staged largely on interior sets, *My Wife's Relations* was the first two-reeler Keaton shot in the new enclosed stage, effectively avoiding rain delays during what was historically the wettest time of the year. Moving on, he embraced the elements in his next picture, shooting two weeks of exteriors in snowbound Truckee, a former logging center and ski resort some five hundred miles north of the studio in the Tahoe National Forest. At an elevation of nearly six thousand feet, the town was a favorite location for movie companies, and there were no fewer than five working locally when Keaton and his crew arrived. The local Southern Pacific Hotel, in fact, was permanently outfitted with a cutting room and screening facilities.

The idea for *The Frozen North* may have come from an experience related by Paul "Scoop" Conlon, Arbuckle's former publicist, who was on the job when Keaton was drafted in 1918. After the war, Conlon joined Famous

Players and went to work for William S. Hart, the stoic western star whose features were released through Paramount.

"He had a big snow story to do," Conlon remembered. "Needed a storm and heavy fall, more than enough for dog teams. Every precaution was taken to insure success. Weather looked fine for the purpose, according to our advance man at Truckee. Bill bought the story and engaged a cast on so many weeks guarantee. Even had our trunks packed and entire studio equipment ready for the train. A few hours before train time we were astounded to get the news that a change had set in and the snow was melting fast. We waited. But the snow never came back. It was near the end of the season, but the snow broke early. The catastrophe cost Bill Hart nearly $25,000—and he never produced the story."

With *The Frozen North*, Keaton burlesqued the kind of northwestern drama Hart had attempted, skewering the former Shakespearean's pretensions in a send-up that just got wilder as it progressed. Hart, who was from New York but spent a portion of his childhood traveling the West, was known for the gritty realism with which he invested his films. His characters were complicated antiheroes who started out bad and sometimes stayed that way, but he was at heart a stage actor whose signature role was Messala in the original Broadway production of *Ben-Hur*. Keaton drove the point home with the picture's first gag, making his entrance into the snowy wilderness by exiting a subway station, the last stop on a line that presumably passed directly through Times Square on its way to the Arctic.

Keaton resembled Hart, a quality that made the film's centerpiece all the more shocking. Walking in on his wife and her lover, seated with their backs to the door, he sees them nuzzle, reacts melodramatically, even sheds a glycerin tear. Then they kiss and it's too much for him to stand. Unholstering his revolver, Buster shoots them both dead, walks over to examine the bodies, and gives a start.

"I've made a mistake," he says. "This isn't my house *or* my wife." Sheepishly he takes his leave, reflexively tipping his hat as he goes.

Keaton claimed to admire Hart's early work in pictures but felt he had "gimmicked up" his later performances. "For some reason he turned ham on us. He was a great actor, but he got hammy at the end of his career. He always looked for the opportunity to cry—even with two guns strapped to his side out in the desert. If the girl turned and looked at another man, tears ran down his cheeks. There's nothing you could do about it. He was his own producer."

Buster's actual wife in *The Frozen North* is once again Sybil Seely, but she
has little to do once she manages to knock herself out with a pot jostled off a
high shelf. He, meanwhile, is fixated on the married neighbor lady and goes
courting. Taxis get hailed, cops give chase, and Buster visits Joe Roberts in
his spacious igloo. The two go ice fishing, but Buster is soon back pursuing
his neighbor with seduction—and possibly even rape—on his mind. (This
point is underscored when Keaton briefly morphs into Erich von Stroheim
as the phony aristocrat from *Foolish Wives*.) As he grapples with the woman's
husband, Sybil appears at the window and shoots her philandering man in
the back. The neighboring couple are reunited, but Buster levels his gun at
the pair and is about to fire when he is awakened by Eddie Cline, playing the
janitor in an empty movie theater. It was, after all, a bizarre dream.

The Frozen North was a sharp stick in the eye of William S. Hart, who
justly regarded it as a merciless parody. "I had a little trouble, but I tried my
best to be Bill Hart," Keaton innocently recalled, "so much so that Bill Hart
didn't speak to me for a couple of years after I made it. He thought I was
kidding him. I said, 'I didn't kid you, Bill. I was just trying to be an actor
like you, and I didn't quite make it.'"

The third Arbuckle trial began on March 6, 1922, and was longer than either
of the previous hearings, consuming nearly five weeks. As before, there was
expert testimony on the state of Virginia Rappe's health on the day of the
party, the defense once more contending that the cause of her death was the
result of chronic bladder troubles and had nothing to do with any actions
taken by the defendant.* Arbuckle, who turned thirty-five during the trial,

* Author-historian Tracey Goessel, M.D., has studied the death of Virginia Rappe and sees
it from a physician's perspective. She says that Rappe's attack of severe pain *could* have been
the result of an ectopic pregnancy, one in which a fertilized egg had attached to a fallopian
tube rather than to the wall of the uterus. But the fact that Rappe survived several days argues
against this. It is more likely, she suggests, that Rappe's pain was from Pelvic Inflammatory
Disease, common even today and much more common in the pre-antibiotic era. Dr. Goessel
also points out that Roscoe Arbuckle's weight could not have caused the rupture of Rappe's
bladder, especially one that was reputedly empty. "Bladders don't rupture that way. They require
a high-velocity, high-force injury, or a fractured pelvis. I'm one hundred percent certain her
death was iatrogenic. The house doctor at St. Francis catheterized the patient after an injection
of morphine, and he observed only a little bloody fluid. I suspect it was peritoneal fluid from a
ruptured bladder. Catheters were either glass or metal in those days, not plastic. *He* caused the
tear with the catheter, and that led to the peritonitis that killed her. Arbuckle had nothing to
do with it. It was the result of an unfortunate adverse effect of treatment."

was put back on the stand, the defense conceding that having his testimony merely read into the record during the second trial was a tactical error. In all, jurors heard the testimony of nearly seventy witnesses before retiring to render a verdict on April 12, a process, based on the two previous trials, that was expected to take at least two days. In fact, they were out exactly six minutes, the actual deliberation having taken less than sixty seconds.

The verdict, rendered by acclamation, was for acquittal. Arbuckle let out a great sigh of relief. Then, for the benefit of the press, the entire jury, including the two alternates, took the extraordinary step of issuing a statement. "Acquittal is not enough for Roscoe Arbuckle," it read. "We feel that a great injustice has been done him. We feel also that it was only our plain duty to give him this exoneration, under the evidence, for there was not the slightest proof adduced to connect him in any way with the commission of a crime. . . . We wish him success and hope that the American people will take the judgment of fourteen men and women, who sat listening for thirty-one days to the evidence, that Roscoe Arbuckle is entirely innocent and free from all blame."

That evening, Jesse L. Lasky, vice president of Famous Players-Lasky, said that a new Fatty Arbuckle feature would be released immediately. "Our contract with Arbuckle expired at the time of his trouble. Whether or not this contract will be renewed will depend on the public. The public makes or breaks all stars."

Around the same time, Arbuckle issued a statement of his own: "For this vindication I am truly grateful to God and my fellow men and women. My life has been devoted to the production of clean pictures for the happiness of children. I shall try to enlarge my field of usefulness so that my art shall have a wider service."

The Arbuckle picture that opened the next day at the New Garrick in Los Angeles was *Gasoline Gus,* the film Sid Grauman prematurely yanked during its premiere engagement at the Million Dollar. The response was encouraging; Arbuckle reportedly drew heavy applause at every performance. On the East Coast, a small theater on Long Island booked one of the old Comique two-reelers and saw turn-away business. Yet, a few days later at a theater in Detroit, an Arbuckle short was pulled within two hours of opening due to complaints from female patrons.

Any groundswell of interest in Arbuckle's comedies was nipped in the bud on April 18, when Will Hays, the newly installed head of the Motion Picture Producers and Distributors Association, officially banned them, at least temporarily, as his first move in an announced campaign to "clean up" the motion picture industry. He did this, he stated publicly, after consulting with Nicholas Schenck, acting on behalf of his brother, and Adolph Zukor, who he said agreed to cancel all showings and bookings of Arbuckle films at his request. "They do this that the whole matter may have the consideration that its importance warrants, and the action is taken notwithstanding the fact that they had nearly ten thousand contracts in force for the Arbuckle pictures."

In Los Angeles, Arbuckle was stunned when given the news by a reporter for *The New York Times*. "Gosh," he said. "This is a complete surprise and I might say a shock to me. It is the first I have heard of it. I don't know what it is all about, for I thought I was well started on my comeback. You see, it's this way. Joseph Schenck of New York, who produced my pictures, will be in Los Angeles tomorrow. He will know all about this matter. As I am entirely at sea, as far as being able to explain it goes, I shall content myself with remaining silent."

Schenck, it turned out, had been boxed in by Zukor, who didn't want the Paramount brand tarnished by its continued association with Arbuckle. The company had already taken a $700,000 write-off on the three completed Arbuckle pictures left on the shelf, and Zukor now saw a threat to the entire program. Years later, Hays admitted as much in his memoirs, revealing that it was Zukor who insisted on Arbuckle's banishment. "So far as he was concerned, the outrage was very real. Arbuckle had let him down—he had let the whole industry down no less than his fans—and Zukor was prepared to take the loss." Hays recalled asking Zukor to issue the necessary statement, but the studio president didn't want his fingerprints all over the murder weapon. "No, Will, let the Association give it out. That will show that the Association means business."*

When cornered by the press, Hays refused to comment on the ban in view of Arbuckle's acquittal and the jury's subsequent statement, but others were more than willing to speak out on his behalf.

"Of course [Arbuckle] is innocent in the eyes of the law," said Dwight Harris, chairman of the Kansas Board of Film Censors. "The baseball players

---

* By 1958, Zukor's attitude toward Arbuckle had softened. "I knew Arbuckle personally very well. . . . He wasn't anything about chasing women or making dates with girls—he wasn't physically or mentally equipped for that. He was a big, heavy, easy-going, three-hundred-pound comedian. He loved life, he loved parties, he loved people to come to his place. In my judgment, whatever happened I don't know, except that whatever happened was an accident."

of the Chicago White Sox, who were accused of throwing the World Series in 1919, were acquitted in court, but you don't read of any of them playing in organized baseball."

Added Mrs. B. L. Short, a member of the Kansas board: "I hope that Arbuckle will not try to force his pictures on a disgusted public very soon."

Similar statements came from exhibitors' groups, women's clubs, and religious leaders across the nation.

Significantly, Joe Schenck had already taken steps to distance himself from Arbuckle, retiring the Comique name and establishing Buster Keaton Productions, Inc., in its place. As with Comique, the principal stockholders were the two Schenck brothers, who jointly owned 40 percent of the corporation, followed by Loew's Incorporated treasurer David Bernstein, Irving Berlin, Sophye Anger, Lillian S. Ullman, David L. and Arthur M. Loew (the sons of Marcus Loew), production executive Albert A. Kaufman, and attorney Leopold Friedman. No apparent effort was made to make Buster Keaton an owner of Buster Keaton Productions; Roscoe Arbuckle never had any ownership stake in Comique. In both cases the men were nothing more than employees, albeit well-compensated ones.

Tommy Gray went back to New York in March, calling it a season after just three months on the West Coast. Having been at least partially responsible for two of Keaton's oddest comedies, he arrived home just as *The High Sign* was making its long-delayed debut on Broadway. *Variety*'s Abel Green, in finding the picture "interesting," seemed to validate its maker's own lukewarm assessment. *The Film Daily* recognized the picture as a Metro release, thus distinguishing it from the more recent First National offerings. "Keaton spent considerable pains on his newest, but it lacks the punch that has put over his newer series. *The High Sign* is much weaker than Keaton's last one, *The Boat*."

With his writing staff back down to two, Keaton opted to return to *The Electric House*, the two-reeler he was making when he fractured his ankle. "We shelved everything I had shot on it," he said in 1958, "and then later on . . . I remade the picture." The task of working out a fully automated version of Ed Gray's old house at Bluffton fell to Fred "Gabe" Gabourie, a former stage carpenter who got his start in New York with George Ade's 1904 comedy *The College Widow*. Gabourie arrived in Los Angeles in 1913 with a touring company of *Everywoman* and decided he liked the climate. In pictures he worked at Inceville, Thomas Ince's sprawling production complex in the Pacific Palisades, and for the Fox Film Corporation. After two years as technical director at Jesse D. Hampton's Fleming Street studios, he moved to Metro as a stage technician and was put in charge of exteriors for *The Four Horsemen of the Apocalypse,* building a French village and the story's Marne Valley castle at the Metro ranch and overseeing the film's depiction of the devastated countryside along the western front. Gabourie joined Keaton when Comique was leasing studio space from Metro and eventually established an independent scenic shop on the property with partner Edward Cushing.

Gabourie must have started with a laundry list of mechanized conveniences, and may even have suggested a few of his own. The setup was simple enough, an accidental mix-up of degrees at the commencement exercises of a state university. The dean (played by Joe Roberts) announces that he needs a technician to electrify his house, and the ideal man for the job presents a diploma in cosmetics and manicuring. The girl next to him has Buster's degree in botany. And Buster himself innocently presents the other guy's sheepskin in electrical engineering. Granted the job, Buster begins to protest, then takes full note of Virginia Fox, the dean's fetching daughter, and relents. As the family pulls away on vacation, leaving Buster to do his stuff, Virginia slips him a copy of the book *Basic Manual of Electricity.*

Finding the dean's house was no trouble at all. Early in the new year, after it was discovered that Natalie was pregnant, Peg Talmadge moved herself in, joining two of her three daughters under Buster's roof. "By April," said Keaton, "the walls were bulging. Nat had said, 'This Westchester Place house will be big enough for anything.' Perhaps it wasn't Sanforized. It had certainly shrunk." Soon the hunt was on for Natalie's "castle of dreams," the home she described in her essay for the *Evening Herald,* something big and roomy with grounds for a vegetable patch and a flower garden. With her sisters and mother pitching in, a three-story Tudor-style mansion was located in the exclusive Westmoreland Place development, a gated community in East Hollywood where Mack Sennett was one of the residents. This rental property conveniently served as the dean's home for Gabe Gabourie's purposes.

The interior sets, fabricated at the studio, were built to reflect the general look and dimensions of the place. The treacherous staircase was reworked from scratch. An electrified bookcase was wired to select and dispense books with a retractable arm that extended six feet into the room. Virginia's suite was tricked out with a mechanized Murphy bed and a traveling bathtub that rolled along on tracks. Sliding doors opened and closed on command. A pool table in the library was served by a conveyor that recovered and reracked the balls automatically. The swimming pool out back instantly drained and refilled with the yank of a lever. The kitchen was equipped to wash and shelve dishes with a minimum of human intervention. And the dining room was serviced by a model train routed through the kitchen and out onto the table, where it would pause and deliver servings at each individual setting. *The Electric House* was the quintessential Keaton invention, a tinkerer's paradise in which every contrivance was blessed with the potential for comedy should anything go wrong.

The first time Buster demonstrates the stairs for the dean, the control sticks and the contraption propels the hapless homeowner through a landing window and into the pool below. At dinner, the track comes undone, causing the train to dump the evening's entrées into the lap of the dean's wife. Then the real electrical engineer sneaks in to take his revenge, crossing the wires in the basement and causing the automated house to take on a life of its own. At the end, Virginia rejects Buster and he ties a rock to his neck, leaping into the pool in another dark climax. Alarmed, she pulls the lever to drain the pool, only to have her father reverse the control, happy to see the cause of the day's mayhem drown at the bottom of one of his own inventions.

The Electric House marked the final appearance of Virginia Fox in a Keaton comedy. At its completion she announced her resignation, weary of being a prop whose principal talent was obedience. "If I was hanging from an elk's head and they said, 'Hold it,' I held it—even if they went to lunch," she said. "I did whatever I was told." Intent upon starring in a series of her own comedy shorts, she managed to make only one, and after a poorly received feature titled *Itching Palms,* she retired from movies altogether. In 1924, she married Darryl Zanuck, Mal St. Clair's writing partner, who was later to gain fame as vice president in charge of production at 20th Century-Fox. The Zanucks had three children, one of whom, Richard, in partnership with producer David Brown, was responsible for a number of successful films, including *The Sting, Jaws,* and *Cocoon.* Late in life, in responding to a fan letter, Virginia Zanuck wrote: "Of all the movies I made, I liked best working for Buster Keaton."

. . .

"Nate is beginning to look like a small popover," Peg Talmadge fretted in a letter to Anita Loos, "and methinks it's a boy. If so, out it goes hot or cold." Peg's middle daughter, who was now seven months along, accompanied her husband to San Francisco in the waning days of the third Arbuckle trial to lend moral support as well as to privately screen *My Wife's Relations* and *The Frozen North* for a conference of First National exhibitors. Reactions to the films were mixed, causing *Variety* to report that "some trouble between Keaton and First National is said to have arisen." The tensions came at a time of consolidation in the world of film comedy. The elfin Larry Semon, whose studio ball team was trounced regularly by Keaton's, was negotiating to end his contract with Vitagraph so that he could produce his shorts independently. Bidding was expected from First National, which would soon be losing Charlie Chaplin to United Artists, as well as Fox. It was known that Chaplin intended to make a serious picture once he had freed himself of First National, a move that would leave just three first-rank comedians in the field—Semon, Harold Lloyd, and Buster Keaton.

Roscoe Arbuckle's three trials for manslaughter left him owing more than $100,000, including a $50,000 payment reportedly due to lead attorney Gavin McNab. Having lived on cash flow for so long, Arbuckle had little in reserve to meet these obligations and began the dispiriting task of dismantling his former life, selling anything of value for as much as he could get. In May 1922, he was said to be flat broke, having sold his Cadillac touring car to Keaton and his Cadillac speedster to Eddie Cline. He deeded his house on West Adams, which he purchased in 1920, to Joe Schenck as security on loans Schenck had made to cover his legal expenses.

In a statement to Lanning Warren of United Press, Arbuckle said he was so heavily in debt that he had no hope of coming back in any line of work until he could once again make pictures. "I'm not sobbing, however. Hays has said my pictures are banned pending an investigation, and I'm sure he'll find I'm the victim of persecution. But until he makes his decision, I'm making no plans for the future." Keaton's first impulse after the Hays edict was to give Arbuckle work behind the camera, and that, it appeared, couldn't happen soon enough. A forlorn, almost ghostlike figure, Roscoe had taken to hanging around the United Studios where he had made his Paramount features. "He has nothing to do," Warren's article reported, "and walks around the studios watching the people who used to work for him. Since his arrest last fall he has had no income whatever, except a check recently received from the Buster Keaton company for a scenario Fatty wrote."

The scenario was titled *The Vision,* and as of June 2, Buster was actually shooting it under Arbuckle's direction. Actress Renée Adorée, who would go on to prominence as leading lady to John Gilbert and Lon Chaney, was the girl in the picture, and in an interview with the French journal *Cinémagazine* she identified Arbuckle as the film's director (as did items in *Variety* and the *Oakland Tribune*). Yet the premise was familiar to followers of Keaton's work: Buster asks a father for the hand of his daughter, and the old man wants to know if he's even capable of earning a living. "I think so," he replies. "To prove it, I'll go to the city and achieve success. If I fail, I'll come back and shoot myself!"

What follows is a series of letters in which Buster paints himself as hugely accomplished, when the reality is something quite different. First, he writes that he is working at a hospital where he cares for two hundred patients. "You wouldn't believe some of the operations I'm performing." Renée imagines him as a great surgeon; then the scene fades in on the gate of a dog and cat hospital. Buster opens it and is greeted by Luke, who accompanies him on his rounds.*

The next letter: "I now work in the financial district, where I am cleaning up in a big way." And Renée imagines him as a prosperous Wall Street tycoon. Fade in on Buster the public sanitation worker. After losing control of a firehose and making a watery mess of politician Joe Roberts' rally, he is summarily dropped into a manhole.

The third segment has him appearing in a production of Shakespeare's *Hamlet,* and Renée envisions him, skull in hand, taking bows for a masterful performance. He is, in fact, a supernumerary in a cheap musical. Costumed as a Roman soldier, he is thrown out by stage manager Eddie Cline and quickly runs afoul of the law.

His fourth letter: "The audience response was so overwhelming, I have been summoned to appear before a police assembly." She pictures him in a reviewing stand as hundreds of blue uniforms march past. In reality he is brought before a judge, but manages to flee before sentencing. The resulting chase quickly mushrooms into a reprise of *Cops,* set this time amid the hilly

---

* Although Arbuckle didn't direct the entire picture, Luke's presence in this sequence, filmed on the grounds of the Keaton studio and its immediate vicinity, further suggests he directed at least some of it.

streets and cable cars of San Francisco. It concludes with Buster leaping onto a ferry leaving port, only to discover it is actually pulling into dock, delivering him back into the hands of his mob of pursuers. Desperate to escape, he hops over a railing and finds himself atop the paddle wheel, momentarily safe until the boat starts moving. Soon trapped inside the thing, he must race like a hamster until he is thrown clear. In the end, a bruised and bedraggled Buster is returned to Renée via parcel post, and her father helpfully offers his pistol so that he can make good on his pledge.

"I used to daydream an awful lot," Keaton once said. "I've done that so often in pictures. I could get carried away and visualize all the fairylands in the world." Buster's natural propensity may have been the reason he settled on *Day Dreams* as the title of the film, his ninth for First National. And, along with the participation of Arbuckle and his dog, Luke, *Day Dreams* also marked Joe Keaton's return to the company as Renée's intimidating father. The year 1922 had kicked off with a family portrait of all five of the Keatons in *Photoplay*, Louise looking winsome, Myra wary, Harry slightly pugnacious. Buster is assuming his trademark deadpan, leaving Joe alone to display a proud smile. But not long after the photo was taken, Joe left the house on Ingraham and moved in with his son and daughter-in-law, an arrangement that was doomed not to last. By the time the Talmadge invasion was complete, Joe had taken a room at the Continental Hotel on South Hill Street, a favorite stopping place for actors and vaudevillians along L.A.'s unofficial Rialto. Downstairs, the walls of the lounge were covered with hundreds of autographed photos of famous guests who had stayed there since the place opened in 1907. Pershing Square was just down the block, the Pantages was right across the street, Bullock's department store was next door, and the Hillstreet Theatre building housed the new clubroom of the National Vaudeville Association, where scores of members congregated.

Buster was shooting *Day Dreams* when Natalie gave birth to a boy at L.A.'s Methodist Hospital on the evening of June 2, 1922. It was an event that brought the entire family together, Norma and Dutch insisting he'd call neither of them "auntie." According to Peg Talmadge, her first grandchild was born at seven minutes past seven and weighed exactly seven pounds. "What's more," said his father, wincing as he walked the floor with the screaming infant, "he was born with seven lungs." There was little debate over what he'd be named. Extending back to Buster's great-great-great-grandfather, the eldest Keaton son was always named Joseph. So the formal birth name was quickly determined to be Joseph Talmadge Keaton. There was pushback on the matter of his nickname, though. None of the Tal-madge women would countenance Buster Jr., and after a standoff lasting several weeks, they got their way. The baby, who scowled in the first picture of him released to the press, would be known as Jim.

When First National exercised its option on a second series of six Buster Keaton comedies, the advance due for each film jumped from $70,000 to $85,000, while worldwide rentals were showing a steady decline.* Keaton, it appeared, was a critics' darling, popular with both exhibitors and audi-ences, but his pictures weren't as profitable as the company—particularly J. D. Williams, co-founder and general manager—thought they should be. Charlie Chaplin, who would soon be completing his contract with First National, thought Williams and his cohorts "inconsiderate, unsympathetic, and shortsighted." Keaton, too, had grown to dislike them, although he didn't have to directly deal with them as much as Chaplin did. Launch-ing into the fourth film of the second series with an absurdist take on *The Sea Wolf,* Keaton left to shoot exteriors in the waters off Catalina Island, dispensing with the usual leading lady and focusing his attentions on Joe Roberts, who had just signed a year's contract with Fox. Big Joe's whaling ship is incongruously named *Love Nest,* and he makes Buster the steward after tossing his predecessor—followed by an obligatory funeral wreath—overboard. In fact, so many crewmembers hit the water at the hands of the menacing captain that a supply of such wreaths is kept close at hand. Buster eventually manages his escape by knocking a hole in the hull of the ship and then patiently waiting in a lifeboat until the water reaches it.

Keaton had completed *The Love Nest* and started on his next picture when he learned from Joe Schenck that First National wouldn't commit to a third series. The telegram from Williams, as Buster remembered it, contained the line WE CANNOT BE BOTHERED WITH HIS SHORT SUBJECTS. "Schenck showed this to me. 'Okay,' I told him, 'I will do them an addi-tional favor. I won't make the last picture for them.'" It was a rare burst of artistic temperament from a man not known for such displays.

"Buster," pleaded Schenck, "your contract calls for you to make twelve

* *The Boat,* the second First National release, generated rentals of $156,124 for all territories, making it the most commercially successful of all the Keaton two-reelers. By comparison, *The Blacksmith* returned $134,715, *The Frozen North* $127,252, and *The Electric House* $129,384.

pictures. I can handle this situation—but not if you refuse to make the final picture for them."

Keaton was unmoved. "But if they say they can't be bothered, my answer is, 'Fine, then I'm doing you a favor in not bothering you with a twelfth picture.'"

He equated what Williams had done with what Martin Beck had done to his father from the wings of the Palace Theater. "How can I make a man laugh who tells me he can't be bothered with my comedies?" he asked. "Why should I want to?"

Williams had chosen to make his move just about the time *Cops* opened on Broadway, drawing lavish praise from all quarters.

"It would take something a lot better than the feature photoplay at the Rivoli this week* to take the honors of the program away from Buster Keaton's new comedy, *Cops*." (*The New York Times*)

"Buster Keaton is traveling high again, scoring a knockout, as it were, with a funny comedy entitled *Cops*." (*Motion Picture News*)

"Don't fail to wait for *Cops*, the Buster Keaton comedy." (*Evening Mail*)

"Buster Keaton is irresistible and you can make no mistake if you show him to your audience. His popularity has grown and is on the ascent." (*Film Daily*)

"A great many kindly people express sincere sympathy for the editor of this department," Robert Sherwood acknowledged in *Life*, "because he is called upon, in the course of his daily duties, to see so many movies."

"'Don't you get tired of them?'

"'Can't you write your reviews without actually seeing the films themselves?'

"'How do your eyes stand the strain?'

"These are samples of the well-intentioned queries that pour in. As a matter of fact, the sympathy is wasted. I am perfectly willing to sit through fifty dull feature films if I know that, at the end of that session, I shall be allowed to see a Harold Lloyd or Buster Keaton comedy. In *Cops*, Keaton develops the old police chase idea to the nth power by staging his antics in the midst of a police parade, and the resultant mob effect is as stupendous as anything in Mr. [William] Fox's spectacles. What is more, it is actually funnier—and that is no faint praise."

J. D. Williams, who retained distribution rights to the Talmadge features,

---

* The feature attraction was *While Satan Sleeps,* a Jack Holt western.

Keaton and crew on location at Truckee during the filming of The Balloonatic, *his final two-reel comedy of the silent era. Co-director Eddie Cline is seated directly behind his star, while actress Phyllis Haver, center, poses with her arm around assistant director Al Gilmore.*

later admitted to Schenck that the wire was merely a ploy intended to counter an expected demand for more money. "That being the case," said Keaton in his autobiography, "Mr. Williams outsmarted himself, for I never did make that twelfth little movie for First National. Just about that time Loew sent word that he wanted me to make full-length features for his company, Metro, to release."

Keaton finished *The Balloonatic,* his eleventh short for First National, with the knowledge it would be his last. Appropriately, the film took on a languid, dreamlike quality that belied its slapstick roots. Creatively, it's Buster putting his feet up, allowing the girl in the story to drive the action for a change. Phyllis Haver, a bright, talented comedienne on loan from Mack Sennett, turned out to be the most boisterous of all of his female leads. He meets her at an amusement park, but the encounter doesn't go well.

"Comedy is best when it arouses the curiosity of the audience," he said, describing the scene to a newspaper reporter shortly after the film's completion. "As an example of the kind of thing I mean, take this situation. A man sees a pretty girl get into one of those 'Old Mill' boats at Coney Island. He gets into the same boat and it passes out of the picture. The action progresses with no sign of the boat for many feet of film. When it reappears, the man has a black eye and other damages. It is simple, but there is nothing that requires more knowledge and has a greater number of rules or technical stunts than comedy slapstick or the other kind."

Buster happens upon a balloon launch and gets trapped on top of the thing after agreeing to attach a banner. In flight, he makes himself at home, and from there the film becomes an idyll. He manages to puncture the balloon while shooting at ducks and lands in a tree. The next morning, he decides to go fishing and comes upon Phyllis doing the same thing. She also swims, chops wood, throws rocks, grills fish, and wrestles a steer to the ground. Rural exteriors, Haver remembered, were shot on the banks of the Truckee River. She described the town itself as having one old wooden hotel, several saloons, and little else. One night she was awakened by shouts of "Fire!" and escaped with her makeup kit and costumes, leaving everything else, and scrambling down stairs "with sheets of flame all around." The fire destroyed the old hotel in fifteen minutes, forcing the company to move to "miserable accommodations" over the Southern Pacific station.

After a scary encounter with a couple of bears, Buster and Phyllis float contentedly down a river in Buster's canoe, unaware that they are rapidly approaching a steep waterfall. Unexpectedly, the boat takes flight, gliding effortlessly on past the edge of the rushing water, Buster having whimsically attached the old patched-up balloon to it. He leans into her, she embraces him, and off they fly into features, leaving the merciless world of two-reel comedies behind.

10

Our Hospitality

WITH *THE BALLOONATIC* cut and titled and his First National commitment at an end, Buster Keaton took his young family to New York for an eight-week respite, the entourage including Lou and Sophye Anger, Eddie Cline and his wife, and publicist Harry Brand. It was common to see Hollywood types stalking Broadway in the autumn, scouting material and catching up with old friends. When the Keatons arrived on the Main Stem, celebrities from the West included one of the Gish sisters, actress Hope Hampton, and actors Huntley Gordon, Montagu Love, and Richard Barthelmess. Joe Schenck, meanwhile, was off touring his native Russia with Norma, Dutch, and Peg Talmadge, and the plan was for the Keatons to remain east long enough to meet their ship.

The Frozen North had gone into release in mid-August, making it the first movie copyrighted in the name of Buster Keaton Productions. "A good time for a snow picture," Keaton commented. "Air conditioning wasn't invented yet." *The Electric House* followed in October. While in Manhattan, Keaton would see *Cops* featured top-line at the Symphony Theater on the Upper West Side, while *My Wife's Relations* was similarly billed on its initial run at the Rivoli.

"The best of the three is *My Wife's Relations*," Robert Sherwood opined, "but *The Electric House* and *The Frozen North* are not far behind. They are all genuinely funny, with occasional thrusts of satire—and they are full of that amazing ingenuity which is a characteristic of every Keaton comedy. Buster Keaton is a distinct asset to the movies. He can attract people who would never think of going to a picture palace to see anyone else. Moreover, he can impress a weary world with the vitally important fact that life, after all, is a foolishly inconsequential affair."

Keaton also sat for interviews. Stifling a yawn during a session with the *Telegraph*'s Gertrude Chase, he was asked about New York nightlife. "Terrible," he answered. "I haven't missed a night at the theatre. Then there are the races, and now the World Series. No wonder I'm underweight. We are seeing as many plays as we can with a view toward getting a new picture for Constance. The one I would like to see her do is *Kiki,* but it may be hard to get."*

When Chase asked if she could see the baby, now four months old, she was told he was airing on Park Avenue and that she could find him when she went out. "You can't miss him," the proud father said. "He looks just like me. He has a black buggy and a white nurse."

Keaton had now starred in nineteen short comedies, three of which were yet to be seen by the moviegoing public. "Next I'm going back to the coast to do a five-reel picture," he told Malcolm Oettinger, who was doing a new piece for *Picture-Play*. "No plots, you know. Just gags. But we'll space our laughs. If we ran five reels of the sort of stuff we cram into two, the audience would be tired before it was half over. So we'll plant the characters more slowly, use introductory bits, and all that. It'll be just as easy to make a five-reeler, because we always take about fifteen reels anyway. Now we'll cut to five instead of two."

Schenck and his party concluded their tour of Russia, which included a pilgrimage to Joe's birthplace on the Sheksna River, in early November. They arrived in Paris on November 6, 1922, and moved on to England a few days later. The order of business there was the judging of a nationwide beauty contest conducted in the pages of *The Daily Sketch,* which drew eighty thousand entries. Of all the photo submissions, one hundred finalists were brought to London to attend a luncheon with the Talmadge sisters at the Savoy Hotel, followed by participation in the fifth Victory Ball (commemorating the end of the Great War) and the making of individual screen tests at the Stoll Film Studios at Cricklewood. The reward for the lucky winner was to be the role of Aggie Lynch, the second female lead in Norma's next picture, *Within the Law.*

---

* Keaton's instincts were spot-on. *Kiki* was indeed hard to get, and Norma ended up doing the picture, not Constance.

In terms of publicity, the campaign was wildly successful, with the newsreel *Topical Budget* (under the same ownership as the *Sketch*) filming contestants in twenty-one regional districts. Norma, Joe, Dutch, scattered First National executives, and members of a Grand Committee of British notables spent hours in an Oxford Street cinema watching the tests and winnowing the entrants until, after much back-and-forth, they finally had a winner. On November 14, the *Sketch* carried a front-page photo of Irish-born Margaret Leahy, who had beaten out all other contenders. Norma pronounced the twenty-year-old shopgirl "a perfect film face" with "splendid eyes, a supple body, and convincing expressiveness . . . her features are so perfect and her character so distinctive!"

Following a quick victory lap, which included the premiere of Constance Talmadge's *East Is West* and a tour of the provinces, Leahy and her mother boarded the *Aquitania* with Schenck and the Talmadges for the long journey to Hollywood where, as *The Daily Sketch* girl, she would surely attain stardom. Buster, Nat, little Joe, and the Angers were among those at the Cunard dock to welcome them when they arrived on December 1, and four furious days of sightseeing and camera tests ensued. "She is of the petite, chic type," inventoried *The New York Times*, "with chestnut hair, blue eyes, and white even teeth and natural pink complexion."

Also meeting the ship that day was *Within the Law* director Frank Lloyd, who would be making authentic exteriors with Norma before accompanying the group home by rail. It was during this brief period that Lloyd got his first look at how Leahy comported herself in front of a camera, and he feared she had little to offer the screen. That fear only magnified when they got to Los Angeles and production on the Metro lot began in earnest. In a diary entry published in the *Sketch*, Leahy described doing a scene for Lloyd fifteen times. "They have taken thousands and thousands of feet of film of me," she wrote. "Mr. Lloyd says he is very proud of me."

Nevertheless, three days in, Lloyd abandoned all hope of coaxing a performance out of her. The girl couldn't act, he concluded. She was hopeless. Norma, the public face of the stunt, was too invested to send her home. Yet Lloyd was adamant and she knew he was right. Joe mustered all the diplomatic skills at his command and told Leahy he had decided he would not be treating her fairly by putting her into a big part without any training, one that would likely expose any "camera faults" she might have. Rather, he said he was extending her contract so that she could watch Lloyd develop *Within the Law* from a directorial angle without the pressure of actually having to appear in it.

"Margaret Leahy has natural ability, is ambitious and beautiful," he said in a statement to the press. "Consequently, if properly handled, she will win fame in pictures. I am determined that she shall have every opportunity at my command to be successful, and for that reason I have decided that she shall be educated for the screen before actually being photographed."

This solved the immediate problem of getting the picture back on track, and the role of Aggie Lynch was hastily recast with the well-established Eileen Percy. Leahy, at least publicly, pronounced herself satisfied. "I realize that stars are not made through popularity contests, but through hard work, perseverance, and experience," she said.

The matter of Roscoe Arbuckle was far from settled. In July it was rumored he would return to the stage—where the ban initiated by Will Hays had no effect—but nothing emerged from reputedly "secret" negotiations. In August, with no prospects, he sailed from San Francisco on a voyage to the Orient. It was the first leg of a long trip that would take him to the Malay Peninsula, the Straits settlements, Egypt, and possibly Paris.

"I need a rest and intend to take it easy and, at the same time, see some other parts of the world," he told the *Oakland Tribune*. "I'll come back to the United States in due time, and then will be my opportunity to decide what I'm going to do. It's entirely up to the people—the people who see the movies and who used to be (and, I think, again will be) my friends— whether I return to the screen or not. Maybe I'll go back to making comedies, but I don't know. San Francisco doesn't make me feel very funny and I can't say right now. Maybe I'll go into the business as a producer."

It was thought that Arbuckle would meet up with Joe and Norma in Egypt, but he suffered an injury on the initial voyage—sliced open a finger after slipping on some steps—and never made it farther than Japan. In October, the trades reported a $400,000 cash offer made by Gavin McNab for the three unreleased Fatty Arbuckle features produced and then shelved by Famous Players. The attorney also indicated that he had access to "practically unlimited" amounts of money from Chicago, New York, and other eastern investors to finance a comeback.

"This money is seeking investment in Arbuckle as a result of a most thorough sounding out of public opinion throughout the United States, with the result that a practically unanimous sentiment favoring his return to film work has been encountered." He added that he felt sure the Hays banishment, which was always characterized as temporary, would be lifted once a personal appeal had been initiated by Arbuckle and his attorney. Nothing, though, ever came of the plan.

In December, *The Film Daily* reported that Arbuckle's friends would make a concerted effort to persuade Hays to let the man work again. How much of an effort got made is unknown, but on December 21, 1922, Hays announced that he saw no reason why Arbuckle should not be permitted to go back to work if he wished to do so. Hays later said it seemed "a relatively commonplace decision to me," but a tsunami of public indignation immediately engulfed him, beginning with the Los Angeles District of the California Federation of Women's Clubs, which, representing a membership of two million, reaffirmed its opposition to Arbuckle's returning to pictures. The mayors of Indianapolis, Detroit, and Boston quickly said they would not permit his comedies to be shown in their cities, and similar statements of disapproval came from the National Catholic Welfare Council, the National Education Association, and club women and religious leaders in Chicago, Philadelphia, St. Louis, Buffalo, and Milwaukee.

All the righteous civic and clerical noise prompted Arbuckle to issue a plea for "American fair play" on Christmas Eve. "It is not difficult," he said in the statement, "to visualize at this time of year, which commemorates the birth of Christ, what might have happened if some of those who heartlessly denounce me had been present when the Savior forgave the penitent thief on the cross with words that have influenced the human race more than any other words ever uttered. Would not some of these persons have denounced Christ and stoned him for what he said? No one ever saw a picture of mine that was not clean and wholesome. No one ever will see such a picture. I claim the right of work and service. The sentiment of every church on Christmas Day will be 'Peace on earth and good will to all mankind.' What will be the attitude the day after Christmas to me?"

When the Keatons returned to Los Angeles, Buster grimly watched as the Talmadge women once again made the house at Westmoreland Place a hive of activity. Even though Norma and Dutch were both making pictures at the nearby Metro studios, the baby, now six months, was an endless source of fascination and brought a steady stream of visitors. "It was not exactly a rest home," Buster conceded. Keen on downsizing—the third floor at Westmoreland was a ballroom where Dutch had learned to ride a bicycle—and eager

At work on the feature comedy that would come to be known as Three Ages *(1923). From left: Joe Mitchell, Clyde Bruckman, Keaton, Jean Havez, and Eddie Cline.*

to own, the Keatons found an eleven-room residence on Ardmore Avenue in the fashionable Normandie Hill tract, a "big tile-roof deal with lawns and clipped yews" for $50,000 with a $35,000 mortgage held in the name of Natalie's mother. By year's end, Nat was planning the move while Buster was preparing to put his first feature comedy before the cameras.

In some ways, *Three Ages* was a feature in name only. Keaton, who said he had D. W. Griffith's *Intolerance* in mind, described the concept in a 1958 interview: "What I did was just tell a single story of two fellows calling on a girl, and the mother likes one suitor and the father likes the other one. And in fighting over the girl and different situations we could get into. And finally winning her. But I told the story in three ages. I told it in the Stone Age, Roman Age, and Modern. In other words, I just show us calling on the girl, the two of us gettin' sore at each other because we were in each other's way. Then I went from the Stone Age to the Roman Age, did the same exact scene with the same people, only the setting was different and the costumes. And the same thing in the Modern Age. So every situation we just repeated in the three different ages."

Griffith's picture was comprised of four interwoven stories, set in four different ages, exploring the theme of intolerance—social, religious, political. When the film failed at the box office, he was able to edit the Babylonian footage into a stand-alone feature called *The Fall of Babylon,* and similarly repurpose elements of the Modern Age story as *The Mother and the Law*—a shrewd commercial resurrection not lost on Keaton.

"Cut the film apart," Keaton said of *Three Ages,* "and then splice up the three periods, each one separately, and you will have three complete two-reel films."

Indeed, Buster was leaving nothing to chance. Not only would he hedge his bets with a modular structure, he would also beef up his two-man writing staff. Accompanying him back to Hollywood was Tommy Gray, having signed on for another tour of duty. Awaiting their arrival was Jean Havez, fresh from a year's sojourn with Harold Lloyd. Added to Mitchell, Bruckman, and Cline, Keaton assured himself of what the *Los Angeles Times* termed "the largest scenario department of any individual star." To play his rival for the love of the girl Keaton selected Wallace Beery, a roughneck character man who had a background in comedy, and for the girl's imposing father he borrowed Joe Roberts back from Fox, where he had appeared in films for directors Slim Summerville and Norman Taurog.

Unsettled until late in the game was the matter of a leading lady. "The cast for our two-reelers was always small," Keaton said in his autobiography. "There were usually but three principals—the villain, myself, and the girl, and she was never important. She was there so the villain and I would have something to fight about. The leading lady had to be fairly good looking, and it helped some if she had a little acting ability. As far as I was concerned, I didn't insist that she have a sense of humor. There was always the danger that such a girl would laugh at a gag in the middle of a scene, which meant ruining it and having to remake it."

Joe Schenck never involved himself in the creative side of Keaton's pictures. "Tell me from nothing," he would say. "Go ahead, what should I know about comedy?" But still needing a feature role for Leahy, Schenck saw an easy out in putting her with Buster. It didn't matter that she couldn't act; Keaton would be helping both Norma and him out of a jam. When it was all settled and arranged, Schenck personally phoned Leahy with the news, laying it on thick. They were entrusting her, he said, with the biggest prize of the year—the lead in the Buster Keaton super-production that all the film fans in America were eagerly awaiting. "I am going to show England what we think of its *Daily Sketch* girl," he declared.

On January 7, 1923, a two-column item appeared in the *Los Angeles Times* announcing the switch in casting: "Miss Leahy was originally chosen for the role of Aggie Lynch in *Within the Law*, but after a week spent in the taking of tests it was agreed that she possessed the talents so necessary for an ingénue and she was chosen to play the important role of Buster Keaton's lead, a part more important than the one for which she was selected as the winner of the beauty contest." Production, it said, would get under way "within another week."

When Roscoe Arbuckle moved from shorts to features in 1920, specifically comedy-dramas like *The Round-up,* Grace Kingsley of the *Los Angeles Times* asked him why. "It's just about a hundred times easier to make a comedy-drama than a two-reeler," he replied, "and you get more for it. Also you get more fame. People go in and laugh when they see you in a jazz comedy, but all the same they think to themselves, 'Pooh, that's nothing! He's just a boob.' Yet you have worked yourself sick and your brain is fagged thinking up new gags for that comedy."

Keaton had wanted to move directly into features after his apprenticeship with Arbuckle, but Joe Schenck was against the idea, probably feeling that Buster needed to carry some pictures on his own first. In the interim, both Chaplin and Harold Lloyd made the switch, Chaplin with *The Kid,* a six-reel subject that made a star out of Jack Coogan's six-year-old son, and Lloyd, unofficially, with *A Sailor-Made Man,* a two-reel picture that blossomed into four, and then officially with *Grandma's Boy.*

"We didn't get William S. Hart, Mary Pickford, or Douglas Fairbanks on the same bill with us," Buster said. "We had second- and third-rate stars on the bill with us. Well, for instance, if the theater, a first-run theater here in Los Angeles, was paying us $500 a week rental for our short, he was probably paying only $500 for the feature. . . . As long as they were going to advertise us above it anyhow—we're the drawing card—we might as well get into the feature field and instead of getting $500 for the picture we take $1,500. It makes a difference."

Creatively, he echoed Arbuckle's reasoning in that he had grown to want longer stories and the room to develop them. "We were knocking ourselves out dreaming up new stuff every six weeks—and gambling each time. A couple of duds in a row and you could slip way down the ladder. With six months—four times as long—to each film, you could give it all you had."

Work on *Three Ages* began in January 1923. Judging from the diary entries Leahy filed with *The Daily Sketch,* Keaton began by puzzling out the Modern Age story, which would then serve as the basis for the Stone Age and Roman segments to come. "It is only preliminary work that we have done so far," she wrote. "Mr. Keaton is not quite sure yet about several points in the picture. It is to be a super comedy, and several of the scenes and incidents are tried out before they are actually taken—that is, we do certain scenes two or three ways before the camera, then we see them run off in the little projection room, and Mr. Keaton finds things wrong with them or gets better ideas, and then we do them over again. When these difficult points are cleared up we will start again, and work the picture right through. There is a scene in which there is a fire—a whole house seems to be burned down, and we have burned it down three times now, and still Mr. Keaton is not satisfied. Of course they do not really burn down an entire house. They build just the front of it. They build it at night, working all night, and then we burn it down in the day time. Mr. Keaton says if he can't get the house to burn down properly he will cut it out of the picture after all."

There was indeed a fire in the conclusion to the modern story, but it engulfed a police station rather than a house. Buster initiates an escape from the cops, desperate to stop Leahy's reluctant marriage to Beery. Climbing a fire escape to the top of a tall building, he must leap from one roof to the next to clear an alleyway.

"We built the sets over the Third Street tunnel—or the Broadway tunnel—looking right down over Los Angeles," Keaton remembered. "Now, by getting your cameras up on a high parallel and shooting past our set in the foreground with the street below, it looked like we were up in the air about twelve, fourteen stories high. And we actually had a net stretched from one wall to the other underneath the camera line so in case you missed any trick that you were doing—one of those high, dizzy things—you had a net to fall into, although it was about a thirty-five-foot drop. . . . So, my scene was that with the cops chasing me, that I came to this thing and I took advantage of the lid of a skylight and laid it over the edge of the roof to use as a springboard. I backed up, hit it, and tried to make it to the other side, which was probably about eighteen feet, something like that.

"Well, I misjudged the spring of that board and didn't make it. I hit flat up against the other set and fell to the net, but I hit hard enough that I jammed my knees a little bit, and hips and elbows, 'cause I hit flush, flat. And I had to go home and stay in bed for about three days. And, of course, at the same time, me and the scenario department were a little sick because we can't make that leap. That throws the whole chase sequence, that routine, right out the window. So the boys the next day went into the projecting room and saw the scene anyhow, 'cause they had it printed to look at it. Well, they got a thrill out of it, so they came back and told me about it.

A breathtaking aerial stunt salvages a missed leap from rooftop to rooftop in Three Ages. *This exterior set was constructed atop the double-bore Hill Street tunnel in downtown Los Angeles to create the illusion of great height.*

'It's a miss.' Sez [I], 'Well, if it looks that good let's see if we can pick it up this way: The best thing to do is to put an awning on a window, just a little small awning, just enough to break my fall.' 'Cause on the screen you could see that I fell about, oh I guess I fell about sixteen feet, something like that. I must have passed two stories. So now you go in and drop into something just to slow me up, to break my fall, and I can swing from that onto a rainspout, and when I get a hold of it, it breaks and lets me sway—sways me out away from the building hanging onto it. And for a finish, it collapses enough that it hinges and throws me down through a window a couple of floors below.

"Well, when we got back and checked up on what this chase was about, the chase was this: I was getting away from policemen and we used the old Hollywood station, which was right next door to the fire department. Well, when this pipe broke and threw me through the window, we went in there and built the sleeping quarters of the fire department with a sliding pole in the background. So I came through their window on my back, slid across the floor, and I lit up against the sliding pole and dropped to the bottom on the slide. I bounced from that to sit on the rear of one of the trucks, and as I hit the rear, the truck pulled out. So I had to grab on for dear life, but I'm on my way to a fire—but the fire was *in the police department.* So we went back and shot the scene where I accidently, not knowing it, had set fire to the police department before the cops started to chase me. Well, it ended up . . . It was the biggest laughing sequence in the picture . . . because I missed it in the original trick."

Keaton shot the entirety of the Modern Age story as if filming a two-reel comedy, and it was that material that formed the backbone of the picture.

"Working with Buster Keaton one has to keep one's wits," wrote Margaret Leahy. "We rehearse a scene and then the director calls, 'All ready. On the set . . . Shoot!' Then we start the scene just as we have rehearsed it. But Mr. Keaton may have a sudden idea right in the midst of the scene and will start doing something entirely different from what we had rehearsed. If I can 'follow' him, or understand instantly what he is doing and what I should do—then everything is all right. But if I am surprised the least bit

Keaton prepares to film a scene for Three Ages *at the Iverson Ranch in Chatsworth. To the right are men poised to catch him with a tarp after he sustains a whack from actress Blanche Payson's club.*

and 'caught napping,' then the scene is spoiled. The director shouts 'Off' and the camera stops and we start over again.

"I went through one whole day splendidly. Mr. Keaton changed every scene right in the middle of it. For example, in one scene we had rehearsed for him to go slowly out of the door, hat in hand, and turn at the door to wave good-bye to me. I was to stand very straight and solemn—angry with him and indignant. Not noticing him at all as he left. Then, just as he pushed up his hat and started to go out of the door he changed his mind. He threw his hat down and came over to me and grabbed me in his arms and kissed me. I hadn't the least idea he was going to do any such thing. I heard him coming up behind me, but didn't know what it meant. I didn't know what to do—what he had in mind. So I 'took a chance,' as they say here, and just picked up a vase that was on the table and smashed it on the floor—to show how angry I was. The director shouted: 'Good girl—hold it—hold it. Get out, Buster, quick—hold it, Margaret, till he's gone—just that way—there you are—Off.'"

Another day, Leahy admitted, she hashed every scene because Keaton changed so much and she wasn't quick enough to follow. "But he expects this."

Used to seasoned Sennett veterans like Alice Lake and Sybil Seely, he plainly saw her as a drag on his momentum. "The scenes we threw in the ash can!" he complained. "Easy scenes! We got a good picture; we could have had a fine one. But, my God, we previewed it *eight* times! Went back and re-shot scenes like mad."

A structure for the Modern Age emerged: rivalry, jealousy, competition,

Keaton shows a double how he wants Margaret Leahy dragged for a traveling shot in Three Ages. *This will free him to direct Leahy as she expresses her newfound love for her prehistoric suitor.*

triumph. "The point of this comedy," Keaton said, "was that love and the relations of man and woman had not changed since the dawn of time." The Stone Age scenes were made among the natural formations of Iverson Ranch, where he had shot much of *The Paleface*. Beery, a club-toting adventurer, makes his entrance on a mastodon; Buster, a "faithful worshipper" at Beauty's shrine, does the same on an animated brontosaurus. Clad in animal skins, the cast goes through the same cultural rituals as before, with Joe Roberts and Lillian Lawrence playing Margaret's parents. To gauge his worthiness, Big Joe gives Beery a few hearty blows with his club and reacts approvingly. A similar wallop sends Buster crashing to the ground. Beery challenges him to a sunrise duel with clubs and seconds, and their rivalry escalates into open battle. At one critical point, he lobs a rock at Buster, only to have Buster assume a batter's stance and whack it back with his club, landing a direct hit.

"Now, Buster accepted the fact that this rock must be papier-mâché," said Clyde Bruckman, who was present that day. "But he wouldn't accept action trickery. It had to be continuous action from the moment the caveman picked it up and heaved it straight through to the moment it homed back and coldcocked him. 'We get it in one shot,' he said, 'or we throw out the gag.' We set up the cameras for a long profile shot—this rock was going to sail for thirty feet—and we worked for hours. Seventy-six takes, all for one little gag. 'Okay,' said Buster, 'now they'll know it was for real.'"

In February, the *Los Angeles Times* carried news that huge sets had been erected at United Studios for the scenes in ancient Rome, specifically seventy-five feet of street and a partial reproduction of the Roman Colosseum. The latter was built primarily to serve as the background for a *Ben-Hur*–style chariot race between Beery and Keaton, the equivalent of the duel of clubs in the Stone Age or a bitterly contested football game in the present. But while Harry Brand's release boasted of an arena 150 feet high, the actual structure was closer to thirty feet, the illusion completed with a hanging miniature—a scale model suspended in front of the camera. When carefully aligned with the partial set in the distance and populated with tiny dolls (some of which could be moved up and down on sticks), the effect was seamless and gave the impression of great size at a fraction of the cost.

For the scenes in Rome, Keaton indulged in visual puns. When he consults his wristwatch, it is, in keeping with the period, a miniature sundial. His chariot has a license plate, the characters, of course, in Roman numerals, and a spare wheel on the back. When he parks, his helmet functions like a modern anti-theft device. "In that film I did take liberties," he acknowledged, "because it was more a travesty than a burlesque. That's why I used a wristwatch that was a sundial, and why I used my helmet the way I did. Fords at that time had a safety device to stop people from stealing the cars, a thing with a big spike which you locked on the back wheel and which looked just like my Roman helmet. So I unlocked my Roman helmet off me and locked it onto the wheel of my chariot. At that time the audience all compared it with the safety gadget for a Ford."

Dropped into a dungeon with a lion, Buster remembers hearing the story of somebody who made friends with a lion by doing something to one of its paws. Gamely, he examines the lion's feet and, in a parody of *Androcles and the Lion,* gives the beast a full-service pedicure. Sprung from the hole, he eludes capture and races to free Margaret, who has been dragged off and imprisoned by Beery. He wrests a long spear from a soldier, commandeers a horse, and vaults to her rescue. "I couldn't just run over a batch of rocks or something to get to her," he said. "I had to invent something, find something unexpected, and pole-vaulting with a spear seemed to be it."

Filming wrapped in March, but the seemingly endless cycle of previews and reshoots continued into May, when Margaret Leahy was finally cleared for travel. In New York, she paused long enough to see George M. Cohan's *So This Is London* and sit for interviews with *The New York Times* and Hearst columnist Louella Parsons. She told the *Times* that picture players were a hardworking lot and that evenings were often spent watching movies in order to get ideas. "She said that Buster Keaton, with whom she was appearing, often came in at night covered with bruises, with splotches of iodine on cuts received in doing his stunts. The task of producing a picture was a revelation to her, far more involved than she had ever imagined. It was just hard work from beginning to end, and a case of getting up early in the morning and staying on the job until four o'clock in the afternoon. Then in the evening came the orders for the next day's work."

Leahy said that she would miss California and showed that she could laugh at the jokes in Cohan's burlesque of the British, even if she did have to have the occasional line explained to her. When Parsons pointedly asked if she was laughing *with* the Americans or *at* them, she replied, "Both."

While the Keatons were settling into their new home on Ardmore, which came complete with Constance Talmadge, their perennial houseguest, Lou

Anger was building a $20,000 place of his own, a nine-room Spanish revival in Hancock Park. Freed from the grind of overseeing six Keaton comedies a year, and ceding responsibility for the Norma and Dutch Talmadge pictures to newly installed associate producer John Considine, Jr., Anger became a man of many enterprises. He owned a petroleum company based on Signal Hill, where "Buster Keaton" was the name of the first producing well, and had his own picture-making entity, Lou Anger Productions.* He was also a partner in Reel Comedies, Inc., which was set up by Joe Schenck to produce two-reelers directed on the q.t. by Roscoe Arbuckle.

At first, Arbuckle attempted to feature himself in a short comedy he wrote with Joe Mitchell called *Handy Andy,* a sort of return to form after the horrors of the past sixteen months. According to *Exhibitors Herald,* shooting began at the Keaton studio the week of January 8, 1923, under the direction of Herman C. Raymaker, who had been Fred Fishback's assistant director back at Keystone. The film was being financed by a group of investors headed by Gavin McNab, and Arbuckle brought Molly Malone, his leading lady from the last five Comique shorts, back as his co-star. Production was expected to take approximately six weeks, but in the face of ongoing protests he called a halt to it all before it was finished.

In May, he was reported as having directed two Al St. John shorts for Fox, and by summer he was back making *Handy Andy* for Reel Comedies, this time directing the great equestrian clown Edwin "Poodles" Hanneford in the part he had originally conceived for himself, that of a hotel handyman who tries to do everyone else's job when the help abruptly quits. Under the title *Front!* the resulting film became the first of five Poodles Hanneford comedies directed by Arbuckle and released through Educational Pictures. Hanneford never caught on with movie audiences, but Lou Anger had somewhat better luck with an Australian-born contortionist and dancer named Clyde Cook, who also appeared in several comedies filmed at the Keaton studio for Educational release.

Costume dramas were all the rage, with Marion Davies topping the popularity polls in the period pictures she made for Hearst, and Joe Schenck encouraging the trend with *Smilin' Through, The Eternal Flame,* and *Ashes of Vengeance,* all hits for Norma Talmadge. On a business trip to New

---

* There was also a racehorse named Buster Keaton, a Futurity winner owned by breeder J. C. McKay. One Sunday, Joe Schenck and the Talmadge sisters accompanied Buster to Tijuana to watch the colt run, and Norma was so amused she bought a half interest in him.

York, he brought back *Secrets* for Norma; *Barbara Winslow, Rebel,* a tale of seventeenth-century England, for Constance; and encouraged Buster to make something along the same lines, convinced that interest in such subjects had reached "fever heat." Indeed, Keaton seemed to acknowledge as much when asked on the set of *Three Ages* what kind of comedy people wanted. "Refined brutality," he said. "Put lace on the slapstick. Gild the club. Don't kill; merely mutilate. That enables the cast to appear in other comedies."

With Keaton's second feature in development, some critical staff changes were announced. Eddie Cline stepped away to direct feature dramas under contract to Sol Lesser, and his replacement was John G. "Jack" Blystone. As with Cline, Blystone had written and directed Fox Sunshine comedies, including, coincidentally, all the Clyde Cook shorts, and had just completed his first feature, the Tom Mix western *Soft Boiled.* Appointed Blystone's assistant was Arthur Rose, and cameraman Gordon Jennings was engaged to grind European negative* alongside Elgin Lessley. Tommy Gray, meanwhile, had left for Universal, where he remained only a few months before joining Harold Lloyd, who was known to pay as much as $1,000 a week for top talent. "All of us tried to steal each other's gagmen," director Leo McCarey said, "but we had no luck with Keaton because he thought up his best gags himself and we couldn't steal *him.*"

In their search for a historic germ of an idea, something that would fit on the back of a postcard, someone hit on the notion of dropping Buster into the middle of a feud on the order of the Hatfields and the McCoys. Tentatively titled *Headin' South,* the resulting story would first go before the public as *Hospitality,* then, ultimately, as *Our Hospitality.* Said Keaton, "On *Our Hospitality* we had this one idea of an old-fashioned Southern feud. But it looks as though this must have died down in the years it took me to grow up from being a baby, so our best period for that was to go back something like eighty years. 'All right,' we say. 'We go back that far. And now when I go South, am I traveling in a covered wagon, or what? Let's look up the records and see when the first railroad train was invented.' Well, we find out: We've

---

* This second camera, generally to the left of the first camera, supplied the first-generation negative that was shipped to Europe for foreign prints. In terms of picture quality, this practice was considered infinitely preferable to making a duplicate negative for Europe. "A dupe negative," explained Keaton, "was always grainy and milky—it wasn't good photography, see. But in later years, they had practically perfected it, so you could hardly tell a dupe negative shot from a real one."

got the Stephenson Rocket for England and the De Witt Clinton for the United States. And we chose the Rocket engine because it's funnier looking. The passenger coaches were stagecoaches with flanged wheels put on them. So we built the entire train and that set our period for us: 1825 was the actual year of the invention of the railroad."

Having settled on an American train with Stephenson's Rocket as its engine, it fell to Gabe Gabourie to fabricate the thing in his shop on the studio grounds using whatever drawings they could locate.

"We did our own research right up there in the scenario room," Keaton said. "We were very particular about details, costumes and backgrounds, props and things like that. And never a script. Because when we had what we knew was a story, and had the material and opportunities to get our highspots, we'd bring in our cameraman, our technical man who builds our sets, the head electrician and the prop man—those boys are on weekly salary with us—we didn't just hire 'em by the picture, they were right there. And we go through what we had in mind on things. They make notes. They know what's going to be built. The prop man knows the props he's got to have and the stuff to be built. The electrician knows what he needs in the way of lights and stuff like that. By the time that we're ready to shoot, there's no use havin' it on paper because they all know it anyhow."

On June 1, while the new picture was taking form, a star-studded fete took place at the Keaton home on Ardmore Avenue. Officially, it was to celebrate Little Buster's first birthday. It was also to commemorate Buster and Natalie's second wedding anniversary. Then there was the matter of Constance Talmadge's divorce from John Pialaglou, the final decree for which had been granted earlier that same day.

"We don't know which event we are celebrating," Dutch blithely told a reporter from the *Los Angeles Times,* "but Baby Buster seems to think it's his party, so we'll let him have all the honors."

And it was around this time that Buster said to Nat, "The kid is a big boy now. Why not come and be my leading lady in my next picture?"

She wasn't at all sure that she wanted to. "She loved her home," wrote Eunice Marshall in a profile for *Screenland.* "She liked to keep house. She liked to take care of the baby herself. A nurse had once let her baby fall ill. Thenceforth she suspected all nurses and took over the entire charge of her son. Screen work would cut in on all this. But Buster insisted. And the thought was not unpleasant."

An official announcement from Harry Brand's office appeared in the

Times later that month: "MRS. KEATON BACK IN FILMS." In Brand's version, it was Natalie who pursued the role, not the other way around. "She went to Lou Anger, executive manager of Buster's studio," the unlikely story went, "and prevailed upon Anger to intercede for her. Between the two of them Buster was won over." The release added that Baby Joe, known within the family as "Winks," was to have a part in the picture too, but in the Keaton tradition he was a seasoned pro at the age of twelve months—he had already appeared with his Aunt Dutch in her upcoming picture *Dulcy*.

Three Ages had its world premiere in London on June 25, 1923, and befitting the enormity of the contest that resulted in the casting of Margaret Leahy, it happened before a capacity audience at Marble Arch Pavilion that included Princess Alice and the Duke of Athlone. Leahy made an introductory appearance, humbly promising to "work very hard to be better and better as my career goes on," and the audience cheered her first appearance on-screen. A private showing hosted by David Lloyd George, the former prime minister, followed for the Duke and Duchess of York, the royal newlyweds of the day and the future parents of Queen Elizabeth II. The British release of *Three Ages* took place on July 2, when it simultaneously opened in twenty-four theaters. Keaton, immersed in preparations for the filming of *Headin' South,* couldn't make the London premiere and was happy to leave the attention to Leahy, who toured the country doing appearances and was perhaps a bigger draw with the British public than Buster himself.

Casting the new movie became a family affair. A year after separating from his wife over his drinking, Joe Keaton had taken the pledge, and with Nat and Little Buster already on board, it was a natural fit to give him the role of the Rocket's high-kicking engineer. Joe Roberts was the obvious choice for the paternal head of the Canfield clan, with New York stage personality Craig Ward and Ralph Bushman (son of matinee idol Francis X. Bushman) as his two trigger-happy sons. Filling out the principal cast were character actress Kitty Bradbury, known for her work with Griffith and Chaplin, and stage veteran Monte Collins, both of whom had appeared with Keaton in the past. Filming began on June 30, initially in Grass Valley, then moved fifty miles east to Truckee, which in the wintertime had served as the setting for *The Frozen North* and would now, in the summer, represent the countryside to which Willie McKay must return to claim his inheritance.

Anticipating a three-week stay, the Keaton company brought two railcars stuffed with costumes, properties, and what appeared to be a miniature railway and track. Having settled on the design of the hybrid train, Keaton effectively made the Rocket a fully developed character in the story, lovingly depicting its many eccentricities in an extended sequence that could serve as a primer on early rail travel.

"They're naturally narrow-gauge," he said, "and they weren't so fussy about layin' railroad track [back then]—if it was a little unlevel, they just ignored it. They laid it over fallen trees, over rocks. So I got quite a few laughs ridin' that railroad. But when [in the picture] I got down South to claim my father's estate, I ran into the family who had run us out of the state in the first place. And the old man of the outfit wouldn't let his sons or anybody shoot me while I was a guest in the house 'cause the girl had invited me for dinner. Well, I'd overheard it and found out. As long as I stayed in the house I was safe."

The rickety train, composed of five cars including a flat, open-air baggage tender and two six-passenger compartments, moves at a deliberate pace, so much so that Willie's loyal dog can easily keep up. The title, which suggests Clyde Bruckman's hand:

Onward sped the iron
monster toward the
Blue Ridge Mountains.

A tramp, caught stowing away, can slow the entire train by merely grabbing hold of it. The track sags and roils as it moves along, and the cars buck roughly as they pass over a fallen tree. A jackass at the side of the track refuses to budge, and it proves easier to nudge the track away from him than to reason with the animal. A field of rocks creates the effect of a prehistoric roller coaster, the passengers' heads banging against the tops of the cars. When the train leaves the track entirely, the only way they can tell is that the ride is suddenly smoother. Up front, the engineer fails to notice because he is busy cooking his lunch in the firebox. Willie, it turns out, has been seated next to the Canfield girl the entire time. She steps off the train and runs into the arms of her father and elder brothers. Willie collects his things and goes off in search of the McKay estate. His dog, hardly winded, has made the entire trip on foot.

If *Three Ages* represented a transitional and somewhat uncertain bridge

Three generations of Keatons on the set of Our Hospitality *(1923).*

between shorts and features, *Our Hospitality* was a mature work of visual storytelling, richly textured and combining the comic and the tragic so deftly it marked an astonishing advancement for a man who had been directing his own films for just three years. "Once we started into features," said Keaton, differentiating between shorts and what he termed "legitimate" stories, "we had to stop doing impossible gags and ridiculous situations. We had to make an audience believe our story." Gone were the anachronistic absurdities of *Three Ages,* replaced by the quaint and charming authenticities of the early nineteenth century. "I don't know why it is, but I know it's a fact, that every gag used in a straight comedy has to be *logical* at bottom. There must be an element of possibility in everything that happens to me or the audience is immediately resentful."

Keaton also returned to a structural convention he first hit upon with *The Paleface,* opening his second feature comedy with a starkly melodramatic prologue in which Buster Jr. played his own father at the age of one.

"I use the simplest little things in the world," Keaton said in a 1965 interview, "and I never look for big gags to start a picture. I don't want them in the first reel, because if I ever get a big laugh sequence in the first reel, then I'm going to have trouble following it later. The idea that I had to have a gag or get a laugh in every scene . . . I lost that a long time ago. It makes you strive to be funny and you go out of your way trying. It's not a natural thing."

It is indicative of the control that Keaton exerted over every aspect of the production that Jack Blystone became disillusioned and asked for his release after just a week on the job. Lou Anger acceded to the request so that Blystone could return to Fox under a new three-year contract, even as Keaton pronounced himself quite pleased with his work. "He was a good man, excellent," he said. Blystone remained with the company through the remainder of the shoot, and would go on to make sure-handed dramas along with comedies, eventually directing Will Rogers, Spencer Tracy, James Cagney, and Laurel and Hardy.

The American premiere of *Three Ages* took place in San Francisco on July 14, and Buster and Natalie trained in from Truckee to witness a Sunday performance. Display ads for Loew's Warfield heralded the "First World Showing of the World's Funniest Comedy" combined with a live prologue titled "Dances of Three Ages." The *Chronicle* reported large audiences on Saturday and Sunday "for Buster is a 'wham' with the public." The paper's reviewer praised "long stretches of splendid fun" and was certain the picture had cost a lot of money. The only sour note was Margaret Leahy's presence in the cast. "She is nice looking, big and healthy, and perhaps could do a good day's washing, but as a beauty! If that's the best England can do, the country had better give up all pretensions to feminine pulchritude."* *Variety* reported a record gross of $17,500 for the week, easily besting Universal's heavily promoted *Merry Go Round,* even with the added advantage of having co-director Erich von Stroheim in town filming his first Goldwyn production, *Greed.*

Location work stretched over much of July, time enough to capture the Rocket's uncertain journey as well as harrowing scenes made on the rapids of the Truckee River. After escaping one of the murderous Canfield boys, Willie is caught in the current rushing toward a deadly waterfall, Virginia Canfield in a small boat paddling desperately to his rescue. But then she is bucked clear of the boat, and in a sequence remindful of the ice floe rescue in Griffith's *Way Down East,* it falls to Willie to try to save her. "For that scene in the rapids, the one where I'm trying to catch Natalie—someone doubled for her in those shots, of course—we picked the best rapids from a pictorial point of view, a two-hundred-yard stretch where the water moves fast and white. I'm supposed to grab onto a sixteen-foot log and float out into the bad water."

Gabe Gabourie rigged a holdback wire around the log and ran it back about sixty feet, where, securely wrapped around a baseball bat, it was held

---

* Similar words had found their way over from England, where *Variety*'s London correspondent characterized Leahy's work in the film as "a distinct screen fiasco."

The waterfall for Our Hospitality *was constructed over a T-shaped pool on the United Studios lot.*

fast by three men. The plan was to get close-ups of Willie in the furiously churning water before adjourning to a calmer part of the river for long shots. With the cameras turning, Keaton could feel the wire give, a break so soft it was barely audible. In moments, he and the log were being swept away, the men hollering and racing through the rocks and the underbrush along the shoreline. "I sure as shooting have to shed that log or it will beat me to death against the boulders. So I kick loose and sprint ahead. Can't look around, but I know that log is right on my tail. I'm hitting boulders now with my hipbones and knees, and a couple I hit so hard on my chest that I go clear up out of the water and over. The main thing is to keep from whirling."

Fighting for breath, he felt the water starting to calm and then found himself submerged in a foot or more of foam. "You don't breathe very well in foam, and you sure as hell can't swim on top of it. I later found that there was three-hundred yards of that foam ganged up at the end of the rapids.

It was a bend in the river that saved me." He caught some overhanging branches and pulled himself ashore, lying facedown and gasping for breath. He couldn't tell how long it took the men to reach him through the underbrush, but it seemed like ten minutes.

"Did Nat see it?" he asked.

Yes, he was told, she had.

"Did you get it?" he wanted to know.

Yes, Lessley responded. Both cameras.

They broke camp at Truckee, returning to Lillian Way to shoot interiors and film Virginia's rescue from the safety of a specially constructed waterfall on the United Studios lot, built over the same T-shaped pool where Buster made his famous dive all the way to China in *Hard Luck*. With Virginia rapidly approaching in the water, Willie anchors himself to the log now wedged in the rocks with a rope around his waist. Perched on a treacherous ledge, he awaits his chance, and as the water carries her to the precipice and begins to pull her over, he swings out and grabs her at the last possible moment. Swinging wildly, he manages to drop her to the ledge below and then struggles mightily to pull himself clear.

Keaton prepares to shoot the waterfall rescue of Virginia Canfield. Elgin Lessley (in cap) shoots the domestic negative while Gordon Jennings exposes a duplicate to be used for European prints. A miniature background lends a striking realism to the effect.

Joe Roberts poses for a still depicting the climactic scene of Our Hospitality. *Flanking him are Ralph Bushman, Monte Collins, Keaton, Craig Ward, and Natalie Talmadge.*

"We had to build that dam," said Keaton. "We built it in order to fit that trick. The set was built over a swimming pool, and we actually put up four eight-inch water pipes with big pumps and motors to run them, to carry water up from the pool to create our waterfall. That fall was about six inches deep. A couple of times I swung out underneath there and dropped upside down when I caught her. I had to go down to the doctor right there and then. They pumped out my ears and nostrils and drained me, because when a full volume of water like that comes down and hits you and you're upside down—then you really get it." The figure he caught was a cleverly weighted dummy dressed in the character's water-saturated clothing. "I think I got it on the third take. I missed the first two, but the third one I got it."

Natalie gave an excellent account of herself in the film, game for a lot of the physical stuff, even though she was aware that she was once again pregnant. Eunice Marshall watched her go through a scene with Ralph Bushman at the studio, costumed in a frock of rose taffeta and a full crinolined skirt: "She was playing a daughter of the Old South and seemed to have gained poise, having learned a thing or two about makeup."

But Natalie, she discovered, was dubious about continuing as Buster's leading lady. "I'm not sure whether I shall do another picture after this one or not. I hate to be away from the baby so much. Of course, he is with Mother and in good hands. But I don't want him to know anybody else better than me. Every morning I bathe him and dress him before coming to the studio. I miss being with him during the day. But it is pleasant here, too. They are very patient with me. It is four years since I have done anything in pictures, you know."

When the baby was photographed for his brief cameo in the prologue of the movie, he developed a case of "Klieg eyes" from exposure to the carbon arcs used in filming. Marked by conjunctivitis and watering, the temporary condition, which afflicted many screen personalities, resulted in his immediate retirement from pictures. Much more serious was a stroke suffered by Joe Roberts on August 17 that brought production to a halt. Roberts had not been well, and it was necessary to double him on multiple occasions while on location in Truckee. He was referred to Dr. Louis J. Regan, who had offices in the Security Bank building on Hollywood Boulevard and saw a number of industry patients. As part of a thorough examination, the doctor drew blood and ordered a Wassermann test, which confirmed a preliminary diagnosis of late-onset neurosyphilis, the infection tracing back some thirty years. There was nothing to be done; Big Joe was dying.

Facing seizures, dementia, and eventual paralysis, Roberts was ordered to bed. Keaton shot around him, but Joe knew the picture couldn't be properly completed without him, and after a brief convalescence he returned to Lillian Way to finish his part. In a severely weakened state, he rested on a couch between shots while others attended to his makeup and wardrobe. Then, mustering his strength and favoring his right side, he managed to hide his infirmities and deliver a strikingly shaded comedic performance in what he now knew would be his final picture. Particularly affecting is his climactic scene in which he comes to the realization that after generations of warfare he must now accept a McKay into the family. Pistol in hand, he registers shock, anger, bewilderment, resignation, and, finally, fatherly love as he kisses his newly married daughter on the forehead and gathers her into his arms, slowly extending a hand of genuine friendship and welcome to his new son. It is a scene that would challenge the most experienced of actors, yet Roberts gives each successive beat a thoroughly natural reading. After years of playing the narrow parameters of low comedy, here he showed in his final moments on-screen what a fine dramatic actor he could be, and the heights he might have scaled had he been permitted a longer life.

With his scenes in the can, Joe retired to the new eight-room house he had built for his wife and family to await the inevitable. When the picture was cut together under the title *Hospitality,* he was too weak to attend a Glendale preview under his own power and had to be carried into the theater. According to Harry Brand, the showing took place on the night of October 27, 1923, and Roberts returned home that evening with the knowledge that he had delivered the finest performance of his career. A few hours later, at just minutes past midnight, a second stroke claimed him at the age of fifty-two.

11

The Navigator

RELEASED NATIONALLY on September 24, 1923, *Three Ages* was a tough sell with exhibitors, who, according to *Variety,* "shied at it to a remarkable extent." Trade notices were mixed, with *Variety* and *Exhibitors Trade Review* delivering solid raves. "On the Sunday night aspect of attendance," wrote *Variety*'s Rush Greason, "the picture will get a big public following and it should, for it is first class screen amusement by a distinct personality and one of the best legitimate comedians we have, either for screen or for the stage." *Billboard,* on the other hand, couldn't discern enough comedy to justify the length: "The picture is really made up of three two-reelers, each the same in story, the only difference lying in the interpretative action in the three ages. After *Three Ages* gets past the half-way mark it becomes acutely boring."

The New York dailies were similarly divided, with the *American, Evening World, Post,* and *Tribune* cheering the picture, and the *Mail, Morning Telegraph,* and *Sun* turning thumbs down. The *Times,* significantly, ignored it entirely. The film did good business during initial stands in key cities, such as Washington, Philadelphia, and Boston, but soon played itself out. Keaton made a quick trip east to attend the World Series, and *Three Ages* went completely unmentioned during an interview he gave the *Telegraph.* "It was difficult to make him say anything," the interviewer, Dorothy Day, complained. "I never saw anybody so unwilling to talk." After a few moments of silence, she asked how he liked the games.

"Oh, the games," he responded. "They were fine."

"Were you satisfied with the outcome of them?"

"Sure. I bet on the Yanks."

"Did you win much?"

"Not much. A couple of dinners and the tickets."

He fumbled with a watch chain and produced a little platinum locket, which he opened to reveal the cherubic face of Buster Jr.

"Does he look like you?" she asked.

"Exactly," he said, finally showing some enthusiasm. "He's a great kid. And there's a vacant space in the other side of the locket, you may have noticed. I'm reserving that."

A British journalist named Margaret Werner detected a similar reluctance unless the subject was parenthood. "The kid is going to be his own boss," Keaton, waxing eloquent, told her, "and whatever profession appeals to him when he grows up, well, that's the profession he's going to ornament. President or plumber, it's what little Buster chooses. That's the way they're bringing them up nowadays. The individuality of the child and all that. The kid's recovering now from a long siege of work. There were three generations of us in *Hospitality*—my dad, my son, and myself."

Back in California, he traveled to San Francisco for the world premiere of *Hospitality*, housed once more at Loew's Warfield, where *Three Ages* had made its stateside bow. Accompanying him were Lou Anger, Jean Havez, Joe Mitchell, Clyde Bruckman, and Roscoe Arbuckle, who was eager to attend the opening-day festivities at Tanforan Racetrack and drew more attention than the others combined. "Just came up with the boys to take in the races," he said, brushing off a reporter from the *Chronicle*. When asked if he had any comment on a divorce action filed October 22 by his wife, Minta, he replied, "No, she said it all."

Hospitality logged even better numbers than *Three Ages* in its opening weekend, near capacity for all showings and another house record of $19,000 for the week. Contributing were wall-to-wall positives in the *Chronicle, Examiner, Journal, News, Bulletin,* and *Call,* all seconded by *Variety's* Frisco correspondent: "The star hangs over cliffs hundreds of feet in the air, rides a log down a seething rapids, and manages to save himself at the brink of the waterfall, which looks a mile high. This scene particularly is a real thrill and kept the audience on edge, gasping with fear one minute and laughing the next."

As Keaton once remarked, "The best way to get a laugh is to create a genuine thrill and then relieve the tension with comedy. Getting laughs depends on the element of surprise, and surprises are getting harder and harder to get as audiences, seeing more pictures, become more and more comedy-wise.

But when you take a genuine thrill, build up to it, and then turn it into a ridiculous situation, you always get that surprise element."

The film's formal release, under the title *Our Hospitality*, came on November 19, 1923. Mirroring the San Francisco dailies, all the New York papers praised it, some extravagantly. The trades were nearly as unanimous, Helen Swenson in *Exhibitors Trade Review* calling it "one of the most humorous pictures ever produced" and going on to praise its comedy as based "on the solid foundation of a good story." The one outlier within the industry was *Billboard*, which inexplicably found long stretches of the picture tiresome. "It is a genuine pity that Keaton ever went into the feature field. His short comedies were scintillating gems of comedy; his features are plain window glass with an occasional glint."

The public embraced *Our Hospitality* wholeheartedly, delivering world-wide rentals of $537,844, a 20 percent jump over the $448,606 reported for *Three Ages*. Late in life, Keaton recalled the costs of his features as being lower than either Harold Lloyd's or Charlie Chaplin's. "I ran around $225,000 to the picture," he said. "That would include my salary. Harold Lloyd, he would go a little more than that, and Chaplin went higher still." Given the consistent profitability of the Keaton and Talmadge features, Joe Schenck ordered no year-end slowdown in their production, despite shutdowns at Famous Players and Universal caused, in part, by huge backlogs of unreleased negative. To the press, he reiterated his intention of going forward with a year's program of nine features budgeted at $3,500,000, with Keaton responsible for two. At the time of Schenck's statement, Constance Talmadge was shooting *The Goldfish*, Norma was finishing *Secrets*, and Keaton was making his third feature comedy, the working title for which was *The Misfit*.

The impetus for *The Misfit* was almost certainly *Merton of the Movies*, a sharp satire of the picture business that opened on Broadway in November 1922. Keaton, who was informally scouting stage properties for Dutch Talmadge, was instantly drawn to the character of Merton Gill—a small-town boob who dreams of Hollywood stardom—and openly said he wanted to play the part on-screen. The sticking point was that the show's star, Glenn Hunter, was under contract to Famous Players, and it was widely assumed that Paramount would have the inside track on any deal for the film rights. While in New York for the 1923 World Series, Keaton had shot a look of disapproval at his questioner from the *Telegraph* when asked if he harbored secret longings to play Hamlet or Macbeth. He did, however, allow as how he would like to play Merton of the Movies.

"Had Buster got the play rights," suggested *Motion Picture* magazine, "we would have had in him a 'different' Merton, but with Famous Players-Lasky in possession, Glenn Hunter will register his delightful version of the pathetic movie hero on the screen. . . . Well, anyhow, Buster Keaton has secured a story on similar lines: *The Misfit*. It tells of a projection machine operator, again a small town hero, who goes to Hollywood to make his fortune and fully becomes a millionaire-producer. Between the first and last exposures appear many scenes of Mertonish poignancy. In the cast are Buster himself and Kathryn McGuire, an ex-beauty of the Mack Sennett tribe."

Kathryn McGuire's presence in the cast resulted from one of the picture's early setbacks, for when filming commenced in mid-November, Marion Harlan, the nineteen-year-old daughter of actor Otis Harlan, was the girl in the story. Harlan apparently shot for several weeks before she had to withdraw due to illness, and McGuire replaced her in mid-December. By then, Keaton had been forced to abandon the idea of bringing his character to Hollywood, and a new device had to be found to set the action in motion. In desperation, he returned to a setup similar to the modern story in *Three Ages:* two suitors for the same girl, one good and one bad. Due to the chicanery of his rival, Buster is unjustly accused of theft and ordered from the house. He must solve the crime to redeem himself, sparking a burlesque of the detective genre most recently exploited by John Barrymore in *Sherlock Holmes*. In fact, it was courtesy of the Barrymore release that the film acquired its permanent title: *Sherlock Jr.*

"I think the reason we started off on that story," Keaton remarked, "is because I had one of the best cameramen in the picture business, Elgin Lessley. He originally was with Sennett. Now I laid out a few of these tricks; [and] some of these tricks I knew from the stage. I seldom did camera tricks. I tried to do the real illusion. (I have done an awful lot of camera tricks too, as far as that goes.) But I laid out some of those gags. And the technical man that builds the sets, I showed him how I have to get them built for the things I had to do. [When] we got that batch of stuff together, [Lessley] said, 'You can't do it and tell a legitimate story, because there are illusions and some of them are clown gags, some Houdini, some Ching Ling Foo. It's got to come in a dream. To get what we're after, you've got to be a projectionist in a projecting room in the little local small-town motion picture theater, and go to sleep after you've got the picture started. Once you fall asleep, you visualize yourself as one of the important characters in the picture you're showing.

[You] go down out of that projection room, go right down, and then walk up onto the screen and become a part of it. Now you tell your whole story.'

"And all I had to round out was that I was in trouble at the start of the picture with my girl's father. He thought I stole his watch. Well, on the screen I became the world's greatest detective to solve this mystery. Of course, while I'm asleep the girl finds out that I didn't steal it, and she was the one who woke me up at the finish. But on the screen I was a son-of-a-gun, the world's greatest detective. No matter how they tried to surround me and kill me or get me, I got out of it."

Putting Buster into the movie itself and having him interact with all the characters on-screen—as well as the conventions of filmmaking—would be Lessley's department. "That was the reason for making the whole picture. Just that one situation: that a motion picture projectionist in a theater goes to sleep and visualizes himself getting mixed up with the characters on the screen. All right, then my job was to transform those characters on the screen into [the projectionist's] characters at home, and then I've got my plot."

Sherlock Jr. started out modestly, keeping to Keaton's policy of never going for big gags at the start of a picture. Buster is sweeping out the theater and finds three dollars in the pile of trash. A young woman appears and says she lost a dollar. Reluctantly, he returns it to her (after having her describe it). Then an old lady comes along and hands him the same story. He forks over another dollar. Finally, a ruffian appears and Buster hands over the third dollar, no questions asked. The man hands it back, then rummages through the pile of trash and recovers a whole wallet with a thick wad of cash in it. Buster takes the one dollar he has left and goes next door to a confectionary to buy candy for Kathryn. Then he marches off to the house she shares with her father (Joe Keaton). Here is where his rival, the local sheik—Keaton's pal Ward Crane—steals the father's watch, pawns it, and pins the crime on Buster.

Jack Blystone having resigned as co-director, Keaton tried shooting the film himself. Then he got to thinking about his pal Arbuckle. ("Roscoe was down in the dumps and broke.") According to Viola Dana, Keaton got Arbuckle to visit him on the set: "He told Roscoe he was needed *in a creative capacity* to get more laughs out of the opening scenes." In terms of credit, they couldn't use his real name, so Keaton jokingly suggested "Will B. Good." Arbuckle himself settled on "William Goodrich," which were his father's first and middle names.

"So we hire him as a director for me," said Keaton, "and at the end of about three days we saw our mistake. He is now so irritable and impatient and loses his temper so easily. He's screaming at people, getting flushed and mad, and of course things don't go so well. In other words, he hadn't recovered yet from those trials of being accused of murder and nearly convicted. It just changed his disposition."

Vi Dana added: "There were never any problems between Roscoe and Buster until Peg Talmadge showed up and demanded to know why Roscoe was there, and who was paying and how much. And then Roscoe would take it out on poor Kathryn McGuire, a lovely girl, a trained dancer. Kathryn was no Mabel [Normand] and she never could do what Mabel could do. Buster, always the diplomat when it came to dealing with Roscoe, thanked him for his help and told him he now had a handle on the film. Roscoe, equally polite, knew better than to question Buster's judgment. It was, after all, Buster's film. It was better to remain friends. Which they did."

Arbuckle went back to directing Al St. John, but a surprising thing happened in April 1924 during a National Vaudeville Artists benefit at L.A.'s Philharmonic Auditorium. During a change of acts the curtain went up by mistake, revealing that one of the volunteer scene-shifters was none other than Roscoe "Fatty" Arbuckle. In overalls, he was a familiar sight moving a piano offstage, and the audience broke into applause, whistles, and finally cheers as he advanced to the footlights to say a few words. The demonstration, in fact, inspired a twelve-week tour of the Pantages circuit, which began the following month in San Francisco. Again Arbuckle was warmly welcomed, with a packed house according him a two-minute standing ovation. In Los Angeles, he was awarded an enormous floral statue of himself—baggy trousers, brown derby—as a gift from old friends in the industry. It was so heavy it required four men to lift it. On his opening night in San Diego, a huge American flag of carnations was presented "in memory of his work during the world war" when he served tirelessly as a celebrity recruiter and godfather of the 159th Infantry, Company C, which he sent off to France with several thousand dollars for their treasury.

The tour progressed to Pantages houses in Long Beach, Salt Lake City, and Detroit, each performance kicked off with a special film made at the Keaton studio in which both Buster and Al St. John help Roscoe break back into show business—and into his dressing room. The Pantages tour was so successful that Arbuckle signed with a new manager, Perry Kelly, who generally toured road companies and who booked him into secondary markets such as Toledo, Grand Rapids, and Milwaukee. When Arbuckle again played San Francisco in November, the act was largely the same—a monologue of reading and answering letters from fans—but still doing turn-away business.

"He looks a little thinner than the last time here," observed *Billboard*'s E. J. Wood, "and he has regained most of his old-time assurance. He made a good short curtain speech and is now thoroughly re-established in this city. Four curtain calls."

"So then I went ahead," said Keaton, "threw the first three days' stuff in the ashcan, started from scratch and made the picture." The big challenge, of course, was how to create the illusion of Buster inserting himself into the movie up on the screen. The first time he jumps into the frame, one of the on-screen characters tosses him back. The second time he makes his approach, the scene abruptly changes from the interior of a large room to the exterior of an ornate entryway and he must struggle to avoid hitting the door head on. A formally dressed character opens the door, steps through it, remembers something, walks back inside. Buster runs up and knocks on

The dreaming projectionist approaches the screen in Sherlock Jr. *(1924). Joe Keaton, in evening clothes, emerges as a character in the movie.*

the door, only to have the scene change to a garden setting and he tumbles off an outdoor bench. Picking himself up, he begins to seat himself on the bench when the scene changes to a city street and he falls backwards, dodging traffic. Walking away, the scene cuts again to a mountain setting and he almost steps off into thin air. Peering over the edge, another cut places him in the midst of a pair of lions. Then a desert with a passing train. Then an ocean reef. Then a snow scene. And so on.

"We built what looked like a motion picture screen," he explained, "and actually built a stage into that frame but lit it in such a way that it looked like a motion picture being projected on a screen. But it was real actors, and the lighting effect gave us the illusion so I could go out of semi-darkness into that well-lit screen right from the front row of the theater [and] right into the picture. Then when it came to the scene changing on me when I got up there, that was a case of timing and on every one of those things we would measure the distance to a fraction of an inch from the camera to where I was standing . . . to get the exact height and angle so that there wouldn't be a fraction of an inch missing on me, and then we changed the setting to what we wanted it to be and I got back into that same spot and it overlapped the action to get the effect of the scene changing."

Moving out of doors, the surroundings of the theater remained, but the screen itself was blacked out so that the film could be rewound and Keaton captured in the unexposed portion of the frame. At times in later years, he said that he used surveyor's instruments to get the effect, but in his 1964 talk with Kevin Brownlow, he specifically said that he didn't: "All we needed was the exact distance, and the cameraman could judge the height. And by using a traveling matte from the other take—which you could do, see—they get me into position here and they crank [a few feet]. They throw [that exposed film] in the darkroom and develop it right there and then and bring it back to [the cameraman], and he cuts out those frames and puts it in [the camera gate]. When I come to change scenes, he can put me right square where I was, as long as that distance was correct."

For the shot on the ocean reef with the waves crashing around him, Keaton described how he matched the transition to the snow: "As I looked down [from the rock] I held still for a moment, and we ended that scene. Then we brought out tape measures, put a crossbar in front of the camera to square it off, and measured me from two angles. That made sure that I was in exactly the same spot as far as the camera was concerned."

The film-within-a-film is called *Hearts and Pearls,* and the characters dis-

Sherlock Jr. is about to go racing down Santa Monica Boulevard on the handlebars of an unmanned motorcycle.

solve into the ones Buster is contending with in real life, again played by Ward Crane, Kathryn McGuire, and Joe Keaton. When a string of pearls is discovered missing, the great detective is summoned to crack the case. What he doesn't know is that the house has been booby-trapped by the thieves. Poison drinks and deadly chairs are offered, and a game of pocket billiards is played with an exploding ball. The action moves outdoors, and here Keaton conjures the stage illusions that prompted Elgin Lessley to tell him they had to come in a dream. With the aid of his assistant, a man called Gillette ("a gem who was ever-ready in a bad scrape"), Buster grabs the pearls in the thieves' hideaway, leaps through a hooped window, and is instantly costumed for his escape as an old woman. Discovered, he is chased into a blind alley, where it is Gillette's turn to pose as an old woman peddling neckties from a display case. Cornered, Buster leaps through the case Gillette is holding in his hands and seemingly vanishes into thin air.

Once again on the run, he is pulled over by a motorcycle cop who turns out to be the faithful Gillette in yet another disguise. Buster jumps onto the handlebars, and they race off to the rescue of Kathryn, who is being held by the mob. The cycle, however, hits a watery hazard in the middle of the street, and Gillette is thrown off.* Buster, still on the handlebars and unaware he's now the only one on the machine, continues on. "The control of the gas is [on the handlebars] for speed, but I've got no brakes. You've got to have a strong arm to get your feet back down there, 'cause it was footbrakes, see. Well, I got some beautiful spills before I could get back. Some beauties. I parked right up on top of an automobile once. I hit it head on, and I ended up with my fanny up against the windshield, my feet straight in the air."

Onward he speeds, dodging traffic, feet in the air, oblivious to the fact that he's entirely alone. "Be careful or one of us will get hurt," he warns the missing pilot as he zooms along Santa Monica Boulevard. In short order he upends a pedestrian, takes a shovelful of dirt in the face from each worker in a line of ditch diggers, plows through an Irish picnic, barrels over an unfinished bridge just as two cargo trucks momentarily complete the gap, is saved by a perfectly timed blast of dynamite that splinters a fallen tree in his path, roars under an elevated tractor, narrowly misses an oncoming locomotive, and goes flying off the handlebars when the bike hits a logged barrier, crashing through the window of a remote shack and hitting the girl's captor feetfirst, knocking him through the far wall. Throughout this astonishing three-minute sequence, the pace never lags, with all the disparate elements as fluid as a single continuous motion.

One of the last scenes to be shot could have proved ruinous. Rule 5 in the handbook *How to Be a Detective* is "Shadow your man closely." So Buster sets off to follow his suspect, generally keeping within inches of the guy. He stalks him onto a train platform and, once noticed, continues right on into a boxcar, only to have the door bolted shut behind him. As it begins to move, Buster emerges onto the roof of the car and starts running toward the rear of the train until it abruptly ends and he's forced to grab on to the rope dangling from the spout of a water tower to break his fall. What Keaton didn't realize at the time was that the stunt and its aftermath had broken his neck.

"Of course all my weight pulls on the rope, and of course I pull the spout down and it drenches me with water. Well, when you're up on top of a freight car you're up there twelve feet high and that water spout is a ten-inch pipe. I didn't know how strong that water pressure was. Well, it just tore my

---

* Donning actor Ford West's uniform, and dressing assistant prop man Ernie Orsatti in his own clothes, Keaton, with his back to the camera, performed this stunt himself.

grip loose as if I had no grip at all and dropped me the minute it hit me. And I lit on my back with my head right across the rail—the rail right on my neck. It was a pretty hard fall, and that water pushed me down. . . . I had a headache for a few hours. . . . I said, 'I want a drink.' I turned at the next block coming back from location—it was out there in the [San Fernando] Valley someplace. I went in to [see] Mildred Harris, Charlie Chaplin's first wife, and I went into her house and she gave me a couple of stiff drinks. During Prohibition, see, when you couldn't just stop anyplace to get a drink. So, that numbed me enough that I woke up the following morning, my head was clear and I never stopped working."

Sherlock Jr. was completed the week of February 4, 1924, and Keaton, as usual, was looking forward to putting it in front of an audience. "One of the main reasons for takin' it out of town was so that none of the carpenters or extra people or anybody connected with studios would be in that audience. Because if we had an outstanding sequence or cute gags or good gags or anything like that, these people would sell it to other studios. Sometimes they'd sell it, and sometimes just to get in good with somebody [they'd say], 'Here'd be a good gag for you.' And we had that happen to us a few times. So our previews—we'd take 'em out to Los Angeles, Long Beach, San Bernardino, Santa Barbara, Riverside, Santa Ana—places like that. And we don't tell the audience they're lookin' at a preview. See, we want a cold reaction. We'd send the print down there to the exhibitor, and he's goin' to have two shows that night, [so] he runs the picture twice. And he advertises a Keaton picture—that's all. So we're in there to get . . . a normal reaction."

According to *Variety*, the first preview of *Sherlock Jr.* took place at a theater in Long Beach. "There," said the trade, "Keaton took in all the comment he heard among the audience and decided that the picture would not do. He tore it apart and started remaking it."

For Keaton, this wasn't as extraordinary as the paper made it sound. "We have never made a picture—I know I never did, and I know Lloyd never did, and I'm sure Chaplin never did—that we didn't go back and set the camera up again. Because we helped the highspots, and redid the bad ones, and cut footage out, and [got] scenes that would connect things up for us. We always put a makeup on and set the camera back up after that first preview. And generally after the second one, also . . ."

On March 4, *The Film Daily* carried an item announcing the completion of *Sherlock Jr.,* and a second preview was held in Glendale. "Again Buster was not satisfied with the picture," *Variety* reported. "Another retake was made. . . ." Keaton blew past Metro's March 10 release date, and a Viola Dana picture titled *Don't Doubt Your Husband* was moved up to fill the hole. For its final preview, *Sherlock Jr.* was brought to a Los Angeles house for a midnight screening. "Keaton and his staff were on hand. The picture looked good to them, the audience laughed heartily. So Buster took it back to the studio, cut it considerably, and then scheduled it for release."

In all, Keaton's trims shortened the feature to just 4,065 feet—scarcely a five-reeler—from the sixty thousand feet exposed, a shooting ratio of nearly fifteen to one. Not that he was counting the amount of raw stock he used. "We never paid the slightest attention to it. But we could generally tell when we were over footage, which we didn't mind, because it was much better to be able to cut and throw things away than to go short." Now more concept than story, *Sherlock Jr.* took on the look and feel of a two-reel comedy, a magician's toolbox of a film. As with *Our Hospitality,* reactions to the picture were largely positive. Released on April 21, 1924, *Sherlock Jr.* quickly made its way to major cities, particularly Los Angeles and New York, where the dailies and trades embraced it warmly. At Loew's State, where the picture opened on April 26, it played to more than twenty-five thousand people in three days, just short of a house record. In New York, the *Film Daily* branded it "The best comedy this year. A riot of laughs. Probably the best thing Keaton has ever done." Even *Billboard* agreed, ranking the Keaton two-reelers among the funniest short comedies ever made. "*Sherlock Jr.,* which is slightly over 4,000 feet long, is funnier than any two-reel comedies Keaton ever made. It is packed with laughable incidents, silly, ridiculous tricks that will cause roars of real belly laughs, and will send them home just a bit ashamed at having laughed so much, just as it did this reviewer—and in a cold projection room, too."

At the other end of the scale, *Variety*'s Fred Schader stood nearly alone in declaring *Sherlock Jr.* "about as unfunny as a hospital operating room." The *Daily News,* the *World,* and *The Brooklyn Daily Eagle* pretty much concurred, while all the other big papers endorsed it heartily. And while Schader sourly predicted economic doom at Broadway's Rialto, the picture actually performed quite well with an estimated gross of $21,000 for the week. The one thing almost universally commented upon was the film's length, which became a particular problem for rural exhibitors, whose audiences expected a full program of entertainment. "A good comedy drama but far from a special," reported a manager from Rossiter, Pennsylvania. "Too short for a feature." The film would accumulate worldwide rentals of $448,337, placing it on a par with *Three Ages* but far behind *Our Hospitality*. Its reputation would continue to grow over the ensuing decades, however, and in 1991, sixty-seven years after its making, *Sherlock Jr.* would become the second of Keaton's features to be enshrined for preservation in the National Film Registry.

"It had always occurred to me that there was a good deal of comedy to be found under the sea," Keaton wrote in 1926, "and I ordered a regulation diving suit that weighed two hundred and twenty pounds. The only variation was that more glass was put into the front of the helmet. The face, even though it is not a smiling one, must be seen in comedy. That was the beginning of *The Navigator*. The story was built up from that diver's suit."

A character under the sea in a diver's suit must be tethered to a ship of some kind—not just a thirty-five-footer, but something of size—and Keaton credited Jean Havez with the idea of making it an ocean liner.

"Well, we went to work right then and there and sez, 'Now, what can we do with an ocean liner?' [Someone] says, 'Well, we can make a dead ship out of it. No lights aboard. No running water. Just afloat.' How could we get it afloat? Well, we set out to figure out how to do that and how to write a story around it. Only to get a boy and a girl alone and adrift in the Pacific Ocean." It was a natural, a real pip of a story. "Now you go back to your first part to establish your characters. Well, if I was a laborer or a poor guy, or something like that, it would be no hardship for me to be on that ocean liner. But if I started out with a Rolls-Royce, a chauffeur, a footman, a valet, and a couple of cooks and [everyone] else to wait on me—and the same thing with the girl—in other words, the audience knows we were born rich and never had to lift a finger to do anything. Now you turn those two people adrift on a dead ship, they're helpless."

Getting the characters stranded on the ship together took some doing, and the setup, as usual for a Keaton picture, wasn't meant to be funny. Buster is Rollo Treadway, heir to the Treadway fortune—living proof that "every family tree must have its sap." Rollo's girl (Kathryn McGuire again) rejects him after he's already purchased two tickets to Honolulu for the honeymoon. "So I tear up one ticket, put the other in my pocket, and I sez, 'What time does it sail?' [My butler] says, 'Nine o'clock.' I sez, 'In the morning?' He says, 'Yeah.' I sez, 'It's too early, so I'll go aboard tonight.'"

"All right. Now we went to the night shot, and we show the night watchman coming out with his punch clock. And I was supposed to go to Pier 2, and we see this watchman come up to punch at this pier. He slid the gate over on 12, but the gate hid the '1.' And I see it from the car and I decide that's the ship. And I go out there and get on this ship. Oh, and here's your plot: We went to a bunch of men in a building overlooking the bay of San Francisco and looking down at the boat at the pier. [One of them] says, 'That boat has just been bought by our enemies, this country that we're on the verge of going to war against. That ship will carry ammunition and supplies. It's up to us to see that she doesn't get there. Tonight, we'll go down there, we'll overcome the night watchman, or anybody else who gets in our way, throw her ropes off or cut them off, set that boat adrift—the wind and tide will do the rest. It's a cinch to go up against those rocks on the other side of the Golden Gate, and it's a doomed ship.' That's the plot.

"So I come down and I get on this boat. Now, there's nobody to meet me. There's no lights. It's a dead ship. There's no water, there's no nothing running. But I finally find my stateroom, and when I get inside I have to light matches to see what I'm doing, but I put myself to bed. About this time, these foreign agents arrive and overpower the watchman, put him in a little room, one of the pier sheds. And they go out to set this boat free. And they no more complete their job—they ignore the gangplank that goes onto the ship—but you could see that the ship is going away from the pier and that gangplank is just sliding.

"The girl and her father [are] all dressed up to go to a dinner party someplace, and she brings the car to a stop—she's driving a coupe—and he says, 'I had to have you drive me down past the *Navigator* because I left some papers in the pilot house that I want. I'll only be a few minutes.' He comes down onto this pier and he runs into these agents. Well, they grab him, but before they can put a handkerchief in his mouth, he yells, 'Help!' She hears it in the car. Well, they drag him into this little shed to bind him up. She doesn't know that, but passes on down and goes over the gangplank onto the ship. And she no more gets onto the ship when the ship is far enough away from the dock now that the gangplank falls. So she's on the ship. And it fades out."

Since *The Navigator* was essentially a drama made comical by the natures of its two characters, Keaton figured he needed a director who was well versed in the staging of serious pictures. Somebody suggested actor Donald Crisp, who had directed more than thirty movies and had just recently made an African adventure called *Ponjola* with Anna Q. Nilsson. "I said,

'I've got a couple of dramatic sequences in this thing, and . . . I want 'em straight. And I'm going to a cannibal island, and I don't want burlesque-looking headhunters and cannibals out there. I want them legitimate.'" Crisp agreed to the assignment, acknowledging it would be "an experience." He was announced as director of *The Navigator* in February 1924, while *Sherlock Jr.* was still in production.

Once Keaton and his crew knew they needed an ocean liner for the story, it fell to Gabe Gabourie to hunt one up. According to Keaton, it was Gabourie who located a former army transport docked in San Francisco called the *Buford*. Under the flag of the Alaska-Siberian Navigation Co., the 370-foot steamer had been converted to a passenger ship for runs to Seattle and the Arctic. On April 17, it returned to port after a sixty-day tour of the South Seas and was due to be overhauled and returned to Arctic service. Keaton traveled north with Gabourie, Crisp, Havez, Joe Mitchell, and Clyde Bruckman, all intent upon giving the vessel a thorough stem-to-stern inspection. "For two whole days the gagmen shot possibilities at each other and at Buster while they built up his story," an article in the *Los Angeles Times* recounted. "A stenographer sat hard by taking down the suggestions. Capt. John A. O'Brien, veteran of fifty-eight years of service on the Pacific, materially aided the scenarists. O'Brien told funny stories of past experiences he had had or of which he had heard, and called in his crew to tell their versions of funny incidents of life on shipboard. At the end of a week of this sort of thing, the stenographer had more than four-hundred pages of single-spaced gag ideas. These ideas were whipped into story form by Buster and his henchmen in several more days of work."

E. B. White, then a Seattle-based reporter, had taken the SS *Buford* to Alaska in 1923 and thought her "a fine little ship . . . She was deep, not overburdened with superstructure, and had a wide, clear main deck." Suitable for filming, the *Buford* was chartered by Buster Keaton Productions for a period of ten weeks at a cost of $25,000. By April 30, it was en route to Redondo Beach, where it would be temporarily outfitted for *The Navigator*. Upon arrival, it was given some cosmetic touch-ups and two portable truck-mounted generators were taken aboard, as were 100,000 feet of raw film stock. One of the staterooms was turned into a cutting room, and the ship's skeleton crew was augmented with thirty production personnel, including Gabourie, electrician Denver Harmon, and cameramen Elgin Lessley and Byron Houck. Within a week, they were anchored off Catalina Island, filming the early scenes of Rollo and the girl aboard the deserted ship.

Donald Crisp directs a scene from The Navigator *(1924). Kathryn McGuire can be seen over Keaton's shoulder.*

Donald Crisp was on the picture nearly three months before filming commenced, and despite Keaton's assertions to the contrary, there exists a thirty-page treatment for *The Navigator* that was likely prepared at Crisp's behest. While in San Francisco, Crisp and Keaton shot Rollo's introduction as laid forth in the document, which was staged on a street in the city's affluent Pacific Heights neighborhood: "The opening gag in that picture with me is one of the most stolen gags that was ever done on the screen," Keaton said. "I think I knew at one time of twenty-seven times it had been done by other companies. With us, the gag was more to establish the fact that I was so helpless, that I went to call on the girl, and I came down and got in my car with a chauffeur *and* a footman. The footman wrapped a blanket around my knees—a big open Pierce-Arrow phaeton—and drove across the street. That's all. I got out to call on the girl. I asked the girl if she'd marry me and she said, 'No,' and I came back down [to the car]. The guy opened the door in the car for me and I said, 'No, I think the walk will do me good.' So I walked across the street with the car followin' me, makin' a U-turn."

Crisp managed the scene beautifully, but now in the waters off Catalina, Keaton came to the realization he had made a mistake: "I said to him, 'You don't have to worry about the gag department. We'll take care of that.' Well, we start and he directed all right, but he wasn't fussy about it. He was only interested in the scenes I was in. He turned gagman overnight on me. He came to work every morning with the goddamndst gags you ever heard of in your life. Wild! We didn't want him as a gagman, for God's sake!" Crisp, he found, had actually bungled some of the serious stuff, permitting the heavies to overact and attempting comedic touches where there weren't supposed to be any. "Nothing to do about it," said Buster. "We carried him through the picture."

Most of the shipboard action was worked out by Keaton himself, particularly a sequence in which Rollo and the girl engage in a series of near misses. Moving around the ship, they can hear footsteps but can't quite catch sight of each other as they climb stairways and walk the various decks and passageways, going increasingly faster all the while. "Then," as James Agee was later to observe, "the camera withdraws to a point of vantage at the stern, leans its chin in its hand and just watches the whole intricate superstructure of the ship as the protagonists stroll, steal, and scuttle from level to level, up, down, and sidewise, always managing to miss each other by hair's-breadths, in an enchantingly neat and elaborate piece of timing. There are no subsidiary gags to get laughs in this sequence and there is little loud laughter; merely a quiet and steadily increasing kind of delight."

As Keaton explained, "We set the camera out on the bow of the ship so it could take in the three decks, and just sit down and talk it over with the girl—tell her how fast to travel, where to look, how to come down stairs and look, go back up, and so forth until we laid out the chase, and then we go ahead and shoot it." There was also an arresting visual in which all the cabin doors were rigged to open and close to the pitch and roll of the ship. "We got a camera with a big weight hanging on there, and we went down underneath [it] with a piece of chalk and marked a figure 8 [on the deck]. Now, this is a free head—a ball head—on the camera. Now this man here just takes this [weighted ball head], and when the scene starts he just follows that [figure 8]. That way you've [got] your [movement]."

In time, Rollo and the girl adapt to their surroundings, making sleeping quarters of the ship's furnaces and improvising an automated galley of pull cords and counterweights. After weeks on the water, land is sighted. Peering through binoculars, they realize they're drifting toward a village of cannibals. "We're safer on the boat," Rollo tells her, but then the stern of the *Navigator* runs aground and they find themselves under attack. Donald Crisp proved helpful in staging these scenes, and took an active role in casting the natives, including the pioneering actor and production executive Noble Johnson. The siege constitutes the entire third act of the film, with the pair fighting off the invaders with everything at their disposal—fireworks, sky rockets, buckets of water, even a miniature cannon that trails Rollo like a tiny attack dog.

"In that particular period of the 1920s," Clyde Bruckman commented, "we were trying to shake the pattern of the final chase. A hard thing to do, it was set in the public mind. 'The chase,' Buster was always saying, 'is just one form of climax. It works so well because it speeds up the tempo, generally involves the whole cast, and puts the whole outcome of the story on the block.' In *The Navigator* we didn't have another liner to chase the one we had. We had to try to come up with another climax."

In July, *The Navigator* company was reported filming in Mexican waters. "We moved our generators and lighting equipment on, and put cooks and assistants on there, and we lived on that boat for a month and shot all around it. We could take it anyplace and drop anchor, or have her out at open sea, or anything we wanted to do." When they returned to Los Angeles, Donald Crisp was unceremoniously let go.

"Toward the end," *Variety* reported, "Keaton decided to handle the megaphone himself and Crisp sat on the sidelines. One day, Keaton informed Crisp that the picture was completed and the latter left the lot. Subsequently, Keaton, it is said, shot the underwater scenes, which, it is claimed, Crisp had never been in favor of doing." Keaton, more to the point, saw no advantage in keeping Crisp on the payroll: "A director can't do anything with an underwater sequence anyway. It's just between me and the cameraman and the technical man."

Originally, the plan had been different. Anchored off Catalina, Keaton anticipated they'd shoot the underwater scenes at the same time as everything else. "But we found that when one walked on the bottom of the Pacific in a diver's suit, he stirred up so much sand that the films became cloudy and indistinct. It was necessary to have clear water into which we could lower our diving bell that contained the cameras." Once back on dry land, Keaton thought they could use the Elliotta Plunge in Riverside, where an enclosed pool, forty by sixty, was continuously fed by natural hot springs, and where his old friend Houdini had shot an underwater sequence for a picture called *Terror Island*. But the pool wasn't deep enough to accommodate the mock-up of the ship's propeller and rudder assembly that Rollo goes down to repair, so it was necessary to add another ten feet to the sides. "Well, we thought that would work out fine because we know the clear water we're goin' to get down there. But the base of the swimming pool is built to only hold seven or eight feet of water. Wouldn't take eighteen. The bottom just went out from under it. The weight of the water pushed the bottom out. So we wrecked that pool. Had to build them a new swimmin' pool."

They finally settled on Lake Tahoe, up near Truckee, where the water was clear but cold and Keaton found he could stay under for only thirty minutes at a time. Stationed in the vicinity of Meek's Bay, the location resembled a marionette theater in which Keaton performed in twenty feet of water while the crew up above manipulated scores of artificial sea creatures. Work went slowly because he could only communicate through a series of clumsy hand signals, the cameramen encased in a stationary diving bell. Several solid gags had been devised, such as when Rollo commandeers a passing swordfish and uses it to fight off another. "Then I started fixing the leak, but a school of fish came by, all going in the same direction except one poor little fish who tried and tried to cross their track and couldn't. I, seeing its plight, picked up a starfish, put it on my chest, whistled, and held up my hand at the school of fish. They stopped, I motioned the little fish to cross, he swam by, then I turned and signaled the school to pass on. They all went by, and I returned to the leak."

Having once estimated that the gag cost over ten thousand dollars to rig up and shoot, Keaton told how it was accomplished in a 1958 interview: "It was perfect. And it was a son-of-a-gun to do. It took us three days to get the gag. We had somethin' like twelve-hundred rubber fish, all around ten inches long—and they had to be solid rubber so they wouldn't float—and hang 'em all with violin string, catgut. And a piece of apparatus built by the Llewellyn Iron Company, and sink four telegraph poles under water up there to operate this apparatus overhead, to control the school of fish. But the gag photographed perfect."

After a week or so at Lake Tahoe, *The Navigator* returned to Hollywood and wrapped in mid-August at a reported cost of $385,000. And because so much of the picture was assembled aboard the *Buford,* it had already been previewed when *Variety* took note on August 28. "The two fish gags," said Keaton, "were perfect—looked real as the deuce—sure for a laugh. We previewed the film at a small movie theater in Hollywood. It went over with a bang—*all except that gag about the school of fish!* The swordfish gag got a laugh, but *not* the other one, which *we* thought was so great. We were at a loss to account for it, for it seemed to us to be funnier than anything else in the picture."

A cold audience wasn't the problem; they were well into the picture by then and loved everything else about it. Moreover, a moment or two later, Rollo stooped over and washed some muck off his hands in a bucket left at the bottom of the ocean, and they laughed at that. "We didn't trust that preview. [I said], 'We'll keep it in for a second [preview]. Somethin's wrong.' We kept it in for a second. And the same thing." They even tried it a third time, but it was just no good. "Could it be that the gag was too tricky—that the audience tried to figure out how it was done? Because as soon as an audience gets interested in technicalities, your laugh is dead. We decided it couldn't be that, because the swordfish gag, which looked much trickier, had got a big laugh. But *why* should they laugh at that and not at the other? At last we struck what we thought must be the reason. We figured it out this way: I had gone down to fix the leak in order to save the girl and get away. The swordfish gag was legitimate because I was protecting myself against them. But there was no excuse for my stopping my work on the leak to go and help the little fish. It was simply illogical, and the public wouldn't have it. So we kissed that gag a sad good-bye."

The original preview version of *The Navigator* reportedly contained about a thousand feet of underwater action, which was sluggish by its very nature, but trims left only about five hundred feet remaining in the final release cut. *The Film Daily* was the first trade to review the picture, its notice appearing in its issue of September 7. "While *The Navigator* isn't as hilarious a comedy number as Keaton's last, *Sherlock Jr.,* it is consistently good comedy and should satisfy those who enjoy a good laugh . . . probably the best bit of the picture is the underwater episode in which Keaton goes down in a diving suit."

A week later, *Moving Picture World* agreed: "Probably it wouldn't be correct to call this Buster's best picture, but certainly it ranks high among his efforts." Ahead of release, *The Navigator* opened locally at Loew's State, where it beat every other bill in town with a gross of nearly $26,000 for the week, shattering the house record for a Sunday and topping the attendance mark set by *Sherlock Jr.* by more than nineteen hundred admissions.

Officially released on October 13, 1924, *The Navigator* opened on Broadway at the Capitol Theatre, which had just recently come under the control of Loew's Incorporated. On Sunday, October 12, the crowds were, in the words of *Variety*'s Sid Silverman, "jammed to the doors" and a record $14,797 flowed into the till. The picture played S.R.O. on Columbus Day as well, delivering a solid $13,185. Powered by great reviews in the New York dailies, the first week total of $60,700 was just shy of a house record, and the decision was quickly made to hold it a second week—a first in New York for a Keaton feature. Similar sales were registered at San Francisco's Warfield, where the film equaled a house record, and at the Stanley Theatre in Philadelphia, where it was held for an extended run. Worldwide rentals would eventually stand at $680,406, making it the most commercially successful of Keaton's features to date.

"The laurels are again going to the comedians," editorialized Edwin Schallert in the *Los Angeles Times,* "and this time it appears as if Buster Keaton were the special victor. His picture *The Navigator* did an astonishing business on the showing in the East and is also rambling into quite a run here. The film is easily one of the most effective in fun that Keaton has yet made, and from all indications it has determined his future as a star in five-reelers. There is a much more human note in the production than many of the others in which he has appeared, and one does not feel the creak of so much machinery as is used to put over some of his productions."

Harry Langdon, Schallert noted, would soon be moving into features, Harold Lloyd was scaling new heights of popularity with *Girl Shy* and *Hot Water,* and carefree Douglas MacLean's light comedies possessed "their own particular spice of humor."

Meanwhile, over on Lillian Way, Keaton was immersed in the making of his next feature comedy, an intriguing prospect in that it was to be made, it had been announced, entirely in Technicolor.

12

Friendless

THE BIRTH OF A SECOND CHILD on February 3, 1924, irreparably altered the marriage of Buster and Natalie Keaton and signaled the beginning of a slow descent into estrangement. The eight-pound boy, born at St. Vincent's Hospital in Los Angeles, had no ready name, even though Dutch and Peg Talmadge were present for the event. The convention of naming a newborn by acclamation was established with Jimmy's arrival two years earlier, but Norma was in Palm Beach with Joe Schenck. "Norma must be consulted," a news item in the *Times* confirmed, "and she is three thousand miles away." There was no mention of the father's role in the matter.

It was no secret that Peg Talmadge exerted tremendous influence over her three girls, a bond forged in childhood when the family was abandoned by the father, an alcoholic sales rep named Fred, and Peg was forced to take in laundry and boarders and sell cosmetics to make ends meet. The girls attended Erasmus Hall in Brooklyn, and when Norma was fourteen her mother started her out as a photographer's model. As the shrewd manager of two and a half careers, Peg made them all rich, but she also fostered a mutual dependency that lasted for the rest of her life. When the subject of Natalie was raised, a family friend was clear: "Norma and Constance are as devoted to her as they are to each other, and they all three unite in worshipping their mother."

Although Natalie did fine work in *Our Hospitality*, her pregnancy nearly scuttled the film. "Before we finished that picture," said Buster, "we didn't dare photograph her in profile. Joe Schenck said, 'Never use Natalie in another picture. You could break this company.'" It was a comment that,

Natalie Keaton cradles Robert Talmadge Keaton as Buster looks on. Little Joseph, age two, stares straight into the camera.

were it to get around, would have turned Peg Talmadge's unruly head of salt-and-pepper hair to bright white. Motherhood was the one distinction Nate had over her star siblings. What if either Norma or Dutch were to decide that they wanted kids too? Particularly Norma, whom exhibitors that year voted the nation's top female star by a wide margin? A couple of careless pregnancies could wreck the family business Peg had worked so hard to build.

"By this time," said Buster, "having got two boys in our first three years, frankly, it looked as if my work was done. I was ruled ineligible. Lost my amateur standing. *They* said I was a pro. I was moved into my own bedroom."

Two children—the second was dubbed Robert Talmadge Keaton—cemented Natalie's status as a homemaker. "I like to cook, to sew, to keep house," she told Julia Harpman of the *New York Daily News*. "Studio life is appealing enough, but somehow I always felt that, as a woman, true happiness for me could be found only in wifehood. When 'Winks'—that's baby Joseph—came, my dream of happiness was fulfilled. Motherhood is the greatest career a woman can have. I know it is trite to say that, but it is so true and there are so many women on the screen who, I am sure, would like to admit it but haven't the courage to sacrifice for motherhood all they have struggled and won in public acclaim."

Despite such pronouncements, Natalie's dream of happiness wasn't all that fulfilled. Buster thought the Ardmore house wonderful, but it wasn't even a year before a move to Hancock Park was mandated. This time it was a fourteen-room mansion on Muirfield Road that cost $75,000. "The Muirfield place was bigger, better, fancier—hell, why argue? We bought it and began housewarming. That meant—for me anyway—two o'clock to bed and up at six, grab breakfast, and off to work." And their bedroom suites, he found, were at opposite ends of the building. Buster knew the source of the trouble and addressed his mother-in-law directly: "I'm just going to let you know right now I am not going to take a mistress and support her, or do anything like that. I will not be spending any money on women and throwing my money around. But if I can't get it at home, I'm going to get it somewhere. And there's a lot of free stuff out there. If you forbid your daughter to sleep with me, I'll go outside and get it."

Keeping Nat happy had always been the prime motivator in each of the moves, even though they had been profitable enough to enable Buster to buy his mother a comfortable two-bedroom home in the mid-Wilshire district. That same year, Myra sold off all but two of the remaining Keaton properties in Muskegon (having disposed of Jingles Jungle in 1923) and found time to visit Frank Cutler in Rockdale, Texas—the first time she had reportedly seen her father in more than twenty-five years.

Up to and including *The Navigator,* all of Buster Keaton's comedies had been made under the terms of the original five-year contract he signed with the Comique Film Corporation in December 1919. Now, after nineteen two-reelers and four well-received features, it was due to expire on December 31, 1924. Not only had Keaton grown in popularity domestically, but his international profile was second only to Chaplin's. In Stockholm, *Our Hospitality* held the screen at the Royal Dramatic Theatre for fifteen weeks, supported by a Swedish version of Buster who walked the streets of the city. "He carried no back banner, and there were no cards on the gripsack," *Moving Picture World* reported. "Everyone knew who he was supposed to be, and the billboards gave the details, if any were needed."

Harold Lloyd was the star for whom British exhibitors were willing to pay the highest price, but it was Keaton who played twenty-one weeks in Belgium, making more money for the distributor on a percentage basis than the company's entire line of films the previous season. And in Paris, *Our*

Hospitality, retitled *Laws of Hospitality*, broke all records at the Madeleine, where it earned 11,500 francs on Armistice Day alone.

"It is a singular fact," said *Billboard*, "that this Keaton feature has been playing in Europe with the greatest success of any American motion picture, not barring even the elaborate spectacles. It has broken records throughout the Scandinavian countries, in Stockholm, Christiania, Copenhagen, and other centers there."

The new contract, signed September 9, 1924, and set to take effect upon release of *The Navigator*, called for "six motion picture feature photoplays of not less than forty-five hundred nor more than nine-thousand feet in length." In terms of compensation, Keaton was to receive $27,000 for each completed feature, payable in installments of $1,000 per week, plus 25 percent of the cumulative net profits. Although not specifically called out in the contract, the *Los Angeles Times* set the approximate value of the new slate of features at $1,800,000, or roughly $300,000 a picture. At the rate of two releases a year, the pact would remain in effect through the spring of 1928.

Seven Chances was a film Buster Keaton never wanted to make. A Broadway stage hit from 1916, the play's principal character stands to inherit a fortune of $12 million if he is married by the age of thirty—and he is due to turn thirty the following day. There is no steady girlfriend, not even one on the horizon, and no real inclination to solicit one. Written by Roi Cooper Megrue (*It Pays to Advertise*), the show drew mixed notices, its undisputed highspot being actor-playwright Frank Craven's droll performance as Megrue's hero, a self-confessed woman hater by the name of Jimmie Shannon.

"[It] was not a good story for me," Keaton explained. "That was bought by someone and sold to Joe Schenck without us knowin' it. As a rule, Schenck never knew when I was shootin' or what I was shootin'. He just went to the preview. But somebody sold him this show that was done by Belasco a few years before. . . . And he buys this thing for me and it's no good for me at all."

The someone who sold Schenck on the play was a writer-director named Jack McDermott, a "local screwball" in Keaton's estimation who had started as an actor, made shorts for Fox and Universal, then moved into features. Keaton considered the $25,000 Schenck paid for the property a waste of money—the material was thin, the characters bloodless, the laughs dependent solely upon dialogue. It was, he said, "the type of unbelievable farce I don't like." Anxious to lose the thing, Keaton tried interesting Schenck in making it with Syd Chaplin, Charlie's half brother, a suggestion that went nowhere. The subsequent idea of making the film in color was an act of desperation, with an article in *Exhibitors Trade Review* noting how Keaton had been "experimenting with the possibilities of color photography for comedy values."*

Having never meddled before in the making of the Keaton pictures, Schenck's actions left his star comedian bewildered, for he was also stuck, he learned, with McDermott as his new director. Could Schenck have been responding to the drop in revenues for *Sherlock Jr.*? Or cost overruns on *The Navigator*? Had McDermott sold Joe on the notion of source material with a commercial track record? Something along the lines of *The Saphead*? Schenck never offered an explanation, and Keaton, apparently, never asked. For the role of Mary Jones, Jimmie's girl, Buster wanted Marian Nixon, who was appearing in westerns for Fox, but found that she had been loaned to Universal for a Hoot Gibson picture. Instead, he selected Ruth Dwyer, who was attracting notice in a romantic comedy titled *The Reckless Age* opposite Reginald Denny.

Filming began on September 16, 1924, the company sharing studio space on the Keaton lot with Roland West's independent production *The Monster* starring Lon Chaney. Keaton and McDermott shot the film's prologue, a courtship exterior stretching over four seasons, in Technicolor, making it the only remnant of the plan to shoot the entire movie that way. Upon learning that he stands to inherit $7 million if he is married by seven o'clock on the evening of his twenty-seventh birthday, Jimmie Shannon races to the home of his longtime girlfriend in a decidedly inventive way—by not driving the car at all.

"I had an automobile, like a Stutz Bearcat roadster. I was in front of [a country club]. Now, it's a full-figure shot of that automobile and me. I come down, got into the car . . . I release the emergency brake after starting it, sit back to drive—and I don't move. The scene changed, and I was in front of a little cottage out in the country. I reach forward, pull on the emergency brake, shut my motor off, and went into the cottage. I come back out after I visit her, get into the automobile, turn it on, sit back there—and I and

---

* Keaton's commercial instincts were sound in that only two widely distributed features had been made entirely in Technicolor, but his typical shooting ratio of twelve to one or greater would have rendered the plan too costly.

Keaton proposes to bit player Jean Arthur in Seven Chances *(1925). She responds by flashing her wedding ring.*

the automobile never moved—and the scene changed back to the [country club]. Now, that automobile's got to be exactly the same distance, the same height and everything, to make that work, because the scene overlaps but I don't. . . . We made sure [it was the] same time of day so the shadows would [be in the same place]. But for that baby we used surveying instruments so that the front part of the car would be the same distance from [the camera], the whole shooting match."

Perplexed, evidently, by the time and care lavished on this seemingly minor transition, Jack McDermott withdrew as director of *Seven Chances* after completing the first week of filming. "You are the star and producer," he told Keaton, "and your version will be the one finally used. You are wasting thousands of dollars having me on the picture." McDermott had come onto the project just a week ahead of production and envisioned a faithful rendering of the play, a farce on the order of *Her Temporary Husband,* a picture he had made the previous year. Although he had supposedly signed a seven-picture deal with Schenck, McDermott vanished, and Keaton went on to direct the rest of the picture himself. By then, *The Navigator* was looking like a hit, and Schenck, evidently mollified, backed off.

Jimmie, of course, botches his proposal to Mary, who angrily stalks off. Now he must find somebody else to marry, and fast. Keaton and his writers jettisoned a tedious first act in its entirety, translating Shannon's increasingly desperate search for a wife into purely visual terms. "When you've got spots in there where you can do things in action without dialogue," he said, "you should take advantage of it. . . . First instructions with the new writers we were getting from Broadway; see, everything with them was based on a joke, funny saying, people shouting. But we'd tell our story, our plot with our characters, and we talk when necessary. But we don't go out of our way to talk. Let's see how much material we can get where dialogue is not needed."

Seven times Jimmie proposes, and seven times he is rejected. (Among the candidates are Doris Deane, Roscoe Arbuckle's fiancée; actress-dancer Pauline Toler; and Bartine Burkett, Buster's leading lady from *The High Sign*.) Finally, Billy Meekin, Jimmie's business partner (T. Roy Barnes), takes charge. "Meet me at the Broad Street Church at five o'clock," he tells Jimmie. "I'll have a bride there if it's the last act of my life." What Shannon doesn't know is that Meekin plans on feeding the story to the *Daily News*. Come five o'clock, Jimmie is in the front pew of the empty church, a bouquet in hand and two tickets to Niagara Falls in his pocket. Wearily, he dozes off, and the church begins to fill, first a scattering, then an onslaught, women of "all shapes and forms with home-made bridal outfits on, lace curtains, gingham table cloths for veils" spilling out onto the sidewalks.

The play *Seven Chances* lacked a strong finish, and by turning the story into one clear progression to an inevitable chase—which grew to constitute the entire third act of the picture—Keaton firmly and indelibly moved it from the cloistered realm of the stage to the limitless expanse of the big screen. Shannon awakens to an unruly mob scene, made all the worse when the minister tells the women they are evidently the victims of a practical joker. They turn their ire on Jimmie, who sinks into the crowd and escapes out a side window, droves of menacing brides flooding the streets in hot pursuit. Here Keaton effectively sets in motion a clever reprise of *Cops* in white lace and heels. The stampeding women trample a football team, commandeer a trolley, invade a scrap yard, flatten a cornfield. Meanwhile, Mary is waiting at her house with Jimmie's partner and a minister as the clock ticks off the final minutes to the seven o'clock deadline.

When *Seven Chances* finished on November 29, Keaton thought the picture "fair" and the conclusion weak. "My God," he said, "we actually hired *five hundred* women, every shape and every size, and bridal outfits on all of 'em. Well, hell, I can outrun 'em. And even if they catch me, how can you end the picture? Can I marry all of 'em? Not even in Utah. Can I fight 'em? So we're crippled. Can't get in any good chase gags, can't end it with any kind of climax. So we simply decided to fade on the chase."

The first preview didn't go well. "I had a bad picture and we knew it, too. And there was nothing we could seem to do about it."

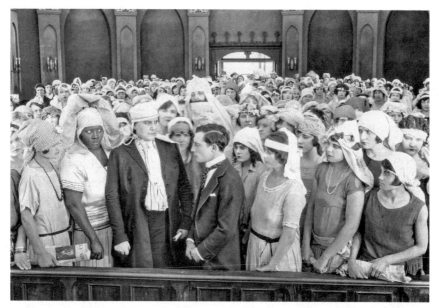

A church full of eager brides confronts Jimmie Shannon in Seven Chances.

Adjustments were made, a second preview was held. Again, it just didn't seem to build to anything. But this time, Keaton noticed something interesting in a portion of the chase in which he ran downhill at a good clip. "I went down to the dunes just off the Pacific Ocean out at Los Angeles, and I accidentally dislodged a boulder in coming down. All I had set up for the scene was a camera panning with me as I came over the skyline and was chased down into the valley. But I dislodged this rock, and it in turn dislodged two others, and they chased me down this hill.

"That's all there was: just three rocks. But the audience at the preview sat up in their seats and expected more. So we went right back and ordered fifteen hundred rocks built, from bowling alley size up to boulders eight feet in diameter. Then we went out to the Ridge Route, which is in the High Sierras, to a mountain steeper than a forty-five-degree angle. A couple of truckloads of men took those rocks up and planted them, and then I went up to the top and came down with the rocks." Not only did the rocks and boulders give the chase an extra dimension at a critical moment, but they had the added advantage of appearing even more dangerous than the blood-thirsty brides. "At least I was workin' with papier-mâché, although some of them . . . for instance that big [boulder], weighed four hundred pounds. By the time you built the framework it weighed something, but you could get hit with them all right." (Keaton was, in fact, briefly pinned to the ground by the faux boulder, resulting in a painful injury to one leg but, fortunately, no break.) "Well, I got into the middle of the rock chase and it saved the picture for me, and that was an accident. It hadn't been framed; it was just an out-and-out accident."

Keaton was reported as making a few retakes in January 1925, and the final preview took place in Los Angeles the week of February 23. Where before he took a series of headers down the side of a dune before scrambling on, he now skidded into a half-dozen melon-size rocks, dislodging them and then tumbling into an entire field of larger rocks and boulders, all bent on overtaking him as he weaved and leapt, picking up speed in a desperate bid to avoid them. The final shots were masterful, his tiny figure on a steep incline amid a vast, seemingly endless field of rocks, a few eight or ten times his size, some dislodging still others until the whole deadly field is in motion.

"When I've got a gag that spreads out," he said, "I hate to jump a camera into close-ups. So I do everything in the world I can to hold it in that long shot and keep the action rolling. When I do use cuts I still won't go right into a close-up: I'll just go in maybe to a full figure, but that's about as close as I'll come. Close-ups are too jarring on the screen, and this type of cut can stop an audience from laughing."

Nothing, however, stopped the preview audience from laughing. The added footage, in fact, whipped them into a frenzy. Metro-Goldwyn executive Edgar J. Mannix wired Nicholas Schenck in New York:

A LAUGHING RIOT. PERSONALLY THINK IT BEST PICTURE HE HAS EVER MADE. THE AUDIENCE JUST ONE CONTINUOUS LAUGH FROM START TO FINISH.

It may not have been coincidental that when Joe Schenck allowed himself to be seduced into *Seven Chances,* he was in talks to join United Artists as a producer with a slate of pictures beyond what just the Talmadge sisters and Buster Keaton could deliver. Industry insiders knew Schenck's properties were in play as early as July 1924, when a break between Schenck and First National was considered imminent, Schenck reportedly unhappy with the way they had handled the release of Norma's feature *Secrets.* Into the fall, rumors had Schenck luring Louis B. Mayer away from Metro-Goldwyn, the new combine of Metro and Goldwyn Pictures Corporation engineered for Marcus Loew by Joe's brother Nick. Loew did shut down the old Metro lot across from the Keaton studio, relocating the plant to fancier digs in Culver City, but Joe had no interest in Mayer as a production executive. Instead, he was being wooed by the partners of United Artists, who were Mary Pickford, Douglas Fairbanks, D. W. Griffith, and Charlie Chaplin. Griffith was on his way out, and the other three couldn't produce enough product to sustain a network of regional exchanges. Pickford was struggling to produce two pictures a year, Fairbanks was down to one, and Chaplin was falling into a pattern of delivering a feature comedy every two or three years.

Bringing the Talmadge and Keaton productions to UA would add another six pictures a year to the company's output. Moreover, Schenck would commit to producing up to six additional films to help fill the pipeline. He hadn't joined UA earlier out of a sense of loyalty to First National, and because Chaplin was against the idea. "Joe was to be made president," Chaplin explained in his autobiography. "Although I was fond of Joe, I did not think his contribution was valuable enough to justify his presidency.* Although his wife was a star of some magnitude, she could not match the box office receipts of Mary or Douglas. We had already refused to give Adolph Zukor stock in our company, so why give it to Joe Schenck, who was not as important as Zukor?"

Nevertheless, United Artists was in the red more than half a million dollars, and the situation wasn't getting any better. It took four days of conferences to bring Chaplin around. The alliance was announced in Los Angeles on October 27 while *The Navigator* was breaking box office records. Nothing with the Talmadge or Keaton pictures would happen immediately; Norma owed four more releases to First National, Constance five, and Keaton was committed to Metro for another two. For the time being, Schenck would have to fill the void with other attractions, and he quickly moved to sign Rudolph Valentino, late of Famous Players, to a contract calling for three films a year, followed by William S. Hart, who would also commit to three.

Upon the completion of *Seven Chances,* Keaton's spring release for 1925, work at the Keaton studio came to a halt for two months and the company's salaried writers were turned over to other producers. Clyde Bruckman and Joe Mitchell were loaned to Mack Sennett, while Jean Havez was allocated

---

* Actually, Schenck became chairman of the board, not president. Hiram Abrams remained president of United Artists following a reorganization initiated by Schenck.

to John Considine, Jr., for a series of pictures featuring a canine star called Peter the Great. The closure, in time, would decimate the Keaton writing staff. First came Tommy Gray's November 30 death in New York at the age of thirty-six. This left an opening on Harold Lloyd's staff, Gray last having been on Lloyd's payroll, and Jean Havez, who had worked previously on *A Sailor-Made Man, Dr. Jack,* and *Grandma's Boy,* was recruited to replace him. Then Havez himself died of a heart attack on February 12, 1925, prompting both Bruckman and Mitchell to go freelance, Bruckman with Lloyd and Monty Banks, Mitchell with Paramount's Raymond Griffith, among others. The result was that when Buster Keaton began work on his new picture, he had to start over from scratch.

Following on the success of *The Navigator, Seven Chances* had its world premiere at the Capitol Theatre in New York on March 15, 1925. As with its predecessor, it led the street in box office, taking in nearly $53,000 for the week. *Variety*'s Robert Sisk summed up the critical response: "It wasn't quite up to the Keaton standard, but at that *Seven Chances* was corking entertainment." The highlight for virtually everyone was the climactic chase sequence, widely hailed as a masterpiece of the form.

"It is the most uproariously funny pursuit picture which has ever assailed our critical diaphragm," Frank Vreeland of the *Telegram and Evening Mail* enthused. "Keaton, who directed for Joseph M. Schenck, starts his comedy effects with the brigade of would-be brides very quietly, and then works the laughter up to fortissimo by a tempo that is as deftly accelerated as if Buster were leading the projection machine operator with a baton. It is a marvelous example of the overwhelming, cumulative effect of repetition on the screen, and Keaton knows just when to poke his spectators in the ribs with his sudden comic thrust. The scenes wherein he dodges an avalanche of boulders that hound him down a hillside very nearly laid us low."

Business for *Seven Chances* was equally strong at the McVickers in Chicago, the Palace in Washington, the Stanley in Philadelphia, and the Warfield in San Francisco, leaving only Loew's State in Los Angeles to report less-than-stellar results, despite raves in the *Examiner, Times, Herald,* and *Record. Seven Chances* would eventually score $598,228 in worldwide rentals, placing it well behind the high-water mark of *The Navigator* but still ahead of all of Keaton's other feature comedies.

.   .   .

Buster Keaton never said where the idea for *Go West* came from, but his affinity for animals was well known. Creatures of all types were naturally drawn to him, and when Constance Talmadge gave Natalie a Belgian police dog as a wedding gift, the dog, named Captain, quickly gravitated to Buster and began spending his days at the studio. Over time, Captain became so protective of his master that he had to be kept off the set when Keaton was shooting rough stuff with another actor. The dog spent his nights sleeping on Buster's bed, and when he went missing one day near the intersection of Gower and Fountain, a classified ad in the *Times* offered a $100 reward for his return. When Captain was struck by a car on April 5, 1923, work on *Three Ages* ground to a halt. Buster was inconsolable, and asked Gabe Gabourie's shop to build a coffin. An all-hands ceremony was held the following day, the workforce in tears, and the dog was laid to rest in a small plot on the studio grounds.

One of the mourners attending Captain's funeral was a former vaudevillian named Lex Neal, a boyhood pal of Buster's who was trying his hand at writing for the movies. Keaton had given Neal work as early as 1921. By 1925, Lex was hankering to direct, so Buster amiably put him in charge of his sixth feature comedy. And when Keaton traveled east to attend the opening of *Seven Chances,* he took Lex Neal along so they could spin story ideas on the train. Neal, fully aware of Buster's natural empathy ("I'm on the side of the animals," Keaton would tell his biographer Rudi Blesh), may have been the one who first had the idea of making his new leading lady a cow.

The western had been a staple of the screen since the very beginning, popular with audiences and cheap to produce. But the genre had gained a new measure of respectability with Paramount's *The Covered Wagon* (1923) and Fox's *The Iron Horse* (1924), big-budget productions that were among the most popular attractions of their respective years. Arbuckle and Keaton had previously burlesqued the conventions of the genre in *Out West,* but now Keaton was aiming for something more, inserting his familiar character into a modern and nuanced version of the western, a satire in the form of a genuine character study. With a rough outline in hand, he hired a scenarist named Raymond Cannon, who was coming off a year's contract with Douglas MacLean, to flesh out the story and help gag it up. He also selected a young Jersey cow from California's vast ranch country as his co-star, a beautiful red-and-white-patterned bovine he named Brown Eyes.

In May, Keaton located five thousand cows in a herd near Fort Worth and applied to the chamber of commerce for permission to drive them through the city's business district for the film's finale. The scene, according to his wire, was to show "about 400 head of cattle stampeding down Main Street and milling about the Texas Hotel, together with other appropriate atmospheric scenes." The city fathers assumed he was remembering the place the way it was back when he was a child in vaudeville, when dirt roads and frame businesses were still common. Keaton's telegram went on to suggest that the shots could be made "on a Sunday when everything is quiet and dull." Now taking offense, the authorities wired back and suggested that he pick some other town for his horse opera, such as Cromwell, Oklahoma. "Besides," they said, "the cows wouldn't like it."

Keaton took great pains in training Brown Eyes for her part in the picture. He began by leading her around the studio on a rope, rewarding her with carrots until she became used to both the rope and the treats. Then he substituted a string for the rope, and finally a thread for the string. "I never had a more affectionate pet or a more obedient one," he said. "After a while I was able to walk her through doors, in and out of sets, even past bright lights. The only difficulty we had was when I sat down and she tried to climb into my lap."

Production got under way in Los Angeles on May 23, while studio carpenter H. B. "Harry" Barnes and electrician Denver Harmon were dispatched to Arizona to oversee the construction of a bunkhouse, blacksmith shop, and various other structures needed for the film's exteriors. Two weeks later, Keaton, accompanied by cast, crew, and three carloads of equipment, arrived in Kingman, establishing an office at the Hotel Beale across from the Santa Fe terminal.* A convoy of cars and trucks then wended its way north about sixty miles to George "Tap" Duncan's massive Diamond Bar Ranch, specifically a portion of the Diamond Bar known locally as Valley Ranch. Brown Eyes got there via truck a few days later, traveling with a long-eared mule Keaton was to ride in the picture and attended by two "valets" and a veterinarian. So distinctive were her markings that Brown Eyes was insured for $100,000 against losses should she have to be replaced.

"I didn't take her on location until I had her perfectly trained to obey my orders," said Keaton. "Everything went fine until we got Brown Eyes out there on the steaming hot desert. There I couldn't do a thing with her, not one thing. We were mystified until a rancher told us, 'That cow's in heat. She won't be a bit of use to you until she's over that.'

---

* The Hotel Beale was owned and operated by a man named Tom Devine, whose nineteen-year-old son, Andy, harbored ambitions to be an actor. While on location, Keaton met the boy and encouraged him to come to Hollywood. "Said he'd get me a job," Andy Devine remembered in 1959, "and he did. I've never been without one since."

" 'How long does that take?' I asked.

" 'Oh,' he said, 'about ten days or so.'

"We had thirty people in the unit on location. . . . I did the only sensible thing. I ordered her let out of the corral so she could find an affectionate and empathy-loaded bull for herself. She picked a bull, but he was not affectionate. In fact he snubbed her by walking away." A second attempt went even worse. "There was nothing to do after that but wait for our cow to get out of heat. We spent our time taking shots of the lovely country all around us, but later never figured out how to use that film. When Brown Eyes finally was ready to turn her attention to movie-making again, we did fine with her."

By Hollywood standards, filming at the Duncan ranch was roughing it. "We were really out in open country . . . four cameramen (that's [including] the assistants), electrician generally takes about three men with him (because we took a generator, which takes a couple of men), technical man takes a couple of dozen carpenters, a prop man must take about four extra helpers with him. . . . Then we house 'em up there, see—we take tents and everything else and a portable kitchen."

The bunkhouse had been built out so that male members of the cast could live in it, while actress Kathleen Myers, even more incidental than usual as the obligatory girl, occupied a suite in the main ranch house. Based at the Beale, Harry Barnes made the daily trip from Kingman to the ranch and back, as did a truck loaded with supplies. Barnes also arranged for the shipment of exposed film to the coast for processing. The days were so hot they had to pack ice around the cameras to keep the emulsion from melting, while winds and flash rainstorms played hell with the schedule. Still, at well over a million acres, there was something inspiring about the Diamond Bar.

"I always preferred working on location," Keaton said, "because more good gags suggested themselves in new and unfamiliar surroundings."

Buster's character is Friendless, a homeless drifter who goes west after heeding Horace Greeley's immortal dictum. He finds work as a ranch hand at the Diamond Bar, where he meets Brown Eyes, a dairy cow destined for the slaughterhouse because she's gone dry. Friendless removes a rock that has wedged itself in her hoof, shows it to her, then dutifully buries it in the dusty soil. Tipping his hat, he walks on, only to catch his foot in a hole. While he's trying to free himself, a menacing bull takes notice and prepares to charge. Racing to his rescue, the Jersey inserts herself between Friendless and his attacker, staring the bull down and backing him off.

Friendless thanks the cow, patting her on the back and giving her a little kiss on the head. Then he's off again, but this time Brown Eyes is right alongside. He notices, stops, is perplexed at first, reproving even, but then he extends a hand and she begins to lick it. As he slowly draws the hand away, he regards it with disbelief. A bond has been formed between these two outcasts, and Keaton's natural economy as an actor makes the moment all the more powerful, a brush with genuine pathos he rarely permitted himself. Caressing her, his devotion to Brown Eyes is now clear, and they become inseparable companions. "I was going to do everything I possibly could to keep that cow from being sent to the slaughterhouse," he said. "I only had that one thing in mind."

Brown Eyes follows Friendless into the bunkhouse—a breach of ranch etiquette—and they are both summarily banished to the barn. He brings her water, cloaks her in a blanket, and when a pair of wolves appear on the horizon, he grabs a rifle and stands guard over her. The next day he is out on chores when she is to be branded for market. He runs to her rescue, hides her in the brush, and when ordered to do the branding himself, manages to fake the job with a safety razor. Still, the rancher must ship a thousand head—he can hold out no longer—and Friendless, increasingly desperate, doesn't have the money to buy her himself.

The loading of the cattle at Hackberry, the major shipping point in Mohave County, had to wait until the stockyards had been cleared of livestock and there was room for the movie cows to take their place. As the train pulls out, Friendless and Brown Eyes stand side by side in one of the open cars, unsure of how to escape a fate dictated by the brutal realities of the marketplace. The train is attacked by a rival rancher's men, and when it pulls away in the resulting melee, Friendless discovers he is the only human left aboard and that it is up to him alone to keep it on course.

Keaton prepares to signal action with a revolver while directing Go West *on location in Arizona.*

After nearly three weeks of location work in Arizona, the *Go West* company returned to the Keaton studio for interiors and to prepare for an epic cattle drive through the streets of Los Angeles that was set to begin shooting the first week in August.

Friendless and Brown Eyes beat a retreat when the train pulls into the Santa Fe depot east of downtown, only to recall that the rancher and his daughter will be ruined if the cattle don't make it all the way to the stockyards.

"I brought 'em up Seventh Street to Spring Street," Keaton related in a 1958 interview. "And we put cowboys off on every side street to stop people in automobiles from comin' into it. And then put our own cars with people in there. And I brought three hundred head of steers up that street. I'd hate to ask permission to do that today."

Staged against a clever mix of city streets and standing sets, the drive builds to a raucous climax as the cattle invade businesses, customers scattering in all directions. Towel-wrapped men escape a Turkish bath just ahead of a particularly large-horned intruder. At a barbershop, Joe Keaton, lathered for a shave, is surrounded by steers, one casually licking the soap from his face. A department store erupts in chaos as dozens of animals arrive, and Friendless is barely able to keep them all moving. "But then I thought that by goin' in a store, and I saw a costume place, and I saw a devil's suit (this was red)—well, bulls and steers don't like red, they'll chase it. 'Course I

To film the cattle drive through downtown Los Angeles for Go West, *Keaton incorporated actual city locations with business district exteriors, such as this one, filmed on the Metro lot.*

was tryin' to lead 'em towards the slaughterhouse. I put that suit on and I thought I'd get a funny chase sequence and have the cows get a little too close to me and [I'd] get scared. Then [I'd] really put on speed tryin' to get away from 'em. But I couldn't do it with steers—[the] steers wouldn't chase me. I actually ran and had cowboys pushing 'em as fast as they could go, and I fell down in front of 'em and let 'em get within about ten feet of me before I got to my feet. But as I moved, they stopped too. They piled up on each other. They didn't mind a stampede at all. But they wouldn't come near me. Well, that kind of hurt when you think that's going to be your big finish chase sequence. We had to trick it from all angles."

The police are dispatched, then the fire department, their hoses soaking the cops as well as bystanders and passing dignitaries. Brown Eyes breaks free of the auto park where Friendless has checked her for safekeeping and overtakes him. He leaps astride her, still clad in his red devil's outfit, and together they lead the herd to its final destination just as the ranch owner and his daughter are pulling up. Friendless unmounts, and the rancher pumps his hand gratefully.

"My home and anything I have is yours for the asking," he says.

After a moment, Friendless gestures in the direction of the girl. "I want her," he says.

The rancher thinks Friendless means his daughter, but then Friendless walks right past her, leading Brown Eyes into view. With the cow loaded into the back seat of the car, Friendless once again at her side, they drive off, rounding a corner, Friendless now deep in conversation with the rancher's daughter, and Brown Eyes gently nuzzling her father's hat.

While Keaton was cutting *Go West,* it fell to Lou Anger and his staff to disperse the cattle leased for the film. Some were returned to the Duncan ranch, others to their owners in Texas. Brown Eyes, meanwhile, was given a permanent home on the Keaton lot, where it was thought she might be starred, like a bovine Rin Tin Tin, in a future production. When it came time to preview the picture, Keaton was certain he had a flop on his hands. His problems with the cattle drive left him convinced it moved too slowly, that he should have been shown "tearing for his life" with the herd furiously at his heels. "We didn't dare speed them up," he said of the steers, "or we would have had a real stampede." Then a gag he thought as surefire as the school of fish in *The Navigator* came up empty, and he was at a loss to explain why.

The scene in question threatened to put Keaton at odds with his public image. Eager to win enough money to buy Brown Eyes from the rancher, Friendless joins in a bunkhouse game of poker. He bets the house, then watches the ranch hand opposite him deal himself an ace from the bottom of the deck. Friendless has no choice but to call him on it, causing the man to unholster his gun and point it directly at him. "When you say that— SMILE," he says, mirroring a famous scene in Owen Wister's *The Virginian*.

"Well," said Keaton, "because I'm known as frozen face, blank pan, we thought that if you did that to me, an audience would say, 'Oh my God, he can't smile. He's gone. He's dead.' But it didn't strike an audience as funny at all; they just felt sorry for me." Later, he decided the audience didn't even necessarily feel sorry for him: "Our mistake probably was that we had counted on something that was outside the picture at the particular moment." The scene was too crucial to cut, and the action was needed even if it didn't draw a laugh. "We didn't find out until the preview, and it put a hole in my scene right there and then. Of course, I got out of it the best way I could, but we run into these lulls every now and then."

. . .

With *Go West* completed, Keaton loaned Ray Cannon to Universal for a Reginald Denny comedy and left for New York with Nat, her sister Dutch, and their mother, ostensibly to confer with Joe Schenck and see to release plans for the new picture, but more directly to shuttle between Washington and Pittsburgh for the World Series. Baseball had assumed an increasingly important role in Keaton's life, and the studio team, known widely as the Buster Keaton Nine, had captured three state championships. The Nine were frequently in the papers, playing municipal teams and athletic clubs as far north as Oxnard and highlighting the standout work of their captain as well as first baseman Ernie Orsatti, who did prop and doubling work around the lot and was trusted with such critical tasks as pumping Buster's air during the underwater scenes for *The Navigator*. Other studios had teams as well: Douglas MacLean's business staff, his writers and visitors, played daily on the FBO lot, and Harold Lloyd had not only a baseball team but a handball crew as well. Yet no Hollywood team seemed to inspire the attention that naturally accrued to the Keaton organization.

Ernie Orsatti was so good that one day in 1925 he arrived at work and found a new set of luggage and a check waiting for him . . . and he was told that he was fired. Keaton handed him a contract to play for the Vernon Tigers, in which he retained an interest, but Orsatti played just six games with the Tigers before he was sent to Cedar Rapids as part of the Mississippi Valley League. By 1926, he would be fielding in the minor leagues for the St. Louis Cardinals, on his way to the majors, where he would enjoy a career lasting into the mid-1930s.

Buster Keaton observed his thirtieth birthday in New York on October 4, 1925. Then he trained to Pittsburgh for the first game of the World Series, leaving Nat and her sisters to immerse themselves in the autumn shopping season. He was back on the sixteenth, the series having gone to the Pirates after seven games, and steeled himself for the opening of *Go West* on October 25. It was the Capitol's sixth-anniversary attraction, and the advance ads played up Brown Eyes over her human co-star, one going so far as to position her as "a new screen vampire." Again, Buster was on hand opening day, and his name on-screen elicited a burst of applause. The theater was jammed, although the week's business wouldn't quite land on a par with *Seven Chances*. While nobody accused director Keaton ("assisted," according to the opening credits, by Lex Neal) of delivering belly laughs, a plurality of reviewers for the trades and the dailies acknowledged the charm and originality of his most personal feature.

One of the strongest responses to *Go West* came from the Pulitzer Prize–

winning poet Carl Sandburg, who was moonlighting as movie critic for the *Chicago Daily News.* "It seems rather silly to say that any screen comedy will leave unforgettable impressions on you," Sandburg wrote, "but that seems exactly what Buster Keaton's *Go West* is likely to do at McVickers Theater this week. Although the theater at times is explosive with hearty guffaws, *Go West* may not be the funniest thing that sour-faced Buster has ever done, but it is by far the most enjoyable bit of humor this writer has seen from the Keaton fun factory. This comedian comes close to the Chaplinesque in his serious comedy. Buster is one of the few comedians of the screen at whom you can laugh without feeling a bit ridiculous yourself."

Keaton always struggled with *Go West,* and in later years tended to distance himself from it. "Some parts I like," he allowed in 1958, "but as a picture, in general, I didn't care for it." He always looked upon the roundup with disappointment, but the picture may also have struck too personal a note with him, something very private in his character that he didn't want revealed. In the end, *Go West* played to $50,300 during an off week on Broadway, a bit less than *Seven Chances.* In comparison, Harold Lloyd's *The Freshman* was in its seventh week at the much smaller Colony, where it took in $30,500 and looked certain to last a full ten weeks. Where Keaton represented an abstraction to American audiences, Lloyd was the real deal, an energetic boy from the Midwest always eager to make good. However popular Chaplin and Keaton were internationally, it was Lloyd who topped the box office polls in the United States and who would remain a big star until talkies and middle age took their inevitable toll.

During Keaton's previous trip to New York, he had acquired an original story by Robert Sherwood, his indefatigable booster in the pages of *Life.* Sherwood, whose first Broadway success, *The Road to Rome,* would appear in 1927, had conceived a *Navigator*-like story that takes place in the middle of Manhattan. "I'm working on top of the skeleton structure of a new skyscraper, forty stories above the ground," Keaton related in a talk with Paul Gallico. "I got the girl, the daughter of the architect, up there with me, only her old man don't know this. We got up there on one of those open elevators which goes down again. And just at that moment there's a strike and all the boys walk off the job. Now the girl and I are up there, no food, no water, no way to get down, marooned on a desert island, kind of, in the heart of New York.

"That's a great situation, only Sherwood hasn't got it solved how to get us out of it. We work and we work and we work on it. And Bob keeps saying, 'Don't worry, Buster. I'll get you down out of there.' Every time I see him he says that. But he never solves it, and eventually we forget about it." The story, titled *The Skyscraper,* was announced as Keaton's next picture in March 1925, but then, with Sherwood unable to crack the story, *Go West* took priority.

"[Nine] years later," Keaton continued, "I'm making a film in England and sitting in the lobby at Claridge's when in walks this guy with the moustache, nine feet tall, and I recognize Sherwood. He recognizes me, too, because he comes over to me and says, 'Don't worry, Buster, I'll get you down out of there . . .' and keeps right on going, and that's the last I ever saw of him."

Keaton made another story purchase in New York that spring, the film rights to a newish musical titled *Battling Buttler,* which had occupied the Selwyn Theatre on Forty-Second Street since the previous October. *Buttler* was a loose Americanization of a British original similarly titled *Battling Butler,* a good-natured stage vehicle for the hugely popular actor-manager Jack Buchanan. Although the contract required screen billing for music and lyrics, Keaton was interested solely in the story line, the tale of two men with the same name, one of whom assumes the identity of the other, a famous prizefighter, in order to get away on alleged training trips from a domineering wife. When he's caught, he has to keep up the pretense, prompting the real Battling Buttler to see to it that he has to fight an actual opponent in a title match.

Ray Cannon stayed with Universal and never returned to the Keaton studio. Though no reason was ever given, Keaton's general dissatisfaction with *Go West* may have been a contributing factor. Lex Neal remained as gagman, story constructionist, and title writer, and, by some accounts, codirector. Still, Buster seemed to value the Broadway credentials that men like Jean Havez and Tommy Gray had brought to the team, and in short order he signed Paul Gerard Smith, who wrote revue sketches as well as the book and lyrics to a show called *Keep Kool,* and Charles Smith, a former vaudeville comic with ties to Joe Schenck through writer-director Roland West. Keaton also brought on a New York–based publicist named Al Boasberg, who was gaining notice as a freelance gagman. In Boasberg's case, Keaton insisted on a probationary period of six weeks with an option for a full year, and although he picked up the option, he remembered Boasberg as a "terrible flop when he tried to do sight gags for us. So were a hundred other writers we imported from New York. It is possible, of course, that we kept sending for the wrong ones."

One of the primary changes Keaton and his new staff made to *Battling Buttler* was to have a spirited girl in place of the wife, the Keaton character never having been particularly suited to the role of a henpecked husband. Actress Sally O'Neill was borrowed from Metro-Goldwyn-Mayer for the part, and filming began the week of January 4, 1926, in Kernville, 160 miles north of Los Angeles, where four weeks of exteriors were made. Keaton's Alfred Butler (reverting to the simpler British spelling of the name) is a rich, pampered twit in the grand tradition of Bertie the Lamb and Rollo Tread-way, all the better to drop him into a situation far removed from anything he's ever experienced. His parents—particularly his disgusted father—want to send him on a hunting and fishing trip. "Yes—get a camping outfit—go out and rough it," the old man tells him. "Maybe it will make a man out of you if you have to take care of yourself for a while." Alfred takes his loyal valet (Snitz Edwards) with him, and is proving thoroughly incompetent at everything he attempts when he meets the local Mountain Girl and is instantly smitten.

"Saturday evening was picture night at the Odd Fellows Hall," William B. Smith reported in *The Bakersfield Californian,* "and we had a good picture, too. But Buster Keaton, who is 'roughing it' in a tuxedo and Rolls-Royce in the brush and woods along the Kern River, had a big battery of powerful arc lights throwing weird effects over the woods and onto the far hillsides. It was snappy cold weather, too, but most of the usual patrons of our picture shows deserted the comfort of the hall to watch the little 'frozen face' comedian work up footage in the brush beside the ice cold river. Mr. Keaton and his company will be in Kernville most of this week."

When the camping and courting scenes were completed, Keaton spent another two and a half weeks in Santa Ynez, north of Santa Barbara, before returning to Hollywood for interiors. A fight between the real Battling Butler and a top-seeded contender was staged at L.A.'s new Olympic Auditorium, while training camp interiors, during which Keaton strained ligaments in his leg and back, were shot at the studio.

"I told the original story that was taken from the stage show," Keaton said, "except that I had to add my own finish. I couldn't have done the finish that was in the show . . . [where] he just finds out in the dressing room up at Madison Square Garden that he don't have to fight the champion and he promises the girl he'll never fight again. And of course the girl don't

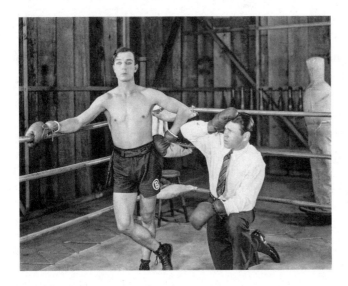

Keaton smugly poses in a gag shot with welterweight champion Mickey Walker on the set of Battling Butler *(1926).*

know but what he did fight. But we knew better than to do that to a motion picture audience. We couldn't promise 'em for seven reels that I was goin' to fight in the ring and then not fight. So we staged a fight in the dressing room with the guy who just won the title in the ring—by having bad blood between the fighter and myself. And it worked out swell."

The scene between Keaton and actor Francis McDonald, who was a pretty good boxer in his own right, was staged at the Keaton studio before a grouping of fight professionals that included welterweight champion Mickey Walker and Walker's manager, Jack "Doc" Kearns. It's McDonald's character, the prizefighter, who corners Keaton's Butler in a fit of jealousy, and Keaton wanted the unrehearsed action as real as they could make it. Covered by two cameras in tight quarters, he saw no way they could completely pull their punches, and McDonald's only instructions were to take a dive, giving the other Alfred a private victory.

Keaton's Butler cowers, pleads, shields himself, as his valet and the fighter's wife watch horrified from the doorway. Finally, he can stand no more and erupts in a furious barrage of punches, aggressively downing his opponent and then picking him up so that he can pummel him more. Keaton, the consummate actor, displays genuine anger in the scene, almost to the point of breaking character. It is a brutal, shocking, merciless display, utterly convincing.

"That's the greatest battle I ever saw outside of a ring," Walker proclaimed when the whole thing was over. "I mean it, too. If Buster and McDonald had put on that scrap before a fight club, they'd have had the crowd on its feet from start to finish."

Kearns, who was famous for managing Jack Dempsey, agreed. "Best fight I've ever seen enacted before the cameras," he said. "The picture Buster was making may be a comedy, but there was nothing funny about that battle. It was a wow. What a beating those boys did give each other."

Keaton completed *Battling Butler* in early March, just as Joe Schenck was announcing United Artists' ambitious slate of feature productions for the 1926–27 season. Included were two pictures from Mary Pickford, one from Douglas Fairbanks (*The Black Pirate*), two from Rudolph Valentino, one from Charlie Chaplin (*The Circus*), three from Samuel Goldwyn, and two from Buster Keaton. *Battling Butler* fulfilled his commitment to Metro-Goldwyn (now M-G-M) and Schenck was moving him to UA at a time when he was assembling the most prestigious roster of talent in the industry. Both John Barrymore and Gloria Swanson were now stars for United Artists, and Norma Talmadge would soon be joining them.

In terms of a picture, all they had from Keaton was a title, and he was encouraged to make it something special, a comedy that would stand up to Chaplin's first movie in two years, to the Technicolor *Black Pirate,* and to such Goldwyn productions as *Stella Dallas* and *The Winning of Barbara Worth*. "We will never have more than fifteen pictures a year," Schenck said in an interview with *Motion Picture News,* "and none of these will be permitted to fall below the present quality. Each picture must have something big about it."

All the New York office knew about the new Keaton picture was that it seemed to have a military theme. UA's two-page display announcement in *The Film Daily* featured the star's profile against a generic pattern of soldiers marching stiffly in parade dress. It was, it turned out, a wildly inappropriate representation of the unconventional comedy Keaton had in mind.

13

The General

THE HOUSE ON MUIRFIELD ROAD lasted eighteen months before it too was consigned to history. Weary of his wife's pattern of elation and disillusionment, Buster Keaton attempted an intervention of sorts. Where Nat was forever on the lookout for the next, seemingly better place to live, her husband arrived at the conclusion that she needed a house she wouldn't find in the local inventory—one that no one else had ever occupied, virgin space rather than, as he reasoned it, "somebody else's hand-me-down." In 1925, he bought a couple of undeveloped lots in Beverly Hills and secretly had a three-bedroom Spanish-style house designed, built, landscaped, and furnished on the smaller of the two. "It cost only $33,000," he said proudly, "but it was on a large lot, had a swimming pool, and was ideal for the four of us. I was so sure of this that I wouldn't let my wife see it until it was ready to move into. I wanted to surprise her."

He imagined they'd drive by the new house, casually stop to have a look, and when Nat exclaimed something along the lines of "It's a dream of a home," he'd tell her with a flourish that it was all hers. But it didn't quite work out that way—principally because the house, with Gabe Gabourie's help, was of Buster's design, not Natalie's.

"In the first place," she said tightly, "it has no room for the governess. Where would she sleep?" Bernice Mannix, wife of Metro-Goldwyn executive Eddie Mannix, was along for the big reveal, and genuinely loved what Buster had conceived and built at 516 North Linden. "If you really want it, Bernice," he said, impulsively throwing in the towel, "it's yours. Have Eddie look at it, and if he likes it I will sell it to you."

The only solution, he conceded, was to build a showplace on a grand scale, something that indulged Nat's every whim. They sold the place on Muirfield for $85,000, pocketing a small profit, and moved into a nearby rental owned by Peg Talmadge. Then they began the arduous process of creating one of the most elaborate estates in Beverly Hills, for which they retained a Canadian-born architect named Gene Verge, who would go on to local prominence as a designer of hospitals, churches, and stately private residences. By the end of 1925, Verge had completed plans for a mansion in the spirit of the Italian Renaissance, ten thousand square feet on three and a half acres of prime Beverly Hills real estate. It would take $200,000 and the better part of a year to build.

Keaton always credited Clyde Bruckman with the idea for *The General*—and Bruckman wasn't even working for him at the time. After Jean Havez's death, Bruck had gone freelance, working at intervals with Monty Banks, Eddie Cline, and Harold Lloyd. A prodigious reader, he had come across *The Great Locomotive Chase,* an account of a daring Union raid into Georgia during the Civil War. The book by William Pittenger, one of the participants in the expedition, had been around for decades in various forms, and it's likely that Bruckman would never have seen the comic potential in the story had he encountered it under its original title, *Daring and Suffering,* or the later *Capturing a Locomotive.* But the apt combination of the words "Locomotive" and "Chase" in the title of the book's third edition, published in 1891, must surely have brought Keaton to mind.

"Clyde Bruckman run into this book . . . and it was a pip," Buster reminisced. "[Bruckman] says, 'Well, it's awful heavy for us to attempt, because when we got that much plot and story to tell, it means we're goin' to have a lot of film with no laughs in it. But we won't worry too much about it if we can get the plot all [laid out] in that first reel, and our characters—believable characters—all planted, and then go ahead and let it roll.'" Of the book's nearly five hundred pages, the story to be told on-screen consumed just 128. "Nothing I had ever heard so fired my imagination," wrote Pittenger, a first corporal in the Union Army. "The idea of a few disguised men suddenly seizing a train far within the enemy's lines, cutting the telegraph wires, burning bridges, and leaving the foe in helpless rage behind, was the very sublimity and romance of war."

Keaton instantly knew his solitary character wouldn't fit in with the twenty-one volunteers under the leadership of James J. Andrews, a Union spy and contraband merchant. Rather, since this was, as he put it, a page from history, it was important to acknowledge up front that the audience would already know how it all turned out for the South. "They lost the war anyhow, so the audience resents it. We knew better. Don't tell the story from the Northerners' side—tell it from the Southerners' side." The character he envisioned for himself would be a Confederate engineer whose beloved locomotive, the General, is the one the spies seize in the raid and pilot northward toward Tennessee.

With such a complex series of events, Bruckman was tasked with the job of getting it all on paper, paring away the many pages of extraneous detail and boiling the book down to its essence. The result was a preliminary 116-page script, by far the most complete scenario with which Keaton had ever started a film. With the document at hand and the book cast aside, he began focusing his mind on the emerging continuity, which would see countless changes. "The moment you give me a locomotive and things like that to play with, as a rule I find some way of getting laughs with it. But the original locomotive chase ended when I found myself in Northern territory and had to desert. From then on it was my invention in order to get a complete plot. It had nothing to do with the Civil War."

In April, with *Battling Butler* cut and titled, and the story for *The General* far from settled, Keaton, Gabe Gabourie, and staff writer Paul Gerard Smith traveled to New Orleans and Atlanta to scout locations. Normally, Buster would have included Elgin Lessley on such a trip, but after five years with Keaton, Lessley had been recruited by Harry Langdon to photograph his first feature comedy, *Tramp, Tramp, Tramp,* and would remain with Langdon for a total of five features—the entire arc of Langdon's career as a first-rank comedian. Shrewdly, Keaton chose to replace him on *Battling Butler* with veteran cinematographer Devereaux "Dev" Jennings, who had more than fifty pictures to his credit, none of which were comedies. *Battling Butler* was a relatively easy picture to shoot; *The General* would be anything but.

"I went to the original location from Atlanta, Georgia, up to Chatta-nooga," Keaton remembered, "and the scenery didn't look very good. It looked terrible. The railroad tracks I couldn't use at all because the Civil War trains were narrow gauge, and those railroad beds of the time were pretty crude.* They didn't have so much gravel rock to put between the

---

* Keaton was under the mistaken impression that Southern railroads during the Civil War ran on narrow-gauge tracks, meaning tracks no wider than four feet eight and a quarter inches.

ties, and then you saw grass growing between the ties every place you saw the railroad, darn near." With the authentic locales ruled out as viable locations, Bert Jackson, Keaton's location manager and chief property man, was dispatched to the verdant lumbering regions of the Pacific Northwest, where rivers and logging trains were plentiful, and where the terrains looked more authentically Southern than the South itself. It was Jackson who identified Oregon's Cottage Grove as the best filming site and, after seeing to preliminaries, such as cooperation from the Oregon, Pacific & Eastern, a local short line railroad, wired the studio to say he had found exactly what they were after.

By the time Keaton and his party, which included Natalie, Bruckman, and Gabourie, arrived in Cottage Grove on May 7, 1926, Jackson had spent four furious days lining up meetings and tours, and sweating the logistical details of a major production based so far from home. *Go West* was three weeks in Arizona; *The General* would be at least two months on the ground in Oregon, possibly more. Fortunately, Cottage Grove was just twenty-two miles south of Eugene, the second-largest city in the state, assuring quick access to supplies not so easily found in a wilderness town of two thousand. Keaton was all business that day, impassively studying the community and climbing over and through locomotives that might be used in the film.

"A person has to work hard if he is going to be successful," he explained to a local reporter, "and we have to keep going all the time." He inspected an abandoned lumber camp that might double as a set, and arranged to purchase two engines, one of which, a wood-burning specimen from the Anderson & Middleton logging camp called Old Four Spot, would be sacrificed by running it across a burning bridge.

"I have looked all over the country for a place like this," he said with a grin of satisfaction. "It is just what I want."

Keaton was a couple of days in Lane County before returning to Hollywood, leaving Bert Jackson to prepare for work at four different filming sites—two on the Row River; one at Dorena, a little village in the foothills of the Calapooya Mountains; and one at a nearby logging settlement called Culp Creek. Soon, representatives of the Dallas Machine and Locomotive Works were on site with plans to bring the engines cosmetically into line with their historic counterparts. Back in Hollywood, Keaton oversaw cast-

However, those in the South during the Confederacy tended to be five feet wide, which was considered a broad gauge.

ing for the new picture, selecting actress Marion Mack for the role of his fiancée, who would come to be known as Annabelle Lee.

"Buster was looking for an old-fashioned girl with long, curly hair . . . because they wanted everything to look just right for the Civil War period," said Mack. "Well, Percy Westmore, who was making up Norma Talmadge for some picture, heard this from her . . . and Percy mentioned that he knew a girl with just the right hair, because he had been my makeup man on [the recently completed] *Carnival Girl*. And Norma said to Percy he should try to find out if I was available, and he called me and the first thing he said was, 'I hope you still have those long curls you had in *Carnival Girl*.' Well . . . this was the year everyone was bobbing their hair, and so, only a couple of days before, I cut my hair short, too, and I told it to Percy. And he said, 'Don't worry, we'll give you a fall or something.'"

In lieu of an audition, Mack sent over a print of her 1923 feature *Mary of the Movies,* and a meeting was subsequently arranged with Keaton, Bruckman, and Lou Anger. "Buster didn't say much," she remembered. "Clyde Bruckman was a nice person. He didn't seem to have a terrific sense of humor. He seemed more like a college teacher-type person. But Lou Anger was very much the executive type, the tummy and cigar type. He didn't seem too impressed with me, Mr. Anger didn't. I wanted to have a hairdresser go along with me. They said, 'Okay, we'll give you the part.' And I said, 'I have to have my own hairdresser sent with me up on location—and that's the only way I'll sign the contract.' And so Mr. Anger [sneeringly] says, 'My, you are demanding, aren't you?' But I got the hairdresser."

Other principals selected for the cast were Glen Cavender as the leader of the raiders, actor James Farley, baseball star "Turkey" Mike Donlin, the great Irish comedian Tom Nawn, and Joe Keaton, all as Union generals. Snitz Edwards, compacted veteran of *Seven Chances* and *Battling Butler,* was chosen for a distinctive cameo. Pressed into service were gagman Charles Smith as Annabelle's father, and construction supervisor Frank Barnes as her brother.

When Keaton returned to Cottage Grove on May 28, Nat was again with him, as were Bruckman, Gabourie, and Dev Jennings and their wives. His hair was grown long in the style of the period, and he had been preceded by eighteen carloads of equipment, some twelve hundred costumes, and an advance party of twenty. Sets were already under construction, while the upper floor of the Long and Cruson Service Garage, formerly a Moose lodge, was in the process of being transformed into makeup and wardrobe departments. Cannons, prairie schooners, wagons, and a stagecoach had been shipped in for the picture. Houses, big and small, were being built in sections so they could easily be moved to where they were needed.

Keaton spent Memorial Day weekend inspecting the filming sites with Gabourie—who had assumed the role of production manager—Jackson, and business manager Al Gilmore, while others picnicked on the banks of the Row River or sampled the fishing. Several spots in Cottage Grove itself were being dressed to represent the town of Marietta, Georgia, including a section of the original settlement called Slab Town, in which many old structures survived.

The last day of May marked the Keatons' fifth wedding anniversary, and a surprise banquet was tendered at the Bartell Hotel by about thirty members of the company. Gabe Gabourie was in charge of the event, and the couple was presented with a pen sketch by the company draftsman. Marion Mack and her husband, producer Louis Lewyn, arrived the following day. Waiting for the first sets to be ready, Keaton stirred up a couple of late-afternoon ball games with the local Methodist church, the first of which was won by the church team 5–3. The local challengers were soon formalized as the Twilight League, while the visitors became known as the Keaton Location Nine.

Frank Barnes had a stretch of Marietta along the railroad line east of town finished on June 3, enabling production on *The General* to begin on Monday, June 7. With the start of filming imminent, a writer for Eugene's *Morning Register* walked the streets of the southern town where the Andrews raid begins, marveling at what Barnes had accomplished in little more than a week:

"The city of Marietta, which has been under construction here, is now completed and a test shot will be made on Sunday. This town site, constructed of new lumber, now has the appearance of having stood for fifty years. The Western and Atlantic railroad station bearing the sign of 'Marietta' in faded weather-beaten letters across the front, its two waiting rooms with conspicuous signs 'colored waiting room' and 'white waiting room,' the faded and dusty blackboard timetable stating No. 3 on time, makes one wonder just a little. A short step or two across the dusty street stands the old Georgia Hotel [and] bar, with shuttered windows of another day. There is the town watering trough, its cracks and joints green with the moss of years, so realistic that one catches himself glancing down to the ground beneath, looking for the puddles in the dust and the steady drip that makes them.

Sauntering on up the street you see the City Hall standing, old fashioned yet business-like, with all its outward appearance of needing paint. There is the tailor shop, the trimmer shop, billiard and pool, blacksmith shop and wheelwright, halls, shoe and harness shop, the Southern hotel, the post office, and numerous other business houses. There is the stage stables from which some long line skinner will reel his string of four or six away and hit the trail for Chattanooga perhaps."

Early scenes captured the arrival of the train at Marietta, the passengers disembarking while Buster, in the character of Johnnie Gray, lovingly inspects the engine, a couple of local boys eagerly miming his actions. "We'd better have a dog or two, lazy ones, in the foreground," Keaton instructed as he composed a shot. "Better give that colored boy a bundle to carry."

A week would be given over to Johnnie's initial scenes with Annabelle, who, with the news that Fort Sumter has been fired upon, sends him off to the recruiting office to be one of the first to join up. His enlistment, however, is denied because he is more valuable to the cause as an engineer. Perceived as a slacker, he is left behind to endure the scorn of the populace, Annabelle's included. Dejectedly, in what filmmaker James Blue would call "a moment of almost pathetic beauty," he sits on the coupling rod that connects the great metal wheels of the General and remains there, frozen in place, as the engine begins to move.

"The situation of the picture at that point is that she says, 'Never speak to me again unless you're in uniform.' So the bottom has dropped out of everything, and I've got nothing to do but sit down on my engine and think. I don't know why they rejected me; they didn't tell me it was because they didn't want to take a locomotive engineer off his duty. My fireman wants to put the engine away in the roundhouse and doesn't know that I'm sitting on the cross bar, and starts to take it in. I was running the engine myself through the picture. I could handle the thing so well I was stopping on a dime. But when it came to this shot I asked the engineer whether we could do it. He said, 'There's only one danger. A fraction too much steam with these old-fashioned engines and the wheel spins. And if it spins it will kill you then and there.' We tried it four or five times, and in the end the engineer was satisfied that he could handle it. So we went ahead and did it. I wanted a fade-out laugh for that sequence. Although it's not a big laugh, it's cute and funny enough to get me a nice laugh."

Spectators drove in from as far away as Seattle, crowding the filming sites and hemming in the actors. When the curious jammed in too close, Gabou-

Keaton, in costume, with his camera crew while on location in Cottage Grove, Oregon, for The General. *Note the parallel tracks in the foreground, which made the extraordinary traveling shots possible.*

rie or Jackson, or even Keaton himself, would walk over and courteously ask, "Will you please stand back so as not to cast a shadow on the picture?" Someone from the *Cottage Grove Sentinel* captured the crush of activity surrounding the star-director as he attempted to squeeze in an interview. "As he answered a reporter's questions, he gave directions for the ball game to start within a few minutes, directed the purchase of balls, gave an order for the entire company to be in the lobby by seven o'clock the next morning, answered half a hundred questions by his production manager or some other official about this and that, described the making of a picture, visited briefly with a stranger who had known him in his childhood and gave the address at which other members of the family could be located, ordered his car, sent for members of the ball team, told the story of the present picture, and a few other things, frequently smiling at something humorous . . ." So focused was Keaton on the making of the picture that he couldn't remember his own room number or how many of his people were on site. "Yes, the slapstick is gone," he acknowledged, reflecting on the dramatic nature of the story. "No longer will folks pay for that kind of stuff. The movie public

The Southern army's retreat and the advance of the victorious Northerners go completely unnoticed by Johnnie Gray.

demands drama, punctuated with comedy. The pictures that go over big are those with comedy situations, and the kind that go over are the kind the producers are going to make. When the public demands something else, something else will be made."

It was estimated that shooting at Cottage Grove cost four hundred dollars an hour, whether or not any film got exposed. On Tuesday, work had to be halted when a two-sided drugstore was blown over in a stiff wind, but the front was quickly righted. Then an onlooker stepped into a shot directly behind Buster as he was oiling his engine, spoiling the take, yet all Keaton could do was to smile and do it over. Later, patiently seated in the doorway of a boxcar during a production delay, he took an empty pop bottle, tossed it into the air, and balanced it on the back of his hand. He repeated the trick several times, then once again sent it skyward, sticking a finger up and catching the bottle by its neck. A crowd of onlookers laughed, and Keaton grinned.

On Wednesday, the company used an old planing mill at Dorena to stage the theft of the train at Big Shanty, the Union raiders uncoupling the passenger cars and pulling away with the General, a tender, and three empty boxcars during a stopover for dinner. Johnnie gives chase, first on foot, then on a handcar, just as the actual pursuers did in 1862. Ahead, the raiders are cutting telegraph lines, pulling up rails, and littering the track with cross-ties. At Kingston, Buster comes across an army encampment and alerts the men to the stolen General, which he thinks has been taken by deserters. They climb aboard a flat car on their own train while Johnnie leaps into its cab and pulls away, unaware the rest of it has come uncoupled, leaving the soldiers stranded at the station. Speeding northward toward Adairsville, he discovers he is alone in his quest to reclaim his engine.

While the company was reconfiguring the town of Marietta to represent Chattanooga and, for later scenes, Calhoun, Keaton turned his attentions to scenes aboard the pursuing engine, the Texas, much of which would be filmed by Dev Jennings and second cameraman Bert "Boots" Haines from a train traveling on a half-mile set of parallel tracks just east of town. These rock-steady images captured brief bits of action, thirty or forty seconds at the most, and then the two trains would have to be backed up to their starting points for another run, a tedious process of stopping and starting until an entire sequence had been completed.*

With the Anderson & Middleton mills closed for their annual Independence Day shutdown, the only other rail traffic to contend with were twice-daily passenger runs, and Bert Jackson was able to get those rescheduled to earlier in the morning and later in the evening for ten consecutive days. Among the crucial scenes to be made during this period was an expertly timed shot involving a rolling cannon Buster uses to fire on the raiders. Bouncing along the track behind the Texas and its tender, the cannon, once lit, adjusts to train itself on Johnnie and the car directly in front of it. He braces for the worst as the engine comes to a bend in the road, taking it out of the line of fire just as the cannon goes off, its shell exploding within feet of the Union men fleeing with the General.

Another sequence inspired by the book, in which the raiders set a boxcar on fire and roll it into a covered bridge, was staged near Disston before hundreds of onlookers. Closer to town, a wheat field became the scene of a Confederate retreat with hundreds of horses, wagons, and soldiers escaping to the South as Buster, traveling north with the Texas and oblivious to the exodus, occupies the foreground, furiously chopping firewood to keep

---

* Marion Mack remembered traveling shots being made from a flatbed truck as well, and the *Cottage Grove Sentinel* reported as much, but for the steadiness of the image, the shots made on the parallel tracks couldn't be beat. Location historian John Bengtson documents many of these in his masterful study of Keaton's filming locations, *Silent Echoes*.

the engine moving. In its sweep and casual majesty, the scene ranks as one of Keaton's most powerful, particularly when the fleeing Southerners are followed by the advance of the Union army, turning the panorama behind him from gray to blue, the ebb and flow of warfare signaling his passage into enemy territory. Topping off the eventful week was a preview of *Battling Butler* at the Arcade Theater, which Keaton had been using to screen rushes. In a gesture of thanks, he arranged to have a print of the new picture sent up for a pair of advance showings, both of which played to capacity audiences. The *Eugene Guard* called it "the best thing we have seen of Buster's."

"I staged it exactly the way it happened," Keaton liked to say of the Andrews Raid. "The Union agents intended to enter from the state of Kentucky, which was a neutral territory, pretending they were coming down to fight for the Southern cause. That was an excuse to get on that train which takes them up to an army camp. Their leader took seven men with him, including two locomotive engineers and a telegraph operator, and he told them that if anything went wrong they were to scatter individually, stick to their stories that they were Kentuckians down to enlist in the Southern army, and then watch for the first opportunity to desert and get back over the line to the North. As soon as they stole that engine they wanted to pull out of there, to disconnect the telegraph and burn bridges and destroy enough track to cripple the Southern army supply route. That was what they intended to do. And I staged the chase exactly the way it happened. Then I rounded out the story of stealing my engine back."

However useful Clyde Bruckman's scenario had been in organizing the contours of the plot, it was remarkably free of the comedy highlights that would distinguish the picture. "The script they took with us they hardly went by at all," said Marion Mack, "except just the next sequence because they had to write the gags that weren't in it." Historically, the Andrews Raid ended at Ringgold, Georgia, when the General ran out of steam some twenty miles south of Chattanooga. But in the picture Keaton and Bruckman kept the engine in play so that Johnnie could come upon a meeting of Union generals and learn of plans for their supply trains to unite with the Northern Division at Rock River Bridge, then advance for a surprise attack.

Throughout the early filming, much was made of a spectacular shot planned for the third act in which Union soldiers attempt to drive a supply train over a bridge Johnnie has set on fire. The weakened span collapses

Director Keaton lines up a shot at Carlton, the Union army supply base where Johnnie and Annabelle steal back the General.

under the weight of the engine, and it plunges into the river below. It was an idea that came from *The Great Locomotive Chase* in which the thieves attempt to torch a bridge on the Oostanaula River near Resaca, Georgia, but the dampness of the structure will not permit it to burn. Keaton was dead set against attempting the effect in miniature, knowing the size and spectacle of the thing would make for a thrilling big-screen experience. He surveyed every existing trestle in the region trying to find one suitable to the visual and logistical demands of the scene, and at various times no fewer than four had been picked and rejected, complicating factors being a necessary elevation of seventy-five to a hundred feet and easy access by a spur from the OP&E. Finally, in desperation, a team of four men, headed by Gabe Gabourie, was dispatched one Saturday into the surrounding counties on a mission to identify the best possible candidate. Their conclusion at the end of the day was that the ideal trestle didn't exist and that Rock River Bridge would have to be built from scratch.

On July 1, a contract was let to begin the design and construction of a 250-foot bridge rising some fifty feet above the jagged rocks of Row River. It would need to be capable of supporting twenty tons of rolling stock, yet collapse into the water on cue. To bring the river up to a depth of twelve feet, a dam at the site near the Culp Creek settlement would also have to be built. By July 7, work had commenced on the span, with a spur five hundred feet in length designed to connect to the main line of the OP&E. The next day, a third engine arrived from Hood River, remodeled to period and renamed the Comet. On July 13, an appeal was made for National Guardsmen from Eugene, Springfield, and Cottage Grove. On July 15, a call went out for five hundred additional men, with tourist sleepers from the Southern Pacific parked on the tracks to accommodate those traveling from long distances. Four days later, confirmation came that the big battle scenes were to be filmed over three days beginning Thursday, July 22, with the collapse of the flaming bridge likely to take place on Friday, July 23.

While preparations went forth, Keaton busied himself playing scenes with Marion Mack, who, as Annabelle Lee, has been held captive by the raiders since the theft of the train. Johnnie rescues her, and the two steal away under the cover of darkness. At daybreak, they discover the General at a bustling army encampment being loaded with supplies. "We've got to get back to our lines somehow and warn them of this coming attack," he tells her. Then he stuffs her into a burlap bag, loads her like a sack of pota-toes, and in a quick, decisive move, clobbers a Union officer and brazenly hijacks the engine from under their noses. Soon, Johnnie, Annabelle, and the General are being chased by the Texas and the Comet, both loaded with Union troops.

Mack quickly learned how unpredictable Keaton could be when the cameras were grinding. Stopping briefly when they had to take on water, she was unexpectedly drenched when he artfully positioned her directly in front of the spout. "It really knocked me down," she said. "It's a good thing we didn't have sound movies at the time." Later, she suggested a gag of her own, where Annabelle, trying to make herself useful, picks up a broom and starts sweeping the cab as the Texas is rapidly gaining on them. Alarmed, Johnnie yanks it from her hands and tells her to add wood to the fire. Compliantly, she picks up a tiny piece, opens the door, and primly tosses it in. Disgusted, he finds an even smaller piece, hands it to her, and watches as she does exactly the same thing. Impulsively, he reaches over and takes her neck in his hands and begins to throttle her. Then, just as quickly, he shifts gears and gives her a kiss.

"I think I got that kiss more for thinking of the gag than anything else," she said.

The General beats the Northerners to Rock River Bridge, giving Johnnie time to set the bridge on fire before continuing on to Calhoun, a Southern stronghold. At division headquarters, he warns the commanding general of the enemy's plan, which sends hundreds of Confederate soldiers streaming northward. Back at Rock River, the supply trains are stymied as General Parker arrives on the scene. "That bridge is not burned enough to stop you," he tells the engineers, "and my men will ford the river."

Thursday, July 22, was devoted to preparations for the fateful crossing. At two o'clock, a train carrying eight hundred men and about ninety horses arrived at Cottage Grove, where they were marched to the wardrobe depot at Sixth and Main Streets. There they were joined by two hundred boys from the local guard company, and all were issued uniforms and battle paraphernalia. Later the same afternoon, the special train, powered by two logging engines, carried them fifteen miles to a camp at Culp Creek. Only a handful of shots would be made the following day. If all went according to plan, one of them would cost $40,000—the most expensive take in the history of the screen. Were anything to go wrong, the added cost of another run would surely break the bank.

Cars began arriving on Thursday afternoon, with spectators planning to camp near the bridge all night. By four on Friday morning, they lined Row

River Road from a quarter mile above the location site to a point about a mile below Culp Creek, leaving hardly any room to get through. Cottage Grove, in fact, cleared out so thoroughly that most merchants closed for the day. Dev Jennings had brought four cameras to Oregon: three Bell & Howells and an Akeley, a versatile camera expressly designed for shooting action footage under field conditions. Two additional camera units were ordered up from Hollywood, making a total of six on hand to capture the fiery crash. Jennings' own crew consisted of Boots Haines, assistant Elmer Ellsworth, and stills cameraman Byron Houck, who was carrying an eight-by-ten Eastman and a five-by-seven Graflex. Jennings' principal cameras were stationed down the river about three hundred yards, while two others were on a platform directly across the river on its south side, high above the far end of the bridge to capture the approach of the supply trains and Union troops.

The atmosphere had grown tense by the time Keaton decided he was ready. Rehearsals coordinated the movements of the key visual elements— the cavalry, the foot soldiers, the two engines. "I marched more there than I did in the army," said Ronald Gilstrap, who belonged to the National Guard and volunteered for picture duty. "We came down this road towards the crossing four times, I think, before they got a shot. The first time some kids were in the road, and another time something else happened. Then Buster Keaton took the engine across the trestle and back." The General had previously crossed over as Johnnie and Annabelle went about the business of starting the fire.

As director, Keaton was ever present, methodically checking and rechecking things as the morning wore on. "Not satisfied to stand on the camera platform and give orders through a telephone with megaphone attachment, he was here and there on all angles of the location," the *Eugene Guard* recorded. Co-director Clyde Bruckman, clad in a red jacket and matching hat, was more conspicuous than useful. "He didn't direct much of it at all," said Marion Mack. "He was more like an assistant in the whole film."

With the timing perfected, the span was weakened by sawing into the timbers from underneath. "There was an awful lot of apprehension about it," said Grace Matteson, whose father worked as a carpenter on the film. "I can remember my father talking about the decisions they had to make in order to get it just right. There was quite a bit of figuring and arguing." They eventually decided that strategically placed dynamite would also help the bridge to collapse on cue. Shortly before noon, the structure saturated with gasoline, Keaton called for camera. "Start your action!" he signaled, but then he decided the flames were no good and aborted the take. A custom water cannon powered by a six-cylinder automobile engine extinguished them before any damage was done.

Dinner was called, and the extras went off to mess as the livestock were cared for and watered. Spectators, estimated at three to four thousand, crowded around the numerous hot dog stands and refreshment booths that sprang up like toadstools. It wasn't until two o'clock that everything was in place for another attempt. The bridge was once again ignited, action again was called, and again the shot was abruptly scuttled as the engine dutifully approached its fate. Down at the far base of the bridge, directly below the flaming timbers, a group of small boys could be seen swimming in the river. The powerful water pump again was trained on the flames, the Texas was once more backed into position, and while the bluecoats retreated with their mounts, Bruckman stormed and fumed at the children. A third attempt was spoiled when some of the soldiers waded into the water at the wrong time, causing yet another half-hour delay.

Before a fourth take was attempted, Keaton had a pile of wood placed at the center of the bridge. Sawdust was strewn all about, and everything was once again saturated with gasoline. Now getting past three o'clock, time was

running short. Silence was politely requested of the spectators, and down-river the temporary dam was opened, causing water backed up some three hundred yards to flow through the gorge. Now all eyes were on Keaton as he took his place on the camera platform and signaled powderman Jack Little. Activating a series of electric ignitions with the press of a button, Little caused the bridge to burst into flames. As the fire built, the smell of gasoline permeated the air. At last satisfied, Keaton called "Camera!" and the words "Start your action!" As the Texas charged toward the burning trestle, Union cavalrymen made for the river. When the cowcatcher on the locomotive reached the exact center of the trestle, Little detonated the dynamite charges at the centermost pilings and the span began to buckle. With the Texas and its tender now perfectly centered over the water and clearing the banks on both sides, it fell and dug deep into the bed below. As it sank, black smoke erupting skyward, steam forced from the boiler caused the whistle to blow a mournful dirge. There was an audible gasp from the crowd, and screams could be heard as realistic dummies representing the engineer and fireman were thrown clear of the wreck. One woman fainted, and another grew hysterical as the papier-mâché head of the engineer floated downstream.

With the bridge and the locomotive now a smoldering mass of wreckage, the horses and infantry waded into the river, where they discovered the dam had left the water deeper in places than they expected. Weighted down with heavy uniforms, rifles, and the like, some of the costumed extras had trouble making it across. "I was pulling them out," said Gilstrap. "I'm a good swimmer, and there were several of us. I pulled four or five fellers up and got them on the bank." Two men nearly drowned when they found themselves in deep water, and a third, a fifteen-year-old, was hospitalized in critical condition. Visibly relieved when the scene was finally in the can, Keaton was, the *Cottage Grove Sentinel* reported, "happy as a kid."

"Come on, gang," he said, "let's call it a day."

Saturday and Sunday were given over to scenes of the climactic battle between the North and the South, pyrotechnic action also under the supervision of Jack Little, who had been in charge of the explosive effects for Metro's drama of the Great War, *The Big Parade*. Little, it was said, ran forty thousand feet of wire at Culp Creek and personally prepared nine hundred "shots" that were either buried, concealed in trees, or fired from behind camera lines from one of three electrical command posts. As many as 150 were detonated in a single take as Southern artillery opened fire on the advancing Northerners and the site of the former Rock River Bridge became a canvas of bloodshed and fury. Then, around two o'clock on Saturday afternoon, sparks thrown off by the Comet started a brush fire along the right-of-way of the OP&E, a conflagration that eventually covered five miles.*

Keaton immediately leaped into action, doffing his trousers and using them to beat back the flames while simultaneously directing the National Guardsmen from Eugene and Corvallis, working in relay, to use the coats of their uniforms as if they were blankets. A number of Confederate extras had already been dismissed for the day, and a contingent was attending a big dance in Eugene when word reached them. "I'd just started to dance," remembered Kieth Fennell, a foot soldier, "and the announcement came over the speaker: 'All those in the Buster Keaton movie get back to camp— there's a forest fire.' So we jumped in this old Model T Ford and away we went. It took us about an hour to get out there, and as we came into camp, [we could see] that [the] fire was out and Buster Keaton was entertaining the boys. He had his pants off, he had his drawers down in the back, and he had a pitchfork and was sneaking up on a little puff of smoke. Just about that time, someone in command gave the order, 'Everybody line up,' so we lined up and they called roll, and we were paid that night for fighting the fire."

Four hundred Union army coats were damaged in fighting the blaze; one of Dev Jennings' cameras, valued at $3,500, was destroyed; and six men were sent to the hospital for exhaustion, smoke inhalation, and minor burns. In all, work was delayed a day, but the company was able to pay off and release all the National Guardsmen from Eugene, Springfield, and other lower-valley towns on schedule. On midday Monday, work at Culp Creek was declared over, leaving it a deserted lumber camp. The company returned to the newly reconstituted Marietta set to stage the picture's concluding scenes with the Cottage Grove National Guard unit standing in for the triumphant Confederate army. "When my picture ended," said Keaton, "the South was winning, which was all right with me."

Work in Cottage Grove was winding down when forest fires unrelated

---

* "Oh, the sparks!" exclaimed Gene Woodward, an actress observing on the set. "When Buster used the General on location, the sparks were flying. The farmers had their haystacks out along the tracks to be picked up. The sparks would set off these haystacks. And so coming back, the crew was met by the farmers, and they paid them twenty-five dollars for each stack that caught fire. And that was a ritual. Going up they'd start the fire, and coming back they had to pay for it."

to *The General* made the air so smoky it became impossible to film. At the Southern Pacific depot, equipment was being loaded for shipment back to Los Angeles, and daily departures had caused the company to dwindle to just twenty in number. On August 5, Keaton surveyed the scene along Row River and made the decision to shut down production until summer rains could overwhelm and extinguish the fires. The next day, accompanied by Natalie, his parents, and Nat's mother, Peg, he left by car for Hollywood, promising to return when the air cleared.

In the beginning, Buster Keaton rarely spoke to Marion Mack. "I had never worked with a leading man like that before," she said. "Usually they were outgoing and chummy, but Buster just stuck to the job and his little clique, and that was all. At first I felt a little bit, I'd say, ignored or slighted, but then he got a bit more friendly as he lost some of his shyness, and he turned out to be a very nice and warm person."

Keaton, she observed, worked hard and unwound just as fiercely while they were out on location, typically rising at six and putting in a twelve- to fourteen-hour day, often slipping in a game of baseball on the side.

"I liked Mr. Keaton, but that first month we were up there, my husband and I didn't drink, and the troupe would meet after they got back from location and they'd have cocktails and highballs and have their dinner about nine o'clock at night. I was sort of left out of the social activity, but it was really my own fault because we just wanted to have our dinner and that was it. . . . Sometimes those parties would go on to twelve or one o'clock. They just didn't stop at nine or ten, not with a group like that together. They would just drink and tell stories." She said she knew she was okay as far as Keaton was concerned when he started making her the butt of his practical jokes.

"One of the first gags he ever played on me was to have a couple of the guys grab me from behind and hang me upside down over a cake of ice as we were on the way to location on the train. I already had my makeup on, which took about an hour to do, and all of it got ruined and I was very uncomfortable, so as soon as they put me down again I went and punched Buster in the eye. It gave him such a shiner they had to stop shooting for a week. This was before I understood that he meant no harm."

After settling into life at Cottage Grove, Marion located a secluded spot on the river and would bicycle there to swim on hot afternoons when she wasn't required on the set. "So he and a couple of his buddies sneaked up after me one day and found where I left my clothes and tied them up in such knots that I couldn't unravel them. And so I had to pedal back to Cottage Grove in my bathing suit, and this was quite a shocking thing to do in 1926. You simply didn't ride a bike in your bathing suit in those days—and a wet one at that!"

Back in Hollywood, Keaton directed *The General*'s few interiors—his courtship of Annabelle, her rescue from the Union raiders, the scene of the Northern generals plotting their surprise attack, and a sequence in which Johnnie goes undercover in enemy territory wearing a black frock coat and stovepipe hat. "The one that gave us the most trouble," Mack remembered, "was the night scene when Buster and I are running away from the cottage [after my rescue]. We were three weeks doing that, and even here in the studio he wanted to do it as true to life as possible, and so we did it on the back lot at night with rain and wind machines. We came in every night at about seven and stayed until maybe one, and this went on for three weeks. And each night we got soaked to the skin. It's a wonder we didn't catch pneumonia."

According to her, not even all the film's interiors were made at the Keaton studio: "Some of the supposed indoor scenes, like the one with Buster in the recruiting office, these were actually done in Cottage Grove outdoors, with fake walls but no ceiling."

Joe Keaton, as one of the Union generals, was as much in evidence at the studio as he was in Cottage Grove, where he gave interviews, consorted with old pals like Tom Nawn and Charley Smith, and, along with such fellow cast members as Glen Cavender, Frederick Vroom, and Earl Mohan, contributed to the reciprocal entertainment during a farewell dance tendered by the locals at the town armory. "Joe?" responded Ronald Gilstrap when asked about Keaton *père*. "Oh boy. He had a beautiful horse, and he looked more like a general than any general I've ever seen. He was something else."

In Hollywood, Alma Whitaker of the *Los Angeles Times* attempted to interview a reticent Buster between shots on the hot, shadeless studio lot, but even with both Roscoe Arbuckle and Lew Cody present, she was able to extract little that could be quoted directly. As the two visitors were ringing up director James Cruze and fishing for an invitation to Cruze's Flintridge swimming pool, it fell to Joe to complete the session with grandly embellished tales of his son's birth and early days in vaudeville.

"There is not a prouder man in the country than Papa," Whitaker concluded. "He isn't afraid of interviewers."

.   .   .

On August 19, word reached Keaton that rains breaking a sixty-day drought had extinguished the numerous fires threatening the Umpqua National Forest, and he wired Harold Anderson of Anderson & Middleton to confirm that he and his people would be back in Cottage Grove as soon as the weather cleared. Ten days later, he stepped off the train in a downpour but appeared "rather jubilant," since the smoke and haze had completely vanished. Traveling with him in a private railcar were Marion Mack, Gabe Gabourie, Clyde Bruckman and his wife, Bert Jackson, Fred Wright (chief mechanic and the star's double), cast member Jimmy Bryant, Dev Jennings and his crew, and Willie Riddle, who served as Keaton's cook and valet. All were eager to get the picture finished, but the company had to wait three days until the rain subsided and the sun began to cooperate.

Keaton's first priority was an enhancement of the scene in which Johnnie and Annabelle set fire to the Rock River Bridge, business incorporating previous footage shot when it was still intact. With a spur logging bridge at Culp Creek standing in for the Rock River span, Johnnie piles wood on the track while Annabelle stands atop the General's tender and helps. Accidentally, she ignites it all, leaving him stranded on the other side of the flames. Unable to get past them, he takes a flying leap over the fire just as she, in a panic, moves the engine off the bridge. He falls between the ties and plunges into the river below.

A few days later, with a section of the Keaton bridge shored up, a shot was made with Mack running the locomotive back out onto the trestle, braking it just short of calamity, and then reversing direction. It was the second time Keaton and his writers had her piloting the General all by herself, although she never got as comfortable with it as Buster did.

"I had to handle it at the top," she said, "but there was a man down there below in case I did something wrong. But I did have to handle the brakes and do all that. I had to do that because they couldn't photograph the man doing it."

Toward the end of their three-week stay, the company lost another two days to weather but were able to finish the morning of September 18, allowing them to leave for Los Angeles the same day. In all, *The General* had been on location in Oregon nearly thirteen weeks, with scarcely a week of filming left to be done in Los Angeles. Exhilarated, Keaton had the train stopped on the way home so that he and the crew could get off and play baseball.

Buster Keaton spent the next four weeks editing and titling *The General,* working with the man he referred to as his cutter, J. Sherman Kell, a former conductor, appropriately enough, on the Illinois Central Railroad. Kell, whom they all called "Father Sherman" because he looked like a priest, made no editing decisions of his own. Rather, he broke the film down for easy retrieval and scraped and glued the pieces together as fast as the boss could hand them over. As far as the intertitles were concerned, Keaton wanted as few as possible.

"There was a fellow called Al Boasberg," Mack remembered. "He was kind of a tall man with a big face, big mouth too. But I didn't think much of his titles. (I hope he hears this.) Charles Smith was kind of nice. They wrote the titles mostly; they weren't around too much."

The General was ready to be screened by the middle of October, and Keaton, wary of showing a rough cut anywhere near Hollywood, arranged its initial preview in San Bernardino, a center of rail and fruit-packing operations sixty miles east of town. The new West Coast Theater seated fifteen hundred, and advance publicity in the local papers, where the title of the film was given as *The Engineer,* ensured a capacity turnout on a chilly Friday night. At eleven reels, Keaton knew it was impossibly long for a feature comedy—approaching two hours at the proper projection speed—but he needed to know what exactly would play before trimming the picture to seven or eight reels.

"Buster himself, present in the audience and watching tensely the reaction, surely must have been pleased with the reception," the *San Bernardino Daily Sun* said in its coverage. "The one fault that might have been found with the picture was its slow beginning, but this was entirely lost sight of when the action, mixed with thrills and heart suspense, came fast and furious after the plot of the story and characters had been introduced. . . . Any minor defects in the raw product, as shown last night, however, could not detract from the certainty that Keaton has completed his very best vehicle. The audience alternately laughed, held its breath, and was momentarily swayed with pathos, with the laughs, of course, predominating. It is this splendid mixture, in the minds of most of those who saw the picture last night, that stamps it as one of the best comedies of the screen, and a production that will do much toward advancing Keaton to the point of displacing Charlie Chaplin as the seriocomic king of the movies."

Buoyed by the reception in the Inland Empire, Keaton spent a couple of weeks tightening the picture, then scheduled a second preview in San Jose, some 350 miles away at the southern end of San Francisco Bay. Shown the first week in November, the event was leaked in Cottage Grove by a local girl attending a San Jose teachers' college.

"It held an audience," Keaton confirmed. "They were interested in it— from start to finish—and there was enough laughter to satisfy."

A few days later, the Bartell Hotel received a telegram from Gabe Gabourie indicating that Keaton, Mack, and a small company of about a dozen would return to Oregon to retake a few scenes with the General and the Comet, work that was not expected to take more than a few days.

It was around this time that Keaton also made the decision to remove the sequence, about a third of the way into the film, in which Johnnie goes undercover in Chattanooga, risking detection and leading to his discovery of the Northern generals' plot against the South. Possibly sensing that it slowed the pace of the story, he covered the elimination with an intertitle, shaving the running time to just under eighty minutes. In that form, roughly thirty minutes shorter than the version seen in San Bernardino, he was confident enough to schedule a third preview at the Alexander Theatre in Glendale, a prominent industry showcase. Within the walls of this atmospheric Grecian garden, he would unveil *The General* before the most jaded of audiences. With him for the occasion would be Natalie, his parents, a smattering of pals such as Arbuckle and Cody, numerous studio personnel—Gabourie, Jennings, Bruckman, continuity girl Chrystine Francis—and, not insignificantly, Norma Talmadge and Joe Schenck, who would be getting his first look at the unlikely comedy that had cost him and his associates more than $400,000.

Anticipation was palpable in part because a dramatic photo of the Texas, lying in the water at Culp Creek, had recently appeared in the Sunday *Los Angeles Times*. The curtains parted on the opening title:

Joseph M. Schenck

presents

Buster Keaton

in

"THE GENERAL"

A United Artists Production

Up on-screen came the train rolling into Marietta, Johnnie Gray proudly at the throttle, basking in the admiration of the young boys as he steps down from the cab. Not only were the early minutes charming, but owing to Keaton's passion for authenticity they had the look of a true period document. Five minutes in, with war imminent, the mood darkens as Johnnie attempts to enlist and is repeatedly rejected.

"If you lose this war," he warns them, "don't blame me."

From an eyewitness account, *The General* clicked 100 percent with the audience that night.

"Every gag in Buster's Cottage Grove comedy registered," wrote Bert Bates, a native of nearby Roseburg then working in Hollywood. "The picture has laughs galore and will set a mark for Chaplin and the rest of the top-notch comedians to shoot at. . . . When the famous bridge crash scene flickered across the screen it obtained all the thrills hoped for, and [for] the first time in many moons we witnessed an audience applauding and whooping when the Confederate army had the Union soldiers in full retreat."

At the fade, Johnnie is issued the uniform he never thought he'd get and, as Annabelle runs to him, a Confederate general gives the order: "Enlist the lieutenant."

A sergeant dips his pen and asks, "Occupation?"

Johnnie puffs his chest. "Soldier," he responds.

The audience was clapping as the lights came up, reflexively at first, and then, as the full realization of what they had just witnessed sank in, their applause intensified and grew more clamorous until Keaton found himself at the center of a thunderous ovation. Some stood, turning and facing him, and within moments the entire house had joined them, up on their feet and cheering. It was an extraordinary demonstration, virtually unheard of for a preview audience. Joe Schenck beamed and said it was undoubtedly the greatest comedy Keaton had ever made. It should earn, he predicted, a million dollars for United Artists. And with that, Buster Keaton knew beyond all doubt that he had created a masterpiece.

14

Steamboat Bill, Jr.

I N MANY WAYS, 1926 was the year of Joseph M. Schenck. His makeover of United Artists was the talk of the industry, with his own productions, up to six a year, helping fill the pipeline for the 1926–27 season. To gear up for such a schedule, he formed Art Finance Corporation to act as the nominal producer of Rudolph Valentino's *The Eagle*. Then Art Finance created Feature Productions, Inc., to function as a production entity, commencing with *The Bat*, a hugely popular melodrama, and Valentino's *Son of the Sheik*. Schenck was president of the Federal Trust and Savings Bank of Hollywood, and a director of A. P. Giannini's Bank of Italy, where he was in charge of all motion picture and theatrical loans. He was also heavily invested in real estate, including an entire neighborhood in San Diego he called Talmadge after his wife, Norma, and her sisters.

In February, Schenck arranged the sale of United Studios to Famous Players-Lasky for $1,250,000 with the intent of moving most UA production activity to the nearby Pickford-Fairbanks lot, which would be expanded accordingly. In July, a profile in the *Los Angeles Times* estimated his personal wealth at somewhere between $40 million and $50 million. In October, *Variety* issued a special "Joseph M. Schenck Number" comprised, in part, of ads and testimonials from friends and associates. "The thing that has impressed me most after over ten years' business, family, and social contact with Joe is his fairness," Buster Keaton wrote. "There is no fairer man than he in the world—and I'm sure the world, assuredly the amusement world, knows that. I have never heard him speak ill of anyone. He prefers to leave many things unsaid. I never really realized the meaning of tolerance until

I became intimately acquainted with the man whom the public knows as a twentieth century business and amusement king, but whom I know as a prince among men. . . . From the day I went into pictures, Joe Schenck has been like a father, brother, pal, and employer, all in one. He advanced me as fast as I deserved. If I ever became discouraged, he snapped me out of it."

Ironically, Keaton wrote these words at just about the time his relationship with Schenck began to unravel. A key element of the strategy to revitalize United Artists was to establish a string of branded theaters in major cities to showcase product on a pre-release basis. Douglas Fairbanks had pioneered the approach with *The Thief of Bagdad*, leasing legitimate theaters where no suitable film theaters could be found and settling in for extended runs before putting the picture into general release. Schenck envisioned twenty such theaters, and in May 1926 formed United Artists Theatre Circuit, Inc., with Sid Grauman and Lee Shubert to build six within the first twelve months. "The problem of sites is the main one that confronts us at the present moment," he told Edwin Schallert of the *Los Angeles Times*, "and I wish that it might be solved as easily everywhere as in Los Angeles."

L.A. was sprawling and not as concentrated or overbuilt as Chicago or New York, where situating a new theater, even an intimate one along the lines of Shubert's 1,600-seat Astor, would require displacing an existing structure. Wary of building new houses outside of established bright-light districts, Schenck felt he needed someone deeply experienced in both real estate and show business for the critical task of scouting sites in such diverse places as Denver and Philadelphia, and in August, while Keaton was working in Oregon, he settled on Lou Anger for the job. Apart from budgeting, Anger's involvement with *The General* had been limited, and he had delegated much of his on-site authority to Gabe Gabourie, who as production manager took on logistical responsibilities while business manager Al Gilmore attended to financial oversight and purchasing. By the time Keaton returned to Hollywood, Anger was in New York and nobody was in charge of the studio other than Keaton himself. Gabourie and Gilmore continued in their roles until October, when Schenck appointed publicist Harry Brand as Anger's replacement.

Keaton had a curious relationship with Brand, who had been with Schenck off and on since the Arbuckle days and was generally well liked. In 1925, Buster compiled an irreverent dictionary of studio personnel for private consumption, and included a wicked dig at Brand, who had worked a stretch for Los Angeles mayor Meredith Pinxton "Pinkie" Snyder and founded the Western Associated Motion Picture Advertisers Society (WAMPAS) in 1922:

> *Publicity man—Impossible person who writes reams of copy for newspapers, most of which is not printed. Member of WAMPAS with no other bad habits, is addicted to showing boss clipping that appeared in metropolitan newspapers with circulation of 150. Admits he's good, but can't prove it. Failure as newspaper man.*

Several months later, while Keaton was away shooting *Go West* in Arizona, Brand transferred to New York to organize an exploitation department for United Artists, and was replaced at the Keaton studio by a man named Don Eddy, who had been Valentino's press agent. Keaton later told Rudi Blesh it was his own suggestion that Schenck make Brand his new studio manager, but why he would do such a thing is unclear. He evidently considered Brand a lightweight, but Brand may simply have been the devil he knew, preferable to some unknown entity Schenck might bring in from the outside. Whatever the reason, Brand arrived back in Hollywood just as *Battling Butler* was looking to be the biggest hit of Keaton's career.

Of all of Buster Keaton's feature comedies, *Battling Butler* was the most conventional, a story any of a dozen leading men* could have managed, if not necessarily with the distinction and acrobatic dexterity Keaton brought to the role. Unlike his other pictures, there were no big ideas, no astonishing chases, no camera tricks to speak of. The comedy was purely situational, the plot accessible to viewers who found *Sherlock Jr.* or *Go West* more challenging than funny. And when it was let out, pre-release, to markets such as Philadelphia and San Francisco, it led all competitors. In New York, where it opened at the Capitol Theatre on August 22, it went head-to-head with *The Black Pirate* and shattered the house record for a Sunday. All the Manhattan dailies gave it a warm welcome, some offering unabashed raves.

"Not since the halcyon days of *The Navigator* has the adamant Buster Keaton appeared in as clever a slapstick comedy as *Battling Butler*," wrote Eileen Creelman in the *Sun*, echoing popular sentiment across the board. "*Go West* and *Seven Chances*, the non-smiling comedian's previous films, cannot be compared with it, and, indeed, there is no reason why they should be, for *Battling Butler* is far beyond them in cleverness, wit, and good robust fun."

---

* Charlie Ruggles, who had appeared in a handful of movies, played the part on Broadway.

Keaton on the grounds of his Italian Villa in Beverly Hills. The mansion and its pool area would later serve as a setting for Parlor, Bedroom and Bath *(1931).*

By the time of its official release on September 19, *Battling Butler* had already played a number of major cities, where it invariably opened strong, reflecting a devoted following for Keaton's work, but sustained itself in no way as dependably as comparable releases from Chaplin and Harold Lloyd, the latter typically enjoying eight- or ten-week runs to Keaton's one or two. In March 1926, Lloyd's *The Freshman* passed $2 million in rentals, an unprecedented figure for a feature comedy. *Battling Butler,* by comparison, would eventually see worldwide rentals of $749,000—a personal best for Keaton but nowhere near Lloyd's career average. Lloyd's greater popularity was also reflected in his annual income, which was estimated in a study for *Motion Picture Classic* to be $2 million, or around $40,000 a week. In the same article, Keaton's annual income was pegged at $200,000 or roughly $4,000 a week.

In August 1926, while he was shooting interiors for *The General,* Keaton's new house in Beverly Hills was being landscaped. Dozens of palm trees, rendered homeless by the widening of Wilshire Boulevard, were moved to the property. "It was a two-story mansion with five bedrooms, two additional bedrooms for the servants and a three-room apartment over the garage for the gardener and his wife, who worked as our upstairs maid," he enumerated. "This made six servants with a cook, butler, chauffeur, and governess."

He had poured $200,000 into the design and construction of the place, and was poised to spend another $100,000 furnishing it to Nat's liking. In size and formality, he indulged a passion for Italian architecture his wife had nurtured since a tour of Europe in 1920, when she and her family visited Rome, Florence, Milan, Venice, and the Lido. ("These old-world storied cities held a particularly potent charm for Natalie," her mother wrote.) And while there can be no doubt that Keaton's home of preference would have been the relatively modest one he designed and built for himself and his family on Linden Drive, he came to enjoy tricking out the Italian Villa at 1004 Hartford Way almost as much as did his wife.

"I designed some of the furniture myself—the king-sized bed that my wife wanted for her room, the fancy bed I put in mine, and a wonderful pair of high bedroom bureaus of dark oak, with a full-length mirror set between them. I had these pieces built by the carpenters at the studio."

One day, Keaton proudly walked Nicholas Schenck through the house, Schenck, of course, being Joe's younger brother, vice president and general manager of Loew's Incorporated, and a major stockholder in Buster Keaton Productions. Nick whistled admiringly as Keaton pointed out such details as the trickling water fountain in the conservatory off the main entrance, the intricate carvings fronting the stone fireplace that dominated the living room, and the imported tiles that made up the checkerboard pattern on the floor of the solarium. In the playroom, with its exposed beams, its projection booth, and its thirty-foot throw to a sliding screen that, when extended, perfectly covered the windows, he had a pool table, gaming supplies, and a hidden room that served as a Prohibition-era bar with access via the booth to a well-stocked cellar. Outdoors, four tiers of lawns, gardens, and white limestone steps formalized by Italian cypress trees descended to a Venetian-tiled swimming pool and a vast expanse of trees and wildlife beyond.

"I hope, Buster, you aren't going over your head on this place," Nick, who knew down to the penny what Keaton was clearing on an annual basis, confided in a whisper.

In December 1926, Arthur McLennan, the new publicity and advertising chief for United Artists, put out word that *The General* would have its world premiere in New York on January 1, 1927. The Capitol had been Keaton's Broadway home since *The Navigator,* and in the wake of *Battling Butler's* sizzling two-week stay, the house and its managing director, Major Edward Bowes, were happy to have it, even though Keaton was no longer releasing through Metro. The plan, however, hit a snag when three M-G-M pictures took precedence in Loew's flagship house—*Valencia,* Mae Murray's final film for the studio, which was slipped in to take advantage of an extraordinarily busy holiday season; *A Little Journey,* an unfortunately titled romance with Claire Windsor and the up-and-coming William Haines; and Clarence Brown's *Flesh and the Devil* with John Gilbert and Greta Garbo, which pulled sensationally and was promptly extended for two additional weeks, giving it the first three-week engagement in the theater's history.*

Effectively shut out of the New York market for the entire month of January, *The General* was left to languish in a no-man's-land of regional bookings. It had its world premiere—such as it was—in Tokyo on December 31, 1926, Japan having emerged from a virtual shutdown of all theaters and nonessential businesses during the illness and eventual death of Emperor Taishō. Stateside, one of the first venues to get it was the Liberty Theater in Carnegie, Oklahoma, and word came back that it landed with a thud. "Amusing," sniffed the house manager, "but not funny. Not one good laugh in the two days' showing."

Portland got the picture next, with a four-week run anticipated, followed by its London opening on January 17. *Flesh and the Devil* was extended a fourth record-breaking week at the Capitol, causing UA's McLennan to creatively point out that *The General* had already achieved a record of its own— for the longest "lobby run" at the theater. Meanwhile, the picture went up against Harold Lloyd's *The Kid Brother* in Kansas City, where the *Star* lent strong editorial support as well as two favorable reviews, and Chicago, where bad weather caused it to slip after a strong opening.

The General finally found its way into New York on February 5, 1927, after *Flesh and the Devil* was essentially forced out of the Capitol. With the mixed evidence already at hand, Schenck and the high command at UA feared it wasn't another *Battling Butler,* although at a negative cost of $415,232 it represented a greater investment. Among the first to register a public opinion was Martin Dickstein, the insightful young critic for *The Brooklyn Daily*

---

* Norma Talmadge held the top two box office records for the Capitol, and Talmadge pictures were twice held over for a second week, but never for a third.

Eagle, who reported an enthusiastic opening-day crowd. "Hardly a foot of celluloid is ground out of the camera but the stoical comedian hasn't some amazing new trick to draw out of his sleeve to the renewed pleasure of the audience. Keaton's gags appear to be spontaneous and perfectly timed, while as much cannot be said for Harold Lloyd in *The Kid Brother* at the Rialto. There is rhyme and reason to Buster's nonsense, as no one would deny if, indeed, time could be found for denial between the hysterical outbursts at the Capitol."

Dickstein's notice was knowing and generous, but it didn't take long for less satisfied voices to drown him out. "*The General* is no triumph as a comedy," judged the same Eileen Creelman who lavished such praise on *Battling Butler,* "but it does not fail as entertainment. Mr. Keaton's special admirers will probably find him funny anyway. Others may receive enough melodramatic thrills to comfort them." Significantly, Creelman classified the film a "historical drama—with comic moments" and lamented what she saw as a trend of feature comedians longing to play heroes, calling out *The Kid Brother* and Raymond Griffith's *Hands Up,* another Civil War story, as examples. "This epidemic of drama among the comedies rouses wonder as to *The Circus.* Will Charlie Chaplin attempt a serio-comic version of [the vivid German drama] *Variety* or, worse yet, *Pagliacci?*"

More withering was *Variety*'s Fred Schader, who branded *The General* an outright flop. "The story is a burlesque of a Civil War meller. It opens with what looks like a real idea, but never gets away from it for a minute. Consequently, it is overdone. . . . There are some corking gags in the picture, but as they are all a part of the chase they are overshadowed. There isn't a single bit in the picture that brings a real howl. There is a succession of mild titters. . . . *The General* is a weak entry for the deluxe houses. It is better geared for the daily change theaters, as that is about its speed."

Within the trade press, *Film Daily* was dubious while *Billboard* cheered: "Keaton's previous picture in no way begins to compare with this one. Book it in spite of cost."*

In *The New York Times,* Mordaunt Hall dismissed it as a "somewhat mirthless piece of work," and of the twelve other major papers, nine clearly agreed while another two straddled the fence. ("The camera work is good,

---

* Distribution of *The General* was hampered by the terms United Artists demanded for new releases, especially in smaller markets. Rural exhibitors frequently complained that it was difficult to make money with them, but terms improved as UA titles aged, extending their lives in the marketplace.

the settings excellent, the gags among the funniest we have seen," hedged the *Telegraph,* "and yet the piece lacks life.") The *Evening Post* stood alone among New York dailies in suggesting it had "a quaint air of quiet thoughtfulness about it which seems to reflect very accurately the attitude and personality of the comedian himself . . . the humor is seldom obvious and never boisterous—an undercurrent rather than a wave of laughter . . . probably lots of people, used to the something-funny-every-second school of comedy, will not think it funny at all."

From his perch across the East River, Martin Dickstein, who endorsed the *Post*'s summary, reacted with astonishment:

Such uncommon comedians as Chaplin and Keaton do not fashion their humor for the delectation of the zanies who must have that humor plastered in custard patties across the screen or driven home with the aid of a pile driver. Buster has made a financial faux pas, perhaps, by preferring to aim *The General* at the lofty-browed minority rather than at the more numerous minds which, for want of a better simile, may be compared to those of taxi drivers. He has, however, demonstrated that he is a facile comedian who prefers to gambol above the heads of sheep rather than to squat upon his haunches and sheer them of their fleece. The idea of *The General* was, in itself, a brilliant one. Few among our more important screen comedians could have visualized the possibilities for humor which lay in that Civil War episode where ten Union soldiers made their way into Confederate territory and kidnapped a locomotive from the soldiers of General Lee. . . . It required no little ingenuity to infuse humor and suspense into a narrative which was necessarily limited in scope to the single-track system of the old Western and Atlantic road through Georgia. . . . These territorial limitations, of course, did not permit Buster to hang hazardously from lofty window ledges, nor did it afford him opportunity to be dragged in the dust while he clung desperately to a horse's tail. I have seen these things done on other screens and invariably they have elicited long and noisy laughter. But Keaton very snootily has proved himself to be above such low business, for which, apparently, he has failed to win the approval of the critical ladies and gentlemen who write about the cinema for the newspapers. However, if you like comedy that is not too painfully obvious, and if you can ascertain a subtle bit of humor without sitting down to mull over it for an hour or two, I give you *The General*—a comedy for the exclusive enjoyment of the matured senses.

Keaton rarely spoke of the critical drubbing he took for *The General*, in part, he said, because he never paid much attention to reviews. "I hadn't because I'd been reading house notices since I was born, and was used to that. This critic likes you and this one don't, so that's that." Typically, he threw himself into his work, having started a new picture, and was deeply immersed in shooting it when the worst of the notices were published. Still, Bob Sherwood's scolding in *Life* must have been particularly wounding, given that Keaton considered him a friend and faithful advocate.

"It is difficult," Sherwood wrote, "to derive laughter from the sight of men being killed in battle. Many of [Keaton's] gags at the end of the picture are in such gruesomely bad taste that the sympathetic spectator is inclined to look the other way."

There had, of course, been other war comedies, most notably Chaplin's *Shoulder Arms* and, more recently, Paramount's *Behind the Front*, but none that had so frankly exploited the horrors of war in the service of comedy.

"Well, he was a little sensitive about that," Keaton allowed. "Because you've had to kill people in comedies. You've done that for years. But as a rule, if we could help it, we didn't." For Keaton, the timing was problematic in that *The General* appeared when the biggest hit of the era was M-G-M's grueling wartime tragedy *The Big Parade*, a near-flawless rendering of the American experience in France that Sherwood immediately felt could be "ranked among the few genuinely great achievements of the screen." The picture was in its sixty-fifth week at the Astor Theatre on Times Square when *The General* was grudgingly afforded its solitary week at the Capitol, and undoubtedly its impact rewired the brains of reviewers and moviegoers alike in terms of what they would tolerate in future depictions of war on the screen. One of *The Big Parade*'s signature sequences portrayed an American advance on enemy positions in a forest, a tense rhythmic march in which soldiers seeing their first action are methodically picked off by German sniper fire. While hardly flippant, Keaton's movie nonetheless caught audiences at a time when they were in no mood to laugh at a scene of a Union sniper targeting rebel soldiers as Johnnie Gray attempts to direct their cannon fire.

The returns at the Capitol weren't dismal, but neither did they soar to the level of *The Navigator* or *Battling Butler*. *The General* finished the week respectably enough with a gross of $51,000 and wasn't held over, while *Butler,* which finished its comparable week at $57,600, was. All the bad luck coming Keaton's way may have persuaded Joe Schenck that a gala premiere was in order when *The General* reached Los Angeles. The venue was Sid Grauman's 3,600-seat Metropolitan, the largest movie palace in the city, and the opening was set for Friday, March 11, with more than fifty picture personalities in attendance, headed by a contingent of United Artists stars that included Keaton and Marion Mack, Norma and Constance Talmadge, Estelle Taylor, and John Barrymore. Heralded by sun arcs and banks of Klieg lights illuminating the theater's Sixth Street entrance, as well as a performance by the 160th Infantry Band of the California National Guard, the film packed the theater "to within an inch from the roof." According to the *Los Angeles Evening Herald,* "uproarious applause" greeted every appearance Keaton made on-screen, and "torrents of laughter" flowed without interruption. "Buster was in the audience last night along with a number of other film celebrities and he received an ovation that must certainly have inspired one of those rare smiles that optimistic fans have as yet failed to see."

Katherine Lipke's lukewarm notice in the Saturday *Times,* headlined "COMEDY IS LOST IN WAR INCIDENTS," was countered by young Louise Leung's perceptive review in the *Los Angeles Record:* "*The General,* especially recommended to theatergoers by Frank Newman, manager of the Metropolitan, indeed is the quintessence of modern movie comedy, renovated and enhanced at every possible turn until virtually the entire slapstick order had been eliminated in favor of a coherent, fast-moving series of mishaps that keep the audience in a state of suspense and laughter until the end. . . . The picture must take its place as one of the best examples of modern comedy construction."

Slipped to Grauman on a flat $5,000 rental, *The General* endured a disappointing week at the Metropolitan, where it grossed about $25,000 and was outperformed by *Slide, Kelly, Slide,* a routine baseball picture, at the much smaller Loew's State. Actress Louise Brooks thought something more basic than the film's quality was at fault, and remembered hearing nothing about the picture prior to its opening. "It was the title *The General,*" she wrote in a 1968 letter to Kevin Brownlow. "We thought Buster was playing a general, a Southern general. Not funny. As an Englishman, you cannot understand that the Civil War killed thousands of Americans fighting against their own families, almost wrecking our country. Nobody connected *The General* with the name of an engine. Many people stayed away. Those who saw *The General* were puzzled."

Once word got around as to what to expect, audiences became more accepting of the picture. Bookings increased in small markets, which had been unusually resistant to it compared to other United Artists releases, such as *The Winning of Barbara Worth* and Mary Pickford's *Sparrows*. A manager in Gunnison, Colorado, actually reported good business and positive comments. "Think it the best Keaton since *Go West*," he wrote. "Sorry we played it during our dull season." Up in Toronto, *The General* was a surprise hit, drawing better than *The Kid Brother*, which was pulled after three lackluster weeks.

There is evidence *The General* had staying power beyond Keaton's other UA features, with more prints in circulation and domestic bookings extending well into 1929. Ultimately, it would log rentals in the United States and Canada of $486,465. Adding in likely foreign rentals in markets such as England, Germany, Italy, and the Far East, worldwide projections easily surpass $800,000, making *The General*, contrary to popular belief, Keaton's highest-grossing feature yet. In 1962, it was a runner-up in *Sight & Sound*'s decennial critics' poll of the greatest films of all time, and in 1972, fifty-five years after its release, it entered the top ten, placing it in the company of *Citizen Kane, Battleship Potemkin,* and *Wild Strawberries*. And in 1989, when the National Film Registry of "culturally, historically or aesthetically significant" motion pictures was established, the Librarian of Congress selected *The General* as one of the first twenty-five titles to be enrolled, along with such other American treasures as *Casablanca, Gone With the Wind, The Maltese Falcon,* and *The Wizard of Oz*.

The General closed at the Capitol on February 11, 1927, and the picture that followed it into the massive theater was M-G-M's *The Red Mill*, a lavish Cosmopolitan production starring Marion Davies. Had he noticed, Buster Keaton would have appreciated the symmetry of having one film bookend the other, for *The Red Mill*, an "A" picture by any measure, was directed by Roscoe Arbuckle.

Keaton himself had brokered the assignment, his pal Roscoe having hit another dry spell after marrying actress Doris Deane, his longtime paramour, in May 1925. (Buster served as best man, Natalie matron of honor.) Early in 1926, while *Battling Butler* was in the works, he drove out to Davies' Santa Monica beach house, took her aside, and pitched the idea.

"Marion sold the idea to [publisher William Randolph] Hearst [who founded Cosmopolitan to produce her pictures]. I think it helped that

Hearst had never believed what his newspapers had printed about Roscoe during his trouble. Once I heard him say he had sold more newspapers with that story than he had on the sinking of the *Lusitania*."

Arbuckle was announced to the trade as the director of *The Red Mill* in March 1926, and he and his wife and the Keatons took a drive north into Yosemite National Park in Roscoe's new Lincoln phaeton to celebrate. The trip didn't go well; they were waved past road repairs being made by convict labor and ran afoul of a state regulation prohibiting women from passing prison work camps. Barred from park roads for fourteen days, Keaton had to charter a train to get them and the car out of the valley. Davies, meanwhile, was wavering on her commitment to the source material, a 1906 Victor Herbert operetta that meant another costume picture tailored to Hearst's tastes rather than the public's. In the end, she went ahead with it, counting on Arbuckle's comedy instincts to get them through it.

Freed from the tensions Peg Talmadge brought to the making of *Sherlock Jr.,* Arbuckle ran a more relaxed and efficient set. Still, Hearst prevailed upon King Vidor, director of *The Big Parade,* to visit regularly and keep an eye on Arbuckle's progress. "But then they didn't like the rushes," said Marion Davies, "so they put George Hill on. Then they didn't like George Hill's work, and they put Eddie Mannix on. And Eddie got fired. That picture had so many directors I can't remember all their names." When filming stretched into a third month, Vidor and unit manager Ulrich Busch were brought on to shoot crowd scenes and minor interiors, reportedly leaving the few remaining scenes with Marion Davies to Arbuckle.

The results weren't well received. *Variety*'s Sid Silverman memorably described *The Red Mill* as "an idiotic screen morsel substantiating the contention that the average intellect of a picture audience parallels an eleven or thirteen year-old youngster." He added: "The Capitol is evidently suffering a reaction from *Flesh and the Devil*. That one lingered four weeks and was doing well enough to have remained another. Then came *The General* and now *The Red Mill*. . . . The adults were up to the neck with boredom, and the morale won't be any different no matter where this one plays."

Prior to the release of *The Red Mill,* Arbuckle landed another assignment, capably directing Eddie Cantor in *Special Delivery* for Famous Players. Yet nothing further came of these two, and with the completion of the Cantor picture, he returned to vaudeville and, briefly, enjoyed a run on Broadway in a revival of *Baby Mine* with Humphrey Bogart and Lee Patrick in support.

.   .   .

As Buster Keaton approached his second picture for United Artists, he was faced with an almost complete shift in his team of writers. Paul Gerard Smith quarreled with him in Cottage Grove and returned to stage work in New York City. Clyde Bruckman went back to Monty Banks, for whom he would direct the comedian's next feature. Al Boasberg asked for his release to take a vacation and get married. And Charles Smith moved on, writing *Naughty Nanette* for Viola Dana, among others. With Lou Anger in New York and Joe Schenck assuming even greater responsibilities with the November 1926 death of UA president Hiram Abrams, Keaton must have felt somewhat adrift, even as he had an idea for his next movie at the ready.

College pictures were in vogue. Mostly comedies or light romances, they radiated youthful energy and beauty, and served as sparkling showcases for new contract talent. More Americans than ever were attending colleges and universities, enrollment having risen 84 percent over the previous decade. Recent film hits included *The Plastic Age, Brown of Harvard, The Campus Flirt,* and *The Quarterback.* A series of two-reelers for Universal, *The Collegians,* was so popular it was extended into a second season. Most successful of all, of course, was *The Freshman,* which ideally suited Harold Lloyd's eager beaver and staked out territory to which Chaplin could never aspire. For Keaton, a college setting offered myriad opportunities for physical comedy, athletics alone suiting him and his unique style of slapstick better than any of his contemporaries. Moreover, a Keaton picture set on a college campus would virtually write itself.

With *The General* essentially finished, Keaton began assembling a new staff to help flesh out a story. In no particular order, he picked up Carl Harbaugh, a journeyman writer with a range of credits, most recently with Hal Roach and Mack Sennett, and Bryan Foy, one of the Seven Little Foys of vaudeville fame who occasionally wrote and directed short comedies. Neither man was of much use to him, particularly Harbaugh.

"He didn't write nothing," Keaton complained. "He was one of the most useless men I ever had on the scenario department. He wasn't a good gagman; he wasn't a good title writer; he wasn't a good story constructionist."

Foy, who would go on to become a producer at Warner Bros., couldn't have been much better. Still, as Keaton reasoned, "we had to put somebody's name up that wrote 'em."

Around the same time, he took on a director named James W. Horne, whose essential background was in making serials, initially for Kalem, later on a freelance basis. Horne was skilled at grinding out footage on a tight schedule, a valuable quality in the mechanical world of chapter plays, where a single project might equal the length of three or four normal features, but of little advantage to Keaton, who adhered to only the vaguest of schedules.

A clash between Keaton and Horne was inevitable, given the instinctive way Keaton developed and refined a scene. Keaton, in fact, found Horne to be "absolutely useless" on the picture, which soon acquired the utilitarian title *College*. "Harry Brand got me to use him for *College*.* He hadn't done very many important—no important—pictures that I remember, only some quickies and incidental things. I don't know why [I used him], as I did practically [all of] *College* anyway. It didn't make any difference to me."

Lacking the support of a Jean Havez or a Clyde Bruckman—his two favorite collaborators—Keaton was effectively left to write and direct *College* by himself. In casting the picture, he knew he would need certain types no matter which direction the story took—the mother, the girlfriend, the rival, the college dean. For the girl, he settled on Anne Cornwall, a no-nonsense brunette who had been in pictures almost as long as he had, and who, at four eleven, was even an inch shorter than Virginia Fox. The part of the mother went to veteran stage and screen actress Florence Turner, arguably the movies' first genuine star, while Snitz Edwards returned to the Keaton studio in the role of the dean. For Jeff Brown, his student rival, Keaton wanted someone who was physically imposing as well as good-looking, and chose Harold Goodwin, who was six two, after a perfunctory interview.

"I was called over to the studio," the actor remembered, "and they said, 'This is Mr. Keaton.' He says, 'Do you play ball?' I said, 'Yeah, I used to play at school.' He says, 'You'll do.'"

Filming began in Los Angeles on January 14, 1927, with the original UCLA campus on Vermont Avenue standing in for the fictional Clayton College. Buster is Ronald, a bookish high school student who is proclaimed "our most brilliant scholar" as he receives his diploma and an honor medal. He is then invited to speak to the graduating class on the subject of "The Curse of Athletics" while his cheap woolen suit shrinks from having been drenched in a rainstorm. Outside, Mary Haynes (Cornwall) angrily delivers a lecture of her own. "Your speech was ridiculous," she tells him, rain

---

* Brand may have been impressed by Horne's work on *The Cruise of the Jasper B*, a snappy farce that incorporated elements of both *Seven Chances* and *The Navigator*.

pouring on them both. "Anyone prefers an athlete to a weak-knee'd teachers' pet." She then delivers the traditional Keaton ultimatum that typically sets the action in motion at the end of the first reel: "When you change your mind about athletics, then I'll change my mind about you."

The rest of the picture is Ronald attempting to prove himself to her, tackling with astounding ineptitude almost every athletic endeavor the school can offer—baseball, track, shot put, discus, javelin throw, high jump, sprint hurdles, hammer throw, pole vault. James Horne was on hand throughout these episodes, most of which were staged on the USC campus or nearby in the Memorial Coliseum, but he really couldn't contribute as Keaton painstakingly worked out the physical business suggested by the trappings and traditions of each event.

"Jimmy Horne—he was probably one of the worst directors in the business," said Harold Goodwin, a veteran of more than fifty films by then, "but Buster had him standing by to direct scenes that didn't mean much. Buster directed most of the show."

While Horne never got in the way, the innocuous Harry Brand was suddenly eager to show Joe Schenck he was up to the job of managing the studio. Brand was always an easygoing sort, famous for his wisecracks and practical jokes. "But once he was on the job he suddenly turned serious," said Keaton. "He was grim. He was watching the dailies—how much is spent on this, how much is spent on that? He worries, he frets, he begins losing sleep. He felt he had to do something, like a guy who has to tear down a car that's running perfectly."

Harold Goodwin recounted a day Brand felt compelled to assert himself: "Well, Snitz Edwards, who played the college dean, was getting $500 a week. I think I was getting $300. Grant Withers was on it and he was getting $200. None of us made much money, but it was a lot of money in those days. And we had one closed stage, and we had an open stage, and we played ball, softball, on this open stage. So, Harry Brand wanted to show his authority and he said to Buster, 'I'd like to get Snitz Edwards off salary.' Buster didn't say a word, he just went to the crew and said, 'Come on, we're going to play ball for two or three days.' And we did. Harry Brand never came back on the set again."

College was a relatively simple picture to shoot—no big set pieces or mechanical effects—but a lot of the action was set out of doors, and it was filmed during the rainy season in Southern California. The opening scenes with Florence Turner were staged in Glendale in a driving rain, but once the

Filming College *on the water at Newport Bay, April 1927.*

interiors had all been made there was nowhere else to go. As in the old days, Keaton would retreat to his dressing room and play cards with the crew, but he typically got itchy after a day or two.

Keaton called on his father to round up a few faces for the new picture. Joe was tickled with the assignment, because he knew a lot of old-timers who would be grateful for a few days' work. He remembered all their names, of course, but didn't have their addresses at hand. So he turned his car over to a guy at the Continental Hotel with instructions to hit all the booking offices and check the registers for "the boys." The result was that fourteen semi-retireds got much-needed jobs. About the same time, a wistful item on "fine old couples" appeared in Nellie Revell's column in *Variety*. She lamented that Harry and Rose Langdon were no longer together, Harry, now a big star, having taken up residence at the Hollywood Athletic Club. "But what caused a really big lump to rise in my throat was the news that Joe and Myra Keaton are no longer sharing the same address. Myra, Louise, and Jingles occupy the handsome home provided by Buster, but Joe lives at a hotel. It is especially poignant when one thinks that now, after so many years of shared vicissitudes, they could be living together with everything they want. And that they are not doing so. But Joe hasn't had a drink for four years."

The highlight of *College* was to be an intramural rowing competition in which Ronald, as the team's unlikely coxswain, manages to save the day when the rudder comes off the boat during the big race. Keaton selected Newport Beach, fifty miles southeast of the studio, as the location for the sequence, having previously filmed there for *The Scarecrow, The Boat,* and *Sherlock Jr.* Specifically, Newport Bay would be the scene of the race, with the landmark Balboa Pavilion, slightly altered, providing a festive backdrop. Keaton gave Harry Brand the job of recruiting sixteen experienced oarsmen, all to work under the direction of Ben Wallis, former coach of the University of California racing crew, while Gabe Gabourie was tasked with rounding up—or having fabricated—six racing shells for the competition. A company of forty-five arrived at Balboa on March 24, some putting up at the Southern Seas Club on the bay front, which would also be feeding the crew, while Buster, Nat, and sister Dutch secured a cottage for the duration of the shoot. Lack of sunshine delayed the start of filming several days, and production stretched into the middle of April, as working on water was always slow going.

Among those Keaton had with him on location was actor William Collier, Jr., a close friend who was also known as Buster, and who was godfather to Keaton's older son. "I worked with Keaton on—not all of his stunts, but a few of his stunts each year that were dangerous," Collier recalled, "and he relied upon me because he wanted to be sure nobody was kidding around. There were always some comedians off screen, you know. And he relied upon me to calm everything down and to get it done, get it right, get him alive. . . . He'd have a water scene, and there were some very dangerous tides. [It was] very badly organized for safety. Nobody else seemed to care about anything but having a good time."

Ronald has triumphed, having tied the rudder to his waist and lowered himself into the water in order to steer the craft to victory. He's alone in the crew's bathhouse when the phone on the wall rings and it's Mary pleading for help. A jealous Jeff, having been expelled, has locked himself in her dorm room so that she'll be expelled along with him. The threat of rape hangs in the air, and the dire circumstances bring the true athlete out in Ronald as he races to her rescue, clearing hedge after hedge and literally pole-vaulting into her room through a second-story window.

For this shot, Keaton faced a dilemma: shut down production in order to master the feat himself, or break a career-long policy of never using a stunt-man. For a comedian, this wasn't a matter of pride or machismo so much as practicality—the professional men and women who did stunts for the screen were able enough but, generally speaking, they weren't funny. "We knew from bitter experience in the old days that stuntmen don't get you laughs. That's why we did most of them ourselves." Thinking it over, Keaton opted to keep the picture moving and sent for USC's Lee Barnes, Olympic gold medalist in the 1924 Paris games, to do the stunt instead.

"I could not do the scene myself because I'm no pole vaulter and I didn't want to spend months in training to do the stunt myself."

Once inside the room, face-to-face with Jeff, Ronald furiously starts pelting his adversary with whatever is at hand—cups and dishes, books, a bust he sends crashing through a window. It's a replay of the fight scene from *Battling Butler*, the character seething with anger, the violence desperate and ragged. As real and as unstaged as it seems, Harold Goodwin remembered a lot of trial and error in getting it right. "We'd make five attempts at the thing and then put a number on it. It was in the college dormitory and Buster's supposed to kick this ball up against the door and it's supposed to come back and hit me in the head. Well, we did that about seventy-five times, and then we abandoned that. Then, in the end, when he catches me in the room with a girl, the ball rolls through the window. I was supposed to start throwing things at him, and he takes this canoe paddle and he's supposed to bat this thing back and hit me, and I go out the window. Well now, he could have done it in cuts, but he wanted you to *see* what the hell is happening. Well, we finally had to abandon *that*. Finally, Buster said, 'If one comes close, just step back and crawl through the window.' So that's the way we got it."

College finished in mid-May after four months before the cameras, and Keaton launched into preparations for his next picture without a break.

The impetus for the film that became *Steamboat Bill, Jr.* came from director Charles F. "Chuck" Reisner, a monologist and song-and-dance man in vaudeville who made the leap to pictures by way of the scenario department at Keystone. In 1918 he joined Chaplin, first as an actor, then as gagman and assistant director, eventually directing Syd Chaplin in five of his feature comedies, including *The Better 'Ole* (1926).

"Chuck's story," as Keaton remembered it, "opened with a rugged old Mississippi steamboat captain reading a letter from his wife. They had a quarrel twenty years before, just after their only child was born. She returned with the baby to her hometown in New England. The letter explains that their baby, now a fully-grown man, is on his way to see his father for the first time. He will arrive by train on Sunday and will wear a white carnation so his father will recognize him. But the Sunday I arrive is Mother's Day, and every man on the train is wearing a white carnation in his buttonhole. Hopefully, my father, Steamboat Bill, approaches one muscular youth after another. But he doesn't find me until the train pulls out because I got off the train on the wrong side. He takes one look at me and groans. I have on a beret and plus fours. I have a ukulele under my arm and a 'baseball moustache,' so called because it has nine hairs on each side. . . . With this for a start, all we needed to get the story rolling and churning was a wealthy menace with a pretty daughter."

For the role of the father, William Canfield, a.k.a. Steamboat Bill, Keaton recruited Ernest Torrence, six foot four, a star heavy in pictures with the face of a battered prizefighter. Torrence's roles ranged from the king of the beggars in *The Hunchback of Notre Dame* to Captain Hook in *Peter Pan.* The wealthy menace, in the person of actor Tom McGuire, became a rival steamboat owner, J. J. King, president of the River Junction Bank and proprietor of the local hotel. ("This floating palace should put an end to that 'thing' Steamboat Bill is running," he boasts.) And Keaton discovered actress Marion Byron, all of seventeen, in the *Hollywood Music Box Revue,* where she played a memorable bit as a child in a sketch with Fannie Brice.

"Miss Byron has never worked before a camera," he said, "but she is a human dynamo and just the right height. In fact, she comes about even with my ears—when she has on high-heeled shoes."

Keaton collaborated on the story with Reisner, who was engaged to direct the picture, while cutting *College* for a July release. Harry Brand, meanwhile, ever eager to justify his existence, appointed Carl Harbaugh, presumably serving out a year's contract, chief of the studio's scenario department "in recognition of his work on the latest Keaton production." By July, Keaton and Reisner were far enough along to make a scouting trip to Sacramento, the state capital, where the winding Sacramento River had previously served as the Yangtze for a Richard Dix epic titled *Shanghai Bound* and the Volga for Cecil B. DeMille's *The Volga Boatman*. Earlier still, portions of James Cruze's *The Pony Express* were filmed there. Accompanied by Brand, Harbaugh, and Gabourie, they cruised the river, confirming it would stand in nicely for the Mississippi, with room to construct the entire town of River Junction on the west bank near its confluence with the American River.

Within days, a huge exterior set was under construction, the King Hotel and thirty-three other buildings lining two fully macadamized boulevards complete with concrete sidewalks, outdoor lighting, and a pair of wharves jutting out into the water. At a cost of around $50,000, River Junction would serve as the backdrop for most of the action in *Steamboat Bill, Jr.*, and then, in a spectacular climax, it would be destroyed by torrential rains and a devastating flood. With typical efficiency, Gabourie and his on-site foreman, Lloyd Brierley, along with 150 local workers and craftsmen, were aiming to have it all fabricated within a couple of weeks so that filming could begin there on July 20. Then portions of the town would be reconstructed a few miles away for the flood scenes in the Sacramento's slow-moving waters. In all, Brierley estimated, 200,000 board feet of lumber would go into the job.

With the town taking shape, a call went out for hundreds of extras, causing the local chamber of commerce to process more than two thousand applicants in the space of a couple of days. A reporter from *The Sacramento Bee* observed "pretty young girls—lots of them—lured by the chance to appear before the camera. There were matrons and mothers with babes in arms, youths, laboring men, well-dressed men, stout men and women and lean men and women. There were a few Negroes too, for these also will be required." The chamber was informed that as many as a thousand people would be needed for some scenes "and that well-dressed men and women and girls and boys are especially in demand." The Keaton company was expected to pay out an estimated $100,000 in wages in just six weeks.

Production started on July 18 when the company filmed Willie's arrival from Boston at the village of Freeport, on the eastern bank of the Sacramento. The old station had been scrubbed and painted for the occasion, and a train from the Southern Pacific, loaded with a hundred extras, was repainted to represent the fictional Southern Railroad. The making of exteriors at River Junction began two days later with the dedication of King's gleaming new boat, hundreds of spectators and celebrants crowding around, while Steamboat Bill watches sourly from the bridge of the aging *Stonewall Jackson.*

"We're having a wonderful time," Keaton told Kay Lane, a feature writer for *The Sacramento Union.* "I always have a good time here. Oh yes, I've been here several times before. That river is great to fish in. We used to start out of here on hunting trips up in the mountains. I'm going again, too, if I ever get time away from the grind."

Joe Keaton, who came up ahead of the company to get away from the city, seconded his son's assessment of the fishing. "I've fished in that river many times," he said. "I've caught lots of bass in there. I fished in that river when the Panic was on and food was scarce."

Leaving the subject of fishing to the Keatons, Dev Jennings praised the river as a photographic subject. "The light here is great, strong, good light," he said. "The color of the river is okay. We're using panchromatic stock, [which] photographs color backgrounds better than ordinary film. This is a good place to shoot pictures."

Buster added: "There's only one thing wrong with your town. I've had a terrible time rounding up bridge players. If you have anybody over there on the *Union* that plays bridge, bring 'em around this evening, or any evening."

Work had scarcely begun when a distraction presented itself in the form of a plagiarism suit filed in federal court against Buster Keaton Productions by the widow of William Pittenger, author of *The Great Locomotive Chase.* In a statement to *The Sacramento Bee,* Keaton dismissed the suit as groundless. "We obtained our source material from the United States War Department records of the Civil War," he said, "and did not use Pittenger's story. He also told the story as a participant in the incident, while we took an entirely different point of view. Investigation has disclosed that the story of the same incident has been written by at least two other participants in the adventure entirely independent of Pittenger's story. We have as much right to use the incident as the basis of a story as two separate authors have the same right to use the World War as plots for stories."

Chuck Reisner turned out to be a good match for Keaton as director of *Steamboat Bill, Jr.* Eight years his senior, Reisner took to referring to his star as "little Buster," his memories of The Three Keatons from his own vaudeville years being so indelible. Reisner traveled to Sacramento with his wife, Miriam, and son, Dean, age nine, who was off from school for the summer.

"They had this great old riverboat," Dean Reisner remembered, "and we all used to fish off the side of it all the time—catching catfish. I remember Buster took a pole one day, and all of a sudden he caught the goddamnedst fish you ever saw. He was fighting it and passing the pole over people and saying, 'Excuse me.' And finally he pulled it up and it was a prop fish that he had."

With Reisner on the job, Keaton was able to make himself available to the press in a way he couldn't during the making of *The General* or *College*. "I'm sort of a long-lost son," he said in giving a reporter for the *Bee* an idea of what the picture was about, "and Ernest is the dad. In fact, we contemplated naming the picture *The Long-Lost Son,* although at present time we have the title *Steamboat Bill.* That's the interesting thing about comedies. You never can tell how they are going to turn out or what they will be named until after they have been finished. Comedies are different from dramas. The detail has to be worked out as the filming of the story progresses. When we get stuck we employ the 'huddle system.' What's that? Why that's what we were doing just a moment ago. We all get our heads together like a bunch of college boys taking football signals. Then we figure out what will come next—whether we will burn up the town or save the heroine."

As was her habit, Natalie Keaton was on location with her husband, but she kept such a low profile she was scarcely noticed. A woman from the *Bee* pursued her for several days, trying to land an interview, but never seemed to be able to get her attention. Finally, Louise Keaton, there to act as script girl and stunt double for Marion Byron, stepped in. Described as "a mannish young person clad in a bathing suit, overalls, and eye-shades," Louise explained that Mrs. Keaton was painfully shy around reporters but that she could and would respond for her: "Although Mrs. Keaton finds Sacramento most charming in every way, most of her thoughts are with her two small boys at home. They are Joseph, aged five, a young Buster, and Bobby, three, who resembles the Talmadge family, of which Mrs. Keaton is the youngest [*sic*] sister."

Buster seemed to enjoy Nat's presence on the set, and she was predictably there, sitting and knitting, every morning at eight thirty. She was also there one afternoon when, while playing a local ball team, Buster removed his catcher's mask in the eighth inning and a few minutes later was pasted by a fast ball, breaking his nose. Still, he was able to keep working, and by August the set was inundated with sightseers from all parts of central California, so many, in fact, they were forced to rope off the camera area.

. . .

College opened at the Metropolitan Theatre in Los Angeles on July 29, drawing a tepid response from Marquis Busby in the *Times*: "While *College* will undoubtedly prove a more popular vehicle for the frozen-faced comedian than *The General*, I am not so sure it is a better picture. *The General* at least had some thrills, but *College* is not particularly exciting. . . . With Buster Keaton the picture passes as mildly entertaining, without him it would be terrible." *College,* paired with madcap bandleader Rube Wolf and a strong Fanchon and Marco prologue, grossed nearly $30,000 for the week, an exceptional performance considering there was a seasonal spell of hot weather. Keaton was still on location in Sacramento when the film came to the Senator Theatre in mid-August, and he took his entire company to see it. Up came the opening title, which then dissolved into the following:

Directed by
JAMES W. HORNE
Story by
CARL HARBAUGH and BRYAN FOY
Supervised by
HARRY BRAND

"I all but jumped out of my seat," he said. "It had gone into the prints after I had okayed the sample. It had been done quietly and with Schenck's permission. The prints—two hundred and fifty of them—were all distributed. The thing couldn't be changed." He was still fuming over Harry Brand's interference when Brand, who insisted on being present on location, objected to Willie being sent into a haberdasher's store for some "working clothes for the boat," only to emerge in a perfectly tailored naval uniform and cap rather than a broadly funny outfit one would naturally expect in a comedy. Chuck Reisner tried to explain:

"Prior to outfitting Keaton in that uniform we had built an unsightly river dock, an old side-wheeler of Civil War vintage, an aging captain, rough, gruff, and tough, and his motley, unkempt, hard-boiled crew completing the picture. And that scene was built and cast that way in order to realize fully upon the contrast Buster would create when he arrived there. But my analysis of the possibility of more and bigger laughs when Buster arrived at that unsightly boat and dock in a neat uniform got me nowhere. The only thing that saved the situation was the fact that we would have to take time off to have a comedy uniform made, and that meant a half day or more lost and an added production cost of probably five thousand dollars or more."

With the remade titles for *College,* the same Harry Brand managed to imply to the world that Buster Keaton was under his personal supervision.

"Now perhaps it sounds like conceit on my part," Keaton allowed, rehashing the incident twenty-five years later. "But besides my own feelings, there were two things. One was the question of interference. A bad thing to get started. The other thing was, the public was already beginning to laugh at this stupid supervisor deal, which had then been going on in Hollywood for about six months. 'Supervisor' was only a job maker, a nothing job, just a title—but it *did* get a guy's name on the screen. Anger never bothered with screen credit. He knew his job and did it."

Rather than rail at Brand or go off and play baseball, Keaton reserved his ire for Joe Schenck. A week later, Schenck arrived in Sacramento, where he toured the River Junction set and huddled privately with his star. Keaton complained about the credit for Brand and the fact that it had been added behind his back. Schenck countered that supervisors were part of an emerging system in the industry, and that he had started giving twenty-eight-year-old John Considine, Jr., a supervisor credit on many of his own productions.

Keaton was unmoved. "There'll be no more supervisors in pictures Buster Keaton makes," he declared. And that was when Schenck told him that Buster Keaton wasn't going to be making any more pictures.

15

Giving In

CLEARLY THE INVESTORS WANTED OUT. The decision had already been made, but to Buster Keaton, immersed in the making of a film, it came as a complete surprise. "So many times I've thought it over," he reflected in the mid-1950s. "Hell, I knew I was a money-maker. And not a big spender. Why, Christ, my pix cost a couple of hundred grand— Fairbanks couldn't make one under a million. It wasn't that." The stockholders of Buster Keaton Productions, Inc., had committed to six pictures for United Artists, yet they were calling it quits after just three. It occurred to Keaton that Joe Schenck, who was still an independent in an age of consolidation, was being squeezed.

"He was too big to knock down, but maybe his brother Nick at M-G-M said, 'Look, Joe, it's hurting the business.' Could be." But not likely— Schenck was one of ten stockholders in Keaton Productions, albeit the managing partner, and he still had big plans for United Artists. While he never explained his reasoning, possibilities present themselves when considering the timing and the justifications that later came out.

The triggering event appears to be the expiration of Keaton's contract. At the completion of *Steamboat Bill, Jr.,* his agreement of September 9, 1924, would be up, and if they wanted to continue, all that Schenck had to do was negotiate a new one. United Artists, however, wasn't reimbursing production costs on the Keaton features; the stockholders of Buster Keaton Productions were on the hook for the entire outlay. After six months in release, *The General* was still inching its way through the market, and it was uncertain whether it would ever break even, much less turn a profit. And although *College* was considerably cheaper to make, its commercial and critical success in New York were anything but assured. Moreover, Keaton was back to spending on the same approximate level as *The General* with the new picture, seemingly unable to work consistently within the $300,000 range anticipated when the 1924 contract was signed.

Keaton always stressed that successful comedies, by their very nature, took longer and cost more to make. "Take any program feature-length picture," he said, "I mean your standard stars such as Gloria Swanson, Norma Talmadge, Rudolph Valentino—not Doug Fairbanks doing *Robin Hood* or those big elaborate expensive pictures—but the average program picture. For instance, Norma Talmadge makes, with an all-star cast, *Within the Law*. The budget of *Within the Law* was $180,000. *The Navigator* with me was $220,000. Our pictures always ran almost a third more in price than the dramatic pictures."

Within the Law not only cost less than *The Navigator,* but it brought in more money—$879,323 in worldwide rentals versus $680,406 for *The Navigator*. So the risk of making a feature comedy was greater, while the return was typically no better than for a comparable drama. The Schenck brothers each owned 19⅔ percent of Keaton Productions, with Loew's executive David Bernstein accounting for another 16⅔ percent. On a profitable film with a cost approximating that of *The General,* Joe and Nick Schenck stood to make less than $20,000 apiece, Bernstein around $15,000 and change. Nobody, in other words, was getting rich on Buster Keaton features other than perhaps Keaton himself, who had his own 25 percent share of the cumulative net profits.

"You are right when you say that a lot of money has been spent on Buster Keaton," UA treasurer Arthur Kelly confided in a letter to Syd Chaplin, "but as far as Mr. Schenck is concerned, no money has been made out of his pictures. As a matter of fact, we did as well with his pictures in foreign territories as we did in the U.S."

With real estate and the stock market booming, there were easier, less risky ways of making money. And if a certain fatigue had set in among the investors, what was the exit strategy for a company formed a decade earlier to make Fatty Arbuckle shorts? One option was to simply shut it down, selling off the inventory and the studio on Lillian Way, cutting Keaton and his staff loose to fend for themselves. Another would be to sell the assets to a larger company, but this would require making a new contract with Keaton—assuming he would go along with such a plan. Here is where the later justifications provide a clue as to what may have happened.

On October 12, 1927, *Variety* published news of Buster Keaton's departure from United Artists, framed in such a way as to imply the move was being made at his own behest. The headline had him "angling" for a four-year contract, which would mark his "return" to Metro-Goldwyn-Mayer. "No reason is set forth for Keaton leaving UA," the item continued. "It may be that Chaplin felt he should be the only screen comedian to provide releases for that organization."

Joe Schenck was a father figure to Buster Keaton, older, wiser, and at five ten and a half, taller and more powerfully built than most of the other picture moguls. He had a presence and a strength of character that earned him the sobriquet "Indian Joe," and even if he wasn't acting in Buster's best interests, he wasn't about to close the company down without arranging a soft landing for the man who was married to his wife's sister and who was father to her two nephews. Keaton had come to require a certain level of income, yet Schenck knew he cared little about money. Operating on his own, he would likely fail as an independent producer. He needed a Lou Anger to keep an eye on operations, and Harry Brand lacked Anger's managerial gravitas. "His pictures have cost, it is said, around $350,000 to $500,000 for UA," *Variety* reported, "with Metro-Goldwyn figuring it can turn out a Keaton comedy for from $225,000 to $250,000."

Beginning with its release of *Three Ages* in 1923, Metro had publicized Keaton as one of its big attractions. When Metro-Goldwyn was created in 1924, and subsequently Metro-Goldwyn-Mayer, he continued to be part of their roster of stars, which had grown to include such household names as Lillian Gish, Marion Davies, Norma Shearer, Lon Chaney, and John Gilbert. So when the Keaton features stopped releasing through M-G-M in 1926, it appeared as if the studio had lost its star comedian to United Artists. A year later, M-G-M was still without a first-rank comic, while UA effectively had two—Chaplin and Keaton. Nicholas Schenck, vice president and general manager of Loew's Incorporated, who would be elected president of Loew's following the death of Marcus Loew, saw a need in the M-G-M lineup for a comedian of Keaton's stature, and with the concurrence of production chief Irving Thalberg, likely made his brother a proposition. He and Thalberg would make a place for Keaton at Metro, where a disciplined production system and organizational efficiencies would bring down the average cost of a Keaton picture. This would enable them to pay Keaton more than he could earn as an independent, and a percentage of the profits would go to Buster Keaton Productions.

Getting the stockholders to agree to such an arrangement would have been a simple matter. Collectively, the two Schenck brothers and David Bernstein owned 56 percent of Buster Keaton Productions—a controlling interest. Moreover, those owners who were also M-G-M stockholders accounted for a 51⅓ percent ownership stake. Going forward, Keaton would still generate income for the company, but without the risk of any capital.

"We loaned [Keaton] out, just like we did with Arbuckle," Leopold Friedman, one of the original shareholders, explained. "It was too much of a risk making these pictures ourselves . . . better to have Metro risk them."

The downside to it all were the conditions under which Keaton would be required to work. Ominously, *Variety* outlined these as well: "According to present plans, it is said that a deal is to be made with M-G-M whereby Keaton will make four pictures a year for that organization with all production to be made on the M-G lot instead of the Keaton studios. The plan also calls for M-G to supervise all pictures, Keaton simply to be starred and an M-G director supervising. Keaton maintained a personal staff while at his own studios, which it is understood will be disbanded should he go over to M-G."

That last condition would have been particularly vexing to Keaton, who saw relatively little turnover in his studio personnel. "His crew loved him," said Buster Collier. "Every luncheon period all the crew ate together. They'd pull the shade and everybody'd go out and spend an hour or so eating or having a drink together. It was fun. He was a very decent, well-behaved guy. Very charitable. If anybody needed anything, he'd be the first one to help out."

As Clyde Bruckman put it, "Buster was a guy you worked with—not *for*."

The discussion that day couldn't have taken much time. Joe simply told him they were shutting down the company and that Metro wanted him to come work for them. The money would be better, the opportunities greater, the audience bigger. Joe's brother Nick would be in charge and would see that Buster was given every consideration. And Thalberg, who had a brilliant story mind, would personally oversee his productions. Predictably, the news left Keaton in a state of shock. Joe, who was a businessman, not an artist, could not possibly have appreciated what taking away the studio and his independence would have meant to Keaton. In Joe's mind, he must surely have thought he was doing his best to ensure Buster's continued happiness and prosperity, yet in reality he had signed his creative death warrant.

There was something else, too. *Steamboat Bill, Jr.* was supposed to end with a spectacular flood, but as Harry Brand pointed out, the year 1927 had seen unprecedented levels of flooding along the Mississippi River, particularly in the Delta. The deadly waters killed as many as one thousand people—estimates were sketchy—and left roughly 640,000 homeless. The waters were just beginning to recede, but the devastation would remain historic in scope, covering twenty-seven thousand square miles. To appear to derive comedy from such an event would invite a backlash that would make the objections to *The General* seem trivial in comparison. Oblivious to the news, Keaton was angry that Brand had once again meddled in the creative side of the business.

"So Schenck told me, 'You can't do a flood.' I said, 'That's funny, since it seems to me that Chaplin during [the war] made a picture called *Shoulder Arms,* which was the biggest money-maker he'd made at the time.* You can't get a bigger disaster than that, and yet he made his biggest laughing picture out of it.' He said, 'Oh, that's different.' I don't know why it was different. I asked if it was all right to make a cyclone, and he agreed that was better. Now, he didn't know it, but there are four times more people killed in the United States by hurricanes and cyclones than by floods. But it was all right as long as he didn't find that out, and so I went ahead with my technical man and did the cyclone."

As Schenck left town, undoubtedly relieved to have the unpleasant business with Buster behind him, he agreeably told *The Sacramento Bee* he probably would shoot another picture in the area in the near future. "I have traveled the state over," he said, "and I am frank to say that I have found no place in California with more picturesque settings for motion pictures." Keaton, meanwhile, set out to quickly revamp the entire third act of the story to remove any hint of a flood while preserving as much of the essential action as possible. And in doing so, he sent to Los Angeles for Clyde Bruckman.

As much as Keaton hated to admit it, the cyclone turned out to be a better option in terms of the possibilities it offered, wind naturally being more cinematic than water. "And a twister could cause the same sort of destruction as a flood," he said. "Either of them could do many things our script called for: blow buildings into the river, fill the little town jail with water almost up to the ceiling, and sink the sleek craft owned by the heavy, my girl's father."

---

* *Shoulder Arms* was released less than a month before the armistice was signed.

Having the town of River Junction blown apart by winds meant that standing sets had to be built out so that their insides could be revealed. Keaton asked Gabe Gabourie how much it would cost to stage a cyclone instead of a flood. "Gabourie, a whiz at his job, said thirty-five thousand dollars. . . . It turned out that the changes we made cost slightly less than that."

They figured out, for instance, how to retain the harrowing rescues planned for the end of the picture by simply restaging them in the river, rather than having the river stand in for the flooded townsite. "The best new gag we invented [was] a breakaway hospital. We used a 120-foot crane set on a barge to pick up this whole structure, leaving only the floor."

The revised sequence opens with commendable understatement:

WEATHER CONDITIONS
Storm clouds in the offing.

Initial gusts send trash and debris rolling down the street, and J. J. King is warned the pier isn't strong enough to hold his boat. As the citizenry scatters and the storm worsens, a car is blown backward down the street, dragging the driver along with it. The corner facade of a two-story building is blown away, and the *Stonewall Jackson* is pulled from its moorings. The King's Fish Palace, a food stand, collapses. As nurses and patients flee, the hospital is blown off its foundation, revealing Willie in one of the beds, an icepack perched squarely on his head. As he grabs his hat and starts for the exit, the building behind him falls to pieces, driving him back into the safety of the bed, which is blown down the road and into a stable. He comes to a stop just long enough for the horses to regard him with benign curiosity, then another set of doors gets blown open and he is again on his way.

For a highlight, Keaton appropriated a gag he had used twice before. In the Arbuckle comedy *Back Stage,* he causes a flat to fall forward as Fatty is serenading his sweetheart while she is perched on a ladder. The window opening lands exactly where the ukulele-playing star is standing, allowing him to remain completely unaware of what has just happened. Upping the ante a bit, Keaton used the gag himself in *One Week,* this time having a two-story wood frame wall falling as the flat did and the window opening once again saving the day. But with neither stunt was there any real sense of weight—and with it danger—so neither gave the audience much of a thrill. The stakes, he realized, had to be even higher, and with whole buildings collapsing around him in *Steamboat Bill, Jr.,* he now had the perfect setup. The design of the structure was crucial, with its facade hinged at the bottom so that it would fall exactly as intended, and with its back built out to reveal rooms and furnishings.

"First I had them build the framework of this building and make sure that the hinges were all firm and solid," Keaton explained. "It was a building with a tall V-shaped roof, so that we could make this window up in the roof exceptionally high. An average second story window would be about twelve feet, but we're up about eighteen feet. Then you lay this framework down on the ground and build the window around me. We built the window so that I had a clearance of two inches on each shoulder, and the top missed my head by two inches and the bottom my heels by two inches. We mark that ground out and drive big nails where my two heels are going to be. Then you put that house back up in position while they finish building it. They put the front on, painted it, and made the jagged edge where it tore away from the main building, and then we went in and fixed the interiors so that you're looking at a house that the front has blown off. Then we put up our wind machines with the big Liberty motors. We had six of them and they are plenty powerful; they could lift a truck right off the road. Now we had to make sure that we were getting our foreground and background wind effect, but that no current ever hit the front of that building when it started to fall, because if the wind warps her she's not going to fall where we want her, and I'm standing right out front."

The rolling hospital bed Willie is riding comes to a stop in front of the house, which was built at the south end of the River Junction set. Willie takes shelter under the bed, while a man appears in the upper window and jumps to safety, landing directly on top of it. It blows away, but the impact leaves Willie momentarily dazed, and it is in this state of confusion that he faces the camera. The front of the house begins to loosen behind him, all four thousand pounds of it. Were he to fail to stand exactly where the nails had been driven, were he to move forward even slightly, he would instantly be killed.

Chuck Reisner couldn't bear to witness the scene. "My father, who was a very religious man, a Christian Scientist, had a practitioner up there," his son, Dean, remembered, "and they were praying all day because here comes this stunt and my father couldn't bear to see it. He and the practitioner were off praying in one corner and waiting to find out whether Buster came through it or not."

Keaton surveys the damage to the town of River Junction in Steamboat Bill, Jr. *(1928).*

With everything in place, the wind machines were started and the cameras began to roll film. Keaton positioned himself precisely where he was supposed to be, rubbing his neck and twisting his head as if to snap himself out of his stupor. Men positioned off camera yanked on a cable to bring the hinged edifice forward, and it landed with a resounding crash, nearly taking the star's right shoulder with it.

"Two extra women on the sidelines fainted," Keaton said in 1930, relishing the memory, "and the cameramen turned their backs as they ground out the film." The thrilling shot, destined to become one of the most memorable ever made for a movie, came off beautifully. "But it's a one-take scene and we got it that way. You don't do those things twice."

Struggling against the powerful winds on a muddy street, Willie races into them, leaps into them, and still he can make no headway. A flatbed truck rolls past, and he is inundated with its cargo of boxes. A tree he grabs onto is uprooted by the wind and blown out into the river. As he clambers aboard the *Stonewall Jackson,* he sees a house floating by with Mary clinging to its side. Springing into action, he tethers the structure using an anchor as a grappling hook and makes his way across the rope, only to have them both plunge into the waters as she clings to him. This was where Louise Keaton came in, for as a child Marion Byron had been caught in a flood in her native Ohio and was deathly afraid of water. Louise hung from her brother's neck in all but the closest shots, expertly obscuring her face, and Buster thought she could have a future in stunt work if she wanted to pursue it.

When the jail holding Willie's father breaks free of its foundation and is blown out into the river, Willie takes control of the aging steamer, ingeniously piloting it from the wheelhouse using a network of ropes hastily rigged in the engine room as if it were Ed Gray's old house back in Muskegon. He rams the sinking building, freeing the old man at the last possible moment, then leaps into the water to save J. J. King, Mary's father, as he clings to the wreckage of his floating palace, the one that was supposed to put an end to the *Stonewall Jackson*. As Mary gives him a grateful hug, he grabs a life preserver and once again leaps into the water, this time to retrieve a minister.

The company left a scene of utter desolation when it closed production in mid-September, and the banks of the Sacramento were cleared to make way for the next Hollywood production to discover the spot. Soon, they were shooting additional water footage at Newport, at first off the jetty, then in the bay that had made such a striking background for *College,* this time disguised and standing in for the Sacramento. Back at the studio, they made the relatively few interiors needed, and Keaton embellished his storm footage with a vignette set in an old theater decimated by the storm. He is beaned on the head with a sandbag, tries running into a scenery drop, encounters a creepy ventriloquist's dummy, finds himself part of a magician's illusion. He escapes the place through a doorway just as the wall collapses inward, and with it completes the final exterior to be shot in the vicinity of the Keaton studio.

It was a measure of Keaton's regard for Chuck Reisner that he agreed to a shot on the fade that he would never have tolerated from another director. "As a gagman, he was his own best," said Clyde Bruckman. "There's only one word to describe his judgment. And that's 'taste.' He never overdid it, never offended, and knew what was right for him. Chuck Reisner once argued him into smiling at the end of a picture—*Steamboat Bill, Jr.* 'You've never smiled, it's a surefire natural gag,' he said. 'It's a misfire gag,' said Buster, 'but I'll try it for you.' The preview audience hissed that ending. Bus never said, 'I told you so.' We simply went back and shot it over."

When *College* opened in New York on September 10, 1927, it wasn't at the Capitol, where M-G-M's pricey spectacle *Ben-Hur* was in its second week, nor was it at either the Rivoli or the Rialto, the two "sister" theaters United Artists had arranged to share with Paramount, both of which were also given over to extended runs. Rather, it was at the Mark Strand, Broadway's first genuine movie temple—about half the size of the newer Capitol—where it posted a respectable week at $32,300. The knock on *College* was that it was one of Keaton's weakest pictures, a conviction that prompted the *Times'* Mordaunt Hall to bluntly label it a "piece of stupidity." Irene Thirer in the *Daily News* thought it a wow, but the reviews overall were more gracious than superlative. As Norbert Lusk suggested in the *Los Angeles Times,* "This is partly attributable to the fact that college films in quantity are rapidly approaching the gravity of an epidemic which is rivaling the steady output of war pictures or pictures with war sequences in them. Enthusiasm cannot be expected of those who perforce must repeatedly view the same background no matter how the treatment may differ." As if to underscore the point, the film that followed *College* into the Strand was First National's *The Drop Kick*—another college picture.

College proved more an audience favorite than a critics' darling, gathering worldwide rentals of $788,554 on a negative cost of $285,771. Factoring in distribution charges, the film eventually showed a profit of $216,814. The dark way Keaton chose to end the picture drew a considerable amount of attention. After Ronald has spent the whole of the story in his dogged pursuit of Mary, whom he throws over his shoulder and then dashes off to a church, there come three lap dissolves in rapid succession. First, to a scene of routine domestic life, Mary darning a sock while Ronald reads a newspaper, both doing their best to ignore three children, the youngest of which is an infant in a basket. Next, to a scene of solitary old age, Ronald bitterly snapping at her between puffs on his pipe. Finally to a pair of graves, side by side, an image that in turn leads to THE END.

"It must have taken either great courage or great faith in the picture to end it with two graves," *Variety's* Nellie Gray commented. "So many comedies reach there so soon, but perhaps *College,* carrying its own, like spare tires, won't need it."

Was Keaton simply stuck for a clever fade-out? Or was this cynical coda inspired by the deteriorating state of his own marriage, which may be seen, particularly in retrospect, as traveling the same trajectory? If so, he never said as much, and these final shots, "as macabre as the end of *Cops*" in critic David Robinson's estimation, still deliver an unexpected wallop nearly a century later.

Leaving the cutting of *Steamboat Bill, Jr.* in Chuck Reisner's capable hands, Keaton left for New York City, ostensibly to negotiate a new contract with

Joe Schenck but in reality to attend the World Series and puzzle over what to do.

He had already consulted with Charlie Chaplin, who disliked everything about the scenario Schenck had laid out: "Don't let them do it to you, Buster. It's not that they haven't smart showmen there. They have some of the country's best. But there are too many of them, and they'll all try to tell you how to make your comedies. It will simply be one more case of too many cooks."

Harold Lloyd felt the same way. "It's not your gang," he said. "You'll lose."

Both Chaplin and Lloyd had something Keaton did not—full ownership of their productions and control over their own destinies. Buster was just as gifted, but he had never made self-determination a priority. Joe Schenck had been with him since his first day before the cameras, and Keaton had always had enough money to do whatever he wished. Now he felt as though he was being bought and sold like a commodity. Yet he never held Schenck personally responsible for the situation in which he found himself.

"He would never say a word against Joe Schenck, in spite of all that happened later on," said writer Bill Cox, a longtime friend. "And I've spoken a hundred times to him about it. He'd go over the history of what happened. I'd say, 'Jesus, Joe Schenck let you down.' He'd say, 'Joe didn't mean any harm.' Or: 'Joe was like my father.' I suppose the thing about Buster [was] he never looked over his shoulder. The past was the past to him. You'd say, 'That person did something very wrong to you.' He'd say, 'Well, most people have a reason.' It's astounding how he stuck to that."

In New York, Keaton went to see Adolph Zukor and proposed to make his pictures for Paramount. "I explained that I wanted to make them in my own studio." Zukor, however, had been releasing Harold Lloyd's comedies for the past year—*For Heaven's Sake* and *The Kid Brother* so far, with *Speedy* still to come. Lloyd had cut a rich deal with Paramount, and Zukor saw no need to add another expensive comedian to the roster.

Keaton attended World Series games at Pittsburgh's Forbes Field and Yankee Stadium, appeared at the opening of Loew's Oriental Theatre in Brooklyn, mourned the death of Marcus Loew on September 5, 1927, and was a pallbearer at the funeral of comedian Tom Lewis, whose last work was as first mate to Ernest Torrence in *Steamboat Bill, Jr.* Keaton was, by his own account, still brooding over the state of his career.

"I got myself thoroughly mixed up," he admitted, "and then I made a mistake, just like in my comedies when I do just one little thing wrong and from then on I'm in the soup up to my neck."

Prior to talking with Nick Schenck, a meeting he later conceded he should never have taken, Keaton had several drinks and, rather than strategically thinking the whole thing through, presented himself at Schenck's office at 1540 Broadway "all softened up."

"What is this thing?" he demanded. "Am I with M-G-M?"

"That's right," said Schenck soothingly. "Your studio is a little place. Our big new plant will give you bigger production, relieve you of producing. You just have to be funny. We got writers and directors out there. The best. Experts. Don't worry. Be happy."

Then Schenck broached the subject of money. He knew that quitting altogether wasn't an option for Buster Keaton, that like so many M-G-M contract players, he needed the cash flow to support his lifestyle. Or, more specifically, his *wife's* lifestyle. What Schenck might not have realized was that Keaton needed to work for reasons entirely apart from the matter of income—that filmmaking for him had become as necessary as breathing, and that he couldn't imagine life without it.

"Three thousand a week," Schenck offered, "and a percentage."

"No percentage," Keaton countered. "If I go with you I want bonuses."

"Bonuses it is. Should we argue?"

"And five thousand a week."

"Three thousand."

"No, four thousand."

"Three thousand a week is just right. And now we go to lunch."

There was no grand announcement, no ceremonial signing of a contract with photographers on hand to record the historic moment. Nothing, in fact, was said publicly for more than a month, and all indications suggest that Keaton balked at finalizing an agreement with M-G-M. Instead, he hit the road for United Artists, supporting *College* with personal appearances, doing his Princess Rajah dance four times a day, five on Saturdays and Sundays. Natalie was with him, but it turned out to be unexpectedly rough duty, Keaton having worked falls and tumbling into the act. After a week in Detroit, he moved on to Pittsburgh in somewhat battered condition, and called a halt to the tour after three days.

Sensing, perhaps, that he needed a nudge, United Artists fed word to the trades that the company would not release *Steamboat Bill, Jr.* "It is stated UA did not want this picture," *Variety* reported, "with the result that if present negotiations are concluded with Keaton to return to the M-G-M fold, that organization will release the film." Three days later, an item in *Billboard* had Harry Langdon dickering with UA to fill the gap left by Keaton's departure.

Both plants underscored the fact that there was no place left for Keaton at UA.

Concurrently, George Shaffer, the Hollywood correspondent for the *New York Daily News,* reported that Keaton had permanently closed his studio on Lillian Way. "The tip is out that if Buster makes more pictures, it will be as a salaried comedian, not for Schenck's United Artists, but for Metro-Goldwyn-Mayer." Keaton, of course, had no direct role in ceasing operations. Buster Keaton Productions, which owned the studio, had simply stopped funding staff and management salaries in anticipation of his move to Culver City.

"In the end," he said, "I gave in." Within days, Keaton was observed touring the M-G-M lot with Nicholas Schenck. *The Film Daily* was first to carry official notice of his "return" along with the news that Irving Thalberg would personally supervise his productions.

There are no accounts of Buster's final day on the Keaton studio grounds, the place where he made eighteen two-reelers and ten features over a period of seven years. If he walked around the compact lot, he would have seen standing sets dating back five years or more, buildings and storefronts and the variegated fence surrounding it all. The great stage where Joe Roberts so affectingly played his final scenes. The laboratory where all the exposed negative was processed, the chemical smells still lingering in the air. The old studio barn, the administration building where Lou Anger had his office and where payroll was made and extras and day workers were processed. Gabe Gabourie's workshop, where seemingly anything could be fabricated on a moment's notice. He may even have paused at the plot of land where Captain was buried. And if he walked past the studio's row of dressing rooms he would have remembered that none of the doors were numbered but rather that each was named for one of the extraordinary comedies he made as an independent. Reading down the line were *The Blacksmith, Convict 13, The Scarecrow, The Haunted House, The High Sign, Hard Luck, The Play House, The Goat, The Paleface,* and *The Boat.*

16

The Cameraman

THE PRODUCING ORGANIZATION known as Metro Pictures Corporation when Marcus Loew bought it in 1920 had come a long way in eight short years. Its 1924 acquisition of Goldwyn Pictures Corporation, which brought with it such troubled productions as *Greed* and *Ben-Hur*, also brought it the larger and more modern Goldwyn studios in Culver City. Originally, the combined company was known as Metro-Goldwyn, but it formally became Metro-Goldwyn-Mayer around the time of *Go West* in 1925.

"In taking this over," said Buster Keaton, "they also took over a few exchanges, picture exchanges that were carryin' the Goldwyn banner. So the name had a value. So changing it from just plain Metro to Metro-Goldwyn was what they were talkin' about, and they liked the title. And they had decided on takin' this independent producer by the name of Louis B. Mayer and puttin' him in charge of the studio and production. And one of the main reasons they wanted him was on account of a young man he had along with him called Thalberg. They wanted him, too—very much—'cause they knew he was not a businessman like Mayer, he was a creator. A good production man, and that was needed badly.

"I was in [Nick Schenck's office, which was connected to Marcus Loew's office at the Loew's State building in New York] when Mayer come there, and he says, 'Why not add my name to it? After all, I'm the head of the studio and production and so forth.' And he says, 'Now look how important this sounds: Hart Schaffner & Marx. It would be Metro-Goldwyn-Mayer. There's class to it, there's dignity.' Brother, what a performance he gave. So

Dave Bernstein, [who] was the secretary of Loew's Incorporated, was in there, so him and Nicholas Schenck walked over to Marcus Loew's office in the next room. Only gone about five minutes, [they] come back in and sez, 'Marcus says okay, you can have your name on there too.'"

The contract between Buster Keaton and Metro-Goldwyn-Mayer, which would nominally place Keaton under Mayer's supervision, was finalized on January 26, 1928. While Schenck wouldn't move on money, he did everything possible to help Keaton feel at home. Where he was originally to deliver four comedies a year for M-G-M, Keaton would now hold to his familiar pattern of two a year—a spring release and a fall release. Every effort would be made to employ his old crew on his productions. And every Friday, Joe Keaton could take the streetcar to Culver City and collect $100. The pact, effective January 15, was for a term of two years.

"When we went down there, Buster didn't want any part of the lot," Harold Goodwin recalled in the mid-1970s. "He wanted to have his own unit. So 'we' moved into a bungalow, about where the Irving Thalberg building is now. There were two or three bungalows. Lew Cody had one for a while, then Bill Haines got one. But they were next to Buster. We didn't go to the studio; they brought our checks over and we got our pay there. We ate our lunch there, and we had Willie, the cook, who was with Buster for years . . . Even Clyde Bruckman had a room in the bungalow where he could work, writing. It really made Louis B. Mayer sore because he was supposed to be the big boss of the studio, but he had nothing to say about Buster. Buster would contact the front office through Nick Schenck or Eddie Mannix."

Mayer, who was vice president in charge of production, found himself completely out of the loop on the Keaton matter. It was between the two Schenck brothers, and Keaton was essentially presented to him as a fait accompli, a situation of no little consequence since the care and feeding of the studio's contract talent, which now consisted of nine stars and twenty-three featured players, was his responsibility. It didn't look good that Buster was maintaining his own digs off the lot, nor that his annual quota of pictures had been sliced in half. Lon Chaney, the company's most profitable attraction, was set to make four films for the 1928–29 season, as were Norma Shearer and William Haines. Greta Garbo and Marion Davies were committed to three each. Only Keaton and John Gilbert were permitted to make just two. More significantly, Mayer lacked an appreciation of Keaton's work and didn't think he was funny. Keaton, in fact, was convinced that Mayer had no sense of humor whatsoever.

When he arrived at M-G-M, Keaton was greeted with an original thirteen-page story prepared at Thalberg's behest by Lew Lipton, a former title writer who served as one of the studio's two full-time gagmen. Lipton proposed teaming Keaton with Marie Dressler, whose *Tillie's Punctured Romance* had convinced a teenaged vaudevillian there was more to film comedy than custard pies and car chases. Dressler, down on her luck, had recently returned to Hollywood on a freelance basis taking character parts at Metro and Fox. She was also in *Breakfast at Sunrise,* the last picture Constance Talmadge owed First National. Lipton's story had Keaton making a transatlantic flight, à la Charles Lindbergh, in pursuit of a $50,000 prize, and Dressler, an aging burlesque queen, making the trip with him.

Keaton thought Lipton's story all wrong but embraced the idea of teaming with Dressler, who was a big Broadway star when he was still ducking the Gerry Society. He went to Thalberg with a proposal of his own. "The story itself was pretty much a switch on *Steamboat Bill, Jr.,*" he said, "except that Marie, as a rugged old aunt, would be playing opposite me instead of Ernest Torrence. The background was Fort Dodge shortly after the Civil War. A wagon train is about to leave for the West. In the rocker on the porch of her little shanty sits Marie Dressler."

Dressler's sister in the East implores her not to make the dangerous trip alone, and is dispatching her son to accompany her.

"I arrive the next day with one carpetbag. I am obviously a weakling, and the absurdity of a scared-looking little guy like me protecting the husky Marie Dressler from Indians, rapists, or even prairie dogs sets up the audience for a big laugh."

It was this kind of setup that sold Keaton on Chuck Reisner's idea for *Steamboat Bill, Jr.* because the potential was so clear. "That's all I have as yet," Keaton told Thalberg. "But I'd like to work on it."

Thalberg, in Keaton's estimation, lacked a true low-comedy mind. "Like any man who must concern himself with mass production, he was seeking a pattern, a format. Slapstick comedy has a format, but it is hard to detect in its early stages unless you are one of those who can create it." Thalberg told him he thought the concept a little frail. "There is really not much to it," he said, but he promised to give it some thought.

Said Keaton: "He was just being polite, of course."

It was about this time that Keaton learned the director of his new picture, whatever the story turned out to be, would be Edward Sedgwick. A native of Galveston, Texas, Sedgwick was an inspired choice. Four years older than

Keaton, he shared much the same background, having joined the family act at the age of four doing a singing specialty as part of the Sedgwick Comedy Company.

"I played child parts and did vaudeville acts until I was seven years old, when I was given my first comedy part—that of an Irish immigrant—in a comedy written by my father called *Just Over*. During this time, however, I was only on the stage during the summer months. Every winter my father took me back to Galveston and sent me to school."

After graduating from a military college in San Antonio, Sedgwick rejoined his parents and two sisters as one of the Five Sedgwicks, playing the circuits in a sketch titled "Jerry the Booby Boy." In time, he had his own musical-comedy company, Ed Sedgwick's Cabaret Girls, which he produced, directed, and managed himself. He made the jump to pictures in 1914, playing comedy leads for Lubin, pulled his first writing credit in 1917, and moved into directing in 1920. Sedgwick joined M-G-M in 1926, where, at six feet and three hundred pounds, he was known around the lot as Big Ed. He made light comedies with Conrad Nagel and William Haines, but it was the Keaton assignment that brought him back to his show business roots.

While Lipton's story was a nonstarter, it did provide the germ of an idea for another try. Screenwriter Byron Morgan, who had a fertile story mind but no background in comedy, recast the Keaton character as a tintype photographer who aspires to be a newsreel cameraman after observing one preparing for the arrival of a VIP. A girl, Sally, works as a featured dancer in a notorious nightclub. The owner of the club is her mother, Maggie, a character Morgan may have drawn with Marie Dressler in mind. Buster manages to shoot film of a gun battle between cops and gangsters, and all the companies bid for it. An organ grinder's monkey is introduced when a drunk hands the animal a heated penny, and Buster, in a throwback to *Go West,* treats the injury, making a friend for life. The third act has Buster and Maggie crossing the Atlantic by air, the monkey complicating the attempt.

"I wasn't in trouble enough tryin' to manipulate a camera as a cameraman," Keaton said, "tryin' to photograph current events as a news weekly cameraman . . . [Thalberg] wanted me involved with gangsters because I photographed somethin' they didn't want me to photograph, and then to get in trouble with this one and that one, and that was my fight—to eliminate those [extra things]."

While Morgan developed a treatment, Keaton went off to Lake Tahoe with Nat, her sister Dutch, and Dutch's occasional beau, Buster Collier. Within days, the studio put out word that Keaton's first picture for M-G-M would be titled *Snapshots,* one of eleven features to be put into production during the month of February.

Byron Morgan produced a forty-eight-page treatment in Keaton's absence and followed up with a draft continuity that was still incomplete when Keaton reviewed it in early March. Judging there were "not enough comedy angles to the story," he kicked it back to Morgan, who responded with a greatly tightened version and a rearrangement of sequences to motivate a new ending. At this point, Morgan was sidelined and the prolific Richard Schayer was brought on, Schayer having been responsible for one of 1927's biggest hits, *Tell It to the Marines.* Working in consultation with Keaton, Sedgwick, and Bruckman, Schayer produced a completely new continuity, some 140 pages in length, which began with Lindbergh's steamer being escorted by a fleet of harbor craft into its New York dock, Buster among the crowd waiting to get a photo with his old-fashioned outfit.

"It's the simplest story you can find," Keaton said, "which was always a great thing for us if we could find it. I was a tintype cameraman down at Battery Park, New York. Ten cents a picture. . . . I saw the Hearst weekly [newsreel] man and a script girl with him [at the ticker tape parade] that I got one look at and fell hook, line, and sinker. Well, immediately I went down and sold my tintype thing to a second-hand dealer and bought a second-hand motion picture camera. And of course I get one of the oldest models there was—a Pathé. And I went to the Hearst offices . . . and they got one look at me and my equipment and sez, 'No.' The girl saw me make the attempt, and she says, 'There's only one way you can do anything. You gotta go out and photograph somethin' of interest. And if they see it and they can use the film you shoot, they'll buy it from you. And if you can do that more than once, then they'll put you on as a member of the [team].'"

The monkey comes into it when Buster accidently trips and falls on him, and a cop makes him compensate the organ grinder for apparently killing the animal. He is, however, only stunned, and Buster is now his owner. Together they film a tong war in Chinatown, an inventive and colorful replacement for the police shootout with gangsters. The script was still considered incomplete when Keaton and Sedgwick, under pressure from the front office, committed to location work in New York commencing April 12. True to their collective word, M-G-M management surrounded their new star with familiar support—Elgin Lessley, having completed his hitch with

Keaton and director Edward Sedgwick arrive in New York for location work on The Cameraman *(1928).*

Harry Langdon, on first camera; Gabe Gabourie as art director; Harold Goodwin playing the heavy; Ernie Orsatti doubling for Buster; Vic Orsatti, Ernie's younger brother, acting as script clerk; and Clyde Bruckman again functioning as gagman after a spell at Hal Roach directing the newly minted comedy team of Stan Laurel and Oliver Hardy.

Keaton and company arrived at Grand Central Terminal on April 7, he, Sedgwick, and Bruckman having talked gags and spun story the entire trip east. Nat and Dutch, meanwhile, contemplated a furious round of shopping and theatregoing. Indeed, Keaton's actual reason for making the trip (according to Harold Goodwin) was to see the groundbreaking musical *Show Boat* at the Ziegfeld Theatre. With the arrival of M-G-M contract player Marceline Day, who would be playing Sally, the love interest at the newsreel office, filming began with shots of Buster making his way to a ticker tape parade for Gertrude Ederle, the first woman to swim the English Channel.

"The first shot we attempted in New York was one of me, carrying my tintype camera, crossing the trolley tracks at Fifth Avenue and 23rd Street. As I was doing this, the motorman stopped his trolley in the middle of the crossing and yelled, 'Hey, *Keaton!*' His passengers looked out of the windows and also began to shout things at me. In no time at all I was surrounded by so many people that the nearest cop couldn't even get near me."

At City Hall Park, scenes were made of Ederle being welcomed by Mayor Jimmy Walker, and again Keaton was mobbed. The following morning, Marceline Day worked a few hours at Battery Park, then Keaton and Sedgwick spent the rest of the day making shots at city hall and the Statue of Liberty.

"Clyde Bruckman knew of [Harold] Lloyd's triumphant location trip there for *Speedy,* taking the center of the city over for spectacular chases," Kevin Brownlow commented. "But Lloyd had one enormous advantage; once he removed his glasses he could melt into the crowd. Keaton merely had to step onto the sidewalk and he created a crowd."

The sheer crush of people made serious work impossible. After conferring by phone with Eddie Mannix—Irving Thalberg was honeymooning in Europe with Norma Shearer—it was decided to trash the problematic scenario altogether and shoot the few exteriors they knew they needed: Buster's race to Sally's boardinghouse and their promenade along Fifth Avenue, early on a Sunday morning before many people were out. Also filmed was an improvised scene in a deserted Yankee Stadium in which Buster mimes a full inning of baseball, pitching, batting, and rounding the bases, then acknowledging the cheers of the invisible crowd, an inspiration destined to become one of the highlights of the movie. In five days, a total of six scripted scenes were shot, while another thirty-eight were captured on the fly. The *Snapshots* company returned to California with a respectable 16,205 feet of exposed film—about three hours' worth.

Back in Culver City, the production office allotted thirty-three studio days to *Snapshots,* with shooting scheduled to begin May 1. Location work with Keaton and Sedgwick had been a profoundly casual process, but it was a whole different world on the Metro lot, with its fourteen stages, its cement-bottomed lake, its French and Spanish streetscapes, and the three-story administration building that loomed over it all. Built in 1916 for Thomas Ince, the plant had expanded under subsequent ownership from sixteen to thirty-nine acres, with five producing executives and fourteen contract directors to turn out forty-four features, seventy-two short subjects, and more than a hundred issues of M-G-M News for the 1928–29 season.

All Keaton had known in his entire life as a comedy star was the modest studio on Lillian Way, and for the first time in eight years he would be working at a facility that did not bear his name. Gabe Gabourie had designed a city hall exterior, built on what was known as New York Street #2, part of a jumble of standing sets that covered the backlot at the southwest end of the property. The call that Tuesday morning was for nine o'clock, and Keaton, typically, was there early.

"I walked on without a care in the world. Automatically start to work as I have all my life. Started feeling around for bits of business and material. I said, 'I'd like to do something with a drunk and with a fat lady and a kid. Get 'em for me.' I was trying for some establishing shots—and a couple of laughs—before we hit the plot."

Over on Lillian Way, the whole studio had been geared to getting Buster what he needed on the double—even if it meant grabbing passersby off the street. But M-G-M was a $10 million operation governed by systems and dictates, and nothing got done without paperwork. ("You had to requisition a toothpick in triplicate," he said.) Sedgwick ordered more extras—146 had already been called—and at 9:25 people waiting outside the casting office were brought down to the set. In the meantime, he requested a private conference with his star.

"I don't think you did it deliberately," he said when they were alone, "but you made a horse's ass out of me in front of my own company."

Keaton was genuinely apologetic. He hadn't meant to undermine the director; he just didn't know any other way to work.

"All right," said Sedgwick, "just so we understand each other."

Back on the set, Sedgwick called for even more people, and another seventy were added. They were ready to shoot at ten thirty, and Keaton waited to be told what to do.

"For a half hour it goes on. 'Do this! No, do that! Shoot this over. Fat lady, *must* you stand in front of Mr. Keaton?' Finally, Sedgwick says, 'Buster, line those goddamn people up and get this fucking shot over with.' 'Me?' I ask. 'You,' he says. That's when we became friends, Sedgwick and I, and I began calling him Junior."

They shot fourteen script scenes and three added scenes that first day, and the added scenes they filmed on a daily basis quickly came to outnumber the scripted ones.* On the fourth day they moved inside, staging the initial action inside the newsreel office, the added scenes now numbering twelve to the scripted five. By the end of the fifth day of production, they had forty-five script scenes in the can, thirty-six additional scenes, and were a full day behind schedule. On Monday, one scripted scene was shot in the newsreel

* What were referred to as "scenes" in the daily production reports were actually individual camera setups.

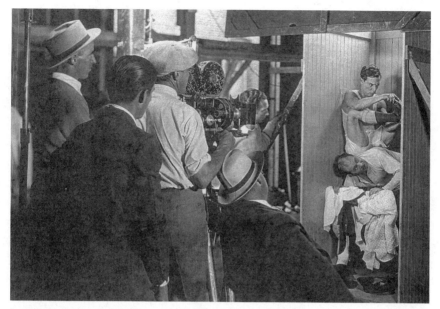

Filming the changing-room scene with Edward Brophy.

office, as were fifteen added scenes and four retakes. By day's end they were two days behind.

And so it went. Unscripted location work at the Venice saltwater plunge took six days and resulted in a memorable scene of two men changing their clothes in a room sized for one.

"Each bathhouse had six hooks on its walls," Keaton said. "We removed four hooks because a couple of men struggling to hang all of their clothes on one hook apiece could be very funny."

Ed Sedgwick wanted to play the other man in the tiny space, but Keaton nixed the idea. "I told him that the audience would expect a man of his size to throw me out of the bathhouse if irritated. What I wanted was a fellow about my size who looked like a grouch but not the sort who dares start a fight." Pressed for time, he enlisted Edward Brophy, Sedgwick's unit manager, who was stockier but about the same height. Back to back, the two men fight over the same hook, dodge elbows, tangle with suspenders, trample each other's clothing—all in a single unrehearsed take. "The scene ran for four minutes," Keaton proudly noted, "which is a very long time on the screen for a string of gags worked by just two men in a single ridiculous situation. Thalberg almost had hysterics when he saw that day's rushes in a projection room."

Back at the studio, Keaton and Sedgwick took to talking story most mornings in Keaton's off-site bungalow, delaying the start of production anywhere from thirty to forty-five minutes. With the company now four days behind schedule, the allotted studio days were increased from thirty-three to forty-seven. On May 22, they began exterior work with a white-faced monkey named Josephine, who was part of wrangler Tony Campanaro's menagerie of animals trained expressly for movie work. The monkey, who would be at Buster's side for the balance of the story, added another unpredictable element to a picture regarded as completely out of control. The following Monday, after some morning location work in Hollywood, and with retakes and added scenes in Venice planned for Tuesday, Eddie Mannix called a halt to filming and spent the balance of the afternoon in conference with Sedgwick, an intervention of sorts. The gist of Mannix's concern was why the hell they couldn't follow the script.

"Now here's the thinking of these people," said Harold Goodwin. "Ed explained—he told this to me, he didn't tell Buster—that oftentimes a situation comes up with potential comedy in it, and we milk it. And they said, 'How can we budget the picture if you don't follow the script?' Big league thinking, you know? Two of the funniest scenes in the picture were not in the script—one of them was Buster trying to put on a bathing suit in a small cubicle, and the other was where he was trying to get his piggy bank open."

The scene with Buster in his spare little room raiding the bank for money to take Sally out for the day had been made the previous week. "You can't ever forget the bath house thing where he gets in with Eddie Brophy . . . they're in there, they just ran out of film, they just let that go. Well, the same thing happened when he was going to take the Day girl to the beach, and he hits the [piggy bank with a claw hammer]. Well, that surprised him, because he hit the thing and it went through the wall and dropped down. They hadn't planned on that. So then, of course, he had to tear out the whole wall to get to it. But he never stopped working it, he'd keep going."

A visual gag that *was* scripted was Buster's rush down four flights of stairs to reach his building's communal telephone. The breakaway set, which extended from cellar to roof, was so tall it wouldn't fit inside any of the dark stages and had to be constructed on the lot. It wasn't diffused, so shots had to be made early in the day before sunlight could spoil the effect. Keaton decided to milk the gag; the first time, the call isn't for him. Sullenly, he trudges back up the stairs, the camera following on an elevator that resembled a dumbwaiter, and absentmindedly finds himself on the roof. Loudly summoned again from below, he madly dashes down the stairs again, zooming straight past the waiting phone and clear down into the cellar below. About the time these stairway shots were completed, the title of the film was officially changed from *Snapshots* to *The Cameraman*.

The loose and collaborative atmosphere that prevailed in Thalberg's absence permitted Keaton to perform his own stunts, such as when Buster and Sally are separated on a double-decker, Buster hustled by the crush of riders to the upper level while Sally is trapped in a window seat directly below. As the bus speeds along, he jumps the railing and perches on the fender next to her, a stunt by a principal rather than a double that would normally have occasioned a heart attack in the executive screening room. A bump in the road sends him thumping to the pavement, whereupon he scrambles to his feet and gives chase, gracefully leaping back onto the fender to continue their talk.

The company repaired to Balboa on June 11 to film climactic action in which Sally is taken speedboating by Hal Goodwin's character, Stagg, as part of a yacht club regatta and is thrown overboard during a sharp turn. This sets up Buster's dramatic rescue of her while the boorish Stagg saves himself, Josephine capturing the heroic deed in full by eagerly cranking the camera from shore. M-G-M advertised for three hundred extras in the local paper, offering five dollars a day and lunch for adults, two dollars and fifty cents for children. A total of thirty-five scripted and thirty-nine added scenes were completed in the space of six days.

Buster is back on the street, peddling his tintypes, when Sally comes to retrieve him. "Everybody's talking about you," she says excitedly. "They're all waiting to give you a great reception!" And with that, crowds surge forward and papers and ticker tapes rain down from above, all seemingly in celebration of Buster's triumph. As he and Sally march down the street, hand in hand, the monkey on his left shoulder, he doffs his cap in acknowledging it all, a rousing bookend to the beginning of the story, taking it all in while unseen just a few feet behind him is the Lone Eagle himself, riding and waving from the back seat of an open car. With the cost of *The Cameraman* approaching $350,000, production closed on June 25, 1928. Editing, titling, and the all-important previews lay ahead.

Since the completion of *Steamboat Bill, Jr.* in September 1927, much had changed for Joseph Schenck and United Artists. Norma Talmadge had very publicly taken up with actor Gilbert Roland, eleven years her junior, and by the spring of 1928 the Schencks were no longer living together. An article by George Shaffer in the *New York Daily News* had signaled trouble in November under the headline "RIFT IN SCHENCK, TALMADGE FILM TIES REPORTED." Shaffer disclosed Keaton's presumed estrangement from Schenck over the closing of his studio. Constance Talmadge's career was on the ropes, and the understanding within United Artists was that her contract with her brother-in-law had lapsed, relieving D. W. Griffith of the onerous task of having to direct her in *Sunny*. And as to the Schenck marriage, Shaffer was as direct as discretion would permit:

"All the social strata of the movie colony have had their ears touched by reports, which Norma Talmadge (Mrs. Schenck) vigorously denies, that personal differences have arisen between her and her important husband. At the United Artists lot, they say nobody can tell until Schenck comes on from New York what course Norma's film future will take. Norma had been scheduled, when she recently returned from Europe, to make a picture called *The Woman Disputed* with Gilbert Roland as her leading man. Whether this plan is to be carried out, no one at United Artists lot now professes to know, although there is no statement forthcoming on an occurrence that may have previously changed the plan. Miss Talmadge and Roland were together on United Artists lot yesterday."

The Woman Disputed did indeed get made, albeit chaotically, at a negative cost of $661,000, roughly 30 percent more than what Keaton spent on *The General*. It broke even, but Talmadge's popularity was slipping. United Artists announced nineteen releases for the 1928–29 season, but some, such as Chaplin's *City Lights* and Howard Hughes' *Hell's Angels,* would be delayed, while others, such as the aforementioned *Sunny,* would never be made. Of Schenck's personal productions under the management of John Considine, Jr., only Roland West's *Alibi* would be an unqualified hit, bringing $1 million in domestic rentals. The troubled *Tempest,* the second of three John Barrymore specials, cost an extraordinary $1,400,000 and couldn't help but fail commercially. D. W. Griffith's *Drums of Love* and *Lady of the Pavements* were both money losers, as was the Corinne Griffith comedy *Garden of Eden*. Of Schenck's entire season, only two clear winners emerged—*Alibi* and *Steamboat Bill, Jr.*

Keaton's picture was set to kick off the season with a July release, but its world premiere actually came on April 5, 1928, when it opened a new theater in Santa Maria, California. Advance word on the film was good, thanks in part to Bob Sherwood's column in the *New York Evening Post*.

"Charlie Chaplin has had more ups and downs than most," Sherwood wrote in a February assessment of top comedians, "due to the fact that he makes fewer pictures than anyone, but only once has his record been marred by really inferior pictures. This was eight years ago. Having scored a great success with *Shoulder Arms,* he slumped badly with *Sunnyside* and *A Day's Pleasure.* Then he came back gloriously with *The Kid;* since then there have been no duds. Harold Lloyd has been as close to one hundred percent consistent as it is possible for anyone to come, but Buster Keaton has been woefully uneven. Indeed, at the moment, Keaton is almost entirely out as a popular attraction, but the reports are that he is due for a grand revival when his next comedy, *Steamboat Bill,* is released."

When *Steamboat Bill, Jr.* opened at New York's Rialto for a two-week stand on May 12, Ernest Torrence was billed above the title in the ads, a first for Keaton in that he had always had the star position to himself—a tacit admission that UA thought his popularity on the wane. "This is the last comedy Buster Keaton made under his United Artists contract," wrote *Variety's* Jack Conway. "It was held back for several months, getting itself concerned in several wild rumors, all of which were a million miles from facts. Whatever may have been the real reason why United Artists took its time about releasing this one, it had nothing to do with quality, for it's a pip of a comedy. Lovers of comedy and picture house regulars will like this latest Keaton film. It's one of his best."

The Film Daily was equally impressed, as were the New York papers, which, with the exception of the *Times* and the *Sun,* thought it terrific. "We cannot remember hearing an audience laugh so whole-heartedly as at the new Keaton comedy" (*American*). "All the Keaton fans should see this one as it will fulfill all their expectations" (*Daily Mirror*). "Buster Keaton hits high with his newest comic offering" (*Daily News*). "Judging by the roars at the Rialto yesterday it will go over in a big way" (*Herald-Tribune*).

Despite all the friendly notices, the resulting business was disappointing, only $38,600 for the fortnight after a bright start. When the picture opened in Los Angeles at the new United Artists Theatre, the pattern repeated itself, with the film starting off great and then losing steam. Still, it managed to better Douglas Fairbanks' *The Gaucho* in its first week at the same venue by $1,000.

In *Steamboat Bill, Jr.,* the funniest part unexpectedly turned out to be an adroit three-minute sequence in which Bill gruffly drags Willie into a haberdasher's to buy him a hat. The boy, drawn to loud, floppy headgear, had shown up affecting a beret, and the old man can't abide the thing. In

In a memorable scene from Steamboat Bill, Jr., *Bill drags his son to a haberdasher's shop to find him a new hat.*

two extended takes, more than a dozen caps and toppers get tried, and as quickly as the father yanks one off his son's head, the salesman replaces it with another, each headpiece imposing a different facet of personality on the otherwise impassive face. (The famous pork pie even makes a cameo appearance while Bill's back is turned.) The classic Keaton payoff comes when Bill finally settles on a Panama, pays the man, and marches Willie out into the street, where a gust of wind catches the new bonnet and sends it bouncing into the river. Willie removes the unsightly beret from his pocket and places it back on his head.

UA felt sufficiently good about *Steamboat Bill, Jr.* to take out a full-page ad in *Variety* heralding the glowing reviews in New York and San Francisco. While the domestic take was less than for either *The General* or *College*, foreign revenues nearly equaled those in the U.S. and Canada, bringing worldwide rentals to $723,400. At a negative cost of $385,643, and factoring in distribution charges of $48,711 to cover prints, advertising, and the like, the film would eventually show a profit of $68,139—a better showing than for most of Schenck's productions that season. In time, *Steamboat Bill, Jr.* would come to be regarded as one of Buster Keaton's greatest achievements, and in 2016, it became the sixth of his comedies to be added to the National Film Registry.

By the time *The Cameraman* was completed, Keaton had settled in at M-G-M. Every morning, weather permitting, he would make the commute

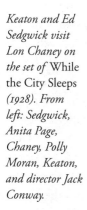

Keaton and Ed Sedgwick visit Lon Chaney on the set of While the City Sleeps *(1928). From left: Sedgwick, Anita Page, Chaney, Polly Moran, Keaton, and director Jack Conway.*

from Beverly Hills to the studio on bicycle, a distance of five miles. His duplex on Grant Avenue opposite the East Gate became a kind of haven for studio expats, where the liquor flowed freely and they were exempt from executive oversight. Ed Sedgwick had his office there, as did Bruckman when he was around, and Keaton had a private gym adjacent to his dressing room. When he did venture across the road, he seemed constantly in motion, and a lull in production usually meant there was time for horseplay. When shooting the tong war sequence—Bruckman's conception—he used a break in filming to barge in on Robert Z. "Pop" Leonard's set, a replica of the casino at Monte Carlo, racing ahead of a band of wild-eyed Chinese extras. Leonard had nearly two hundred dress extras of his own on the stage, and they were sent scattering amid all the whooping and gunfire, Keaton ducking and dodging and finally taking a fast dive across the studio floor and sliding for cover between Leonard's legs.

"Can you speak Chinese, Bob?" he croaked. "For gawd's sake then tell these Chinks the scene is over. They can't distinguish one set from another and the whole gang's been chasing me all over the studio!"

Keaton made a more conventional entrance to visit his pal Lew Cody on the set of *The Baby Cyclone*. Cody's character was about to take a fall and they had two stuntmen present. One of the doubles tried the fall, but director Eddie Sutherland wasn't getting what he wanted.

"Finally I said, 'Sedgwick wouldn't need me for a while. Give me Cody's clothes.' So, there was no stage dressing room in those days; I just went behind a piece of scenery and put on his full dress suit, that's all. I come down [the stairs], step on the cake of soap, and . . . The trouble with the other stunt men doing it is that they each did good falls, but they weren't funny. And he didn't want a big, dramatic straight fall—it had to look funny or he couldn't use the scene. So instead of hitting the piece of soap and both feet going out from under me that way, I did it the other way. I hit the soap and took my feet out that way so that it threw me onto my head. And as I came down, I threw a neck roll and lit with the tails of the coat over my head, and I was on my knees like that with the tail of the coat over here, which is an ideal cut with the camera right there. For a double, it hid me immediately when I hit, see. So all I had to do was to move Cody in there, into the exact same spot, move the camera up just a few feet, and he just rose up, got the coattails back off his head, shook his head like that, and went on with it. Now, they did it without putting a number board up on the camera or anything. So it was a continuous scene on the screen except for the one little quick blur moving the camera."

In the projection room, Thalberg was watching the dailies when the scene came up. "You must never let Cody do a thing like that," he told Sutherland. "Do you realize the chance you took? Cody could be laid up for weeks!"

All Sutherland could manage without breaking Keaton's cover was a weak, "Well, he wanted to do it."

Thalberg could only see dollar signs, unaware that someone far more valuable than Cody had actually done the trick. "Well, never let him do anything like that again!" he ordered. If word ever reached him that Keaton was issued a $7.50 stunt check for the fall, he never let on.

Keaton pulled the same sort of prank on director Allan Dwan's *Tide of Empire* without even telling him. "It was a western," Dwan told Peter Bogdanovich, "and we were shooting on the street at M-G-M one night when suddenly we heard a commotion and wham! a fellow came flying out the saloon doors. It wasn't part of the scene at all—I didn't expect it. He did two or three somersaults—amazing flops—slid down the street, sat up and looked around. It was Buster Keaton. He did the stunt to amuse the Talmadge girls—he was married to Natalie Talmadge—who were on the set. And I kept it in—bit of atmosphere, a bum who's thrown out of a saloon."

Socially, Keaton also had time on his hands, and life at the Italian Villa took on the look and feel of a perpetual party. "He loved to barbecue and have people at his house to spend Saturday and Sunday and enjoy themselves," said Buster Collier. "Big laugh, the whole thing." Keaton would draft Collier and Ed Brophy to help with eighty or so invited guests every Sunday between May and October.

"Many others came uninvited," Keaton said. "They had heard about our wonderful barbecued chicken, steaks, and English lamb chops. Wilson Mizner, the country's greatest wit, had a standing invitation. He boasted that he could smell my cooking even in Santa Barbara, ninety miles away."

In the winter months, the Keatons hosted elaborate costume balls on the order of the parties that Marion Davies and William Randolph Hearst gave. Buster admitted he enjoyed staging these as much as his wife did.

Keaton was also out and around town a lot, usually with Nat, and even put in an appearance at a party for the newly married Thalbergs at Eddie Mannix's house, the same home he had designed and built for himself on Linden Drive. In September, he was part of the opening-night festivities at the Plantation, a Culver City restaurant that constituted Roscoe Arbuckle's latest enterprise, in which the waiters were all costumed as two-hundred-pound replicas of the proprietor. After a few cabaret acts, Keaton joined Arbuckle, Al St. John, and Tom Mix in an informal exhibition of head spins, flip-flaps, and intricate falls, with Buster making a high dive for Mix's outstretched arms. Arbuckle and comic Jack Pearl performed a mutual face-slapping routine, and then a waiter caught the boss with a custard pie for a finale. As was frequently the case in such environments, Keaton's natural reserve was mitigated by a steady flow of alcohol.

"Keaton was a very quiet guy," Collier said. "He loved the outdoors and loved the barbecue and loved the home and loved the kids. . . . Natalie was a very good mother and the two kids were very well brought up. But Buster never stayed home very much. He was always out playing ball, or hunting, or fishing. He wasn't a family man, particularly. Natalie had no personality, but I liked her very much."

Previews of *The Cameraman* took place in July, and a number of minor fixes and embellishments were identified. The frantic sequence with the criminal Wung Fa Tong particularly needed work, and on August 1, Lew Lipton dictated five new pages of action, calling for machine-gun fire, a few handy light bulbs that could be thrown to the pavement to simulate gun-shots, and heroics on the monkey's part when he knocks out several tong henchmen with a hammer. Previously, Keaton had submitted to live gunfire when a studio marksman shot all three legs of his tripod out from under him, and now he would do so again with a live machine gun taking out a window directly above his head.

The tong sequence had another problem that needed fixing. In the final reel, Buster is cornered by killers in a fortified den overlooking the street. "I didn't seem to have any choice but to just leave my camera and dive out the window into a fire escape to get away from 'em. And then go ahead and round out the story. We previewed it and we thought the last reel was a good reel . . . and the last reel just died the death of a dog. It dawned on us what that was. I deserted that camera. [The audience didn't like it.] So I had to go back and remake that—even with the trouble of tryin' to get away from those wild Chinamen in the tong war I still kept my camera. Then it was right. It was okay."

Three days of retakes were made commencing August 4, beginning with careful rehearsal of the footage requiring the real bullets. The scene in Buster's room with the piggy bank was refined and remade, as was the action on the four-flight staircase on the back lot. In all, there were some forty added scenes, bringing work on *The Cameraman* to a close on August 6, 1928. In the final tally, there were 395 scenes added to 307 scripted scenes. A total of forty-nine camera days yielded 192,255 feet of exposed film, representing a shooting ratio of roughly twenty-seven to one—virtually unheard of for a Metro-Goldwyn-Mayer production.

Management lost no time in getting another Keaton comedy into the pipeline. Everyone seemed to agree that *The Cameraman* was a good picture—Thalberg thought it hilarious—but the time it took to make didn't reflect the contention that big studio efficiencies would bring the cost of a Keaton comedy into line with the studio's other star vehicles. *The Cameraman* came in at a final cost of $362,000. In comparison, the Lon Chaney melodrama *West of Zanzibar* cost $249,000 to make, and Chaney's films were typically bringing in close to a million apiece in worldwide rentals. Another hit in the current season, Greta Garbo's *The Kiss,* cost $257,000, would bring in about the same as *Zanzibar* worldwide, and be even more profitable.

Keaton, for his part, couldn't understand the institutional obsession with schedule and budgeting. "We didn't shoot by no schedule at all," he said of the old days. "We didn't know when we started whether we was goin' to have the camera up five weeks or ten weeks. And it didn't make any difference. We owned our own camera. We're not paying rent on anything. All our people are on weekly salary anyhow. . . . We've just got two pictures a year to make and that's all there is to it."

Following the pattern that led to *The Cameraman,* Lew Lipton was assigned to come up with a new story for Keaton which, under Eddie Mannix's supervision, would be considerably cheaper to make than its predecessor. Lipton's solution, which took the form of a sequential treatment, was a backstage story about an actress who marries a besotted fan when jilted by her leading man. Circulated on August 28, suggestions and comments, principally from Keaton and Sedgwick (as Clyde Bruckman had rejoined Harold Lloyd's staff), were incorporated into a September 13 revision.

Lipton was at work on *Spite Marriage* when *The Cameraman* opened in New York on September 15. Business was robust—the film was accompanied by an onstage appearance from the cast of the popular Our Gang comedies—and the notices were mostly laudatory, with even Mordaunt Hall registering approval. "One feels quite sorry for the imperturbable creature, who, to put it mildly, is just a trifle absent-minded when it comes to either love or work. He, Mr. Keaton, is the type of chap who will never grow up, for he never permits a wrinkle to come to his face."

Highlighting Keaton's pantomime baseball improvisation, Martin Dickstein, his steadfast champion at *The Brooklyn Daily Eagle*, declared it "undoubtedly one of the funniest things the screen has brought forth this season."

Box office for the week at the Capitol was a solid $70,400, more than enough to merit a holdover week for *Battling Butler* two years earlier, but *The Cameraman* was boxed in by the house converting to sound, counter-programming Al Jolson's part-talking *The Singing Fool* at the Winter Garden with *Our Dancing Daughters* offering Joan Crawford with music and sound effects, a Fox Movietone newsreel, and an M-G-M talking short. *The Cameraman* moved out into the world, reaching Los Angeles in October, where the big attraction on the bill at Loew's State was Texas "Hello, Suckers!" Guinan in a noisy nightclub-themed vaudeville. The opening-day advertising had Keaton and *The Cameraman* second-billed to Guinan, but the calculation didn't pay off at all, and Guinan withdrew after the first day. Newly elevated to the top position, *The Cameraman* beat out every show in town that wasn't *The Singing Fool,* going on to worldwide rentals of $797,000, with foreign revenues besting domestic by nearly $75,000. It returned a profit of $66,932, meager by Metro standards when profits on less expensive films (such as *The Kiss*) could soar past $400,000. As preparations went forward on *Spite Marriage,* it became imperative to keep a lid on costs.

Compared to *The Cameraman,* the development process for *Spite Marriage* was streamlined. With the participation of colleague and fellow "comedy constructor" Ernest Pagano, Lipton completed a draft continuity by the end of September. Mannix was still the line producer, but an increasingly ineffective one because he was weak on story. Also, he had been given the monumental task of overseeing the studio's conversion to synchronous sound recording, a responsibility that was consuming a great deal of his time. Mannix weighed in on Lipton's ninety-page screenplay but knew he was being gently moved to one side. As with *The Cameraman*, Richard Schayer was brought on to write the final script, and Irving Thalberg stepped in to lend a firmer supervisorial hand. In late October, Mannix was dispatched to New York, where it was announced he would be scouting stage talent for several talkies he planned to produce. In short order, he would be advanced to general manager of the studio, a position he would hold for more than twenty-five years.

A problem with Lipton's story line for *Spite Marriage* was that it veered wildly off track in its third act, putting Keaton's character, Elmer, and the girl, an actress in the story named Trilby Drew, together on a yacht, then stranding them on an island teeming with cannibals in a throwback to *The Navigator*. At first, Schayer was unable to fix this, although he did add a fire in the engine room as the motivation for abandoning ship. It was in the final draft of the script, okayed by Thalberg on November 7, that a solution appeared. As in *The Cameraman*, the girl's love interest saves himself at a time of danger, leaving it to Elmer to actually rescue her. With the two of them now stranded alone on the ship, there was no longer any need for the scenes on the island, although an echo of *The Navigator* stubbornly remained.

Thalberg's reputation as a genius with story was well-earned, and Schayer's 134-page continuity would be the best-constructed script of Keaton's career. A week later, with Mannix still in New York, Thalberg passed supervision of *Spite Marriage* to his new brother-in-law, a former publicist named Lawrence Weingarten. Brought in the previous year as an assistant to production executive Harry Rapf, Weingarten was producing the studio's Tim McCoy westerns when he married Thalberg's sister, Sylvia, a writer, in June. Officially, Thalberg would still be the producer of *Spite Marriage*, but Larry Weingarten, uncredited, would handle the day-to-day responsibilities of the job.

With the release of *The Cameraman*, M-G-M formalized its agreement with Buster Keaton Productions. In exchange for turning Keaton over to them and allowing a contract to be negotiated, Metro would pay the company 25 percent of the net profits of each film, less distribution costs estimated at 30 percent. In addition, each picture would carry the credit "A Buster Keaton Production." In October, Keaton signed over to Natalie all future sums due under his contracts with Comique and Keaton Productions, possibly as a tax strategy, but more likely to give her an income stream of her own after an attack of insecurity. "My wife was forever hearing stories about my over-friendliness to this bright-eyed starlet or that leading lady," Keaton said in his autobiography. "Most of these stories had not a grain of truth in them. Most, I say, not all. The only comment I care to make on this is that I would like to see the healthy, normal man in my spot at M-G-M who could resist more feminine temptation than I did. But Mrs. Buster Keaton kept seeing rivals everywhere."

One of the better-known rivals was actually chosen by Thalberg to be Keaton's leading lady in *Spite Marriage*. Alabama-born Dorothy Sebastian had previously made the short list for *The Cameraman*, but was beaten out at the last moment by Marceline Day. She ended up in *Our Dancing Daughters* instead, paired in a sisterly fashion with Joan Crawford, who at twenty-four was nearly the same age and coloring. "She couldn't act for beans," Sebastian later said of Crawford, "but she screwed everybody at M-G-M but Leo the Lion."

Sebastian had been in the chorus of *George White's Scandals of 1924* with Louise Brooks, Dolores Costello, and Ruth Wilcox (later Selwyn), all of whom went on to picture careers. In Los Angeles, she crashed the guard gate at United Studios, walked into the office of director Henry King, and told him she had decided to become a movie star. He liked her style enough to give her a screen test, and then cast her in a picture. On the strength of her scene-stealing work in *Sackcloth and Scarlet,* she was recruited by M-G-M and signed a contract in 1926. The daughter of a clergyman, Sebastian had a honey-laced drawl and a bit of a wild streak. When Keaton met her she was engaged to director Clarence Brown.

Brown had proposed while she was making a Tim McCoy western called *Wyoming*. "I remember the day Dorothy Sebastian arrived on the set wearing a ring in which was set a diamond seemingly only slightly smaller than a goose egg," McCoy wrote in his autobiography.

" 'He asked me to marry him,' Dorothy explained before any questions could be posed.

" 'Will you?' I asked.

" 'Hell, no!' she laughed, and then recounted how her beau had given it to her the previous evening, pressing his case and adding rather gratuitously

Keaton with actress Dorothy Sebastian on the set of Spite Marriage *(1929). Their on-again, off-again relationship would continue for more than a decade.*

that even if Dorothy rejected him she need not return the ring. Gazing appreciatively at the glittering stone, she murmured warmly, 'You can bet your sweet ass I won't.'"

Spite Marriage began filming in the midst of the most sweeping flu epidemic the state had seen since 1918. District-wide school closures were mandated, and production schedules were disrupted with the illnesses of such industry figures as Jack Blystone, Hal Roach, Hoot Gibson, producer Benjamin Glazer, and Paramount's David O. Selznick. At M-G-M, both Eddie Mannix and Harry Rapf were laid up, and phone-ins from stars, directors, and featured players became a daily routine. Keaton, who was rarely sick, showed up forty minutes late the first day, had a five-minute conference with Ed Sedgwick, then sent to wardrobe for a hat and asked for a barber to come trim his hair. Ready and rehearsing at 10:10, he completed fourteen script scenes and only two added scenes, a clear indication the *Spite Marriage* script was in considerably better shape than the one for *The Cameraman*.

The company spent eleven days in a theater interior on M-G-M's Stage 14, working around the illnesses of both Keaton and actor Edward Earle, who was playing the caddish Lionel Benmore, Trilby's leading man. In keeping with Thalberg's involvement, the picture emerged as more conventional and plot-driven than most Keaton features, another *Battling Butler* rather than another *Sherlock Jr.* Now on the cusp of a talking-picture career, Keaton was giving a talking-picture performance. Knowing the film would be released with a synchronous musical score and sound effects, his charac-

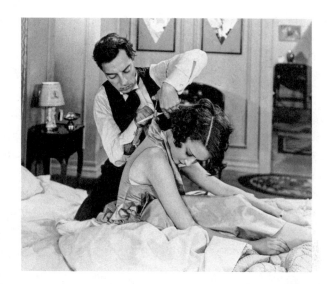

Elmer struggles to put a drunken Trilby to bed in Spite Marriage.

ter, Elmer, was speaking through intertitles as little as possible. There were routine delays while he and Sedgwick talked story and figured out physical business, and by the first of December they were four days behind.

The next five days were spent on interiors and location shots that were needed only briefly. On December 8, the company converged in a bridal suite erected on Stage 2 to capture the film's most memorable sequence, in which Elmer brings a drunken Trilby back to their hotel and attempts to put her to bed. The script provided minimal direction, calling simply for "a series of Rube Goldberg poses in his efforts to take her dress off and still keep her from falling on her nose or ear." Keaton and Dorothy Sebastian spent nearly an hour working out the mechanics of the scene, which had its basis in the deck chair gag from *The Navigator*. They both went to makeup at 9:20 and were back on the set at 10:35.

Elmer enters with his arm around the exquisitely plastered Trilby, who proceeds to crumple onto the floor as he steps away to pull the door shut. Turning back, his coat over one arm, he trips over her inanimate form and falls flat on his face. She rouses momentarily, then passes out, leaving him to work her into a chair, her perfectly limp body fighting him every inch of the way. After a half-dozen attempts, he lays the chair sideways on the floor, fits her into it, and rights both of them as a unit, only to find that she can't even then remain upright. She oozes out of it like quicksilver, so he throws her over his shoulder and lands her on the bed. Then he tries undressing her, starting with her shoes. While probing for a zipper, he rolls her over, and once again she continues onto the floor. After contemplating cutting her dress off her with a pair of scissors, he gives up entirely and just heaps the bedclothes over her. As he walks away, the bed collapses, which doesn't rouse her in the slightest.

Cut together, it's four minutes of superb physical comedy, Dorothy Sebastian proving herself a wonderfully gifted comedienne, even though, unlike most of Keaton's girls, she never worked for Mack Sennett. Eighteen days in, the company adjourned to Long Beach to take exteriors aboard a yacht, a grueling twelve-day shoot on choppy waters marred the first day by seas so rough they stood the boat on its end and made everyone seasick. Two days later, *Screenland*'s Helen Ludlam came aboard and found the crew roping the yacht to a tugboat that was to carry four cameras and wind machines for a shot of Keaton climbing over the rigging, getting tangled in the ropes, and plunging into the water.

"Buster came up from his dip in the sea looking quite happy and as though he really liked it. It was terribly cold, too. 'Oh, I always cover myself with goose grease when I have water stuff to do,' he said. 'It keeps the heat in the body and prevents one from feeling cold.' The sun came out so there could be no more work for a while. 'Isn't it the limit?' asked Buster. 'Most companies have to wait around for the sun, but this sequence calls for a stormy sky so we have to wait for clouds! We were lucky to strike that storm the other day, though the boat pitched so everyone was too seasick to work. We really had a close call. And if we hadn't made the harbor just when we did, there would have been a few lives lost. As it was, we had to anchor because the sea was too heavy to land.'"

The crew that day included Reggie Lanning on first camera, Elgin Lessley having retired due to ill health; Ernie Pagano as on-site gagman; and Ernie Orsatti, who, having returned to the fold in the off-season, represented the last vestige of Keaton's original team. Ed Sedgwick was a flamboyant presence on the set, part cheerleader, part cast member, part exasperated parent with a low boiling point. Yet he could also be easygoing and philosophical after nearly fifteen years in the movie business, spending the inevitable delays on the set composing popular songs with an accordionist named Norman McNeil and singing them in a beautiful tenor voice.

He told Helen Ludlam he went into pictures because he was tired of rehearsing and spending so much of his time indoors. "And now these sound pictures have come along and disorganized a profession that was just beginning to sit pretty! I'm not for sound pictures. Life won't be worth living if they go at those things one-hundred percent. Imagine what it's going to be like with actors who don't enunciate properly, and there are plenty, don't make any mistake about that. Take the line, 'Charles, will you ask the Duke to step this way?' 'No, no,' from the director, 'not Dook, but Duke.' Once more the actor tries. 'Charles, will you tell the Dewke to step this way?' 'No, no, no! Not Dook, not Dewke, but—Duke.' Holy mackerel! Right back to what I got out of! Not for me. I'd rather hunt up a good baseball team and umpire that!"

Sebastian performed like a champ, even as she was clad for plot purposes in summer clothes and the chill December winds had her teeth chattering. "Eddie," she wailed to Sedgwick as Keaton threw an overcoat over her shoulders. "Eddie, I want to go back. Look how far out we are, Eddie!"

A squall comes up and Elmer must change the sails, but the boom carries him out over the water with only Trilby on deck to help him. The mainsail collapses, and she becomes trapped herself. A boat carrying a gang of rumrunners approaches, and when their leader, Scarzi, tries forcing himself on her, Elmer must take the entire crew out by himself. The picture's climax becomes a life-and-death struggle between Elmer and Scarzi that plays across the entire length of the 135-foot vessel, Elmer eventually gaining the upper hand. With the action captured by the cameras aboard the adjacent tug some fifty feet away, Keaton performed one of his most spectacular stunts, in which he fell overboard from the bow of the yacht and was carried away by the current, recovering only by grabbing hold of a yawl being pulled in real time by a rope trailing from the stern. He clambered aboard, grappled up the rope to the deck, and resumed the battle, engaging in a desperate fistfight with his adversary until he wearily triumphed and collapsed in Sebastian's arms.

Spite Marriage returned to Culver City on December 22, 1928, and wrapped six days later, exactly thirty camera days into a thirty-day schedule. Budgeted at $264,493, it was brought in at a negative cost of $282,215, nearly $80,000 and nineteen days less than *The Cameraman*. As far as the studio was concerned, Keaton was now on the right track. It was precisely the wrong time for talkies to interfere.

Montreal, Quebec

SEPTEMBER 5, 1964

B USTER KEATON indulged a lifelong fascination with trains. He grew up on them, making jumps from city to city during his years in vaudeville, and he used them in his films, beginning with the Roscoe Arbuckle shorts he co-directed in California. "It was a great prop," he said. "I did some awful wild things with the railroads."

Now it is his first day shooting *The Railrodder,* and the setting is the sprawling Taschereau railyard that occupies a huge swath of the City of Côte-Saint-Luc. Keaton is in his element. He knows trains, their rhythms and dynamics. As a diesel locomotive glides into place on a track alongside where he is standing, he reaches out, grabs the handrail, and expertly mimes pulling the 150-ton engine to a halt.

"He knew by the sound of that engine that the thing was about to stop dead," marveled director Gerald Potterton, recalling the moment a half century later. "It was a remarkable act." Moments later, sensing it is ready to back away, Keaton convincingly reverses the feat, sending it on its way and watching with satisfaction as it gains speed, its bell sounding.

Surveying the great Canadian National yard with its eighty-one strands of classification track gives Keaton an inspiration. Parking an ever-present cigarette holder between his teeth, he produces a piece of scratch paper and a pen and begins to diagram some action.

"Three tracks are moored, like that," he says to Potterton, drawing it out. "You're comin' along this way [on the speeder], and an engine just with a caboose [is approaching] with a big locomotive. Camera's behind you travelin' with you. So that you got the thrill of that being on the same track with you, comin' right at you. Just about the time he reaches this switch is when you see him, and all you do is this." And chuckling, he waves the oncoming engine aside with an outstretched arm.

"He goes onto that track and you go to this one," he says, selling the gag with unmitigated glee. "See?"

"Great," says Potterton. "Yeah, it's great."

"And it's as sure as—" He hands the paper over.

"Yeah, that's a surefire."

"The suspense is that you don't pay any attention to it," Keaton says, laughing, and the others join in. "That's all there is to it. Wave 'em off." He gestures, his hands gracefully following the divergence of the two machines. "Get out of the way."

They all love it. "I think," mused Potterton, "he was the film director again, you know? We were in awe of that sort of situation, and he would do little arrows while smoking a cigarette in his holder."

As the camera crew wheels into position on a truck fitted with track guides, Keaton copes for the first time with the younger man's concern for his safety. "And I don't want you to worry about it," he tells Potterton, a fatherly hand patting his shoulder. "I'll miss 'em."

"I'll worry about it if you worry about it. But if you don't worry about it . . ."

Keaton shakes his head and turns away.

"You think you'll miss him all right?"

Keaton doesn't catch him, his hearing still compromised from the war.

"You're going to miss him, okay?" the director probes.

"Oh, I'll miss him," Keaton assures him, nodding.

"Otherwise," says Potterton, "it'd be a very short movie."

Keaton backs the speeder into position as the oncoming train prepares to make its run. There is perhaps twenty feet between the two switches that will clear the track, the speeder going off to the right, the locomotive to the left. Traveling behind him is the crew, the camera holding the locomotive dead center in the frame. As it bears down on Buster, he waves it off, but the timing isn't right, and the near miss isn't nearly near enough. They try again, but takes two and three aren't any good either. Finally, take four gives them the shot they're after. The rest of the afternoon is spent making a tracking shot of Buster from the other side of the train he has just missed, appearing between the cars as might the image in a zoetrope, standing in profile for the first flash, then head on for the second, then in profile again for the third, and finally with his backside to the camera as he fishes a spyglass from the boot.

Thus begins production on yet another film to feature Buster Keaton, one of well over a hundred, a body of work encompassing shorts and features, industrials and epics, silents and talkies, cameos and star turns—the entire range of what the medium could offer a well-known figure over the span of half a century. Keaton is an old hand at this, more in demand than he thinks he would like to be, but the intricate process of filmmaking engages and invigorates him as nothing else can.

"He's been insisting for the last three or four years that he is at least partially retired and intends to retire completely—until the phone rings," his third wife, Eleanor, says. "But then he'll turn right around and tell somebody he's retired." She chuckles. "It wouldn't work out. Because if the phone didn't ring for a month he would feel terribly neglected and abused because nobody wanted him anymore. Nobody loved him anymore. Nobody wanted him to work anymore. Deep down, I know darn well he enjoys working or he wouldn't say yes."

Gerald Potterton, meanwhile, is experiencing the same pangs of self-doubt that all new directors, with the possible exception of Orson Welles, felt at the start of their careers. Over the next five weeks, he will take Keaton across the entire span of Canada, through eight provinces and five time zones, from Halifax to Vancouver, amid some of the most spectacular scenery in the world. "On that first day of shooting on our little epic," he would write, "that face . . . was looking at mine. I remember thinking, 'My God! We're about to shoot an outdoor movie across one of the largest and coldest landmasses in the world with a few scraps of paper for a script, an aging star who should be enjoying a well-earned retirement, and on top of that, do I really know what I'm doing?' "

Part Three

YOU STUDIO PEOPLE WARP MY CHARACTER

17

The Gag Day Is Over

THE TALKIES had dogged Buster Keaton even before they were known as such. Marion Mack would vividly recall seeing *The General* in New York during its solitary week at the Capitol and noticing that *Don Juan* was in its twenty-seventh week at Warners' Theatre across the street. *Don Juan* itself wasn't a talkie, but it had a synchronous Vitaphone score performed by the New York Philharmonic, a few sound effects, and John Barrymore in the title role. It was, however, garnished with a selection of talking, singing, and instrumental shorts, the cumulative effect an intoxicating brew of pretense, hokum, and technological advancement, correctly heralded by the producing studio as "motion picture history in the making."

College opened just ahead of the double whammy of F. W. Murnau's *Sunrise* with its orchestral accompaniment courtesy of Movietone, and the gala world premiere of *The Jazz Singer* with Al Jolson delivering a couple of minutes of improvised dialogue in addition to six showstopping songs. By the time *Steamboat Bill, Jr.* made it into release, Warner Bros. had announced that all Warner pictures would include Vitaphone sequences, and the race was on to produce the first all-talking feature. It wasn't, as anticipated, a prestige affair but rather an impossibly stagey gangster melodrama, not even an hour in length, called *The Lights of New York,* and in July 1928, it knocked the industry on its collective ass.

"*The Jazz Singer,*" said Darryl Zanuck, Jack Warner's second-in-command, "turned them to sound, *The Lights of New York* to talk. It turned the whole goddamn tide."

Within the industry there was a lot of resistance to talking pictures—from stars whose speaking voices had to be vetted by engineers, from writers and directors who appreciated the flexibility intertitles gave them, and from executives who saw only the costs involved in soundproofing stages and acquiring delicate new recording equipment. One of the most prominent naysayers was Joe Schenck, who considered talkies a novelty whose vogue would pass in six months. In August 1928 he acknowledged that United Artists would be releasing a few talkies during the upcoming season, but they would be done only to satisfy a passing fancy.

"No talking picture is any good," he said with some justification. "They are uniformly uninteresting."

Scarcely a month later, Schenck changed his mind. One night, he accompanied Mary Pickford and Lupe Vélez to Paramount to see and hear voice tests the two actresses had made and to view rushes from the studio's first all-talking picture, *Interference.* "I have never seen anything like it," he raved. "The tests of Miss Pickford and Miss Vélez are marvelous, the voices were perfect, and the scenes shown of the Paramount picture were astounding for their naturalness." Perfectly aware of having to eat those earlier words, he added: "Here I have been panning talking pictures; now I am going to make them."

Louis B. Mayer had a similar epiphany when persuaded to see a Vitaphone short featuring operatic tenor Giovanni Martinelli. Mayer and Thalberg had famously resisted talking pictures to the point where M-G-M had fallen to the rear of the pack, allowing Warner Bros. and Fox to assume leadership positions, Warners with the sound-on-disc Vitaphone and Fox with the sound-on-film Movietone. By February 1929, theaters were being wired at the rate of 250 a month and, according to Western Electric, more than a thousand jobs were on back order. Yet only about half of M-G-M's feature output had a sound component. In fact, as late as June 1929, when Nicholas Schenck announced the company's new season, sixteen pictures were still being set aside as silents.

Even as the studio embraced sound, however tepidly, management faced the reluctance of two of its biggest stars to speak on-screen. To Lon Chaney it was a matter of business; his contract didn't require him to talk, and he expected a generous bump in salary were he to do so. To the Swedish-born Greta Garbo, it was less about money than insecurity over her command of the English language. Both would come around, and both would make their talking debuts in 1930, but both were stage-trained actors and there was little doubt that they would eventually speak on-screen. Buster Keaton belonged to a far more exclusive group of artists, and there was more consternation expressed over that group than any other. In March, Bob Sherwood devoted an edition of his "Motion Picture Album" in the *New York Evening Post* to the question of whether the great silent comedians would—or even should—talk.

Even those of us who are extreme in our confidence in the talkies are inclined to be dubious as to the future of comedy on the screen. It is true that the new Noise Era has been productive of several worthy comedies; in fact, the general quality of the two-reel gag-fests have been elevated to an incalculable extent during the past year. . . . Nevertheless—and no matter how humorous the screen dialogue may become—there is one thing certain: No one ever has achieved, or ever will, in spoken or printed words, the heights of comedy that were reached in the old days of silence by Charlie Chaplin, Harold Lloyd, and Buster Keaton, or by Harry Langdon, Mabel Normand, Chester Conklin, Raymond Griffith, Douglas MacLean, Hank Mann, Clyde Cook, Syd Chaplin, and other unforgettable clowns of the film.

It is in the field of comedy that the moving picture has been most surely and indisputably an art. One may argue that it is inferior to the play or the novel as a means of expressing tragedy, fantasy, irony, ruthless realism, or even melodrama. But no one can possibly say that there has ever been, in all the history of creative thought, anything so gloriously funny as a Chaplin comedy. No one can say it, that is, unless he speaks from the depths of ignorance and pretense, in which case he does not deserve to be heeded. . . . Through no medium less pitiable, less broad, less absurd than the moving picture could the art of Chaplin and Lloyd and Keaton be expressed. Where but on the screen would a chase be possible? And what scene in any play or what passage in any literary composition has caused as much hilarious laughter that was provoked by the chase in *Girl Shy?*

It is impossible to guess how Chaplin, Lloyd, and Keaton will be affected by the talkies, but I am certain that if they go too heavily for humorous dialogue they will lose something that is priceless and irreplaceable. For they have achieved by means of grotesque physical actions an eloquence that is far beyond the limitations of any language. Their comedies have never been restricted by frontiers . . . If the talking pictures are going to kill the fine art of movie comedy, then I take back everything I have ever said in their favor.

Harold Lloyd had already moved to embrace the talking screen, producing the tentatively titled *T-N-T* (later *Welcome Danger,* directed by Clyde Bruckman) in Movietone, but conservatively hedging his bet with a silent version as well. Chaplin, conversely, had no use at all for the talking screen, having witnessed a badly produced sound test made by Warner Bros. Then M-G-M released *The Broadway Melody,* ominously advertised as "All Talking, All Singing, All Dancing," and Chaplin found it "a cheap dull affair" that was nevertheless "a stupendous box office success." It was that success, he felt, that marked the twilight of the silent film.

"It was a pity, for they were beginning to improve," he wrote in his 1964 autobiography. "Murnau, the German director, had used the medium effectively, and some of our American directors were beginning to do the same. A good silent picture had universal appeal both to the intellectual and the rank and file. Now it was all to be lost. But I was determined to continue making silent films, for I believed there was room for all types of entertainment. Besides, I was a pantomimist, and in that medium I was unique and, without false modesty, a master. So I continued with the production of another silent picture, *City Lights.*"

Keaton was in a different place from Lloyd and Chaplin, having unwittingly sold his soul to Metro-Goldwyn-Mayer. When *Spite Marriage* opened at the Capitol on March 24, 1929, it was advertised as "with sound," which the public was beginning to understand meant music and effects, not dialogue. In many instances, the films that talked on big-city programs were not the features, but the one- and two-reel shorts that showcased vaudeville comics, musical acts, and news. Vitaphone was the dominant technology of the day, but the cleaner, simpler Movietone was making inroads, and M-G-M was starting to produce musical subjects in the sound-on-film format even as some of their major stars remained voiceless. One such short, featuring tenor William O'Neal, star of the Broadway hit *New Moon,* accompanied *Spite Marriage.*

Spite Marriage had a troubled release that was ultimately bolstered by good notices and the reach and power of Loew's Incorporated. In New York, it was unceremoniously dumped into the Capitol when the new attraction, an ineptly filmed stage play titled *The Great Power,* fared so poorly it was pulled after a single day. Reviewers were caught off guard, and it took a while for word to spread. Mordaunt Hall was first out of the gate, publishing his verdict in Monday's *Times* after giving over fully half the review to the unusual circumstances of its early appearance. "Words can hardly tell of the relief it was to look at Mr. Keaton's imaginative but silly silent antics in his latest farce, *Spite Marriage*. The theater that had been filled with pain and gloom was aroused to a state of high glee, and whether Elmer (Mr. Keaton) endeavored to help a girl who had imbibed more champagne than was good for her, or he bailed out of the engine room of a yacht in a foolish but apparently successful manner, there were waves of laughter from top to bottom of the house."

Others quickly caught up, although the stigma of a non-talking comedy was baked into even the most favorable of reviews. "*Spite Marriage* is a silent picture—as silent as any movie ever was except for the orchestral score—and it is a successful, amusing, entertaining, and enjoyable film," said Creighton Peet in the *Evening Post*. "Who says the silent film is all washed up? I think people will be crowding into the Capitol for two reasons—to enjoy themselves, and to shed a tear for the complete and utter passing of the familiar old-time silent movie."

Everyone had praise for Dorothy Sebastian's comedic chops, even more so in some cases than for Keaton's. "Although the frozen-faced Buster isn't quite as comical as he has been in past performance, his acrobatic sense is in great form," wrote Irene Thirer in the *Daily News,* "and his leading lady, Dorothy Sebastian, gives you the surprise of your life via this film. Dorothy is not the perfect clothes horse you've always seen on the screen. She's a comedienne, and a swell one. Director Edward Sedgwick gives her a chance to play an actress who has had much too much champagne. And she truly convinces you that it wasn't property liquid in the bottle—although we presume it was."

Audiences and critics alike praised the scene of Elmer putting Trilby to bed, and it immediately found a place in the pantheon of Keaton's most memorable on-screen exploits—right up there with the falling facade in *Steamboat Bill, Jr.* and the boulder chase from *Seven Chances.* Indeed, the bit of Keaton fitting Sebastian into the chair was so original and screamingly funny it brought a spontaneous salvo of applause from the audience. Even the normally sour Roy Chartier from *Billboard* called the scene "a knockout for laughs," but in a chilling glimpse of things to come, this modest little masterpiece of a scene almost didn't make it into the picture.

Larry Weingarten had little direct involvement in the making of *Spite Marriage,* but Louis B. Mayer kept telling him that M-G-M was a producer's studio, so he naturally felt he should take ownership of the finished product. One day, Weingarten viewed the rushes of the scene in the bridal suite—Keaton was on location off the coast of Long Beach—and chose to ignore the fact that the two characters were married and that the scene was in the script Irving Thalberg had okayed. "Don't bother to tear that sequence down," he told editor Frank Sullivan. "I don't like that type of thing in *my* pictures."

"I talked like a Dutch uncle to save that scene," said Keaton. "It was only the biggest laugh in the film." He was, of course, vindicated by all the reviewers who singled it out, and by reports in the trades of applause from jaded Broadway audiences who rarely clapped for movie gags. "I'm afraid that Larry Weingarten was plenty sore, especially when the putting-the-bride-to-bed was such a success. But, God almighty, I'd fight for the darndest things that I knew were right, and they'd brush me off."

Spite Marriage was, as *Variety* put it, "sacrificed to emergency" in New York and doubtless did less at the box office than it would have done had advance publicity given it a proper ballyhoo. It wasn't held a second week, and didn't reach Los Angeles until May, where it was relegated to the Fox Boulevard, a large neighborhood house, Loew's State having gone all talking in the interim. With the headwinds, domestic rentals were held to just $345,000, but foreign markets, not quite as enamored of talk as the Americans, embraced it solidly, delivering another $556,000.

"The silent film is giving its dying kick just to show it cannot be pushed out so easily," James N. Stephens, London film correspondent for *The New York Times,* commented, "and its kick has taken the form of Buster Keaton in *Spite Marriage.* This is so funny and so human that it has broken even the box office records held by its sometimes noisy sound rival at the cinema where it is being shown."

By July 1930, worldwide rentals amounted to $991,000 and M-G-M was showing a net profit of $196,785—making *Spite Marriage* the most profitable of all of Keaton's silent features.

The chemistry between Buster Keaton and Dorothy Sebastian didn't just exist on-screen, and they formed a bond that extended far past the completion of *Spite Marriage.*

"He had quite a crush on Dorothy Sebastian," said Harold Goodwin. "She [had one on him], too."

As Keaton attended year-end holiday parties and western star Fred Thomson's funeral, at which he was an honorary pallbearer, Sebastian and

Clarence Brown could still be seen around town, their engagement having extended sixteen months from its announcement in August 1927. But true to her word, Dorothy would never commit to a date, even as Brown made flamboyant gestures of devotion, such as borrowing a plane during the *Spite Marriage* shoot to deliver an emergency load of raw stock via parachute while they were filming fifteen miles off the coast of Long Beach.

Sebastian was being featured in Brown's *A Woman of Affairs* about the time she brought their engagement to an end, although the public announcement, such as it was, didn't come until later. Meanwhile, a syndicated profile by NEA's Dan Thomas likened her to Mabel Normand in looks and talent, a comparison she eagerly embraced.

"I would give anything in the world to be allowed to play the same kind of roles that Mabel used to," she said. "I have been on the screen for a little more than three years now and during that time I have portrayed almost every type of character, but I really didn't find myself until my last picture. That was with Buster Keaton in *Spite Marriage*. My role in that was similar to the ones Mabel used to play. I loved it and think it was the best work I ever have done."

It's easy to see what Keaton found attractive about her. Dot, as she liked to be called, was widely known as a good time, easygoing and pretty much the complete opposite of Natalie.

"Dorothy was sweet, funny, and sentimental, and I liked her," wrote Charles Francis, a tenant of hers in the late 1940s. "She had a collection of strange headwear and would spring a new one on us at our weekly boozy house parties. She could play the ukulele and sing nonsense songs. This charming lady also possessed an inexhaustible repertoire of bawdy limericks."

She didn't, however, hold her liquor very well, which led Buster, with his penchant for nicknames, to call her Slambastian.

"Buster was very sexy, very relaxed and easy with women," Louise Brooks said, "the first sign of a man secure in his performance. I think he was capable of love, but like me he was possessed rather than choosing to possess. I knew Dorothy Sebastian very well. She was adorable and adored by him, but neither was possessive."

They discreetly spent time together over the summer of 1929, when Keaton was largely inactive and Dorothy seemed to be working all the time. That fall, she was lent to Pathé for a picture opposite William Boyd, who had come to prominence under the direction of Cecil B. DeMille, and moved into his orbit. Boyd was a heavy drinker himself, and one picture quickly led to another. Both divorced, Dorothy and Bill could be an item without the subterfuge, and their engagement was announced in September 1930.

With the completion of *Spite Marriage,* there was no avoiding the fact that Buster Keaton's next picture would have to be a talkie. Silents—even very good ones like *Spite Marriage*—were being relegated to second-class status, blocked out of first-run theaters that had necessarily, due to popular demand, gone all talking. Keaton had two 1928 releases in *Steamboat Bill, Jr.* and *The Cameraman,* and his first release of 1929 was already in the can. Now he had a full six months to develop and produce a second, this time making shrewd use of a soundtrack that would incorporate not just music and effects, but his actual speaking voice. At first, this did not unsettle him in the least. "We talk when we're supposed to talk," he reasoned, "but we lay out material that don't call for dialogue."

This was easier said than done. Weingarten had little experience in script development, and virtually none in talking pictures. And Thalberg, with overall responsibility for the entire season's schedule of releases, was too distracted to be of much help. What followed was a semester of on-the-job training in which Keaton ran up against a struggling producer's absolute authority.

"New York stage directors, New York writers—dialogue writers—and musicians' union all moved to Hollywood," Keaton said. "So, the minute they started laying out a script, they're looking for those funny lines, puns, little jokes, anything else. And my fight with Thalberg at M-G-M was [to say], 'Lay out a script with me the same as you always did. You come to that sequence where a man's working here on this part of the thing and I'm working on something else. We don't talk back and forth, we work. Now, you go out of your way when you have us talk. Work the same as we always did. We avoid talking when it's not necessary.' "

What followed was a flood of ideas, most of which were utterly hopeless, but many of which were considered and then abandoned simply because Weingarten had little sense of what he was doing. Keaton counted twenty-two writers during this period: "And it wasn't only the twenty-two writers who were eager to help me out. The executives and studio big shots also turned into gagmen overnight, adding greatly to the confusion. With so much talk going on, so many conferences, so many brains at work, I began to lose faith for the first time in my own ideas."

Keaton must have wondered if he was in some sort of a miasma at M-G-M in which he had been acquired and then forgotten. The only actual production he saw during this period was in April 1929, when he was added to the studio's first complete musical picture, an all-star affair directed by Chuck Reisner called *Hollywood Revue*. It was designed to feature all of M-G-M's top contract talent, and it very nearly did, with only Greta Garbo and Lon Chaney opting out. Keaton did a variation of his old Princess Rajah routine, which required neither scripting nor dialogue. Then in June he was back to appear with all the other principals in the film's Technicolor finale in which they sang "Singin' in the Rain."

In May, Thalberg and Weingarten briefly settled on a musical-comedy called *His Royal Highness* as Keaton's first talkie. A month later, Ed Sedgwick dictated an original of his own, a backstage story he called *The Three Act*. Somewhat Chaplinesque in tone—Sedgwick referred to the Keaton character throughout as "The Little Fellow"—they probably went with it because time was running short to get a fall release into production. Richard Schayer was again brought on to write the scenario, which had endured two rounds of revisions by the time Thalberg okayed it on August 23. Still, it wasn't right. Schayer was tasked with coming up with an entirely new story line, and the incomplete draft of September 17 was made up of "sections taken out and put in." Yet another story line was developed in early October; then the decision was made to scrap the theatrical background altogether and set the picture in a Hollywood studio with a character and plot reminiscent of *Merton of the Movies*. With Al Boasberg, who had earlier contributed to *Battling Butler* and *The General*, fashioning dialogue, the final version began taking shape as *On the Set*. Now Thalberg stepped away, and when *On the Set*, soon to be known as *Free and Easy*, was finalized on November 22, it was okayed for production by Larry Weingarten, not Irving Thalberg. For Buster Keaton, the transition from Thalberg to Weingarten was now complete.

Keaton had little involvement in the scripting process, no more than, say, Ramon Novarro or Joan Crawford had in the shaping of their pictures. At Metro, it was the supervisor's responsibility to bring the story along, and the star only got in the way until it came time to commit the thing to film. The rationale was that most screen personalities had no clue as to what the public wanted from them. Keaton realized he was now regarded by the corporation as an actor—not a writer or a gagman or a director or even a fully vested member of the creative team, but simply an actor. As Douglas Fairbanks said the first time he stepped inside a tomb-like stage that had been wired and blanketed for sound: "The romance of picture making ends here!"

Keaton remained sequestered in his off-site headquarters, busying himself with the establishment of a permanent field for the studio baseball team, the Metro-Goldwyn-Mayer Lions. ("I don't think M-G-M knew he was there," Buster Collier commented.) When Hearst reporter Harry Brundidge interviewed Keaton, he found him, as Brundidge put it, in a "talkie mood," forever on the move, "standing up, sitting down, climbing on furniture, and laughing."

What little news he had of the script development process came from Ed Sedgwick, whom Weingarten had to involve since the story was still officially his. What Weingarten proudly lacked was any understanding of Keaton's screen character or the qualities that made his comedies unique.

"If Buster Keaton had been still a big commercial thing for Joe Schenck," Weingarten said dismissively, "he wouldn't have turned him over to Metro-Goldwyn-Mayer." Weingarten was well steeped in the workings of the M-G-M story machine and considered plotlines for their stable of stars interchangeable. "We found stories and if they suited . . . they might not suit one, they'd suit the other, or we make them suit."

Keaton's character, Elmer Butts, was conceived as the bumbling manager of Miss Gopher City, a small-town beauty queen brought to Hollywood for a chance at the movies. As written, Butts is just a boob who takes no initiative at anything, robbing Keaton of one of the signal traits of his past screen characters. Life happens to him, and he's powerless to do anything about it. But if Keaton objected to the story on these grounds alone, it likely went no further than Sedgwick, who was as concerned with the technical aspects of the show as he was the ever-changing details of the script.

To Buster, Weingarten had even less of a low-comedy mind than Thalberg. "Right from the start of talkies they were fascinated by the new equipment, new techniques," he said in a 1961 interview. "Everything was different. They threw the old casting in the ash can. 'What kind of voice does so-and-so have?' the casting director would ask. Before that, they hadn't thought about voices. It was just how somebody could act, or do comedy, or how he looked."

For a leading lady, Keaton was given Anita Page, who had just turned nineteen and had been in *Our Dancing Daughters* with Joan Crawford and Dorothy Sebastian. Unlike Sebastian, Page was no comedienne, and she lacked the sophisticated good looks of Marceline Day. Her principal qualifications for working opposite Keaton was that her voice recorded acceptably and she was five two. Otherwise, the only cast member of any consequence was Trixie Friganza, a veteran vaudeville and musical-comedy star cast as Page's overbearing mother.

Production began on November 21, 1929, with an incomplete script and a writer named Paul Dickey feverishly retooling the dialogue as they went. The first day's work at the studio's main gate, where Elmer tries to get past the guard, didn't go well due to an equipment breakdown that limited Keaton and Sedgwick to five setups for the day. The next day didn't go much better, but by the third the script was at least considered complete with 144 scenes. Still there were frequent delays while the cast and crew, ready to shoot, sat around waiting for dialogue. And when Dickey's pages finally arrived, Weingarten would disappear into a huddle with Sedgwick while the rest of the company continued to wait. "He rushed on the set, overseeing the works," Keaton complained. "Rode the writers, rode the director, rode me." And so the man who had made *The General* just three years earlier was reduced to the role of a spectator in the making of his first talking picture. And for the first time in his life, the joy of filmmaking left him.

The actors had to hold their lines until whoever was speaking ahead of them was finished—overlapping dialogue was thought to confuse both the recording equipment and the audience. The result was that any verve or pacing the scene might have was completely destroyed, and the practice played hell with comic timing.

"Everything got so technical when sound came in," said Anita Page, who was used to the live mood music that was standard on the sets of silent pictures. "When the microphones began, everything on the set changed. Musicians were gone, and everything had to be still and quiet. Nobody could talk together or make anybody laugh. That was out. And you had to speak with such *precision*. If my dress rustled or my feet made any noise, we had to shoot the scene all over again."

When it came time to shoot the film's musical numbers, work was suspended while Keaton and the other principals rehearsed with choreographer Sammy Lee. ("I don't think he enjoyed that part of the picture," Page confided.) Keaton managed his natural baritone well, but was noticeably uncomfortable letting the movie go for so long a stretch without a single laugh. The nadir of all this was a scene in which Elmer is strung up like a giant marionette and bounced around the stage wearing a grotesque clown's makeup that turned his distinctive features into a Death's mask of hapless

Keaton hated the clown outfit and makeup he was forced to wear in Free and Easy *(1930).*

abandon. And in the end, when, for the first time in his feature career, he loses the girl, he is made to appear to be reaching for Chaplin's mantle of pathos in the crassest possible way. Keaton apparently shot this scene without protest, showing at best that he was making a game attempt to follow the studio's dictates in the hope that they would see how miserably they were missing the mark. As Keaton's friend Loyal "Doc" Lucas said, "He thought that clown-face thing was the most ridiculous thing he ever did."

Free and Easy was not only the worst picture Buster Keaton had ever made, it was also the most expensive. Estimated at $439,782, it finished $33,000 over budget. Yet the fact that it wrapped with more than 200,000 feet of exposed film—a shooting ratio of twenty-four to one—was more a reflection of technical troubles than added scenes or last-minute inspirations. Of the 134,000 feet of soundtrack—the balance was silent—only 18,000 feet were deemed to be technically acceptable. Yet the picture finished in just twenty-four camera days—three days ahead of schedule—attesting to Keaton's cooperation throughout.

Keaton never said publicly what he thought of *Free and Easy*—not at the time, not later. He seemed, in fact, to avoid talking to the press. And in the film's aftermath, his contract with M-G-M was allowed to lapse, prompting *Variety* to conclude that Metro was turning him loose. It is likely, however, that Keaton was holding out for better terms; he had made his first talking picture their way, and now he wanted to make one *his* way. The authority Weingarten exerted over *Free and Easy* was evident in the statistics—only eleven added scenes were made as compared to *The Cameraman,* on which nearly four hundred were unscripted additions. Now Keaton went to Thalberg, asking once again to be given his own unit. "I kept pleading, 'Give me Eddie Sedgwick to direct, two or three writers, my own prop man, electrician, wardrobe woman, and a few technicians, and I will guarantee to deliver pictures as good or better than *The Cameraman.*'"

Predictably, Thalberg wasn't persuaded, but he was sufficiently in sympathy with Keaton's predicament to permit him more room in which to work. Buster would have more voice and latitude in the writing of his next picture, and Weingarten would be told to back off and give him his head. On January 27, 1930, Keaton signed a new contract commencing January 15 and continuing for the amount of time services were required to make one photoplay. As a trade-off, he would also be required to make one or more foreign-language versions of *Free and Easy,* for which he would be paid an additional $12,500 each.

Keaton's picture under this contract, which would come to be known as *Doughboys,* began as an original story from actor-director-playwright Willard Mack, who was under contract to Metro at the time. Primarily the author of stage melodramas such as *The Dove, The Noose,* and *A Free Soul,* Mack had a tin ear when it came to comedy. His story, *Fix Bayonets,* had little to recommend it, and even the author's foreword signaled trouble: "In writing this story for Buster Keaton, I have tried to fashion a yarn which fits him in the new field of Talking Pictures. You have—and you could—and you did depend upon a series of gags in the silent picture—but the 'gag day' (existing on gags alone) is over. A comedian must today extract laughs from his lines, provided those lines contain a medium of humor."

While Willard Mack was at work on his story, Al Boasberg and Paul Dickey were on a parallel track with a comedy titled *War Babies.* Notes, synopses, threads, changes, and outlines followed, and then Dickey fell away from the project, replaced in late January by Boasberg's sometime collaborator, a former magazine writer and dialogue specialist named Sidney Lazarus. Boasberg and Lazarus took a fresh pass at the story, generating at least five different versions, some under the title *Fall In,* before Richard Schayer was brought aboard in April to sift through the remnants and, in collaboration with Keaton, produce a draft continuity.

Buster's character, again called Elmer, reached back to the rich twits he played in pictures like *The Saphead, Seven Chances,* and *Battling Butler,* young men born into wealth and privilege without a clue as to how the rest of the world functioned. Keaton's influence over the story could be seen in the setup, the character itself, and the circumstances that lead to his mistakenly enlisting in the army. Moreover, the love interest is clear from the outset, a pretty girl named Mary who rebuffs all his efforts to woo her. When they both end up based overseas, he in the infantry, she in the entertainment division, the stage is set for Elmer to save the day and win her hand—in other words, the classic Keaton formula for a six-reel comedy.

With his newly won authority, Keaton would make the film as he and Sedgwick had made *The Cameraman,* using the script as a starting point and sharpening the comedy as they went. Weingarten would still be the supervisor, but he'd hold back and not stifle the creative process. The film, in other words, would be allowed to evolve as all the best Keaton pictures had. And Buster was determined to show that *Doughboys* could be brought in for a lot less money than *Free and Easy.* It was, in many ways, a necessary course correction after the artistic debacle that preceded it. With a budget of $265,000, *Doughboys* was given a twenty-four-day schedule and a start date of May 13, 1930.

Buster Keaton took his first taste of whiskey in Bluffton one summer. The occasion was the rejection of his pal Lex Neal by the town beauty, who was the daughter of the commissioner of the Muskegon County Water Works. "I'll prove I am your true friend by not letting you get soused alone," Buster told him. "I'll get drunk, too." They got an adult, who ran a tourist camp, to buy a bottle for them, and the two boys sat and took alternate pulls from it.

"When darkness fell," remembered Keaton, "I was blotto." In no shape to go home, Buster was taken back to Lex's house, where he was nursed through the mother of all hangovers. Chastened, he didn't take another sip until he was a soldier in the war.

That time, the glow stayed with him, and when he returned to Los Angeles in 1919, he was ready to indulge in the Prohibition era's favorite pastime. Alcohol softened his defenses and loosened him up. At work, he was comfortable, contained. After hours, he was reticent outside the protective bubble of show business. Dance nights at the Hollywood Hotel were spent in Viola Dana's suite drinking pure-grain alcohol flavored with mysterious additives, while other evenings took place at the Palm Court of the Alexandria Hotel, where diners brought their own rotgut in hip flasks, or at the Ship Cafe in the open city of Venice. As the twenties wore on and enforcement grew laxer, the supply of genuine or slightly cut goods increased, and it seemed that fully half the mechanics, doormen, chauffeurs, and office boys at the various studios were dealers. Following Roscoe Arbuckle's example, Keaton always had a well-stocked cellar in any house he owned, and the Italian Villa was designed and built with a bar hidden off the playroom.

"Buster Keaton needed excitement," said Buster Collier. "But deeper than that, he loved to make everybody happy, liked his gang around. So it became two drinks in the evening, then four, then the sky's the limit. Whereupon you move it down into the daytime, and soon you have a bottle beside the alarm clock."

Pressures of work, changes like the loss of the studio, and the cold center in his marriage took their toll. At his studio, he'd admit to taking a drink with the crew over lunch, but he never allowed it to interfere with filming, especially when there were stunts to do and he needed his wits about him. Then came the move to M-G-M. There is no evidence of dissipation in either *The Cameraman* or *Spite Marriage,* both of which were as physically demanding as his independent features. But *Free and Easy,* piloted by Ed Sedgwick and a crew of audio technicians, was largely beyond his control, and he found himself with nothing to do. Frequently, he retreated to his off-site bungalow, where he nursed a resentment far greater than he realized. And the effects began to seep into his work. It shows in some of his later scenes in *Free and Easy,* where his speech is noticeably thick in an exchange with Anita Page. In March, when he filmed his scenes for an all-Spanish version titled *Estrellados,* he was stone sober, his time spent carefully mastering the phonetic Spanish lettered on cue cards held out of camera range.*

"I never liked the idiot cards," he said. "I preferred memorizing one simple sentence or two or three while the scenes I wasn't in were being made."

Free and Easy was released on March 22, 1930, and had its first West Coast showings in Los Angeles and San Francisco. Philip K. Scheuer, the acerbic young critic for the *Los Angeles Times,* framed it as "a noisy trip through Hollywood and environs" and cut it more slack than it deserved. "Funny

---

* German and Italian versions were made as well, but these were essentially silent films with music, effects, and intertitles in place of dialogue. However, two English-language musical numbers were left in.

enough to merit recommendation on this score, the picture is handicapped by a too-great abundance of extraneous material. At one time it hovers perilously close to emotional drama, at another displays all the earmarks of going *Hollywood Revue*. It all comes from trying to make a Pagliaccio out of Keaton." Ed O'Malley of the *Hollywood Filmograph* approvingly described Buster's voice as "very much like that of Dante's Satan—sepulchral, low, baleful and unmelodious, and through all his spoutings and guttural exhalations he still maintains the famous frozen face."

The picture performed well in these initial engagements, particularly in Fog City, where it upped the gate at the five-thousand-seat Fox for the first time in weeks. It opened in New York a month later, agreeably pulling a $70,000 week at the Capitol while drawing a range of mostly tepid reviews. To *Variety* it was "strictly a routine programmer"; to *Film Daily* "just one of those things."

No reviewer commented on the film's most glaring fault, that there was nothing Keatonesque about it. But to Martin Dickstein it was something akin to a cinema event: "Keaton in the talkies reveals himself, if anything, a more entertaining comedian than he was in silent pictures, and his many uproarious comments before the microphone promise numerous treats yet to come. It all goes to prove, probably, that the talkies no longer hold any terror (if they really ever did) for the old favorites of the silent days."

All this seemed to validate the studio's approach, which couldn't have made Keaton very happy. As a comedy, he knew the picture was a stiff, contrived and tedious and unlike anything his fans had come to expect of him. It offered only brief, fleeting moments of amusement, and could have top-lined any of a dozen male stars with no discernible difference in the outcome. It was in this frame of mind that he began work on *Doughboys* with training camp exteriors and an incomplete script. The first few days went smoothly, with some exuberant physical comedy recalling Keaton's silent days and Ed Brophy's eruptive drill sergeant energizing the early action. Better still, there were twenty-seven added scenes, attesting to the fact that Keaton was back on solid creative ground. In contrast to the generic blandness of *Free and Easy*, *Doughboys* promised some of the character and precision that exemplified his better work.

On the fifth day of production, a Saturday, they were already a day behind schedule. The script called for Elmer to play a romantic exchange with Mary at the hostess house. All went well in the morning, with Sedgwick concentrating on scenes with actress Sally Eilers and Cliff "Ukulele Ike" Edwards.

Keaton was drunk when he played this dialogue scene with Sally Eilers in Doughboys *(1930). His condition went unnoticed by audiences, but studio management took note.*

Keaton himself played a short bit at a pay phone talking to his father. ("No, Father. I don't think I'll stay in the army. The other chaps don't seem to recognize my social position.") The company broke for lunch. There was nothing remarkable about the day until Keaton returned to the set glassy-eyed, weaving and slurring his words.

He was drunk.

Sedgwick got through the rest of the day as best he could. There were seven retakes, but the star's condition was painfully obvious in the rushes, which were viewed by Thalberg and Weingarten. Keaton continued to drink for the next several days, the effects clearly showing on film, until he could barely stand for a daytime exterior involving an exchange between Elmer (as part of a guard detail) and a corporal enacted by a day player. Judging that Keaton would be unable to carry the scene, Sedgwick concocted a substitution with Ed Brophy, positioning Keaton with his face away from the camera, his only line a perfunctory "Is that all, sir?" They broke early, putting the film another half day behind. Presumably something got said, for Keaton cleaned up and shot nineteen script scenes the next day, not only bringing the picture up current but putting it a full day ahead. The following day, a Friday, he filmed another sixteen interiors and finished the week with the picture up two days on the schedule.

Four days of battlefield exteriors were filmed at Lasky Mesa, northwest

Supervisor Lawrence Weingarten, Ed Sedgwick, Keaton, and Edward Brophy on the set of Doughboys.

of Los Angeles. On location, actor-stuntman Gil Perkins observed Keaton butting heads with Sedgwick. "I would say [on] *Doughboys* he was kind of sulking. He would try to contribute and they wouldn't accept it. . . . We all felt sorry for the situation, and we also felt sorry for the director because it's tough for a director to have an actor who had decided ideas on what he wants to do. In many cases when that happens, they discuss it and resolve [it], but it never seemed to be resolved with Buster. Buster always seemed to be upset about the situation." There were also accounts of his drinking, which was regarded on the set as an open secret. "In talking with the sound men and cameramen and assistant cameramen and prop men, they all felt that he was very unhappy with the situation there, and that that contributed to not only his drinking but his depression."

While still at work on *Free and Easy,* Ed Sedgwick decided that talking comedies should still be 40 percent silent, and seemed to be striving to achieve that balance with *Doughboys.* "Audiences are still used to the methods of silent comedy," he said, "and we have to give them pantomimic gags in with the new talking technique to have them really satisfied."

The problem with physical comedy was that it often had to be worked out on the set, and sometimes they came up empty-handed. Stymied one day, Keaton, Edwards, and Sedgwick improvised a two-minute scat number, Buster on his uke, Ike singing and drumming, Ed, as the company's cook, sawing at his rifle as if it were a bass fiddle. It was a delightful interlude, but when they finished, Keaton was done for the day. He wasn't drunk, but with the added scene and four retakes in the can, he was intent upon leaving and did so at three forty-five. Apparently he had an exchange with Weingarten on the matter, but it made no difference. Knocking off early would have been perfectly normal back at the studio on Lillian Way, but at the factory known as M-G-M it drew a written rebuke from Irving Thalberg in the form of a telegram. The wire instructed him to report to the studio at ten o'clock the next morning.

> YOU ARE FURTHER ADVISED THAT YOUR REFUSAL
> TO COMPLY THIS AFTERNOON HAS CAUSED US
> CONSIDERABLE LOSS, AND FURTHER LOSS WILL BE
> CAUSED IN [THE] EVENT YOU FAIL TO COMPLY AND
> RESUME YOUR SERVICES.

Chastened, Keaton appeared as required and shot twenty-nine script scenes, two added scenes, one retake, and still finished early. The last few days of production were given over to a troop show on the order of the Sunshine Players in which Keaton, in drag, performed a French dance with a male partner to Jacques Offenbach's "L'Amour de L'Apache." Production closed on June 9 at a final cost of $275,949—almost $200,000 less than *Free and Easy*.

If Keaton had shown he could make a better picture that was considerably cheaper, he had also shown he could be irresponsible—at least by the standards of a major studio. L. B. Mayer would happily have cut him loose, but Thalberg valued Keaton's standing as the only star comedian on the M-G-M roster. "Without stars," he once wrote, "a company is in the position of starting over again each year." Instead of a scolding, Thalberg would give Keaton a show of support and time to pull himself together. On July 2, with the completion of *De Frente, Marchen*, the Spanish-language version of *Doughboys*, Keaton's single-picture contract was terminated. A week later, he signed a new two-year agreement with the studio, which Thalberg made effective October 16, 1930. This gave Keaton his two releases for the year, plus a three-month holiday, during which, Thalberg told him, he should take Natalie to Europe. "Have a good time for yourselves," he said.

. . .

Perhaps Thalberg sensed that Keaton was overextended. In April, inspired by the experience of filming *Estrellados* in phonetic Spanish, Buster hit on the idea of remaking some of the Fatty Arbuckle comedies for foreign markets where the demand was still strong. He looked at three—*The Cook, The Bell Boy,* and *The Garage*—and thought they held up so well he told Louella Parsons he'd partner with Hal Roach to make a Spanish version of *The Garage* as a pilot. His extracurricular love life was the perennial subject of studio gossip, and his off-site bungalow had become so overrun with old vaudevillians and hangers-on that he was forced to move to new quarters on the studio lot just to get rid of them. Then there was the entertaining—the barbecues and parties and the like—and the gambling (bridge and poker and weekends at Agua Caliente, the Mexican Monte Carlo). And, of course, the seemingly endless stream of practical jokes.

Maybe, too, it was that Buster Keaton, approaching his thirty-fifth birthday, had simply burned himself out. "It's just like the candymaker who handles sweet stuff every day of his life," he said. "He sees so much sugar that he loses all taste for it. That's my fix. I used to be able to laugh at anything funny. But thinking comedy, playing comedy, and making work out of humor have taken away my taste for laughter. People seem to feel it a sort of duty to tell me funny stories. I used to hear about a hundred stories a week which would give me a good laugh. Now if I hear three or four new ones, I feel lucky."

The Keatons sailed from New York on July 15 with plans to visit England,

Gilbert Roland, Norma Talmadge, and Keaton on holiday in France.

France, and Germany. The *Los Angeles Times* reported that Buster planned to purchase a car in Europe with the intent of touring some of the out-of-the-way places that vacationers typically missed. "While the comedian is away, a new story will be prepared, and he will return to plunge immediately into production."

The timing of Keaton's departure was significant in that he made sure he was out of town when *Doughboys* (under the working title *The Big Shot*) was previewed locally at the Belmont Theatre. Had he remained a few days longer, he might have been surprised by the crowd's reaction. The film was "a riot of cross purposes, ludicrous situations, and diverting extravaganza," according to the *Filmograph*'s Ed O'Malley, who covered the screening. Keaton's Apache dance, O'Malley reported, brought forth "dynamic bursts of laughter," while Ed Brophy's drill sergeant nearly stole the show.* "*Big Shot* is sure to go over with a wham—make no mistake."

In September, columnist Frank Scully noted that Keaton was about the only celebrity who passed up Antibes that summer in favor of Biarritz in the French Basque Country, Buster and Natalie having met up with Nat's sister Norma in Paris. As they were settling in, Gilbert Roland came up from Antibes to join them, and as a foursome they ate, drank, and took in the sights. Roland, who was born in Mexico, wanted to see Oscar Wilde's tomb at Père Lachaise. "It was abandoned, forgotten," he wrote, "lizards crawled all over it, it depressed me, and at the Castiglione Bar with Buster Keaton we got drunk. Buster because he was having trouble with Natalie, and I because lizards crawled on Oscar Wilde's tomb."

Norma, Roland recorded, was in bed with the curse, and Natalie stayed with her as the two men crossed into Spain at San Sebastian to attend a bull-fight, Keaton's first. "The standing ovation he received brought tears to his eyes. Then Marquez [the matador] dedicated the bull to him, flung up [his hat], the montera. 'Great honor, Keaton,' I said." Not knowing what to do, Keaton was advised to offer a gift. Cash, he was told, would be considered an insult. Stuffing a wad of bills back into his pocket, Keaton took out a gold cigarette case purchased at Cartier, placed it inside the montera, and threw it back down to Marquez. "Everyone in San Sebastian was happy about Buster Keaton's gesture except Natalie. She had given him the expensive cigarette case, and he in turn had given it to some 'lousy bullfighter.' Buster laughed.

---

* In a scene reflecting one of Keaton's own experiences at Camp Kearny, Brophy conducts bayonet drill in such gruesome verbal detail the men faint dead away.

It was wonderful to see him laugh; deadpan on the screen, in real life, a happy, humorous, generous man. Natalie at times made his life miserable, was extremely jealous, often unreasonable. I loved them both, refused to interfere with their personal problems, but [it] made me uneasy when she quarreled and cried."

The Spanish, Keaton discovered, had a name for him—*Pamplinas*. The word roughly translated to "nonsense," but even that wasn't terribly accurate. Twenty-five years later, he would ask the renowned flamenco dancer Jose Greco what he thought it meant, and an animated discussion between Greco and his manager and troupe ensued. Finally, Greco turned back to Keaton and explained, "Pamplinas, in English, means 'a little bit of nothing.'"

M-G-M released *Doughboys* on August 30, 1930, while its star was still out of the country. It opened in New York on September 19 to lackluster notices and disappointing business, most everyone acknowledging laughs while considering the idea of a comedy about the war old hat. Even Cliff Edwards as the live act on the bill at the Capitol didn't help. "The picture is moderately amusing until an hour's worth has been unreeled," Irene Thirer allowed in the *Daily News.* "Then it gets so funny for the remaining twenty minutes that the audience reaction is all favorable." In the *Sun,* John S. Cohen, Jr., seemed to detect the scenes in which Keaton had been drinking. "There is a mechanical quality about him now, instead of the air of spontaneity that he used to have." There were also the inevitable comparisons to Chaplin's *Shoulder Arms,* now more than a decade old.

Keaton arrived back in Brooklyn on September 22, but steered clear of the Capitol and avoided the press. All he offered the *Times* was that he had hurried back to see the first two games of the World Series, in which Ernie Orsatti would be batting for St. Louis. He said that he saw pictures in England, Germany, France, and Spain. There was, he found, continuous propaganda in the British newspapers against American films, and readers were urged to see only the domestic product, which was largely inferior. Yet in Germany there was no effort to keep American pictures out of the country because the Germans could make pretty good ones themselves.

Back in California, he figured he ought to see *Doughboys,* but approached the experience with dread. "Keaton I got to know," said M-G-M publicist Robert M. W. Vogel, who had recently joined the company. "He missed the preview and he was coming into a projection room to look at it and invited me to join him. Why that came about, I don't remember. But we came out with our chins down to our knees, and then found out a day or two later that the picture was a big hit."

As it turned out, the audience for *Doughboys* was not in the big-city movie palaces, but in the neighborhood houses (what *Variety* called "the nabes"). And it all came down to cost. *Free and Easy,* with the $100,000 price of *Estrellados* factored in, carried a total negative cost of $572,557. Worldwide rentals amounted to $875,000, delivering a net profit of $32,208. On the other hand, the combined cost of *Doughboys* and *De Frente, Marchen* was just $348,816. So while worldwide rentals were $814,000, less than for *Free and Easy,* the lower price tag enabled the picture to show a profit of $160,051. For Keaton, it pointed a way forward in the challenging new medium of the talking film.

"We were desperate," said Larry Weingarten. "We didn't know what to do. Sedgwick, the director, and I were riding down Hollywood Boulevard by the old El Capitan Theatre. . . . We saw a play, a matinee, an old Avery Hopwood play with Charlotte Greenwood. It said: *Parlor, Bedroom and Bath.* I said, 'Eddie, let's go in and see this.' We saw it and it appeared to be the genesis of an idea."

After three pictures with Buster Keaton, Weingarten was no better at developing stories for him than he had been at the outset. Sam Marx, a former critic who joined M-G-M as the studio's story editor in June 1930, saw the problem. "He really did not want to do movies based on plays or books," Marx said of Keaton. "[Weingarten] was a little more sophisticated producer of comedies, and Buster was, of course, anything but sophisticated. Larry [later] did very well with the [Spencer] Tracy–[Katharine] Hepburn pictures, and that was his métier. But I think he was lost in the Buster Keaton pictures."

Parlor, Bedroom and Bath was indeed an old play—it dated from 1917— but it wasn't a Hopwood. The authors were C. W. Bell and Mark Swan, and it was a considerable hit on Broadway around the same time as *Seven Chances.* The local revival starring Charlotte Greenwood opened at the El Capitan on September 22, just as Keaton's arrival in New York was intensifying Weingarten's search for a new story. When the idea was first broached with Keaton, he reacted as he had to *Seven Chances:* "It's a farce—not my kind of story." But then he capitulated, as he did with *Seven Chances,* and set out to make the best film he could. Technically, *Parlor, Bedroom and Bath* would be a remake, Metro having done a version with Eugene Pallette in 1920. But M-G-M had inherited only silent picture rights, necessitating the purchase of talking-picture rights for $11,500. Keaton was encouraged to see the play during its L.A. run and apparently did, as it was likely his enthusiasm for Charlotte Greenwood's performance as the society columnist Polly Hathaway that led to M-G-M signing her for the picture.

"Farce comedy, as a rule, is based on a simple misunderstanding or a mistaken identity," he said. "There's always a couple of characters in that show, that if they come out and say, 'Hey, wait a minute. This is the case,' all the problems would be solved. And [there's] a farce tempo. In all farce comedies, everybody works automatically faster than they do when they're telling a legitimate story. They take things bigger. People get hysterical easy." Keaton's comedy, for all its demented logic, was more sober and contemplative, less frenzied. "I shouldn't have been put into anything that was a farce, because I don't work that way. Life is too serious to do farce comedy."

Although *Parlor, Bedroom and Bath* had the principal character of Reginald Irving, a young husband who, with modifications, could be credibly played by Keaton, he wisely saw his best opportunities coming from his standing outside the play and adding in gags that served to open it up. Sedgwick worked directly with Dick Schayer on the adaptation, a first temporary of which was ready on October 22. A second draft was delivered in mid-November, and Weingarten okayed a shooting final, its dialogue sweetened by Robert E. Hopkins, a former title writer and gagman, on November 24. Production began two days later with Keaton's own Italian Villa posing as the exterior of the Embrey estate, the palatial residence on Long Island where the smart set surrounds a glistening swimming pool and stirs the sexual tensions at the core of the story. Casting was extravagant for a Keaton feature, with Sally Eilers, Cliff Edwards, and Ed Brophy retained from *Doughboys;* Reginald Denny, formerly a star comedian for Universal, as the plotting Jeffery Haywood; freelancers Dorothy Christy, Joan Peers, and Natalie Moorhead as the women complicating Reggie's life; and the aforementioned Charlotte Greenwood re-creating her triumphant stage role.

Sedgwick got the film off to a snappy start, the poolside banter giving the audience a quick resume of the various relationships. Then the retooled Reginald Irving comes into the picture, a humble, unmarried sign tacker who gets struck by a car on the periphery of the estate. Keaton executes an expert

Reggie fends off the insistent Polly Hathaway (Charlotte Greenwood) in Parlor, Bedroom and Bath *(1931).*

back flop, then is hustled into the mansion, where he becomes embroiled in Jeffery Haywood's romantic hustle. ("Have you ever had anything to do with women?" Jeffery asks. "Oh, I used to sell vacuum cleaners," says Reggie.) In the play, Irving is a swaggering fabulist full of tales of his own lurid past, while in reality he's a man "with all the passion of an infuriated clam." In the movie, it falls to the Hayward character to contrive such legends to make Reggie intriguing to the girls, one of whom, Angelica Embrey, must be married before he can claim his own bride, Angelica's fetching sister, Virginia.

Placed in charge of her $8 million estate, Reggie sits stamping envelopes with the aid of Angelica's Pekingese, who eagerly licks each stamp. The script is full of clever exposition, which Keaton and Sedgwick leaven with wordless interludes of physical comedy, striving for the sixty-forty balance Ed liked to espouse. The third act of the play takes place in a parlor, bedroom, and bath surreptitiously reserved by Hayward for "Mr. and Mrs. Smith," giving Keaton the chance to devise a riotous on-screen transition. Stuffed into a little Austin Roadster with Nita Leslie (Joan Peers) and a gigantic suitcase, Reggie pulls away from the Embrey estate, mistakenly taking the wrong woman to a supposed rendezvous at the Seaside Hotel.

Racing down the road, the car's rear wheel comes off, forcing it to a stop at a railroad crossing, where Keaton proceeds to reprise his climactic train gag from *One Week*. Reggie sees the train bearing down on them, can't budge the disabled vehicle, pulls Nita and the suitcase away at the last possible moment, only to watch as the train roars past on a second track, completely missing the car. Relieved, they turn away, and a second train appears from the opposite direction, totaling the car. Stranded, they try to make the rest of the trek on foot, manage to flag down a hay wagon, and arrive at the hotel in a driving rain. Dripping and dribbling onto the glassy tile floor of the lobby, Keaton registers and drags bellhop Cliff Edwards into a ballet of slips and falls that eventually leaves a total of five people in a heap. It's as funny and artful as anything Keaton has done on-screen, another unscripted highspot in a film that, for all its verbal sophistication, contains more first-rate silent comedy than the previous two films combined.

All this leads up to the tremulous encounter between Reggie and the long-limbed Polly Hathaway, bent on seducing him for appearance's sake, which gives the film its slapstick apogee. ("You're just as safe with me as you would be in jail," she soothes.) At five ten, Charlotte Greenwood towers over Keaton, and their mating dance is not unlike that of an octopus and a sea otter.

"Clinch," she instructs. "Will you clinch? Get a half nelson!" It's all she can do to ignite a spark in him, and she's left breathless and panic-stricken once she does. Pushing and yanking at each other, they are the Astaire and Rogers of cross-purposes, one of those rare comic pairings that was just meant to be.

As Greenwood recalled, "We did one of our scenes in such a realistic manner, and it seemed to be going so well, that nobody on the set was astonished when the director suddenly yelled out, 'Cut!' But after the cameras had stopped grinding we found out why. My lips were bleeding where they had come in contact with Keaton's teeth, and my always uncontrollable hands had made his eye into a sorry-looking sight!"

Sober and rested, Keaton was at the top of his game in *Parlor, Bedroom and Bath,* and the film was finished in fourteen camera days, an all-time record for a Keaton feature. Previews mandated six days of added scenes and retakes, but the film still finished in just twenty days, one day under schedule, at a negative cost of $186,368—an astounding $36,967 under budget. When Welford Beaton, the iconoclastic editor of *The Film Spectator,* encountered Keaton on the M-G-M lot one day, Buster told him he thought his latest picture would be "a good laugh-getter," causing Beaton to hie himself over to the publicity department and ask if he could see it.

When Metro put Keaton in *Parlor, Bedroom and Bath,* it provided him with a vehicle which had places in it for the logical introduction of his comedy antics, and it surrounded him with a cast that could be relied upon to add to the entertainment of any picture. All this has resulted in the production of one of the funniest comedies I ever saw. I always regarded Keaton as one of the most accomplished actors on the screen, but in the silent days I felt that he had carried his absolutely expressionless face about as far as he could without losing his popularity. I advised him to smile occasionally. However, now that an ability to talk has been added to his other methods of expression, I can find no fault with the continuance of his stony countenance quality. His voice adds to his characterization a suggestion of liveliness that was missing before the screen went talkie. He still maintains his place among the two or three finest pantomimists on the screen, and in no picture in which he has appeared does he put such talent to better effort than this one.

Keaton was on the verge of a whole new chapter in his troubled relationship with the talking screen and, in particular, with Metro-Goldwyn-Mayer. Relaxed, he and Natalie attended a small party hosted by Irving Thalberg and Norma Shearer at the Notre Dame–USC football game, and made plans to spend New Year's at Agua Caliente with Buster Collier and his current girlfriend, the actress Marie Prevost. For Buster Keaton, 1931 would be a year to remember, but for all the wrong reasons.

"There I was," he said, "on the top of the world—on a toboggan."

18

Running Around Loose

KATHLEEN KEY was a well-known presence around Hollywood—better known, in fact, than she was to audiences, who saw her too fitfully to form much of an impression. Her friend, the actress and columnist Dorothy Manners, described her as "a strange little kid with huge eyes, the brow of a madonna, and the temperament of a prima donna." Along with dark hair, a pointed nose, and the kind of lips that invariably got her the vampire parts in the pictures she landed, she was subject to the black moods of the Irish. "I think I'm a little crazy," she confided in a 1926 interview. "Not much, you understand, but just a little nutty in the head."

She got her start in *The Four Horsemen of the Apocalypse,* then made the notoriously troubled *Rubáiyát of Omar Khayyám,* on which she met Ramon Novarro, who would become a devoted friend. Named a WAMPAS Baby Star the same year as Margaret Leahy, Key got her big chance in 1923 when she was cast in Goldwyn's *Ben-Hur.* She subsequently spent two years in Rome making the film, not the best of career moves in that it kept her out of the public eye at a critical time. When the film finally appeared in 1925, her smoldering performance as Tirzah, sister to the title character, had been trimmed to the bone. "Two years off the screen," she groused, "just to fill up the background when they ran out of extras."

She met Buster Keaton around the time she was an M-G-M contract player and he was a Metro star by virtue of the independent features they released. As Keaton's marriage to Natalie Talmadge withered, Key became a paramour of sorts, although she traveled a great deal and spent a year living in Paris immediately following her talking-picture debut. When she returned to California early in 1930, her career had taken all the self-administered abuse it could, and she was without either means or prospects.

"She was no good," said Harold Goodwin. "We did a picture with Ramon Novarro called *The Midshipman* in 1925, and she went back to Annapolis with us. We had a couple of ingénues [in it]. She'd leave herself wide open for a pass and then renege, so they sent her back. We got rid of her quick." As Key herself remembered: "After working one day in the picture, I found out they didn't need me anymore for academy scenes. They immediately sent me back to New York and told me I was to leave for the coast in a few days. And I was under the impression that we were going to make all the interiors in the East!"

At some point, she took up with Keaton again, and he may have slipped her money on occasion. What happened between them during the year 1930 is open to speculation, but significant clues emerged when an incident on the Metro lot landed them both on the front pages of the nation's newspapers. It happened on the afternoon of February 4, 1931, the scene being Keaton's new white frame bungalow wedged in between a rehearsal stage and John Gilbert's stucco hacienda on the Washington Boulevard edge of the lot. Buster dubbed the little building "Keaton's Kennel" to commemorate the residency of a 170-pound Saint Bernard named Elmer.

"Miss Key came back from Europe a year ago," he told a reporter for the United Press as he nursed a face swollen with scratch marks. "We had been friends for many years. Recently she came to me and complained that she was in dire straits financially. I told her she was getting too stout—she weighed 130 pounds—and that if she could get her weight down she would become a big bet in talking pictures. She said, 'I'll bet you $500 I can take off twenty pounds in ten days.' I told her it was a bet. At the end of the ten days she came back, but she had only lost six pounds instead of twenty. I told her, 'You tried hard enough. You've won the bet.' And I gave her a check for $500. She had a photostat copy made immediately, cashed it and spent it, holding the photographed copy over my head to collect more money. After that she made numerous threats and caused a lot of gossip."

Keaton's spin on the story made little sense. If Key were in such dire financial straits, what was she doing proposing a $500 bet? And if she was overweight, what precipitated the weight gain? Charles W. Lyon, a local attorney, provided more details. "Another attorney came to see me last November or December," he said to the UP. "He told me quite a long story about Miss Key and Keaton. I am a friend of Keaton. I assume this attorney wanted me to inform Keaton and his associates, and that is just what I did."

Proof of an innocent bet over weight loss was not something that could be held over a celebrity's head in order to extort money—unless the check was in payment for something else entirely. Had Kathleen Key gotten pregnant? And could the $500 have paid for an abortion rather than a bet? Whatever it was, it was threatening enough to prompt Keaton to pay her off.

"She said she needed $4,000," he recounted. "I finally agreed to give her the $4,000—and $1,000 on top of that for her to buy a ticket to China or any other place just so the gossip would be stopped."

Key, however, decided her silence was worth more than $5,000 to a man who made $3,000 a week. When she called at Keaton's bungalow that February afternoon, Cliff Edwards and a publicist named Clarence Locan were present, as was Willie Riddle, Keaton's cook and valet. Apparently, he wanted witnesses to the transaction.

"I offered the check for $5,000 to her, but she demanded $20,000 more. I resolved not to give her another cent and tore up the check for $5,000 in her presence and threw it on the floor." It was the shredding of that check that set her off. "She blew up. She manhandled me something terrible. I had hold of her wrists, but when she got loose she clawed me like a tiger."

The melee sent Edwards and Locan scrambling, because Key, who once rode opposite Tom Mix, knew how to take care of herself.* She shattered the windows in the narrow building, punching and kicking and screaming all the while. It was Riddle who summoned security, and it took two members of the studio constabulary, one the M-G-M police chief himself, to subdue her. "Keaton's dressing room looked as though a cyclone had passed through it by the time Culver City police arrived to drag away the angered Miss Key," the *Los Angeles Times* reported. She was still cursing and yelling at the top of her lungs as the patrol car rolled off the lot.

Keaton declined to press charges, and had a sign nailed to the bungalow's door: CLOSED FOR REPAIRS. Key refused to talk to the press, merely saying, "Call up Mr. Keaton and see what he has to say about it." To one reporter, she admitted she was irked when she saw Keaton strolling with his wife at Agua Caliente and he pretended not to know her. To another, she

---

* Returning from a year's work in Australia, Key and a fellow actor had amused the other passengers on their ship by giving boxing exhibitions "in which," said an eyewitness, "the girl did not get the worst of it by any means."

dismissed the whole thing as a joke. Natalie, meanwhile, said nothing when confronted by a reporter at the house. "*That* helped," said Buster.

The press cast a knowing eye on Keaton's account, even as the details were necessarily left vague. Mollie Merrick, Hollywood correspondent for the North American Newspaper Alliance, filed a particularly droll version of the event. "Hollywood this morning is trying to find the key to the Keaton situation," she said in her lede. "But Kathleen Key, brilliant brunet beauty who is alleged to have landed one on Buster Keaton's jaw and wrecked the studio dressing room yesterday afternoon over a little discussion about money, has disappeared from the scene." Merrick characterized the whole matter as a "slight disagreement" and freely used the word "blackmailing" in describing what Key was up to. She had Edwards and Locan diving to safety as Keaton and Key "remained to close the deal amid a shower of broken glass, resounding smacks, and shrill cries and scratches."

Both the *Los Angeles Times* and the *San Francisco Examiner* ran their stories with cartoons attached, the *Times* depicting Key furiously chasing Keaton and shouting, "Give me that $25,000 check!" The *New York Daily News* used a shot of him in caveman garb from *Three Ages* with Margaret Leahy slung over his shoulder. Sidney Skolsky, columnist for the *News,* sent Keaton a telegram: HEAR YOU ARE OFF KEY. The *Boston Globe*'s headline: "ACTRESS MAULS BUSTER KEATON."

"What a joke!" exclaimed Harry Carr in the *Los Angeles Times.* "Miss Kathleen Key explains she wrecked Buster Keaton's dressing room and all but tore the eyes from the sad face of the comedian 'for a joke.' Dear, dear, there's nothing like a sense of humor, is there? Answer: No. Buster explains, however, that it wasn't a joke at all; it was something about a photostatic copy of a check for $500 and something more about another check for $25,000. So there, you see, it is quite a simple affair after all. But why did she wreck his dressing room anyhow? I get all mixed up over these Hollywood affairs."

The worst repercussions were at home, where Buster had been in the doghouse for more than a year. In January 1930, there was a fire at the villa while he was away on a hunting trip with Buster Collier, Gilbert Roland, and four others.

"They served my brother and I liver one time," Jim Talmadge explained, "and no kid liked liver. That was verboten. So we threw it down the heat ventilator, and eventually it caught fire." The boys' tutor smelled the smoke not long before midnight and hustled them and the dog outside, with Nata-

The former Keaton studio at the corner of Lillian Way and Eleanor Avenue awaits demolition in 1931.

lie and a retinue of servants following. The blaze was quickly extinguished, and damage was held to $10,000. (The *Los Angeles Examiner,* in its coverage, referred to the absent father as "the should-be hero.") Three days later, it came out that the hunting party had been snowed in at Lake Arrowhead, and that Marie Prevost, Collier's girlfriend, was among them. "There was no other girl along," said Keaton, "but nothing I could say could convince my wife of that. Once or twice she threatened to leave me."

At the studio, Thalberg and Mannix told Keaton he had to settle with Kathleen Key and settle fast. Claiming that Buster had broken her jaw, she was demanding a $10,000 payoff.

"If she doesn't get it," said Mannix, "she'll bring the whole mess into court."

Keaton resisted, knowing he couldn't have fractured her jaw, but the decision had already been made, and he eventually forked over the money. "Needless to say, it was a long, long time before I heard the last at home about this depressing incident," he said. "But eventually everything seemed to be patched up. I was told I was being forgiven only for the sake of the children."

Exhibitors coping with Depression-era gloom were appealing for feature comedies at a record rate. "Demand for comedies is considered here a reaction to the blood and thunder of the recent gang cycle," *Variety* reported, "and the gradual dropping from programs of the feature rib-ticklers that used to go out on a ratio of at least one to three." Following the completion of *Parlor, Bedroom and Bath,* Thalberg asked Keaton, "Now what was the story you wanted to do with Marie Dressler?" By then, Dressler, who had secured an M-G-M contract on the basis of her performance in *Anna Christie,* was a genuine star, billed over the title with Wallace Beery in *Min and Bill* and soon to collect an Academy Award.

"It's too late for that story," Keaton responded, believing that "no one was using two stars in comedies like mine." Nevertheless, M-G-M let out word, possibly at Thalberg's behest, that an original comedy was in the works, purportedly to star Keaton and Dressler, with Cliff Edwards, Polly Moran, Jimmy Durante, and others in support.

Meanwhile, Larry Weingarten had set about developing a new story for Keaton while his star was away from the studio. It grew from the combined efforts of staff writers Lou Edelman and Edgar Allan Woolf, as well as a newspaperman named Gilmore Millen, whose novel *Sweet Man* had briefly brought him to M-G-M. The untitled original had Buster once again cast as a wealthy twit with a butler and a Rolls-Royce, this time romancing a woman who can't marry him as long as he won't attend to his business affairs. Figuring it a misfire, Weingarten passed the material to two men more familiar with Keaton's past work, Paul Gerard Smith, who contributed to *Battling Butler* and *The General,* and George Landy, who was married to Kathryn McGuire, Buster's love interest in *Sherlock Jr.* and *The Navigator.* In collaboration, Smith and Landy produced a twenty-five-page treatment that put a clueless slumlord amid a group of rowdy kids on Manhattan's Lower East Side.

"I read the story," said Keaton, "which was called *The Sidewalks of New York,* and told Larry it was impossible. The plot required me to cope with a gang of juvenile delinquents. I might have done that. What I couldn't cope with, I said, was the plot. . . . I felt this so strongly that I went over his head and appealed to Irving Thalberg to help get me out of the assignment. Irving was usually on my side, but this time he said, 'Larry likes it. Everybody else in the studio likes the story. You are the only one who doesn't.' In the end, I gave up like a fool and said, 'What the hell?' Who was I to say I was right and everyone else wrong? I'd been wrong about my marriage, hadn't I? That was the way I reasoned."

Keaton busied himself shooting the French- and German-language versions of *Parlor, Bedroom and Bath* ahead of the film's domestic release on February 28, 1931. In Los Angeles, the short-lived trade paper *Inside Facts* caught a showing at Loew's State. "The house chuckled and chortled, roared and guffawed its approval of each and every line and situation that offered any possibility for such display," Vi Hegyi, the paper's reviewer, wrote. "*Parlor, Bedroom and Bath* starts with a bang and ends with a whoop and has a great line of fast-moving entertainment in between." *Modern Screen, Photoplay, New Movie,* and *Screenland* all accorded it raves, with the normally reserved *Photoplay* naming it one of the best pictures of the month.

In New York, the notices were uncommonly good for a Keaton talkie, and with strong competition from *The Front Page,* Chaplin's *City Lights, Skippy,* and Metro's *Trader Horn,* the picture held its own in a week's stand at the Capitol. Apart from its exceptional quality, the big takeaway for *Parlor, Bedroom and Bath* was its extraordinary commercial success. Performing better at the box office than any of Keaton's other M-G-M talkies, it pulled in worldwide rentals of $985,000. With a yield of $299,000, it became the most profitable of all of Buster Keaton's features, silent or sound.

Parlor, Bedroom and Bath was a happy accident, but Larry Weingarten seemingly learned nothing from it. In March, with the success of the new picture not yet fully apparent, Keaton again was adrift, his fate in the hands of two men who had made their mark at Metro with a series of short subjects that featured dogs in place of human beings. The Dogville comedies included parodies of popular movies bearing such titles as *The Dogway Melody* and *So Quiet on the Canine Front.* Impressed with these sound novelties, which were called "barkies," Weingarten tapped Jules White and Zion Myers to co-direct *Sidewalks of New York* while Ed Sedgwick was on loan to Howard Hughes. Also gone from Keaton's creative team was Richard Schayer, the man who had written the shooting finals for all of his M-G-M features, but who had left to take the job of story editor at Universal.

No longer comfortable contributing to the script as he had with Schayer, Keaton maintained a distant relationship with White and Myers as they set out, with the aid of novelist Eric Hatch, to produce the final screenplay themselves. As Keaton remembered: "They'd say, 'This is funny.' And I'd say, 'I don't think so.' They'd say, 'This'll be good.' I'd say, 'It stinks.' It didn't make any difference; we did it anyhow. I'd only argue about so far and then let it go." When the script for *Sidewalks of New York* was okayed for production on May 1, it bore the fingerprints of thirteen different writers, among them Willard Mack, the playwright who, at the time of *Doughboys,* said a modern screen comedian had to "extract laughs from his lines" rather than from gags. "I knew before the camera turned on the first scene that we had the perfect foundation for a stinker," Keaton said. "And by now I couldn't tell anyone anything."

The script was still being massaged into shape when filming began on the studio's New York Street exterior where Keaton had shot the tong war scenes for *The Cameraman*. The early action, in which his man Poggle (Cliff Edwards) is rushed by a gang of kids as he attempts to collect the rent, leads Keaton, as the impossibly rich Homer Van Dine Harmon, to attempt doing the job himself. Mired in too much dialogue and a surfeit of plot, Keaton found he was straitjacketed by the material in a way he never was when he was in control of his own studio. Then White and Myers "alternated telling me how to walk, how to talk, how to stand, and how to fall—where and when, how fast or slow, how loud or soft. I was Trilby with two Svengalis— M-G-M had gone to the two platoon [system of baseball] with unlimited substitutions."

Keaton's character was poorly drawn, prissy and ignorant and completely lacking in the resourcefulness he had shown in his best work. The script left him little room to improvise, and he found himself compensating with minor bits of business—falls and knocks and the like—where the film screamed for bigger effects. There was a boxing match remindful of *Battling Butler*, but the only genuinely clever gag in the entire picture—the recording of a marriage proposal composed entirely of song titles—was handed over to Cliff Edwards to play.

"[Buster] was unhappy about the amount of creative input he was allowed in *Sidewalks of New York*," said Anita Page, who appeared opposite him as she had in *Free and Easy*. "We spoke of that over lunch in his bungalow." He would, she said, "have a whole group of us over to his bungalow for lunch." With the damage inflicted by Kathleen Key quickly repaired, another sign greeted visitors to Keaton's Kennel: OPEN UNDER NEW MANAGEMENT.

Jules White found Keaton's attitude puzzling. "Buster was an introvert and he would eat himself," he said. "He'd never come out and tell you what was in his mind. But you could just tell from looking at him that he was unhappy. So I learned much about him on this picture and finally got him to come around. He was really unhappy at the start because Eddie Sedgwick had been directing all his films, and for some reason, I don't know why, M-G-M wanted me to do it. Zion and I." The third act devolved into an amateur play performance with Keaton's bumbling character in drag and a painfully contrived subplot had his girlfriend's younger brother being ordered by a local hood to literally shoot him to death on stage. He is rescued by a gang of young toughs, inept and hapless to the final frame.

Inferior to *Parlor, Bedroom and Bath* in every respect, *Sidewalks of New*

York was no model of efficiency either. Scheduled for eighteen camera days, it actually took twenty-six with another full week devoted to retakes. Similarly, while *Sidewalks* was budgeted at $204,000, it came in at $279,000, putting both White and Myers behind the executive eight ball. They continued to generate cutting notes and suggestions into August, but the film laid a sizable egg when screened in advance.

"At the preview," recalled Keaton, "it did not get a giggle, something that was blamed on me."

Ultimately, though, it was White and Myers who were made to walk the plank. "L. B. Mayer fired us," said White. Then it again became Weingarten's job to find a better way of monetizing the corporate asset known as Buster Keaton.

When asked about the Talmadge women, Louise Brooks said: "They loved each other very much." But it was, she clarified, much more pervasive than that.

> The Keaton house was "their" home. . . . The most extraordinary home in Hollywood! No films were shown—nor talked about. There was no tension, no conflict. The Talmadge women were the most natural, comfortable people I ever knew. Connie may have suffered briefly with English Royalty fever, but she remained naturally delightful; Natalie was a very comfortable lump; Norma, curled up in a chair, was very comfortably bored (even with Gilbert R.). And Peg—old Buddha— was kept comfortable, as she surveyed the scene, by her attentive daughters. (I suppose that is why I don't remember the kids—they came and went as they pleased—without fuss.) In this family nobody "made" anybody do anything. Connie had practically quit films— marrying very rich men was much more fun. Norma forced herself to do her last films in order to get richer. At worst, Buster might fall on his head, leaving Natalie a Wealthy Widow. The teaching of Old Buddha was sound: Get money and then get comfortable. People don't really matter. You can see how this completely secure and serene family left Buster in creative freedom. There was never any "make, make, make" when he got home. If the loss of his own production unit, and of Joe as his manager, opened the door to his ruin, the loss of the Talmadge family let it in. He seemed unable to deal with people in the

real world. That is when, I suspect, booze ceased to be a creative release and became his solution to wretched reality.

Natalie and Buster Keaton celebrated their tenth wedding anniversary in May 1931, but when news of the Kathleen Key affair landed, their marriage entered a death spiral from which it couldn't recover. Buster always maintained that he loved Natalie: "I know of no woman in the world who could have taken me from Natalie—except Natalie herself. I tell you truthfully, I may not be a strong character, but I was strong enough for that."

Myra Keaton agreed. "I know my son," she said firmly, "and I know that he loved Natalie Talmadge."

Still, it was becoming increasingly clear that the end was in sight. In July, Peg Talmadge was diagnosed with cancer and underwent surgery at Cedars of Lebanon. With Norma in Hawaii and Dutch—now Mrs. Townsend Netcher—in Italy, it fell to Natalie to see her through the ordeal, suddenly aware as never before that nothing in her meticulously ordered life was destined to be permanent.

Buster was off-screen that summer, other than briefly appearing in an all-star musical-comedy known variously as *Hollywood Revue of 1930*, *Toast of the Town*, and *March of Time*, for which he contributed two days of material. Released in a German-language version titled *Wir schalten um auf Hollywood!* (*We Switch to Hollywood!*), it had its Berlin opening in July 1931 with the well-known comedian Paul Morgan in the lead. Along with Keaton, the film featured cameos from John Gilbert, Ramon Novarro, Adolphe Menjou, and a gathering of German stars then working in California. "It was all very gay, with plenty of wisecracks and pep," Curt Heymann reported in *The New York Times*. "Nevertheless, the reception was mixed—we expected better jokes from Morgan and better sketches from the Americans."

Keaton spent a lot of time at the studio, where his father, Joe, was a regular fixture and where his drinking accelerated. Buster made light of the Key fracas, asking any woman entering the Kennel to sign a release stating that she was there at her own risk and would under no circumstances sue for damages arising out of "any injury, broken limbs, or any other mishap" that took place. A partial list of signatories, their slips adorning the walls, included Marie Dressler, Polly Moran, Charlotte Greenwood, Marie Prevost, Lili Damita, Leila Hyams, Marion Davies, Ruth Selwyn, and Lola Lane. Keaton and Cliff Edwards whiled away their time playing bridge at ten cents a point. Occasionally he and Nat were seen out on the town, at the Cocoanut Grove or the Blossom Room of the Hollywood Roosevelt, or yachting to Catalina with Norma, who had by this time taken a dislike to her brother-in-law. Frequently, he was away from the house, sometimes overnight, and as liquor gave voice to his frustrations, he was known to reduce Natalie to tears.

In terms of a new picture, Larry Weingarten reverted to the formula that resulted in *Parlor, Bedroom and Bath,* although his choice of a play this time was decidedly less serendipitous. In 1928, Weingarten's first full year at the studio, one of M-G-M's big pictures was *Her Cardboard Lover,* based on a French farce and starring Marion Davies. Weingarten remembered it as one of Davies' more successful movies, and apparently envisioned it as a suitable property for Robert Montgomery, a rising young contract player who had served as the romantic lead in *Free and Easy.* The talking-picture rights were secured for $10,000, and playwright Laurence E. Johnson, author of the Broadway comedy hit *It's a Wise Child,* was put to work on the adaptation. Then Montgomery fell by the wayside, and Weingarten went about retooling the material with Keaton in the role Davies had taken in the original. "That was an old trick," he said, "to take a story about a man and change it to the woman and vice-versa."

This seemed a good idea to somebody. Predictably, Keaton was not receptive to another farce, even as he acknowledged that *Parlor, Bedroom and Bath* turned out pretty well. *Her Cardboard Lover* had starred Jeanne Eagels and Leslie Howard on the New York stage, actors well suited to the play's sly Parisian intrigues, and he couldn't fathom how he would fit into such a thing. "If they had known that I was still essentially a slapstick comedian, they would not have bought for me the sort of stories they did," he said.

Keaton's boozing while in residence at the studio, coupled with the vague notion that he was somehow slipping as an audience favorite, led Louis B. Mayer to have him paired with the cacophonous stage and nightclub comedian Jimmy Durante for *Her Cardboard Lover.* New to Metro, Durante had appeared in two M-G-M features, neither yet released, and Keaton heard that Mayer was out to build up Broadway's acclaimed Schnozzola at his expense. Suddenly, Johnson's script had to be pried apart to insert a new character, and the job was given to Sennett veteran Ralph Spence, a celebrated title writer who would essentially function as gagman for the newly minted comedy team of Keaton and Durante.

"It was," said Keaton, "entirely wrong for me."

While all this was going on, *Sidewalks of New York* was released on Sep-

tember 26, 1931. Five days later, it opened at the Fox Theatre in San Francisco, eliciting a friendly review from the *Examiner* ("The current week at
the Fox promises to be a great one for the kids") and respectable opening-
day receipts. But whatever enthusiasm the film generated was short-lived,
and it was pulled after six days, scarcely drawing more than the John Gilbert
disaster that preceded it. In Chicago, the movie performed better, even as
it received an anemic welcome in the *Tribune* and the display ads curiously
billed Anita Page over Buster. Prior to its New York opening, it faced a
censorship struggle over scenes showing young toughs being schooled in
crime, but after an adjusted print was previewed, it was cleared for exhibition. Still, unlike all of its talking predecessors, *Sidewalks of New York* was
deemed unworthy of the premium showcase that was the Capitol Theatre,
and for the first time since 1923 a Keaton feature had no home on Broadway.
Instead, it was relegated to the Loew's 83rd and 175th Street houses, a gloomy
milestone that did not go unnoticed.

"In Buster Keaton's heyday, *Sidewalks of New York,* with its routine comedy and slapstick, would have been only a little bit below first rate," *Variety's*
Joe Bigelow noted. "Today it is so outdated, so elementary, that prospects
for money are anything but bright. The B and C houses, in preference to
the As, in situations where all exist, as well as double-billers, is the picture's
fate. Bookers of big houses wouldn't chance this one."

Universally met with derision and disappointment, *Sidewalks of New York*
might reasonably have been expected to be an unqualified commercial flop,
but when it got outside the big cities its outlook brightened considerably.
In the end, domestic and foreign rentals were evenly split, amounting to
$855,000 worldwide and a profit of $225,000. Not as good as for *Parlor,
Bedroom and Bath,* but in what was widely believed to be, financially, the
worst year in the history of the movies, not too dusty. In terms of profitabil-
ity, Keaton was outranking John Gilbert, William Haines, Ramon Novarro,
and Marion Davies. As the filming of *Her Cardboard Lover* approached, he
noted at least one positive result of the picture's utter lack of critical appeal:
"It came out such a complete stinker, such an unbelievable bomb, that they
gave Sedgwick back to me."

As story editor, Sam Marx could see that Keaton was growing unhappier,
saddled as he was with a tone-deaf producer and material like *Sidewalks* and
Cardboard Lover. "Buster used to have a group around him. Several were
writers who were working in my department. Men like Al Boasberg, Ralph
Spence, a few other comedy writers, strictly gag writers sitting around, push-

ing an idea across a table like you were playing Ping-Pong. Somebody comes up with a notion—'How about this?'—and then they expand on it, and then they think about it. The sight gags came out of that. . . . Buster's coterie of directors, friends, various advisors, and particularly the gag writers, had changed a great deal. Many had moved on. Buster himself was no longer the young kid who used to fall out of buildings and off moving cars. Times had changed."

When filming began on December 1, there were some twenty other features shooting on the M-G-M lot, including *Tarzan the Ape Man, The Beast of the City, Arsène Lupin,* and Tod Browning's *Freaks.* From the outset, it was clear to Keaton that he and Jimmy Durante lacked chemistry: "He tried hard and I tried hard, but our styles, our timing, didn't jibe." Each extended the utmost courtesy to the other, Durante making no attempts at upstaging, and Keaton giving him all the room he needed, even to the point of suggesting retakes on scenes where the Schnoz appeared to be overshadowed.

Keaton resolved to do the best he could with *Her Cardboard Lover* because an infinitely better picture was in the offing, one that could help him break out of the rut of progressively worse comedies. Thalberg and producer Paul Bern were assembling an all-star cast for the movie version of Vicki Baum's *Grand Hotel,* and director Edmund Goulding thought Keaton would make inspired casting for the role of Otto Kringelein, an aging German bookkeeper with only weeks to live.

"In almost every picture I've made," Keaton told Goulding, "I make it a rule to become very serious about the fourth reel or so. That is to make absolutely sure that the audience will really care about what happens to me in the rest of the picture." Thalberg, especially, knew what a good actor Keaton could be, and multiple tests were made that stretched into the early days of *Her Cardboard Lover.* Keaton was so pleased he drove home one night in his costume and makeup, bedeviling Jimmy and Bobby, neither of whom could tell it was him. With his heart set on playing the role, he nonetheless knew there was very real concern that audiences conditioned to laugh at him might wreck the picture, something that had happened the previous year to comedienne ZaSu Pitts, who had to be replaced as Paul Bäumer's dying mother in *All Quiet on the Western Front* after an unruly preview in San Bernardino.

Almost immediately, he heard that actor George E. Stone, who wasn't burdened with a history of comedy parts, was in contention for the role. The final cast began falling into place. Joan Crawford and Wallace Beery were set, then John Barrymore, at the end of his lucrative contract with Warner Bros., came on as Baron von Gaigern, prompting Greta Garbo, who had declined the role of the Russian dancer Grusinskaya, to reconsider. With Lionel Barrymore, who had just won an Academy Award, confirmed for the part of Kringelein, the film at last had its five major names to go above the title. And over on the set of *Her Cardboard Lover,* Buster Keaton was once again tipsy before the camera, his timing off, his delivery blunted.

Keaton's drinking drove yet another wedge between him and Natalie, and as Christmas approached they separated for the first time in their marriage, Nat fleeing to her mother's house on Angelo Drive. Back in October, amid rumors she would finally be seeking a divorce from Joe Schenck, Norma Talmadge, in the spirit of family unity, had given a birthday party for her brother-in-law, presenting him with a cake "the size of the Yale Bowl" and ablaze with at least seventy candles. Invited to make the first cut, Buster refrained from falling into it as he had the previous year. Now the fan magazines zeroed in on Norma and Joe, portraying the Keatons' long marriage and Dutch's third as exemplary contrasts to the hollowed-out shell that was left of the Schencks' storied union. In *Modern Screen,* a December profile conspicuously titled "Family Man" was illustrated up front with a picture of Keaton and his two boys. On New Year's Day, he chartered a bus to ferry a load of friends to the Rose Bowl for a game between Tulane and USC, but Nat remained aloof, spending the day with her children and the rest of the Talmadge clan at the Santa Monica home of her sister Dutch.

Retakes on *Her Cardboard Lover,* wisely retitled *The Passionate Plumber,* extended into January 1932, putting the film four days over schedule. It was previewed to a weeknight audience a couple of weeks later, the *Filmograph* acknowledging "a laughfest" while harboring serious reservations. "Buster is funny in spots," the notice allowed. "Jimmy Durante yells too much and should be toned down before he bores people." As a way of discouraging more pairings with Durante, Keaton lobbied the studio to buy the screen rights to a play called *The Unexpected Husband,* in which Edward Everett Horton was appearing at the Hollywood Playhouse. Thalberg reportedly approved the purchase, even as Weingarten was closing in on another property that would accommodate both Keaton and Durante as a team. "Durante just can't keep quiet," Buster complained. "He's going to talk no matter what in the thunder happens. You can't direct him any other way."

The Passionate Plumber opened in Los Angeles to what *Variety* characterized as "fair" business. It did better in San Francisco but was pulled in St. Paul after five days to make way for Paramount's *Shanghai Express*. In New York, the critical consensus was that the film got laughs, but that Durante tended to overpower Keaton in the scenes they shared.

In *Variety*, Bigelow saw that Keaton was once again boxed in by the material, and that Durante's crowd-pleasing performance was all shtick, no character. "There is some comedy of merit in this flimsy scenario, stretched from a natural two-reel length to fill a full-length spool, and it isn't necessary to gaze beyond the cast to find the source. But the cast and the laughs are constantly obliged to fight the plot and motives; unfortunately the plot wins the battle, contrary to the picture's best interests, and the result is another lay-me-down-to-sleeper for box office."

The Passionate Plumber spent a lackluster week at the Capitol while at least restoring Keaton's stature as a Broadway attraction. It went on to pull domestic rentals of $413,000, not as good as its predecessors, and its talkiness limited the foreign take to $366,000, the lowest figure yet for a sound Keaton feature. At a cost of $263,000, it showed a profit of $186,000, a drop of more than $100,000 from the career high claimed by *Parlor, Bedroom and Bath*. Yet it seemed to validate the idea that Keaton was losing his commercial mojo and that keeping him and Durante together made good business sense. And so *The Unexpected Husband* was quietly put to one side.

Keaton was seen in public only sporadically during this period. In February, he and comedian Joe E. Brown assembled squads of big-league ballplayers to square off at Wrigley Field for the benefit of the American Olympic Finance Committee, a game that was mostly a burlesque played before a crowd of eight thousand. In March, Buster was spotted at Agua Caliente in the company of Gilbert Roland and the Schenck brothers watching the Australian gelding Phar Lap win the $50,000 handicap. But mostly he withdrew, bewildered by the wilting of his career and what, if anything, could be done about it.

"I got to the stage where I didn't give a darn whether school kept or not, and then I started drinking too much. When I found out that they could write stories and material better than I could anyway, what was the use of my fighting with them? It only takes about two bad pictures in a row to put the skids under you."

Claude Autant-Lara, who directed the French-language versions of *Parlor, Bedroom and Bath* (*Buster se marie*) and *The Passionate Plumber* (*Le*

Plombier amoureux), recalled spending considerable time working in the "American sumptuousness" of the Keaton bungalow. "Buster arrived there in the morning around nine o'clock in a tiny Austin, a toy car, that made the Americans laugh and laugh it was so small. The second seat, at his side, was nearly always occupied by the huge Saint Bernard Elmer, who was constantly drooling. From nine in the morning in this great room, the Filipino who was at his service was continuously placing in front of the workers—authors, directors, and Buster—long drinks of fairly high alcohol content which very quickly, although they were iced, evaporated into the atmosphere. In two hours' time, Buster, who had the capacity to absorb double, triple, or quadruple ours, would go from his normal pink to scarlet. By midday he was apoplectic, very funny, and his voice would become hoarse."

Keaton reached the depth of his malaise in late March 1932 when he was asked by Mayer's office to appear for work on a Saturday afternoon and pretend to shoot a scene so that a group of visitors would think they had witnessed some actual moviemaking. This was a fairly common practice when exhibitors, politicians, influential civic groups, and the like descended on the studio and expected to be treated like big shots. Keaton had drawn this sort of duty before, as had most contract players whose names weren't Barrymore or Garbo, but he legitimately had other plans that day. The big California–St. Mary's game, in which the Bears would make another bid for the State College Baseball Association championship, was set to be played on the St. Mary's campus in Moraga, and he had committed to being on the home team's bench serving as their mascot, a thrill for someone whose passion for the game was as great as his.

Mayer's office was brooking no excuses, and although Keaton declined as diplomatically as he could, there was no way he was going to miss that game. St. Mary's was an eight-hour drive north of Los Angeles, and he was on the road by the time an ultimatum came down: be there or face disciplinary action. California's varsity pitchers beat St. Mary's Gaels three to one that weekend, a bad omen since Keaton was met with a piece of mail from the studio when he arrived home on Tuesday. Signed by Mayer, the letter instructed him to report to Mr. Mannix's office the following afternoon, presumably to receive the obligatory dressing-down. When he ignored the demand, he received written notification via registered mail that he had failed to render services as required under his contract. "This is to advise you that, pursuant to the provisions of paragraph 10 of said contract, we shall refuse to pay you any compensation commencing as of March 30, 1932, and

Keaton with his beloved dog Elmer, circa 1931.

continuing thereafter until you are ready, willing and able to render your required services for us in accordance with the terms of your said contract."

Keaton had not been seen on the lot since March 3, about the time his dog Elmer went missing.* Taken off salary, he proceeded to get into it with Natalie, who didn't want to pull the kids out of school and take an extended holiday in Mexico. Rebuked, he retired to the playroom, where he stewed, fuming at his impotence at home as well as the studio. He passed the next three days in an alcoholic haze, sullen and argumentative. One night, he had a few friends in, and sometime after midnight, invited Buster Collier and Louise Brooks to accompany him on a drive to the studio.

"He was drunk," said Brooks, "but I didn't know it. Buster Collier didn't know. He was driving a car, but he had marvelous coordination. We walked in, locked the door, and turned on the lights. All around his bungalow were these built-in bookshelves with glass cases. And for no reason at all—see, you never knew what Buster was going to do anyhow; he was always thinking up gags—he picked up the baseball bat, and we're just standing there and nobody was thinking about anything, and he goes to each bookcase and

---

* As was his master, Elmer was an independent soul, known for wandering off. Mindful of his predecessor's fate, Keaton fretted extravagantly when the dog disappeared, checking all his usual haunts. It was only after an ad was placed in the classified section of the *Times* that Elmer, having visited his veterinarian and a butcher where the family had an account, was identified and returned.

smashes out the glass in each one. In other words, there is that feeling that *I am ruined, I am trapped, I'm caught at Metro-Goldwyn-Mayer, I'm finished, I'm done.* And I don't think he was aware of it, and, of course, we didn't know it either. He didn't say a word about anything. He didn't talk a lot, ever. No, he just broke all the bookcases, and then we turned out the lights and left."

This act of "trying to break out of his cage" (as Brooks put it) left the perpetrator with a corneal abrasion from a tiny shard of flying glass. After the eye was washed out by a doctor, he was told it was so badly scratched it needed repeated applications of hot towels in order to heal properly. That night, a Friday, Natalie disappeared, leaving Buster and their sons in the care of staff. "We had quarreled all night," she remembered, "and I had gone home to Mother." His sister, Louise, stayed over on Saturday to tend to the eye, and Myra Keaton did the same on Sunday. Early Monday, he was feeling well enough to rouse the boys, determined to fly off to Ensenada with or without Nat's approval. They left the house at nine, had lunch at the studio, then were driven to Clover Field by the family chauffeur. Keaton borrowed Hoot Gibson's plane and hired a pilot to take him, the two boys, their governess, and Willie Riddle to San Diego. During a brief stopover to get clearance to cross the border, the boys went off to the restroom with their governess and never returned. Keaton discovered that all three had been detained for questioning by the police.

Natalie, who had a morbid fear of flying, raced downtown when she caught wind of her husband's plans and, accompanied by her sister Dutch, tearfully invaded the offices of District Attorney Buron Fitts, alleging her husband had kidnapped the children and pleading that they not be allowed to reboard the plane.* Fitts placed a call to the San Diego chief of police, M. M. Scott, who personally drove out to Lindbergh Field to make the arrest. Incensed, Keaton told Scott the children and he were en route to Ensenada, where he expected to "rest up." After talking with his sister-in-law on the phone—Natalie wouldn't speak to him—and promising they'd motor back in the morning, he and the others were released.

"I don't care to make any trouble, so I guess I'll saunter on back to Los Angeles tomorrow morning," he told a reporter. "It was just a little family difficulty. There's nothing to the whole thing—it's so trivial."

They were home before lunch, but Natalie was nowhere to be found. "I

* Family lore has it that Fitts and Constance Talmadge had at one time been lovers, and they apparently remained on good terms.

just went to show Nat who is boss around here," he huffed to a guy from the *Examiner*. "She is peeved at me because I've been sort of running around loose for the last couple of weeks. She left the house Friday night and went over to her mother's or down to Constance's house at the beach. She knows I love her. I adore her. She knows I haven't been doing anything wrong—just having a little fun." Then he turned contrite: "I've been a bad boy, I guess, but, gee, I wish she'd come home. I've called Constance's home but got no answer and I can't get an answer at her mother's place. This is my punishment, I guess."

For the news cameras, he and the two boys posed for pictures, seated, pondering, gloomily "waiting for Mama to come home." He was also observed rehearsing a comic scenario with the kids and staff. "She'll look at me and say, 'What's the meaning of all this?' I'll just give her a deadpan." He turned to Willie. "Then she'll ask you, and you say: 'Everything went black—black—and I don't remember what happened. Maybe it was two other fellows.'" And then the children were given cues of their own to recite.

Not sure what to do next, he selected a phonograph record from the dozens they had lying around the house—Cab Calloway singing "Between the Devil and the Deep Blue Sea"—wrapped it, and had it delivered to Peg Talmadge's house as an appeal for reconciliation. No response. A few hours later, a second, "All of Me," was dispatched. Again nothing. A third, "Can't We Talk It Over?" did the trick. Nat phoned her sister Dutch to say that she was going home to have dinner with Buster and the boys, and reappeared around eight.

"It was just stubbornness that caused it all," she admitted in the press the next day. "For a month Buster has been talking about taking the boys up in an airplane. Naturally, I was nervous. I didn't want him to do it, so when I heard he had taken them and started to Mexico I asked the police to stop them. When they came home yesterday, Buster and I talked it over last night and settled everything. He wanted to take the boys camping, and I agreed. He took their governess and his man and they went down on the beach somewhere. They'll be home soon and then everything will be all right again."

Their time at the beach did him no good. He came down with grippe a few days later and had to spend the balance of his suspension confined to quarters. When he arrived back at the studio on April 14, the scripting of his new picture, done entirely without his participation, was nearly complete. Derived from Clarence Budington Kelland's novel *Speak Easily*, it offered

Keaton the role of a stuffy college professor who is duped into believing he's inherited $750,000. Eager to leave campus life behind ("I'd love to rub elbows with the outside world"), he gets mixed up with a traveling company of actors and decides to use his supposed wealth to take them to Broadway. The original material had been submitted in galley form to Metro's New York office, where it was enthusiastically covered by a reader named Alexina Brune:

"This is a perfect story for Buster Keaton. Couldn't be better. Much more interesting plot than [Booth Tarkington's play] *Clarence,* which was such a success. The character of the professor is delightful, his language amusing, and in contrast to the slangy theatre crowd, gives ample opportunity for amusement. It will make a fast-moving, delightful picture, and the dialogue is all in the book. There is plenty of action. It would be a shame to miss it, for nothing I have seen lately so completely fills the bill for Mr. Keaton."

Brune's endorsement found its way to Weingarten, who liked the story well enough and saw a part that could be tailored to Jimmy Durante. As with *The Passionate Plumber,* the ditchdigging was assigned to Laurence Johnson, with Ralph Spence working in behind him and gagging it up as best he could. But, as with *Plumber* and *Sidewalks of New York* before it, their work left little room for Keaton to do what he was so uniquely able to do, and what M-G-M seemed not to want from him.

"Sound comedy is a different thing entirely," Weingarten contended. "Sound comedy is about what people say, mostly, not what they do. We tried to combine both." Keaton himself thought *Speak Easily* at least had a "sound comedy plot," something that couldn't have been said about his two previous pictures.

Relations were still tense with the studio, Keaton contending he was owed $150,000 for the year if he completed two pictures, regardless of the suspension, and M-G-M insisting he was a salaried employee compensated at the rate of $500 a day. He was paid for the five days leading up to the suspension but returned the check, as he did the checks issued in the weeks following his reinstatement. "On the way out after I get my coin," he said, "I *bite* it!"

Speak Easily began filming on May 9 with Ruth Selwyn, Nicholas Schenck's sister-in-law, as Pansy Peets, Keaton's love interest; comedienne Thelma Todd as the conniving Eleanor Espere, a Broadway veteran; and Jimmy Durante as the head of a struggling company with more spirit than talent. Keaton gamely embraced the role of Professor Timoleon Zanders

Post of Potts College, giving it an earnest reading and contriving modest gags, including a reprise of sorts of the bedroom scene from *Spite Marriage*. A standout, improvised when *Speak Easily* was away on location, had Post retrieving his trunk as his train is pulling away, grabbing on to the handrail of the passenger car and being dragged alongside it as it picks up speed, dust billowing in his wake, Durante and Ed Brophy frantically trying to pull him inside. There is no record of the exchange that undoubtedly took place when Thalberg and Weingarten viewed the rushes the next day, as both could clearly see it was Buster himself risking his neck and not a stunt double. In fact, with its abundance of location work, Keaton truly seemed to enjoy the making of *Speak Easily* and, blessed with a spell of relative serenity at home, remained stoically sober.

Keaton thought Durante got over in the new picture because the character he played "was very much like the real Jimmy Durante." But with Durante now an integral part of the package, and not simply a guest star as he had been in *The Passionate Plumber,* he continued to overshadow Buster, essentially grabbing the audience by its lapels and demanding its attention. The third act of the picture was the troupe's disastrous debut in New York City, in which Post unwittingly injects himself into the performance and makes a shambles of the proceedings, much to the delight of the first-nighters out front. This, especially, required time and inspiration on the part of the creative team, and while the sequence never reached the sublime heights of the silent Keaton comedies, such as *Back Stage* or *The Play House,* it was, given the lowered expectations engendered by the studio's assembly line mentality, something of a miracle in how well it turned out. Even so, Keaton, on location at L.A.'s Mason Opera House, inexplicably showed up drunk on a Saturday, midway through production, and had to be sent home. Two full days were lost before he was able to resume. Then he and Sedgwick blew past their deadline, delays and story trouble adding another nine days of overhead to the original twenty-three-day schedule. Filming finally ground to a close on June 17, 1932, and Buster persuaded Natalie to join him on a romantic jaunt by train up the coast to Seattle.

What ensued was an example of the growing disconnect between himself and his wife of eleven years, for what he had in mind was a gift so spectacularly at odds with her personal tastes and desires that he might as well have given her a private plane. Feeling unusually good about the new picture, Keaton had received word through a broker of a ninety-six-foot diesel-powered yacht called *Canim,* the motivated seller being Colonel Clarence B.

Blethen, publisher of *The Seattle Times*. Commissioned in 1930, the boat's interior was all teak and mahogany with a master stateroom as well as two guest cabins and crew quarters. Inspecting the craft in dry dock, Keaton and a subdued Natalie learned that Blethen had spent $100,000 on it, but in the pit of the Depression, buyers actively seeking yachts being scarce, he was willing to part with it for $25,000. The deal was closed on June 22, and Keaton, oblivious to the fact that she probably feared the open seas as much as flying, grandly declared that he was renaming the boat *Natalie* and taking both it, and her, on a cruise of the Mediterranean.

Unimpressed, Nat, in a replay of the debacle of the house Buster had secretly built for her, refused to join him on the trip to San Pedro, unsure of his skills as a seaman and unwilling to take his word for it. So while her husband and a friend, actor Larry Kent, sailed the boat on the first leg of the trip south, she followed in the comfort of a Pullman car, agreeing to consider joining the voyage home only if and when the two men made it to San Francisco without mishap. Arriving at her hotel, her mood softened as she spoke to the press, characterizing the yacht as "a little reconciliation gift" and laughingly dismissing recent reports of marital disharmony as "nonsense." When Buster and his crew of one actually did arrive on schedule, she relented and agreed to accompany them the rest of the way, prompting her husband to outline a whole new lifestyle to a reporter from the *Oakland Tribune*.

"We'll make the ship our floating home," he said effusively. "We'll visit all the beauty spots on the Pacific coast—and maybe go to Panama too."

That's when Natalie cut in. "Let's see first if the sea suits me," she said.

The boat's maiden voyage under its new name was the twenty-three-mile run to Santa Catalina over Independence Day weekend. Constance Talmadge; her mother, Peg; and pal Mae Sunday, ex-wife of Billy Sunday, Jr., son of the famous evangelist, were along for the christening, but the trip didn't go well. Buster's simmering resentment of Nat and her dislike of the new yacht came bubbling out after a few drinks, and both Dutch and Peg, pleading seasickness, abandoned ship, arranging to take a plane back to the mainland. Natalie, meanwhile, gave him the silent treatment and headed for Dutch's house as soon as they docked. She consulted attorney Jerry Geisler but cautioned she had "no immediate plans." A week later, the Keatons' third separation in eight months was confirmed in the press.

While Natalie was away from the villa, "thinking it over," Buster was morosely contemplating the end of his marriage and a 35 percent cut in pay proposed at the studio, a corporate survival tactic until an "economic recovery." Word of the trim, to apply to any M-G-M employee earning more than $1,500 a week, came as something of a shock since the studio had weathered the downturn better than the other majors, all of which had already made similar reductions and, in some cases, imposed full operational shutdowns.

On Saturday, July 16, a meeting took place at Geisler's offices on West Fifth Street, Buster pressing for another chance, Natalie a property division. Later that day, Louella Parsons reached Nat at her sister's Santa Monica spread and confirmed that another try at saving the marriage was out of the question.

"There isn't the remotest chance of Natalie and Buster Keaton becoming reconciled," Parsons reported. "Natalie will sue for divorce in Los Angeles, asking for the custody of the two boys and the family home. Jerry Geisler has not yet determined what grounds will be stated in the complaint as Mrs. Keaton does not wish to have any unpleasant publicity over the divorce."

When confronted with Parsons' column, Keaton made a statement of his own. "Mrs. Keaton is giving me the air," he said mournfully. "There is no one else. She doesn't want anything. She doesn't want me any longer. She has decided I am useless. She has decided I am incompetent. I am unreliable. I am just a washout. The kids are being put into a military school."

The next day, he reported to the studio for six days of retakes on *Speak Easily*, and Ed Sedgwick once again found himself having to cover for his friend's drunkenness—the halting delivery, the quivering of the head, the way he leaned in, crowding his fellow actors.

Officially, the divorce was still up in the air, but by Thursday a property settlement was in the works. "I don't mind losing the boat," Buster said, "but I left my old ukulele on it and I wish I could get that back."

On July 23, Natalie signed away all interests in a group of investment properties, granting her husband full ownership of unimproved lots and homesites in Beverly Hills, El Segundo, the Union Pacific expansion, and the Hollywood High School tract. Two days later, she filed a petition for divorce in the superior court on the grounds of "extreme mental cruelty" causing "grievous mental suffering." Specifically, she charged that on numerous occasions Buster stayed out late or did not come home at all, refusing to say where he had been; that when visiting the homes of mutual friends he conducted himself in a way that caused "great humiliation and suffering"; that while on the voyage to Catalina he had behaved unconscionably; that he had flown the children to San Diego against her specific wishes and with the intention of taking them into Mexico "for some period of time"; and that all these events caused her "grievous mental distress, suffering, and anguish." No adultery was alleged in the complaint, although the Kathleen Key incident was recalled in much of the news coverage. The complaint indicated that Buster had already agreed to give her custody of the children (with reasonable visitation) and to pay support of $300 a month.

Buster moved out of the house on August 3, taking only his personal belongings, and Natalie promptly put the estate up for rent with an eye toward disposing of it as soon as possible. For both, the place had become a symbol, a metaphor, of the growing dysfunction within the marriage—a big, extravagant mistake. She also put the boat in her mother's name, again with the intent of seeing it sold. The trial took place on August 8, 1932, with Buster a no-show, leaving it to just Natalie and Constance to give their testimony.

"My husband was impossible," Nat testified. "He would stay away from home, many times all night, and would not tell me where he had been." She was asked by her attorney how that conduct affected her.

"I was terribly upset," she answered. "I would walk the floor most of the night." This occurred two or three times a week, she stressed. "Social engagements caused a lot of trouble. I would accept invitations for dinner and he wouldn't show up." When questioned on her husband's attempt to fly the boys to Mexico, she repeated what he told her: "He said they were his children as much as mine, and he would take them wherever he pleased." In corroborating testimony, her sister remembered that Natalie would frequently phone her in the middle of the night to say that Buster was missing, and that she would go over and stay with her. She added that after the airplane trip her sister was ill in bed for several days. Buster Keaton, she concluded, was an "incorrigible rounder," a man who drank to excess and spent money freely.

It was all over in fifteen minutes. The judge granted an interlocutory decree of divorce for the plaintiff, together with the care, custody, and control of the minor children.

The newly retooled *Speak Easily* was previewed before a Los Angeles audience on July 31, and Sidney Skolsky, visiting from New York, happened to catch it. "*Speak Easily* is another very funny Keaton-Durante picture," he judged. "It gives Jimmy a chance to strut some of the stuff that made him a Broadway favorite. He plays the piano and sings a couple of ditties. The crowd had never seen Jimmy in a night club, so they went big for his manner of delivering a song. The studio is now looking for a story to star Durante and let him open his bag of cellar tricks."

Released on August 13, *Speak Easily* proved a favorite of both crowds and reviewers, drawing solid notices and posting the best domestic numbers for a Keaton picture since *Parlor, Bedroom and Bath.* That Durante was a major component of its appeal was beyond doubt, and exhibitors in major markets, unhindered by the contractual billing requirements the studio had to adhere to, began billing him above Keaton's name in their display advertising. Similarly, Keaton's foreign figures continued to plummet, wiping out any advantage the jump in U.S. box office conferred. *Speak Easily* took longer to make and cost more than any Keaton talkie since *Free and Easy.* The net result was that it showed a profit of just $33,000, better than a loss in tough economic times but reinforcing the dubious notion that Keaton was slipping at the box office.

It was just a year earlier that *Sidewalks of New York,* Keaton's last solo feature, had amassed $113,000 more in worldwide rentals. Had the poor quality of *Sidewalks* precipitated the drop? Or did Durante's discordant participation not sit well with Keaton's core audience? A clue lies in the steady decline of foreign revenues, which reached a high-water mark with *Parlor, Bedroom and Bath* and were cut nearly in half with *Speak Easily.*

"I think the audience started to go wrong," Buster Collier suggested. "The people who were watching pictures, seeing comics, started to move away. Different stars were born. Buster wasn't as popular as he should be. He got some bad pictures all of a sudden. It could hurt anybody. Metro had a lot of people hurt. Some of the most important M-G-M pictures didn't make a dime. Buster was starting to take the slide. He should have had strong script supervision. His scripts were very bad. Buster got a little tired, too, of working, I think."

Collier could sense where all this was leading, and conspired to have a long talk with his friend. They settled on a duck-hunting trip to Bakersfield, but Collier was chagrined to find that Keaton had brought along a distraction, a starlet under contract to Paramount. Collier saw his chance when they were out alone on an early-morning duck hunt but didn't get very far.

"Listen," said Keaton. "If you were sent up here to me to have this big thing out with me and tell me how I'm doin' wrong, you're just wastin' your time. I know the only person in the world who can cure me of that is me." It was the beginning of the end of their friendship.

Keaton poses outside his land yacht,
The Good Will, *with sons, Robert and*
Joseph, while Jimmy Durante and
Lew Cody look on.

"I saw it begin to happen," said Collier. "I loved and admired the guy too much to stick around and watch it. We drifted apart."

In a garage on Ivar Avenue in the heart of Hollywood, a large powder-blue bus was being renovated and painted and turned into what the *Citizen-News* called a "hotel-on-wheels," a thirty-two-foot response to the dismantling of Buster Keaton's home life. Having lost a seagoing yacht in his recent divorce, Keaton decided to replace it with something a bit more unusual, a similarly styled craft appealingly known as a land yacht. Originally commissioned at a cost of $52,000 by Edward F. Carry, the president of the Pullman Company, it had changed hands after Carry's 1929 death for $17,000 and was badly in need of work when Keaton acquired it for $10,000 in borrowed money. Luxuriously fitted for transcontinental travel, the cruiser had twin motors on the chassis of a Fifth Avenue bus, twin drawing rooms, observation deck, galley, bar, shower, and on-board electrical generator. Christened *The Good Will*, it also slept eight people, making it ideal for a personal appearance tour Keaton had in mind.

"I had as much fun with my land yacht as a man can whose main purpose is to forget that his whole private world had fallen apart," he said.

Buster Collier having receded as a fixture in Keaton's life, Lew Cody now stepped into the void, the two men tooling around town in high style, Willie Riddle, whom Keaton took to calling "Carruthers," at the wheel;

the destination sign above the windshield read DAMFINO. With Keaton clad in a ceremonial admiral's uniform trimmed in gold braid and epaulets, and Cody in his idea of a captain's dress blues, they took to arriving at parties conveniently soused, two adventurers presenting themselves as carefree playboys while both in reality were deeply in mourning, Keaton for his family and the relatively stable life he had known, Cody for his wife, Mabel Normand, who had died of tuberculosis in 1930. It was a lifestyle that portended no happy endings, but the potted crew of *The Good Will* attracted nationwide press attention, prompting the lieutenant governor of Nebraska, Theodore Metcalfe, to send Buster a commission appointing him an admiral in the "Great Navy of Nebraska."

In September, Keaton and Cody took *The Good Will* northward, stopping off in Monterey on their way to San Francisco. Ordering Carruthers to "cast anchors fore and aft," Keaton emerged in full costume, responding, "No time for golf," when asked if he would be playing in the amateur tournament at Pebble Beach.

"We would park it in front of the St. Francis Hotel in San Francisco and pay fifty cents a day for parking," he reminisced. "They even strung a telephone line to us from a second-story window, and it was the only bus in town with room service."

The men were docked in Yosemite National Park when news of Paul Bern's suicide reached them. Bern was the beloved "Little Father" of the film colony, newly married to Jean Harlow when he inexplicably shot himself in the head at the age of forty-two. Keaton and Cody interrupted their "voyage" across the Sierra Nevada range, electing to return to Los Angeles.

At the studio, the idea of permanently teaming Buster Keaton and Jimmy Durante had gained currency, while Larry Weingarten's health had taken a serious hit. Due to general dissatisfaction with Weingarten's work on the Marie Dressler–Polly Moran comedy *Prosperity*—a chaotic affair shot by Paramount's Leo McCarey and then completely remade by director Sam Wood—as well as the troubles and cost overruns incurred on *Speak Easily*, Weingarten suffered a nervous breakdown and was placed on leave of absence. With no other supervisors to turn to, Irving Thalberg teamed two writers, Lou Edelman and Frank Davis, and put them in charge of the Keaton-Durante picture, a comic murder mystery based on an old play called *The Rear Car*. Screenwriter John Goodrich was put to work on a script while a new contract was being drafted for Keaton, whose current two-year pact was up in mid-October.

Without an agent, Keaton, a pale, dissipated shell of his former self, was left with whatever was put on the table. At the completion of *Speak Easily*, studio business manager Milton Greenwood concluded that two production days had been lost due to Keaton's absences at an estimated cost to the company of $3,000 a day. Now management would incrementally claw that back, assessing a penalty of $600 a week until the losses attributed to Keaton were fully recovered. The new one-year contract, signed on October 5, 1932, also permitted the studio to co-star him for the first time since the release of *One Week* in 1920. From Metro's standpoint, this was simply a matter of catching up with exhibitors who had taken to billing Jimmy Durante alongside or even ahead of him in their display ads. Within days, M-G-M let it be known they were grooming Durante for stardom with *The Rear Car*, which would be directed by Chuck Reisner, and that the studio "may" try to write in a part for Keaton as well.

In desperate need of money, Keaton was in no position to argue. And with Thalberg locked in a battle of his own with Mayer and Nicholas Schenck over the state of his fragile health, the only reliable advocate Keaton still had in the front office was Eddie Mannix. In early November, Mayer, a rabid Republican, pressed Keaton into appearing, along with Conrad Nagel and Lew Cody, as a master of ceremonies at an all-star rally at the Shrine Auditorium in support of President Herbert Hoover. A few days later, the wire services carried a photo of a beaming Natalie, stylishly dressed and flanked by her two boys in uniform at the Black-Foxe Military Institute. Keaton and Lew Cody, meanwhile, could frequently be seen having dinner together at the Brown Derby. One night, it was reported the two men stormed out of a party where they claimed the host was being stingy with the refreshments. It only later dawned on Keaton that he himself had been the host in question.

One of the more memorable characters on the M-G-M lot was Bob Hopkins, a writer who never seemed to put anything down on paper but still received dialogue credits on a number of films, including two of Keaton's features. "Hoppy," as he was known to just about everyone, was the closest thing to a handyman they had when it came to script, and when he wasn't on a set somewhere, he was lurking in the studio commissary or standing on the corner—"the crossroads" they called it—ready to nab a producer and shout an idea at him.

In the wake of Franklin Delano Roosevelt's landslide election on November 8, 1932, it was Hopkins' idea to have a picture ready for the inevitable amendment to the Volstead Act heralding the eventual repeal of the Eighteenth Amendment and the end of Prohibition. His pitch likely consisted of fewer than a dozen words, but one of those words was undoubtedly "beer."

The concept seemed such a natural that Thalberg put M-G-M stalwart Carey Wilson, who had authored everything from *Ben-Hur* and *He Who Gets Slapped* to Marion Davies' *Polly of the Circus,* on it. Wilson, who worked faster than practically anyone, had a nineteen-page synopsis titled *Happy Days* ready within ten days of the election, and an eighty-eight-page draft continuity called *Beer* a few days after that. Conceived from the start for the team of Keaton and Durante, *Beer* had the two of them trying to revive a shuttered brewery in order to get a jump on all the pent-up demand. With filming set to begin in mid-December, it took the place of *The Rear Car* on the M-G-M production chart. Keaton thought the script awful, a "one hundred percent turkey." Going to Thalberg would be futile though, and when filming began on December 17, he dutifully played his first scenes with Durante, toward whom the story was heavily weighted.

"I was trying to drink away my sorrow and woe every night," he said in his autobiography. "It was the only way I could go to sleep. But one weekend when I absorbed unusually large quantities of whiskey I was unable to sleep at all. I came to the studio that Monday so woozy from lack of sleep that I hardly knew what I was doing. Somehow or other I got the crazy idea that the one thing in the world that would wake me up was a bottle of beer. I'd tried coffee and everything else that I could think of, and none of them had helped. Instead of waking me up, of course, the beer put me to sleep. I laid down on my studio couch for a cat nap. But my exhaustion was so complete that when the assistant director came to call me to the set he couldn't rouse me. Eddie Sedgwick . . . summoned doctors who worked on me and then took me home. There was no shooting that day."

The rushes revealed a man who was waxen and lifeless, paralyzed by drink and depression. Production on *Beer* stretched for what seemed an eternity. "Most pathetic happy man I know," Gilbert Roland recorded in his diary, "my friend Buster Keaton." On December 29, halfway through the ordeal, Irving Thalberg suffered a heart attack, forcing Mayer, the executive head of the studio, to take on Thalberg's responsibilities as production chief. As far as Mayer knew, *Beer* was on track to finish on schedule, but Carey Wilson had no ear for comedy, and Sedgwick had humorist Jack Cluett, who had written for *Judge, Life,* and *The New Yorker,* on set to punch up the dialogue. A song by Harry Tobias and David Snell was added for Durante, but nothing seemed to bring the material to life.

Keaton spent New Year's at Caliente—supposedly with his mother—and was in no condition to shoot the following week, costing the company a total of six camera days. His absence was publicly laid to a bout of the flu, or, as Louella Parsons had it, "a few days' rest." He rallied on occasion, such as the day when Joe and Louise Keaton visited the set, and George Shaffer was on hand for the *Daily News* to observe two men he described as "the happiest couple I have seen around any of the studios in weeks." With Buster's sister looking on, they rollicked during lulls in production, thrilling the normally jaded cast and crew with a reminder of just what it was like to see The Three Keatons in their prime.

"Buster started it with the old vaudeville trick of balancing a broom upside down on his toe and kicking it the length of the movie stage into his father's face. Only it didn't quite reach his father's face. The father reached forward just as if he had been practicing for weeks and grabbed the hurtling broom. Then the pair improvised an act in which Buster chased his dad off the set. The father ran, carrying the broom, but the broom wedged lengthwise in the doorway, and the gag ended with the dad bouncing back into the room and whacking Buster a full wallop in the face with the broom. 'He's losing his wallop,' Buster laughed as he got up from the floor. 'He's getting afraid to hit hard; he pulled his blow with that broom.' Then the pair of them set to work to see which could simulate the most natural fall over a rolling barrel. The barrel was supposed to convey them—and if you don't think riding a rolling barrel is a hard stunt, take out life insurance and try it—right out the door of the room."

It was a joyous interlude in an otherwise gruesome work pattern, but Buster's renewed sense of fun couldn't sustain him for long. Living under his mother's care at her house in the flats of Beverly Hills, he fell asleep one night with a burning cigarette in his hand and was too drunk to notice when it lit the bed on fire. Smelling smoke, Myra burst into the room, rolled him to safety, then wrestled the smoldering mattress out onto the lawn, where she doused it with the garden hose. Neighbors called the fire department, the commotion rousing the entire block. Without Thalberg to protect him, a termination notice was drafted in the legal department citing intoxication as the cause. Keaton had parked the land yacht on the backlot during the making of *Beer,* and Sam Marx, who tended to refer to it as a "trailer," remembered it fondly.

That trailer was the greatest party place I've ever known. It rocked back and forth day and night with the drinking that was going on, the carousing. They were having guests. It was a great place to drop in on, and it was like New Year's Eve every day.

M-G-M was not happy about that, but then Buster was very unhappy about M-G-M. . . . Finally, Mayer had it drawn to his attention. Mayer was a highly moral man, no matter what people may say about him, and he did not want a potential scandal erupting within the studio. They were having a lot of girls show up, there was a tremendous lot of drinking, and there was probably some gambling. And so, consequently, Mayer sent Eddie Mannix to go down there and stop all the carousing. Unfortunately, Mannix was one who joined in half the time. So it was not exactly the right thing to send a fire bug to put out a fire. After Mayer realized that Eddie wasn't getting anywhere, he went down himself and had a tremendous confrontation there with Buster. He finally reached a point where Buster ordered him out of the trailer, and Mayer ordered him out of the studio.

Beer finished after thirty-two days, and Mayer ordered it previewed as quickly as possible. At eighty-six minutes, it was impossibly long for a comedy, and *The Hollywood Reporter,* which covered the screening, pronounced it dull. "The picture needs plenty of trimming—which it will undoubtedly get—to bring the laughs closer together. But there is no denying that, while the laughs are there, they don't exactly grow in bunches, and brother, they never build to anything resembling a good roll in the aisles."

Two frantic days of retakes were made, but there was no salvaging what was widely regarded as a complete disaster. Retitled *What—No Beer?* it finally closed on February 1 at a negative cost of $266,785. The following day, February 2, 1933, the two producers of the picture, Lou Edelman and Frank Davis, handed Keaton a terse one-sentence dismissal "for good and sufficient cause" signed by Louis B. Mayer.

He was fired.

19

Crash in to My Life

THE ORDEAL WAS OVER. There was no contentment in what came next, no lasting sense of relief. If the corporate entity known as Metro-Goldwyn-Mayer had set out to degrade him in its collective ignorance, to destroy him in the only profession he had known since the age of five, he would now finish the job as if his life was one of his own grand-scale comedies in which a sense of disaster pervaded the third act and only the hero's newfound mettle and ingenuity could save the day.

It was said that Buster Keaton wept when he got the notice his services were no longer required. However sick the situation had grown, it was still a bitter blow. Posterity would redeem him, but that would have been cold comfort had it occurred to him as he surveyed the wreckage of his life in the early days of 1933. Natalie had not asked for alimony, just child support, and what she did take—the house, the boat, the cars—she wanted only for whatever cash value they had in such diminished times. She had spent their money freely in an obsessive one-sided competition with her sisters over clothes, status, and family. Her husband never saw the bills, never looked at a bank statement, never handled a paycheck. Over time, he had been conditioned to assume there would always be enough money, and so all the income and all the expenses went directly to John B. "Jack" Codd, who was an estimator at Metro when Buster first met him, and who later came to work as an auditor at the Keaton studio. As their business manager, Codd handled all the messy details of day-to-day living for the Keatons, paying the staff, seeing to repairs to the house and the cars, and materially facilitating the entertaining so central to their lives.

Gambling was the only transactional thing in which Buster Keaton regularly indulged—the races at Caliente, wagers at sporting events, and, most significantly, bridge, which, apart from polo, was the industry's favorite pastime. Keaton, who enjoyed the mechanics and the problem-solving aspects of the game, was considered a top player, as were Zeppo and Chico Marx, actor Ralph Graves, and actress Bebe Daniels. For the public, he won his greatest fame playing for comedy on the radio against Chuck Reisner and Bob Vogel, announcing his surprise partner as Oliver Hardy (with an assist from Stan Laurel). The exhibition was presided over by referee Jimmy Durante.

Buster recalled having no real interest in bridge until he found himself traveling east on a train with Nicholas Schenck and Hiram Abrams and his wife in 1925. Upon learning that neither he nor Schenck played, Mr. and Mrs. Abrams offered to teach them. "Like so many old pinochle players trying bridge for the first time, I was reluctant to sacrifice my hand for the sake of my partner. Mr. Abrams kept telling me that I was stupid and became more abusive as the day wore on."

Keaton was so put off by the experience, which came close to a physical altercation, he spent the next six months reading everything he could find on the subject of bridge. He started playing again at a quarter of a cent a point, working his way up to twenty-five cents. Eighteen months later, he was again in a game with Abrams—this time opposite him—and after two weeks' worth of such meetings, accepted the UA president's check for $3,400.

"I was anything but a great gambler," Sam Marx said, "but I liked to play bridge, and they knew about it—at least my friends at M-G-M knew about it—so I was invited to Joe Schenck's home in Beverly Hills and, subsequently, Buster Keaton's home.

They used to play bridge [because] it was a means of letting off steam after the tension of making movies all day. There were two kinds of games: There were the high-stakes games, which Joe Schenck and Buster Keaton were part of, and there was the low-stakes game [for] their little friends who didn't want to play for twenty-five cents a point—which is a high bridge game, or at least it was then and I suppose it can still be considered so. Joe Schenck and Buster Keaton were in those [high-stakes] games, and then right alongside would be the smaller games with people like myself and producers like Larry Weingarten and Harry Rapf. . . . But the high stakes were Joe Schenck, Buster Keaton, Eddie Mannix, and men like Thalberg . . .

I would show up at this massive Beverly Hills place. I never met the lady of the house; Buster or a valet or butler or someone would answer the door, and I'd go upstairs where my friends were assembling to play, and I would be ushered to the smaller game. I got to know Buster and watch him, and I think he was under a strain of heavy gambling. I think he liked to gamble and that he got drawn into a bigger game than he might have wanted, and it's not uncommon. I saw it happen in poker and, later, I saw it happen in rummy as we have progressive card games that take over the population. I saw people wiped out by those games. I played one poker game where Joe Schenck was playing in which [Paramount general manager] Ben Schulberg got $48,000. I won $200 [but] I had no place being in the game in the beginning.

Well, I am positive that a lot of Keaton's money went down the drain due to those bridge games. He was in the big games, and I would never have cast him as a top-rank gambler of the type that Joe Schenck and Eddie Mannix were, or Ben Schulberg, or any of the high, high producers or studio executives who were dealing with money like it was coming out of a pump. And, therefore, they didn't care much how they threw it away—the higher the stakes, the more excitement they got. I never saw Buster seemingly excited in this bridge game. He played it methodically, quietly, and I'm sure he lost his shirt when he was doing it.

Keaton gave up the high-stakes bridge marathons when he left the mansion on Hartford Way, never sure how much he had won or lost over the years. He retreated to a six-room bungalow he had purchased on Queensbury Drive in the Cheviot Hills neighborhood of West Los Angeles. While he was burrowing in on the day after he was sacked, most of the trades and all the wire services were reporting in a face-saving sort of way that the decision to part with Metro had been his alone. Only the upstart *Hollywood Reporter* went its own way, telling readers in its lede that Keaton "is finished at M-G-M, a letter from the business office of the studio informed him yesterday." The break happened so quickly that industry-based ads and some editorial content were still pushing the notion that Keaton would appear with Durante in a picture called *Buddies,* written by Jack Cluett and co-starring ten-year-old Jackie Cooper. He told the press himself that he and

Lew Cody would sail for Honolulu in a few days but, as was usually the case, it wasn't quite that simple.

Mae Elizabeth Scriven, a California native, was born into a family of farmers and ranchers. She grew up in Merced, at the gateway to Yosemite National Park, and on her father's ranch in Orange, not far from where Walt Disney would later situate Disneyland. It's clear she didn't see a future for herself in agriculture, and in 1925 she was a nineteen-year-old nursing student fascinated by the Hollywood scene and hankering for a piece of it. To get away from rural Orange County, its orchards and walnut groves, she married an auto mechanic named Frank Hawley and set up housekeeping in a Venice duplex, four blocks from the famous boardwalk and a million miles from the farm life she had known. An attractive brunette with rock-gray eyes and exotic tastes, she was divorced by 1930, living in Hollywood and looking for work. With her nursing credentials, she landed a job as a physician's office assistant, taking an apartment off Wilshire Boulevard in the Westlake area of Los Angeles. It was while living there in October 1932 that she met Buster Keaton for the first time.

Having "fallen ill" at a lavish party hosted by adventurer and millionaire playboy John Brandeis, who was in the throes of a very public divorce of his own, Keaton was transported from Brandeis's Open Diamond Bar Ranch near Chatsworth to the Beverly Hills Emergency Hospital, a place that seemed to have a direct line to M-G-M. At the studio's behest, he promptly found himself under the care of Dr. Harry Martin, an old friend who had been prominent in industry circles for years, and who had grown even more so with his 1930 marriage to Hearst columnist Louella Parsons. A urologist by specialty, Martin was known for performing abortions, treating sexually transmitted diseases, and generally attending to the needs of the major studios whose employees required delicate handling and the utmost in discretion. He was a famous drinker himself, an easy, congenial drunk who knew the ins and outs of addiction treatment and had seen it all since coming to Los Angeles in 1919. For Keaton, he prescribed the steam caves at Arrowhead Springs, sending along a young associate physician to attend his drying out, and with him a freelance nurse who turned out to be Mae Scriven Hawley.

"When we returned, Dr. Martin was not satisfied with my condition and insisted that the nurse remain with me a couple of weeks longer to make sure I completed the cure. She had her orders of just the right amount of whiskey to give me so I wouldn't go nuts, also hypodermics to put me to sleep."

On August 22, Keaton emerged from seclusion to attend a star-studded program honoring George M. Cohan at the Cocoanut Grove, where he was photographed dancing with a non-professional. He began talking up the idea of replacing the yacht he lost to Natalie with another oceangoing vessel, only to emerge at the end of the month with *The Good Will*, a purchase that signaled the end of his brief flirtation with sobriety.

Keaton and Lew Cody spent the month of September drunkenly rolling around the state in the new land yacht, only coming to rest so that Buster could sign his new M-G-M contract on October 5. The following night, he and Cody attended the seasonal opening of the New Frolics café in Culver City, Cody escorting actress Phyllis Crane and Keaton with an unknown brunette on his arm who more than likely was Mae Scriven. What followed was characterized by friends as a "hectic" romance, with Mae regularly seen out on the town with her former patient, dancing in fashionable restaurants and generally putting on the dog. When the filming of *Beer* commenced on December 17, 1932, Keaton, according to his autobiography (in which the chronology is somewhat at odds with the historic record), was still taking the cure under her care, but this seems unlikely. Then, when the holidays rolled around, he decided he wanted to spend them at Agua Caliente with his mother and sister. While there, he was photographed dancing with actress Eileen Bramley, and was home again on January 2, 1933. He returned, how-ever, in no condition to shoot, causing the film to shut down in his absence. He and Mae would later claim they were married in Ensenada on January 8, 1933, but the judge of the local court, who would have performed the ceremony, denied any knowledge of it. After the alleged marriage, Keaton returned to the set of *Beer,* which was now suddenly six days behind sched-ule, and moved in with his mother, who saved him from incinerating him-self a few days later. By February 4, he was estranged enough from Mae to say he would travel to Hawaii with Cody to regain his health, but the trip never took place. He dropped out of sight for the rest of the month, surfac-ing in El Paso on February 27.

That evening, fortified by strong drink and using a tablecloth as a veil, he reprised his Princess Rajah dance for the amusement of Cafe Central patrons, his hat serving as the head of John the Baptist and his necktie inter-preting the role of the snake. Then he collapsed after ripping his undershirt in a burlesque attempt to vamp the orchestra leader. "I'm just out for a good time," he said with a wide grin. "The crowd at the café was appreciative and human, and I'll do anything if it pleases them. I couldn't get away with it in Los Angeles."

The next morning, he spoke to a reporter from the *Herald-Post* at the Hotel Paso del Norte, Mae conspicuously at his side. "I had admired Buster on the screen," she stated. "Then a mutual friend introduced us, and we fell in love. We are very happy."

The story was picked up by the wire services, prompting comment from friends in Hollywood, one of whom thought he was "either kidding or not fully aware of what he was saying." Lew Cody and Gilbert Roland were amazed at the news, given they both thought the hectic romance had run its course. At his home on North Canon Drive, Buster Collier received a telegram from Texas:

SOMETHING BEAUTIFUL HAS COME CRASH IN TO MY LIFE=

BUSTER K.

It never occurred to Buster Keaton to consult a lawyer when he was let out at M-G-M, even though his contract had eight months left to run. "By that time I was drinking more than a bottle of whiskey a day," he said, "which neither improved my mental processes nor lessened my sense of humiliation." And to many of those around him, those who had sadly observed the steady process of disintegration, his leaving Metro was actually considered a positive development.

"I always thought that Buster had a wonderful exit line," said Sam Marx, "because he said: 'You studio people warp my character!' Which was literally true, of course."

What—No Beer? was rushed into release in anticipation of repeal votes in the House and Senate, which doubtless supercharged the film's timely appeal. In New York, where it opened at the Capitol, it was supported onstage by Ed Wynn and a big revue called *The Laugh Parade,* which in itself added $20,000 a week to house overhead. Aggressively edited and shorn of twenty-two minutes, the picture didn't impress many reviewers, who gave whatever honors there were to Jimmy Durante. At $53,000, business at the Capitol fell short of expectations, but the program was held a second week, which delivered a little less than $40,000—not so good, yet true to pattern. Overall, *What—No Beer?* continued Keaton's slide, pulling $115,000 less in domestic rentals than *Speak Easily* while slightly improving on its foreign revenues. At a negative cost of $267,000, *What—No Beer?* returned a profit of $135,000, vastly improving on the performance of *Speak Easily* where it really counted.

What the picture ultimately demonstrated was that Keaton remained commercially viable as long as his pictures were made for a price. In the bracket of $200,000 to $300,000 a feature, he was a reliable moneymaker; at $500,000 per he probably wasn't. All this fed his conviction he would be picked up by another studio, where he wouldn't be managed so foolishly as he was at Metro.

"Losing out at M-G-M made me poison at the other major Hollywood studios," he said. "None of them seemed to want or need me. I don't know what wild rumors went around about my unreliability and alcoholism. But in that tightly knit one-industry town there were then seven major studios in a position to spend on a picture the sort of money that my comedies cost. No offers came from the other six: Paramount, Columbia, Warner Bros., Universal, Fox, or RKO."

"We tried to keep our marriage quiet," Keaton said in El Paso. "I met Miss Scriven and fell for her hook, line, and sinker. And she's just as much in love with me. We haven't hurt anyone, taken advantage, or cheated anyone. We are happy together, and we'll face the world in that knowledge. She would rather be with me, no matter what the past or the future, and I with her."

They caught a plane for Mexico City on March 3, Buster characterizing the trip as a honeymoon and a much-needed vacation. "I'll be around a month or so," he predicted, "or maybe more." He busied himself making personal appearances at Mexican theaters and talking of making bilingual comedies as an independent producer. He was still drinking heavily and skipped out on a commitment to officiate at a comic bullfight, drawing jeers and catcalls from an angry mob that had turned out to see a famous American movie star. He and Mae caught a plane for Tijuana that day, Keaton telling the press he was headed to Los Angeles to "attempt to straighten out financial matters."

Back home on Queensbury, the Keatons cavorted for the cameras, Buster grimly presenting his bride with a posy from his garden and she telling dreamily of how he serenaded her one night in Mexico City.

"Of course we are not legally married in the United States," he acknowledged. "We will be as soon as my divorce becomes final in August. Valentino did the same thing. Those who don't like it aren't my kind of people anyway." He said he might return to Mexico before then to make an independent picture. "Everything is hunky-dory," he insisted.

"Wonderful," Mae agreed.

They proceeded to spend the next couple of months showing each other off. For the world premiere of *King Kong* at Grauman's Chinese, Buster, sporting evening clothes and a silk topper, arrived at the red carpet astride a motorcycle, with Mae, wearing a white fur stole and matching hat, riding in the sidecar. She, in turn, brought him to a party at the home of developer Carl Benning, a Scriven family friend, making a grand entrance on his arm with a live snake draped around her neck.

"She was the talk of the family," said Glenn Scriven, whose father was Mae's cousin. "The scuttlebutt in the family was that Mae married Buster to take advantage of him."

The story persisted that Mae got Keaton drunk in order to get him to marry her—or to convince him that he had done so after the fact. And that she maintained her control of him through the strategic use of alcohol. In April, she was sued by a wealthy acquaintance who accused her of wrecking an imported cabriolet she had "wrongfully converted to her own use." An attempt to drag Buster into the suit as co-defendant, and a subsequent demurrer filed on his behalf, caused tension in the relationship, and when he applied for a passport toward the end of the month, anticipating a working trip to England, it was Lew Lipton who would be joining him on the voyage, not Mae. To reporters covering the story, he had two words: "Forget me."

The opportunity in England never materialized, but in its place came a seemingly solid offer from Aubrey M. Kennedy, who had a long executive résumé from silent days and the funding to establish a studio at St. Petersburg, the peninsula city on the western coast of Florida. Keaton dispatched Lipton to assess the situation, and on May 29 Kennedy announced that Keaton had agreed to a deal that called for three pictures a year for two years, with an option for three additional years. Kennedy also noted the start of construction on a twenty-one-thousand-square-foot soundstage and carpenter shop, the two forming the hub of a studio development on Weedon's Island called Kennedy City. He claimed he had contracts in hand to make twenty-four movies for a startup called United Pictures, as well as releases for the pioneering producer Pat Powers. He indicated, in fact, that the first title for Powers' Celebrity Productions was already in production with former Fox star Olive Borden in the lead.

Keaton had high hopes for the arrangement, and Kennedy's proposed soundstage must have revived thoughts of how casual production was back in the days of the old studio on Lillian Way. "Think of it—having to get an OK to do a retake!" he said of the M-G-M way of doing things. "It's like a painter having to get a permit to do a painting over. If I thought I was going to need a retake, I'd just tell the actors not to shave their beards off until I'd looked at the rushes."

He and Lipton worked out the story for a picture titled *The Fisherman.* "I was determined to stay off the booze, do a great job, and show everyone that I was anything but a dead duck." He leased a house on Tampa Bay, played baseball as part of a team from the local Coca-Cola bottler, welcomed Mae, Elmer, and his brother, Harry, to town, and set about putting together a production company. Kennedy, it seemed, was full of big plans, but the disconnect was over money.

Kennedy's sole source of funding was a local engineer and sportsman named T. C. Parker, who had pledged somewhere north of $100,000 to get the enterprise rolling, and who had absolutely no experience in moviemaking. Kennedy hoped to get two or three inexpensive features made with the money, then use them to sell the viability of the idea to others. But then the size of the proposed soundstage got cut in half, and the personnel he attracted were all has-beens, names from back when Kennedy was a studio big shot, all, with the exception of Keaton himself, long since out of work. In addition to Olive Borden, there were Molly O'Day, Sally O'Neill's sister, and Marshall Neilan, who had directed Mary Pickford, Colleen Moore, and John Barrymore in his prime, but who drank himself out of a top-rank career and was now virtually unemployable in California.

In an effort to take control, Keaton formed the Flamingo Film Company with himself as president, Neilan as vice president, Lipton as secretary-treasurer, and Aubrey Kennedy taking a seat on the board. There was, however, no possible way he was going to make a releasable feature for $41,000, which is what Neilan's poverty-row effort, *Chloe,* cost. Kennedy was either unaware of what Keaton's M-G-M talkies had been costing or, more likely, thought the Keaton name and track record would attract other backers, maybe even Keaton himself. With the downsized soundstage still under construction, Keaton, Lipton, and Neilan traveled to Havana as guests of the Cuban president, "who insisted on getting the fleet out for review—all four ships." Scouting locations for *The Fisherman,* this was where Keaton was on the morning of June 29, 1933, when Roscoe Arbuckle slipped into a bed at the Park Central Hotel in New York City and suffered a heart attack at the age of forty-six.

After years of neglect, Arbuckle's career had been on the upswing. Newly married to actress Addie McPhail, who served as his onstage partner in their loosely scripted vaudeville appearances, he had returned to movies under his own name for the first time in more than a decade, signing a six-picture contract with Warner Bros. to make two-reel comedies at their Vitaphone studio complex in Brooklyn. The first of these, *Hey Pop*, was released on November 12, 1932, and signaled the comeback for which he had long striven. Arbuckle had just completed the sixth picture in the series and signed a contract for a starring feature when he failed to respond to his wife, who thought he was merely sleeping. Stuck in Cuba, Keaton couldn't get to New York in time to attend the July 1 funeral, nor even send a floral tribute.

"All who have ever known the real Roscoe Arbuckle will always treasure the memory of the great, generous heart of the man—a heart big enough to embrace in its warmth everyone who came to him for help, stranger and friend alike," Joe Schenck said in a statement. "It was this quality which led to his downfall after he had struggled from poverty to a fame in which the children throughout the world worshiped him. Those who knew him for the great artist he was admired him. His was the tragedy of a man born to make the world laugh and to receive only suffering as his reward. And to the end he held no malice."

On the day of the funeral, humorist Arthur "Bugs" Baer put it more succinctly: "He died eleven years ago and he was buried today."

Met with political tensions, which would culminate in the September overthrow of President Carlos Manuel de Céspedes y Quesada, Keaton and Lipton returned from Cuba to announce a two- or three-week delay in starting the picture. On July 7, Buster visited the set of *Playthings of Desire* to observe some location filming, posing for photos with Molly O'Day, who was to play the love interest in *The Fisherman* as her sister had in *Battling Butler*. With no place to film interiors, Keaton went off to New York with Neilan and Kennedy to arrange for rental space, determining the company would film about 20 percent of the picture at the former Paramount Long Island studio, 40 percent in Cuba, and 40 percent in and around St. Petersburg. He made the rounds of nightspots, talking up the picture, but no work got done, no contracts signed.

Finally, tired of Kennedy's specious claims, T. C. Parker bought him out, taking possession of all the assets Kennedy had amassed in St. Petersburg, including ownership of *Chloe* and *Playthings of Desire*. In New York, Keaton took the opportunity to say he wouldn't be back, blaming "misrepresentations" made by Kennedy. The collapse of the setup in Florida dealt a severe blow at a time when he saw no options for himself in Hollywood. Production money was scarce for independents, several of the majors were flirting with insolvency, and even Harold Lloyd was on the ropes, his last picture registering what *Variety* termed "a startling low in grosses." Yet it was Lloyd who might have provided a way back for him.

As Harold Goodwin related, "Clyde Bruckman directed a picture that I did with Harold Lloyd, *Movie Crazy*. And Harold said to me, 'I'd like to get Buster to direct me.' He wanted Buster to direct him, and Buster wouldn't do it. I don't know why. I think Buster was so timid he didn't like to order people around. Of course, I'm prejudiced, but I think Buster knew more about comedy than any of the others."

Keaton had put Bruckman's name as co-director on *The General* in order to give him a promotion, he said, a reward, presumably, for discovering *The Great Locomotive Chase*. "Lloyd didn't know any better and kept him for about four pictures.*. . . But he turned out to be good for Lloyd, so there was no harm done. Made him a good director. But up to then he had no experience directing at all."

Now Lloyd was readying a new picture, *The Cat's Paw*, but if he and Keaton ever discussed the matter, it is lost to memory. Keaton, moreover, suggested it was a time when he was in no condition to direct anything: "I really started to hit the bottle hard after returning from Florida, and in a short while I had a bad case of the D.T.s."

Irving Thalberg arrived back at M-G-M on August 19, 1933. In the more than eight months he had been absent, the studio had switched to a straight unit system, eliminating the position of production chief he had occupied since the studio's founding in 1924. Now in charge of his own unit, Thalberg would be responsible for eight or ten pictures a year, working with a small group of associate producers. Keaton had been gone for six months but had left behind a story idea that Ed Sedgwick was desperate to make. It was likely Sedgwick, in fact, who related the idea to a columnist at the *Hollywood Filmograph*, which ran the following item in its issue of February 25:

---

* Bruckman actually directed three Harold Lloyd features: *Welcome Danger* (1929), *Feet First* (1930), and the aforementioned *Movie Crazy* (1932).

Maybe you think there won't be a lot of the old merriment out at M-G-M when the new flicker *Gland Hotel* gets under way. As a wise-cracking burlesque of *Grand Hotel,* the show should pack a good-sized twitter. . . . Buster (Ice-Pan) Keaton will impersonate Kringelein, the Lionel Barrymore role, and our old friend Polly Moran will do Flaemmchen, the hotsy little secretary. What we want to know is— who's going to do a Garbo?

Now, six months later, Sedgwick was approaching Thalberg with the details as Keaton had related them. The setting would be a fleabag hotel where the best rooms rented for fifty cents a night. Oliver Hardy would play the Wallace Beery part, a manufacturer of front-collar buttons trying to arrange a merger with Stan Laurel, who makes back-collar buttons. Polly Moran would indeed play the Joan Crawford part, inspiring a passionate seduction scene with Hardy. Comic character actor Henry Armetta would play the room clerk enacted in the original by Jean Hersholt, Jimmy Durante would take on John Barrymore's role as the bogus count, and Marie Dressler would serve as the picture's Garbo. "Let them release this parody of *Grand Hotel* six months after their big picture is released," Keaton told Sedgwick, "and I'll bet anyone on the M-G-M lot anything from a Ford to a Cadillac that my take-off will out-gross their all-star movie."

Back in Los Angeles, Keaton was mourning the Florida deal, unshaven and deep in a hole when Sedgwick came to him. "He said he had told Irving Thalberg about my *Grand Hotel* take-off and that Thalberg wanted to make it. 'He can't make it,' I said. 'It doesn't belong to M-G-M. It belongs to me.' 'Irving knows that,' Eddie replied. 'That is what he wants to talk to you about.'"

But Keaton wouldn't go back to M-G-M, wouldn't even set foot on the premises unless Mayer himself invited him back. "It was also true that I was in no shape to go back. In no mental shape, that is." And so he stubbornly ignored the hand Thalberg extended. "Everything might have been different if I had gone back. Doing a picture I was so eager to do might have enabled me to stop drinking and re-establish myself as a man whose only business was making people laugh. Eddie Sedgwick, like any successful director, was a master of persuasion. Yet he could not talk me that day into doing the sensible thing and eating humble pie. So nothing ever came of that bright notion."

·   ·   ·

In 1961, Keaton faced the microphone of broadcaster and columnist Shirley Eder for a brief radio interview. Their talk started off with pleasantries and the fact that he was touring in a Broadway musical. But Eder had a way of getting under a subject's skin, and the session took a dark turn.

"Well, Buster Keaton," she said as their talk was winding down, "do you have any friends today that you had when you were big in pictures?"

"Oh, sure," Keaton responded. "Sure."

"Out in Hollywood, did they stick by you when things got a little tough for you? The ones who were still up there? Were they loyal to you, or did they each go his own way because of the caste system?"

"I was left pretty much alone for a while," he admitted. "Now that *did* happen to me."

"Was that a terrible hurt when it happened?"

"Yes, you're doggone right it was."

Keaton always said the years 1933 to 1935—the years he was married to Mae Scriven—were the worst years of his life. On August 10, 1933, Natalie's divorce from him became final. Almost immediately, speculation was that she would marry Larry Kent, who had been her frequent escort and traveling companion over the previous year, although she denied there was any romance. Then came the death on September 29 of her mother, Peg Talmadge, putting the brakes on wedding plans of any sort. Kent, along with Gilbert Roland and Buster Collier, served as an usher at the funeral held at Hollywood Memorial Park, an event that took place while Buster and Mae were on the road.

The one positive career move Keaton made during this period was to finally secure himself an agent. When he started in pictures, agents weren't common, and he always felt that Joe Schenck had his best interests at heart. When he moved to M-G-M, it seemed that Joe's brother Nick would treat him fairly as well. Thalberg reassured him in terms of production, and it was only after he was co-opted by Larry Weingarten that he grew sullen and unhappy. Once he left Metro, the top-rank agents, such as Myron Selznick and Edward Small, wouldn't touch him, not wanting to invest considerable time in smoothing over his absences and his drunken antics. Fortunately, a New York transplant named Leo Morrison was willing to take him, a testament to the enduring power of the Keaton name. Morrison had nearly a hundred clients, but many were featured or contract players such as Mae Clarke, Leo Carrillo, or the young John Wayne. The number of genuine stars Morrison handled could be counted on the fingers of one hand— principally Spencer Tracy, Colin Clive, and, now, Buster Keaton.

Morrison's roots were in vaudeville—he had once booked the Palace—so he began by setting up a series of personal appearances for his new client. Fortunately, Keaton was still on the nation's screens, either in playoff engagements of *What—No Beer?* or in a well-received edition of *Hollywood on Parade,* a series of themed short subjects independently produced by Louis Lewyn for Paramount release. This wasn't anything Morrison arranged; Lewyn was the husband of Marion Mack and had used Keaton before in the series, as well as in its predecessor, *The Voice of Hollywood.* The twelve-minute film, entirely hosted by Keaton, opened with him conducting a band with his back to the camera, then looking around for the big reveal. A second Buster shows up in period garb, accompanied by Marion in her first screen appearance of any note since *The General.*

"We're the spirit of 1902," Buster announces, and he and Marion launch into a duet of "Bicycle Built for Two." He speaks in couplets throughout, introducing a succession of real couples (such as Mr. and Mrs. Clive Brook) in period costuming. He is at his best, clear and lively in a charming reminder of how good he could be when left to his own devices.

The tour kicked off in Baltimore on September 1, with Keaton performing a sketch in a company of five titled "The Field of Honor," to be followed by RKO and Warner dates into the fall. In New York, he guested on NBC's *Fleischmann's Yeast Hour* with crooner Rudy Vallée, going over better with the studio audience than with the listeners at home. Then it was on to Cleveland, where he fell off the wagon in spectacular style, managing to take a dive offstage, bumping his head and curtailing the performance. The Associated Press blamed the episode on an attack of "nervous indigestion," but poor word of mouth brought the monthlong tour to a premature conclusion after a scheduled stop in St. Louis, during which he observed his thirty-eighth birthday.

Mae drove in from New York with Elmer, meeting up with Buster and his brother, Harry—who was briefly part of the act—in Chicago. The tonic he needed, he decided, was a visit to Bluffton and the old Actors' Colony, where memories of carefree summer days were still fresh and a dozen of Frank Pascoe's fried perch awaited. Excitedly, he chartered a plane to get them across Lake Michigan, landing unheralded at the county airport on the afternoon of October 6. They slipped down to William "Mush" Rawls' place, where they were invited to spend the night. After stopping at Pascoe's—"Oh, they were good!" he said of the perch—and getting a couple of hours' sleep, Buster was off visiting old friends and swapping stories, at ease in a way he

Keaton casts a wary glance at Mae Elizabeth Scriven on the day of their wedding in Ventura, California.

hadn't truly been in years. It was Mush and his wife Ella's idea for him to dress up as a plumber with an outsize wrench and have him pay a call on the Kruegers—their son, Keith, was a great pal—offering to fix the pipes. Ma Krueger wasn't fooled, and so he spent the next few hours spinning tales at their Edgewater home.

On Saturday, Keaton visited Jingles Jungle with Mae, Harry, and the Rawlses, the little green cottage perched on a sand hill where he passed some of the happiest days of his life. He sought out others in the quiet neighborhood, seasonal residents who had retired and built out their places for permanent occupancy. They were set to leave at noon that day, but he was enjoying himself so much they stretched the visit into Sunday before heading home.

In the afterglow of the trip to Muskegon, Keaton took steps to make his marriage to Mae Scriven legal in California. Accompanied by friends from San Francisco, they appeared at the county courthouse in Ventura and applied for a license. Three days later, on October 21, 1933, they were married there, Mae wearing a gray silk dress, a gray cape trimmed in gray fur, and matching pumps. Buster, in a conservative brown business suit, joked and danced a few steps as he took her arm and led her into the judge's chambers. Then they returned to the house on Queensbury Drive, where a dinner was given that evening. Leo Morrison, who was among the guests, fed Louella Parsons a tip that he was negotiating with both Gaumont British and Germany's UFA for a pair of features, the first to start almost immediately. "A personal appearance tour is also on the book," she reported, "which will put Buster right back in the money-making class. And Buster is being a good boy, according to his friends, who say he looks much better."

Keaton's good spirits lasted for a while, but he went back to the bottle when the deals in Europe didn't pan out and he was hit with a $14,000 tax lien by the Internal Revenue Service. Morrison told him frankly that he'd continue to be a hard sell unless he cleaned himself up, and Keaton voluntarily submitted to the Keeley Cure, a treatment that had its roots in the tradition of patent medicines into which he had been born himself in the 1890s. Named for Dr. Leslie E. Keeley, whose study of alcoholism supposedly dated from the Civil War, the original "cure" involved injections of Keeley's own formulations of what he called the double chloride of gold remedies, which were used to treat opium, liquor, and tobacco addictions. Founding the Keeley Company, he franchised Keeley-branded institutes around the country, but subsequent investigations found the secret formula contained no chloride of gold, just concentrations of morphine, cocaine, alcohol, and cannabis.

The Keeley name retained its commercial appeal, even when the famous "cure" did not. The Los Angeles branch of the Keeley Institute still existed on Pico, west of downtown, promising "a method of quick relief" ending "misery and unhappiness due to liquor." Keaton described the treatment as he experienced it: "It starts with three days during which the nurses and doctors do nothing but pour liquor into you, giving you a drink every half hour on the half hour. . . . You get your favorite snort, all right, but never twice in a row. Instead they start you off on whiskey, and on succeeding rounds they give you gin, rum, beer, brandy, wine—before they get around to the whiskey again."

The impact of mixing all these on an empty stomach was a classic aspect of aversion therapy, forever buffeting the patient between acute intoxication and severe nausea. "When you plead, 'Oh, no! Take it away *please!*' all you get from your bartenders and barmaids in the white coats is a friendly smile. . . . 'Just one more,' they say, for their purpose is to make the hurt in your stomach grow until it becomes unforgettable. And, being a weakling, you take that one more just as you did in a thousand barrooms. The Keeley Cure may have worked wonders for some alcoholics, but it did nothing for me that first time."

Having dropped out of sight for a month, Keaton resurfaced in Mexico, where he had fallen into a small volcano while hunting alone near Mexicali. Two locals heard his yells and pulled him out, his clothes reportedly singed by the sulfur. But where the Keeley Cure hadn't had any effect on him, a deal closed by Leo Morrison perhaps did in that it promised to return Buster Keaton to the American screen nearly a year after getting sacked over at Metro-Goldwyn-Mayer. The contract wasn't for features though. It was for his first two-reel comedies in more than a decade.

"Buster Keaton celebrating his new contract with Educational by calling his pals and telling them the good news," Louella Parsons reported. "Buster is drinking only beer these days."

Educational Pictures had its beginnings in the teens, when it was a distributor of short scenic and entertainment movies, its trademark an Aladdin's lamp and the slogan "The Spice of the Program." In the twenties, the company started releasing short comedies, and in 1927 it reorganized to produce as well as distribute one- and two-reelers under the direction of Jack White, the elder brother of Jules White. Roscoe Arbuckle directed movies for Educational, many starring the hard-drinking Lloyd Hamilton of "Ham and Bud" fame. When Keaton signed on, the company was releasing between seventy and eighty films a season, two-reelers with such established stars as Moran and Mack ("The Two Black Crows"), Andy Clyde, and Ernest Truex, as well as one- and two-reel subjects with up-and-comers like Bob Hope, Milton Berle, and Shirley Temple. Keaton's contract was initially for two shorts, with an option for four more at a rate of $5,000 per.

"A writer we had, Ernie Pagano, was friendly with him," said director Charles Lamont, "and he talked him into coming over and making two-reel comedies for us." Adding Buster Keaton to their roster was a big deal for Educational, and they trumpeted the news in trade ads that laid out their programming for the rest of the season. Keaton's pictures would go out as Star Comedy Specials, and Educational's production chief, a former actor named E. H. "Ed" Allen, pledged all the creative room he needed to deliver the goods. For writers, Keaton was given Pagano, who had gravitated to shorts since his work on *Spite Marriage,* and Ewart Adamson, a Scottish-born novelist and short-story writer whose Hollywood credits dated to the early twenties. Three scripts were initially commissioned, two from Pagano and Adamson and one from Keaton himself. Directing would be Lamont, whose vaudeville background was similar to Buster's—he was born into his family's act in a San Francisco dressing room—and who had casually known him for nearly a decade. It was almost too good to be true, and as the start of the first picture loomed, the pressure began to wear on him.

"Buster Keaton is ill again—stomach trouble," George Shaffer obliquely warned in his column for the *Daily News*. "Keaton's friends are beginning to worry about his condition."

The Gold Ghost did get off to a rocky start—the star was visibly intoxicated while filming a nighttime exterior—but the picture had all the hallmarks of a classic Keaton comedy. He is Waddy, a rich nincompoop, and the girl lays down an ultimatum. ("Until he proves himself to be a man, I'll have nothing to do with him!") Left to his own devices, Waddy motors from the wealthy enclaves of Boston to the ghost towns of central Nevada to toughen himself up. The dialogue was minimal, the physical business more plentiful than for many of the M-G-M talkies. Moreover, the production values were good—not always a given with Educational comedies—and the supporting cast solid. Warren Hymer, late of Fox features, took the role of the heavy, a gangster named Bugs Kelly; Dorothy Dix, having come up in shorts and feature westerns, was Gloria, the girl of Waddy's dreams; and industry veterans Lloyd Ingraham and William Worthington played the respective fathers in the story.

Keaton liked to refer to the new film as "a silent picture with talk," an idea he could never get across to the executives at Metro. "Let the others talk their heads off," he said, preferring to remain as silent as possible.

Associated Press columnist Robbin Coons visited the set the first day on location and observed that *The Gold Ghost* was being made much as a silent comedy would have been. "They have a script and dialogue, but it is, to say the least, subject to change as they go along. Somebody invariably has an idea that's brighter than some previous bright idea in the script. And yet the whole picture is to be finished in four or five days—or less."

Even with the time and cost constraints—which enforced a practical limit on retakes—the level of inspiration far exceeded what prevailed at Metro, as Keaton's thoughts were welcomed for a change, and he was given the creative elbow room that was so often lacking at the larger studio. Educational was too small an operation to micromanage anyone, much less a man of his stature.

"He was practically his own boss," said Charles Lamont, who was the company's top director, "and he was real friendly. He liked Mr. Allen. He liked Ernie Pagano, and he liked me. He was a great joker. I mean it was bread and honey one day, champagne the next."

Keaton and crew during the filming of The Gold Ghost *at the Trem Carr ranch in Newhall. Director Charles Lamont is seated to the right of the camera.*

Much of the film was made at the Trem Carr ranch in Newhall, where a rustic street exterior served as background to countless low-budget westerns, including Lone Star programmers with John Wayne. Waddy's roadster comes to a rest at Vulture City, where he sounds the horn to raise a populace that has long since vanished. With no response, he collects his bag and his golf clubs and makes his way to the local hotel, the Waldorf Astoria, its dusty interior seemingly frozen in time, cobwebs everywhere. With no dialogue imposed upon him, Keaton is free to roam the decrepit town at will, mining every sight gag the standing set can suggest. He finds an old sheriff's badge in an abandoned desk and pops it on his vest. After the collective insult of the years at Metro-Goldwyn-Mayer, it's exhilarating to watch.

He borrows a shooting gag from *The High Sign,* then saunters into the saloon, where he flips a coin onto the bar and pours himself a drink. Another coin brings a piano roll to life, and the evocative music summons a ghostly dance hall girl. As he approaches her, an equally ghostly gunfighter appears and pulls her aside. Waddy utters a single word: "Stop!" And the spirit draws his gun. Waddy fires, the outlaw returns it and falls dead. The girl retreats, and three more transparent gunfighters walk into the scene, Waddy blasting away and leveling them all. The girl spreads her arms in gratitude and vanishes on the staircase as he bows deeply in return. It's an astonishing effect, spine-tingling and funny and completely unexpected, Keaton the master filmmaker at his finest.

Another scene finds Waddy doing his wash in the middle of the deserted street, the watering trough elevated just enough to suggest he is in the raw. Drawn by news of a gold boom, traffic begins to appear behind him as he remains oblivious to all the potential onlookers he suddenly has. He turns, panics, and flees for cover, revealing that he was wearing boxers all along. Set upon by a gang of crooks, Waddy and Bugs are scarcely holding their own until he spies a supply of small kegs and starts rolling them into the melee, knocking the attackers over like bowling pins and keeping score on a handy blackboard. An ancient slot machine pays off, and Waddy wins the girl, stretching the film's running time to a copious twenty-one minutes.

Everyone at Educational loved *The Gold Ghost,* and a preview audience seemed to think it was great. The company commissioned a full-page ad in the trades to herald "the triumphant return of Buster Keaton in a two-reel comedy masterpiece." It was, judged *The Film Daily,* "a finely executed short comedy starring Buster Keaton in the style of material that he can handle to perfection. . . . Filled with delightful Keaton touches, it will go over big with his many admirers."

Harry Burns of the *Hollywood Filmograph* hailed the return of "the Buster Keaton of old" in a film "which will, to our way of thinking, give theatergoers plenty to laugh over."

Once it was set for release on March 16, 1934, exhibitors were encouraged to treat *The Gold Ghost* as an event booking, positioning it as Keaton's return to the form of comedy that made him famous. In Los Angeles, Loew's State, the city's longtime home of his feature work, added *The Gold Ghost* to a weak double bill and promoted the whole package as a "Big Three-Unit Holiday Show," according the two-reeler equal standing with M-G-M's *Lazy River* and Fox's *Murder in Trinidad.* Advance coverage in the *Los Angeles Times* gave Keaton the headline emphasis over feature stars Robert Young, Nigel Bruce, and Heather Angel, creating an air of excitement over what might normally be considered a sweetener to the main bill. In New York, it gained a booking at the 6,200-seat Roxy, where it was paired with the English-made *Constant Nymph.*

"Buster Keaton is almost a forgotten story," conceded *Variety's* Wolfe Kaufman, "but if he can turn out more shorts as consistently funny as this one, he doesn't have to reach for a back seat."

Booked widely, *The Gold Ghost* was a hit for Educational, elevating the entire season and ginning up interest in the next Keaton comedy. Across the board, exhibitors had nothing but praise for the film.

"I wish a half-dozen other Educational comedies were a third as good as this one," said a manager in Cedarville, Ohio. "Oh, well!"

The inspiration for Keaton's second for Educational was the song "The Daring Young Man on the Flying Trapeze," which dated from the turn of the century but had been given new life by a 1933 recording from Rudy Vallée. Ernie Pagano and Ewart Adamson, who sketched the story, called it *Allez Oop,* and again the director would be Charles Lamont. With most of the Educational pictures finished for the season, they would have the entire lot and its three stages to themselves. An added attraction would be Dorothy Sebastian in the female lead, Lamont just recently having made a two-reeler with her called *No Sleep on the Deep*. Still married to Bill Boyd, Slambastian's career had dwindled to cheap independent features and she was glad to have the work. Their reunion was enough to justify a lead item in Louella Parsons' column.

Where *The Gold Ghost* was spread over an entire town, *Allez Oop* was as contained as the modest clock shop operated by Buster's character, Elmer. The gags start out as small precision affairs—watchmaker gags—then expand under the big top with the spectacle of a center ring trapeze act. When Paula becomes infatuated with Apollo, the lead aerialist, Elmer decides to develop his own set of skills with a makeshift setup that relies on tree branches from which the fly and catch bars are suspended. Mounting a ladder, he narrowly avoids breaking his neck as the contraption has its way with him. The real crisis comes when Apollo attacks Paula in her apartment. A fire starts, and in a familiar Keaton device, the heavy saves himself, leaving it to Elmer to perform a daring third-floor rescue by swinging on a clothesline, Tarzan-style, Paula grabbing on to his feet and dropping safely into a life net.

With the cast's trapeze stunts expertly doubled by a circus troupe known as the Flying Escalantes, *Allez Oop* proved that *The Gold Ghost* was no fluke. At the film's completion, which fulfilled Keaton's commitment to Educational for the season, Leo Morrison disclosed a deal for his client to travel to Paris to make a feature. The job, projected to take four weeks, would pay $15,000, but getting there would prove a challenge. According to Buster, personal and tax obligations had left him flat broke, and the producer had advanced nothing for travel expenses. On the evening of May 30, he attended a beach party thrown by Lew Cody, who owed him $2,000. He may have contemplated touching Cody for the money—Arbuckle had died owing him $2,500—but nothing apparently got said. Cody retired about 1:00 a.m., and was found dead the next day at the age of fifty-one.

Keaton never recorded his reaction to Cody's death, but their closeness was widely noted in the press. "Buster Keaton will take the loss of Lew heavily," said newspaperman Jerry Hoffman. "They were the last of the Three Musketeers. Porthos went with Arbuckle, Lew Cody was the dashing, debonair d'Artagnan." During the brief service held at the Pierce Brothers chapel, Keaton was described as unashamedly tearful as he sat among Cody's closest friends and drinking buddies—Norman Kerry, Lowell Sherman, Marshall Neilan, and actor Frank Mayo.

That same day, Educational picked up the option for four additional Keaton comedies, announcing the first would start sometime in August. With their output for the 1933–34 season completed, the studio on Santa Monica Boulevard was shuttered, and the Keaton contract became the first order of business after a three-week hiatus. *Allez Oop,* meanwhile, secured a prestigious booking at Radio City Music Hall, bringing forth another round of raves from the trade press. Its star still had to sell some old war bonds to manage the trip to Europe, settling on the cheapest possible way of getting himself and Mae across the Atlantic. They left port at San Pedro on June 13, two of fifteen passengers aboard the new motor liner *California Express,* a fruit carrier offering service to Glasgow via the Strait of Magellan, a journey that would take twenty-five days to complete. After landing in Scotland, the Keatons made their way to London, where a night at the Grand Palace brought a wonderful surprise—a letter from Joe Schenck with a $1,000 check enclosed.

"He wrote that this covered my share of the sale of some leftover equipment at the Keaton studio. I could not remember any leftover equipment and suspected this was Joe's tactful way of extending a helpful hand. I was in no position to question this."

He arrived in Paris to the news that there had already been trouble with the picture, which was titled *Le Roi des Champs-Elysées* (*The King of the Champs-Elysées*). The project represented the combined efforts of a trio of German refugees—producer John Blochert, writer Arnold Lipp (née Lippschitz), and, eventually, director Max Nosseck, a wild-haired little man who always managed to keep one step ahead of Hitler. Blochert established a production company, Les Films Margot, and had Lipp's screenplay as a starting point. It was apparently his idea to bring Keaton to France to play the dual roles of an inept fellow who distributes flyers for a living and a ruthless mobster who is almost his identical double. Then his funding fell through, and in the ensuing scramble the package was taken over by the newly reconstituted Nero Film, Seymour Nebenzahl's famed company that was known for such German classics as *Pandora's Box, The Threepenny Opera, M,* and *The Testament of Dr. Mabuse.* Now based in Paris, Nebenzahl secured the financing for *Le Roi des Champs-Elysées* and arranged for its distribution through S.A.F. Paramount, raising hopes the picture would find an international audience.

As Keaton was awaiting the start of filming in France, a law firm he had retained in Los Angeles filed a petition for voluntary bankruptcy in federal court. In it, Keaton stated his willingness to turn all assets over to creditors, with the exception of property valued at $3,400 he claimed as exempt under the law. He scheduled debts of $303,832, including $15,708 in tax obligations and $2,100 he owed Natalie for child support. Of assets valued at $12,000, he allowed $2,600 for items of real property, $5,000 for promissory notes, $1,000 for household goods, and $2,500 due to open accounts. Meanwhile, *The Good Will,* the famous land yacht that Keaton and Lew Cody had cruised in in happier times, was being offered for sale at a bargain price on a used car lot in Los Angeles.

The papers and wire services immediately picked up on the move, with a United Press item in the *New York Daily News* headlined "BUSTER KEATON SAYS HE'S BROKE." When word reached Paris, there was hell to pay with Mae, who handled the household accounts, had no advance knowledge of the filing, and was humiliated that the entire world knew of it. Angrily, Keaton made a statement to the press. "A Los Angeles report of a bankruptcy petition in my name was a complete surprise to me," he claimed. "Evidently my attorney filed the petition without my authorization."

Picking up on the news, Louella Parsons was inspired to include a particularly sharp-edged item in her column of July 18: "I wonder what Buster Keaton's chances are in coming back into screen popularity in Europe? Buster has gone into bankruptcy here, burned his bridges, and settled himself in Europe with an idea of trying to regain his lost prestige. His first picture, *The King of the Champs-Elysées,* goes into production August 3rd at the Paramount Studios at Joinville, outside of Paris. Then he moves on to England to accept a job there. England has always liked the sad-eyed Buster and perhaps, who knows, he may be able to come back to his former prestige."

According to Jean Delannoy, who edited *Le Roi des Champs-Elysées,* its first director was Robert Wyler, the elder brother of director William Wyler,

Keaton's performance as a hardened criminal in Le Roi des Champs-Elysées *(1934) stood in stark contrast to his characterization of Buster Garnier, a little man who passes flyers for a living.*

who had signed films in Europe but was repeatedly taken off assignments in Hollywood, where he was under contract to Universal. Wyler leaned heavily on Delannoy for advice and was quickly replaced by Max Nosseck, who had directed one of Arnold Lipp's earlier screenplays, *Dance into Happiness*. Delannoy would remember Keaton's drinking, and the efforts they would make to prevent it, but in front of the camera he was on his best behavior, sober and thoughtful throughout. The picture was completed in just twelve camera days, and although Nosseck's habit of undercranking the action couldn't have been to Buster's liking, the story was well-constructed, yielding an entertaining and frequently funny result. At its core, the strength of *Le Roi des Champs-Elysées* would lie not so much in the gags as in Keaton's own expert performance as Buster Garnier, the naïf, and as the grim-faced killer for whom he is mistaken. The two roles are largely silent turns, and Keaton makes the latter as distinctive and menacing as the former is warmly familiar—even when, as contractually required, he smiles broadly at the very end, overcome with joy at having finally won the girl.

With the completion of *Le Roi des Champs-Elysées,* the Keatons returned to London for a second picture, a last-minute affair thrown together by a big-talking producer named Sam Spiegel, a card-playing chum of Seymour Nebenzahl's who was also involved on occasion with Paulette Dubost, the French actress who appeared opposite Keaton in *Champs-Elysées.* Earlier in the year, Spiegel had formed a company in London called British and Continental Films Ltd. with the intent of making pictures in both French- and English-language versions. With just two features to his credit, Spiegel grandly let the trades know that British and Continental's first movie, *Le Gentleman,* would be directed by Jacques Feyder and star the great German actor Emil Jannings. Spiegel claimed a capitalization of $500,000 and spent lavishly, but after several months word went around that he was having the script refashioned for Clive Brook in the lead role. After all the flash and braggadocio, *Le Gentleman* turned out to be a puff of smoke. Spiegel's credibility was on the line if he couldn't pull together another picture—a cheap one with international appeal. Keaton's availability presented an obvious solution, and a deal went together quickly with Leo Morrison at the other end of a transcontinental phone line.

A script was commissioned from writer-director Edwin Greenwood, while Adrian Brunel (*The Constant Nymph*) was engaged to direct. Brunel charitably remembered Sam Spiegel as a flashy man struggling with his own "peculiarities" which, to his mind, included "financial recklessness, writing phony checks, police charges, lack of sexual control, and other disturbing addictions."

In his autobiography, Brunel portrayed the future Academy Award–winning producer of *Bridge on the River Kwai* and *Lawrence of Arabia* as argumentative and ignorant, a guy not to be trusted. "There was trouble from beginning to end," he wrote. "When our third general flare-up had been provoked at two o'clock in the morning—this was while Edwin Greenwood was writing the script—I asked [Spiegel] if it were really necessary to be so offensive to everyone. He answered that it was, and that films which ran smoothly were colorless—only those which were produced in strife had any outstanding merit. If he had really been experienced, we might have allowed him this opinion, but as he was then utterly ignorant of all aspects of film production, we were not impressed by this theory."

A chilling message written on a half sheet of notepaper was passed to Brunel during the initial production meeting: *Don't let him drink!* Filming, which took place at Worton Hall, Isleworth, began on September 6 with

Greenwood's script, based on a story credited to Keaton himself, carrying the title *The Invader*. The setup was true to the Keaton formula, with Buster as the wealthy Leander Proudfoot, "the sort of boob who goes on stage when the magician wants someone." Proudfoot docks his yacht at a Spanish waterfront and immediately qualifies as the stooge in a matrimonial murder plot. The idea had possibilities—Greenwood was a crime novelist as well as a screenwriter. And Keaton took his job seriously, but was sabotaged by factors beyond his control. The German cameraman, Eugen Schüfftan, was brilliant but unsuited to the demands of slapstick. As Brunel wrote, "After having feasted myself on his lighting effects—many of them dark and atmospheric—I realized how inappropriate much of it was for a broad comedy of this kind."

Knowing that Keaton was prone to tippling on the set, Leo Morrison sent over a man named Hank Hartman to keep an eye on him. Schüfftan's camera operator, Eric Cross, remembered Hartman as "a big American football type, and Buster was paying him to keep him off the booze. Every now and then I'd catch Buster and him round the back of a flat, and Buster was paying him to let him booze. He was paying him twice."

Keaton wasn't obviously potted on camera, but he was tipsy enough to throw his normally faultless timing off. The rushes lacked energy and were sluggishly paced. The film was also padded with a tedious dance number that consumed, Brunel estimated, about 20 percent of the budget. "Buster was ill most of the time, but he was a grand trouper; it was bad luck that he should have got into this galère." Filming took longer than expected, as Spiegel remained true to the mission of making English- and French-language versions of the picture. Getting the film off the ground was a trial as dialogue had to be refined and rewritten between takes. Then the same had to be repeated in French, with Hartman, who spoke it like a native, coaching the star word-for-word, explaining the gist of a sentence and giving him the correct words to emphasize.

The Keatons lingered nearly three weeks in England after finishing *The Invader*, and there was talk of coming back in the spring to make an English-language version of *Le Roi des Champs-Elysées*. On a tip from Leo Morrison, Louella Parsons praised Keaton for "being a very good boy and paying strict attention to business."

But, of course, he hadn't been as good a boy as she had been led to believe. "In between these professional mishaps," he admitted, "I kept on drinking like a fish."

Buster, Joe, Louise, and Myra Keaton reunite in Educational's Palooka from Paducah *(1935). Perennial screen heavy Dewey Robinson is to Buster's left.*

As soon as they embarked on *Île de France,* where their fellow passengers included Maurice Chevalier, radio comedian Jack Pearl, and actress Ketti Gallian, Buster was in a social mood and remained so for much of the voyage. During the crossing, one of the passengers remembered that he had been taught how to extricate himself from a straitjacket by Houdini, and so he was placed in one during a wine tasting and promptly forgotten about. Chevalier was awarded a silver cup while Keaton, hidden behind a screen, remained typically stoic for an hour and fifteen minutes. Then someone remembered he was there and got him out of the thing.

By the time the ship docked in New York on November 6, he and Mae were quarreling. ("The Buster Keatons have stopped throwing kisses," Walter Winchell reported, "and have started throwing anything.") Mae loudly declared that she wanted a divorce, and on November 22, celebrated the decision at the house by inviting the press in for food and drinks. Buster, meanwhile, distracted himself by preparing his first two-reeler of the new season. Ernie Pagano had left Educational after nearly three years on the job, and Keaton was left to break in a new man, writer-director Glen Lambert, who had been knocking around the industry since 1912, most recently at Vitaphone. Lambert, working with Charles Lamont, had conceived a story about a tight-knit family of moonshiners put out of business by the repeal of Prohibition, and Keaton saw a chance to cast his own family, particularly his father, who had gone back to work taking day jobs in pictures.

The Continental Hotel, where Joe Keaton had lived since his separation from Myra, was demolished in 1933 to make room for an addition to the adjacent Bullock's department store. Joe followed proprietors Pat Shanley and J. C. Furness to the Hotel Yorkshire, one block over on South Broadway, but the Yorkshire lacked the theatrical cachet of the larger Continental, and with just a Pig 'n' Whistle on its ground floor, there was no place for Joe to hang out and swap stories. "I got so tired doing nothing I simply had to get a job," he said. Joe landed a bit part at M-G-M in *What Every Woman Knows* and followed it with another in *Evelyn Prentice*. On November 30, 1934, The Three Keatons regrouped on a stage at Hollywood's General Service Studios for the first time in a generation, a reunion so historic even the Associated Press took notice.

Sporting a crepe beard, as were all the men of the Diltz clan, Joe was instantly in his element, proud to again be on-screen with his famous son. But the real revelation of *Palooka from Paducah* was Myra Keaton's wry comic performance as Ma Diltz, puffing a corncob pipe and delivering her backwoods dialogue as if she were a seasoned veteran of the talking screen.* Filling out the cast were Louise Keaton, hulking Dewey Robinson, and actor-wrestler Bull Montana, whom Robinson, as Elmer "Hill Billy" Diltz, meets in a title match that Buster referees. The days were long, but having his family around gave Keaton a measure of comfort he seemed to need at a time when it was so elusive at home.

"Speaking behind the camera, he was a pretty dull man," Charles Lamont said. "There was no conversation with Buster. And moody—tremendously moody. But, well, he had a lot of trepidations which were not monetary. It was love affairs, personal life."

With the picture finished, Buster and his wife reached an accommodation that brought the marriage back from the brink of divorce. Mae, who had experience as a hairdresser, would use the $5,000 he earned making the film to equip and open her own beauty salon. It seemed an ideal resolution, giving her a separate income at a time when every dollar counted. But if it was meant to permanently restore marital harmony, the move was of

---

* Myra would go on to appear in three additional Educational shorts before calling it quits in 1937.

questionable value. As the holidays rolled around, Buster had the house on Queensbury Drive to himself while Mae spent Christmas with friends at the fashionable Hotel del Tahquitz in Palm Springs.

As the possibility of another picture in England continued to loom, Leo Morrison thought it prudent for Keaton to complete the remaining three comedies he owed Educational as soon as possible. *The Palooka from Paducah* was released on January 11, 1935, and continued his winning streak as a top attraction in shorts, *The Film Daily* pronouncing it hilarious. It was booked into the Rialto Theatre for its Broadway debut, supporting the Martin Johnson adventure *Baboona,* and the combination did well enough to be held a second week. All the talk about *Palooka* diverted attention from the Paris opening of *Le Roi des Champs-Elysées,* which laid an egg as far as *Variety* was concerned: "Picture contains a certain number of laughs, especially in the early reels, but gets tiresome toward the end. First showing in Paramount here rated a moderate amount of whistling and booing from the audience." The film, the correspondent concluded, was "weak."

Fulfilling the Educational commitment for the 1934–35 season got off to a late start, prompting Keaton and Charles Lamont to knock out the remaining subjects at the prodigious rate of one a month. *One Run Elmer* was released on February 22, *Hayseed Romance* went out on March 15, and *Tars and Stripes,* filmed entirely at the U.S. Naval Training Center in San Diego, wrapped up the season on May 3. The two men by then had arrived at an agreeable and effective method for fleshing out a story.

"The two of us would work together," Lamont remembered. "Once in a while we'd bring in another writer for additional gags. We got along great together. He'd think of a gag, I'd think of a gag. We'd put them down, and then we would write a script, which generally amounted to about two pages. None of the other guys would read it, except myself or Buster. And we started from there."

Once filming began, Keaton was laser-focused on the picture to the exclusion of all else.

"Keaton was a perfectionist. With this guy you didn't need a rehearsal ninety percent of the time. It was all perfect. I never asked him to do anything twice. He always did it right the first time unless something didn't work which wasn't in his control."

Educational, which had now shifted its base of production to the General Service Studios, concluded work for the season in April, with *The Palooka from Paducah, One Run Elmer,* and *Hayseed Romance* already in the marketplace. *Hayseed Romance,* which had elements of *My Wife's Relations,* was followed by *Tars and Stripes,* which similarly owed its origins to *Doughboys.* *Tars* merited a New York opening at the Roxy, causing the feature attraction, RKO's *Laddie,* to wither in comparison. With the Keaton comedies now clearly leading the Educational program, it was a no-brainer for president E. W. Hammons to sign him for yet another series, which he did prior to leaving for a Fox sales convention in Chicago.

A planned trip to England fell apart just short of departure, and with little to do, Keaton took to hanging out in the new cocktail lounge at the Holly- wood Knickerbocker Hotel, where Mae had situated her salon, the Buster Keaton Gold Room. She showed little interest in actually working the place, and her manager quit after a few weeks. Spring afternoons would find her seated among her husband's idle cronies, who included other remnants of silent picture days such as Marshall Neilan, Mae Murray, and H. B. War- ner, as well as the more current Gertrude Michael and, sometimes, Thelma Todd. Buster played in a charity baseball game, comedians versus leading men, at Wrigley Field, where the players included Benny Rubin, Frank McHugh, and Al St. John, while among the opposition were James Cagney, George Raft, Ricardo Cortez, and Hoot Gibson. Then the Keatons headed to Santa Barbara for a July 4 rendezvous with friends that would bring their benighted marriage to an end.

The prelude to it all was an innocent bridge game at the Beverly Hills home of Mrs. Barton F. Sewell, who was seeking separate maintenance at the time from her sportsman husband, the beneficiary of a family trust fund worth $28 million. Leah Clampitt Sewell was well known to newspaper readers, who gobbled up accounts of her adventures with other women's husbands. In 1929, her first husband sued a man for alienation of affections. She later married the guy, who in turn sued Bart Sewell for the same thing in 1931. She married Sewell the following year, and although the union was longer than her first two, it wasn't necessarily any happier. In 1934, when the rupture between her and her husband emerged, it was alleged by the wife of actor-writer Walter Emerson that Mrs. Sewell was the instigator in a wife-swapping scheme in which she paired off with Emerson while Mrs. Emerson voluntarily went off with Mr. Sewell. The resulting divorce action was unsuccessful when the judge decided all four were equally culpable.

Somewhat overweight with a plain, almost matronly, face, Leah Sewell had people wondering what the attraction was, other than, presumably, availability. Mae, possibly sensing a kindred spirit, decided she liked her enough to accept her offer of a ride up the coast in her limousine. They were meeting up with separate parties, it was reported, but everyone was staying at the same hotel, which made what happened next unusually convenient.

"When the festivities were over," said Mae, "we took adjoining rooms. We visited back and forth. Then I discovered Buster . . ." Depending on who was telling it, Keaton either leaped onto Leah Sewell's bed in one of his misguided attempts at being zany, or was buck-naked and caught in flagrante delicto with the other woman. "I was humiliated beyond words when I saw them together in Mrs. Sewell's bedroom," Mae continued. "Distraught, I returned to Los Angeles—but Buster did not follow until two days later. Still I had no drastic action in mind, but last Saturday and Sunday he was away from home. My nerves were shattered. I was disillusioned. I had to go to a hospital. It was only then I decided upon a divorce."

Of course, it's also possible she had tired of the marriage and was looking for the exit when a third party with loose morals and deep pockets wandered onto the scene. Thinking strategically, all Mae had to do was set the trap and then play the role of the wounded spouse for the benefit of the press. Significantly, she waited until Buster was knee-deep in making his first Educational under the new contract, a story called *The E-Flat Man,* to spring her surprise, filing suit for divorce, charging infidelity and naming Leah Clampitt Sewell as corespondent. Simultaneously, she also filed suit for $200,000 in damages against Mrs. Sewell, charging she had "willfully and wrongly enticed" her husband away from her.

"It is the most ridiculous thing I ever heard," said Leah Sewell. "I'm going out to the hospital as soon as I can get away from court and see her. Of course I knew the Keatons, but we were only with them six or eight times. I heard that Mae had threatened to bring this suit, but it is so ridiculous that I never thought she would. I've had a hard time keeping my name clean, and I don't intend allowing anybody to besmirch it now."

Mae had already moved out of the house on Queensbury Drive, taking much of what could be considered the couple's community property with her. "Friends of my husband are beseeching me to forgive and forget," she said dramatically, "but I cannot. Buster hurt me more than words can convey when he shattered the happiness that had been ours for almost two years. Never before had there been any other women in Buster's life. True, he danced with our friends at parties, and was constantly thrown into contact with pretty girls in his film work, but always he was loyal to me—I was his constant companion."

Said Buster: "I don't want a divorce; I have asked my wife to forgive and forget. But now that she has decided to go ahead with divorce plans, I shall not stand in her way. She is the sweetest person in the world."

If her motivation in suing the corespondent was the money she knew she was unlikely to get from Buster, Mae underestimated how willing to go on the attack a woman like Leah Sewell would be. Soon after the Keatons' marriage, Mrs. Sewell charged, misunderstandings and quarrels broke out in the Keaton household "through Mrs. Keaton's association with other men, all the while she was married . . . she persisted in keeping company with men other than her husband." Mrs. Keaton, she contended, kept her husband "under the influence of intoxicating liquor . . . and arranged bridge games in order to keep him occupied, so not as to arouse his suspicion."

She denied improprieties with Buster Keaton, asserting instead that Mae did not leave her husband due to misconduct but rather to rendezvous with another man. At four o'clock on the morning of July 5, her answer continued, Mae Keaton and a man "not her husband" entered the Keaton house and, shortly thereafter, all the lights were extinguished. "Decedent alleges that no affection existed between the plaintiff (Mrs. Keaton) and Keaton at any time."

The intertangled lives of the Sewells, the Emersons, and the Keatons

made rich fodder for the press into the fall of 1935. On October 10, an interlocutory judgment of divorce was granted, awarding Mae the sum of $500, plus additional $500 payments after the completion of each of his next three pictures for Educational. Buster, however, maintained that Mae had effectively cleaned out the house, taking all business and tax records, and emptying their joint savings and checking accounts. Then she took a powder, stiffing one of her attorneys in the bargain. Her actions seemed calculated to inflict maximum injury on her bewildered husband, who was only seeking a fair and equitable parting of the ways. For instance, there were two sets of silver flatware, and rather than taking one complete set for herself, Mae took half of each set. She also did the same with two sets of tableware, but whatever their value, they were just things, easily replaceable and of no real interest to the defendant.

Then she did the unthinkable—she took her husband's beloved dog, Elmer. Keaton was devoted to that long-haired Saint Bernard, a canine aristocrat who had the run of the M-G-M lot, who protectively accompanied Greta Garbo on her lunchtime strolls, who dined daily with Marion Davies, and who was arguably as famous within the industry as his master. Keaton hired a private detective to find Mae, not because he ever wanted to see her again, but because he wanted Elmer back. He first sent the man up to Fresno, thinking she might have gone to where she had family, but there was no trace of her anywhere. Keaton never did see the dog again, and for the rest of his life, until the day he died, every dog he ever owned was a Saint Bernard. And all, apart from a single female known as Myrtle, were named Elmer.

Amid all the personal chaos swirling around him, Keaton still managed to produce a winning short for Educational with *The E-Flat Man,* but it was all he could do to complete the thing. When it hit the papers that Mae was suing him for divorce and asking "reasonable support, maintenance, and alimony" and counsel fees, Natalie Talmadge blew a fuse. If he was capable of making monthly payments of support to Mae, he should be working to bring himself up current with the money he owed for support of his own children. Since their divorce, Nat had gone to court twice with the purpose of unraveling connections with her former husband. In 1934, upon the news that Buster had made his two sons beneficiaries of a $40,000 life insurance policy, she asked that she be named their guardian. Then she petitioned to have her maiden name restored. Of the $300 monthly support the court had ordered, Keaton had paid $6,900 and was delinquent $3,300. He was ordered to appear on September 12, 1935, to show why he should not be held in contempt of court, an action that was continued until September 23 because he was making another picture.

By then, Buster Keaton was incapable of appearing anywhere. Maybe it was Mae's theft of the money, maybe it was her stripping the house bare, maybe it was Natalie's piling on at a critical time, or maybe it was simply not knowing what had happened to Elmer, and the dreadful suspicion that she may have had the dog put down. It was all too much for him to handle, and he passed his fortieth birthday in an alcoholic stupor, too drunk to take notice. Flat on his back, he deteriorated rapidly. Myra came to take care of him, but she could do nothing to snap him out of it. He was stricken with influenza, which settled in his eyes, and then his breathing grew labored. His physician, Dr. John Shuman, diagnosed pneumonia and told him that his continued drinking would likely kill him. On October 20, his condition was reported in the press as serious, but Keaton stubbornly remained at home until he began coughing up blood. Shuman told him he was going to the hospital, but Buster would have no part of it. He was, said the doctor, in "a very confused mental state." Help was called in, and on the evening of October 21, fighting mad and struggling against a set of camisole restraints, he was admitted to the psychopathic ward of the National Military Home at Sawtelle.

20

I've Got Lots of Time

B USTER KEATON is suffering from a nervous breakdown brought on by family and financial worries," Dr. John Shuman explained in a statement to the *Los Angeles Times*. "His condition is very grave, and it was necessary to remove him from his Los Angeles home to a hospital for complete isolation."

With the press carrying news of Keaton's condition nationally, it took exactly one day for Mae to emerge from hiding. She told the Universal News Service she was ready to forget the past and go to his bedside. "I know I can help him," she said. "I nursed him through a similar collapse three years ago and I can do it again. If he is worried about financial matters I'll take care of him until he can return to his studio. I'm able to do so. I want to tell him I love him and that the divorce was too hasty. I know I can help him."

She appealed to Colonel Thomas A. Mattison, medical director at the soldiers' home, but was told Buster was under sedation and could only be seen by the two attending specialists. (Myra and Harry Keaton were told the same thing.) She left a note: "Darling—Please tell the nurse when you feel like seeing me. Elmer and I are waiting. Oodles of love, Mae."

Buster Keaton had always exhibited remarkable recuperative powers, and on October 24, 1935, he was reported as improving. "Buster spent a comfortable night," Mattison said, "and during waking moments is rational. He sleeps quietly most of the time."

The daily condition updates subsided. Seven days into his hospitalization, Keaton was up and around, eating well and submitting to tests. "They won't release you out of that until they've x-rayed everything you've got," he told

Kevin Brownlow in 1964. "If you've got dandruff, they'll keep you there. The doctor calls me in and says, 'When did you break your neck?' I said I never broke my neck. He said, 'Look at this x-ray. This callus has grown over the crack; it's next to the top vertebra.' I didn't know it. I said, 'How long ago was this?' 'That looks like it could be somewhere between ten and fifteen years ago.' That's how old the scar was. I started thinking back. 'I know when it happened. It's that goddamn fall on the track [during the making of *Sherlock Jr.*]. It cracked this vertebrae.' I never stopped working, never knew it. Well, that's luck. No nerve pinched or anything in the healing—and I never knew it."

On October 31, ten days into his hospitalization, Keaton was temporarily released so that he could belatedly celebrate his fortieth birthday. The house on Queensbury was festively decorated; Myra had baked a cake and was roasting a chicken. Joe was present, as were Harry and Louise. By design it was a quiet, private affair. And at the end of the evening, Buster was driven back to the hospital, where he would submit to an exit exam in the morning.

Mae never did get to see him but told the *Times* she was ready to go to him in her capacity as a nurse. "It all depends on him. If he wants help I'll go to him. I know he needs me. I know I can help him."

Keaton, however, told the paper his marital troubles had contributed to his breakdown. "I'm not interested in marriage anymore," he said. "I've got to go to work next week. I just folded up on account of all my troubles hitting me at once. Mrs. Keaton is a nice girl, but patching things up is out of the question. They've got me on a milk diet and I feel one hundred percent better. There'll be no more sickness if I can help it."

Mae, who had offered to drop her alienation-of-affection suit against Leah Sewell, didn't take the news well. "Apparently Buster wasn't suffering as much from worry over domestic troubles as I had been led to believe," she said tartly. "He hasn't seen fit to acknowledge my visit to the hospital or the friendly note I sent him. So things inevitably remain as before, and I intend to go ahead with the alienation suit which I had been willing to drop if it would ease his condition. But I'm grateful that he is well again, and I wish him every success in his work."

Two months later, Mae skipped over the border to Tijuana and married a publicist and aspiring screenwriter named Sam Fuller, who was seven years her junior. In this, history repeated itself in that it would take another nine months for her divorce to become final. In the papers, both she and Fuller vowed to occupy separate homes.

In Grand Slam Opera
*(1936), Keaton hijacks
Colonel Crows' Amateur
Night while bandleader
Harold Goodwin gently
attempts to restore order.*

Keaton was still not out of the woods. For the picture he went back to make, *Three on a Limb,* he was drunk through much of the shoot. He was, however, among friends—Charlie Lamont and Hal Goodwin were both on the picture—and the film turned out well, its chaotic climax, an ever-shifting combination of bride and groom, being one of the best farcical turns he ever pulled off. He held himself together for *Grand Slam Opera,* his final film of the season, a minor masterpiece of comedy in which he delivered an inventive parody of Major Edward Bowes' *Original Amateur Hour,* which had become a national obsession on network radio. People were traveling from all over for their chance at stardom, so Keaton, who shared a writing credit with Lamont, envisioned a musical opening to the tune of George M. Cohan's "So Long, Mary" with the townspeople forcibly loading him onto the back of the Western Limited, eager to get rid of him.

"Awfully good of all you boys to see me to the train . . . ," he sings.

"So long, Elmer!" they respond.

"I didn't think you'd care should you ne'er see me again . . ."

"You're *right,* Elmer!"

Keaton was so tickled at the prospect he paid $300 out of his own pocket for the rights to the song. Later in the film, he performed a parody of Fred Astaire's "No Strings" number from *Top Hat,* the phonograph blaring as he clambers around his tiny room, leaping onto a bureau, a chair, a side table, up onto the mantel, where he manages a clumsy tap routine, then crashing down onto the bed, anticipating in some respects Astaire's own ceiling dance

("You're All the World to Me") from *Royal Wedding*. When the picture was finished, Keaton came away knowing he had to get serious about drying out. Despair at Metro was one thing, but Educational had been more than good to him, and he loved the work he was doing. So in December he submitted once again to the so-called Keeley Cure, this time with a renewed sense of purpose.

Keaton's modest home looked out onto the California Country Club, where a converted ranch home served as the clubhouse. "After taking that cure the second time," he recounted in his autobiography, "I was taken home and immediately went for a walk on the golf course. I walked over the entire eighteen holes and, on reaching the clubhouse, I walked to the bar and ordered two manhattans. I drank them one after another. They not only tasted great, they stayed down. That was in 1935 and, after proving to myself I could drink if I felt like it, stop if I felt like it, I did not touch a drop of whiskey or any other alcoholic drink for five years."

It was on Christmas Day 1935 that Keaton took the pledge. Once he regained his health, he made a renewed commitment to filmmaking, signing for six more comedies with Educational and two proposed features for independent producer I. E. Chadwick. Concurrently, he was on the nation's screens in *The Timid Young Man, Three on a Limb,* and a Technicolor confection from Louis Lewyn titled *La Fiesta de Santa Barbara,* which afforded him particular prominence among "a galaxy of screen stars" that included Robert Taylor, Harpo Marx, Gary Cooper, and the singing Garland Sisters. Then *Film Daily* caught a preview of *Grand Slam Opera* and pronounced it "a laugh riot," building industry and exhibitor anticipation ahead of its February 21, 1936, release date.

Somewhat poisoning the well amid all this good news was the long-delayed appearance of *The Invader,* the Sam Spiegel epic Keaton had filmed in England in 1934. Released in its country of origin by Metro-Goldwyn-Mayer, it was widely seen—and derided—as the second feature on a bill with *The Hands of Orlac,* an American-made thriller starring Peter Lorre and Colin Clive. The problem, according to director Adrian Brunel, was that the completed film was deemed too short by its distributor, and so a new editor was hired to put back "every cut-out piece of film she could find until the picture was 6,000 feet in length," thus yielding an even more sluggish result than the movie's deliberate pacing alone could achieve. "The staging is cheap, and the direction obviously handicapped," concluded *The Kinematograph Weekly*. "It is impossible to assess the entertainment value of this film—there is none."

Control of *The Invader* fell to a broker called Interworld Films, the head of which, E. R. Gourdeau, brought it to New York in January 1936 with hopes of finding an American distributor. In the end, there was little interest, and the movie was picked up by J. H. Hoffberg, who specialized in foreign product and vintage silents. Hoffberg proceeded to offer the Keaton picture, retitled *An Old Spanish Custom*, on a state rights basis, placing it in such regional markets as Georgia, Texas, Ohio, and Kansas. The closest it ever got to New York was a Skouras house in Newark, where it was one of four features holding down the bill for a single week.

Once again Keaton was at the head of the Educational lineup with *Grand Slam Opera*, which debuted at the Roxy in support of the Gaumont-British feature *Rhodes*. "This is a wholly funny two-reeler," said *Variety*, "showing Keaton as a small town lad from Arizona who juggles and wants to make good on the air. He finally gets on Major Crow's [*sic*] program, gets the gong quickly but refuses to take it, and winds up nearly wrecking the studio. There's a stock shot of the RCA Building in Radio City to cinch the resemblance just in case audiences don't get the 'Major Crow' billing. It's pretty near good enough to be sold as a baby feature."

As the new season's schedule was taking shape at Educational, the decision was made to base all future production at the Eastern Service Studios (formerly Paramount) on Long Island, effectively severing ties with Hollywood at a time when more filming than ever was taking place in California. Keaton arrived in New York by air in May, where he discovered he wouldn't have the support to which he was accustomed in Los Angeles. The threadbare script for *The Fourth Alarm*, his eleventh comedy for Educational, was the work of one of the top radio writers of the day, David Freedman. It was Freedman who pioneered the technique of compiling extensive joke and situation files, and combining those resources with an assembly line of "assistants" who could turn out custom material for individual clients and agencies on demand. In Keaton's case, the Freedman contribution tended to be dialogue rather than action, the overall idea being little more than a simple setup with a predictable payoff—Keaton as Elmer, an incompetent firefighter, who triumphs despite his ineptitude. Raymond Kane, a former production manager who had been with Al Christie since his days as an independent producer, was an efficient director who lacked Charlie

Lamont's gift for gags and plot turns. Keaton, in other words, was pretty much on his own.

The result was a comedy more situational than usual, with stock clips and exteriors shot on streets proximate to the Astoria complex giving the film a New York flavor. Once Elmer's bleak future as a firefighter was established, Keaton, free to take as many risks as he pleased, took a spectacular fall off the back of a racing fire engine as it rounded a corner, the kind of stunt neither Freedman nor Kane could ever envision, but one that clearly declared the star's independence from the banalities of the script.

Retitled *Blue Blazes,* the picture was finished in time for Keaton to spend Independence Day in California and fulfill a commitment to play in a charity baseball game. Around town, he was no longer a figure of dread, turning up, for instance, at a party thrown by Eddie Mannix and doing his waiter routine for an appreciative audience. Usually at such affairs he was accompanied by Betty Ann Logan, a blond bit player to whom he was rumored to be engaged. He returned to New York just ahead of the Labor Day weekend to tackle two more Educational two-reelers, a Freedman story titled *The Chemist,* directed by Al Christie, and another for Raymond Kane, *Mixed Magic,* in which Elmer, nicknamed "Happy," makes a shambles of a sideshow magic act. The three films made in the east weren't bad, but they lacked the level of inventiveness apparent in the comedies made in Hollywood, where Keaton had Charlie Lamont as his principal collaborator.

It was during the filming of *The Chemist* that Natalie Talmadge brought an action in the Supreme Court of the County of New York to attach Buster's earnings for the picture, claiming the amount of $4,500, the aggregate of fifteen missed support payments of $300 each. Yet when she applied to the Superior Court in Los Angeles to collect the money, Keaton and his attorney responded by pointing out that when the original order was made in 1932, she was, without his knowledge, in possession of $12,000 she had taken from a joint bank account, community property she never disclosed in the settlement. He therefore maintained that he was not in arrears at all, but rather due $6,000 from the plaintiff as his share of the money. He also took the opportunity to ask that the monthly child support payments be reduced to $100 a month, given that his employment situation had changed dramatically since 1932, and that he had earned just $15,000 since January 1, 1936. Finally, he asked that he be given custody of their two boys, alleging that Natalie had not maintained a home for them, but "has kept, and continues to keep, them in a boarding school, which is expensive and beyond the means of affiant to provide, and that affiant, at all times, has been willing, and is now willing to support said boys to the best of his ability . . . so that they may attend the public schools and higher educational institutions of this county and state."

The matter of the boys had long stuck in his craw, since he had made repeated attempts to see them at the Black-Foxe Military Institute and take them out for weekends, only to have them ordered not to go at—he believed—Natalie's direction to "further embarrass" him. (The institute's president, actor Earle Foxe, went back a long way with the Talmadges, having played a featured role in Norma's breakout picture, *Panthea.*)

"The boys adored Buster," said Louise Keaton. "He was upset when Natalie wanted to put them in pictures. He tried to get them back. He wanted them to have a normal childhood, but he didn't have the money to go against the Talmadges in court."

It was as if Natalie wanted to clear her life of all reminders of her marriage to Buster Keaton, including the children who were the products of it. "My mother was very vindictive," Jim Talmadge said. "She had nothing but the worst things in the world to say about him. He never said anything bad about her in his life." Jim and his brother, Bobby, hated Black-Foxe, as did the sons of other famous figures who parked their kids there, such as Samuel Goldwyn, Jr., Charles and Sydney Chaplin, and Harry Carey's son, Dobe. "That was a prison as far as I was concerned. I escaped from there five times."

Following one particularly bold attempt, the boys were sent to live for a year with their aunt Norma in West Palm Beach, where Jim was permitted to drive her Rolls roadster at the age of twelve. Meanwhile, their mother was seen out on the town with Charlie Chaplin and was courted by the likes of Randolph Scott and Howard Hughes.

In his motion to vacate the warrant of attachment in New York, Keaton said he was a poor man whose reversals had rendered him unable to live up to the terms of the original settlement. "It is my belief that the persecution tactics indulged in by the plaintiff have been motivated by her sister, Norma Talmadge, who for years has evidenced a violent dislike for me. The plaintiff has always been dominated by the advice and guidance of her sister." He estimated that he gave Natalie allowances totaling $254,800 during their marriage, as well as the house and furniture, the yacht, and other California property valued at $30,000. Since the divorce, he said he had lost $30,000 on his investment in the Hollywood Roosevelt Hotel and another $30,000 in the Talmadge residential development in San Diego. "There is a claim against me by the United States government for $28,000 in income tax arrears. I now live in a small six-room bungalow in Culver City, California, with my mother, sister, and brother. I have no servants, cooks, valets, or chauffeurs." By comparison, Natalie lived in a town house she rented for $470 a month, and had multiple servants on her payroll. The kids, he added, were each beneficiaries of $35,000 trust funds. She waited, he charged, until he came to New York to bring about the present situation, which left him struggling to raise money to cover his hotel expenses and his fare back to Los Angeles. "In this action I am being persecuted by a wife who is attempting to make it appear to the public, from which I must make my living, that I have failed to support her and her two sons. Nothing could be farther from the truth."

The battle continued into December, when Natalie filed a lengthy affidavit in response to her ex-husband's. She disputed his claim that he had "no regular means of livelihood" and provided details of his income for the years 1932 through 1936. For his last full year on salary at M-G-M he was paid $145,200 by the studio and another $2,100 as his share of the profits from Buster Keaton Productions. For 1933, the year he was fired, his income from Metro, personal appearances, and Aubrey Kennedy dropped to $47,400. In 1934, he had income from Educational of $17,500, the $15,000 payment for appearing in *Le Roi des Champs-Elysées,* and another $12,000 fee from British and Continental for *The Invader.* For 1935, his compensation from Educational amounted to $42,500, and the estimated total for 1936 was $15,000 for the three pictures produced in New York, with another $15,000 coming in 1937 for the balance of the contract.

She recounted his problems with the Internal Revenue Service, which, having signed a joint return, affected her as well, and denied that she lived as extravagantly as he claimed. The only real estate she owned was a three-story house on Las Tunas Beach, between Santa Monica and Malibu, which she received as part of a trade for the estate on Hartford Way. Yet the waterfront house had turned out to be a liability, as it could only be rented in the summer months and stood vacant much of the year. With upkeep and taxes, she cleared only a few hundred dollars a year in rentals. She was also the beneficiary of a trust established by her younger sister, Constance, that paid her $200 a month, which amounted to all the income she had. She drove a 1934 Packard coupe, a gift from the same sister, and employed only one maid, who was paid $25 a month. The monthly rent for the apartment she lived in was $85, and it had an extra bedroom for her sons when they came to stay over weekends and holidays. In terms of savings, she had $3,700 and change left from the divorce settlement. The trust funds for her kids were established by their grandmother. She disputed the business about the $12,000 in unreported community property.

The gambit over the kids didn't work, and Keaton admitted he was mistaken about the $12,000. In a stipulation between the parties dated December 8, 1936, Natalie agreed to dismiss the attachment of the funds in New York, and Buster agreed to pay back and future child support totaling $5,900 on a scheduled basis over a period of seven months. Natalie would take no more actions against him, and the court would continue the matter of reducing the monthly support payments until July 1, 1937. Thereafter, whenever the kids came for a court-ordered visit, they were accompanied by an armed guard.

Buster Keaton's next two shorts for Educational were made in December 1936 at the General Service Studios in Hollywood. Reunited with Charlie Lamont and producer Ed Allen, he secured the services of writer Paul Gerard Smith, who dated back to *Battling Butler* with him and knew his formula as well as anyone. Together, they produced a model of economy called *Jail Bait,* condensing enough material for an entire feature into nineteen compact minutes. In Smith's story, a newspaper copy boy is persuaded to confess to a murder to help a pal, but can't get himself arrested until he's caught walking on the grass. He confesses, is sentenced to death, then discovers his friend has been killed in a plane crash. He busts out during a jailbreak, intent on finding the real killer and proving his innocence. With Hal Goodwin as the doomed friend, the film is full of morbid plot turns and rich in clever gags.

"He had a subtle way of getting suggestions in," Goodwin remembered. "He'd say, 'Oh, how about . . . Let me try . . . '"

Jail Bait was quickly followed by *Ditto,* which took advantage of the availability of identical twins, eighteen-year-old Gloria and Barbara Brewster, who had been scouted by 20th Century-Fox. Given the opportunistic nature of the picture, it played more like a sketch than a story, as far removed from *Jail Bait* as it could possibly be. Keaton had earlier explored the notion of unwittingly courting twin girls, and here the farce played itself out between a pair of duplex apartments. The idea quickly ran out of steam, and the ending, recalling the surrealistic turn of *Hard Luck,* was set fifteen years into the future, where planes fly with teardrop trailers attached and the next girl he meets turns out to be one of a set of quintuplets.

As the final film of Keaton's contract came due, it was clear with the tightening shorts market that Educational couldn't afford its costlier stars any longer, the most expensive of whom, at $5,000 a picture, was Buster himself. For his sixteenth and final two-reeler for the company, he brought his series of Educational comedies to a close with *Love Nest on Wheels,* based on a story by William Hazlett Upson of *Earthworm Tractors* fame. For Keaton, it would be a kind of farewell to the two-reel comedies in which he began exactly twenty years earlier. With him would again be his family, in a sort of reprise of the Diltz clan from *Palooka from Paducah,* Myra as the corncob-puffing matriarch, Louise as her indolent daughter, and, in lieu of Joe, Harry Keaton as Elmer's younger brother. In form and substance, *Love Nest* would emerge as a hillbilly remake of *The Bell Boy,* with many of the same gags incorporated into Upson's story. This time, the elevator in the dusty Van Buren Hotel is powered by an old mule, and Bud Jamison, who holds the mortgage on the place, gets his head caught between floors when the car stalls, prompting Elmer to try and dislodge it with a wooden plank. And like Alice Lake before her, Louise Keaton seesaws twelve feet into the air, landing on a moose's head overlooking the hotel lobby. Adding to the valedictory tone of the film is the presence of Al St. John as Elmer's bewhiskered Uncle Jed, a turn not unlike the scruffy sidekicks he was playing in B-westerns.

Ahead for Educational would be a gradual lessening of its output, with figures such as Iris Adrian, Willie Howard, and Tim and Irene Ryan starring in place of the likes of Keaton and Bert Lahr. The company would file for bankruptcy in January 1940, leaving a mixed legacy that included a body of work by Buster Keaton in which he demonstrated precisely how well he could do in talkies when permitted the autonomy he was largely denied at M-G-M.

With the completion of *Love Nest on Wheels,* Keaton was again at liberty. Briefly, he was up for a part in an Eddie Cantor feature at 20th Century-Fox and, more substantially, Leo Morrison was dickering with Hal Roach, who was planning to put him into a feature called *Road Show* with Oliver Hardy and Patsy Kelly. Nothing came to pass, though, and he filled his days spinning story ideas with Lew Lipton, one of which, *Marooned in Mojave,* was registered with the Copyright Office in April 1937. Still, no money was coming in.

Joe Schenck was now chairman of the board of 20th Century-Fox, having partnered with Darryl F. Zanuck in 1933 to form 20th Century Pictures. "Schenck knew Buster was in a bad way," said Harold Goodwin, "because every nickel that Buster would make, Natalie would grab. . . . Schenck told him to come over to the studio, that he wanted to see him. He got over there, and Schenck had a check, a blank check for him. He says, 'Fill that in.' Buster says, 'I don't know how much.' He says, 'Well, is a thousand dollars enough?' Well, a thousand was a lot of dough. But Schenck always loved Buster."

The money was deeply appreciated, but it wasn't a job. In desperation, Keaton phoned Eddie Mannix at M-G-M and asked about prospects. Irving Thalberg was gone, having died of pneumonia the previous year, so Mannix connected him with Jack Chertok, who ran the short-subjects department and was amenable to bringing him on. The job paid $200 a week—a far cry from the $3,000 he was getting just four years earlier.

"Buster Keaton, former star of the slapstick school, and who in the days of silence was one of Metro's luminaries in comedy features, is returning to that lot as a director," *The New York Times* reported. "According to an agreement reached today . . . Keaton will be assigned to the two-reelers with the hope that he will be handed features after his initial endeavors."

Keaton went back on the M-G-M payroll on June 24, 1937, joining the ranks of shorts directors David Miller, Leslie Fenton, Jacques Tourneur, and Fred Zinnemann, all of whom would advance to features. What happened after that is unclear, for three months later he was still without an assignment. A clue emerged in October, when it was reported that he, Ted Healy, and Buddy Ebsen were being groomed to replace the Marx Brothers, who had been brought to M-G-M by Thalberg, and who were moving to RKO after fulfilling a two-picture commitment. For Keaton, the good news was that their first picture was to be produced by action specialist Nat Levine, whose background was in serials, and not Larry Weingarten. By the end of the month, Ed Sedgwick had been added to the mix, and it seemed likely that production would get under way before the end of the year.

Keaton was preparing to direct a short for Chertok titled *Life in Sometown, U.S.A.,* a catalog of obsolete laws to be shot silent and dryly narrated by Carey Wilson. He worked with writers Richard Murphy and Carl Dudley in visualizing how such laws could be portrayed on-screen, and even dug up a few examples of his own. Filming began on December 18 with a cast that included silent stars Francis X. Bushman, Betty Blythe, King Baggot, Phillips Smalley, and Jules Cowles. When queried about his own work in silent pictures, Keaton feigned indifference, even though *The Navigator* had just been shown by the Museum of Modern Art as part of a series of screen classics.

"Well, I guess that stuff kind of got passé," he said. "But it will come back. It always does. I'm going to stay off the screen until my kind of comedy is good again. In the meantime, I hope to turn director. This little picture, *Sometown in the U.S.A.,* is a step toward feature comedies. I'm a young man—only forty-two—so I've got lots of time."

Keaton finished the picture in the six days allotted, but the feature comedy with Ted Healy and Buddy Ebsen never materialized. On December 21, while *Sometown* was in production, Healy died following a drunken altercation outside the Trocadero nightclub, forever scotching such plans. The following year, the Marx Brothers rejoined Metro-Goldwyn-Mayer after making just one picture for RKO.

Keaton directed two additional shorts for the studio in 1938, both for Louis Lewyn and both showcasing songwriter Leon Rene's Original Sing Band, a black vocal group that mimicked the instrumental sounds of a small jazz ensemble. *Hollywood Handicap,* released in May, cast the ten Originals as stable boys at Santa Anita, while *Streamlined Swing,* released in September, had them turning a private railcar into a Hollywood nightspot. Both were rich in "the music of tomorrow" but Keaton's boredom was evident in the straightforward staging of the numbers. In between shorts, he occasionally consulted on features. For *Love Finds Andy Hardy,* he showed Lana Turner how to get a laugh by spilling coffee on Mickey Rooney. And on a Weingarten show called *Too Hot to Handle,* he worked out the mechanics of an opening that had a cynical newsreel cameraman, played by Clark Gable, faking war footage with miniatures.

In September, with just three one-reelers to show for fifteen months' employment, Keaton left M-G-M for 20th Century-Fox, where he joined producer Sol Wurtzel's B-picture unit at a rate of $300 a week. Under Wurtzel, he was assigned to work with associate producer John Stone on the Jones Family pictures, which were among the few comedies issuing forth from a studio that seemed to lose its funny bone with the death of Will Rogers. Helping to develop stories for the ongoing series, Keaton received screen credit on *The Jones Family in Hollywood* and *Quick Millions.* He was clearly out of his element though, and the arrangement didn't last six months.

In February 1939, Leo Morrison approached Jules White, who was by then in charge of short subjects at Columbia Pictures, and told him that Keaton was available.*

"Well," said White, "I grabbed him. I just sent a wire to New York and said, 'I'm signing up Buster Keaton. Are there any objections?' Quite the contrary." The item in *Variety* was headlined "KEATON'S COMEBACK."

White, who assumed the post at Columbia in 1934, had built the studio's short comedies program to twenty-six two-reelers a year, eight with the Three Stooges, many of which he directed himself. Charley Chase and Andy Clyde contributed six each, and an All-Star series served as a catch-all for other prominent comics—Harry Langdon, Smith and Dale, Walter Catlett, and now Buster Keaton. White initially contracted with Keaton for two pictures, with options for more. Compensation would be $2,500 a picture—half of what it had been at Educational—but the market for short subjects had continued to narrow.

"All the shorts were in trouble," White said. "This was the double feature and vaudeville era. It was hard to get a short booked into a theater because they had to have double features, and they had to have vaudeville acts, they didn't have to have the short and it cost them money for a rental and extra projection time."

For Keaton's first Columbia short, which came to be known as *Pest from the West,* he was paired once again with Clyde Bruckman, who had been writing comedies for Columbia since his run as a director ended in 1935. Together, they tackled the missed opportunity of *The Invader,* which was essentially a two-reel story stretched to a sixty-one-minute feature. The resulting twenty-seven-page script was in the established house style with the gags written out in considerable detail, leaving little room for improvisation. Still, this was a do-over for Keaton, a remake where he knew exactly what had gone wrong the first time. Moreover, the director assigned to the picture was Del Lord, who was White's best man at Columbia.

"Del, at Mack Sennett studios, had progressed from stunt man to stunt driver—he drove the Mack Sennett paddy wagon and did crazy gags with it—and progressed to director," said Ed Bernds, whose sound crew was also on the film. "When Frank Capra worked at Sennett's as a gagman in the pre-sound era twenties, he described Del as Sennett's top director. . . .

---

* "I think an agent came to me and told me that Buster Keaton was available," Jules White told me in 1975. In 1979, he told Edward Watz that Clyde Bruckman made the connection. Either version is plausible.

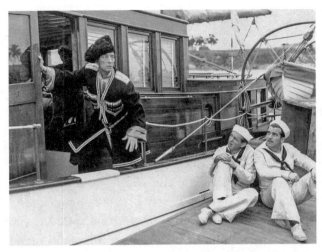

Keaton's first two-reeler for Columbia, Pest from the West, *was a superior reworking of* The Invader, *written by Clyde Bruckman from Keaton's original story and directed by Del Lord.*

I worked as sound man on a couple of the pre-Del two-reelers [with the Three Stooges] and on many that Del directed later. In my opinion, Del was the man responsible for the Stooges' success."

With contract player Lorna Gray cast in the role played by Lupita Tovar in the original, waterfront filming began March 29, 1939, at Balboa. A running gag had Keaton repeatedly dashing from his yacht to the dock and plummeting into the cold water, each time in a different costume. "He was playing the ukulele and singing," Gray remembered, "and it broke me up watching him. What also broke me up was watching him fall in the water. He'd look like he was walking on air for a while, then he'd just fall straight down."

The company repaired to the studio for the remainder of the shoot, which was scheduled and budgeted at four days. "Buster gave every indication of being dedicated to making the film as good as he and Del Lord could make it," said Bernds. "They got along very well."

Compared to the Educationals, the slapstick was of a crasser nature, with sound effects carried over from the Stooges films. Overall, it was a snappier take on the material, a superior job in every respect.

"Buster was not chummy with the crew—not standoffish or snobbish as some actors and actresses were—he was just immersed in his work," Bernds added. "But on one occasion I did tell him that I thought that *The General*

Keaton confers with Groucho and Chico Marx during his brief tenure as gagman on At the Circus *(1939).*

had probably the greatest sequence of thrills and gags ever filmed, or ever *would* be filmed. That great stone face broke into the warmest smile you ever saw and he said, 'Thank you. Thank you very much.'"

It was producer Mervyn LeRoy's idea to hire Keaton as a writer on *At the Circus,* the new Marx Brothers picture at M-G-M. Keaton began work on May 3, drawing $300 a week, but found it a frustrating experience. "The Marx Brothers—it was an event when you could get all three of 'em on the set at the same time. The minute you started a picture with the Marx Brothers, you hired three assistant directors, one for each Marx Brother. Get two of 'em, while you went to look for the third one and the first two would disappear. . . . They never worried what the next setup was going to be or what the routine . . . or anything else. 'We'll ad lib it when we get there.' Chico always had his bookie on the phone. Groucho had some other excuse to be missing. Harpo was visiting the other sets to see who was workin'."

Since Groucho and Chico were essentially verbal comedians, Keaton spent more of his time devising business for Harpo, the silent one, which may have aroused Groucho's ire. "You think that's *funny?*" he demanded after Keaton described a particularly inventive gag in which a single straw causes a camel's knees to buckle. Another idea had Harpo selling helium-filled balloons with the assistance of a midget who found himself airborne whenever he took charge of the inventory. Keaton's stretch on *At the Circus* lasted ten days.

He returned to Columbia for the second of his two-reelers, a Civil War comedy with echoes of *The General* titled *Mooching Through Georgia*. This time his director was Jules White, whose style was so firmly influenced by the Three Stooges he could direct no other way. Although written again by Bruckman, many of the knockabout gags suggested the essential brashness of the Stooges rather than the cool polish of Keaton at his best. As with *Pest from the West*, it was scheduled for four camera days and budgeted at $15,000, but the process of shooting it wasn't as smooth as with Del Lord, who made few changes and only minor eliminations. White fussed over the script a lot more, making many cuts and changes. What emerged was a good picture, just not as good as the first.

Meanwhile, over on the Fox lot, Darryl F. Zanuck was developing an idea that was near to his heart but stubbornly resisting the transition to screenplay. It was a comedy-drama covering the early days of Hollywood, centering on composite characters drawn from actual personalities of the time. One of those was Mack Sennett, on whom the protagonist was loosely modeled, and whom Zanuck envisioned Spencer Tracy playing. Then he fixed on Alice Faye as the female lead and began reimagining the story as a dramatic musical. After assigning and rejecting multiple treatments, he trashed one by a writer for the fan magazines named Hilary Lynn: "Lousy—finish hoke of the worst sort—if we are to make a film of our own industry let us at least be honest and legitimate." The story finally began to gel when poet and playwright Ernest Pascal was brought on and the title became *Falling Stars*.

Zanuck's concept was to salt the cast with real faces, such as Ben Turpin and Sennett himself. Keystone veterans Chester Conklin, Hank Mann, and Jimmy Finlayson were added, but Zanuck also wanted someone easily recognized by modern audiences as the principal comedian in the picture. In notes dictated on April 26, 1939, he said: "We are going to write Buster Keaton into the picture—if we can get him—and he will play himself. He will appear in the following episodes: (1) PIE EPISODE. Keaton is the bashful boy, with the turned-up hat, whom Mike bawls out, etc. (2) SANTA MONICA ROCK. Keaton is the "messenger" who tells Mike [that] Stout wants to see him right away. . . . (3) COPS. Keaton featured. He can be the one that Molly carries down the ladder. (4) ANNIVERSARY PARTY. Keaton makes the speech." Filming in Technicolor began on May 31 under the direction of Irving Cummings, with Alice Faye and Don Ameche in the leads. By the time Keaton joined the cast in mid-June, the title had been changed to *Hollywood Cavalcade* and Mal St. Clair was directing most of the footage in which he would be appearing, particularly a sequence establishing him as one of the originators of the pie fight—an innocent fiction that would dog him for years.

"I had the studio's bakers make the pie according to our original 1917 recipe," Keaton said. "No custard was used, and with a blonde the target the filling is a mixture of blackberries, flour, and water, garnished with whipped cream. . . . Two crusts are cooked, one inside the other, until brittle. The double crust prevents crumbling when your fingers slide across the bottom. . . . The shortest throw, across a distance of from three to six feet, is called a shot putt, and this was the custard pie surprise I was to heave at sweet-faced Alice Faye."

St. Clair deferred to him almost completely in the shooting of their scenes, and Keaton had a wonderful time on the picture. Surviving outtakes reveal a party-like atmosphere on the set, black and white footage shot silent with Faye giving as good as she got, Buster and she breaking up as they drip with crust and filling.

"She," said a friend, "was crazy about him."

Pest from the West was released on June 17 to wild praise from the trades, particularly *Film Daily,* which rated it a wow. "One of the funniest shorts of the season. In fact, of any season. . . . When a comedy shown cold in a projection room can make trade press crits howl in their seats, you can bet your mortgaged theater that it's FUNNY."

Once the film got out into the marketplace, exhibitors chimed in as well. "Here is a comedy that is a comedy," came a report from Indiana. "Why not give us more of this type? Has anything skinned a mile that Columbia has made this season. Just a knockout that had them in stitches the entire performance. Excellent."

Pest accrued domestic rentals of $23,000 in its initial release, and a 1948 reissue would surpass even that figure. *Mooching Through Georgia* was released two months later, and while the notices were more restrained, the two pictures together more than justified White's commitment to another pair for the 1939–40 season.

The Columbia shorts were still in circulation when *Hollywood Cavalcade* had its gala premiere in October. Despite leaden dialogue and Cummings' sluggish direction, most reviewers gave it a pass on good intentions, many praising the slapstick sections in which Keaton was prominent. The pie throwing sequence with Alice Faye was a crowd-pleaser, even though it has Don Ameche talking Buster through a scene, as ludicrous a notion as the depiction of him stunting in front of a process screen.

"After all these years, Mr. Keaton still has a way with a custard pie," Frank Nugent commented, "and we never guessed that Miss Faye could make such a perfect target."

Faye also took Keaton's place on the handlebars of a driverless motorcycle, a necessity of plotting even as the real story, minus the aforementioned process screen, would have been infinitely more interesting. "They were making a picture about the old days of pictures," said Hal Goodwin, who had a small part in the film, "and so many of these people were new. They didn't know that we didn't have slates with numbers on them then. One side said NG and the other side said OK. They let the cutter worry about putting the picture together, and I had told the prop man that. He said, 'Mind your business.'"

The greatest value of *Hollywood Cavalcade* was as a showcase for old-timers, principally Mack Sennett, but it was Keaton who got more favorable exposure from the picture than anyone else. "The biggest surprise of the year was the way the fans all over the country applauded Buster Keaton in *Hollywood Cavalcade*," Louella Parsons said in her column of October 25, "proving what I've said so many times—that the public does not forget old favorites. What Darryl Zanuck did for Buster when he gave him that break cannot be overestimated. It's brought him back with a vengeance. Today the deadpan Keaton conferred with Boris Morros, who is trying to get him to do a talkie of *The Navigator*, his greatest silent success." And so with Parsons' benediction the "comeback" of Buster Keaton was official.

21

One of the Skeletons
in the M-G-M Closet

BORN ON HOLLYWOOD BOULEVARD in 1918, Eleanor Ruth Norris grew
up surrounded by the film industry. At age five, she attended the Vine
Street Elementary School, a block south of the Keaton studio, while
scenes for *Sherlock Jr.* were being filmed on adjacent streets. Her father,
Ralph, a studio electrician, was killed on the job when she was ten, and her
mother went to work as a seamstress, doing alterations at one of the big
department stores. With her younger sister just starting school, Eleanor had
to grow up in a hurry. She had studied dance from an early age and began
performing at women's clubs and parties, doing what she loved while helping to put food on the table.

"I was never young," she said. "I never went through that giggly teen-age
thing; I went from child to adult overnight."

At the Hollywood Bowl she was part of Theodore Kosloff's ballet company, at fourteen she got her first movie work by lying about her age, and
at fifteen she was in *The Gay Divorcee* with Fred Astaire and Ginger Rogers.
At sixteen, she dropped out of high school and, using her aunt's passport,
toured the Orient as one of the Six Hollywood Blondes. In Bombay, she was
scouted for stardom before Bollywood was Bollywood, in Miami she was in
the chorus of a lavish revue starring singer Harry Richman, and back in Los
Angeles, again with Richman, she was a featured dancer in *The Hollywood
Restaurant Revels of 1937.*

Eleanor Norris was strikingly photogenic, with Hepburnesque cheekbones and blue-gray eyes that would sparkle in Technicolor. Metro put her
under contract in 1938. At five three, she was tall for a pony—which is what
they called the dancers in the chorus—but she caught the eye of Albertina

Rasch, one of the studio's dance directors, who appreciated her work as a toe dancer and used her in a couple of Eleanor Powell musicals.

"Being under contract at M-G-M was fun," she said. "It's like a family. They had, I think it was, thirty-two dancers because they had different productions going on, and sixteen boy dancers, and sixteen or eighteen singers, and we all worked together in different films. . . . You worked pretty much all the time, you almost didn't get any days off, because all the productions were waiting in line."

One day, she was standing around a set with a dancer named Art Whitney. "The kids used to sit behind the scenery and play cards all the time in between shots and setups, and I used to watch them play bridge, and it looked fascinating. I said, '*I* want to learn to play that. What is that?' Because I used to play cards. I'd played cards all my life—goldfish, gin rummy, all kinds of games, pinochle, whatever there was to play."

Whitney, it turned out, was Harry Keaton's best friend. "Well," he said, "I know where there's a card game and a good teacher all day every day. When we're through, I'll take you up there."

Eleanor had seen Buster Keaton around the studio, knew his name and that he was famous, but had never watched him on-screen. "My first impression of him was before I ever knew him, 'cause we were both at M-G-M. And normally I wouldn't see him except at lunch in the commissary. He used to have a whole series of slacks and shirts—he had 'em made—in tans and grays. And when he wore the gray ones, he used to sort of blend in—he looked like this little gray thing going by. He blended right in. And that was my impression: I wish he'd put some color on, or some makeup or something, because he blended into his clothes."

True to his word, Whitney took her to the house on Queensbury Drive, and she was allowed to watch as the others played bridge. "I met the whole family en masse. I imagine Harry was probably there, and I met Louise and Myra at the same time because they were playing bridge. They played bridge all day every day."

She estimated it took a full year, coming two or three times a week, before she felt confident enough to play on her own without someone standing behind her and kibitzing. Conversation wasn't encouraged, but she had the chance to observe and form impressions.

"The whole family looked pretty much alike. They all looked like Myra, not Buster, except that the coloring would vary. Buster was hazel eyes and dark hair, and Harry had bright blue eyes with blond hair, and Louise was

Dining with Dorothy Sebastian at the Beverly Hills Brown Derby, September 1939.

Buster's coloring. Louise had dark eyes, and Myra had the hazel eyes like Buster. Joe had dark eyes. Buster and Louise got Joe's coloring except for the eyes."

As far as women were concerned, Buster had kept his distance since the debacle of his marriage to Mae Scriven. Those who made the columns were all casual acquaintances, even Betty Ann Logan, who under the name Betty Andre was the briefly seen girl in *Jail Bait*. Marlyn Stuart, who appeared in all three of the New York Educationals, was an occasional date, as was actress Dorothy Lee, who was brought to Keaton's Italian Villa for the first time at the age of eighteen. More often than not, a favorite partner was his own sister, Louise, whom he would take to the Cocoanut Grove and throw around the dance floor.* Still, the woman most frequently associated with him was Dorothy Sebastian, who was divorced from William Boyd, by now the movies' Hopalong Cassidy.

"The reason I was given for that," remembered Gil Perkins, "was that Bill used to go away to Bishop and Lone Pine on location for Hoppys. He had a beach house as well as the Beverly Hills house. There were always some Hawaiian beach boys around his place there, and he came home and found Dorothy in bed with one of the beach boys. That's what wound up that marriage."

Keaton clearly enjoyed Sebastian's company, and they were spotted together at places like the Grace Hayes Lodge, Slapsy Maxie's, and the Hollywood Brown Derby. Yet it was hardly a committed relationship. She drifted off from time to time, as did Buster, who generally waited for the

---

* Louise had studied acrobatic dance at the Dinus School in Hollywood.

girls to come to him. Eleanor's main interest was in the game and the cards; she never paid much attention to him as an individual.

"He said the first time he ever paid any attention to me at all was [when] I used to have somebody stand behind me to help me when I started, and one day somebody—I don't know who—was sitting on a chair or standing behind me watching, and I did something and he yelled, 'That's stupid!' Y'know, one of those kind of things. And I reared back and I said, 'I don't know this game very well, but I'm damned if I'm stupid!' And I yelled back at him. And Buster suddenly says, 'Who was that?'"

It wasn't exactly love at first sight; it had been six months at least. "It was a gradual thing," she said. "There was no big awakening; it just sort of grew into a friendship. He was aware of it before I was—that he wanted to do something about it—but he'd been with [Dorothy] for two or three years, I guess. And he had to find a new boyfriend for her 'cause he couldn't dump her. We used to go to the wrestling matches all the time. There was this young, good-looking 'hero'—not a villain, a hero wrestler—real nice, stupid, good-looking son-of-a-gun, and he had a manager or whatever. We knew a lot of the wrestlers to speak to 'cause we used to go in a group. Five or six of us would go to the matches. So he invited the boy and his manager out for dinner, to spend the afternoon and have dinner, and just let nature take its course. He did find her a new boyfriend, and then he asked me to go out."

The third two-reeler for Columbia, *Nothing but Pleasure,* was on a par with *Mooching Through Georgia,* a contrived but frequently effective treatise on the trials of owning a new car that introduced actress Dorothy Appleby to the series. It was with Keaton's fourth Columbia short, *Pardon My Berth Marks,* made in January 1940, that the generic flavor of the Columbia comedies began to overtake whatever distinctive qualities Keaton and Clyde Bruckman could contribute. *Berth Marks* was the first Keaton comedy into which another Columbia star, such as Charley Chase or Harry Langdon, could easily have been dropped with minimal adjustments. The story, in fact, would be remade in 1947 with radio announcer Harry von Zell in the lead.

"When Buster started," said Jules White, "after about two pictures he became the old Buster and warmed up."

Bruckman was the writer on the show, but the man firmly in charge was White.

"Jules was the kind of guy [where] somebody would sit down and jump up, and then he'd take an insert of a pin cushion," said Harold Goodwin. "That was his idea of a laugh. Well, Buster hated inserts. He said, 'You've gotta show what you're doing without an insert.' Charlie Lamont knew comedy pretty well, and he was as different as night and day from Jules White. *He* would avoid an insert to get a clean shot. Like Buster used to say, 'Just get me in trouble and let me find a clever way of getting out.' That's the way he thought, and it paid off."

Completed in four camera days, *Pardon My Berth Marks* was the first Keaton short to finish under budget, and it set the tone for what was to come at Columbia. Around the same time, Keaton completed work on *New Moon,* an unwieldy costume musical with Jeanette MacDonald and Nelson Eddy for which he was paid $750 a week to serve up comedy relief alongside actor Nat Pendleton.

"They were like the featured comics all through the film," said Eleanor, who remembered he was on it for weeks and weeks. "But the picture got away from them, and they were so busy with Nelson Eddy and Jeanette MacDonald's songs and everything that they wound up practically being cut out of the picture."

Though the film was carefully edited to remove as many traces of him as possible, Keaton could still be glimpsed as one of the king's rebels, particularly in the opening minutes in the hold of the *Joie des Anges* and during the rousing march in which Nelson Eddy sang "Stout-Hearted Men."

Nineteen forty was a busy year. Columbia committed to another pair of shorts, the first of which, *The Taming of the Snood,* was built around an acrobatic dancer named Elsie Ames, who toured vaudeville and worked nightclubs in a knockabout comedy act called Ames and Arno. For *Snood,* Keaton stepped in for husband Nick Arno, as Elsie, a drunken housemaid, leaped about the room, taking pratfalls, doing splits, and generally bedeviling the innocent milliner who's just there to make a delivery. Rehearsals for this scene stretched the schedule to five days, but never before had Buster gained a female partner who could match him fall for fall. A delighted Jules White, who loved the sort of broad physical comedy Ames trafficked in, would use her repeatedly over the next couple of years.

In March, Keaton drew another feature assignment, one that reunited him with Eddie Cline for the first time in seventeen years. The film, which was frankly regarded as an experiment, was inspired by a local theatrical phenomenon called *The Drunkard,* which opened in 1933 and was still running at L.A.'s Theatre Mart. The show itself was an old-fashioned temperance melodrama, *The Drunkard: Or, the Fallen Saved,* first presented in New York in 1850 by P. T. Barnum. The producers shrewdly re-created not just the original Barnum staging, but also the music hall atmosphere in which audiences of the time experienced it. Free beer and sandwiches were served during performances, people were encouraged to hiss at the villain and cheer the hero, and an olio was offered at the conclusion.

From the beginning, the show attracted the movie colony and won endorsements from the likes of Mary Pickford, Billie Burke, and W. C. Fields, who saw it more than thirty times and incorporated aspects of it into his 1934 feature *The Old Fashioned Way.* Now an independent producer, Harold B. Franklin, proposed to film the whole thing, camping it up in the same manner as onstage. A longtime theater executive, Franklin had dabbled in production but really didn't know what he was doing. He gave his son Elbert the job of writing the screenplay, and filled the cast with comics and character actors, all familiar faces but no big stars. Keaton, as the hero's earnest friend William Dalton, took fourth billing behind Hugh Herbert, Anita Louise, and Alan Mowbray.

Cline approached the job with a what-the-hell attitude that made the actual shooting of the picture more fun than what eventually made its way to the screen. He had his actors take it up big, throwing broad asides to the audience and shamelessly mugging for the camera. The atmosphere was so loose that ad libs and blowups were left in, and Keaton, in the spirit of the thing, quickly learned to tame his impulse to rib the man he always referred to as E. Francis.

With villain Mowbray sprinting away, Buster said to the others, "Come, we must catch him," only to take off in the opposite direction.

"That's a great piece of business!" Cline whooped. "It stays in the picture!"

Keaton's next Columbia short, *The Spook Speaks,* continued the series' descent into the commonplace, with Jules White exploring the comedic possibilities of arming Elsie Ames with a polo mallet and strapping roller skates onto a penguin named Orson. Keaton would have been astonished to discover that *The Spook Speaks* became the most successful of all his Columbia comedies, pulling domestic rentals of $28,500 upon its initial release, and another $24,000 from a 1949 reissue.

"He hated them," said Eleanor of the Columbias, "but they paid the bills."

. . .

Keaton manages a rare smile for the camera on the occasion of his 1940 marriage to Eleanor Ruth Norris. Superior Court Judge Edward R. Brand, who was himself a comedian before turning to law, presides.

It was Eleanor who proposed to Buster. It was New Year's Eve, and she and he were out on the dance floor in Palm Springs. "I took the bull by the horns," she said.

"When are we going to get married?"

"How about tomorrow?"

"Well, maybe not . . ."

"How about May 28? Because that's when I was married the first time, and I'll be able to remember it."

"Take your May 28 and shove it. I don't need that."

As a compromise, she picked May 29, 1940. "He said afterwards that the reason he hadn't asked me himself was that he was afraid he was too old for me." But Eleanor Norris had always dated older men: "It wasn't a boy I went to school with or anything because I didn't know any of those. So it was probably somebody at least ten or fifteen years older than I was. So the fact that Buster was twenty years older didn't dawn on me or make any difference. I knew it, but I didn't care."

Revisionist texts to the contrary, Keaton, at age forty-four, had weathered the difficult years admirably.

"He was still beautiful. He still had great bone structure and very few wrinkles . . . he didn't even look his age."

Buster's friends were horrified. Two of them, one a rabid bridge player named Freud, the other Jack Shuman, his doctor, spent hours trying to talk her out of it. "The doctor and the other friend on two separate occasions lectured me severely about how wrong this whole thing was going to be. It wouldn't last, all of that. And the fact that if I was marrying him for his money—forget that. He didn't have it. And I, very polite nice little girl, I sat and listened to everything they had to say very carefully, all of it, and ignored them. And then we went and got married."

He was, she said, "just a kind, gentle, wonderful soul. He never had an enemy. Everybody loved him. And I suppose I just joined the group." They appeared at the Los Angeles County Clerk's office on May 22, a Wednesday, and applied for a license. Eleanor, described in the papers as a statuesque blonde, gave her age as twenty-one and said that she lived with her mother and sister in North Hollywood. Buster gave his age as forty-four and listed the house on Queensbury Drive as his residence. To reporters, he admitted the occasion called for a smile. "And I feel like smiling, but the studio won't allow it—not in public anyway." He added: "I have not smiled since Dewey captured Manila."

They were married a week later in the chambers of Superior Court Judge Edward R. Brand, the younger brother of Keaton's former nemesis, Harry Brand. Eleanor, attended by her sister, Jane, wore a powder-blue chiffon gown with white accessories and an orchid. Buster, whose best man was his brother, Harry, was in a blue serge suit. Others present for the ceremony were Eleanor's mother, Jessie M. "Dot" Norris, and Joe, Myra, and Louise Keaton, all of whom were conspicuously absent from Buster's first two weddings.

"I wanted to finish up the ceremony, then take Eleanor for a rowboat ride in Westlake Park, a roller-coaster ride at Ocean Park, and a bridal dinner in a drive-in," Buster said. "But the folks all turned thumbs down on that idea."

They went back to the house for a reception, the station wagon packed for a camping and fishing trip to June Lake, about 250 miles away. A few more guests arrived.

"They were all busy getting drunk and having a wonderful time," Eleanor said, "so we just changed clothes and left. We put the traditional cut in the wedding cake, and I think we took a piece with us."

When they got back, the Keatons discovered their Saint Bernard pup had gotten onto the dining table and eaten the rest of the cake. She was sick for three days. Myra rescued the little bride and groom off the top; it was the only thing left.

When Eleanor first arrived at Cheviot Hills, Myra, Harry, and Louise were all living with Buster under the same roof. "The only practical thought I had on the whole thing was whether the rest of the family was going to be there the whole rest of my life. As it turned out, Myra says, 'Up and at 'em, we're going to move. We're going back to my house.' She had people renting, and she gave them notice. They got out, and she moved back and took Harry and Louise with her. She said, 'They deserve to be alone.' And she packed them up and took them."

The new couple settled in, Eleanor making no real changes other than to clean the place up and throw out old bank statements and the like. Built in 1931, the house reflected the solid craftsmanship of the era with tongue-and-groove floors and Spanish tile work—two bedrooms and two baths on a landscaped lot with mature citrus trees in the back.

Times were good. By all accounts, Eleanor was the best thing that ever happened to him. She was beautiful, supportive, a tireless worker, and a bright, plain-spoken companion. The contrast between her and his two previous wives could not have been more pronounced. Yet it was over the summer of 1940, when everything seemed to be going so gloriously right, that Keaton's five years of sobriety came to an abrupt end. What exactly triggered it is a mystery, but the one dark event that would doubtless have affected him deeply was the sudden death on July 4 of his boyhood chum Lex Neal. As Harold Lloyd's career wound down, Neal had found it hard to find other work. In 1936, he was diagnosed as an insulin-dependent diabetic, a condition exacerbated by acute alcoholism.

Buster, of course, shared his first bottle of whiskey with Lex. The two of them co-founded the Bluffton sandlot ball team, the Juniors. And it was Lex who was likely the driving force behind *Go West*. As a writer, he contributed to five of Lloyd's feature comedies, beginning with *The Kid Brother* in 1926.

According to Eleanor, he was in and out of their home a lot. "He used to come to our house and pass out on the couch and vomit in the middle of the floor—wonderful things like that."

He was admitted to St. Vincent's Hospital in a diabetic coma, and died three days later at the age of forty-seven.

Buster, fortunately, was not working at the time, but Eleanor had to figure out how to handle him. It couldn't have helped that *The Villain Still Pursued Her* inspired catcalls, wisecracks, and raspberries among the bored participants at its press preview in Glendale. The picture, his first feature appearance since *Hollywood Cavalcade*, was DOA by general consensus. He didn't venture out in public again until August 8, when he played in a big charity game at Wrigley Field, the greatest showing of star power yet for Mount Sinai Hospital. He drew a big hand from the crowd of 25,000 as he took the field as catcher for the comedians' team and obligingly took a stiff pratfall at the sight of Boris Karloff approaching home plate as Franken-stein's monster.

When it came time to report for *Li'l Abner,* based on the United Features strip by Al Capp, Louise Keaton was detailed to accompany her brother to make sure he didn't drink. The character he was to play was Lonesome Polecat, a grim-faced Indian of the Fried Dog tribe who, with his colleague Hairless Joe, was purveyor of Kickapoo Joy Juice, a moonshine of legendary potency.

"We wrote down the description in a meeting of what he should look like," recounted director Al Rogell, "and after we wrote all the adjectives down everyone agreed [and] said automatically: Buster Keaton. Deadpan, straight-faced, good gags, an athlete—there was no one that could play it like Keaton. So when we called him and asked him to come out, he said, 'For what role?' Because he had read the comic strip. We [told him] and he came out just as he was with the pork pie hat, and the only change that he'd made was to put one goose feather in the hat."

Polecat's utterances were limited to ceremonial whooping and the pidgin English common to such characters ("Me call great spirit, makeum fire like ances-tor"). Working with a script that left plenty of room for embellish-ment, Keaton spent as much time on the picture developing gags as he did playing his part.

"He not only did a great deal to help himself with his own situations and gags as a gag writer as well as an actor," Rogell said, "but if he could contribute to someone else's success with a good gag or a laugh, he was one of the first to come in with, 'Hey Al, here's an idea.' And he'd play it out, and if it was good we used it and thanked him very much and everyone was very happy."

Keaton finished with *Li'l Abner* in September and committed, without enthusiasm, to another three shorts for Columbia, bringing his total to nine for the studio. *His Ex Marks the Spot* was another for Jules White, a rowdy nightmare of a domestic comedy written by Felix Adler, who was respon-sible for many of the best Three Stooges comedies. The next, *So You Won't Squawk?,* offered a respite from the White school of knockabout by briefly returning Del Lord to the director's chair. *Squawk?* recalled the smoother contours of *Pest from the West,* taking a bewhiskered plotline about a mob of gangsters moving in on a rival gang and invigorating it with an abundance of inventive new gags. Buster unwittingly takes the place of upstart hood Louie the Wolf, and Slugger McGraw's boys repeatedly try rubbing him out, only to have their increasingly desperate efforts turned against them. For a rousing conclusion, Buster rallies the police in such numbers as to recall *Cops* from eighteen years earlier, only with motorcycles and squad cars racing after him instead of patrolmen on foot. Enlivened by the clever use of stock footage, *So You Won't Squawk?* was completed by Keaton and Lord in just four days.

It was as if the new picture challenged Jules White to up his game, since *His Ex Marks the Spot* was largely shot on a single set. White's next Keaton comedy, written in tandem by Adler and Clyde Bruckman, would be a semi-remake of *Doughboys,* updated to reflect the new realities of the peacetime army. White arranged to shoot the camp exteriors at the Columbia Ranch in Burbank and commissioned three songs from Adler and composer-arranger Paul Mertz for the picture, which carried the working title *The Private General.* As in *Doughboys,* Keaton would play a rich twit, in this case Peter Hedley Lamar, Jr., or, more succinctly, Hedley Lamar, a name dangerously close to that of one of M-G-M's newest stars. The induction exam from the earlier picture was extended and improved upon, and White permitted Keaton and Elsie Ames unusual latitude in developing their flirtatious duet, which comes while Hedley, who lusts after Dorothy Appleby, is stuck polishing spittoons.

"Though you're low in the rank," Elsie sings, "you've got dough in the bank. That is why I am falling for you." And then, of course, she literally does.

Keaton got another feature role in April 1941 when he signed on as comedienne Judy Canova's boyfriend in *Puddin' Head.* It wasn't a large part, but the early scenes director Joseph Santley shot were so impressive, and the chemistry between Keaton and Canova so good, that producer Albert Cohen had the early footage junked and the part of Herman considerably expanded. Keaton was set to resume production on May 9 when he came down with a stomach ailment, possibly the flu, and was ordered to bed for two weeks. There was no hint of alcoholism in the sketchy reports that emerged, and comic Chick Chandler replaced him.

"This was my first good part in six years," Buster groused. Apart from an unpaid cameo in a picture to benefit British War Relief titled *Forever and a Day,* his only subsequent work came from Columbia.

May brought word that the play Keaton and Lew Lipton wrote in 1937, *Marooned in Mojave,* was up for a possible Broadway production under the title *Lambs Will Gamble.* Director Ralph Murphy collaborated with Lipton on a rewrite, and a deal was brewing for actor Brian Donlevy to star in a production underwritten by Paramount production chief B. G. "Buddy" DeSylva. Fittingly, the entire summer of 1941 was given over to stage work. The so-called straw-hat circuit of rural theaters was a lucrative sideline for a lot of Hollywood figures, and the cumulative roster for 1941 included Harpo Marx, Fay Wray, Ruth Chatterton, Luise Rainer, C. Aubrey Smith, Ramon Novarro, and Elissa Landi. Keaton went east to star in *The Gorilla,* Ralph Spence's comedy-mystery featuring a couple of dimwit detectives that enjoyed a brief stay on Broadway in 1925 and a longer life on tour and in stock. The Keatons' arrival in New York for a few days of theatergoing sparked a flurry of press coverage.

"He giggles," Eleanor admitted when the subject inevitably turned to the deadpan. "And he nearly rolled out of his seat at *Arsenic and Old Lace* the other night."

The Gorilla, with Keaton as Detective Mulligan and Harry Gribbon as his partner, debuted at Brighton Beach, Brooklyn, on July 8, moving to Cedarhurst, Long Island, the following week. "Because much of the talk was dated," said Keaton, "we cut it out. That left a first act only twenty minutes long, so I filled it out with action." Guaranteed $500 a week plus expenses, he found business disappointingly thin at first. Yet he and Eleanor enjoyed the jumps they made from town to town in their wood-paneled Ford station wagon, Eleanor gayly likening the experience to a picnic, "making money having fun." They continued on to places like Marblehead, White Plains, Toledo, and Worcester before heading home in September, where another short for Columbia was in the offing.

Columbia had contracted for another Keaton two-reeler nearly a year earlier as part of a plan to stretch the number of All-Star comedies to eighteen for the 1941–42 season. Keaton, however, was growing weary of working for Jules White, who increasingly seemed to think that all his comics were interchangeable. The nadir of the series was reached with *She's Oil Mine,* in which White attempted to turn Keaton, Elsie Ames, and comic Monty Collins into an ersatz Three Stooges with gags that were drawn almost entirely from the Stooges' playbook. Based to some extent on *The Passionate Plumber,* one of Keaton's worst features, the third act of *She's Oil Mine* became a lift of the dueling sequence from the conclusion of *Plumber,* and it's indicative of Keaton's antipathy that the picture was finished in just three eight-hour days and nearly $1,600 under budget. Clearly, he could see where this was going.

It was the routine use of stock footage, recycled material, and stuntmen in the Columbia two-reelers that caused Keaton to deride them in later years as "cheaters." Jules White commissioned another script from Felix Adler, *What a Soldier*, but Keaton declined to make it. "I just got to the point where I couldn't stomach turning out even one more crummy two-reeler," he said. *She's Oil Mine* became the forty-fifth and final theatrical short to star Buster Keaton. From now on he would stick to feature roles, stage work, and writing. At the age of forty-six, he was done.

Japan's attack on Pearl Harbor brought the entire picture industry into the war effort. Many of its workers were considered serving by just doing their daily jobs creating the entertainment that helped sustain the nation's morale. Actor Robert Montgomery spent time in England as naval attaché at the American embassy and had earlier volunteered as an ambulance driver in the war zone before the fall of France. Screenwriter Robert Riskin also went to England to serve as public relations counsel to the British Ministry of Information. Writer-director Garson Kanin was drafted, then mustered out when the army discharged those over twenty-eight. So Kanin joined the Office for Emergency Management Film Unit to make civilian defense pictures. John Ford took up duties as lieutenant commander in the naval reserve, making highly classified films with the help of *Citizen Kane* cinematographer Gregg Toland. Douglas Fairbanks, Jr., had a reserve commission in the armed forces and went on active duty. Actor Jimmy Stewart won a commission as a lieutenant in the army. And 20th Century-Fox production chief Darryl F. Zanuck served as a lieutenant colonel in the Signal Corps, in charge of at-cost production of military training films.

Locally, two private organizations were ready for volunteer duty in the Pacific danger zone. The fifty-two men of Victor McLaglen's light horse troop, based at the actor's sports center on the outskirts of Hollywood, were sworn in as special emergency police, while the eighty-three members of McLaglen's women's auxiliary committed to Red Cross duty. Then there was actor Lewis Stone's station wagon brigade, established in August 1941 under the aegis of the L.A. County Sheriff's Department for use in civil emergencies. Starting with about sixty privately owned vehicles, the brigade formally became the First Evacuation Regiment of the California State Guard in November. After Pearl Harbor, Keaton was among one hundred new applicants inducted, a group that included actors Raymond Hatton, John

Miljan, Jack Holt, and Robert Young. Their vehicles would carry firefighting equipment, medical kits, and stretchers, as well as six to eight passengers in the event of an evacuation. Assuming the rank of colonel, Stone, at age sixty-two, served as commander of the unit. Soon, Donald Crisp was recruited, as were Rudy Vallée and Cesar Romero, both of whom were commissioned lieutenants.

The regiment grew to number more than a hundred vehicles and approximately three hundred volunteers, both drivers and aides. Stone, a major in the last war, conducted training every Tuesday night—foot drills, first aid, driving in the dark, repair work. He turned one of the unused stages at the old Warner Bros. studio on Sunset Boulevard into an armory, equipping it with twenty-four-hour phone service and cots to sleep the entire regiment should the need arise. Women who owned station wagons were welcome to register their cars, but were prohibited from joining themselves.

It was perhaps Keaton's involvement with the First Evacuation Regiment that convinced him that the house in Cheviot Hills was too close to the ocean for safety in the event of an invasion. In December, nine Japanese submarines had been positioned off the coast, attacking eight American merchant ships and actually sinking two. Myra, meanwhile, was alone in her house on Victoria Avenue, Harry and his wife and child and Louise having decamped to Las Vegas "because there was a big war plant opening up there."* It was, said Eleanor, "a much safer place to be . . . because it was a good fifteen, twenty miles inland. He got frightened about leaving his mother alone in her house, and she wouldn't pack it in and come back and live with us. So he says, 'Well, we'll have to go there then.' So we put our little house up for sale and moved in with her."

Before moving to Myra's house on Victoria, Keaton took a job at the nearby Fox studios, where the making of an unusual movie was in progress. The idea for *Tales of Manhattan,* which follows a formal tailcoat through six otherwise unrelated stories, apparently came from an old German film called *Der Frack.* Screenwriters Billy Wilder and Walter Reich knew of the film and suggested it, possibly as a joke, to the perennially penniless Sam Spiegel. It took form at Paramount, where co-producer Boris Morros had a two-picture deal, then moved to Fox when projected costs spiraled out of control. The cast was stellar: Henry Fonda, Ginger Rogers, Edward G.

* This was the Basic Magnesium plant, authorized by the federal government in July 1941 but not completed until after the attack on Pearl Harbor. It operated through November 1944.

Robinson, Charles Boyer, Rita Hayworth, W. C. Fields, Paul Robeson, and Charles Laughton. At one point, Keaton was set to play Hiawatha in the picture, but eventually he was engaged to consult on the Fields sequence. Julien Duvivier, the renowned French director of *Pépé le Moko,* became attached to the project when Morros abandoned his original plan to have six top directors make the various segments.

After a false start, the Fields sequence was scripted by Bill Morrow and Ed Beloin, two of Jack Benny's writers, who cast the Great Man as a phony temperance lecturer working the gullible society circuit. Duvivier, who was described by one of his actors as "a humorless man, very serious," was judged to be the wrong guy to direct a low comedian with a penchant for ad-libbing. Mal St. Clair was asked to take charge instead and, according to Fields, it was St. Clair who brought Keaton along with him.

"Buster was assigned an office next to mine," editor Gene Fowler, Jr., remembered. "One day, I heard such a commotion I went next door to see what it was. Buster was repeatedly throwing himself against our common wall. I said, 'What are you doing?' He said, 'I'm writing!'"

The house on Queensbury was the scene of a signal event in Keaton's life when he was reunited with his elder son. "I knew where he was all the time," said Jim Talmadge. He was eighteen when a close friend, who couldn't understand why he wasn't in touch with his father, took him over to the house and reintroduced them. They said hello, shook hands, and Buster said it was one of the thrills of his life. Later, Jim brought Bobby, then sixteen.

"From that day on," said Buster, "I had my own boys back again."

But Natalie wasn't yet finished with him. In May 1942 she filed a petition to legally change the boys' names from Keaton to Talmadge, although they had informally gone by the name Talmadge for nearly a decade.

"Everybody knew the name Keaton, but very few knew the name Talmadge," Jim said. "At school, nobody knew who my father was. . . . It was a lot easier to get along with the name Talmadge than it was Keaton."

And so, with the signed consents of both, Joseph Talmadge Keaton became James Talmadge and Bobby Keaton became Robert Talmadge.

That fall, at age twenty, Jim joined the Coast Guard. In July 1943, having achieved the rank of seaman second class, he eloped to Ventura with Barbara Jane Tichenor, an eighteen-year-old student at Santa Monica City College who was also a top-ranked junior tennis champion.

"I had some very strict parents," Barbara explained. "He was in the service. Everybody was worried about the war. All these boys were going to go fight, and they might not come back." She kept the marriage a secret while she went east to play as a member of the Whiteman Cup team, the women's equivalent of the men's Davis Cup, at Forest Hills. The announcement finally appeared in the *Los Angeles Times* on October 4, shortly before Jim left for Florida to attend officer's training school.

Walking away from Jules White imposed a heavy financial penalty. Keaton's income for the year 1941 was almost $8,000, much of which came from the two Columbia shorts he made that year. But in 1942, without the money from the two-reelers rolling in, his income dwindled to just a few hundred dollars. There were still Eleanor's earnings as a dancer, and true to her frugal ways, she made sure the proceeds from the sale of the house in Cheviot Hills were set aside for another once the war was over. In September 1942, he went to see his old friend Eddie Mannix at M-G-M.

"I told him how I felt about what I'd been doing and asked if he could put me on the payroll as a gagman and comedy constructionist." Mannix told him he could put him on at $100 a week. "It's a deal," said Keaton.

He went back on salary on October 2, 1942, and was immediately assigned to the Wesley Ruggles comedy *Nothing Ventured,* already in production.* It was Keaton who devised the film's snappy meet-cute between Lana Turner and Robert Young in which Turner, working a drugstore soda fountain, bets a colleague she can do the job blindfolded. And, contrary to Keaton's comedy instincts, she proceeds to flawlessly build a jumbo banana split before getting called on the carpet by her new manager for attempting such a stunt. "When Eddie put me on at $100 a week I thought it was darned nice of him," Buster said. "We could live on that, and I was sure M-G-M would raise my pay once I started giving them gags and comedy ideas they could use."

There wasn't a lot for him to do at Metro, at least not at first. To Lewis Jacobs, a writer in the shorts department, he was a vaguely pathetic figure: "It seemed to me that they were buying off their own consciences—at a hundred bucks a week. He was one of the skeletons in the M-G-M closet."

One thing that may have affected Keaton's demeanor was the knowledge that producer Jack Cummings was preparing to remake *Spite Marriage* as a vehicle for comedian Red Skelton, and no one had bothered to consult

---

* Released as *Slightly Dangerous* (1943).

him about it. On December 14, 1942, an M-G-M transportation order was issued:

> Take Buster Keaton home to 1043 Victoria Ave. L.A.
> Drunk per JTR

Keaton passed the war working for M-G-M and volunteering at the Hollywood Canteen, then operating out of an old livery stable off Sunset Boulevard on Cahuenga. ("I was doing magic tricks for the troops," Orson Welles remembered, "and Keaton was washing dishes.") Over much of 1943, he was involved in the development of a screenplay for Stan Laurel and Oliver Hardy titled *The Home Front*. The original idea, which came in the form of an eleven-page story from producer-director Sam Taylor, was, in Taylor's words, "a satire on the present civilian war-time situation in which it is almost impossible to get help of any kind, either business or domestic. . . . The picture will unfold exclusively from the viewpoint of Laurel and Hardy, two likable but very stupid bums who haven't held a job in ten years, and soon find their services at a premium—with employers fighting madly to give them a job and to keep them on the job."

Keaton was one of four writers contributing to the draft screenplay, which was completed in July with the notion of simply putting Stan and Ollie into a situation they could screw up. In September, Taylor signed

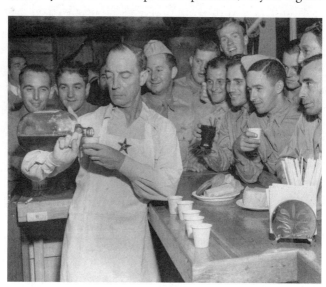

Keaton serving drinks at the Hollywood Canteen, circa 1943.

off on a revision in which Keaton had the pair fooling around with their employer's microcopter, nearly getting themselves killed—but demonstrating the machine's viability to the extent that it sells to the government. Taylor stepped away as producer in October, and B. F. "Bennie" Zeidman took over. Zeidman, a former publicist, had scant history with comedy, but was presumably considered qualified for having supervised the team's previous feature for the studio, the sluggish and unfunny *Air Raid Wardens*. It was on Zeidman's watch that the device of a boy king whose life needed saving was introduced, a needless subplot that effectively killed any chance the picture had of being good.

Gamely, Keaton continued to offer material. In April 1944, he fashioned a section of script that had Stan slicing up a beehive with a hatchet as if he were cutting a piece of cake. Another had the boys, as tree surgeons, going from home to home, faking damage and then repairing it. (At the second house, Keaton called for an "iron-jawed character woman.") By the time Taylor began shooting in June, it had taken the combined efforts of fifteen writers to create one of the weakest scripts Laurel and Hardy ever tackled. Fittingly, it would be Zeidman's last credit as producer.

Keaton alternated his work on the Laurel and Hardy picture (released as *Nothing but Trouble*) with *Mr. Co-ed,* a Technicolor musical starring Red Skelton and Esther Williams. "Buster worked with Red Skelton a lot," said director George Sidney.* "Skelton did some of the routines that Buster had done in silent films and updated them."

Keaton also worked out problems left unsolved on the page, such as when Skelton finds himself in Williams' house and encounters her dog. "Red was trying to get out and the dog wouldn't let him," said producer Jack Cummings. "He put on Esther's clothes. The dog wouldn't let him out. He had to get out somehow, and we didn't know how to work it. So I said, 'Well, call Buster.' And Buster came down and he looked at it. He said, 'I tell you what you can do. Just take the pins out of the hinges. As the dog comes inside this way, he can turn around and put the door the other way.' That's exactly what we did. But it was like magic."

When it was decided the picture, with a water ballet as its centerpiece, needed a more marketable title, Keaton helpfully suggested *The Fatal Breast Stroke.* (Throwing the spotlight on Esther Williams, it went out into the world as *Bathing Beauty,* making a top star of the twenty-two-year-old com-

---

* Keaton first worked with Skelton on *Du Barry Was a Lady* (1943).

Jon Hall, Louise Allbritton, and Keaton share a magical bus ride in San Diego I Love You *(1944).*

petitive swimmer.) In a similar spirit, Keaton proposed a gag for Tay Garnett's romantic drama *Mrs. Parkington* in which Walter Pidgeon casually drops a banana peel for Greer Garson to slip on. Later, assigned to the Bud Abbott–Lou Costello comedy *Lost in a Harem,* he was reminded of his experience with the Marx Brothers and their seeming aversion to anything that smacked of preparation.

"Abbott and Costello never gave the story a second thought," he said disdainfully. "They'd say, 'When do we come and what do we wear?' Then they find out the day they start to shoot the picture what the script's about. Didn't worry about it. Didn't try to. Well, that used to get my goat because, my god, when we made pictures, we ate, slept, and dreamed them!"

Keaton took a much-needed break from M-G-M courtesy of Ernie Pagano, who had last worked with him at Educational. In 1943, Pagano and his writing partner, Michael Fessier, were awarded contracts as writer-producers at Universal, and their third production under the agreement was *San Diego I Love You,* a whimsical wartime comedy about civilians caught up in the California resort city's housing shortage. A running theme of the picture was people breaking out of their everyday routines, so the team tailored the role of a downtrodden bus driver for him, his first on-screen appearance in a couple of years.

The sequence had a charming Capraesque quality, not unlike the famous bus trip in *It Happened One Night.* Actress Louise Allbritton, cast as a failed inventor's daughter, goads Buster into deviating from a route he has driven for a decade.

"For ten years I've been drivin' this route," he tells his passengers, "and for ten years most of you have been ridin' with me through billy-be-cursed backyards and I'm sick of it. I'm gonna drive along the beach, and the Consolidated Bus Company can go shoot itself!"

At dusk, they cruise along, waves breaking romantically on the shoreline, the soothing melodies of a quartet of handy musicians emanating from the back. At the end of the evening, he drops the two lovers (Allbritton and top-lined Jon Hall) at her family's house.

"Lady," he says poignantly, "what happened tonight never happened before, and it'll never happen again. And I'll never forget a minute of it." He takes her hand. "Thanks." And he smiles.

Scheduled for three camera days, Keaton's seriocomic turn in *San Diego I Love You* was completed in just one, Leo Morrison having negotiated a week's guarantee regardless. At a rate of $1,000, it would take him ten weeks to make as much at M-G-M as he cleared in a single day at Universal. Fessier and Pagano stuck with Keaton as a kind of talisman for their next two productions. In *That's the Spirit*, best described as a supernatural musical-comedy, he played the harried proprietor of a heavenly complaint department atop a cloud of spun glass. Clad in a white suit with a white satin band around the pork pie, he is approached by a deceased Jack Oakie, who petitions for a return to earth to make amends with his wife.

"Oh, that's the trouble with fellas like you," Buster complains. "You believe your own obituaries. Think the world can't get along without you."

When Oakie proves his case, Keaton grudgingly awards him a seven-day pass as a ghost. "I'm going to send you back down there," he says. "But I warn you—don't go around clankin' chains. It's absolutely forbidden. Besides, it's corny."

In the team's next picture, *That Night with You*, Keaton's profile dwindled to a perfunctory cameo as a dyspeptic counterman at an all-night diner, a part that barely required his presence. Back at Metro, he obligingly delivered another cameo—this time gratis—as a bellboy in the feature comedy *She Went to the Races*. He consulted on *Abbott and Costello in Hollywood* and developed a running gag with actor Dave O'Brien for a Pete Smith short titled *Equestrian Quiz*. (O'Brien's character, Horace, tries different mounts—such as a flying mount—in a catalog of ways someone can fall off a horse.) It was after finishing with the Smith short that Keaton sat for a six-minute radio interview with future film producer Irwin Allen, who was a Hollywood columnist and broadcaster at the time. It must have come as a shock when Keaton found that Allen's station, KMTR, was located in a rustic mission-style building that stretched along the western edge of what had once been his own studio lot.

"You and I just met before we came to our broadcast booth in here," ventured Allen. "Didn't you tell me something about your old studio being right here on this very site?"

"This very site," said Keaton.

"And if we can believe what we were told just before we came in, some of the old Buster Keaton pictures are buried here in an old vault, somewhere below ground."

"Well, I doubt that the pictures are," said Keaton good-naturedly. "You might find some old gags down there."

22

A Comedy Sequence Here and There

WITH THE WINDING DOWN of the war effort and its related industries, the Keaton family converged once more at 1043 South Victoria. Originally a two-bedroom, one-bath layout, a third bedroom had been added, and this was where Buster and Eleanor slept. To reach it, they had to walk through the original back bedroom that Myra now occupied, or through an exterior door that opened onto the backyard. Harry Keaton; his wife, Ernie (short for Ernestine); and their son, Harry Jr., shared the front bedroom. And Louise, who remained in Las Vegas, would eventually return and settle in the den off the front room. It was under these familiar boardinghouse conditions that the family began the year 1946 with the death of Joe Keaton.

"Joe was a wonderful character," said Eleanor. "I just loved him. By the time I knew Joe, he hadn't had a drink in thirty years. He was a sweet, darling man. We used to have on the front door of our house one of those door latches you push down. . . . He never opened that with his hand in his life. He'd walk up and go *chunk!* with his toe and open the door. He did all kinds of silly, funny things like that."

Joe was still doing extra work, reporting income of $1,716 for the year 1939, working as much as forty-eight hours a week. And he was still living downtown at the Yorkshire Hotel, driving his own car and squiring around a lady friend of long standing. Every Sunday he would drive out to the house in Windsor Square for dinner, greeting his elder son, now approaching fifty, with a bellowing "How's my little Bussy?"

Joe's world began to fall apart with the woman's death in the early days of

Joe Keaton, late in life, with a lithograph from his "The Man with the Table" days in vaudeville.

the war. Then in February 1944, at the age of seventy-six, he was struck by a car while crossing Broadway at Eighth Street. Although his injuries were considered minor, a fog began to come over him. He was moved from the Yorkshire to Camarillo State Hospital in July 1945.

"The last time I went over to visit him it was summer," remembered Eleanor. "I had a white dress on and he kept calling me nurse; he had ceased to recognize me. But it was a strange mental thing. He digressed. He went from—this is 1945 we'll say—he went back to the thirties and he'd tell stories, and they were true, they were things that happened, and he went back and back. Before he finally died he went back to when Buster was a baby. . . . He lived inside his head by then."

Officially, Joe Keaton died of pneumonia, with senility as a contributing factor, on the evening of January 13, 1946. Unofficially, Myra got another story from inside the hospital. "She told me he had prostate cancer," said Barbara Talmadge, "but he was afraid of doctors so he operated on himself. She said he bled and he bled."

The services took place at a funeral chapel near M-G-M on the morning of January 16, with burial following at Inglewood Park Cemetery. Buster never got around to purchasing a headstone, and the grave would remain unmarked for more than seventy years.

·   ·   ·

Gradually, Buster Keaton established his worth to M-G-M after a shaky start. Not only did he consult on more films as word got around that he was available, but he played occasional parts, directed when the need arose, and even generated original story material. In February 1944, he told a story idea to screenwriter Irving Brecher, who wrote it down. It was called *G.I. Casey Jones,* two or three pages that seemed to have real potential as a feature comedy, and it evidently inspired management to raise him from $100 to $250 a week, retroactive to the approximate date he first conceived it. But such a steep increase needed the approval of the regional War Labor Board, and it fell to M-G-M talent executive Benjamin Thau to make the case.

Thau laid it on thick, recounting how Keaton had once made $3,000 a week at the studio and how it had always been his practice to work with the directors and writers in the development of his movies. He further explained that, because of drink, Keaton could no longer be used in pictures and eventually came to the point of "being destitute," at which time he was benevolently put back on salary at the rate of $100 a week. "For the past year Keaton has not been drinking and consequently has made very valuable suggestions to our directors and writers in the way of gags, etc. We therefore wish to compensate him for his increased value to us and it is our desire to pay him $250.00 a week." On the matter of making the raise retroactive to February 14, Thau added that Keaton had assumed the burden of taking care of his father (because of the automobile mishap), "who has been in the hospital for some time and as a result has contracted bills of around $1,000 to $1,500." The increase was granted on May 15, 1944, and Keaton received a lump sum payment of $1,950 in back wages.

The extra money would come in handy with the newly reconstituted family on hand, since Buster insisted on supporting his sister as well as his mother, and his brother, Harry, refused to work.

"He was a *leech,*" said Eleanor of Jingles. "And he was mother's spoiled baby, and she protected him with her life. Louise was the youngest, but she wasn't the spoiled baby—Harry was. So I had no respect for him whatsoever."

Over the years, Buster had used his influence to get work for his brother, either in front of the camera (as in *Three Ages* and *Love Nest on Wheels*) or behind the scenes in a studio training program for sound technicians.

"That wasn't good enough for Harry. I never worried about it, but people who knew him well said that he always wanted to be a big star like Buster, and if he couldn't do that he wouldn't do anything."

Louise Keaton did play occasional parts in films, but her brother had been deeply wounded by Natalie's public inferences that he wouldn't support his sons. "Buster wrecked what could have been a good career for her," Eleanor said, "because she was a *funny* lady. She could have been as funny as Buster with the proper material and direction . . . and Buster practically put a stop to it because he didn't want people to think he wouldn't [or] couldn't support his family. . . . He thought it was a reflection on him that Louise would have to go out and go to work. It never dawned on him that she wanted to."

Now partnered with Ed Sedgwick, who was doing as much uncredited writing as he was directing, Keaton consulted on a Jack Cummings production titled *Easy to Wed,* a musical remake of the screwball comedy *Libeled Lady.*

"I got Buster principally to work on the block comedy scenes," Cummings recalled. "It was my habit in trying to make musicals to have a man like Eddie Buzzell to do the book, somebody else to direct the dances, and somebody else to do the block comedy scenes. And in that way we could kind of collapse the cost of making the picture. With Buster, the first thing really that he asked was, 'Well, what is the character of the man?' Which is revealing of Buster's character. And once Buster knew this then he shaped his material. He worked with Ed Sedgwick. When they started working together they had a view of the entire motion picture business from its start, its conception, at least from the comedy point of view, because their knowledge of gags was incredible."

In the picture, Van Johnson played an undercover reporter who was posing as an avid duck hunter. "It wasn't enough to say that he was an amateur. We have to show that he's an amateur. And in showing it, show it with fun. And it's got to be interesting fun. And there was nobody better in my mind than Buster Keaton at that sort of invention. I watched him at work, putting the whole thing together and deciding that it was to be told from the dog's point of view, and that the dog was suffering because of this complete amateur. Through an accident, however, he finally kills a big duck and in the next scene, of course, the dog is snuggled up to him, adoring him. But the whole idea and the interplay was all Buster's. He had the idea and he just lit up. He got up and played the dog and then he played Van Johnson—it was a great experience. He laughed all the way through it, except when he was being the sad-eyed dog, of course. But he was hilarious. Every move he made was a comedic move."

Writer-producer Richard Goldstone, former assistant to Jack Chertok and an associate producer in the M-G-M shorts department, returned to the studio in 1946 as a features producer after four years in the Signal Corps. "They assigned us to a whole row of little offices in an old wooden building," he remembered. "Little tiny offices, like a *railroad* car. Like compartments. And my office was next to Buster's. Buster had been a *huge* star at M-G-M in the silent days, and now he was pensioned off as a comedy consultant. And nobody ever consulted with him. He was a very sweet *angry* little man, and he spent his time in the office next to me. . . . He would spend his couple of hundred bucks a week buying Meccano sets, and he would put together these Rube Goldberg contraptions! He built a cigarette lighter that was *yay* high, and *so* big, and he'd put a cigarette in it, and it traveled through Ferris wheels and merry-go-rounds . . . round and round, came out at the top. An American flag went up on a flagpole, a picture of Louis B. Mayer went up on a flagpole, and the thing handed you a lighted cigarette. I'll never forget that. It was a *real* picture of Hollywood!"

Originally, Keaton's creations weren't products of his exile to the old writers' building, but rather a hobby plied at home in the days when his chief source of income was the series of shorts he was making for Jules White at Columbia. In fact, the cigarette lighter, three feet in height and composed of 567 separate parts, was exhibited at San Francisco's Union Label and Industrial Exhibition in 1940. "I built this thing in my spare time from one of those mechanical sets you give children," he said at the time. "I wanted to take a crack at those inventions of Ed Wynn and Joe Cook I'm always hearing about. The difference between my invention and Rube Goldberg? Mine works, while his are crazy!"

Six years later, Keaton was sharing an office with Sedgwick they called the Boars' Nest. Buster had taken to embroidery to pass the hours, and was at work on a project when Philip Scheuer of the *Los Angeles Times* paid a visit. "Just a purse I'm making—for the missus," Keaton explained, casting it aside. "But here—I don't believe you've seen my Erector sets. This one I'm working on is an assembly line for a ham and cheese on rye." After Lucille Ball looked in with a cheery greeting, Keaton proceeded to give Scheuer a comprehensive tour of his inventions. The first contraption, designed "to let in more light," worked splendidly. "A little car ran down one incline and up another, at the top it tripped a weight; the weight dropped, and all hell broke loose. Simultaneously, it seemed, a Venetian blind clattered open, a pin-up picture of Mme. Ball (her honorary title) slid down one wall to eye level, and a cowbell clanged against another."

Keaton beamed and activated the cigarette lighter, which strangely mal-functioned when called upon to perform. He moved on to the next, a wal-nut cracker. "This," he announced, "is my best engineering job." But the weight dropped before the walnut had moved into position on its platform, spoiling the effect. "Keaton muttered something about janitors who won't leave things alone, and we sat down to talk over old times." In a garrulous mood, Keaton pointed out that there was only one actor on the lot who had been with the company longer than he (Mitchell Lewis, by then an extra) and that he even predated Louis B. Mayer by virtue of Joe Schenck's 1920 distribution deal with Metro.

"What do I do now? A comedy sequence here and there . . . Last thing we did, Sedgwick and I, was to make a duck hunter out of Van Johnson for *Easy to Wed.* We wrote it and shot it, too. I even turned prop man, working those trick wires for pratfalls. Scared Johnson, I'm afraid; the younger generation doesn't understand these things." Keaton said he was committed to making a picture in Mexico City, but what really interested him was the upcoming production of his play *Lambs Will Gamble,* which was finally due to go into rehearsals ahead of a projected run on Broadway.

The inspiration for the play was a famous restaurant and casino on the outskirts of Palm Springs known as the Dunes. Built by a Cleveland mob-ster named Al Wertheimer, it was one of Joe Schenck's favorite hangouts, a place of dark wood, plush carpeting, and crystal chandeliers where the patrons wore dinner jackets, dined on steak and Maine lobster, danced to a live orchestra, and enjoyed the card and dice games on offer in the back.

"The Dunes must have been three or four hundred feet, at least, back in a grove of trees off a two-lane blacktop highway, fifteen miles from *anything,*" said Eleanor. "And it probably had a blacktop driveway going in, but that's about as close as you'd get to civilization. They had their own wells, they had electric wires coming in from heaven knows where, and Buster was *there* in a heavy rain one time where they had trouble getting in or out of the club. And he said, 'What would happen if it got a little worse?' And he just went from there."

The authors envisioned a police raid, a flash flood, and the murder of a Hollywood producer who is caught with loaded dice. As a comic *Grand Hotel* of the desert, it had all the elements of a good lowbrow evening at the theater. But, as revised and directed by Ralph Murphy, it was a stiff from the outset, a vanity project in which the principal backer, *Denver Post* heir-ess Helen Bonfils, claimed one of the featured parts for herself. The show opened in tryout at the Shubert Theatre, New Haven, on April 25. After three days of brutally bad business, Murphy withdrew as director and was replaced by Bonfils' husband, George Somnes, who had co-directed a handful of movies. As the company made its way to Pittsburgh, Keaton was hurriedly summoned from Hollywood to see what he could do with the script. Opening night at the Nixon Theatre was equally grim.

Kaspar Monahan of the *Pittsburgh Press* thought the dialogue trite, the characters shallow, the climax forced and artificial. "It's from a story by Buster Keaton, whose face was as solemn as it ever was in any of his hilarious silent films as he sat in a back row seat." Monahan said he applauded the handsome sets rather than the show itself.

Lambs Will Gamble was due to move to the Walnut Street Theatre in Philadelphia on May 6, but Keaton wouldn't follow it there.

"The whole play took place within the dance floor, tables around the dance floor, the kitchen, the gambling room and the bar," said Eleanor. "They were marooned with flash floods, and they slept on the crap tables with sheets and napkins for blankets and pillows and all. It was written as a comedy, and a very good, funny comedy. Buster wasn't involved with it until they were within three or four days of opening and knew they had a total bomb on their hands." *Lambs Will Gamble* folded in Philadelphia on May 11, 1946, following a week of record-low grosses. The expensive sets were sent to Elitch Gardens, home of Denver's resident stock company, as a gift from the producers. Walter Winchell reported that Bonfils lost $100,000 on the show.

The appeal of the picture to be made in Mexico—at least initially—was that Keaton would be starring in a feature comedy for the first time in more than a decade. He knew it was unlikely he would ever get such a chance again in Hollywood where, during the war years, comedies were in high demand. The producer of the Mexican picture was a German-born émigré named Alexander Salkind who, at age twenty-five, had exactly one movie to his credit, a romantic comedy based on a Spanish operetta called *Marina*. Having established a base of operations in Mexico City, Salkind made his first trip to Los Angeles looking to sign an American name.

"A third-rate agent came to me, to the hotel, and presented me with a list of different names, and I found in the long, printed list the name of Buster Keaton. I asked the man if that was the famous Buster Keaton. 'Yes, that's the one.' Then I said, 'Could I get him for a film?' He said, 'Of course.'"

The deal called for a fee of $5,000 plus 12½ percent of the gross. Keaton would co-direct, co-write, and star in the picture, which would be produced in both Spanish- and English-language versions. Filming was set to begin in February 1946, but script and funding delays pushed the start back to July. When M-G-M studio executive L. K. Sidney granted an extended leave of absence commencing July 17, Buster and Eleanor headed south. It wasn't until he got a look at the actual sets and learned the capitalization was just $50,000—roughly the cost of three Jules White shorts—that the reality of another Spiegel-like experience began to sink in.

Titled *El Moderno Barba Azul* (*The Modern Bluebeard*), the story had an American soldier landing in a Mexican jail, where he is mistaken for a serial killer. There, he and a cellmate are conscripted by an eccentric scientist to man a newly completed rocket ship on a mission to the moon. What they don't realize is that the ship has doubled back and returned to Earth, and what Buster thinks is the moon's surface is actually just another patch of Mexican soil. Keaton spoke English in the picture and a few basic words of Spanish, but kept as wordless as possible during most of the action, which was studded with modest gags and his trademark acrobatics. As with *The Invader,* its pacing was sluggish and its funding inadequate.

El Moderno Barba Azul was not without its minor charms. It was widely seen in Mexico and, according to Salkind, "was sold for very high prices all over Latin America and all over Europe, including England." It also played Spanish-language theaters in places like Phoenix and Albuquerque.

"As a comedy I must say it was a little childish," the producer admitted. "But the final result was economically very pleasant. I made a very, very good profit of maybe ten times what it cost." In fact, Salkind announced that he would make another picture with Keaton, but it never came to pass. *El Moderno Barba Azul* found its way to American television in 1975. By then, Alexander Salkind was famous for producing Richard Lester's *Three Musketeers* and its sequel, and would gain even greater prominence with his four *Superman* epics starring Christopher Reeve and Margot Kidder.

Back at M-G-M, Keaton served as "technical advisor" on a pie-throwing sequence for the third screen version of *Merton of the Movies,* but the title role, which he had once coveted and pursued, was played by Red Skelton. Keaton devoted more of his time to a picture titled *Cynthia,* a coming-of-age story which was to be fourteen-year-old Elizabeth Taylor's breakout film. On October 23, he contributed some physical business to a sequence set at a high school prom:

CLOSE SHOT—DONI AND WILL DANCING

Doni's chin is well up. Will is doing his best to look dignified, too. But his stiff shirt front is bulged out a little too far. Doni's hand slides over from his shoulder and flattens it. This causes one end of his collar to come loose and fly up. They keep dancing or keeping time, that is, until he has it fixed. He then puts his arm back around her only to discover that his cuff has fallen down over his hand until just the ends of his fingers can be seen. He puts the other arm around her and tries to shove it back in place. This confuses and smothers her a bit. And when the shirt front pops up and hits her in the nose, she pushes him away. This causes the collar to come loose again. On account of long sleeves both cuffs have fallen and they don't help him much when he tries to fix his collar. Doni doesn't know whether to help him or not when she sees the loose end of his suspender hanging. She just stares.

Note: CLOSE-UPS of Rosie, Mrs. Brady, Cynthia, and Ricky staring at them may add to Doni's embarrassment.

On January 25, 1947, following some work on a problematic film for Frank Sinatra called *The Kissing Bandit,* Keaton's contract with M-G-M was

Keaton observes the rehearsal of comedy business he contributed to Cynthia *(1947) as director Robert Z. Leonard works with actors Carol Brannon and Scotty Beckett.*

terminated. According to Eleanor, it was a "blood purge" in which a lot of longtime employees lost their jobs. A week later, the announcement was made that Ed Sedgwick would be leaving as well. Sedgwick, it seemed, was happy to be taking some time off, but Keaton, whose mind was always turning, was thrown by the sudden spell of inactivity and the boredom it brought.

"He was a deliberate drunk," said his brother-in-law Walt Kelly, who was married to Eleanor's sister, Jane. "He'd get to a point where, as Eleanor would say, he'd 'get excited' and all wound up and he'd want to party, and he was going to party come hell or high water. And that's what got him into trouble throughout the years. It was several days of imbibing and out of control, and nobody really wanted to put him under control because he was a lot of fun. And he paid the bills. . . . Eleanor could contain him most of the time, except when he really made up his mind and there was no containing him. Then she'd pick up the pieces, and that's when, lots of times, she'd take him down to Santa Ana to the Reed Ranch. It was an old Spanish land grant, beautiful place. She'd take him there and dry him out. It took age and Eleanor to get him down off it."

Keaton clearly enjoyed drinking, and sometimes needed it as an avenue of escape. But then there were the times when alcoholism was lonely, and it was all he could do to hold himself together.

"Buster started to drink a little," said Dean Reisner, who encountered him around this time. "It's a good man's failing. I had it myself, you know. I remember going into a bar one day about ten o'clock in the morning. This wasn't the 'Oh, let's all have a toddy on Christmas' [sort of thing]. This was real drinking people's time. There he was, and there I was. I made the mistake of speaking to him, and he wasn't overjoyed to see me. But I wasn't overjoyed to see him, either."

Keaton had never considered working in a circus because the thought of making a live appearance before five or ten thousand people unnerved him. Circuses in Europe were more intimate affairs, and no more so than in Paris, where permanent buildings had been constructed to house such famous Parisian companies as the Médrano, the Olympique, and the Cirque d'Hiver.

"For a long time," said Jerome Médrano, "I had the idea of bringing over American artists, especially comics, and with Buster it was easier for me because he did not speak, so he could be understood by every one of the

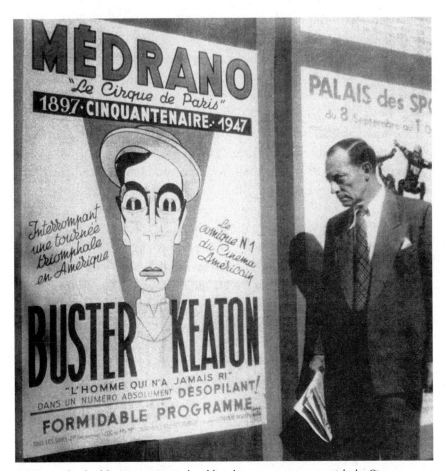

Keaton studies his likeness on a poster heralding his 1947 engagement with the Cirque Médrano in Paris.

audience everywhere." Keaton was also pleased to know that the circular building that housed the Médrano, a Paris landmark on a little street in the Montmartre district, was designed to seat just fifteen hundred people.

Buster and Eleanor flew to Europe in August 1947. They planned to spend six weeks at Cirque Médrano, opening the season and commemorating the show's fiftieth anniversary. Arriving at Orly Field, Keaton still hadn't settled on what he would do to justify his star slot next to closing.

"At the last moment, he had this duel sketch and I was afraid by it," said Médrano, "because this is a sketch that has been done so many times by the clowns. But this time there was Buster. It was completely different."

Originated for *The Passionate Plumber* and condensed for *She's Oil Mine,*

Keaton stretched the material to a boisterous twelve-minute turn packed with adroit physical business. As *Variety* described it, "He first comes on in the ring as intending to 'do big moments of big plays' and soon gets into an argument with the orchestra leader as to the kind of musical introduction he should receive. After that, a 'duel' is arranged, all donning big black cloaks. Keaton is told to choose the pistol and leave the sword to his opponent. It's all plain pantomime and clicks up to his trick exit."

Since average French citizens had no money for luxuries such as shows in the aftermath of the war, Parisian nightlife, with only a couple of exceptions, was pretty much dead. The opening-night crowd at the Médrano was largely composed of visiting Americans such as Chico Marx and actress Joan Fontaine. Fortunately, Keaton was still a well-known and affectionately remembered figure in France.

"When we got to Europe he was big, big, big," said Eleanor. "With the American public being so blasé—and they forget everything within twenty minutes—it shocked him more at how popular he still was over there, more than it did me. He felt wonderful about it. People would line up for autographs. It startled him."

The act went over as well with local audiences as it had on opening night, drawing capacity business twice a day that rivaled the cirque's top prewar attraction, an act with four elephants. "And," the show's manager added, "we had to feed the elephants."

"Things were very scarce," said Eleanor. "Meat was very scarce. They were still eating that dark brown ersatz bread that I'm quite sure had sawdust in it. . . . All the bomb holes and everything were still very evident, never filled in. What little damage was done to Paris was still there. They hadn't had time to repair anything."

Keaton's salary was $3,500 a week, and a law forbidding foreigners from taking more than half out of the country required them to live royally in their suite at the George V. Earnings were subjected to a 12 percent income tax, but there was still plenty of money to spread around.

"The American Graves Association* was there collecting bodies and putting them in the right places, and they had a PX. We used to go out there and we'd buy jam and jelly and bread and candy and all kinds of stuff the French couldn't get, and then we'd take them to work and give 'em. We

* This would have been the Graves Registration Service, the part of the U.S. Army responsible for the permanent interment of American war dead in Europe.

took a whole carton of soap, little soaps, not as big as you'd buy, and took them to the Cirque Médrano when we were working there and gave them to everybody. There was a little Italian dance act, a boy and two girls, and Mama, and they got [one square piece] of lye soap, that would blister you, for a whole month for all of them. We gave her a half a dozen bars of soap. She stood there and cried. Just unbelievable."

From Paris, the Keatons traveled to Bordeaux to fulfill a three-week commitment. They landed back in New York on October 14, and an AP photo of them disembarking their TWA flight made papers around the country. Buster had a new picture taking shape, a live action *Tom Thumb* for producer George Pal in which he was to be teamed with actor-comedian Mischa Auer, to be followed by a six-week stage engagement in Buenos Aires. Nothing seemed to pan out—Pal's financing dried up—and the first months of 1948 yielded little in the way of activity or income. The industry had contracted after the boom years of the war, and work was scarce. It was only when a new Red Skelton picture bombed in previews that Keaton once again found himself on the Metro-Goldwyn-Mayer payroll, this time at $350 a week.

Producer Paul Jones, who had a long history at Paramount with the W. C. Fields, Preston Sturges, and Hope and Crosby "road" pictures, had been lured to M-G-M expressly to mollify Skelton, who felt he was being mishandled. Once there, Jones was pitched a story by the writing team of Norman Panama and Melvin Frank. Fleshed out to a seventy-page original, *The Spy* was a Civil War comedy with hints of *The General* in its central character's exploits behind enemy lines. Veteran screenwriter Harry Tugend wrote the script, which he titled *A Southern Yankee*, but Skelton, unhappy with the pictures and directors he had been handed since his return from the army, staged a work slowdown in hopes of breaking his contract. Shot in early 1948 by S. Sylvan Simon, who had directed three of Skelton's earlier pictures, the star "deliberately dogged it" according to Tugend. "But the odd thing was, even when he was dogging it he was brilliant and nobody even noticed." When the picture was finished, it previewed poorly and Jones feared he had a disaster on his hands when he asked Keaton to have a look.

Buster watched the film and told the producer he had a whale of a story, but that a couple of mistakes had been made. "One was having Red behave like an imbecile in the opening scenes. As the comedian and leading man, Red lost the audience's sympathy by behaving too stupidly. If you act as screwy as he was doing, the people out front would not care what happened to the character you were playing." Subsequently, Keaton was teamed with Nat Perrin, another comedy veteran who had co-written films for the Marx Brothers, Abbott and Costello, and even Buster himself (the execrable *Sidewalks of New York*).

"I was working at the studio," Perrin recalled, "and they felt the picture needed a lot of work on it, so they asked me to stop what I was doing and come on this for retakes, added scenes. Keaton was also around to work on it. So I'd go to lunch with him and see him, and I liked him. He was a very, very nice guy . . . but he was *dull*. I can't say 'dull' in the sense that he said dull things—he didn't say *anything* much, you know."

Keaton wasn't outgoing with Perrin, in part because he didn't know him, but also, perhaps, because he bore some responsibility for what Buster considered his worst picture at M-G-M. Working pretty much on his own, Perrin created a new outline, revised sections of the script, and generated notes for Paul Jones, all without a clue as to how to work effectively with his temporary writing partner. In April, Jones wisely brought Ed Sedgwick back to the studio, and he and Keaton paired off to develop new material on their own, particularly a sequence in which Skelton ducks into a dentist's office to elude capture, has a healthy tooth forcibly pulled, and ends up in a store-room stocked with Confederate uniforms. Perrin took the bits Keaton and Sedgwick generated and incorporated them into the forty pages of revised script he was fashioning. Director Simon had long since left the picture, so when it came time to shoot the added scenes and retakes in early May, Ed Sedgwick, with Keaton at his side, became the director of record.

"They wrote a whole chase with a horse and buggy," remembered Gil Perkins, "with all kinds of gags going on. Also Skelton riding in a chase sitting backwards on a horse—I had to do all that." In addition, Keaton contributed a memorable gag up ahead of the dentist bit in which Skelton calms a fierce battle between North and South by simply walking between the lines carrying a flag, causing both sides to hold their fire. Skelton was wearing half a Union Army uniform on the side facing the Northern soldiers and half a Confederate uniform facing the other side. "Both sides cheer him wildly," Keaton recounted, "until a sudden gust of wind reverses the flag, showing both sides the game he is playing. As Red turns around to straighten the flag they discover his half-and-half uniform."

"These were the kind of things he wrote," said Perkins, "and always when we shot them he would be out there on the set with Sedgwick. Sedgwick

was the official director for the second unit. It might have been Roy Rowland directing the first unit—or Chuck Walters or somebody—but it was
always Ed Sedgwick with the second unit. And any time I saw Buster go to
Sedgwick and say, 'Look Ed, I think for this scene we should change it and
do it this way,' Ed always listened and nearly always did it the way Buster
suggested."

Keaton spent a total of nine weeks on *A Southern Yankee*. The revised
picture was released in August to glowing reviews and returns that covered
serious budget overruns and still delivered a profit in excess of $250,000. As
a result, *Variety*'s Florabel Muir reported the studio had commissioned an
original comedy from Keaton, but nothing ever came of it. In June, Keaton
generated a three-page scene for *Neptune's Daughter*, again for Skelton, part
of a six-week stint on that production. According to Eleanor, he also contributed to the Gene Kelly–Frank Sinatra musical *Take Me Out to the Ball
Game*. He was set to play another six weeks at Cirque Médrano in the fall
when work intervened and he found himself cast once again in a major
M-G-M musical.

Monologist Joe Laurie, Jr., had a prolific career as a writer and showbiz historian. He authored more than a hundred vaudeville sketches, doctored a
number of Broadway shows, wrote for Eddie Cantor and Al Jolson on radio,
and was responsible for the first words Fred Astaire ever spoke onstage.
Nobody knew more about the standard acts on the old two-a-day than Laurie, and it may have been Joe Keaton's death in January 1946 that inspired
him and *Variety* editor Abel Green to propose the lightly fictionalized history of The Three Keatons as the basis for a movie. Their original story idea,
carrying the title *Barbary Host*, was purchased by Warner Bros. on April
16, 1946, the two authors splitting $5,000 for their trouble. Not that they
troubled all that much. The story line had Joe and June Tyme, the married
proprietors of an old-fashioned act called the Two Tymes, getting nowhere
until their twelve-year-old son throws in with them. Suddenly, the new act,
called the Three Happy Tymes, is a solid success. In New York, they run up
against the Gerry Society and the act is shut down. Joe is so upset he takes
to the bottle. And the name of the boy in the story is Buster.

Remarkably, producer William Jacobs, whose own father was stage
manager at a Chicago vaudeville house, saw nothing fishy in this. He put
screenwriter Peter Milne on the job—the two men frequently worked

together—and the script that emerged deviated little from the Keaton story other than the Tymes' act being of the song-and-dance variety, not the rambunctious acrobatic spectacle that Joe and Buster made famous. In January 1947, the husband-and-wife team of Henry and Phoebe Ephron were brought in to do a polish on the Milne script, but found there was little they could do for it.

"Brightening the dialogue couldn't help this one," said Henry Ephron. "It was too heavy a story for a musical—a father jealous of his young son who has more talent than he has. It was impossible to get any sympathy for the father."

Filming began in August 1947, with Jack Carson as Joe, Ann Sothern as June, and fourteen-year-old Robert Ellis making his screen debut as Buster. The result, as directed by James V. Kern, is best described as quaint. The picture was released in March 1948, and although it was widely reviewed, nobody fingered it as the Keaton story, not even the mugg from *Variety*, who surely should have known better.

"We were sitting home one day and the phone rings," remembered Eleanor. " 'Is this Buster? This is Joe.' Buster says, 'Yeah, how are you?' And so forth. 'Haven't seen you in years.' He says: 'You've got to sue Warner Bros.'

" 'I do? Why?'

" 'I wrote a film for them starring Jack Carson and Ann Sothern called *April Showers,* and it's the story of The Three Keatons. I wrote it. And I wrote it with The Three Keatons in my head all the time I was writing it. It's now filmed. It's in the can. It's in release. They've just opened it. Sue the hell out of them!'

"So Buster went to our attorney and said, 'Joe says so forth and so on . . .' And the attorney says, 'Oh, good!' "

Keaton was coached to play it up big in the columns, so in May he alerted Louella Parsons, Sheilah Graham, and Sidney Skolsky to Warner's alleged perfidy.

"Buster Keaton stops me in the Metro café to tell me that his lawyers will demand fifty percent of all the profits from the Warner picture *April Showers,*" Skolsky reported, "which the old non-smiling comedian claims is his own life story. I understand that the movie starring Ann Sothern and Jack Carson is cleaning up."

In July, it was announced that Keaton would graciously settle the suit out of court, and in October, he and Myra executed a general release in exchange for a one-time payment of $3,500. "So Joe Laurie wrote the thing, he called

Buster and said, 'Sue 'em!' And Buster wound up with a $3,500 check from Warner Bros. to shut up and go away—and we never would have known the difference otherwise."

In February 1948, Keaton had a visit from Pop Leonard, one of his favorite directors on the Metro lot. Leonard, who was a stickler for story development and famous for conferences that ran on for hours, was preparing a musical version of the sly Ernst Lubitsch comedy *The Shop Around the Corner* and had encountered a problem. A running gag in the script had the proprietor of a music store, a mediocre violinist, cherishing a Stradivarius he had no business owning. At a crucial point in the story, the Strad had to be destroyed. "And he didn't know how to break it," said Eleanor, "because it *had* to be an accident, couldn't be vicious or deliberate . . . And he didn't know what to do with it, didn't know how to do it, or how to get at it. So he came down to Buster's office and said, 'Take this damn thing home and read it and tell me how to break this violin, will ya?' And Buster said, 'All right.' So he brought it home and read it, and mulled it around over the weekend."

Keaton told Leonard he couldn't break the Stradivarius even if it was staged as an accident—the audience wouldn't stand for it. But it would be okay for the characters to *think* it was the Strad as long as the audience knew it wasn't.

" 'Now, be careful, because if you get a stuntman that looks like he's doing a stunt it's going to look phony.' It's got to be done so it's an accident. 'Make sure it doesn't look like a trick.' And Bob said, 'Okay, good.' And he went away. About four days later, he called Buster and said, 'I've got the whole thing figured out. It's all solved.' Buster says, 'Good.' He says, 'You're going to be in the picture. I'm going to put you to work in the music store so that you'll be in and established all through [the movie] so *you* can break it—because I know it will be done *right* if you do it.' "

The screenwriting team of Frances Goodrich and Albert Hackett took a minor character, a fawning yes-man named Hickey, and reimagined the part with Keaton in mind. Hickey would grow to become the inept nephew of the store's owner, a prim little man who is always in the background but has a crush on the film's star, Judy Garland. He also serves as an occasional sounding board for Van Johnson, who ends up with Garland at the fade. Awarded a ten-week contract as actor, writer, and gagman at $500 a week, Keaton began work on *In the Good Old Summertime* on October 28, 1948,

Judy Garland and Van Johnson collide under Keaton's direction in the musical remake of The Shop Around the Corner, *retitled* In the Good Old Summertime *(1949).*

devising bits of business in consultation with director Leonard, including an intricate first encounter between the two stars that establishes their tense relationship through most of the story. Production commenced on the studio's Fifth Avenue exterior on November 22.

As Garland, resplendent in her turn-of-the-century finery, rounds the corner to the steps of the post office, Johnson, engrossed in a letter he's just received, collides with her, knocking her to the ground. Mortified, he helps her to her feet and tries putting her hat right before she shoves him away. What follows is a tangle of good intentions, the hat catching on her parasol, her hair disheveled, the white dove on her hat replaced by a live pigeon, the hat and her hair now an irreparable mess. The parasol collapses, the faux bird tumbles repeatedly to the ground, and, as Johnson apologetically takes his leave on a bicycle, the thing catches on the hem of her dress and tears it away, leaving her reeling on the sidewalk in her bloomers.

Keaton took all morning to stage the scene, which in the picture would consume two minutes of screen time. When columnist Harrison Carroll arrived on the set, he saw Keaton lying on his stomach, out of camera range, coaching Johnson on how to hook one of the ribs of the parasol on Garland's hat, sending it—and her hair—aloft.

"Sounds easy, but it isn't," Carroll noted. "After several tries, director Leonard calls a halt to give the stars a breathing spell."

Garland, in high spirits, came over. "Isn't this something?" she laughed. "This is my first day on the picture and I started out very nervous. But already I feel like I have been working for two weeks."

She was called away by her hairdresser, and Carroll engaged Keaton for a moment. "Think Judy would have made a good Mack Sennett star?" he asked.

"Sure, with a little training," Keaton replied. "Of course, in the old days this would have been a simple scene. We wouldn't have rehearsed it. We would have talked it over. Then we would have started shooting and let nature take its course."

A few days later, Louella Parsons was surprised to happen upon Keaton "busy as busy could be" working with Leonard on the film's music store interior. "See?" said Keaton, proudly showing off a canvas director's chair. "This is my name. That's the first time I've had my name on a studio set in a long time."

Filmed in Technicolor on a forty-day schedule, *In the Good Old Summertime* would be Judy Garland's penultimate musical for M-G-M, management no longer willing to abide the delays and illnesses and fits of temperament that came with a Garland picture. For Keaton, the assignment inspired the usual stale talk of another comeback, and the crawl of progress when Garland was unavailable made for a drag of a shoot.

"He was just bored stiff most of the time," said Eleanor. "Because *if* she showed up, okay, sometimes she's late, sometimes she'd get there and then she'd quit in the middle of the day. Sometimes she wouldn't show up. . . . Anybody who was interested in the money, who was in the business strictly to get the money, they *loved* to get on Judy's films because they went on *forever*. And they'd be on salary for weeks and weeks and weeks and weeks and weeks—more than they should have been. But that *bored* him. Fortunately, being on the M-G-M lot, he could always go to his own office and they knew where to find him. If they needed him they'd call him at the office because he was there with Sedgwick and they were doing their own thing."

When it finally came time for Buster to shatter the violin, an inexpensive substitute secretly swapped with the Strad, he did so with aplomb, tripping on one of the steps to the bandstand, losing his balance, falling backward, then slipping on the polished floor, pitching forward with his full weight, and landing squarely on the fragile instrument. Accomplished in a single take, it was fluid and convincing, and no stuntman could have performed it nearly as well. With his time on the picture drawing to a close, and Ed Sedgwick allocated to a remake of *The Cameraman* with Red Skelton, Keaton accepted an offer of a one-day cameo at Fox, effectively appearing as himself, and then arranged to appear in an independent feature titled *The Great Speculator* with Charlie Ruggles in the title role. He finished up at M-G-M on January 27, 1949, and checked off the lot, presumably for good.

23

Diggin' Up Material

WITH *IN THE GOOD OLD SUMMERTIME* awaiting release, the only film work Buster Keaton could muster was a one-day cameo at Paramount. The picture was titled *Sunset Boulevard*, and it starred Gloria Swanson as an aging movie queen who keeps a struggling young screenwriter played by William Holden. The scene in the script was of a card game taking place inside Swanson's run-down mansion, depicting her "and three friends—three actors of her period. They sit erect and play with grim seriousness." In his voice-over narration, Holden describes them as "dim figures you may still remember from the silent days. I used to think of them as her Wax Works."

Producer Charles Brackett had no trouble securing Keaton and H. B. Warner for the picture, but was turned down "with hauteur" by Theda Bara and Jetta Goudal. When director Billy Wilder shot the scene on May 3, 1949, the foursome consisted of Swanson, Warner, Keaton, and Swedish-born Anna Q. Nilsson, a major star in the twenties who had lately been doing extra work.

"She looked well, by the way, the ghost of a beauty," Brackett recorded in his diary. "H. B. Warner and Buster Keaton were somber relics of the past. And Gloria, looking absolutely sparkling, full of the sense that she'd beaten the years far better than they, made a great fourth." As he took his seat at the table, Keaton was heard to mutter, "Wax Works is right," sending the others into howls of laughter.

Keaton returned to the stage in 1949, embarking on his first summer stock tour since *The Gorilla* in 1941. The play this time would be George

On the set of Billy Wilder's Sunset Boulevard: *Anna Q. Nilsson, Gloria Swanson, Keaton, William Holden, Erich von Stroheim, and H. B. Warner.*

Abbott's Broadway hit *Three Men on a Horse,* a perennial favorite on the straw-hat circuit but one that would burden him with dialogue. As they had eight years earlier, Buster and Eleanor made the drive east on their own, this time planning a two-day stopover in Muskegon to get some fishing in. Having not been there in sixteen years, he was astonished at all the growth.

"I thought I was in the wrong place," he said. "One-way streets with traffic lights had me confused. Back thirty-five years ago, there wasn't much traffic in Muskegon and there were only a few policemen and I knew them all. Now there's traffic all over, and everywhere I look there's a policeman."

His first act upon arrival was to head for Pascoe's, where he introduced Eleanor to the wonders of fried perch. "Most people don't know how to cook perch," he once averred. "You have to skin 'em, roll 'em in half corn-meal and half flour, and fry 'em in half butter and half lard." That day, he sensed that Pascoe's had been short-listed for extinction, the founder, Frank "Bullhead" Pascoe, having sold the place during the war.

"There was a young man there who never heard of him or me or anybody else," remembered Eleanor. "It was about 3 p.m. and he had to have that perch. So the young man fixed it for him, and we sat on those front steps and ate it."

Said Buster: "I must have eaten two dozen perch. They had the best fish I've ever eaten."

*With Frank Buxton in the
Berkshire Playhouse production of
Three Men on a Horse.*

He and Eleanor stopped by the Muskegon Elks lodge, where Buster was a life member, and were rushed from one place to the next as word spread. ("They organized a parade of cars to take us on a tour.") He fished off the dock at the Muskegon Yacht Club early the next morning and caught three pike. They visited Jingles Jungle, the old family homestead, and Keaton Court off Lakeshore Drive. And they were guests for dinner at the Edgewater home of Mr. and Mrs. E. W. Krueger, where Buster had held court back in 1933. It was a satisfying, and ultimately nostalgic, visit, doubtless tinged with regret for all the familiar figures who had passed from the scene—Big Joe Roberts; Max Gruber; Lex Neal; the Kruegers' son, Kurt, who looked so much like Buster they were often mistaken for each other; his father, Joe, of course; Kate Millard (Mildred's mother); and even Pascoe himself, who had died just prior to the Keatons' arrival. Buster would come close to Muskegon again in the future, particularly to Detroit and Chicago, but never again would he make the familiar trip along U.S. Route 12 to the only hometown he had ever known. Too many ghosts now, too many to count.

Keaton's tour of *Three Men on a Horse* began on June 20 in Stockbridge, Massachusetts, where it inaugurated the Berkshire Playhouse's eighteenth season. Actor-director Frank Buxton, who was spending the summer as a nineteen-year-old member of the resident company, recalled that Buster, despite a generous rehearsal period, was not letter-perfect that first night. "There were several moments when those of us on stage with him had to ad lib to get him back on track, with the audience none the wiser." As Erwin Trowbridge, an unassuming man with a knack for picking racehorses, Keaton managed to work in some signature bits. "Billy Miles, the director, was smart enough to incorporate Buster's shtick into the play because people expected it. Buster, of course, said, 'I can do this here . . .' And Billy said, 'Certainly!'" Keaton put comedienne Janet Fox to bed as he had a drunken Dorothy Sebastian in *Spite Marriage*. "At another point Erwin gets mad at his meddlesome brother-in-law. To chase him off the stage, Buster ran from one side of the stage to the other, leaped in the air, landed on the back of his neck, and did one of his famous acrobatic twirls, finally landing on his feet."

In three acts and two intervals the show ran long, not ending until half past eleven, causing *Three Men on a Horse* to draw a mixed notice in the *Berkshire County Eagle*. As Buxton remembered it though, they had a successful run: "We had great houses and great response." The Keatons moved on to Hoboken in good spirits, but there were places where the Keaton name wasn't the drawing card it had once been. As the tour wound down in Norwich, Connecticut, Keaton was wondering if he had a future in television, since the picture business seemingly had so little need for him.

Then something extraordinary happened. *Life,* in its issue of September 5, 1949, carried as its cover story an immense essay stretching over eighteen richly illustrated pages under the title "Comedy's Greatest Era." Its author, James Agee, former film critic for *Time* and *The Nation,* cast a broad net in researching this masterwork, then slowly narrowed his focus to the pioneering slapstick of Mack Sennett and the four comedians "who now began to apply their sharp individual talents to this newborn language." These were Harold Lloyd, who "wore glasses, smiled a great deal, and looked like the sort of eager young man who might have quit divinity school to hustle brushes"; Harry Langdon, who "looked like an elderly baby and, at times, a baby dope fiend"; Charlie Chaplin, who "was the first man to give the silent language a soul"; and Keaton, who "carried a face as still and sad as a daguerreotype through some of the most preposterously ingenious and visually satisfying physical comedy ever invented."

A vintage photo of Buster in costume, teetering on a diving board during the making of *Hard Luck,* dominated the initial two-page spread, and a section of the essay devoted to him carried the subtitle "THE GREAT STONE FACE."

"Keaton worked strictly for laughs," wrote Agee, "but his work came from so far inside a curious and original spirit that he achieved a great deal besides, especially in his feature-length comedies. . . . He is the only major comedian who kept sentiment almost entirely out of his work, and he brought pure physical comedy to its greatest heights. Beneath his lack of emotion he was also uninsistently sardonic; deep below that, giving a disturbing tension and grandeur to the foolishness, for those who sensed it, there was in his comedy a freezing whisper not of pathos but of melancholia. With the humor, the craftsmanship, and the action there was often, besides, a fine, still, and sometimes dreamlike quality. . . . Perhaps because 'dry' comedy is so much more rare and odd than 'dry' wit, there are people who never much cared for Keaton. Those who do cannot care mildly."

Life enjoyed a weekly circulation of 5.2 million, and its publisher figured that it reached one in five Americans—meaning that "Comedy's Greatest Era" put Keaton before an audience of nearly thirty million readers, enshrining him as part of comedy's Mount Rushmore and making the case for his continued relevance. Moreover, of those with whom he was ranked, Keaton was the only one still ready and eager to work. Langdon was dead; Chaplin, beset by personal and political woes, was nearing the end of his time in the United States; and Lloyd was firmly retired, even as he considered ways of putting his old pictures in front of new audiences. The timing, for Keaton at least, could not have been better.

During the war, Jim Talmadge and his brother, Bob, served in the OSS as underwater demolition experts, based in Ceylon. Afterward, Jim settled in Pacific Palisades with his wife, Barbara, and their young family. Following the birth of their second boy in 1948, Norma, Jim's aunt, said, "You won't get out very much. I'll buy you a little GE."

When Jim's father and stepmother came over, Buster was immediately transfixed. "We had one of the very first television sets in the whole area," Jim said. "There was a ten-inch screen and a big console that weighed a ton, and my dad sat there and looked at that thing all afternoon." Barbara finally had to force him to come to dinner.

"*That*," Buster concluded, "is the coming mode of entertainment!"

Keaton had already settled on television as his new medium of choice when the appearance of "Comedy's Greatest Era" reminded a broad swath of the public that he was a natural fit in a half-hour format. Immediately, he canceled plans to stop in New York to make some TV guest appearances and returned to California, where he huddled with Clyde Bruckman over the notion of making some "television shorts." Leo Morrison instinctively went after a network deal, and soon arrived at a general understanding with CBS. Buster would go on the air December 14, 1949, with a weekly series called *The Keaton Komedy Kollege*. Ahead of that, he would soften up the

Keaton performing the "Butcher Boy" sketch on The Ed Wynn Show, *which was widely believed at the time to be his TV debut.*

audience with a guest shot on Ed Wynn's network show, which would be promoted as his TV debut.* The broadcast would originate live from the KTTV studios in Hollywood, with kinescope recordings of the show going to network stations in New York and Chicago, covering thirteen other eastern and midwestern markets. Keaton's reserved demeanor could not be more unlike the flamboyance of the Perfect Fool. There were concerns the two wouldn't mesh well, but in rehearsals Wynn wisely let Buster take the lead. On Thursday, December 9, at 9:00 p.m., Wynn took the stage in a sleigh pulled by a quartet of shapely young women and the show was on.

The first half was typical of Ed Wynn's brand of befuddled nonsense, while the second half, introduced by the host as "silent television," recalled Keaton's screen debut in *The Butcher Boy* some thirty-two years earlier. The scene was a general store. Keaton entered and adroitly picked a broom up off the floor with his foot. He mimed a line, then held up a card with the intertitle: GIVE ME 25 CENTS WORTH OF MOLASSES PLEASE.

---

* Actually, Keaton had already made at least two TV appearances, including one on KTTV's *Pantomime Quiz Time.*

Wynn mimed an equally elaborate response and produced a card of his own: OKAY. The sketch was at once a send-up of silent-movie technique and an affectionate homage. The coin in the bucket, the molasses in the hat, the feet stuck to the floor—it was all there. The audience ate it up, delivering by far the biggest laughs of the evening. Wynn called Keaton back to take a bow, and the crowd gave him a rousing ovation.

"One of the most delightful gifts the televiewing public got for Christmas was Buster Keaton making his TV debut," Larry Wolters proclaimed in the *Chicago Tribune*. "For all we knew this great comedian of the silent-film era might have been dead. Then he bobbed up without advance warning on the Ed Wynn show. For middle-aged persons it was sheer delight to again see this sad-faced little man with the wonderfully expressive eyes. And for generations of young Americans, who had missed him entirely in the pre-sound era, he proved just as funny. . . . Not one word was spoken in the whole twelve-minute skit and yet it was one of the funniest bits that TV has offered to date."

And there was something more, an embellishment to the skit that brought the biggest laugh of all. It wasn't Keaton's invention—he always gave his father the credit—but it was an idea that took the pratfall to the level of high art, a signature bit that would remain in the collective memory of an entire generation of viewers. As Wynn used a kettle of boiling water to loosen the grip of the molasses on his shoes, Buster hoisted one leg onto the counter, then the other, and seemingly paused in mid-air before plummeting to the floor—where the sticky stuff proceeded to saturate the seat of his pants.

"It looked like something off an animation board," Keaton said, "the kind of thing an animator would draw—the four key positions—and leave the rest for in-betweeners to fill in."

The public had seen it before—he did a crude, early version of it in *Hollywood Revue of 1929* and reprised it in *Three Men on a Horse*—but now it advanced the action and enhanced the payoff. How he did it without breaking his neck was a mystery to many, but to Keaton himself the technique was elementary.

"When he did the 'Butcher Boy' fall," Eleanor explained, "his feet were high enough that when he crashed, all his weight fell on the shoulders, which is where it should be. He's got that heavy muscle structure [and it] acted like a pad. The spine, the tailbone—nothing like that ever touched the floor. You could get hurt. But if you held your breath and tensed the muscles, it doesn't even knock the wind out of you."

When no national sponsor came forward, the start of the new Keaton TV series was pushed back to December 22. Now simply titled *The Buster Keaton Show*, it became a production of KTTV, the CBS affiliate in Los Angeles, with plans to syndicate the show to other stations. With high hopes, management budgeted the series at $3,000 an episode, unprecedented for a sustaining program in a local market. The surrounding cast was assembled with actor-musician Leon Belasco, perennial heavy Ben Welden, blustery Dick Elliott, and radio's Alan Reed, who would go on to fame as the voice of Fred Flintstone. Former child actor Philippe De Lacy signed on as director, with freelance producer Joe Parker pulling it all together.

The second revision of the script by Clyde Bruckman and actor-writer Henry Taylor was finalized on the day of broadcast. Advance press said Buster would speak just two words that night: "Ladies and . . ."

From the review in *Daily Variety:*

> An old-timer came into his own last night over a new medium. And it looks like television has a new "must-see" program, very likely to become a permanent fixture. Buster Keaton is the old-timer and the new *Buster Keaton Show* is the vehicle. Keaton has lost none of his touch with the passing years. Little Sad-Face is still one of the really great pantomimists of the era, and the television camera proves a perfect medium to catch those mannerisms and expressions, if last night's work was a criterion. . . . Opening show was built around ad agency topper (Elliott) hiring players for a show for a macaroni sponsor. Keaton is hired as star, Reed as emcee, and Belasco as maestro. Ben Welden is a temperamental prop man. Keaton delivered his best pratfalls and twisted his magic face to the howls of studio audience as rehearsals on show got under way.

The Buster Keaton Show came off so well that the Studebaker Dealers of Los Angeles County signed on as sponsors commencing with the January 5 broadcast. Keaton was pleased. "One of the reasons I stopped making movies [back in the thirties] was because there were too many cooks in the kitchen," he told United Press' Alice Mosby. "In the old days only three of us made my movies. Any more people and it's poison. . . . Arbuckle, Lloyd, Chaplin, Langdon—all their pictures were made by only three men, too. It's not that way today. On television I can go back to creating my own show. Only three of us are working on it."

the
BUSTER KEATON
show

thurs 8 pm

channel 11 KTTV

Despite the rosy outlook, the sixteen-week run of *The Buster Keaton Show* was roiled by departures and station politics. Alan Reed withdrew after four weeks due to "contractual differences," producer Joe Parker left after "strong words" with management, writer Al Manheimer came in to replace him but lasted only a week, the show itself was moved ahead an hour on the program schedule and relocated to the El Patio Theatre on Hollywood Boulevard, Parker returned after the show limped along for five weeks without a producer, and the show's proposed syndication plan never got off the ground. Through it all, Keaton struggled to come up with twenty-five minutes of weekly content.

"The biggest thing that any comedian has got in television is diggin' up material," he said. "I'll give you an idea: It's that I used to make eight two-reelers a year. Well, a two-reeler was a half-hour show. Well, now when television comes along, they want thirty-nine of those a year. Well, there's only one way you can get material. I mean just hiring writers and gagmen don't solve the problem. You've got to start repeating and stealing. Anything you can think of. Like, 'Well, we did that three or four weeks ago in a drug store; the next time we'll do it in a butcher shop.' And we change the backgrounds for gags or steal gags right and left!"

Bruckman and his various collaborators—Taylor, Ben Perry, Elwood Ullman, Jay Sommers—did the best they could, but they could only hint at the physical stuff, the specifics of which generally fell to Keaton to work out. As to dialogue, it turned out the two words he spoke on the first show were about all he cared to say. "And on future shows I'll kill dialogue whenever I can," he vowed. "I don't go out of my way to talk."

In desperation, Keaton recruited Harold Goodwin as his writing partner. "They were paying the writers to write the stuff that we'd ignore," Goodwin remembered. "There was one show where he gets his diploma [and] he's a private detective. It was a funny show, and we wrote it over at Buster's house—Buster, Eleanor and I. This was a pip. And when the writer came on to see his rehearsed show he said, 'That's a rewrite of a rewrite!'"

The final broadcast took place on April 6, 1950. "Buster got into this straitjacket. It was a haunted house thing. . . . Buster'd had a little too much to drink, and he fell on the floor in the straitjacket and cut his head. We had to go right on with the show and rush him off stage. That was the last show we did."

It wasn't the end of the road—everyone agreed the show would return in the fall—but something had to be done about the weekly grind. "It's the quickest way to Forest Lawn that I know of," Keaton said. "Trying to dig up material for that weekly show. The first few are easy. Then it starts to get tough."

A hopeful sign was KTTV's ten-year lease of the Nassour Studios at Sunset and Van Ness, a small but modern independent movie studio suited for production of the kind of filmed programming needed for syndication.* The deal was worked out by Norman Chandler, publisher of the *Los Angeles Times,* which owned 51 percent of the station to CBS's 49 percent. The first two shows on the production docket at the new facility would be the second season of the Keaton series and *Pantomime Quiz Time,* which was already being seen via kinescope in New York. As if to underscore the importance of the show's continuing, the March 13 issue of *Life* devoted three pages to a photo layout of Keaton at work, including a traditionally verboten shot of him breaking into a broad smile.

Keaton was still at liberty in June when he came across a funny hat he thought Ed Wynn would like for his collection and took it over to him at the CBS Playhouse.

"Where do you keep your stage wardrobe?" Wynn urgently wanted to know. He had no finish for the show that was to go on that night and needed Buster's help. They had booked five silent comics to pose as the original Keystone Cops for a pie-throwing finale, but nothing his writing staff—which included Hal Kanter and Seaman Jacobs—came up with was working. As Keaton raced home, he considered how Wynn usually ended his show by coming out in a nightshirt and nightcap and getting into bed. That night, after Wynn had personally displayed the credits for what would

---

* In the days before videotape, the only way to record a live broadcast was to aim a 16mm camera at a video tube and capture it that way. The quality, of course, left much to be desired. It was widely felt a kinescope couldn't deliver the detail necessary to put Keaton across on a TV screen when shot in full figure, which is what he always insisted upon.

be his final show of the season, Keaton appeared, unannounced, to say he had another credit: PIES BY HELMS BAKERY.

"What pies?" asked Wynn.

"The pies," responded Buster, "that we're going to teach you how to throw."

The curtain behind Wynn and his bed rose to reveal all five cops with pies in their hands.

"All kiddin' aside," Keaton assured him, "there's a science to pie throwing. There's an art to it." He called for a volunteer, and Hank Mann, the only member of the group who was legitimately one of the early Keystone Cops, stepped forward. Keaton proceeded to demonstrate "the slow burn," a deliberate shove straight into his face. Next came Keystone veteran Chester Conklin, who received a "shot put," fast and messy. Then Roscoe "Tiny" Ward, who never worked for Sennett but whose towering frame forced Keaton to back away ten or twelve feet so that it was "like a throw to second base." Finally, Heinie Conklin—no relation to Chester—stepped forward as Buster coached Wynn into delivering "a walking thrust." The payoff came when a man stepped into the line of fire and Wynn landed the pie squarely in the face of CBS Chairman William S. Paley (as impersonated by Hal Kanter). Though hastily assembled, Keaton's four-minute segment inspired more laughter than the entire show that preceded it.

Later that month, plans were announced for the continuation of the Keaton series on 35mm film. Norman Chandler was driving the creation of a loose network of twenty stations owned by major newspapers. Production bids were being solicited from outside producers for the making of a pilot, which was to be filmed in July. Then Chandler changed course and formed a company of his own, Consolidated Television Productions, to produce the pilot at a reported cost of $25,000. Mal St. Clair was set to direct the show, with Clyde Bruckman in the role of writer-producer. KTTV, being controlled by the *Times,* which was in turn controlled by the Chandler family, gave Consolidated first refusal on all of the station's shows that could be shot on film. Contracts between the station, the packagers, and Leo Morrison, representing Keaton, were signed on August 7, 1950.

Frustrated by all the delays, Keaton signed another week-to-week contract with M-G-M, specifically to consult on a new Red Skelton picture titled *Excuse My Dust.* He worked with director Roy Rowland and screenwriter George Wells to gag up specific scenes in the script and to help visualize a road race staged with antique cars. (Toward the end of the race, Skelton gets a sudden thought and tells actress Sally Forrest: "Throw out the tool box," explaining that his gas mobile will go faster if it's not carrying so much weight. She throws out tools, then gets the idea of throwing herself out too.) The Skelton job took fifteen days, and Keaton went off the Metro payroll for the final time on September 15.

The pilot for the filmed version of *The Buster Keaton Show* was shot in early October at the new KTTV studios. The setup had Buster working for a tyrannical boss in a sporting goods store. Ineptly, he attempts to wrap a fishing pole and assemble a tent, and manages to get himself challenged to a grudge match with two popular wrestlers of the day—Lord Jan Blears, a snobbish monocle-wearing Brit who invented the Oxford leg strangle, and George Scott, better known as the Great Scott, a Canadian grappler who wore his hair long and blond and bounded into the ring wearing plaid trunks. Frequently seen on TV, Blears and Scott made inexpensive guest stars as well as durable foils for a burlesque tag team match in which Killer Keaton and Sluggy Slugger (stuntman Harvey Parry) faced the two men with predictable results. With a pilot finally in the can, the Keatons left for New York, where a round of TV appearances awaited them.

On November 5, 1950, Buster was on Ed Sullivan's *Toast of the Town,* the first of several guest shots he would make on the program. Sullivan, who was a New York newspaperman and Broadway columnist in Keaton's heyday, was a genuine fan and wanted his viewers to be as excited as he.

"You know, back when I was a youngster, one of the great comics of show business was called Buster Keaton. Now your fathers and mothers will remember him—I know you youngsters won't—but Keaton had a very unique style of comedy. In the first place, he was a poker face. (When I speak about a poker face, I feel that I'm in charge . . .) But on top of that, his pantomime, his understanding of comedy and his timing set him apart in what was then an infant industry, just as TV is now. So it's with the greatest sense of pleasure that tonight—making not his TV debut because he was on Ed Wynn's show out on the coast and he was a tremendous hit—a great sense of pleasure that *I* present him on this stage. And I want to call him out here before he goes on and have you meet him formally. And I want you to give him the biggest hand that's ever been given to a great performer—Buster Keaton, come on out here! I want you to meet the folks!"

Keaton emerged, acknowledged the audience, and spoke a few words. Sullivan asked him what he was going to do. "Oh, I'm not goin' to do anything," he replied. "I'm goin' fishin'." Whereupon the curtains parted to reveal a small pond. He took his place on a platform and proceeded to fuss with his pole, his hook, and his bait, taking several hard falls into the water (and onto the floor) while progressively drenching himself. Keaton had previously done the sketch on TV in Los Angeles, where the pond was bigger and more realistic-looking. (In New York it looked more like a children's wading pool.)

"Only when he toyed with a splinter, climaxing with his donning an enormous bandage which entangled his gear, was there some of the brilliance of the silent film comedies," *Variety* commented. If the bit wasn't particularly strong, at least it was new to most of the country, and it heralded his return to the public eye in a big way.

The following week, Keaton was the uncontested hit of the Sullivan show as he reprised the famous scene from *Spite Marriage* with Eleanor, perfectly limp, as the woman he tries to put to bed. Having cleared a contractual blackout period, he was on Garry Moore's afternoon show the following day, Ed Wynn's *4 Star Revue* on Wednesday, and *Stop the Music* on Thursday.

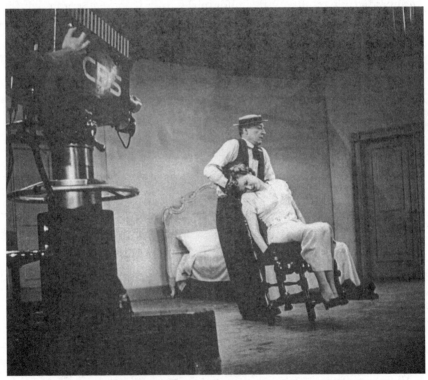

Performing the Spite Marriage *routine with Eleanor on Ed Sullivan's* Toast of the Town *in 1950.*

"I averaged two shows a week," he said of their New York sojourn, "with the lowest pay $750 a shot (when rehearsal was necessary) and $2,000 a Sunday from Sullivan." For his third *Toast of the Town* appearance, on December 10, he offered an atypical bit of pathos as a department store Santa laboriously donning his shabby costume in hopes of finding seasonal work.

"He was going crazy trying to write all these things all by himself and get it organized," said Eleanor. "They're sketches, one or two he repeated, but mostly he's trying to work out sketches to do on these shows. There might have been a couple of interview things, but mostly it was sketch work on the show. And he had to do everything by himself, work with the prop man to get all the props ready, everything. So by the time we got down to December, he was a basket case. We finally left New York and got home Christmas Eve. He was exhausted. With good reason."

As Keaton put it: "I became, I think, the year's No. 1 guest star."

The decision to put *The Buster Keaton Show* on 35mm film made it imperative to sell the series into other markets before going back into production. Norman Chandler and Consolidated president J. Bert Easley had covered the cost of the pilot but were unwilling to front the money to make another twelve shows when shooting on film added as much as $5,000 an episode to the budget. Twelve stations were lined up in November 1950, grouped as Publishers Television Syndicate, but capitalization of $1 million wasn't finalized until February 1951. The first series to go before the cameras would be a quarter-hour children's show, with a soap opera to follow and some religious fare for the Protestant Film Commission. Keaton and Bruckman went back to work, preparing scripts to be shot at the rate of one a week. The great advantage of the new arrangement would be a consistent level of picture quality, infinitely superior to kinescope. The big drawback: no studio audience.

Filming began in April 1951, with Bruckman serving as producer under an executive producer named Carl K. Hittleman, a writer whose résumé consisted almost entirely of cheap westerns. With no background in comedy, Hittleman nevertheless imposed himself on the writing process, pushing Bruckman aside. Things did not go well from the start. Harold Goodwin, who was in some of the live shows, was present for the shooting of the pilot with the two wrestlers.

"We shot that in one day, that whole show," Goodwin remembered. "So then, after the show got a sponsor, Hittleman wanted us to make them *all* in one day. *One day* . . . and this is comedy, this is not just stuff where you stand and read dialogue. That caused a lot of trouble because we went into overtime. My God, we were working from eight o'clock in the morning until eleven or twelve o'clock at night. They were pretty bad."

The British-born director, Arthur Hilton, had been an editor at Universal, where he cut the W. C. Fields comedies and was nominated for an Oscar for editing *The Killers*. Hilton knew how the shows were going to go together, but he was of little help to Keaton in the staging of gags.

"Buster knew the shows weren't good," said Goodwin. "And I was partly responsible for talking him into it . . . Clyde Bruckman and I . . . but Clyde was through. He'd lost his creativeness. We made some horrible things—some turkeys. Buster hated Carl Hittleman. He said, 'I won't work with him on the set.' He just took a dislike to the guy, and this same fellow said to me: 'Here's a comic who's been in show business forty-five years and doesn't know why he's funny.' Now that was a pretty dumb statement."

The filmed series burned through material at a worse rate than the live shows because it lacked the considerable advantage of an audience. "It didn't look up to date," said Keaton. "It just looked old-fashioned, but the same material done in front of a live audience. . . . You're looking at just a dead machine when you do it with just a silent camera.* And the canned laughs are absolutely no good at all. . . . But the live audience, that's a different proposition. And the same material, I only need two-thirds of it—I can eliminate a third of the material—to do a half-hour show. Work it to a silent camera . . . all right, now do the same material to a live audience and I can throw one-third of that material away and save it for the next show . . . Their reaction will make you work to 'em, which you don't do to a silent camera, but you do to an audience . . . They space it for you. When you spy a laugh is going to come up, you don't hurt that laugh, you help build it. I slide right past it to a silent camera."

The stories put Buster in the Wild West, in a time machine, in a haunted house, and in the army once again, but the physical comedy in which he had no peer was supplanted by labored verbal exchanges. An air of desperation

---

* The problem in working to a single camera was solved a few months later when Desi Arnaz envisioned three cameras covering the action simultaneously, making it practical to film before a live audience. The show, of course, was *I Love Lucy*, which went into production in September 1951.

crept into the proceedings, as if all they were really doing was just grinding film.

"They weren't spending any money on them," said Eleanor, "and they gave us a director and editor who didn't do much but stand around. Buster and the script clerk were the ones who really made those shows. The script clerk was a dear lady who had been around for years and knew what she was doing."

The second season of *The Buster Keaton Show* debuted in Los Angeles on May 9, 1951, while the series was still in production. Reaction varied; Walter Ames of the *Los Angeles Times* caught an advance screening of the pilot and thought it "one of the funniest shows on the airwaves."

The detective episode, which was actually the first televised, was caught by *Variety,* which had a vastly different reaction: "These are the kind of film quickies that give Hollywood a bad name. For a town that aspires someday to be the television capital, this is a sorry trailer."

The show was still well-enough regarded to attract a regional sponsor in the American Vitamin Association, which secured five stations in Ohio for the run of the series, and in Vanity Fair Tissues, which covered a run over WNAC in Boston. The show was also cleared for Pittsburgh, where it was sponsored by the Duquesne Brewing Company. By the last of June, *The Buster Keaton Show* was airing on seventeen stations.

Keaton no longer appeared to care. He turned in the final show of the series on June 2 and, ignoring plans for another set of thirteen, left the same day for an eight-week variety tour of Great Britain under contract to Stoll Theatres. With options, he and Eleanor would be gone for three months, time enough, he hoped, for Consolidated Television Productions to forget all about him. The tour began on June 18 in Leicester, with Buster and Eleanor doing the *Spite Marriage* scene that went over so well on the Sullivan show. Other stops were made at Chiswick, Wood Green, Manchester, Derby, Cardiff, Shepherd's Bush, and Hackney.

Upon conclusion of the Stoll tour, Keaton was recruited by impresario Bernard Delfont for an old-timers' show called *Do You Remember?* that carried him, and such British favorites as George Robey, Hetty King, and Wee Georgie Wood, through most of August. In Newcastle, Keaton faced a decision to remain with the thriving show—in which he was top billed—or to return to New York, where he had TV offers lined up, including another *Toast of the Town.* To Buster, it wasn't a hard call.

"I could never get a hot meal," he said of the provinces. "It was either too early or too late in every hotel I stayed at. I had cold sandwiches for ten weeks. And they never seem to have heard of room service." And it irked him to be bunched in with the geriatric set when he was only in his mid-fifties. "It's like walking on your own grave."

Buster Keaton was once asked how it felt to get back into pictures under Charlie Chaplin's direction. "Oh, old home week," he said warmly. In December 1951, Chaplin sent for him to discuss a scene in his new film, a drama of the English music halls called *Limelight*. The two men embraced; there was always great affection between them.

"He seemed astonished at my appearance," Keaton recalled. "Apparently he expected to see a physical and mental wreck." Fresh from his tours of Britain and a round of guest shots in New York, the man before him was feeling rested and prosperous, hardly someone on his uppers who hadn't worked in years.

"What *have* you been doing, Buster?" Chaplin asked. "You look in such fine shape."

"Do you look at television, Charlie?"

The answer, of course, was no. Chaplin wouldn't have one in the house. And he couldn't understand how working in such a lowly medium would be of benefit to anyone. "But, Buster," he pressed, "tell me, how do you manage to stay in such good shape? What makes you so spry?"

"Television."

Abruptly, the subject got changed. "Now," said Chaplin, "about this sequence we're going to do together . . ."

Charlie Chaplin had abandoned his tramp character after *The Great Dictator*, released eleven years earlier. In the interim he made only a single feature, a sardonic comedy about a serial killer titled *Monsieur Verdoux*. James Agee considered it a masterpiece, but it had gone begging at the box office, Chaplin's first commercial failure. And now, four years hence, he was preparing to spring a stark drama with comic interludes on a moviegoing public that had lost its taste for him. In the story, Chaplin's character is Calvero, an aging comedian with a history of alcoholism. When he is discovered performing on the streets, he is offered a benefit performance, which he sees as a chance at a comeback. On the evening of the show, he does several of his classic routines to great acclaim. Then comes the encore, a two-hander with another old-timer, and together the pair manage to bring down the house.

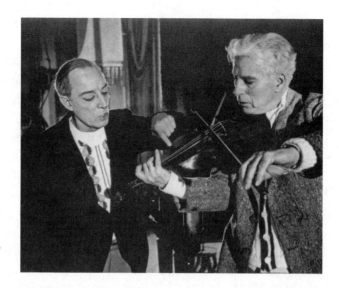

*Working with
Charlie Chaplin
during the filming of*
Limelight *(1952).*

"Charlie was debating throughout the picture," said Jerry Epstein, one of Chaplin's two assistants. "He knew he had to get someone for the part [of Calvero's partner]. He kept seeing someone on the set who was Sydney Chaplin's stand-in . . . and he kept saying, 'That guy's got something. I bet he can play it.' But he wasn't too certain." They had been shooting for several weeks when Keaton's name came up. "I think the production manager on the picture [Lonnie D'Orsa] suggested Buster Keaton, and Chaplin heard he was a little hard up at the time and said, 'Yeah, bring him in.'"

Once Keaton was set, Chaplin sketched a wordless routine that, when typed, ran to slightly less than a page and a half. Much of what he envisioned amounted to business—Keaton's elderly, nearsighted pianist struggling with a slippery stack of music, Chaplin's rusty fiddler dealing with limbs that retract and have to be yanked back to length, piano wires that stubbornly refuse to be tuned and seemingly snap at will. It amounted to a scripted improvisation, something to serve as a starting point for two master pantomimists when they got on the set.

"That sequence was a very, very difficult sequence to do, the two of them together," said Epstein. "Buster came on the first day wearing his Buster Keaton hat, ready to go, and Charlie took him aside and said, 'Buster, this is not [that] kind of picture. We're playing different parts now. We're not playing the old thing.' And he said, 'Yes, Charlie, of course. Sure. Of course. Anything you want.' [Which is] what was sweet about him. It was like his first picture. He had all this enthusiasm of starting in pictures again, and that was terribly endearing. . . . The crew just loved it, seeing Keaton and Chaplin working together."

Keaton joined the picture on December 22, playing a brief dialogue scene with Chaplin in Calvero's dressing room. Others working that day included actress Claire Bloom, a Chaplin discovery making only her second appearance in a movie; Sydney Chaplin, Charlie's son; and veteran actors Nigel Bruce and Norman Lloyd. The company broke for the Christmas holiday, and Keaton subsequently occupied the background in theater scenes shot on a standing set at the RKO-Pathé studios in Culver City.

"His reserve was extreme, as was his isolation," wrote Claire Bloom. "He remained to himself on the set, until one day, to my astonishment, he took from his pocket a color postcard of a large Hollywood mansion and showed it to me. It was the sort of postcard that tourists pick up in Hollywood drugstores. In the friendliest, most intimate way, he explained to me that it had once been his home. That was it. He retreated back into silence and never addressed a word to me again."

Keaton had been on the film twenty days, some of them on holiday, others on hold, when Chaplin was finally ready to shoot the routine at the core of the picture's final act. Arrayed in antique formal wear, musty and ill-fitting, they determinedly take the stage, Buster stooped and plodding with thick glasses and moustache, leaves of music stuffed under his arm, Charlie a portly, grotesque figure with bow and instrument in hand. And even though Chaplin was ill with the flu, running a fever and dripping with perspiration, it took just two days to get the entire sequence in the can.

"There was this kind of unconscious communication that went on," said Norman Lloyd. "Not much talk. They would look and do something, then do it again. No talk. No Stanislavsky. There was a kind of communication between them that was unspoken. But it happened as they would adjust the routine—maybe more music or maybe Charlie wanted to pull the pants up higher or whatever. But then—'No, we'll do it again.' And Buster would keep adding stuff at the piano with having more music falling all over the place."

The routine ends in applause and death, Calvero working himself into such a lather he tumbles off the edge of the stage and lands in a bass drum, from which he continues to play. They haul him up and carry him off, drum and all, to the laughs and the cheers of the audience. He has hurt his back, he thinks, but as he lies on a couch in his dressing room, the doctor determines he's had a heart attack. While an ambulance is summoned, he asks to be carried to the wings to watch the performance of a ballerina he's mentored. And there he dies. As the body is covered with a sheet, the camera pulls back to include those surrounding him, principally Keaton, Sydney Chaplin, Norman Lloyd, and Nigel Bruce. It continues out onto the stage where Claire Bloom, in mid-performance, twirls into the shot.

It was a deceptively complicated movement that momentarily summoned the filmmaker in Keaton. "The camera," said Lloyd, "was on Charlie—centered on him—and, as we were going backwards, with no dialogue, just music, I heard a voice, very quiet, just above a whisper, saying, 'It's okay, Charlie. You're right in the center of the shot. Yeah, you're fine, Charlie. It's perfect. Right in the shot. Right in there . . .' That was Buster. He just volunteered that. He had nothing to do with the making of the shot at all, but he was directing that scene. He wanted to make sure that camera never got off Charlie. And he's making certain that Charlie gets his shot."

Keaton finished his part in *Limelight* on January 12, 1952. Chaplin wrapped the film thirteen days later, and began the lengthy process of winnowing more than 200,000 feet of exposed footage down to the 12,600 feet that would comprise the final cut. Keaton, recalled Claire Bloom, was "brilliantly alive with invention. Some of his gags may even have been a little too incandescent for Chaplin because, laugh as he did at the rushes in the screening room, Chaplin didn't see fit to allow them all into the final version of the film."

As Jerry Epstein clarified, "I was with him every second in the cutting room. He shot enough for ten films of material in that sequence. I used to say, 'How can you cut your gags when they were so funny?' He said, 'We've got to keep it going. You can't put in everything.' And it was always the narrative that meant more than anything else—no matter how funny the gag is. . . . Sure, he cut stuff of Keaton's out, but he cut just as brilliant stuff of his own out because he knew it had to be sharp and fast."

Ben Pearson, Keaton's agent for the last fifteen years of his life.

When the deal for *Limelight* was made, it was through an agent named Ben Pearson, who had been involved in packaging the syndicated *Buster Keaton Show* for a firm called Stempel-Olenick. Formerly a writer for radio, Pearson took over for Leo Morrison after Morrison lost Spencer Tracy as a client and decided to close up shop. "He was ready to retire," Eleanor said, "and he knew absolutely nothing—or wanted to know—about television coming in."

The Federal Television Corporation was formed as a talent agency and packager with Buster Collier serving as president for a time and Pearson as vice president. It was Pearson who told Keaton he thought Chaplin's offer—$1,000 for either one or two weeks—was on the cheap side for a billed appearance, but Buster said he would have done it for nothing. With the completion of *Limelight,* Keaton did something that would have horrified Chaplin. He made a flurry of live television appearances, managing six guest shots in the space of two weeks. The highest profile of these was Ken Murray's "Salute to Movietime, U.S.A." over on CBS, on which he reprised the molasses sketch, this time with comic Billy Gilbert in the role of the proprietor, and once again incorporating the "Butcher Boy" fall.

There would be more TV in the coming months, but nothing to rival the impact of an appreciation by *Herald Tribune* drama critic Walter Kerr that appeared in the May issue of *Harper's Bazaar.* Its title was "Last Call for a Clown."

"This is a love letter," Kerr began, "some years late. But if I don't get it off now, it may come altogether too late to do anyone much good. The curator of the Museum of Modern Art film library will tell you that the print of Buster Keaton's *The Navigator* is wearing out. Unless an additional print can be uncovered in some unlikely vault, or unless a great deal of money is forthcoming to make possible a transfer onto fresh stock, no one is ever again going to see one of the two or three best films Keaton made. No one is ever again going to see one of the funniest—albeit one of the shortest—sustained shots in the history of the films. Keaton is the object of this love letter."

While taking nothing from Chaplin, Kerr went on to deconstruct Langdon and, particularly, Lloyd, whom he saw as a symbol of his time rather than of the present. "We look at the man without very much recognition. The American image of itself has altered too profoundly in the intervening years for us to make spontaneous connection with this figure who was once so appealing, and Lloyd is somewhat trapped—as art, in its universals, is never trapped—in a passing phase. Keaton emerges the artist."

The Keaton "mask" in Kerr's estimation had a meaning. "It stood for stubbornness in the face of a tricky, hostile, and oversized universe. . . . Behind the mask is an alert mind. It is a suspicious mind which expects the worst and is constantly on the *qui vive* against the next unpredictable, but inevitable, blow. But it is not a panicky mind; it is in full control of itself, unwavering, steady. When the blow falls, neither the mind nor the body recoils in terror."

Kerr admitted his own rediscovery of Keaton came late, and that he was dubious about it. He recalled seeing *The General* as a teen and thinking it was good but not sensational. "A few years ago, through the services of the Museum of Modern Art, I saw *The General* again. I couldn't believe my eyes. It not only hadn't dated; it was funnier than it had been the first time." Distrusting his own objectivity, Kerr tried the film out on a group of graduate students he was teaching, mixing in examples of Langdon and Lloyd as well. After a reel or so, they had abandoned their notebooks and forgotten completely they were watching a twenty-year-old comedy. "*The General* was, quite literally, the funniest film these people weaned on talking films had ever seen."

Which brought him full circle to the point he made at the beginning. "The Museum of Modern Art, in its film footnotes, speaks of the 'brilliance' of Keaton's style—an estimate it is impossible not to go along with once you have renewed acquaintance with the work—but in most quarters Chaplin is revered, Keaton forgotten. Keaton's point of view is as defined as Chaplin's, and every movement he makes, every frame of film in which he appears, belongs to it. If Chaplin was the little man doomed to be crushed, Keaton was the little man who *couldn't* be crushed. . . . His imagination is everywhere stamped on the work: in the story, in the direction, even in the subtitles. The unity that followed from this practice of pursuing a single vision—the comedian's—raised the best silent comedies to a level of art no longer possible in the collaborative manufacture of the large studios. Hollywood became an assembly line, went in for piecework. Chaplin maintained his integrity, at a certain cost in technical proficiency, by holding onto his own studio and his own releasing organization. Keaton got lost in the vast shuffle of Metro-Goldwyn-Mayer.

"A lot of Keaton is already gone for good. A laboratory fire wiped out his two-reelers and some of the early features, *Three Ages* among them. *The Navigator* may not be long for this world. Better hurry around next time the Museum is showing *The Navigator, The General,* or *Our Hospitality.* A great man is slipping away from you."

Montreal, Quebec

SEPTEMBER 16, 1964

T IS THE KIND OF GAG Buster Keaton was known for in his prime—bold and mechanical, with an element of danger to it. Gerald Potterton thought of it and had drawn it up as a storyboard.

"The cameraman, Bob Humble, and myself, we took a trip out together," he recalled. "We researched as much as we could. Went from coast to coast checking out some key places and thinking: We could do this at this point, and that at that point. Things like this big sight gag I wanted to do."

Completed in 1959, the Saint Lawrence Seaway extends from the Port of Montreal to Lake Erie, the critical portion of a waterway designed to connect the Atlantic Ocean to the Great Lakes via a system of locks, canals, and channels. The Saint Lambert Lock is the first of seven locks in the Saint Lawrence River, and over it runs the venerable Victoria Bridge, more than three kilometers long, that links Montreal to the south shore city of Saint Lambert. At the entrance to the lock, the south end of the Victoria becomes a vertical lift bridge to permit oceangoing ships to pass through, and this is where Potterton has visualized his gag.

"Where the railroad crosses the bridge, with all these iron girders and skyscrapers in the background, there is this huge [elevator] which lifts up, high into the air, nearly two hundred feet up, to allow the big ships to go underneath. After I'd storyboarded the sequence for Buster to actually stop on that little piece of track—he runs out of gas or something—and the next thing we know, he's going up into the air, well over a hundred feet up on this thing, so that a ship can pass underneath. Well, the Saint Lawrence Seaway people wouldn't let us do it. They said it was too dangerous and blah, blah,

blah. And Buster said, 'God, I could have done that in my sleep.' So that was a problem for us. We had to panic and find something else."

They must settle for shots of Keaton shooting across the Victoria Bridge on the speeder, Montreal in the background. Then, on the other side of the river, they locate a little-used swing bridge, built in 1915, that spans the Lachine Canal and connects Montreal's Central Station to the railyards of Pointe-Saint-Charles. Here is where Keaton can come to a stop and fuss with his vehicle, never noticing that the bridge is slowly swinging open. He peers under the hood, wields a gigantic wrench, produces a stick from his pocket and checks the fuel level. As a tug passes through he is cranking away, oblivious to the action around him. The bridge begins to move back into position while he is picking through the contents of the boot. The tracks meet once more, and he is off without the slightest delay.

"It always amazes me when those tracks come back again for him to continue his journey. If you check that, as soon as that track clicks into place, he boots the machine up and clicks over. His timing is so . . . it's magic."

To Potterton, however, the gag is not what he envisioned, and the substitute, however deftly accomplished, is not as satisfying. "It was fine," he allowed, "but it was sort of a disappointment for me because, you know, us animators, when we storyboard something, we like to see it at least get as close to the real thing as we can."

Three days later, at Wakefield, past Ottawa, Potterton has his chance to pull off a gag exactly as illustrated. Rounding a turn, Keaton passes a fine dining establishment overlooking the Gatineau River. Shot from inside the restaurant, he can be seen through the windows looking in, standing motionless on the speeder as it trundles past. It's a still life in motion, with nobody paying the slightest attention. Inspired, he decides it's time for dinner and lays out his place setting, tablecloth and all, as the speeder continues on down the track. "That particular section was actually on the Canadian Pacific line. They kindly let us use their line; otherwise it was all Canadian National from east to west. I knew exactly what I wanted with that, and it worked very well."

Coming together, The Railrodder is a gentle film, whimsical and contemplative, with none of the comic violence that characterized Keaton's work as a young man.

"He was known as 'the Little Iron Man' around the studio," Eleanor Keaton tells the documentarians. "Nothing stopped him. Or there wasn't anything he didn't try. He slowed down, and come around to the line of thinking that he can do other, smaller-type things, or less dangerous things, that can be *almost* as funny. Why, he might not consider them as funny as falling off the whole top of a building or something, like he might have done earlier, but they're funny enough to get by. . . ."

Part Four

THE BIGGEST STAR
IN THE PICTURE

24

Along Came Television

A ND SO IT BEGAN.
　　If James Agee's 1949 essay was a broad historic appraisal tinged with nostalgia, Walter Kerr's 1952 bookend was a hard-nosed reconsideration wrapped in a clarion call to action. To Kerr's understanding, one of the great treasures of the silent screen was on the verge of extinction, and something had to be done. There were small, imperceptible moves at first, but they were important first steps in an effort that would, over time, snowball.

Buster Keaton Productions, Inc., successor to the Comique Film Company, was dissolved in 1940, two years after Keaton himself signed away all rights and claims for the sum of $1,000. At that time, all the holdings, which consisted mainly of copyrights and the residual rights to stories and plays, were transferred to Loew's executives David Bernstein and Leopold Friedman, two of the original stockholders, as trustees under a trust agreement. Bernstein, vice president and treasurer of Loew's, Metro-Goldwyn-Mayer, and a hundred subsidiaries, died in 1945, leaving Friedman, Loew's general counsel and secretary, the sole surviving trustee.

The last distribution to the owners and their heirs had taken place in 1944—based on the sale of some old equipment—and the trust that resulted from the liquidation of Keaton Productions and its assets came to life only once thereafter when, in 1948, M-G-M briefly contemplated remaking *The Navigator* and sought Friedman's permission to copy the Museum of Modern Art's print, the one Walter Kerr feared was unique. Around the same time, Joe Schenck advised Friedman that Buster Keaton was hopeful of selling Warner Bros. on the idea of remaking the same property with Danny Kaye.

"I gave Buster an option on *Navigator* for $5,000 for 6 months," Schenck wrote. "Know it's low, but want to give him an opportunity to make some money."

Friedman, possibly out of loyalty to M-G-M, promptly put the kibosh on the deal. "I cannot consider giving Keaton an option on *The Navigator*," he responded, "as there is no provision for the stockholders."

On September 4, 1952, five months after *Harper's Bazaar* hit the stands, Friedman made an inquiry regarding pictures he hadn't given a thought to in years. In a memo to M-G-M attorney Mark Avramo, he asked about the status of the copyrights to the Keaton features distributed by the studio. Four days later, Avramo responded with data "gleaned from the copyright cards in our files." *Three Ages,* he reported, had been registered with the Copyright Office in 1923 but not renewed when it became eligible in 1951.* *Our Hospitality, Sherlock Jr.,* and *The Navigator* had all been renewed, and *Seven Chances* was currently eligible for renewal. For all the others, Avramo provided the dates they would become eligible.

Friedman then asked assistant secretary Harold Cleary to assemble "all of the information regarding Buster Keaton pictures and what the rights are of the corporation as well as Buster Keaton individually." It was Cleary who turned up documents showing that pictures made by Buster Keaton Productions and distributed by Metro reverted to Keaton Productions after five years. He also discovered that Keaton was personally entitled to 25 percent of the profits, although he wasn't yet aware that Keaton had signed away all rights in 1938. As Buster and Eleanor sailed for Europe to fulfill a three-week engagement with Cirque Médrano and attend the London premiere of *Limelight,* they were completely unaware that any of this was happening.

Buster Keaton's uneasy relationship with television continued. He adored the live broadcasts, particularly the ones with audiences that took on the look and excitement of theatrical turns, but hadn't yet solved the puzzle of delivering a weekly half hour of physical comedy.

---

* At the time, the initial term of copyright protection was twenty-eight years from the date of publication. In the twenty-eighth year, the copyright owner could apply to the Copyright Office for a renewal for another term of twenty-eight years.

Keaton with Lucille Ball and Desi Arnaz on the set of I Love Lucy. *In 1950, he helped Ball get an act together that she performed during a brief vaudeville tour with husband Arnaz. The routine, in which she played a "loaded" cello, was incorporated into the show's unaired pilot as well as episode six of the series' first season.*

"With a million writers in Hollywood, there aren't two left who can write for me," he lamented. "When sound pictures and radio came in, they switched from situation writing to joke telling. Pantomime writers are a vanished breed."

Consolidated Television Productions had ceased operations after reportedly sinking $500,000 into twenty-six weeks of children's programming and *The Buster Keaton Show*. Mercifully, the filmed series received scant exposure. Yet from a business standpoint, it refused to go away. After Consolidated folded as a production entity, another firm, Crown Pictures International, came along and bought all thirteen of the Keaton films, with the idea of mastering a relaunch. Under its former name, Exclusive Distributors, Crown had been one of the pioneers in bringing theatrical features to TV. Now the company wanted to develop original filmed product for video and saw the Keaton series as a bridge between distribution and production. It was an audacious plan. Rather than merely picking up the series and giving it wider distribution, Crown would pretend the earlier series, under the title *The Buster Keaton Show*, never existed, and that the old episodes were, in fact, new episodes. Freelance editor Stuart O'Brien was assigned the job of repackaging the films, which he did by giving the series a new name, *Life with Buster Keaton,* and coming up with rudimentary titles for the individual episodes. Once the initial thirteen were successful, Crown would seek financing to make another twenty-six.

Keaton, meanwhile, thought he had a better idea for a series that could inspire a full season's worth of material. Earlier, he had scribbled out a concept for a show called *School of Acting,* which would be done in the style of *The Drunkard.* The host would be a combination director–leading man who would select a cast from the studio audience and have them perform a one-act melodrama. Now he massaged that idea into a format for himself. He would be the actor-manager of a little theater company in the San Fernando Valley and play the lead roles in parodies of old stories like *Count of Monte Cristo, Human Hearts, Mutiny on the Bounty,* and *Ben-Hur.*

"I will, of course, play Ben-Hur," he said. "We'll put the chariots on treadmills. I'll race either Ed Wynn or Jimmy Durante."

Crown's gambit with the old Keaton series almost paid off. Under the title *Life with Buster Keaton,* the show was picked up by the Du Mont network affiliate in New York, where it premiered on December 4, 1952. The pilot episode was given the title "The Collapsible Clerk," and the trades obligingly reviewed it as if it were brand-new. But the show proved to be an even tougher sell the second time around, and markets that formerly had the series under its original title wouldn't bite again. Keaton was more widely seen in the early weeks of 1953 in *Paradise for Buster,* a thirty-eight-minute industrial he made at the old Essanay Studios in Chicago for the John Deere company. Directed by Del Lord, it was the sharp and funny story of a city dweller adjusting to farm life after inheriting a spread from his uncle, and it delighted rural audiences gathered for the company's annual showcase known as John Deere Day.

Life with Buster Keaton was such a flop for Crown Pictures International that the company attempted to recoup its investment by using the footage to cobble together a short feature titled *The Misadventures of Buster Keaton.* Released by British Lion, *Misadventures* was widely shown in the United Kingdom during the latter half of 1953 and was nominally released to television in the United States. For the rest of Keaton's life, the series that began as *The Buster Keaton Show* would pass through multiple owners and keep popping up on TV. It became, in fact, one of the most frequently seen things Keaton ever did, a dubious introduction to generations of film enthusiasts who might otherwise have been exposed to some of his silent classics.

. . .

Keaton's times with Cirque Médrano opened the whole of the European market to him, an audience more responsive to his work and seemingly more eager to see him than the domestic audience he once saw as primary. Buster and Eleanor began spending more time there, sometimes making multiple trips in a single year. In July 1953, they arrived in Italy for a series of dates, starting with a summer revue at Milan's Teatro Manzoni and working their way down to Livorno, a three-month tour in all. And the year 1954 began on the *Île de France* bound for Paris.

"He clowned spontaneously on the ship during a dance one evening out of sheer exuberance," the author Paul Gallico, a fellow passenger on the voyage, recalled. "Suddenly we saw him pantomiming the washing of the great plate-glass doors to the lounge. Then he continued on and polished the empty space where there wasn't any door. Such perfection of pantomime is rarely seen anymore today. With one accord, the passengers stopped dancing and burst into applause."

Buster was headed to his third stand with the Cirque Médrano, and then on to the Cirque Royal of Brussels. As they settled in at the George V, a reporter from the *Evening News* requested a short interview. Eleanor confirmed they would be staying a month, then moving on to Belgium. "After that, nothing is definitely decided, and we'll see what turns up."

She also seemed surprised to find that it was winter in Paris: "We haven't had time to see much of it, but I find it mighty cold."

Buster concurred: "Do you know when we got into Le Havre it was snowing? Not so funny."

Keaton opened on Friday, January 8, doing a "park bench" act, a sort of miscellany of bits kicked off when he entered the ring carrying a black evening suit on a hanger. The pompous red-coated ringmaster was in the midst of singing a song and ignored his attempts at making the delivery. As he continued, Buster circled him, receipt pad in hand, trying to get his attention. Soon, the garment was in a dusty heap on the ground, and the audience was choking with laughter. A window box full of flowers appeared. As Buster bent over to pick one, he was confronted by a menacing policeman. He tried to hide an enormous stolen balloon from the cop, then did battle with a gumball machine and an octopus of a newspaper. When he sat at the edge of the ring and attempted to watch the performance of another song, a burly stagehand motioned for him to move.

"The ringmaster chased him," remembered Billy Beck, an American-born clown at the Cirque, "and then the stagehands got into the chase, and Keaton began to run—first of all a circle-circuit of the ring, then out one of the entrance ways. One, two, three, four entrances into the ring, and that meant that he would run through the corridor, round underneath the seats, and come in through another entrance way to the stage. This went on, back and forth around, in and out entrance ways, into the seats, sitting in the seats, hiding behind the people in the seats while the stagehands were supposedly looking for him and couldn't find him. He finally disappeared and ended up among the [players in] the band, which is situated above the principal entrance where the artistes come in—which meant he had to run back through the corridors again and up a rickety old spiral staircase to where the band was situated. . . . When they discovered him in the band, the stagehands went up there and actually manhandled him from one to another down to the ring and then booted him out."

Gallico made a point of catching a performance: "I shouted with laughter for this was the Buster Keaton of my youth, now sixtyish, who could still fall backwards off a bench or trip on the ring's edge and end up in a flying forward somersault. This was my deadpan boy, hero of a hundred movies, frustration's mime, pursued, put upon, persecuted by humans as well as by objects suddenly possessed of a malevolent life and will of their own. The oldsters in the audience of Frenchmen laughed too, a double compliment because of what he had been and what he was. But there was another sound that rose above it all, the joyous screaming of children, and I thought that this was the greatest achievement for this wholly American clown in a foreign circus. For the small fry had never seen him or heard of him before, and wave upon wave of love and laughter went out from their hearts and throats to him."

Again he was a hit for the Cirque, filling the house twice daily. Yet when Jerome Médrano learned about the subsequent engagement in Brussels, from which Keaton would be collecting no traveling expenses and would be accepting less money, he was incensed. "He suggested I get off the hook by reducing my salary to the Brussels figure," Keaton recounted. "When I refused, he offered to book me for two weeks more on the condition that I cancel the Belgian engagement. This, of course, I could not conscientiously do, and monsieur's next move was to go to the police."

Médrano alleged breach of a 500,000-franc-a-week contract and had the Keatons' luggage impounded. "It was my agent's fault," Buster explained.

"I was booked two places at once. When the case came up, I was given a woman lawyer who figured it would be smart if I pleaded I was broke." He went to court the next day, saying he had received 100,000 francs on arrival but nothing since. "I have not got a cent to my name."

Médrano's leverage was a one-month contract with an option for an additional month. He had never exercised the option before, but this time he said that he would.

"I think he sued, or wanted to sue, or was going to sue the Cirque Royal in Brussels for stealing Buster," said Eleanor. "I don't know. It was a whole drama; it was terrible. . . . Médrano was a bastard. He always was."

Keaton got out of the scrape by reducing his rate to what Médrano demanded, but the resulting publicity paid an unexpected dividend. In England, the press coverage the incident provoked alerted Douglas Fairbanks, Jr., to the fact that Buster Keaton was nearby. He sent Keaton a telegram:

I AM MAKING A BIG SERIES OF HALF-HOUR FILMS FOR TV. WOULD LOVE YOU TO PLAY THE STAR PART. DEADLY SERIOUS. NO COMEDY BUT LOTS OF PATHOS.

"I'll do it," Keaton responded. "Of course I'll do it. But why does he tell me it's 'deadly serious'? Have I ever been anything else?"

The Keatons flew into London on March 8, 1954, and were immediately driven to the British National Studios at Elstree, where Buster would spend five days making an adaptation of Nikolai Gogol's influential short story "The Cloak." The syndicated anthology series produced and hosted by Fairbanks was in its second season, and Keaton's casting was serendipitous in that most episodes featured, with the exception of Fairbanks himself, British actors.

"It struck me as a beautiful idea, a novel idea, to put him in a straight part," said Fairbanks, "because he was such a beautiful actor and a great talent. It worked out very well; he gave a marvelous performance."

Larry Marcus' script, titled "The Awakening," took the premise of the aging bureaucrat whose life is transformed by a newly tailored overcoat and gave it a totalitarian setting with an Orwellian figure known as the Chief at its center. The clerk doesn't die as he does in the original, but instead dreams of confronting the Chief, whose supposed benevolence cloaks a brutally regimented society. The Chief's solution to the citizen's loss of his coat is to purge the officials of the departments dealing with the case.

Douglas Fairbanks, Jr.,
welcomes Keaton to the
British National Studios,
March 1954.

"Successful action has already been taken," he announces.

"And they'll still say my report has been properly filed and duly processed," Keaton's nameless character charges. "You can keep dismissing them, stripping them of all power, disgracing them, and replacing them until the end of time, and it still won't get my overcoat back. And when I protest they'll still throw me into prison—because it's not 'they.' They're just part of a machine, a machine that was to give us so much happiness. This machine that reduces a broken heart to a number in a catalogue, that says a hungry child is nothing more than 26583-Y. A machine that's forgotten what kindness, warmth, and pity mean . . ."

Keaton delivers the speech with startling intensity, the character's words and demeanor fitting him so well it was as if Marcus had written it expressly for him. Eleanor thought both he and the film great, but she didn't consider Buster's first serious part to be much of a stretch.

"He'd done a lot of TV," she said. "It was easy. In comedy he had to create everything. In drama you just learn your lines and let someone else do the worrying. Buster always had a dramatic quality about his work. He was always very serious."

Buster and Eleanor Keaton were stopping at the Hotel St. Moritz on New York's Central Park South when, on October 6, 1953, a man named Rudi Blesh paid a call. Blesh was primarily known as a jazz critic, having served in that capacity for the *San Francisco Chronicle* and the *New York Herald Tri-*

bune. He was also the author of two books on the subject, *Shining Trumpets*, published by Knopf in 1946 and, with Harriet Janis, *They All Played Ragtime*, published in 1950. Now, possibly inspired by the Walter Kerr essay, Blesh proposed to write a third—a full-scale biography of Buster Keaton.

"B. met me," Blesh recorded in a composition book, "shy and reticent at first—looks older, but still slender—hair only slightly gray but has bald spot at back. Came around to idea of book slowly, but when he did said, 'This won't be a book about the movies, but about vaudeville . . . K. said he only knew 1st run vaude. Played best houses—openings (?) of B. F. Keith's $1 million theatres, Boston and Philey (about 1902). Says, 'People say they would like to see vaude. come back—but it can't come back because there's no school anymore. Vaude. isn't just standing on the stage getting chummy w/the aud. (monologue)—it is variety (then named a variety of top acts).'

" 'Why did all those wonderful old minstrel shows go out?' he cont. 'Because vaude. could pay better + draw off the best talent from the minstrels. Then musical comedy began drawing off the best vaude. talent [about 1912 on—Fannie Brice, Bert Wms., Cantor, Jessel, Ed Wynn, W.C. Fields, etc.]. Then about 1917, the movies took the rest. That's what happened to vaude.' "

Offering 25 percent of the author's royalties for Keaton's cooperation, Blesh would proceed to research and write a biography he would come to call "The Two Worlds of Buster Keaton." He'd spend endless hours sitting with his subject in the breakfast nook of the house on Victoria, even living with the Keatons for a time. He'd interview Myra Keaton, Clyde Bruckman, Al St. John if he could find him.

"I hesitated a long time," Keaton said. "I've never wanted to make my life an open book. But now that I've finally decided to have a biography, it's no holds barred."

The ranks of those closest to the story were thinning at an alarming rate. Lou Anger and Mal St. Clair were already dead, as were, of course, Arbuckle, Lew Cody, Ward Crane, Jean Havez, Ed Sedgwick, Al Boasberg, and Gabe Gabourie. Blesh would work hard, cranking miles of microfilm and poring over papers and scrapbooks, but the book would never see publication—at least not in its subject's lifetime.

From the challenge and prestige of "The Awakening," Keaton did a one-eighty and opened at the Silver Slipper Gambling Hall in Las Vegas, where he was slipped into an ongoing revue hosted by house comic Hank Henry. He was so well received that his residency was extended to four weeks, but the big hit of the show was vocalist Gogi Grant, whose chart-topping single "The Wayward Wind" would follow in 1956. There was more TV in the fall of 1954, principally in New York, where Keaton was added to the all-star cast of *The Man Who Came to Dinner* and did guest shots on shows like *Life Begins at Eighty* and *I've Got a Secret*. (His secret on the latter: "I'm sitting on a custard pie.")

When he wasn't on television, Keaton was dreaming up sketches and ideas for pilots, often with Hal Goodwin, who had replaced Clyde Bruckman as his principal collaborator. Bruckman had gone off to write for Abbott and Costello on a syndicated series of their own, but by the end of 1953, work on the second season of *The Abbott and Costello Show* was over and there would be no third. Bruckman tried stirring up work by writing spec scripts for the likes of Danny Thomas and Stu Erwin, and he approached Stan Laurel about doing a filmed Laurel and Hardy series to alternate with new Keaton episodes. But his efforts were tainted by a history of alcoholism and the loss of a plagiarism suit filed by Harold Lloyd that made everything he wrote suspect. Bruckman had, said Eleanor, written himself out. "He had long since given up trying to think of anything. All he did was remember back and pluck and steal. . . . He never once *ever* came up with anything original or new." In November 1954, Bruckman was reduced to borrowing money from director George Stevens, who had been his cameraman back in their days with Hal Roach.

Along about New Year's, Bruckman phoned Keaton and told him he was driving up north to do a little fishing. He knew Buster had a gun permit and asked if he could borrow his army .45 automatic for protection. Keaton lent him the pistol and thought nothing more of it. On the afternoon of January 4, 1955, Bruckman drove to Bess Eiler's, a restaurant not far from the Santa Monica apartment he shared with his wife. He went inside and ordered a drink in the lounge. A few minutes later, he disappeared into the men's room, settled into a stall, and shot himself in the head. In a note tucked into his jacket pocket, he asked that his body be donated to "some medical school for clinical examination because I have no money to provide for my burial." Clyde Bruckman was sixty years old. The Keatons learned of his death when the police traced the gun back to Buster. They tried to return it, but he didn't want it.

Shaken by Bruckman's suicide, Keaton didn't work much over the first half of 1955. He spent the month of July and part of August in England, where he consulted on—and appeared in—a pilot for a commercial TV series titled *The Adventures of Mr. Pastry*. The bumbling Mr. Pastry was the invention of stage and film actor Richard Hearne, a natural acrobat whose working methods were not unlike Keaton's. The American-born producer Hannah Weinstein, who had settled in London in 1952, conceived of bringing the two men together for a string of thirty-nine episodes, having previously created the series *Colonel March of Scotland Yard* and *The Adventures of Robin Hood* for the U.S. market. With Keaton initially proposed as co-director, the matter had to be put to the General Council of the Association of Cine Technicians, but there was no trouble about it. "ACT welcomed so distinguished a person as Buster Keaton working here," the council's report said, "and would not oppose a permit for the pilot, especially as an ACT member would co-direct."

Keaton's co-director turned out to be Ralph Smart, whose feature credits included *Bush Christmas* and an episode of W. Somerset Maugham's *Quartet*. The resulting collaboration was slick and funny, with Mr. Pastry arriving for the first time in London to try out for the International School of Drama and finding its proprietor, the threadbare Colin Dingle, contemplating suicide. It's not Pastry's audition that excites Dingle so much as his pension, and the two become roommates. The business of Dingle trying to sneak out of his boardinghouse, Pastry steadying the ladder and then losing control of it, became one of the show's comic highpoints, as did the chaotic ending in which Keaton and Hearne as supernumeraries lay waste to a performance as Buster once did in *Speak Easily*. Hearne, for whom Keaton had tremendous affection, tended to dominate the action when it came to the rough stuff while Buster graciously deferred.

"It didn't sell," said Eleanor, "so that was it."

While Buster and Eleanor were in Britain, word came from California that Myra Keaton had died at the age of seventy-eight. Having contracted pneumonia, Myra was admitted to a hospital the day before she passed. "Just bones," said Eleanor, who estimated Myra's weight at sixty-three pounds. "She practically died of malnutrition. She used to get to the point where she wasn't interested in food. You couldn't get her to eat."

In her final years, Buster's mother subsisted primarily on whiskey. "She drank a pint of Four Roses a day," her grandson Jim Talmadge recounted, "rolled her own Bull Durham cigarettes, had a little gold cigarette holder that fit on her finger, and she drank and smoked 'til the day she died. And under her bed, after she died, was a pint of Four Roses."

Stuck in England in the middle of production, there was little Buster could do. "We sent a cable," Eleanor recalled, "and said, 'It's impossible. Do as you see fit. Do what you need to do. We'll pay the bill when we get home.'" Louise's best friend from school, who came from a large family, stepped in and helped with the arrangements. Harry Keaton got a deal on a couple of plots at a new cemetery in Sylmar, leaving Joe Keaton, still at Inglewood, permanently separated from the rest of the family. At the time of her death, Myra had three grandchildren and six great-grandchildren, of which only one, Melissa, was a girl. "She was Buster's favorite," said her mother, Barbara Talmadge. "Whenever we went over to play bridge at their house, which was every Sunday night, we'd have dinner and play bridge and the kids would go to sleep on Eleanor and Buster's bed. And then we'd pick them up and put them in the car and take them back home. *He* had to carry her. Nobody else could carry her out to the car except Buster."

Prior to leaving for London, Keaton had been approached by a screenwriter named Robert Smith, who proposed to write and produce a film of his life. Keaton gave Smith an option for $1,000, never thinking it would come to pass, and left for the United Kingdom. While he was gone, Smith announced to the trade that he planned to make the picture as an independent production. By the time Keaton returned, Smith had acquired a partner in fellow screenwriter Sidney Sheldon, and the two men had formed a production company to make the picture with Smith producing and Sheldon directing.

Eleanor was dubious from the start. "From the moment they came over, and whatever they said at the house, [Buster] knew it was going to be a disaster. . . . They didn't know what they were talking about. You *know* when you've got a couple of idiots in the place, you know that. You don't have to wait for eight days to find that out. And Buster could spot those things."

Had Eleanor seen the pitch document, which put forth the idea of making a movie of her husband's life, her worst fears would have been confirmed. "This is the story of a man who made the world laugh," it began, "who lived in fabulous times among fabulous people, who made millions and then did something much worse than die broke—he lived broke . . . Most of it is true in fact, and all of it is true in spirit." Then came one of the first lines in the story itself: "Buster grew up in the circus."

In September 1955, the Keatons traveled to Durango, Colorado, where Buster would play one of the twenty-four star cameos in Mike Todd's pro-

Keaton talks with Mario Moreno, better known to the world as Cantinflas, while on location in Colorado for Around the World in 80 Days.

duction of *Around the World in 80 Days*. His casting in the picture was the idea of Michael Todd, Jr., who became a tremendous fan of Keaton's pictures while a student at Amherst.

"Mike Todd called me up one night from RKO, told me what I would have to do," Keaton recounted. "He was so enthusiastic that I agreed right away and without a signed contract."

When they arrived on location, Eleanor observed that the three stars—David Niven, Cantinflas, and Shirley MacLaine—had their own trailers, while the character people, a group which included John Carradine, Keye Luke, Philip Van Zandt, and Buster, were left to fend for themselves.

"It was bitter cold," she said. "Each day you'd almost expect snow. It didn't quite make it, but it was down in the twenties every morning."

In the middle of the first day, they were sitting around in the weak sun, huddled together, when Eleanor heard the explosive Todd giving somebody hell. "My big ears are hanging out. I like to pick up all the little tidbits I can. He says, 'I don't give a goddamn where you have to go, [even if] you have to go to Denver and have it flown in. He will have the trailer here by tomorrow morning, or I will know the reason why.'"

The next morning, a fourth trailer, bigger and more richly appointed than the other three, appeared—and it was assigned to Buster Keaton. Quietly, Keaton caught the head man's attention.

"Mr. Todd," he said, "I think there's been some mistake. I've been assigned the biggest trailer."

"There's no mistake," Todd replied. "You're the biggest star in the picture."

Humbled by Todd's largesse, Keaton threw open the doors to Van Zandt and Luke, and all three men proceeded to use it. His role as a conductor on the Denver & Rio Grande Western's narrow-gauge train must have reminded him of shooting *The General* some thirty years earlier, particularly when the engineer is goaded into crossing a spindly bridge he doesn't think will hold, and it collapses as the last car clears the span. "For a bit part, it certainly took a long time," Keaton remarked. "We were in Colorado three weeks for just the part I played on the train."

Scenes of Phileas Fogg and his man Passepartout in the American West had to be made without benefit of rear projection, as no equipment could yet accommodate the Todd-AO wide-screen system that required 65mm film running at thirty frames per second.

"There was no process," said director Michael Anderson, "so the whole side of the train had to come off. The cameras had to be put on platforms, and the actors had to be put on the open train. You'd get the train up to forty or fifty miles an hour, bring the actors in, and start rehearsing with the train going at full speed and the camera crew hanging on for dear life."

Keaton turned sixty on October 4, 1955, and observed the occasion by preparing a nostalgic nod to The Three Keatons for an all-star TV spectacular. "Just give me enough money for a couple of acres in the valley and I'd chuck the whole works," he told the AP's Bob Thomas. "You really can't make much out of European tours. I've done more TV guest shots than most stars. I've been on Ed Sullivan's show four times, the *Comedy Hour* five times, and I'm the only one who has been on *What's My Line* twice. But you do a shot and then lay off two months. You can't save money that way."

In "Show Biz from Vaude to Video," which originated live from NBC's new Color City studios in Burbank, Buster was an inept janitor trying to clean up the stage while a magician (Harold Goodwin) is attempting to do his act. They quickly get in each other's way and begin trading blows, Buster whacking the magician on the backside with a broom while his adversary hits him over the head with a big roll of paper. They quickly fall into a rhythm and, of course, the orchestra strikes up "The Anvil Chorus." It was an exceptional appearance, energetic and funny, and for a finale, the entire cast, including Groucho Marx, Bert Lahr, and Buster, joined Eartha Kitt in singing "Shake, Rattle and Roll."

On November 19, Keaton appeared in Rochester, New York, to accept the newly instituted "George" award given to industry veterans by George Eastman House. A committee chaired by Jesse L. Lasky conducted balloting among players, directors, and cameramen to select five each of actors, actresses, directors, and cameramen from a roster of more than four hundred who were active during the formative period 1915 to 1925.

"Comedy is comedy," Buster told a reporter for the local *Democrat and Chronicle*. "The same things get laughs no matter what the setting. You remember those old chases we used to have in the silent picture days? They'd still knock 'em dead. The only trouble is that it would cost just about eight times as much to prepare and film them today as it did in the old days." Asked about television, he said it had "put greasepaint back on me. I was spending my time for the last fifteen years as a writer for some of the modern comics. Along came television and I was back in business."

Other recipients attending the First Festival of Film Artists at the Eastman Theater were Lillian Gish, Mary Pickford, Mae Marsh, Ronald Colman, Harold Lloyd, Richard Barthelmess, director Marshall Neilan, and cameraman Hal Rosson. Gloria Swanson sent regrets from Paris, Charlie Chaplin, in England, didn't reply at all, and no one, it seemed, could locate Norma Talmadge. A duplicate ceremony was scheduled for Los Angeles on December 7, 1955. Immensely proud of the award, Keaton was planning to join his contemporaries once again when, fighting a chest cold he caught on the trip, he ruptured two varicose veins in his esophagus during a coughing fit. Medicine had no effect on the hemorrhaging, and the doctor told Eleanor to get him to the hospital if he wasn't better by eight that evening. He was still coughing up blood as he was wheeled into surgery at the veterans' hospital on the night of December 3, but the doctors could do nothing to stop the bleeding. He fell into a coma, and on December 5 his condition was reported as "very grave." Eleanor was advised to gather the family. Two nights later, after clips from some of his greatest films flashed on the screen during the Eastman event at the Screen Directors Guild, Mary Pickford appeared onstage and asked the audience to pray for Buster Keaton.

25

The Worst Thing Ever Made

ELEANOR PHONED US," said Barbara Talmadge, "and he was at the VA hospital there in Sawtelle. They couldn't stop the bleeding and they needed blood for transfusions. Could Jim come down? Jim got there, and they told him they didn't have enough of the blood [type] for the transfusion." Jim Talmadge wasn't eligible to give blood himself because he contracted dengue fever, which is similar to malaria, during the war. "So he called, possibly, four of the fellows that he'd been overseas with in the OSS. They all went, and what [the doctors] told him was that they were trying to stop the bleeding before they started the transfusion. It took six orderlies in the hospital to hold Buster down, he was so strong, because he was fighting. He wasn't really conscious [of] what was going on and they were trying to get this tube down his throat and, finally, to [inflate a balloon] down there and get it up against the bleeding and stop the bleeding."

The headline in the *Los Angeles Examiner* was stark: "BUSTER KEATON FIGHTS FOR LIFE." The accompanying copy summarized his career as would an obituary. On December 7, 1955, he was still on the critical list but "slightly improved" and conscious enough to recognize Eleanor. He showed a slight gain the next day, and by December 12 he was "improved and feeling much better." His room was flooded with messages and good wishes from the likes of Clara Bow, Louise Dresser, and Mrs. Darryl F. Zanuck—the former Virginia Fox. On December 14, Jesse Lasky visited his bedside with an AP photographer to again present him with his George Eastman Award. Buster, clad in his robe and slippers, made newspapers around the country. He returned home two days later, and was formally discharged on December 23.

"Yes, it was a tough time," he acknowledged. "But I didn't know any-thing about it. I was fighting the anesthetic when they put me under. Every time I started to come out of it, I'd be fighting again. So they kept me out cold for four days. They pumped ten pints of blood into me in fourteen hours. Ten pints—that's as much as I had in me, so you can see how much I lost. They cut a hole in my trachea so I could breathe and were feeding me intravenously in my ankle. At one time I had six tubes stuck in me. . . . I had nine doctors working on my case and the best of equipment and facilities. It was the kind of care I couldn't have begun to pay for. That's what saved my life."

The night before he was discharged from the hospital, Keaton was once again before a national audience as the star of "The Silent Partner," an epi-sode of NBC's *Screen Directors Playhouse*. Heading a cast that included Joe E. Brown, ZaSu Pitts, Snub Pollard, and, in a cameo, Bob Hope, he played Kelsey Dutton, an anonymous little man who stops at a bar in Hol-lywood on the night of the Academy Awards. Nursing a beer, he watches as a veteran director accepts an honorary Oscar and recounts the time the two men met in 1916 and began making comedies together. Flashbacks return them to the days of their youth, and at the climax they're reunited with the prospect of once again working together. Directed by George Marshall, "The Silent Partner" was one of the best received episodes of the series and a poignant showcase for Keaton at the end of an eventful year.

It is not clear what initially brought actor James Mason and Buster Keaton together—or if, in fact, they were brought together at all. What is known is that when the estate on Hartford was built in 1926, a film vault was included in the plans. Specifically, there was a garden shed on the property, and hidden behind a wall of shelving inside that shed was a concrete vault built into the side of a hill. It's been speculated that Keaton used the small structure as a cutting room, and that the vault held work prints as well as copies of all of his shorts and features. After he left the house in 1932—and Natalie disposed of it—it passed through an assortment of owners and ten-ants. Woolworth heiress Barbara Hutton leased it prior to her marriage to Cary Grant, and Marlene Dietrich and actor Jean Gabin occupied it for a time. In 1949, James and Pamela Mason acquired it from the widow of John Raymond Owens, son of glass industrialist Michael J. Owens, who leaped at a lowball offer of $86,000 for what was widely considered to be a white elephant.

"Buster Keaton called once," said Pamela Mason, "and asked if he might come to see the house and show it to his new wife. And I said no because I thought it would break his heart to see what we'd done to it. I had corked the floors, the halls and the marble, because we had children—and eighteen cats—and I had done everything to make it convenient and comfortable for a lot of children." They had also auctioned off some of the custom furnishings and subdivided the property to create three additional parcels, consigning the great swimming pool and its majestic staircase to another owner. "Everything was horrific by his standards."

In a way, though, Eleanor had already seen it. "It was about 1938, I think. Buster and I were out for a drive. We had just started going out together. Maybe he wanted to impress me a little. Suddenly, Buster drove up the driveway to the front of the house and said, 'I used to live here.' We sat for a moment, looking at the house and the grounds . . . Buster pointed out where he raised his prized pheasants. Then he just put the car in gear and back down the hill we went. Buster wasn't a big talker, and he was pretty quiet on the way home. But he did say one thing: 'It took a hell of a lot of pratfalls to build that dump.'"

If the film vault was indeed concealed behind shelving, nobody would have tried opening it in the intervening years because no one would have known it was there. The late Bart Williams, an actor who inspected it in 1998, described the surrounding structure, then in an advanced state of decay, as "a sort of gardener's cottage, part greenhouse, potting shed, hothouse, and tool shed. This white-painted building, made of lattice, glass, and wood, was set against the original cement retaining wall on the east side of the property." The vault itself, which was the size of "a small basement room," resembled a bank vault. "A combination dial lock and large chrome door handle worked a thick, vertical lock bar on the inside of the door."

Keaton spoke on the record about it twice. In an interview with Joe Hyams of the *New York Herald Tribune,* he said he had been asked by the Museum of Modern Art if he had a print of *Sherlock Jr.** According to Hyams, Keaton called at the house and requested permission to go into the vault and retrieve the cans. The Masons' butler relayed the message and the answer came back: "No." Keaton explained to the butler that it was for the museum, and thereupon Mason relented. With plans for *The Buster*

---

* This would have been an odd request, since it was well known that the museum already had a print of *Sherlock Jr.* in its collection.

Keaton Story going forward, Hyams suggested that Keaton must now have "everything he wanted" out of life.

"Not everything," Buster returned. "I won't feel I've really arrived until I can go to my old house and get permission to go into the film vault for my own films from Mr. Mason himself, without mentioning the Modern Museum."

Two months later, Keaton told much the same story to Jim Cook of the *New York Post,* and this time he was quoted directly: "He sold off most of the ten [*sic*] acres, and the crowning indignity came when I went to the house . . . to get one of my old films which was still in the vault there. Mason wouldn't come to the door and the maid said I couldn't get the film. But I played a trump card—I told her to tell Mason that the Museum of Modern Art in New York wanted it. I got it then."

James Mason, who would later claim he was out of town when Keaton appeared at his door, apparently summoned a locksmith to open the vault. Inside were nine of the ten features Keaton made for Joe Schenck, and seven of his best two-reelers. Mason was conflicted, since technically he was the legal owner of the abandoned films.

"A dilemma presented itself," he wrote. "Should I make a respectful humane gesture towards this great artist? Or should I guarantee the preservation of the films? I knew that Keaton could not use the films to his personal advantage and that he did not command the facilities for preserving them. Anyway, right or wrong, I chose [to donate the films to] the Academy." And so in January 1956, the Academy of Motion Picture Arts and Sciences took delivery of the entire contents of Buster Keaton's former vault, which included 35mm prints of *The General, The Navigator, Three Ages, Go West, Cops, The Boat,* and *Sherlock Jr.** For his trouble, Mason awarded himself a $10,000 deduction on his federal income taxes.

While the largest single collection of Buster Keaton's films in the world was being inventoried and examined in Los Angeles, the long-dormant holder of the copyrights of those films was continuing to move ahead in New York. In July 1955, Leopold Friedman requested a complete report on Buster Keaton,

---

* Since *Our Hospitality* was the only Schenck feature missing from the inventory, this was probably the title requested by the Museum of Modern Art, not *Sherlock Jr.* It was likely copied by the museum and, at Mason's request, passed on to the Academy, which later had possession of it.

covering his picture history prior to M-G-M, his two-reelers produced by Comique, the shorts and features made by Buster Keaton Productions, his pictures as a salaried actor, summaries of all his M-G-M employment agreements, and his assignments of all rights. In October, Friedman also asked for a summary of Keaton elements on hand, both negatives and prints.

In time, a fuller picture developed of what existed and where. Metro's rights to *The Saphead* had lapsed in 1930, but the Academy had a print. M-G-M had a negative and print on the silent version of *Spite Marriage,* and an incomplete negative on *Battling Butler.* Studio records showed they had destroyed the negatives of *Three Ages, Our Hospitality, The Navigator,* and *Seven Chances,* presumably after distribution rights to those titles had lapsed. They claimed no elements whatsoever on *Sherlock Jr., Go West,* or *The Cameraman.* Over at Fox, where Joe Schenck's personal prints were stored, there were copies of *Our Hospitality* and *Battling Butler.* The Museum of Modern Art had *Sherlock Jr., Go West,* and *The General.* Their print of *The Navigator,* about which Walter Kerr had written so passionately in 1952, was thought to be the only one in the country. (M-G-M's print had come from this.) George Eastman House held a 16mm print of *Go West* made from the M-G-M negative in 1952. The British Film Institute distributed *The Navigator* and *The General* in the United Kingdom.

Of the trove of reels donated to the Academy, many were in a state of decomposition since they had all been printed on nitrate film stock. When stored under less-than-ideal conditions, nitrate stock tends to decompose, generally through shrinkage and discoloration, then with the emulsion and its base becoming a gummy, flammable mass, sticky, runny, and beyond rescue. In the final stages of decomposition, all that remains is a rusty brown powder. Of the Keaton features received from Mason, only *Battling Butler, The General, College,* and *Steamboat Bill, Jr.* were intact. Three reels of *Sherlock Jr.* survived, but a fourth reel had to be destroyed. One reel of *The Navigator* also had to be junked. *Three Ages, Go West,* and *Seven Chances* were total losses.

With Myra Keaton's death in 1955, her elder son could finally divest himself of the house at 1043 South Victoria. Louise Keaton, then working as a bookkeeper, moved out and got her own apartment, but Harry Keaton never acknowledged the plan and remained steadfastly entrenched.

"There was a bar up the street where he used to spend his evenings," said

A family gathering at 1043 South Victoria, circa 1952. From left: Melissa Talmadge, Louise Keaton, Eleanor Keaton, Buster, Barbara Talmadge, and Myra Keaton.

Eleanor, "and that's the way he lived." Several months passed until *The Buster Keaton Story* was set up at Paramount. Keaton's first payment would amount to $19,000, enough, combined with savings, to buy the modest house he had always wanted.

It wasn't the first time the Keatons had yearnings for a place of their own. In 1949, Eleanor had managed to put enough money away to build a house near Culver City, where they found a four-acre lot for $10,000. They began by planting a row of pine trees across the back, drenching them with water during their weekly visits. Then a friend, John S. "Jack" Fredericks, who had been a star fullback for UCLA and was at one time the owner of the Los Angeles Bulldogs, offered to go in with them, taking half the acreage for himself and giving the Keatons the wherewithal to start construction. After the foundations were laid, Buster and Eleanor had to go east for *Three Men on a Horse*. In their absence, they asked Fredericks to keep up the payments on the land, promising to square everything when they got back. But unbeknownst to anyone, Jack Fredericks was terminally ill. No payments got made that summer, and by the time the Keatons returned, the property had been lost to foreclosure. Less than a year later, Fredericks was dead of a brain tumor at the age of thirty-nine.

When the money from Paramount came through on April 16, 1956, Keaton knew exactly what he wanted—a small, manageable place with enough land to plant trees and keep animals. Hal Goodwin, who was working in real estate when not before the cameras, took him around.

"When I sold him this house [in Woodland Hills], he was ready to settle down. What he wanted [was] a farm. Well, that was a pretty big place, you know—a hundred and twenty feet by three hundred feet with barns in the back for horses."

One of Buster's criteria was that he wanted a semi-rural setting, away from the noise and density of Los Angeles. The bedroom community of Woodland Hills was at the southwestern edge of the San Fernando Valley, running up along the northern slope of the Santa Monica Mountains. There Buster took a fancy to a ranch house built in 1947, two bedrooms, one bath.

"I walked him through the house and into the den, and there was a pot-bellied stove in the den. That sold the house. I took him, put him in the car, and he says, 'Where you going?' I said, 'I'm going to show you some more houses.' He says, 'I want this one.' So he had made [up his mind]. . . . He paid cash, $29,000."

Eleanor was fine with the house. They moved in June, she remembered, "and Harry stayed, hanging on to the bedpost until the day we moved the furniture out from under him."

There was a surge of biographical pictures in Hollywood as *The Buster Keaton Story* made the rounds. *The Eddy Duchin Story,* with Tyrone Power as the late bandleader, and *Somebody Up There Likes Me,* starring Paul Newman as the middleweight champ Rocky Graziano, were awaiting release. Also shooting or in development were *Man of a Thousand Faces* (Lon Chaney), *The Wings of Eagles* (Commander Frank "Spig" Wead), *The Spirit of St. Louis* (Colonel Charles A. Lindbergh), *The Helen Morgan Story,* and *The Best Things in Life Are Free* (songwriters Buddy DeSylva, Lew Brown, and Ray Henderson)—more than thirty such properties in all. Robert Smith and Harry Essex had settled an original western called *The Lonely Man* at Paramount, and both men were seeking deals for separate biographical subjects, Essex with *The Benny Leonard Story,* concerning the former lightweight champion, and Smith with Keaton. The studio already had several other biographical stories in the works, including *Beau James* (with Bob Hope playing Mayor Jimmy

Walker), *The Five Pennies* (Danny Kaye as jazz cornetist Red Nichols), and *The Joker Is Wild* (Frank Sinatra channeling nightclub comic Joe E. Lewis).

Smith, whose writing and producing credits tended toward low-budget independents like *Quicksand, 99 River Street,* and *Invasion, U.S.A.* pitched Academy Award–winning screenwriter Sidney Sheldon, who was already under contract to Paramount, in order to get the Keaton story off the ground. Sheldon, who had moved into directing with the Cary Grant misfire *Dream Wife,* wanted another picture to direct when Smith, whom he didn't know, showed up at his office one day. Sheldon took the idea to production head Don Hartman, who embraced it and suggested Donald O'Connor for the title role. Keaton himself had been thinking of TV's George Gobel, but readily approved of O'Connor playing the part. "Gobel would get more laughs," he said, "but O'Connor would be better for the action. He's a dancer and could handle my kind of knockabout comedy."

Buster, according to Eleanor, didn't particularly care how the script turned out. "It all boiled down to the fact that they had just made the Lillian Roth story about a drunken woman [*I'll Cry Tomorrow*] and it was very successful. It made a lot of money, so they said, 'Okay, if one drunk is good, a bunch of drunks will be fine. So they came to Buster and said, 'Can we film your life story?' And Buster said, 'Be my guest,' because, you know, he got that twice a week [and] nothing ever happened. And darn if they didn't go through with it. They never asked him question one, they never talked to him, they didn't do anything until they were ready to shoot, and then: 'Here's the script and we're ready to go.' He never read the script. . . . He said, 'I'm not going to like it, and the fact that I have script approval is not going to make any difference. They're not going to change anything no matter how loud I scream, so I see no reason to grow a new ulcer.'"

Smith and Sheldon had some Keaton films shipped in from MoMA, dug up others through private sources, and built their script around spectacular physical gags they felt could be re-created with Buster's help.

"Some of the prints were in terrible condition," Smith lamented. "A shameful waste of great art."

After the screenplay was finalized, Smith, with a straight face, assured *The New York Times* that Keaton was "very pleased with the script." In the run-up to the start of the picture, Buster assumed the role of personal trainer for their twenty-nine-year-old star, holing up with him in the studio gymnasium and practicing moves from some of his cleverest comedies as Fred Astaire might do in rehearsing a number.

"You've got to learn how to fall," Keaton told him. "I never take the impact of a fall on the back of my head, the base of my spine, my elbows or my knees. That's how you break bones."

Donald O'Connor regretted the fact that the budget wouldn't permit some of Keaton's most spectacular gags, such as the house fall from *Steamboat Bill, Jr.* or some of the traveling shots in *The General.* "I said, 'Why don't we grain down the film?' And they said, 'What are you talking about?'" What O'Connor was suggesting was to use actual clips of Keaton from the original pictures, with O'Connor entering and exiting the scenes as he might before handing them off to a stuntman. The new footage would be shot to match the grain of the old footage as closely as possible.

"Get me walking into a scene," he said, "and then you show Buster, because we did look an awful lot alike at the time. . . . They didn't understand what I was talking about, but that would have helped open it up."

What they began filming on June 25, 1956, bore little resemblance to Buster Keaton's actual life, even though Donald O'Connor had insisted on at least some rudimentary adjustments. "Donald did so much screaming that they did change two or three *basic* things," said Eleanor. "First of all, they thought it would be more colorful if he was born and raised in the circus and he was a trapeze performer. And Donald screamed like a maniac until they put *that* where it belonged."

As conceived from the outset, the highlights of the film would be the Keaton gags re-created for the high-resolution wide-screen process known as VistaVision. Deprived of the size and scale of some of Keaton's signature stunts, the filmmakers fell back on smaller moments of comedic virtuosity. Scenes from the shorts and features were sprinkled throughout: the game with the wet playing cards from *The Navigator,* the soda fountain business from *College,* the attempt at ice fishing from *The Frozen North,* the part from *The Paleface* where the Indians attempt to burn him at the stake. Keaton liked to say the launching of *The Boat* cost Paramount more money than it took to make the whole film back in 1921.

Buster oversaw all the comic action in the picture, effectively directing much of it and making sure it was all staged correctly. When re-creating a portion of *Cops,* he grew dissatisfied with how a stuntman was doing a 108—a pratfall where the comic goes straight up and then lays out flat as he hits the ground. And, as he had done so often back in the silent days, Keaton donned the uniform himself and, running straight into another cop, got the shot. The chase from *Cops* was augmented with the magician's

Donald O'Connor, Cecil B. DeMille, and Keaton during the filming of The Buster Keaton Story. *DeMille played himself in a cameo.*

vanishing act from *Steamboat Bill, Jr.* and the blind alley escape into thin air from *Sherlock Jr.*

For the latter, Keaton had to reveal the secret of the trick to Sidney Sheldon and his crew, and coach Donald O'Connor on how to make the precision leap into the void. In the original, actor Ford West posed as an old woman peddling neckties from a display case. Cornered, Buster leaped through the case West was holding in his hands and seemingly disappeared. The secret, O'Connor learned, was that an opening in the wall behind him permitted the actor holding the case to be suspended parallel to the floor while his head and arms remained visible inside the costume. With the man's body out of the way, O'Connor could leap through the opening in the case and disappear behind the wall. The man's body is then lowered back into position, allowing him to walk away while leaving no visible trace of the escapee.

"I worked with Buster on that," O'Connor said, "and they brought in three stuntmen to do it. And I guess I was more nimble because I'm the one who finally did it. The stuntmen couldn't get through that hole. . . . The wall was made of rubber and there was a T [opening]. The 'lady' was supposedly a hawker on the street holding a cigarette tray—cigarettes and candy and what have you—and that's what I dove through. But the legs were up into this black hole behind the wall, so as I went through this box . . . I disappeared. They put the legs of the feller down, the stunt man, and he walked away. And they had buckshot in the skirt at the bottom to make it look like it was on the ground. . . . It was a marvelous trick, and it was very dangerous. [The person doing the jump would] have to go from sunlight into this dark hole and lay out straight—there was no way to tuck in and roll out of it—and worry about catching the back of your head going through the hole. But we did it and there was no problem. Because with Keaton around, standing and watching you, you had this feeling nothing's going to happen to you."

Toward the end of production, the company put out word that Buster wanted to gather his leading ladies for a luncheon at the studio. The idea was actually put forth by Sybil Seely, who heard about the movie and sent Keaton a box of orchids and a note wishing him luck. She was, of course, married to screenwriter Jules Furthman and living in Culver City. Virginia Fox's whereabouts were also well known, since she was married to Zanuck. Keaton, however, wasn't sure what had become of some of the others and specifically mentioned Anne Cornwall (*College*), Marion Mack (*The General*), and Kathryn McGuire (*Sherlock Jr.* and *The Navigator*). Cornwall, it turned out, was divorced and playing bit roles in films like *Destry* and *The Search for Bridey Murphy*. Unlike the others, she needed the work, and so Sidney Sheldon awarded her a speaking part in the picture as a fan from Elmira, New York, who, accompanied by her husband, encounters Buster on the street and asks for his autograph.

When *The Buster Keaton Story* finished on August 8, it was ahead of schedule and under budget. Keaton went over to Sheldon and said, "I want to thank you."

"What for?"

"I was able to buy a house."

As part of his deal with Paramount, Keaton was committed to supporting the release of *The Buster Keaton Story* with a ten-city tour and as much press as he could squeeze in. Neither Buster nor Eleanor looked forward to this, as they both knew the picture was a dud, a suspicion only confirmed when they attended a Glendale preview.

"For God's sake," exclaimed Eleanor, "it's the worst thing ever made. . . . My stomach turned over, it was so awful! We sneaked out of the theater practically on our hands and knees. It was just trash. It had nothing to do with him. Of course, he knew ahead of time that was going to happen. The only things that were halfway decent were the comedy sequences that he and Donald had re-created and copied."

The publicity push kicked off on April 3, 1957, two weeks prior to the film's gala opening in New York City. That evening, at a couple of minutes past seven, an elevator door opened at the NBC offices in Burbank, and Keaton stepped out into the harsh lights of a remote television hookup. Host Ralph Edwards took his hand, shook it, and told him he'd been a big fan of his from way back. "You're on television coast-to-coast," he explained as Buster hurriedly moved to button his collar and cinch up his tie. "America's waiting for the story of one of the immortals of the silent screen—you, Buster Keaton—for tonight, *This Is Your Life*!"

As per the show's usual format, the subject was ushered into NBC's Studio 1, where a parade of old friends and fam-

Ralph Edwards, Buster, and Eleanor Keaton during the live telecast of This Is Your Life *on April 3, 1957.*

ily paid tribute. First was Louise Dresser, his sister's namesake, remembering him as a child, and seventy-nine-year-old Mush Rawls, representing the old actors' colony at Muskegon. When Louise and Harry Keaton emerged from the wings, Buster wrapped his hands around his sister's neck and pretended to throttle her. "Did you help them frame me?" he demanded.

The glory days in Hollywood were represented by Eddie Cline and Donald Crisp, a bad case of bronchitis having forced Virginia Fox to cancel at the last minute.

"Say, do you remember the time she saw the smoke coming outside her dressing room window?" Cline prompted. "And she yelled, 'Fire!' And she tried to get out the door and it was locked. She went to the phone—no answer. And you rescued her before she really fainted? Then she found out about you lightin' those smoke pots out there?"

Keaton nodded broadly, warming to the memory. Typical of the period, the clips were atrocious—murky fourth-generation dupes so washed out the hurricane action from *Steamboat Bill, Jr.* had to be narrated by the unctuous host.

Then came the talkies, and Edwards tried to draw out the details of a career on the rocks and the why of it all.

"Oh, it just came to a stop," was all Keaton, clearly uncomfortable, would volunteer.

For the years spent behind the scenes, a jovial Red Skelton was summoned, making some dubious claims about not realizing what Keaton had contributed to his pictures. The wrap-up brought a beaming Eleanor to the stage, Donald O'Connor in full drag as the subject of the new picture, and sons, Jim and Bob.

"Well, this is your life, Buster Keaton," Edwards concluded. "You gave the world the sunshine of laughter. Better still, through good luck and bad luck you were able to laugh at yourself and at the comedy of life. Keep on making us laugh, Buster, and God bless you."

According to Eleanor, Buster was "dumbfounded . . . and then pleased." There were portions of the program where he appeared to be close to tears. Helping to arrange it all while keeping it a secret was a monumental undertaking. "I went through six weeks of hell," she said.

Five days later, Dorothy Sebastian, fifty-one, died of cancer at the Motion Picture Fund's hospital in Woodland Hills, a distance of less than three miles from Keaton's new home. Sebastian had played her final movie role, a bit in *The Miracle of the Bells,* in 1946. The same year she married a hospitality executive named Herman Shapiro, and together they ran a small hotel in Miami Beach. As far as anyone knows, the last time she and Buster were together was in February 1950 when they reprised their famous drunk scene from *Spite Marriage* for a benefit at the Shrine Auditorium. Keaton was in New York when her funeral took place at a Catholic church in Playa del Rey on April 11, 1957. The industry she had known was represented by actor Monte Blue and actresses Ena Gregory, Yola D'Avril, Greta Granstedt, Mona Raye, and Lorrie Larson. Eddie Mannix and M-G-M publicity director Howard Strickling were among the pallbearers.

The Buster Keaton Story opened April 20 at the Mayfair Theatre in Times Square with the Keatons in attendance. The next night, Buster once again appeared on *The Ed Sullivan Show,* where he successfully demonstrated the blind alley escape from *Sherlock Jr.,* an astonishing feat for a sixty-one-year-old man.

"Of course, it is no camera trick," he said. "You do it in full view of the audience and on a full-lit stage. There's no lighting effects, no mirrors or anything. And it's really a great trick and it shocks an audience. And after the show was over, Sullivan sent for me. And I went up to his dressin' room and he says, 'So I can sleep tonight—how'd you do it?' I wouldn't tell 'im."

The reviews of the *Keaton Story* were mixed, generally with praise for the gag re-creations and groans for the phony plotline. And as good as he was, Donald O'Connor proved a poor substitute for the real thing, his acrobatics more like a slick dancer's moves than the work of the hardscrabble genius whom the film was about. "He taught me how to do a lot of the things he did, falls, tumbles, and so on," O'Connor said, "but nobody has his comic timing. Nobody can do Buster the way he did."

Business was tepid, even as the picture moved into wider release after two lackluster weeks at the Mayfair. In speaking to the press, Keaton did his best to avoid talking about the film, deflecting instead with anecdotes, reflections, and occasional thoughts of the future.

"I'm a little dizzy," he admitted as he met up with Mel Heimer of the King Features Syndicate at a saloon called Danny's Hideaway. "This is quite a merry-go-round, isn't it?"

Heimer recalled the lean, youthful Keaton of *The Cameraman* and thought the 1957 version, a bit thicker around the middle, resembled somebody's uncle. He suggested it must have been unsettling to have reporters, due to the movie, constantly asking him about his meteoric rise and fall.

"It's funny," Keaton responded, sipping an orangeade. "I'd just about dropped out of circulation before all this." He lit a cigarette, his hands a little unsteady. "I drank myself right out of pictures. I guess it's as simple as that."

In Oklahoma, where they claimed him as a native son, the *Keaton Story* was booked to open in a hundred theaters following a "world premiere" in Perry on May 7. The local chamber of commerce threw itself into preparations, the city council declaring Buster Keaton Day, and the Keatons were driven around town in a new Oldsmobile sedan provided by the local Olds dealer. Buster was silent for the most part, leaving it to Eleanor to be the outgoing one, and confided to their host he didn't remember much about living there.

"I was interviewed in almost every town," Eleanor said. "The ladies' department would come and interview me, y'know, while Buster was being interviewed, and it was awful to sit there with a straight face and not say, 'For God's sake, it's the worst thing ever made, and don't go see it.' You don't dare say the truth. You've gotta sit there with a smile on your face. It's hard work."

The morning after the event in Perry they were gone, headed back to California and their spread in Woodland Hills. "I'm just a farmer now," Keaton told Mel Heimer. "I've got this little farm in the San Fernando Valley with nine walnut trees . . ." And as he trailed off, he leaned back comfortably and he smiled.

26

Merton of the Movies

WAS BORN IN 1923," said actor James Karen, "and I was reading by the time I was three years old, very well. My father, who was born in this country, ended up working in the coal mines when he was six years old in Pennsylvania. [He] worked for six years until his older brother made enough money to buy a horse and wagon, and they became hucksters. But my father never really learned to read or write. He could do little things with numbers and stuff, but he was not a reader. But he loved movies, so he took me to the silent movies because I could read the titles for him. I became enamored with Buster Keaton. I saw all the others; I saw Chaplin, I saw Lloyd, I saw all the movies at the time. I believe I saw *Steamboat Bill, Jr.* when it first came out, and *The Cameraman* I remember very well.

"I just was constantly trying to figure out how to meet him. And Rudi Blesh was a friend of mine from the Players Club [in New York's Gramercy Park]. I loved Rudi. He was a marvelous guy, he was a wild man. He was his own worst enemy. I think he drank a lot. He was also a gambler, and he owed everybody. He also lived big. The reason he owed me money was he bought six chairs from me, six antique chairs that he *had* to have, and he got them into his station wagon and said, 'I forgot my checkbook.' And I said, 'Oh . . .' And I just didn't have the heart to say, 'Take them out, put them back where you got them.' I said, 'Well, you'll send me the check.' And, of course, I never got a check from him. He owed everybody. But I liked him. I knew his jazz books. Charming man, and Buster liked him a lot.

"So Rudi owed me money. He owed me three hundred and fifty bucks, and I saw him at the Players Club one day and I said, 'Rudi, could you give me Buster Keaton's phone number? I'd like to talk to him about something.'

I was trying to do a theater piece, and he said, 'Oh, no, I couldn't do that. That wouldn't be right. I don't think that would be right.' I said, 'What about three hundred and fifty bucks' absolution?' 'Oh,' he said, 'his number is . . .'

"So I called Buster. I said, 'Boy, I had trouble getting your phone number. It cost me three hundred and fifty dollars. Rudi Blesh owed me money, and I had to tell him it was okay and he gave me the number.' He said, 'That was dumb. It's in the phone book!'"

Like a lot of actors, Jimmy Karen wanted to work with Buster Keaton. At the time, Karen was mostly doing summer theater, occasionally producing, and knew all the managers on the straw-hat circuit. He began talking up the idea with other actors and directors, and a loose grouping of friends and associates embraced it. With all the TV work he had done, and with *The Buster Keaton Story* nearing release, Keaton was arguably more famous than he had been in twenty-five years. A Yale-trained director named Alan Harper, who thought Keaton "the greatest name in show business," came up with the idea of casting him in Molière's *The Imaginary Invalid*.

"That would be superb," Harper said excitedly. "That would be ideal. We could trim some of the words, and there's all kinds of opportunity for his particular genius."

A partnership between Harper, his wife, Paula Hays, and actor John Bennes was formed to produce the show. When Buster arrived in New York to promote the *Keaton Story,* they contacted him and arranged to see him at his hotel and make the pitch.

"He was kind of vague," Harper remembered. "We suggested the Molière, and he was kind of intrigued by it, but it was all sort of unsatisfactory. We left with the feeling, had he said yes or no? John pointed out: 'What can he say no to? We haven't told him [when] we'd like to start . . . and, also, we hadn't mentioned at all, but we figured to be able to *pay* him.' And in the lobby of the hotel, we said, 'Well, we gotta call up there.' We got on the house phone and called back and said, 'By the way, we can offer so-and-so (whatever the figure was) plus a percentage of the gross.' 'Oh, yeah, well okay. I'll go for that.' *That's* what he was waiting for."

The Imaginary Invalid sounded too highbrow for stock audiences, and it was when tossing around other properties for Keaton's consideration that Buster himself suggested *Merton of the Movies.*

"There was a meeting [of stock managers]," said Karen. "We went to that meeting and said, 'Would anybody be interested in Buster Keaton?' You had to get ten separate summer theaters to book because they would pool the money for the production and then you would play in each of their theaters. Sometimes you couldn't get ten; you'd do it with eight. Ours was a very inexpensive piece of theater because we carried six people and picked up all the others. We'd send an advance person. We would be playing in one theatre and the advance person would be there setting up the play. We'd close on a Saturday night, travel on Sunday, and Sunday night we would do a dress rehearsal in the new theater.

"I used to spend a lot of time at the bar at the Players Club, and I played pool. I was a big pool player there. The table was in the barroom. So I was there almost every day. I wasn't working, and Marc Connelly [co-author of *Merton* with George S. Kaufman] came in. I had read the script, of course. I just wanted to work with Buster. So I said to Marc, 'Jesus, you got a problem.' Buster picked *Merton* because he had seen it in 1923, and he was never able to grab it. The guy who played it on Broadway, Glenn Hunter, played it in the movie, and it always rankled Buster that he hadn't done it. So when this all came up he said, 'I'd like to do *Merton of the Movies*.' Reading the script, you know, it was a young nineteen-year-old man who was working in the Gashwiler's grocery store in Illinois. And he comes to Hollywood. So I told Marc the problem. And he said, 'Oh, we must do anything we can to permit Buster to play the part.' And he wrote out a letter saying 'You can do anything you want' so Buster could play the part. It was on Players Club stationery; he just took it off the bar."

And so, carefully, and with Keaton's participation, a play from 1922 was adjusted so that a man of Keaton's years could play the title role. "I became the romantic," said Karen, "and we teamed Buster up with the trouper, who was a beautiful young girl in the play but became an older character woman [for our purposes]. We got Jane Dulo, who was an actress who did a lot of nightclub work and who was funny as hell. She and Buster fell madly in love—I mean, they were terrific together. We made it into a more chaste relationship, and I was flirting with all the girls. We changed a line. I played the assistant director, Weller. I'm looking for a guy to do a little piece of business, and Jane just pushed him out. Buster was startled, and I said, 'You. What do you want to be an actor for at your age?' And Buster looked and said, 'Hey, it ain't my fault movies was invented when I was old.'" With Keaton, Jane Dulo, Karen, and John Bennes already set, the cast was completed with TV's Robert Gibbons and Pearl Pearson, Ben Pearson's wife, whose aunt was the influential acting teacher Stella Adler.

During a week's rehearsals in New York, Keaton made the play his. "He'd say, 'I got to move from Gashwiler's Grocery Store to Hollywood. I wouldn't just go out there,'" Karen remembered. "And so he worked up a thing, a fake mirror at a dressing table. You could see there was no mirror—you could see right through it—but he was sitting facing the audience and we used it as a scene change from Gashwiler's Grocery Store to the casting director's office. That was behind the curtain going on and, down in one, there was Buster, just brilliant. He'd say, 'How much time do you need to make that change?' 'Well, we need about eight minutes.' 'Okay.' And he did eight minutes' worth of business making up, putting on a toupee which kept slipping over his face. He put on a girdle and got all dressed up to go to Hollywood. And all through the play he did those things."

The company made its way to Spring Lake on the Jersey shore, where the show opened at the Ivy Tower Theatre on July 15, 1957. The first performances didn't go well; attendance was light and the laughs spotty. For a scene in the second act where the studio people watched rushes of Merton making a fool of himself, Alan Harper used some vintage clips of the twentysomething Buster that were shown out of context. They didn't go over at all.

"Buster was embarrassed," said Karen, "because it was this beautiful young man that's up there and we're supposedly doing [the play in the same period]. He said, 'No damn makeup could cover this face and make me look like that.' He had gotten this 16mm camera from the glorious Ralph Edwards, and so we went out and shot [our own film] . . . and we kept adding to it. It got better and better. Wherever we were we'd go out for a day's shoot, and we started in Spring Lake. As a matter of fact, Buster did a fall over the edge of a dock, and it was a murky kind of lake we were shooting in, with a lot of flora in the lake. And he came up out of the water . . . and the wig was gone. I dove for two hours to find that wig; I was going through all that stuff, the muck. And finally, I couldn't tell for sure, I was the prop man on it. Eleanor was the cameraman, and Buster was the actor. And I think John Bennes helped out on it too."

The word of mouth at Spring Lake wasn't good.

"Buster Keaton didn't draw at all," said Rea John Powers, the producer at the Ivy Tower. "People who like him thought he was tremendous. But some of our regular customers weren't even interested. The show was so old it was new, with no reputation. Many people asked about Keaton: 'Is he still alive?'"

Amid the confusion resulting from a last-minute reshuffling of touring

James Karen,
Keaton, and Jane
Dulo in the 1957
touring production
of Merton of the
Movies.

companies, they lost their slot at a theater in Pennsylvania and had to lay off.
More film got shot, but with a weekly nut of twenty-five hundred dollars,
the show was already in the hole and new theaters weren't exactly lining up
to take it.

Merton of the Movies did better at the Southern Tier Playhouse in Binghamton, New York, where the show was tighter and audiences fell into the
mood of the thing. To a reviewer from the *Press and Sun-Bulletin,* the only
dull spots came when the plot needed attention: "At one point, [Keaton]
employs a pack of cigarettes in some buffoonery which is pure comic genius.
At another, he dons a musketeer costume which is so funny in itself the
audience applauded and laughed at the same time. Then he gets involved in
a pantomime piece of swordplay which not only breaks up the audience but
breaks up half the set and winds up with a custard pie toss which, hackneyed
as it sounds, is hilarious."

They opened at the Hinsdale Summer Theatre outside Chicago on August
19, and it was there the show threatened to close after a run of just five venues. The audiences at Hinsdale were large and responsive, and the notices
excellent. "Buster Keaton is more than durable," declared Seymour Raven of
the *Chicago Tribune.* "He is regenerative. To see this comedian renewing at
Hinsdale the ancient art of still movie pantomime while crossing the bridge
to spoken theatre is an experience of pure pleasure."

It was a two-week stand at Hinsdale, time enough to do some maneuver-
ing, and John Bennes saw a chance at a reprieve. "We never stopped working
on it for the entire six weeks until we got to Chicago," said Karen, "and then

John said, 'You know, I hear . . .' He was from California—most of us were from New York—and he said, 'Huntington Hartford [the A&P grocery heir] has got a theater that he hasn't got anything to put in. I hear he's in Chicago, I'm going to call him.' He called him and Huntington Hartford answered the phone. John said, 'Listen, we're doing a great show here with Buster Keaton. You ought to come see it. You might want to put it in your theatre.' Huntington Hartford came and bought it, and we all went on to California to do the show."

While *Merton of the Movies* was in Chicago, Paramount Pictures was slapped with a $5 million libel suit filed in New York by a woman called Jewel Steven. In an earlier life, she said, she had been married to Buster Keaton under the name of Mae Elizabeth Scriven. It was a Hail Mary pass, an opportunistic demand for money from a deep-pocketed defendant based solely on the presumption that any film of Buster Keaton's life would have to portray her in a disparaging light. In her complaint, Mae charged that the film contained libelous elements, showing "that the plaintiff married said Buster Keaton while he was in a drunken state . . . that she took undue advantage of his inebriate condition . . . that she married him for his name . . . and that said Buster Keaton was also of the foregoing opinion."

Sidney Sheldon and Robert Smith had anticipated the danger of portraying two ex-wives who were still living by creating a composite character played by Ann Blyth that incorporated aspects of all three of Keaton's marriages. The entirely fictional Gloria Brent first meets Buster while she is casting director at the studio he crashes, just as Natalie worked in a somewhat similar capacity at Comique. Later, the well-meaning Gloria marries the drunken Keaton with the aim of reforming him. Finally, he hits the comeback trail with the supportive Gloria as part of the act, as did Buster with Eleanor. At no time is the character portrayed as anything other than dutiful and loving.

The years since Mae's divorce from Buster hadn't been good to her. After her Mexican marriage to Sam Fuller fell apart, she wed a Los Angeles insurance broker and, in 1940, a grocer in Fresno, a union that lasted just seven months. By 1942, she had relocated to New York, where she was writing plays under the name Jewel Steven. *Satan! Pull Up a Chair* was registered with the Copyright Office that year, and *Desk Clerk* followed in 1943. Down on her luck, she applied to the Salty Peters Traveling Carnival, Roadshow, and Burlesque Revue as Mrs. Buster Keaton, suggesting she could sign autographs for the celebrity-starved rubes and double as the company's nurse and hairdresser. By December 1944, she was working as a real desk clerk at a hotel in New York City.

After the war, Mae surfaced in Delaware as a concert promoter, again using the name Jewel Steven. Then she formed the Saratoga Players in Saratoga Springs, New York. Operating the Spa Theatre, she promoted a season of summer stock in 1946, bringing in star talent like Elissa Landi, Edward Everett Horton, and Jane Cowl. She returned to Wilmington in 1947, presenting Robert Merrill, the Don Cossack Chorus, and Vincent Lopez and his orchestra. In a bankruptcy hearing the following year, it came out that she had married Edward Van Nierop of the Shepherd Steamship Co., a limited partner in the Saratoga Players, in 1943. They divorced in 1947, but he continued to contribute to her support. In 1948, she went into partnership with Fred Kelly, Gene Kelly's brother, in producing TV shows, and was listed as president of Steven Televised Presentations, Inc. In May 1953, she was involuntarily committed to the observation ward of the Kings County Hospital, and subsequently to Creedmoor Psychiatric Center.

"I lived in Hell," she wrote in a bylined article for *Confidential*. "This time it was a real snake pit. I was given electric shock treatments—the 'electric chair'—twenty-eight times and I suffered the torments of the damned. I worked many months at hard labor. I slept in a ward with fifty women, the beds only ten inches apart. I was allowed to bathe twice a week under showers with eighty other women." By her own account she was released in October 1955 and found work as a beautician. When she filed suit against Paramount in 1957, she was living on West Seventieth Street and giving her age as forty (it was actually fifty-two). Keaton, who had no love for *The Buster Keaton Story*, was bewildered by the suit, since the story had been scrubbed and so thoroughly fictionalized. "You never do find out which wife was depicted in the movie," he told the *Tribune*'s Herb Lyon. "Actually, it was Natalie Talmadge, my first. The picture ends in 1930—I didn't marry Mae until 1933."

Nevertheless, Mae's suit went forward, if for no other reason than she had the time to make a nuisance of herself. She even appeared on the Joe Franklin show to press her case. Paramount, in its response, dismissed the action as frivolous, suggesting she hadn't even seen the film, and got it thrown out. In 1959, she took aim at an even larger target, suing the State and City of New York for $50 million over her treatment in the mental health system, another scheme that was doomed to failure. Clinging to the name and persona of Jewel Steven, she faded back into obscurity.

. . .

When *Merton of the Movies* closed in Chicago, the Keatons returned briefly to New York so that Buster could fulfill a TV obligation for the Goodson-Todman people. Dick Cavett, who was a twenty-year-old English major at Yale, was on hand on the night of September 1, 1957.

"All the guys at Yale went to Smith, Vassar, and Wellesley on the weekends," he said, "and I went to New York and sneaked into [Jackie] Gleason's show rehearsals, and famous people's dressing rooms, and stuff. I had gone to the Garry Moore show, and then I realized that *What's My Line?* was the next night, and so I went to *What's My Line?*

"I was a little late, and I was standing outside when it started. They had a practice of hiding the celebrity [mystery guest] in a little restaurant right next door. The odious autograph crowd [was there], led by two star figures: Dave, a refrigerator repairman from Brooklyn—a big, oafish lout with an ear-flap cap—and Sheila, who was queen of the autograph mob, a snaggle-toothed, skinny, lengthy-haired girl from Brooklyn [with] her toothless mother. . . . So I'm outside the *What's My Line?* studio, way over in the West Fifties somewhere. I see the autograph people, and somehow they apparently had gotten the celebrity into the little restaurant before the autograph folks got there, because they were all speculating. The week before it had been Gary Cooper. And the week before that Bob Hope. So they were all abuzz, and out comes the little troop from the show with Buster Keaton. And the group went, 'Ohhhhhhh . . .' And he heard it. It was quite clear. They didn't even bother to come up and get his autograph."

Warmly greeted by the studio audience, Keaton wasn't much of a match for the show's four panelists—columnist Dorothy Kilgallen, comedian Ernie Kovacs, actress Arlene Francis, and publisher Bennett Cerf. He tried giving his answers in a high-pitched voice, but the questioning quickly narrowed the possibilities down to "the school of comedians of Harold Lloyd." It fell to Cerf to ask, "Was there a picture recently made based on—allegedly—the story of your life?" Pointedly, Keaton scowled as he answered, in a significantly lower voice, "Yes." And then he dashed offstage, shaking hands with the panelists as he went, before moderator John Daly could ask a single question.*

---

* With the picture's fate more or less settled, Keaton became increasingly candid in his opinion of *The Buster Keaton Story*. "The only thing I liked about it was O'Connor," he told the *Arizona Republic*. "But I'm the last one in the world to judge. All I did was to supervise the comedy sequences."

"I don't think I got in," Cavett continued. "[The reaction of the auto-graph people] was very sad, and I made a point afterwards when he finally came out of saying, 'Mr. Keaton, I just want to say this is the thrill of a lifetime for me.' He seemed very pleased."

It took two months for *Merton of the Movies* to make the transition to Hol-lywood, where it would occupy the thousand-seat Huntington Hartford Theatre, formerly the CBS Radio Playhouse, on Vine Street. Hartford, who was funding the move, was anticipating a possible Broadway run for *Mer-ton* if the show got over well, and certain changes were made. New settings were commissioned, and Keaton's weekly fee, which on the road had been $1,000, was bumped to $1,500. Most of the traveling cast remained intact, their commitment to the show unshakable. And the little film of rushes Keaton had made for the second act continued to grow until it was eight minutes in length.

"We ended up [in California] shooting out at Lake Sherwood," said James Karen. "We shot a wonderful sequence out there with a duck. We built what we called 'Doughnut Island' and I guess we got a big truck tire and covered it over with the grass and branches and stuff. Buster was out hunting, and he sees a duck out on the water. And he sees this little island, and he jumps over from the bank to the island and goes right through it. And he disappears into the water. There's a space of ten seconds, and Buster's hat shows up, and then Buster . . . and he's right in front of the duck with a gun. He points the gun at the duck, and water came out of the muzzle of the gun. And the duck suddenly attacked the muzzle of the gun—*Bite!* It's one of those marvelous accidents that only Buster could create."

Making the film with a pickup crew of three took Keaton back to his earliest days in the movies, when the process wasn't nearly as regimented and sound wasn't even a consideration. He directed easily, naturally, show-ing Eleanor where to place the camera and what the frame should contain. When processed, he tried editing the footage on a rewind with a viewer—a home movie setup—but nothing looked right to him. John Bennes mar-veled as he held the film up to the light, as he had back in the twenties, and tore it by hand. The finished product had all the verve and heart of one of his classic two-reelers, particularly when Keaton flawlessly reprised the gag from *The Frozen North* where, once again suggesting William S. Hart, he believes he's come across his wife with another man. Again he registers shock and dismay, and again tears are shed. Then they kiss, and the sight is too much for him to bear. He draws, shoots both of them dead, then realizes he's in the wrong house.

The scene shifts to Rodney St. Clair—a "man's man" according to the intertitle—who attempts to fish off a little dock and manages to fall in. Recovering his toupee, he wrings it out as one would a washrag and plops it back atop his head. Then comes the business at Lake Sherwood with Doughnut Island, the hunting rifle, and the scene-stealing duck. In the final segment, he returns with a little boat, which sends him face-first into the water as he attempts to board while the ducks look on placidly. He clambers back into the boat, weighs the rock he uses as an anchor, attempts to row, and clobbers himself in the face with one of the paddles. A duck appears, and in his haste to get in a lucky shot, he capsizes the tiny vessel, slowly disappearing into the water as he did in *The Boat,* leaving only his pork pie hat to mark the spot. It was an eight-minute interlude of utter delight for Los Angeles audiences, the premiere of a brand-new Buster Keaton comedy some thirty-five years in the making.

With the film finally completed to his satisfaction, Keaton began working out new bits of business for the play itself. "We did a thing where I hire him," Karen recalled. "I say, 'We're going to shoot this tomorrow—so you be here tomorrow.' And I leave him. I'm walking away, and there's a beautiful girl going by, and there's a little chair on stage right. I would put my foot up on the chair and talk to the girl. The set, in perspective, was of a town with a street, and Buster was checking everything. He was on a movie set at last! And he's checking, and he's following this street, and there's a ladder in front. He gets to the ladder, and he's walking up the ladder not realizing he's on a ladder. When he got to the top he would fall. And he would kick the top and do a front 108. My job, when I heard the click, was to kick the chair away with my foot. It was on domes of silence, so it slid, and Buster set it every night. And everybody knew they were not to touch that chair. I said, 'Jesus, Buster, I'm very nervous about this.' Because I just kicked it, and he caught it with his behind as it was rolling toward him. He just stopped it. He would fall into the chair and he would whip out a newspaper and pretend to be reading so that anybody who saw him [wouldn't know that he hadn't intended to do that]. I thought it was a terrible idea. I mean, I always kept saying, 'He's going to kill himself.' But he was always in control. He was *always* in control."

Merton of the Movies opened in Hollywood on October 8, 1957, but the Huntington Hartford was far from full. Mary Martin and John Raitt were drawing the big crowds downtown in *Annie Get Your Gun,* while the invitational premiere of M-G-M's *Raintree County,* a $6 million Civil War romance likened to *Gone With the Wind,* was taking place in Beverly Hills. The notices the next day lamented the creakiness of the thirty-five-year-old play while praising its star unreservedly.

"Keaton's sense of timing remains split-second perfect," the *Times'* Philip K. Scheuer reported. "Hilarious are such scenes in which he struggles with a wig in making himself up and in which he attempts to perform his first 'big' scene in a society set—not to mention those sequences shown on the screen."

But *Daily Variety,* which the industry crowd would see, warned them away: "The vast difference between acceptable silo fare and good road or Broadway material has rarely been pointed up as effectively. . . . Keaton played the citronella circuit with it last season and the results were sufficiently strong to encourage Huntington Hartford to mount it for key city presentation. It's a mistake."

Merton never found its footing. The first seven performances brought in just $10,000, less than half the house potential and $2,000 below operating costs.

"It was badly publicized," said Jane Dulo. "People thought it was Buster in an old silent film. If they could have hung on a few more weeks we could have built it up." The closing notice was posted before the first week was up, trimming the scheduled run from three weeks to two. Still, there was a steady stream of admirers eager to witness a live Keaton performance, including professionals who never went away disappointed. "I remember one time," said Karen, "Burl Ives and Roald Dahl and Roald Dahl's wife, Pat [Neal] were there. . . . They came backstage, and I used to makeup with Buster at the Huntington Hartford. They came in and Buster was taking off his makeup, and they were talking. Finally, Roald Dahl said, 'Jimmy, did you ever miss?' [meaning the gag with the ladder and the rolling chair]. I said, 'No,' modestly. 'Oh no, never missed.' And Buster said: 'Try it with an untalented butt some day, Jim.'"

Keaton continued to do television, by now limiting himself to one appearance a month to avoid overexposure. *The Rosemary Clooney Show, Playhouse 90, You Asked for It, The Betty White Show,* an occasional commercial. At first, he resisted the idea of selling aspirin and detergents and such, but found the money too good to ignore. One of the first things he did in the realm of advertising was a 1956 spot for Colgate toothpaste. Then in March 1957, he posed for photographer Bert Stern in a classy series of print ads for Smirnoff vodka.

"When it came time for me to negotiate for his services," said Ben Pearson, "Buster would always say, 'I'm not a commercial actor so price me out of the market.' I would forthwith quote some ridiculous fee, and I usually got it."

By August, Keaton was thinking of TV commercials as little comedy shorts akin to the two-reelers he made for Joe Schenck. "I've got an idea I'm going to try and sell," he told a reporter. "I'm going to create some thirty-second comedy commercials which I hope to film on my ranch just outside Hollywood. Farmer Keaton will be the pitch, and I think I can make people laugh and maybe sell some products at the same time." Why commercials? "Every time they show one of them, I get a check."

Nineteen fifty-eight brought two exceptional opportunities. The first was a set of five sixty-second spots for Alka-Seltzer in which Buster, in various guises, interacted with the brand's animated ambassador, Speedy Alka-Seltzer. The second, in which he was given more creative latitude, was a group of twenty-second spots for Northwest Orient, a regional airline based in Minnesota. These minimalist films were built around the company's jingle with Buster taking various approaches to sounding its trademark gong. Produced at the Desilu studios, Keaton could film eight of these in the space of two or three days. Actress Dorothy Lee, who was one of his occasional girlfriends after the bust-up of his second marriage, was a neighbor in Woodland Hills. She was driving by Buster's house one day just as he had pulled into the driveway. She stopped to say hello, and he pulled a check from his pocket.

"Hey, Lee, look at this! A thousand bucks for doing nothing!"

She asked him what it was for.

"I made a commercial today. It only took a couple of hours."

She frowned, shaking her head in mock disapproval. "Oh, Buster!"

He laughed. "I'll be dead in ten years, so who cares?"

The year 1958 also put Keaton back onstage, this time with a company of contemporaries in a revue originally conceived for TV. *Newcomers of 1928* was the brainchild of a writer-composer named Jackie Barnett, protégé and creator of special material for Jimmy Durante. The show was a sly gathering of performers who were all major show business figures just prior to the

Keaton onstage in Newcomers of 1928 *with Paul Whiteman, Rudy Vallée, and Harry Richman.*

Great Depression. The cast consisted of bandleader Paul Whiteman, singing star Harry Richman, crooner Rudy Vallée, French bombshell Fifi D'Orsay, and Keaton, who was accorded fourth billing in the ensemble. Backed by thirty-five singers, dancers, and showgirls, *Newcomers* opened at the Desert Inn in Las Vegas on February 25 and was an immediate hit. At the conclusion of the first night's performance, Barnett was called to the stage, where he was hailed by the cast and showered with bravos for creating a show that didn't lean too heavily on nostalgia for its punch.

For Keaton, it couldn't have been a more carefree engagement. Freed of the responsibility of carrying a show like *Merton of the Movies,* he participated in the initial "Newcomers of 1928" number with Whiteman, Richman, and Vallée, then took a long break in his dressing room, sometimes emerging during Rudy Vallée's number to fence with Whiteman behind the curtains using breadsticks. He went on next to closing with the pantomime duel he perfected at the Cirque Médrano, his opponent Whiteman, his second Vallée, his referee Richman. There was a dinner show at eight fifteen and a cocktail show at midnight. Without an intermission, the entire performance was in and out in eighty minutes, about the outside limit in Vegas for keeping the customers away from the gaming tables. Immediately, the hotel tried extending the show's six-week run by another four weeks, but most of the headliners had booking conflicts.

After a planned hiatus, *Newcomers* opened in Los Angeles for two weeks at Frank Sennes' Moulin Rouge. Again, the press was enthusiastic, and again Keaton's duel routine was celebrated as the show's comedy highlight. Then, heading into summer, he was again cast in a major dramatic role, having previously appeared in a relatively minor capacity in an all-star *Playhouse 90* called "No Time at All." Perhaps due to the broad exposure "The Awakening" gained in syndication, he found himself more prominently displayed in another *Playhouse 90,* this one a psychological thriller by Tad Mosel (*Other People's Houses*) titled "The Innocent Sleep."

Rehearsals for the live ninety-minute telecast stretched over a week, Keaton, as a deaf vagrant named Chas Blackburn, voicelessly popping in and out of the drama at critical moments, balefully regarding actress Hope Lange, who has taken a young lover (John Erickson) while in a marriage with a much older man (a Barrymore-ish Dennis King). Having once taken a cake knife to his father, the guilt-ridden Blackburn is a masochist who doesn't sleep and can't tolerate the regard of others. "He feels he must cadge his drinks," a character explains, "and even then accepts only dregs. Every summer, Charles Blackburn takes a booth at the bazaar. He hangs a piece of canvas painted like a target, cuts out the center, puts his head through. Ten cents a throw. Now that's conscience carried to criminal lengths." In time, Lange's character, Alex, comes to see herself in him.

Directed by Franklin J. Schaffner, "The Innocent Sleep" originated from CBS Television City on the night of June 5, 1958. Keaton displayed little in the way of nerves as he prepared to give a characterization unlike any he had ever attempted. There were aspects of Lon Chaney in his spare performance, and in the gripping climax, he riveted viewers as Alex placed a butcher knife in his hand and invited him to kill her.

Keaton had long been held in greater esteem in Europe than in America, and when major appreciations were written, they tended to come first from foreign shores. In June 1948, more than a year before "Comedy's Greatest Era" appeared in *Life,* Maurice Schérer (later the French director known as Éric Rohmer) placed him on a par with three of the screen's greatest stylists, F. W. Murnau, Sergei Eisenstein, and Orson Welles, in his first important article for *Revue du Cinéma,* "Le Cinéma, art de l'espace" ("Cinéma, art of space"). Schérer contrasted Keaton with René Clair and, more directly, with Chaplin, proclaiming him "not only one of the biggest comics of the screen, but one of the most authentic cinema geniuses."

Broad critical appreciation of Keaton was hampered by the scant avail-ability of his best films, and the maddening proliferation of some of his worst. In America, the release of his M-G-M talkies to television in 1957 compounded the damage done by the continued syndication of *Life with Buster Keaton*, which was now officially classified as a children's program and seemingly in all the major markets. Yet nowhere could *Sherlock Jr., The Navigator,* or *The General* be seen except for regional museum showings supplied by the Museum of Modern Art. Then in August 1958, prompted by the European release of *The Buster Keaton Story,* he appeared on the cover of *Cahiers du Cinéma* riding the cowcatcher of the No. 5 engine, a compo-sition reflecting the "elegance, skill, courage, and spirit of geometry" that distinguished his artistry. "We had been looking for a long time to talk about Buster Keaton at length," wrote Schérer, now the editor of this famous successor to *Revue du Cinéma*. "Why not take advantage of the calm of the summer and the release of Sidney Sheldon's mediocre film *L'Homme qui n'a jamais ri* [*The Man Who Never Laughed*] to celebrate one of the greatest actors in the history of cinema?"

Inside were twenty-three pages devoted to Keaton, the writing and analytical chores divided between critic André Martin and the magazine's American correspondent, John Schmitz. "Countless studies are devoted to the origins of today's great comic cineastes: Chaplin, René Clair, or Jacques Tati," Martin wrote in his introduction. "The films of Laurel and Hardy are regularly presented to the public. Every three years, Chaplin authorizes us to find, alternating with his new works, some of his former successes, while it is impossible to see Buster Keaton again when you want, or even to see his work evoked in reviews and magazines . . . The Seventh Art is, however, not so rich in comedians-auteurs-cineastes of this importance. Every day the complete work of some less amazing pioneers is piously exhumed and celebrated. Stupidly eclipsed, that of Buster Keaton is not a collection of aborted projects. Comprising at least ten films whose qualities escape the cinema of today, it is almost worth that of Chaplin for the number, and equal to the poetic and cinematographic value."

In preparing for the issue, Schmitz made the trek to the Keaton home to conduct a two-hour interview. "Mr. Keaton met me in the front of his ranch house with a watering hose in his hand. At once he smiled and said, 'Let me show you around my house.' I followed him as he showed me new trees he had just planted and a red chicken house in the form of a miniature schoolhouse which he had built. Baby chickens were climbing out of its doorway. He then took us through his house into the kitchen and gave me some Coca-Cola. We were directed into his study and sat around a poker table. On the walls were many pictures from his early days in films and portraits of his sons. 'They're both in their thirties,' he said, 'and I have six grandchildren.'

"I had typed out many questions that I had intended to ask him, but once we began talking I had little time to watch him and listen to his conversation. An enormous St. Bernard came into the room and Mr. Keaton petted him as he spoke. During our conversation he would sit down periodically, but very soon would be on his feet again, walking about as he talked, gesturing with a deftness that filled the room with imaginary properties and characters. His voice has resonance and authority, he speaks with precision and candor. His wife, Eleanor, entered the room and after a simple introduction entered the conversation in a natural informal manner."

Schmitz asked him about his deadpan expression. Did he consciously create it? "It never entered my mind," Keaton responded. "I was concentrated on what I was doing—it never occurred to me until people commented on it and I saw the films projected."

How did he show he was happy? "I had another way of telling the audience when I was happy."

How did he feel about *The Navigator*? "The greatest for laughing matter."

Did he have prints of his films? "No. Joseph Schenck owns all my early films. M-G-M took *The Navigator* and *Sherlock Jr.* with the idea of using them for a television show, but it didn't work out. The pictures are tied up by stockholders—without their consent they can't be released to anyone. If I had prints of my pictures I wouldn't hesitate to put them on television—I wouldn't mind going to court against any of those outfits [who control the negatives]."

It didn't take long for Keaton to settle into the community scene in Woodland Hills. He and Eleanor had purchased the property on Sylvan Way before the Ventura Freeway went through, and so any trips into Los Angeles were on surface streets, making the place seem even more remote than the thirty miles it took to reach downtown.

"It's rural," he said, "and the most peaceful place in the world." There was a barn on the parcel already, and lots of walnut trees. His first construction project was the chicken coop out back of the barn whose occupants—a dozen red hens and a rooster—were all named after the reigning glamour

Eleanor and Buster at home in Woodland Hills, California.

queens of the day—Ava, Marilyn, Jayne, Zsa Zsa. It had a small flagpole on it, and Keaton made a ceremony of running the flag up the pole every morning and lowering it at sunset.

"The chickens seem to like it," he said.

"My favorite memory of Buster," said Eleanor, "is doing his gardening out in the backyard. We had about an acre and a half, like a baby farm, and he used to put in a garden, and that was his favorite thing to do when he wasn't working. In fact, he could do a lot of writing while he was doing that. He'd come in from working in his garden, whatever, and he would have half a sketch organized."

Louise came out every Friday, and the guest bedroom was always kept waiting for her. On Sunday, when it was time to go home, Buster would take her to the market and buy more than enough food and supplies for the coming week. "She never had to buy food; she always had a car loaded with food to go home."

Melissa Talmadge's earliest memories of her grandfather were those of his distinctive chicken coop. "It looked like a little red schoolhouse," she said, "and you would go into the back, and there were boxes along the edge. When I was visiting over there, and he knew we were coming, he would let me go in and collect the eggs."

The kids' grandmother wasn't as much fun—she wasn't the sort to get down on the floor and play games with them—but her white stucco

Natalie Talmadge in 1949 with grandchildren Jim, Melissa, and Michael Talmadge.

house on Santa Monica's famed Gold Coast, where the neighbors included Harold Lloyd, Darryl Zanuck, George Jessel, and Peter Lawford, was. "I have very fond memories of going to Grandma's house to visit. She lived a couple of miles away on the beach, and my brothers and I would often spend the night there. It was a great house for kids and the backyard was all sand with a gate opening onto the beach. We each got to choose a bedroom to spend the night in, and mine was in the upstairs back with the view of the ocean. Grandma Natalie liked to tip the Four Roses, but my mother never would have let us go down there if it was in any way unsafe or if she wasn't capable of watching us." Natalie was, however, a heavy smoker, and Barbara worried that she might drop a lit cigarette and send the house up in flames.

Around Natalie, the bitter topic of Buster never came up. ("For heaven sakes, Natalie, they were not born by immaculate conception," Dutch Talmadge once exclaimed. "Will you *please* wise up?") Jim Talmadge built a house in nearby Pacific Palisades, and Natalie would come to dinner once a week.

"We had a breakfast nook in the kitchen," remembered Barbara. "We were sitting there having dinner, and all of a sudden [our eldest son] Jimmy pipes up. 'We don't tell Grandma Natalie about Grandpa Buster, do we?' This is out of a three-year-old mouth! Jim slid down underneath the table; I think I probably sat there with my mouth open. Natalie, she got bigger and bigger because she was little, and she got up and she said, 'Take me home now.' She didn't say another word. She was furious. He took her home, and she never said a word on the way. She got out of the car and slammed the door and stalked in. That was the first information she had that we had been seeing Buster."

On an evening in 1958, Buster took Eleanor to a screening of *The General,* a picture she had heard much about but had never seen. The showing was at a small theater in Beverly Hills known as the Coronet, the 267-seat home of the Society of Cinema Arts, which had been programming the venue since 1950. At the door, they were greeted by a man named Kristian Chester, who recognized Keaton and escorted them in. Chester then excused himself and raced up to the projection booth, where he advised Raymond Rohauer, the projectionist and founder of the Society of Cinema Arts, that Johnnie Gray himself was in the house.

"He came down," recalled Eleanor, "and said, 'Hi, I want to talk to you after,' and he went back up."

Rohauer was an interesting character. Born in Buffalo in 1924, he moved to Los Angeles with his mother, a seamstress, at the age of eighteen. While a drama student at Los Angeles City College, he wrote scripts, acted, and worked odd jobs, even pulling a stretch on the grave-digging detail at Hollywood Memorial Park. He met Kristian Chester when the older man picked him up while hitchhiking on Wilshire Boulevard. The two probably became lovers, and Chester threw in with him in his goal of making an amateur feature in 16mm. Rohauer completed the seventy-two-minute *Whirlpool* in 1947, drawing admiring coverage in *Hollywood Review* and the magazine *Home Movies* (which titled its illustrated story "Hollywood Genius"). Rohauer formed the Society of Cinema Arts the following year and began a brief career as a concert promoter, presenting coloratura soprano Miliza Korjus, Ethel Waters, contralto Eula Beal, and pianist Soulima Stravinsky in recitals at L.A.'s Philharmonic Auditorium.

With his move to the Coronet, Rohauer aggressively programmed avant-garde, experimental, animated, and documentary films in addition to domestic and foreign classics. In 1956, he served as a source for Robert Smith, who asked him to help locate some of the shorts and features that he, Sidney Sheldon, and Donald O'Connor wanted to study for *The Buster Keaton Story*. In 1957, Rohauer was credited as producer on a pair of shockers imported from Finland and Sweden, and in October of that year, he was arrested for showing two homoerotic films—one of which was Kenneth Anger's *Fireworks*—and charged with "exhibiting a lewd play." By this time, Rohauer had developed a reputation as slippery and untrustworthy, even as he made the Coronet one of the most important film showcases on the West Coast.

What Rohauer wanted to know that night was if Keaton had prints of any of his pictures, but Buster had to tell him no. James Mason had transferred all of his personal prints to the Academy. Did Keaton own the rights? Rohauer pressed. No, he told him, Joe Schenck owned them. It was, however, a momentous meeting for both men. In Keaton, Rohauer would find the vessel for his ambitions to become an owner and distributor of important films. And in Rohauer, Keaton would find an obsessive champion for his legacy as one of the world's great filmmakers. Eleanor was dubious. To her, Rohauer was the strangest man she had ever met.

What Keaton gave Rohauer that night was a target. The mother lode of Keaton properties was close at hand—the Academy of Motion Picture Arts and Sciences was within walking distance of the Coronet. All Rohauer, an inveterate film collector, needed was access to those prints, presumably all pristine 35mm originals. An association with Keaton himself would confer legitimacy, but it wouldn't go far enough toward Rohauer's eventual goal, which was a degree of ownership.

"The first thing I did was send Buster over to see Joe Schenck, to get Schenck to help Buster get the rights to Buster Keaton Productions," Rohauer told Edward Watz, a business associate, in 1977. "Buster knew that Schenck had a stroke, but I told him he recovered. Schenck lived at the Beverly Hilton in the penthouse, so we went there and I waited in the lobby. Buster came down and said, 'I don't know if he recognized me.' So I had to find another way to get somebody on our side."

Said Eleanor: "Raymond knew Joe Schenck was in bad shape, but he lied to Buster. He said, 'He's fine! He wants to help.' When Buster came home he was still upset. He felt like he was tricked into bothering his sick old friend. We didn't talk to Raymond for a while after that happened. He knew to leave us alone."

If the man behind Buster Keaton Productions was an invalid, Rohauer assumed there would be no opposition to a newly created entity also called Buster Keaton Productions. On September 24, 1958, papers were filed establishing it as a California Domestic Corporation. This time, Keaton would be the president, Rohauer vice president, and Eleanor secretary. Now that he was formally in business with the Keatons, Rohauer could approach the Academy on something other than bended knee. What he didn't know was that the surviving trustee in the liquidation of the original company, Leopold Friedman, was breathing new life into the old, original entity. In a letter to Irving Berlin, one of the initial stockholders, Friedman advised him of an offer from Robert Youngson Productions, which had a deal with 20th Century-Fox. Formerly the Academy Award–winning producer of one-reel shorts for Warner Bros., Youngson had the idea to produce a theatrical feature made up of scenes from silent comedies, dressed up with music and narration and condensed for modern consumption. Warner rejected the idea, and Youngson struck out on his own. The result, the seventy-eight-minute *Golden Age of Comedy*, was a surprise hit, pulling in more than $500,000 in domestic rentals, exclusive of foreign and TV sales.

"They intend to produce three pictures (primarily for theater exhibition) in which they may use footage from these old Buster Keaton silent pictures," Friedman advised, outlining the deal. "They have offered to pay $500 as an advance royalty for the use during a period of seven years, of material from these old Keaton shorts in the making of three planned photoplays, against 40% of the producer's net profits (after certain deductions) of the three pictures, if the entire new pictures are made up of material from the old two-reel shorts. This percentage of the net profits may be less if the footage of the new picture is not comprised in its entirety of the material from the old films. However, in no event can it be less than 27½%."

He added: "In developing the foregoing deal I have had the assistance of . . . the law firm of Bautzer & Grant, who represents Mr. Joseph M. Schenck (founder of the Keaton company and its principal stockholder). With their assistance I hope to develop a market for the further use of the foregoing pictures and will keep you advised from time to time of the result of our efforts."

27

Once Upon a Mattress

R UDI BLESH'S BIOGRAPHY "The Two Worlds of Buster Keaton" was at
a standstill by 1958, finished but unpublishable because the author
refused to make any cuts. "We were kind of out of touch," said Eleanor Keaton, "because Rudi, for a finish, wound up back in New York. I'm
not sure, but he had a place in Vermont and lived up there for a long time.
We really didn't see him that much." So the door was wide open in November of that year when a professional writer and novelist named Charles Samuels came along. Samuels, who had written numerous books, including a
biography of boxing promoter Tex Rickard and as-told-to autobiographies
with Ethel Waters and Boris Morros (*My Ten Years as a Counterspy*), had a
tentative deal with Doubleday to bring Buster Keaton's story to the reading public. Offered a $1,000 advance against a percentage of the royalties,
Keaton invited Samuels to Las Vegas, where he was due to open in a reboot
of *Newcomers of 1928*. Armed with a portable typewriter, Samuels spent five
weeks in Vegas debriefing his subject, poised to turn whatever Keaton told
him into a generic version of the authorial voice, scrubbed clean of collo-
quialisms and color. Samuels already had an appropriately banal title for the
book: *My Wonderful World of Slapstick*.

"He never talked to anybody," Eleanor complained. "He didn't even talk
to me. And he and Buster would go off by themselves up in the room, and
they'd talk and he'd take it right on the typewriter. That's the way he always
worked. . . . He and Buster would work together all day, every day, and then
afterwards he came and stayed at our house for three weeks. And we were
together all the time, but he never asked me a question. He didn't want to
know anybody's opinion."

As was Keaton's habit when he was approached directly, he made the deal without consulting Ben Pearson. Now seven years into his business relationship with Keaton, Pearson was resigned to Buster's impulses. "He wouldn't always get the right terms," Pearson said. "I could've done better for him when he did some of those commercials but he would sell himself cheap. He'd usually pay me a commission even on the jobs he'd set up himself. But I could've helped him get better terms. . . . He made that bloody deal with that guy that wrote the Ethel Waters book—Charles Samuels—without consulting me. Nor did he give me any money. He made that deal with Samuels when he was out in Las Vegas in the Paul Whiteman show. And he made that deal with Raymond Rohauer without consulting me. I didn't get any money out of that, and that's all right, but Rohauer is one awful guy."

In September 1959, Rohauer persuaded Keaton to sign over any rights he might still retain to his old pictures in exchange for a half share of the profits. In turn, Rohauer assigned those rights to Buster Keaton Productions, Inc. "What I don't understand," Keaton said to James Karen, "is what the hell's all this about these films? Who the hell wants to see a picture that's forty years old?"

It took a year, but now Rohauer was ready to make his move with the Academy of Motion Picture Arts and Sciences. On October 26, 1959, he met with assistant executive director Sam E. Brown as a representative of Keaton Productions. The following day, Benjamin D. Brown, a Los Angeles–based attorney representing the newly established corporation, wrote the Academy to confirm that Sam Brown had agreed to loan their print of *Cops* for screening purposes. The Academy cautioned that no such oral agreement had been reached, so the next day, October 28, a formal request for the loan was made in writing by the attorney. On October 30, executive director Margaret Herrick recommended the loan be made, but with the stipulation that the print be accompanied by an Academy employee "to get out of a difficult situation."

Cops, of course, was copied, and it became the first 35mm Keaton subject in Rohauer's inventory. Two months later, on December 31, attorney Brown wrote again to indicate that Keaton wanted to borrow *The General* and *Our Hospitality,* also for screening, and that the prints would be picked up on January 6, 1960. New 35mm negatives of *Cops, The General,* and *Our Hospitality* would give the corporation three of Keaton's most important titles. This time, however, the process didn't go quite so smoothly. On January 29, Rohauer advised the Academy that *Our Hospitality* had "deteriorated considerably" and that it was impossible to run all the reels. Both it and *The General* would be returned the following week, at which time Keaton Productions wished to borrow *The Saphead*, *The Navigator*, and *Sherlock Jr.*

In order to cover the fact that all the loaned prints were being duplicated, Rohauer conceived the fiction that Keaton had prints of many of his old pictures stored in the garage of his old house on Victoria. It was, he maintained, these prints that were being copied, not the prints that had come to the Academy from James Mason. He also made the claim that he met Keaton in 1954, and that he first examined the films, at Keaton's invitation, before the Mason prints ever came to light. Shrewdly, Rohauer never made an outright claim to the copyrights of the films he was borrowing, trusting that the name of the new corporation and Keaton himself would give him all the credibility he needed. When the films were returned to the Academy in late February, Rohauer told them that *The Navigator* and *Sherlock Jr.* were each missing a reel, which was consistent with the records the Academy kept as to which reels had been lost to decomposition. Not knowing this though, Rohauer hopefully added that he was sure the missing reel to *The Navigator* had simply been misplaced in the Academy's vault.

It was perhaps all this activity surrounding the Academy's Keaton holdings that raised Buster's profile among the organization's small administrative staff and occasioned an entirely unanticipated result. The Academy Awards ceremony was set to take place in Hollywood on April 5, 1960. At a celebrity-studded pre-event supper given by Louella Parsons and songwriter Jimmy McHugh, Keaton was invited to impersonate a waiter, one of his favorite practical jokes, and hector the TV hosts, actors Tony Randall and Betsy Palmer, by spilling drinks and plates of hors d'oeuvres as they attempted to interview the nominees.

"They set it up at the Hollywood Brown Derby, right [down] the street from the Pantages theater where they did the Oscar show," Eleanor remembered. "All the names like Hedda Hopper and Louella Parsons, all the big name–type people were there in the restaurant as guests, and they interviewed around from table to table. And they got Buster and Bob Cummings and a couple more to be the waiters. They dressed in the waiters' uniforms and they waited on tables for all of this whole show, and that's how they got Buster to go. Because Buster wouldn't go to the Oscar show; what did he know from that? They said, 'Come and be a waiter . . . and we'll save you seats.'"

At an all-star supper prior to the thirty-second annual Academy Awards, Keaton waits on songwriter Jimmy McHugh and actress Jane Russell.

As editor Henry Hart would report in *Films in Review,* "Keaton was in and out of camera range throughout this half-hour show at the Brown Derby and stole the show."

The awards ceremony itself was unremarkable, with Metro's *Ben-Hur* picking up eleven statuettes, including Best Actor, Best Director, and Best Picture. Yet the clear favorite of the evening was actress Simone Signoret's win for *Room at the Top.* Afterward, the winners and nominees and all the participants converged on the Governors Ball at the Beverly Hilton, where Buster and Eleanor were seated at the main table with Bob and Dolores Hope. Academy president Benjamin Kahane rose to announce the presentation of two honorary awards. The first went to Dr. Lee de Forest, the eighty-six-year-old Father of Radio, "for historic achievement in the science of sound pioneering, and for inventing the vacuum tube that gave voice to the screen."

Then Kahane announced that the night's final Oscar, "for having made pictures that will play as long as pictures are shown," would go to Buster Keaton. The response from the crowd was instantaneous. People leaped to their feet, applauding fervently, a joyous, thundering ovation that swept over him in waves of affection. Gary Cooper, Olivia de Havilland, Billy Wilder, Charlton Heston, Ginger Rogers, William Wyler, Elizabeth Taylor, John Wayne, Jack Lemmon, Susan Hayward, hundreds of others. And then came the cheers. It was, said Harrison Carroll, "the most spontaneous standing ovation I ever saw."

Later that same evening, he is presented with an honorary Oscar by Academy president Benjamin Kahane.

Startled by the commotion, it took Keaton a moment to overcome his natural reticence and get to his feet. This was not just for him, he decided, but for some of the better pictures he had brought to the screen—*The Navigator, Steamboat Bill, Jr., Our Hospitality, The General,* most of all. Slowly, he made his way to the microphone, fighting back tears as he attempted to speak.

"It wasn't on the air," said Eleanor, "but he was thrilled about that. Stood up there, crying, and all he managed to get out was 'Thank you.'"

Robert Youngson's picture, the one that occasioned his deal with Leopold Friedman, was called *When Comedy Was King.* Placed into wide release just prior to Keaton's honorary Oscar, it put him before modern movie audiences in scenes from one of his greatest achievements, *Cops.* Youngson's formula was to treat the old two-reelers he showcased with respect, using the best-quality materials and presenting them at their proper speeds. The narration was learned and sympathetic, at times poignant. And Youngson dispensed with the cliché of the tinkling upright piano, opting instead for the raucous sound of a pit band, returning often to the familiar theme of Chopin's Étude opus 10, no. 3 for the sentimental heft it conveyed. Keaton, busy promoting *My Wonderful World of Slapstick,* consulting on TV pilots and commercials, and rehearsing a *Sunday Showcase* special titled "After Hours," failed to notice.

Small wonder. In New York, columnist Earl Wilson asked him for the name of the TV special. "What the hell is the name of it?" said Buster, looking to Eleanor for help.*

---

* Keaton's memory was notoriously bad when it came to names and titles. "One day in a New York elevator," Ben Pearson recounted, "a guy greeted him like a long-lost brother, pumped his

"Maybe it's on the script here," she suggested, taking a look. "No-o-o, all it says here is Act One."

He shifted to ticking off his commitments. "We go back to do a coffee commercial, and one for somebody's cigars."

"That'll be his sick day," Eleanor interjected. "He doesn't smoke cigars."

He mentioned that his silent pictures were to be rereleased in Europe, that they wanted him to tour in the musical *Once Upon a Mattress,* that his autobiography was out, and that Jack Webb had hired him to help direct a couple of new TV comics.

"But you can't think of the name of the TV show?" Wilson pressed.

"'Long Chance' or something . . . I play Santa Claus. You know I did a movie recently—accidentally." He meant *The Adventures of Huckleberry Finn,* on which he worked exactly one day.

"Buster's incorporated," Eleanor said brightly, referring to the entity Rohauer established.

"What network is your TV show on?" Wilson asked.

"I don't know what the devil they call it" came the answer. "You can probably find it."

Wilson did, but with no thanks to one of its stars. Keaton played a nice opening cameo in "After Hours" as a sidewalk Santa, but the show, a droll comedy of modern psychiatry, really belonged to principals Christopher Plummer, Sally Ann Howes, Philip Abbott, and Natalie Schafer.

When Comedy Was King opened in Hollywood on May 18, 1960, but by then Raymond Rohauer was already well aware of Leopold Friedman. Rohauer had assured Keaton the new corporation had gained outright ownership of the ten silent features he made for Joe Schenck and twelve of his two-reel comedies, principally those distributed by First National, but the truth of the matter was more complicated. Schenck was never vigilant about his copyrights, and his old pictures, particularly the silent ones, seemed to interest him not at all. Once the initial registrations had been filed with the Copyright Office, they were good for twenty-eight years. All were eligible for renewal in the twenty-eighth year, extending protection for a total of fifty-six, but by 1948, when the first of the Keaton two-reelers came up for

---

hand and slapped him on the back. As we left the car, Keaton said to me, 'Who's that fellow? I cooked him barbecue at my house once.' I told him it was Noël Coward."

renewal, they were, for all practical purposes, played out, and even Friedman failed to keep track.

And so the Keaton pictures began to fall into the public domain, available for commercial exploitation to all who could secure prints. The exceptions were the shorts and features distributed by Metro, Metro-Goldwyn, and Metro-Goldwyn-Mayer. The studio had a team of lawyers that made sure the great M-G-M backlog, which included such classics as *Grand Hotel, The Wizard of Oz,* and *Gone With the Wind,* remained protected for as long as the law allowed, and few renewals escaped their notice. *One Week* and *Three Ages* slipped by, and both entered the public domain in 1949 and 1952, respectively, but all the other Metro shorts and features were renewed on schedule, and these formed the basis of the rights claimed by Friedman and the remnants of the original Buster Keaton Productions.*

This, of course, left a number of copyright-free subjects for Rohauer, Keaton, and the new company to exploit, including a majority of the shorts and at least two of Keaton's strongest features. But Rohauer couldn't legitimately assert ownership over these to the extent of preventing others from profiting from them. So how to turn back the copyright clock? Rohauer hit on a strategy: Modify the films with changes and embellishments and then copyright the *new* matter. He embarked on a process of rewriting the intertitles, adding canned music, and altering crucial edits made by Keaton and his original cutters. To act as a pilot for this approach, Rohauer selected *Steamboat Bill, Jr.,* one of the features he borrowed from the Academy and copied. On April 13, 1960, two 16mm prints containing new matter ("revisions") were received by the Copyright Office. The "new matter" was registered in the name of Buster Keaton, falsely claiming a publication date of June 6, 1956, two years before Rohauer and Keaton actually met.

Armed with the new copyright registration, Rohauer and his attorney filed suit against two well-known organizations in the Bay Area, where a 16mm print of *Steamboat Bill, Jr.* was known to have been floating around. One sought to enjoin three area men and several John Does associated with the San Francisco Film Society from exhibiting the film, and asked they be ordered to surrender the print. The other targeted the Berkeley Cinema Guild, seeking $150,000 in damages and requiring the manager of the the-

---

* It's interesting to note that *Cops* was one of the First National releases that had fallen into the public domain, but the deal Friedman made with Robert Youngson was probably for a blanket license and may have left Youngson to his own devices in securing prints.

ater, Pauline Kael (later the renowned film critic for *The New Yorker*), to turn over copies of *Cops, The Balloonatic, The Haunted House,* and *The General,* among others Rohauer suspected they owned.

This flurry of activity on the part of Buster Keaton Productions, Inc., was summarized in an item in *Variety* headlined "BUSTER KEATON SUES FRISCO FILM SOCIETY." By then, Leopold Friedman had learned that Rohauer had exhibited his newly minted print of *The Navigator* at the Coronet Theatre in March 1960. Foreshadowing Rohauer's own hardball tactics, Friedman promptly brought an action against him in the district court seeking damages for the alleged infringement and a preliminary injunction against further showings. Rohauer countered by asking that the injunction be denied, and the battle was joined.

On July 6, 1960, the Copyright Office received duplicate prints of five Buster Keaton shorts—*The Blacksmith, The Boat, My Wife's Relations, The Paleface,* and *The Play House*—and three additional features, all claiming revisions and bogus publication dates and seeking to have them registered in the name of Buster Keaton. Significantly, all the shorts and two of the features (*College* and *The General*) were among those films received by the Academy from James Mason in 1956 and subsequently borrowed for "viewing" by Buster Keaton Productions. And since these were all titles that were otherwise in the public domain, Leopold Friedman could do nothing to stop it. He would have to concentrate on the seven shorts and six features still protected by virtue of the M-G-M renewals.

On July 14, the Keatons and Rohauer left for Europe aboard the *Queen Mary,* destined for Munich. Keaton told *Variety*'s man in Paris, Gene Moskowitz, that he was there to put sound to some of his pictures, which had finally reverted to him "after years of legal battles." He said he intended to rerelease them theatrically and to sell them to television. "The success of Charles Chaplin and W. C. Fields reissues here, as well as that of the early U.S. comic pic compilations *The Golden Age of Comedy* and *When Comedy Was King* augur a good future for Keaton's pix," wrote Moskowitz. "Rene Clair is now prepping the French version of Keaton's *Our Hospitality.*"

While in Germany, Keaton was so focused on business he was caught unprepared when asked to make a public appearance. "They wanted me on a television show there," he related, "and I sez, 'Well, the first thing I gotta do is have a hat. Where's a hat store?' They point to one across the street. I went over there. Nobody in the place speaks English. I don't speak German. So I went down and found the type of fedora I wanted, start tryin' them on until finally they came to my aid and they found one that fit me. When I found one that fit me, [I] took the price tag off, then took the money out of my pocket and held it out and let them take the money. Well, it was kind of an expensive hat—it amounted to about ten dollars. So now I ask 'em for a pair of scissors, [miming the scissors with his fingers]. They don't know what the hell I want scissors for, but they go get me a pair of scissors. I immediately started to cut down the brim. Then I reached in and pulled out all the insides of the hat—threw it away, tore it out. Then started to break it down. Well, these people look at me as if I'm absolutely going out of my mind. I pay ten dollars for a hat, an expensive hat, then cut it to pieces, tear out the insides. But when I finally get it down like that, where I wanted it, and put it on, looked in the mirror, all three in the store threw their hands up and said: 'BOOSTER!' "

The European trip was brief in duration because rehearsals were due to begin in New York for *Once Upon a Mattress,* the hit musical-comedy derived from Hans Christian Andersen's tale *The Princess and the Pea.* "They tried to get me to do the part [of King Sextimus] when the show was being produced here," Keaton told the Associated Press. "But it was planned for an off-Broadway theater, and I was having too much fun making television commercials on the coast." Jack Gilford played the character instead, and actor Will Lee (later Mr. Hooper on *Sesame Street*) assumed the role when the show moved to Broadway. Before leaving for Europe, Keaton was able to catch one of the final performances at the St. James Theatre. According to Eleanor, seeing the show on its feet was part of Buster's rehearsal process, after which he "cleaned up a bunch of stuff to make it precise."

The national tour of *Once Upon a Mattress* commenced at the Erlanger Theatre in Chicago on September 1, 1960. Starring opposite Keaton as Princess Winnifred, the role originated in New York by Carol Burnett, was comedienne Dody Goodman, prominent for her frequent TV appearances with Jack Paar. Also in the cast: Harold Lang, Fritzi Burr, Cy Young, and, as Lady Mabelle, one of the ladies of the court, Eleanor (who chose to be billed as Mrs. Buster Keaton). As he had with *Merton of the Movies,* Buster tried injecting some broad slapstick into the initial performances, only to find the rough stuff fell flat with audiences worried, at his age, that he'd injured himself. Director Jack Sydow gently discouraged him from keeping in such things, and Keaton settled into the role of the king henpecked into silence

Keaton as King Sextimus in Once Upon a Mattress.

by the shrewish Queen Aggravain, wordlessly mastering a pair of musical numbers, "The Minstrel, the Jester, and I" and, particularly, the delightful "Man to Man Talk" in which he mimed the birds and the bees to his gawky son, Prince Dauntless, the Drab.

"Mr. Keaton is Mr. Keaton," cheered Claudia Cassidy of the *Chicago Tribune,* "and how we could do without him this long is more than I can reasonably understand." Business was respectable in the show's first week, better in the second week, stronger still in the third. "The thing that always impressed me about Buster," said Sydow, "is that most actors will elaborate on a role as they go along. What Buster did was he pared everything down to absolute minimum. When he started to lose the laughs, then he goosed it up a little bit. He always pared down; he never added to. It was always the most simple and the most direct way to get the laugh. It was always very precise and very clean and very consistent."

Acting the king became second nature to him, but Germany was never far from his mind. Five days into the Chicago run of *Mattress,* he sat for a forty-minute conversation with WFMT's Studs Terkel. "I'm just back from Europe and went through to Munich," Keaton told him. "And then passing through Paris I found out that this *When Comedy Was King* was playing in four theaters there. And then I found out that they were playing at six theaters in London, about three in West Berlin, and even down into Munich, which is one of their big labs, their studios. An exhibitor says, 'Have you got any pictures we can have? I mean the silents?' I sez, 'No, but I'm going to make sure you get 'em.' So in Munich I made arrangements to give them dupe negatives because I found prints. The original negatives . . . practically gone, but finding good prints of all these old pictures that I could get a good dupe negative off of, and give 'em to them there in Munich. They will make new prints, some with the subtitles . . . in French, some in German, some in Italian, some in Spanish, and some in English. And all we would do is put a full orchestration music track to those silent pictures, with no moderator, and leave the old-fashioned subtitles in, but a good musical score behind 'em, and re-release 'em. And this is going to happen within the next couple of months. . . . Start in Europe first, because television hasn't wrecked all the neighborhood motion picture theaters there. So you got an awful lot of theaters. Well, soon as I see what they are going to do there, then I'll have prints made for here."

Once Upon a Mattress moved on to San Francisco, where it was booked into the Geary Theater for a four-week stay. As in Chicago, the box office started out slow and then built, powered by reviews and word of mouth and the slightly risqué nature of the title.

"It's a clean show," Keaton insisted, "a musical fairy tale. That's probably why they wanted me. I guess I'm the last living comedian who's never had any censorship trouble. I'm not a nightclub comedian." Still, a lot of pinching and goosing helped define his character as a randy old soul. "Somewhere along the line," recounted the *Examiner*'s Charles Einstein, "Mr. Keaton, John Baylis as the minstrel, and the redoubtable Harold Lang, as the jester, sing a duet for three people, if you can imagine such a thing—and if you know Mr. Keaton, you can. 'What's good for the gander,' they sing, as Mr. Keaton disappears momentarily from view, 'is good for the—' Piercing off-stage scream."

Keaton celebrated his sixty-fifth birthday on October 4, a day he shared with Damon Runyon, Charlton Heston, and Rutherford B. Hayes, at Chinatown's Kuo Wah Cafe with a magnum of champagne and a three-tiered chocolate cake. Dody Goodman and guests helped him finish off the champagne, while the cake was whisked back to the Geary for the cast's enjoyment.

With the years weighing on him, he again told a reporter he was going to retire. "I've had it," he said. "When I finish this play, there'll be no more." In Los Angeles, the Keatons savored a respite from the road, four weeks at home in Woodland Hills and a welcome break from hotel lobbies and restaurant food. ("All we know is the hotel and the theater—back and forth," Buster said.) They had the entire company of twenty-eight out to the house one night for a spaghetti dinner. (Keaton was fond of cooking for guests; his specialty was lobster Joseph.) The local notices were fine, even laudatory, but business at the Biltmore Theatre took a sharp drop in the third week, a dip that drove the L.A. engagement into the red.

It was during the company's five-day stopover in Denver that Keaton made one of his best-known and most fondly remembered television appearances. Allen Funt's *Candid Camera* grew out of a radio series titled *Candid Microphone* and had been on television, off and on, since 1948. The series had just debuted on the CBS network, paired with *What's My Line?* on Sunday nights, and Funt was recruiting familiar faces such as Van Johnson, George Gobel, and singer Dorothy Collins to pull hidden camera tricks on random victims. "We were in the process of finding unusual people to add to the *Candid Camera* series," Funt said, "and he was one such—the perfect introduction of a new type of comedy for us. So we sought him out—and he was."

With Keaton's penchant for practical jokes, the assignment held special appeal for him. The setting for the stunt was a roadside diner, and he was seated at the counter. "We went out in those days with no clear idea of what we would do," said Funt. "We knew it was going to be a diner location, and [that we would] have maybe two or three ideas that we'd try. . . . The first thing he said was, 'I could do some funny things while I'm having breakfast.' I said, 'Well, that's wonderful. Do you need any props?' And he said, 'No, nothing, zero.' I said, 'Why don't you try it once and I get an idea what it looks like?' We rolled that camera. He sat down and he was in trouble for twenty minutes. And the people alongside of him were trying so hard to be polite and not look at him, you know. But they just couldn't keep their eyes off."

Clad in a seasonal overcoat, civilian hat, and thick glasses, Buster is virtually unrecognizable as he enters and sits next to an unsuspecting woman. Lighting a cigarette, he orders a bowl of soup. He tastes, and as he adds pepper the top comes off the shaker. Fishing it out of the soup, his watch comes loose and falls in after it. While cleaning the soup off his watch, he drops the handkerchief in as well. And, of course, he spills his coffee in his lap. In another vignette, he has ditched the hat for an ill-fitting toupee. Again with the pepper, which causes him to sneeze—propelling the cheap misshapen rug into the soup. Then the glasses go tumbling in. He spills coffee on his sandwich, saturating it, then wrings it out like a dish rag. Reaching behind the counter for the sugar, he catches his jacket on something and the entire sleeve pulls away.

"One gag right after another," marveled Funt. "And one take, one take, and that was it. He was truly a genius."

While Keaton was on the road with *Once Upon a Mattress,* Raymond Rohauer had a series of court dates with Leopold Friedman. Rohauer had been successful in getting a federal judge to deny Friedman's writ for a preliminary injunction against further showings of *The Navigator,* but when the judge who issued that denial suddenly died, Friedman renewed his request, hoping another judge would see it his way. This second attempt was no more successful than the first, a judge holding that Rohauer's claim that neither Loew's nor M-G-M ever held the copyright to the picture was credible enough to justify a denial. He set a pre-trial hearing for October 3, when Keaton would be in San Francisco with *Mattress.* Finally, on November 22, district court judge William Mathes ruled in Friedman's favor, granting his request for an injunction against future screenings at the Coronet Theatre, awarding nominal damages of $250 and $600 in attorney's fees.

Rohauer correctly contended that the old Buster Keaton Productions was an independent production entity, and that Metro had only a limited distribution deal for *The Navigator* that had expired by the time Loew's Incorporated renewed the copyright in 1952. But then he claimed that since Loew's was not the copyright proprietor at the time of the renewal, the renewal was invalid and the picture was in the public domain, a stretch the court found unpersuasive. Friedman countered that Loew's copyright renewal was valid on behalf of Keaton Productions, since Nicholas Schenck, as Loew's president, was a principal stockholder. Judge Mathes' decision applied only to *The Navigator,* but both sides knew it set a precedent for all the Keaton films renewed by Loew's. Nevertheless, Rohauer, through his attorney, vowed he would appeal all the way to the U.S. Supreme Court.

The Keatons spent Christmas with the company of *Once Upon a Mattress* in Detroit, riding the city buses around town, loaded down with trees and packages during a week's holiday break. The show opened there on December 26, playing into the new year. In Columbus, an old vaudevillian sought him out, as they did in many of the cities in which they stopped. Jenny

Crotty, formerly of the Crotty Trio, brought photos and clippings and memories of playing Tony Pastor's at about the same time as the Keatons. They stood outside the stage door in the weak winter sun, stagehands milling about.

"Jenny," he said, his expressive hands doing much of the talking, "it's been a long time since I played the old Keith's here on East Gay Street. Burt Cutler, my uncle, was the bandleader of the Al G. Field Minstrels and we always stayed at his house."

There were stops in Cincinnati, Louisville, and Baltimore, the show chugging along at a deliberate pace, its income flat and predictable, its reviews praising the actors and the overall level of production while bemoaning the thinness of the material. The tour came to a conclusion in Boston, where it closed at the Colonial Theatre on March 18, 1961. Losses were well in excess of $100,000, with some of the slack taken up by a bus-and-truck company headed by Imogene Coca and Edward Everett Horton that played split weeks in places like Tacoma and Salt Lake City. The Keatons lingered in the east, Buster appearing on the Jack Paar show, and then they made their way back to Detroit, where he picked up a new Cadillac at the factory, a yearly ritual and a favorite indulgence. They had scarcely been home a week when a call came from Horton, who had been offered a part in Frank Capra's new picture, *Pocketful of Miracles*.

"He said, 'Would you come and take my place? So I can do this Capra movie?'" Eleanor remembered. "'We only have [a] one-week stop and then go into Washington, D.C., for eight weeks,* so you wouldn't be doing all that traveling.' He looked at me and I looked at him, and he says, 'All right.' So we went and we did a week somewhere in Ohio and then went into Washington, D.C., and finished Edward Everett Horton's tour."

Keaton loved playing the show, and did so one final time at Tonawanda, near Niagara Falls, for two weeks in August, his first and only time working in the round. He told a reporter for a Buffalo paper it was going to be his farewell to touring. "I'm going to stay home on my thinking man's farm and only make a few commercials a year."

Eleanor wondered if he had the resolve, since he had tried to retire two or three times before. "I have my fingers crossed about him not touring anymore," she said. "Staying home sounds fine, but it usually lasts about three weeks."

---

* It was actually for six weeks.

Keaton chats with veteran comedy director Norman Z. McLeod during the filming of "Once Upon a Time," a 1961 episode of Rod Serling's The Twilight Zone.

Apart from a few commercials and an industrial filmed for a planned community in Arizona called *The Home Owner,* Keaton's two major projects for the remainder of the year were both for television. *The Scene Stealers* was a one-hour special teaming him with Ed Wynn in an all-star push for the 1962 March of Dimes campaign, notable primarily for a brief reunion with host Jimmy Durante. More significant in terms of posterity was a third-season episode of *The Twilight Zone* written expressly for him by series regular Richard Matheson, titled "Once Upon a Time." Matheson's idea was to take a disgruntled citizen from the year 1890 and transport him, via time machine, to the clamor and expense of the modern world. The job returned him to the desolate M-G-M lot in Culver City, where filming began on September 8, 1961.

"They gave me a certain framework and let me do what I felt like," he said.

"Here's a legend in his own time, for goodness' sake, and he was exactly as reported," said producer Buck Houghton. "He was very sober about comedy. He'd take me out on the street and say, 'Buck, you can't do it that way. If I start *here,* then the gag works, but if I start *there* you can never make it work.' Such things as walking behind a policeman in step and disappearing down a manhole just before the bird comes, you know, those Rube Goldberg devices that the picture was full of. He knew right down to the jot what made it work."

Matheson, who envisioned the show as one long Keatonesque chase, was disappointed in the result. "I realized later that the cost would have been prohibitive, of what I wrote," he said. "My script went very rapidly from beginning to end—extremely rapidly—and they took out some of the really quick scenes, and then put a scene, what I thought was an interminable scene in a repair shop where they just kept kvetching back and forth."

Still, "Once Upon a Time" was warmly received when it went out over the CBS network on December 15. "A much older clown attacked the sight gags and pratfalls with real courage, allowing for some fine nostalgia," *Variety* said approvingly, while the *Los Angeles Times* simply pronounced it "weird and wonderful."

Once he finished with *Once Upon a Mattress,* Keaton happily returned to what he called his "thinking man's farm" (because there wasn't too much work to do). He only ventured into town for commercials, occasional TV work, and funerals, as many as half a dozen a year. For a print campaign, he endorsed Country Club Malt Liquor. He sold cigarettes (Marlboros) for Philip Morris and gas for Phillips 66. In 1958, he was asked to be master of ceremonies for the Woodland Hills Fall Festival, a four-day celebration of suburban life that resembled a county fair with a parade, a festival queen, booths and judgings, and a program of live entertainment. This led to his being named honorary mayor by the chamber of commerce, a post he officially assumed in January 1959.

"He was a happy person; he had a gag for everyone," said Loyal Lucas, who frequently house-sat for the Keatons when they were away on tour. "You could never tell when he was going to do something. He had eyes like an eagle. He could walk across the yard, reach down and pick up a four-leaf clover." Along with the Earl twins, Ruth and Jane, a pair of young dancers the Keatons met during the *Newcomers* tour, Buster officiated at the gala opening of the Ventura Freeway, Woodland Hills being at the western terminus of the first phase of construction. In his capacity as honorary mayor, he presided over store openings, ribbon cuttings, parades, groundbreakings for parks, bowling alleys, schools. In April, he threw out the first pitch when the Dodgers met the champion Cincinnati Reds at the Los Angeles Memorial Coliseum, where nearly forty years earlier he had filmed Roman exteriors for *Three Ages.* He was on hand for Christmas parties and Easter egg hunts, photo ops of all kinds.

"After all," he said, "it's a big job. Who else would open YMCAs and Little League seasons?"

"He had electric trains," said Eleanor. "He had tracks that ran out from the garage, out around the swimming pool, around the back, and made a giant circle around the picnic table and then back into the garage again. It was all freight train. One car would carry three hard-boiled eggs and another would carry a hot dog. And each one was the size for one bottle of Coca-Cola. He had pickles and radishes and all kinds of things. He would take this whole freight train out around the picnic table and stop it so that everybody could take what they wanted, and then take it back in and load it up again. The last car was a bottle of Alka-Seltzer tablets."

It was an innovation straight out of *The Electric House,* engineered and fabricated nearly four decades after it first was conceived but very much for the same purpose, which was to automate and amuse, with the emphasis on the latter. "I want you to look at my cocktail train," Keaton would say when welcoming a new guest, pointing out the tracks running along the fence out to the swimming pool. "These engines will pull fifteen cars crammed with food," he said proudly. "My next plan is to have a train big enough to carry me in."

In 1960, Keaton took on the job of directing a series of whimsical 7-Up commercials featuring the Kingston Trio. Yet, the greatest demand among television advertisers was to have him in front of the camera, not behind it. And through it all there was Eleanor, usually in the background but always in complete charge of any given situation. Sharing late-night sandwiches with Norman Nadel, a Columbus newspaperman, she instinctively knew when to speak up. "For a while, Buster ate while Eleanor talked. . . . Even while talking she watched, to make sure that Buster had the cream for his coffee, that he was comfortable—perhaps that he would know, subconsciously, that he is loved. It was a silent communication of much warmth."

As James Karen said, "She did everything for him. I mean, she just was there every single moment. 'Father. You need some rest! Father, sit down!' Always ordering him around. 'Sit down, Father.' But it was always done with love and affection. There was never anything mean about it, you know, or even ballsy. It was just . . . she just loved him."

"He was a project," her nephew Rick Kelly acknowledged. "I don't think you can see him as anything but a project because he was always up to something. I mean, he'd walk across the living room and he'd flip his hat, catch it with his foot, flip it back up with his foot, and catch it. My mother, me, and a couple of other people were sitting at the kitchen table one time, and he walked in and he stood right there in front of us, and he put one foot on the table, and then he reached out and lifted the other foot and he put it [on the table] and stared at us for a second. And then fell down."

Once they settled in Woodland Hills, and particularly after he had become honorary mayor, Eleanor made it her job to follow Buster's purchases among the local merchants and settle up, since he never carried any money of his own. "I'd hand him a five-dollar bill when he was working at the studio and I wasn't going. I said, 'Here.'

"He said, 'Well, I'll lose it.'

"'You might run out of cigarettes, you know. You might want lunch or something.'

"'Oh, all right.'

"He never had any money, but he'd take off and go in the car, and the next thing I know he's back. He needed some nuts and bolts at the hardware store, and he comes back with [something else besides]. 'I saw this and thought it would look good.' He saw something that would look good on the kitchen wall. I'd say, 'Where'd you get it?'

"'Oh, you know. The one down at the corner of Topanga.'

"'And you didn't pay for it.'

"'I didn't have any money.'

"'Okay.'

"And then I'd have to check out where he'd gotten them, because I had to trail around the next day and pay for all of it. It was not like we had charge accounts with any of them. They'd give him anything he wanted in many of those stores . . . They were all wrapped and bound with a little ribbon. It's not like he's shoplifting. He legitimately bought them; he just didn't pay for them. They'd just write *Keaton* on the register tape and shove it in the drawer. And every time I went by, they'd pull all the tapes and I'd write out a check."

For Eleanor, one of the more amusing aspects of being married to Buster Keaton was that people expected her to be in the same general age range as her husband. In her early forties, she looked thirty-five, with a dancer's poise and boundless energy. The people assembling the *Once Upon a Mattress* tour were shocked when they first met her.

"He came east [for *Merton of the Movies*]," remembered Karen, "and we started rehearsing. And he was closed off at first, and part of that was Eleanor protecting him. She didn't let people get too close. He had a problem with a lot of people [around him]; he would get panicked. I remember one time we were at a party, and people were kind of closing in on him. He broke away, ran out, and Eleanor said, 'Let's follow. We've got to get him. He's sick.' There he was in the bushes, puking. Eleanor was one of those perfect people. She protected him like crazy, but she had a great sense of humor. She'd say, 'Let's go get Father. I think he has to take a leak.'"

On October 13, 1961, Buster Keaton, along with Jimmy Durante, George Burns, and Groucho Marx and all of his surviving brothers, attended the funeral of Chico Marx at Glendale's Forest Lawn. In an interview the previous year, Keaton had, with a rueful smile, lamented not seeing cronies from his earlier days "except at funerals." In 1947, Chico had been on hand when Buster opened for the first time at the Cirque Médrano, and it was he who acquainted him with a nearby restaurant seemingly exempt from food rationing, where no coupons were necessary and where plenty of butter, olive oil, and meats were there for the asking.

Nine days later, on October 22, Keaton was rocked by the death of Joe Schenck at the age of eighty-two. In 1941, Schenck had been convicted of evading payment of $413,000 in income taxes for the years 1935 to 1937, a charge he laid to carelessness over a complicated stock-loss deal. Then it was found that both Joe and his brother Nick, acting for their respective companies, had been paying off Willie Bioff and George Browne, racketeers who controlled the stagehands union, to the tune of $50,000 per organization. In exchange for his cooperation in prosecuting Bioff and Browne, Joe was allowed to plead guilty to a perjury count, taking the fall, it was widely acknowledged, for the entire industry. A sentence of one year was imposed, along with a $20,000 fine, and Schenck ultimately served four months and five days in federal prison. In 1945, he was granted a full pardon by President Truman.

Schenck tried to step down as executive head of production at 20th Century-Fox in 1949, but his resignation was declined by the board on the grounds he was indispensable. The next year, he resigned as board chairman and president of the United Artists Theatre Circuit. In 1953, he finally made the break with Fox, was reelected chairman of United Artists, and also became chairman of Magna Theatre Corporation, which was built around the new Todd-AO wide-screen process. He suffered a heart attack in 1955, prompting him to withdraw from all his corporate responsibilities at the age of seventy-six. Then, in September 1957, he suffered a debilitating stroke and lingered in a kind of netherworld. He was left unaware when Norma Talmadge died in Las Vegas three months later at the age of sixty-three.

Sadly, Keaton was one of the few on-screen personalities to attend the funeral at the Wilshire Boulevard Temple. In earlier times, Norma would certainly have been there, Jack Barrymore, Valentino, Doug Fairbanks, Ronald Colman. The executive ranks were out in force, led by Samuel Goldwyn, Sol Lesser, Harry Brand, and David O. Selznick, along with directors Henry King, George Seaton, Leo McCarey, and, as one of his oldest friends, Irving Berlin.

"Joe Schenck never waited for anyone in trouble to come to him for help," said Y. Frank Freeman, longtime senior executive at Paramount. "If he knew about it, he went to them. . . ."

Burial would take place in New York following another service at the Frank E. Campbell Funeral Chapel, which gave Constance Talmadge and brother Nick an opportunity to represent the family. Lillian Gish, Richard Barthelmess, Spyros Skouras, Adolph Zukor, Barney Balaban, and Albert Warner attended, as did hundreds of others.

"I had never met a finer man in show business," Keaton told Charles Samuels in 1958. "I haven't yet."

28

The Laughter of the World

P OSSIBLY INSPIRED by a British film production proposed in 1960 under the title *The Optimists of Nine Elms*—an idea that didn't go anywhere at the time—Buster Keaton conceived of his own transatlantic production, a sort of modern remake of *Sherlock Jr.* called *Flannelfoot*. Expressed in the form of an eleven-page synopsis, the story began in New York, where Buster delivers dry cleaning and devours all "the top true-detective magazines." He is mistakenly chased by the police and, hiding, finds himself loaded onto an ocean liner bound for England. In London, he encounters a colorful array of supporting characters as he decides to show his ability as a detective in order to catch a cat burglar and aid a friend.

MISS LILLY is described as "a bit of age but lots of life, plenty of money" ("A younger Bea Lillie," Keaton specified). SGT. MONTGOMERY is burly, stern, a perfect policeman ("Jack Hawkins type"). And FLANNELFOOT is "a jolly crook so elusive we never see him until the last scenes of the picture." He is also a bit of a gourmand. "He always raids the icebox of its dainties tidbits."

To be made in wide-screen and color, *Flannelfoot* was a genuine bid to resume the motion picture career Keaton involuntarily stepped away from in 1933, an attempt to place himself on an equal footing with Peter Sellers, Terry-Thomas, and Alec Guinness in the field of modern motion picture comedy. But as with *The Optimists of Nine Elms,* it proved to be impossible to get backing for such a project with Keaton as its star, despite the vividness of the concept. Writer-director Anthony Simmons finally got *The Optimists* made in 1973 with Sellers as the old street busker originally conceived for

Keaton, an unusual and compelling film that was nonetheless
a commercial failure.

The groundwork laid during the
1960 trip to Munich paid off
in 1962, a year that for Keaton
would represent a collision of
high points and missed opportunities. As an omen of sorts, the
year began in tragedy with the
death of video surrealist Ernie
Kovacs at the age of forty-two.

Keaton always swore he would
never do another TV series, yet
late in 1961 he signed on for a
pilot at Screen Gems, seduced
by the promise of easy money

*Keaton and Ernie Kovacs during the shooting of
the* Medicine Man *pilot in January 1962.*

and limited hours. Working with Kovacs was also a lure, since the younger
man, who adapted silent-film techniques to the electronic medium and
stretched it as far as it would go, plainly idolized him. Both had similar
comedic sensibilities, what Kovacs liked to call "the humor of the anomaly,"
the art of leading the audience to expect something and then to deny them
what they are expecting. It could have been a creative match made in heaven
should anyone have been insightful enough to give them an empty studio
and all the resources they'd need and simply tell them to go at it.

Instead, it was a single-camera comedy called *Medicine Man,* which had
Kovacs traveling the West as Doc, the proprietor of an old-time medicine
show peddling Mother McGreevy's Wizard Juice. Keaton was cast as Junior,
Doc's mute Indian confederate, with braids down past his shoulders and a
feathered derby on his head. Written by radio veterans Jay Sommers and
Joe Bigelow, it was a listless piece of work, completely unworthy of its two
extraordinary leads. Richly larded with an insistent laugh track, *Medicine
Man* still looked as if it could land a spot on ABC's fall schedule, and the
company worked a full day on Friday, January 12 to get it all in the can. As
Keaton headed back to Woodland Hills, Kovacs drove off to an editing session at ABC to fine-tune his eighth special for the network. After stopping

by his house on Bowmont Drive to change, he arrived late to a baby shower at the home of Billy Wilder. In high spirits, he swapped cars with his wife, comedienne Edie Adams, and sped off in her Corvair station wagon to meet a friend for a nightcap. Reaching for one of his trademark cigars, he took his hands off the steering wheel, lost control of the car on a rain-soaked street, and wrapped it around a utility pole.

The industry awoke the next morning to the sight of the wreckage on the front page of the *Los Angeles Times* and the shocking headline "CRASH KILLS ERNIE KOVACS." With Adams under sedation, it fell to actor Jack Lemmon to identify the body.

"We've lost a good friend," he said somberly, "a lovely and dear man." The simple Presbyterian funeral took place the following Monday within sight of the street on which Kovacs died. Keaton attended, as did, it seemed, every A-list figure in Hollywood. Pallbearers included Wilder, Lemmon, Frank Sinatra, and Dean Martin. The minister said that Kovacs once summed up his life in two sentences: "I was born in Trenton, New Jersey, in 1919 to a Hungarian couple. I've been smoking cigars ever since."

Within days, the Keatons were en route to Europe, where *The General* was to be shown commercially for the first time in more than thirty years. The rerelease was part of Raymond Rohauer's strategy of legitimacy as he waged his ongoing battle with Leopold Friedman. His first salvo came the previous year when, in a move widely reported in the press, he had Keaton make a symbolic demonstration of proprietorship by pledging prints of twenty-five of his pictures to the Hollywood Motion Picture and Television Museum, then in the planning stages. Now, piloting a hundred-year-old engine found in Vienna by the film's distributor, Buster began a triumphal tour of West Germany that commenced on February 6, 1962.

"We hit all the major cities in Germany in about seven weeks," Eleanor said. "At each stop we'd show Buster's films. We started in Munich and hit half a dozen different cities like Essen and Bonn and Hamburg. We flew into Berlin and had MiG jets flying on each side of us—I guess to make sure we didn't stray off the path. He drove a train into the station of every town. It scared the wits out of the German engineers. They thought he was going to wreck the train. They couldn't believe it when he would just step in and say, 'Okay, let's go!' We'd get it up to speed and then we'd come into the station exactly where we needed to be."

The first performance in Munich had all the trappings of a Hollywood premiere and Keaton wanted no part of it. "Raymond and I went to the opening night," said Eleanor, "but he stayed back at the hotel. It was a roaring success. I think it was just that he didn't want to be disappointed. He used to say, 'When we made these films, we made them to play for approximately a year and a half and hoped they'd make money. By then we would have made one or two more.' The fact that they have come back after all the years and have been such a success all over again—he just couldn't believe it! And he hated crowds bearing down on him. He was paralyzed by crowds."

The program that first night included a selection of shorts.

"We—Ray and I—were standing in the lobby talking with the manager when all of a sudden I heard this . . . just absolute screaming laughter. And I thought: What in the name of God is going on? *The General* is not that funny in the beginning. We had reserved seats in the balcony, and I went charging up the stairs to see what was going on, and it was *Cops*. They had opened with *Cops*. I didn't know what was causing all this hysteria. When we went back to the hotel we told Buster and he was pleased."

The German reissue was hugely popular, drawing rave reviews and big audiences wherever it played. "In ten towns at a time, and everywhere a terrific success," Keaton said. "Turning people away. Tens of thousands of spectators every day."

In West Berlin the honorary mayor of Woodland Hills shook hands with mayor Willy Brandt and signed the city's Golden Book. By then it had been announced that he would be honored with a full two-week retrospective at the Cinémathèque Française in Paris, where, naturally, the celebration would lead off with *The General*. This time he agreed to show up, but wasn't any less affected by close quarters and the press of the crowds. "At a showing of one of his films . . . the lights went up and he took off up the aisle in as close to a dead run as he could get," said Eleanor. "When I finally caught up with him, he was in an alley upchucking his dinner."

The screenings proved extraordinarily popular, with enthusiasts crowding the theater nightly and many seeing the films, gathered by curator Henri Langlois from sources as far flung as the Museum of Modern Art and Czech Film Archive, for the first time. The record-breaking tribute had local distributors and art house exhibitors lining up to book Keaton features for first-run reissues, with demand particularly strong for *Our Hospitality, Sherlock Jr.,* and *The Navigator*.

"Nothing could be nicer than taking bows for something you did thirty-six years ago," he said happily. "The nice part is that the biggest percentage of the audience are school kids."

In an expansive mood, he told the Associated Press the experience took him back forty years to when silents were new and not something people saw on the late, late show. "I looked around and half expected to see Gloria Swanson and maybe even Chaplin in the crowd. If someone had driven up in an old Stutz Bearcat and said, 'Come on, Buster, let's go up to a party at Valentino's,' why, I'd have been in the rumble seat faster than Tom Mix could draw his six-gun."

The glow lingered as he returned to New York for what would be his first starring feature in years, a musical-comedy about an aging TV veteran knocked off the air by an upstart rival—a Lassie-like dog named Nellie. Originally, Ed Wynn was to have played the part, but as the start date neared, Bert Lahr assumed the role.

"They came to me," said Lahr. "I read the script. It wasn't good. They were giving me a three-week guarantee for a tremendous amount of money. When I read the script, I realized they couldn't get it done in twenty weeks. It was a real amateur situation."

When they needed someone to play another comic part in the picture, Lahr suggested Eddie Foy, Jr., who accepted without reading the thing, regretting it later. Keaton was added independently of the other two, and the part of Casper Dan was expanded to accommodate him. All three men converged at Grand Central Terminal to make the trip north. Lahr's twenty-year-old son John was permitted to carry Buster's ukulele to the train.

The producer, a former publicist named Ed Gollin, formed Am-Can Productions Ltd. to produce feature pictures in Canada with American talent for considerably less than what they'd cost in Hollywood. The final component of the principal cast was teen idol Dion DiMucci, late of Dion and the Belmonts but by then pursuing a solo career with hits such as "Runaround Sue" and "The Wanderer." DiMucci had appeared in Sam Katzman's hugely profitable *Twist Around the Clock*, and Gollin thought he had screen potential as another Tommy Sands. He figured the entire picture could be shot at the Toronto International Film Studios in Panavision and Eastman Color for a cost of around $200,000. Under the title *Ten Girls Ago*, the picture was picked up for distribution in the United States by Universal.

Filming began on March 12, 1962, but the movie immediately took on the look of a jinxed project. "There were budget constraints," said stills photographer John Sebert. "Every once in a while things would slow down until somebody came running in with some more money."

Within days, Joe Harnell, the film's musical director, was injured in an automobile accident, sustaining a fractured collarbone and a broken shoul-

Keaton stares down the camera on the set of Ten Girls Ago.

der. Foy kept blowing takes, unable to master his lines. Keaton bit his tongue during a scene, spitting blood as film captured the moment. Then Bert Lahr had to leave the set with a 104-degree fever and was laid up for a week with pneumonia. Keaton, meanwhile, directed some chase footage and spent his time working out physical business that might never be caught on camera.

Committed to touring, DiMucci had to quit the movie before his scenes were completed. As production wound down, the three comics, certain their paychecks were going to bounce, spent their time on the set trying to break each other up.

"I wonder how this movie will work out," Keaton said. "I'm dying to see the ending."

The cost of *Ten Girls Ago* swelled to more than twice its modest budget, with editing and scoring yet to come. What remained to be shot was the final chase sequence when the picture shut down on April 13, appropriately enough a Friday. Producer Gollin assembled a nine-minute sizzle reel to pull in the funding needed for completion, but the action, overplayed and underwritten, did nothing to help sell the picture. In June, *Variety* reported it was "almost completely cut" and only needed soundtrack work.

Final word on *Ten Girls Ago* came in June 1965, when the Am-Can shareholders reportedly decided to put up $275,000 for postproduction and a little more shooting. It was the last anyone ever heard of it.

After spending the first third of the year away from Woodland Hills, Keaton told Ben Pearson he was taking the summer off.

"When we got home," said Eleanor, "that's where we wanted to be. We'd call all of our friends and say, 'Come on out.' We'd have barbecues and we'd swim, but at our house so we wouldn't have to go anywhere."

With his mind always turning, it didn't take long for Buster to start spinning stories with his friend Bill Cox, a prolific writer of pulp stories, paperback novels, and episodic television whose wife had been the script supervisor on the Keaton TV series. Earlier, the two men had collaborated on a story for *Wagon Train,* for which Cox had co-written the series pilot.

"Buster had this idea of journeying the wagon train with a miniature kind of wagon and jackasses or ponies carrying it," he said. "That was his idea, and immediately I said, 'Well, if you do that you'll have to have a mission.' I made [him] an undercover Pinkerton detective looking for a murderer who he suspected was on the wagon train and we carried the plot from there."

The idea for *Wagon Train* never sold, possibly due to the death of series star Ward Bond, but Cox saw that Keaton had a keen sense of story. "Bus had a great definition of story. He said a plot is like a clothesline, and a story is like the wash you hang on the clothesline—which is very good for a fellow who never went to school." It is unclear whose idea it was to pitch an idea to *Route 66,* the popular CBS drama about two guys looking for meaning on the open road, but the series format left wide latitude for development. Each week was a new locale and a new cast, often rich with Hollywood veterans. The notion was to offer Buster as a backwoods jinx—an accident-prone character who gets tangled up with stars Martin Milner and George Maharis, an outright comedy for a series that had never done one. Underscoring the redemption theme of the story, the turn of fortune for Jonah Butler coming when he finds, as Keaton often did in real life, a four-leaf clover, Cox titled it "Journey to Nineveh." The resulting episode represented a true collaboration between Keaton and Cox, who turned in a script so tailored to Buster's strengths it would be impossible to make it with anyone else. Having created a second role for another seasoned comedian, Cox recommended Joe E. Brown for the part of Sam Butler, Jonah's older brother, and the surrounding cast was fortified with such stalwart character people as Edgar Buchanan, Guy Raymond, and John Astin. Filming began on June 16, 1962, in Calabasas, a rural enclave only four miles west of the Keaton homestead.

Working along the shore of Lake Sherwood, Keaton was in his element silently attempting to thumb a ride to Gladstone Landing, a fictional outpost in the Missouri Ozarks. Jonah is well known to the locals, none of whom will risk stopping for him. He spins, falls, races for a door as a car

With George Maharis and Martin Milner during the filming of the Route 66 *episode "Journey to Nineveh."*

speeds off. He tips his hat to a woman driver to no avail. Finally, he lies down on the pavement, spread-eagle, determined to stop the next passing auto at all costs. A station wagon pulls to a halt just feet away from him, and he springs to life as the driver exits. Scrambling through the passenger door, the man hot on his tail, Jonah exits through the other side, somersaulting back onto the pavement as the vehicle roars off. It's all exquisite, wordless action with Keaton in full command of his gifts. As Buz Murdock and Tod Stiles (Maharis and Milner) approach in their Corvette, he is attempting to fish off a small dock. He gets his line caught and takes a flying backflip into the water. Buz rushes to his aid, leaps to a newly reconstituted Doughnut Island nearby, and disappears into the lake himself.

The ensuing action is played to the roaring laughter of Milner as the two men struggle to reach the dock. "Keaton worked with me on all the physical business," said George Maharis. "He knew exactly how it should be played, exactly how it should be done. We had to shoot that scene when I try to pull myself out of the lake by holding on to him three or four times because I couldn't stop laughing."

According to Eleanor's notes, "Journey to Nineveh" took nine days to shoot, even though the individual episodes were routinely scheduled for six. The last day's location was the Iverson Ranch, familiar territory where Keaton filmed a crucial scene for *The Paleface* and, later, the Stone Age exteriors for *Three Ages*.

The scene is a small pond, where Jonah and Buz are taking an undersized boat out for fishing. Again Keaton uses a rock for an anchor, and again the boat is supposed to fill and sink. In order to achieve the effect in one take, a cable had been run to an off-camera station wagon. With film rolling, Maharis climbed into the tiny boat, Keaton clambered aboard after him, and the overloaded craft did its sinking chore without waiting for its cue. With two wet actors and no usable footage, they had to be dried off and given a change of clothes before attempting the stunt again. On signal, Milner waded into the shot to save the day, and Keaton and his two young co-stars drew a spontaneous round of applause from the crew. It was only in viewing the rushes that Keaton realized that director David Lowell Rich, who had little experience shooting comedy, had broken away from the action in the water to film a reaction shot from the canine actor playing Jonah's dog.

"Nothing should be said against David Lowell Rich, a fine director," said Bill Cox. "He just did not understand comedy routines. He was not that kind of director. He could direct the comedy on the road and that sort of thing, but he didn't know about routines. . . . Buster was doing the *Merton of the Movies* routine with a rowboat and a rock for an anchor, and he sank the boat and put himself in the water, and was scrambling around doing all kinds of things with the fish. And the director took the camera off him and put it on a dog! You just don't do that. When a comic is doing a routine, you never take the camera off him. If they wanted a shot of the dog, they [should have made it with] another camera. And then if they wanted to interpose it, they would have to pick a spot.* Buster and I were watching it. He said, 'Where are the outcuts?' And they said, 'Well, there are no outcuts. We were only using one camera.' And Buster just got up and walked out. He didn't say anything. I walked around a long block with him and he said, 'Well, that's the way it is.' All the time we were walking he was telling me about it. Not angrily, though. Just saying how these people were so stupid."

Misgivings aside, "Journey to Nineveh" stands as one of the finest things Keaton ever did for television, a constant delight in which he had complete artistic control over the slapstick, and the director's miscues were not fatal to the comedy. When cut together, his wordless gag sequences accounted for

---

* Ironically, David Lowell Rich's younger brother, John Rich, was one of TV's most honored comedy directors.

nearly 25 percent of the total footage in a forty-nine-minute episode. George Maharis, who over the two previous seasons of *Route 66* had grown used to high-caliber guest stars like Lee Marvin, Sylvia Sidney, Walter Matthau, and Douglas Fairbanks, Jr., recalled Keaton with particular affection. "He was the kind of guy who could just walk into a room and you'd smile."

Keaton remained inactive the rest of the summer, only taking a couple of day jobs that held special appeal for him. For *Candid Camera,* he posed as a service station attendant bent on eradicating a stubborn spot on a victim's windshield. He determinedly shoots it with water, scrubs it with a long, soapy mop, and ultimately takes the gas hose to it. Then, on August 15, he reported to the Oxnard location of *It's a Mad, Mad, Mad, Mad World* to take his place among the fifty or so name comedians populating the film, playing a waterfront character known as Jimmy the Crook. Stanley Kramer's epic had generated a lot of ink since he announced the project in July 1960, in no small part because the producer-director was known for socially signifi- cant dramas like *The Defiant Ones* and *Inherit the Wind,* and a $6 million comedy was widely thought to be firmly outside his wheelhouse. Keaton's call was for eight o'clock that morning, and when he arrived on the set, he beheld an array of star talent such as he had never before seen on a single pic- ture: Milton Berle, Mickey Rooney, Buddy Hackett, Terry-Thomas, Eddie "Rochester" Anderson, Dick Shawn, Jonathan Winters, Phil Silvers, and Sid Caesar, among others. "When Buster worked," said script supervisor Marshall Schlom, "the comedians were toast. They fell apart."

The start of filming was delayed due to fog, and Keaton sat by himself as the comics kept a respectful distance. When the fog lifted, the rest of the day was given over to stunt drivers and stunt extras stuffed into a pair of yellow cabs, as well as some fleeting action involving the principals. It was two thirty in the afternoon when Kramer's top-billed star, Spencer Tracy, appeared, and he and Keaton proceeded to play two scenes together, one a crucial phone conversation telling the audience that Tracy's Captain Cul- peper was planning to take $350,000 in stolen money and skip over the border in Jimmy's boat, the *Natalie Anne.* They were finished for the day by four fifteen, and Keaton collected $1,000 for his work on the picture. It would be more than a year before he'd see the final result.

· · ·

In December 1962, the Keatons returned to Rochester, this time for an industrial Buster was to make for Eastman Kodak. One evening, the curator at George Eastman House, James Card, brought Louise Brooks, then living in the city, to the Sheraton for a reunion. It had been thirty years since Keaton and she had seen each other, and Brooks, at age fifty-six, had long since stopped wearing her hair with the bangs that defined her look in the twenties. Famously mercurial, she took offense when Buster failed to recognize her. An alcoholic, Brooks convinced herself he was drunk, and said as much in a 1983 interview.

"He was not supposed to be drinking. In this big suite he was in, they had a regular kitchen. He was in there with a couple of reporters. Jimmy Card and I and his wife noticed that Buster would pour himself a beer, then he would walk into the sitting room, into the bedroom, and then he would disappear into the can. So obviously he was pouring a little bit of booze into his beer. You know, the boilermaker. Getting himself soused."

If Keaton was jolted by Brooks' appearance after three decades of hard luck and dissipation, she was equally affected by how the years had impacted the face she remembered as flawless back when he was in his thirties. "No one could have that beautiful a face and not be beautiful inside. He pretended not to know me when I went to his room there at the hotel. He stared at me for a long time. Because he connected me, of course, with Buster Collier and Constance and old Peg and the whole thing."

Years earlier, Brooks had written of the same meeting in a letter to Keaton biographer Tom Dardis, and managed to completely ignore the alleged slight. "When Keaton was in Rochester in 1962 for the Kodak commercial. I was shocked and betrayed by a Keaton destroyed and then invented again by his cult and the lugubrious tales of journalists weeping over genius destroyed by heartless Hollywood. But Hollywood never destroyed anybody. If, like Chaplin and Lloyd, he had held to his own magic world, he would have remained great. (Perhaps that was what he was doing the night he took a baseball bat to the glass doors of the built-in bookcases in his bungalow at M-G-M—trying to break out of his cage, escape to creation.) But he never made it. He had lost his magic power over booze."

In March 1963, Buster's bronchitis worsened and Eleanor drove him to the hospital, where he was admitted late on a Saturday night. It was pneumonia, she was told. "The first morning when I talked to the doctor, he says, 'If he lives five days, I'll let you know what I think.' On the sixth day, that was it. He was ready to go home looking like an octopus with all the tubes and attachments here and there."

Fully recovered, Keaton did an extraordinary thing. In April, he flew to New York to participate in a two-hour tribute. The occasion was a Friday-morning edition of NBC's *Today,* already a network institution, with a new host in broadcaster Hugh Downs. The show's producer, acclaimed novelist Al Morgan, had instituted a policy of occasional theme programs, specials devoted to such cultural giants as George Gershwin, Robert Benchley, and Jerome Kern. Now it was time for Keaton to be celebrated in all his silent glory for an audience largely unfamiliar with his work. Since the episode, titled "Buster Keaton Revisited," was to air on April 26 when the *Today* team would be in Holland for a week of remotes, the Keaton segments, apart from the show's frequent news updates, would be taped at the NBC studios on April 17. For all the good intentions that day, the staging couldn't have been cornier.

Announcer Jack Lescoulie was dressed as a silent-screen cameraman, Hugh Downs as a producer, and "Today Girl" Pat Fontaine as a leading lady of similar vintage. The film clips were 16mm and of variable quality, the accompaniment an old-time piano. Buster made his entrance in a Ford Model T pushed by Lescoulie. Downs climbed in on the passenger side as Buster fiddled with the controls. Downs introduced a clip from *Cops* that moved into another from *My Wife's Relations.* Buster must have been mortified as the gags were shown out of context.

Downs forced a few weak laughs. "I don't know how you can be that funny," he said, "and never smile."

Keaton replied: "It was darn serious work!"

The brawl from *The Butcher Boy* was shown, and Lescoulie equated the flour throwing with pie throwing.

"As a rule," said Keaton, "you don't throw a pie unless somebody annoys you." An entire segment was devoted to the business of pie throwing. Buster hit Lescoulie with a lemon meringue pie. It didn't stick very well, so Downs asked him to do it again. There were scenes from *The Boat* and *The General,* and Keaton's microphone was left open so that he could comment as he watched.

Brendan Gill of *The New Yorker* was invited to witness the taping, and he had a few minutes with Keaton when it was all over.

"I was pretty proud of it at the time," Keaton said of *The General.* "Right now, it's playing all over Europe, and people are laughing harder at it today than they did in 1927 when it came out." He wandered over to a studio monitor to watch a murky print of a two-reeler as it was being run off. "In the picture," went Gill's account, "he is being chased by what looks like hundreds of frantic cops; they are about to capture him when a car goes by and Keaton reaches out, grabs the brace supporting its canvas top, and is jerked into momentary safety. At that point, something astonishing happened in the TV studio. On the screen was a mournful little man running lickety-split down the streets of long since vanished Los Angeles; in the studio watching him was the same mournful little man, forty-two years older, and now, instead of being deadpan, the face was smiling."

While in New York, Keaton paid a call on Leopold Friedman, the first time the two men had been face-to-face in decades. "It's not M-G-M that's trying to stop you from releasing your pictures," Friedman explained. "They are just the releasing organization. But they were protecting the Joe Schenck estate. They have declared themselves cut in on them, or they will stop you from showing your films." The meeting was cordial, even if Friedman saw the *Today* gambit as a fresh shot over the bow in his continuing battle with Rohauer. The new sound version of *The General,* over which Friedman had no control, had opened at two theaters in Paris to "sock reviews and biz" (*Variety*) before breaking wider throughout France. Meanwhile, Friedman's claim as the valid copyright owner of *The Navigator* had been reaffirmed by the Ninth Circuit Court of Appeals, which upheld the lower court's judgment that Rohauer had indeed infringed by exhibiting the film without proper authorization.

Emboldened, Friedman initiated an exhaustive search of all registrations and renewals through the offices of copyright attorney Julian T. Abeles. The results acquainted him with Rohauer's registrations of doctored versions of Keaton pictures otherwise in the public domain, as well as rights assignments Rohauer had obtained from Eddie Cline and Keaton himself. About the same time, Friedman was able to report income of $55,800 that had accrued to the former shareholders of Buster Keaton Productions since October 4, 1944, the date of the last distribution, primarily reflecting money paid by 20th Century-Fox in the form of royalties for the use of *Cops* in *When Comedy Was King.*

Both parties had unique advantages in the ongoing struggle over Keaton's legacy of nineteen two-reelers and ten features. Friedman controlled the rights to seven of the shorts and six of the features released and renewed by

Metro-Goldwyn-Mayer—a position effectively confirmed and underscored by the appeals court ruling—but he had no prints. Rohauer, on the other hand, had no rights to the remaining films, but through an aggressive—and oftentimes deceptive—campaign to acquire prints, had amassed an impressive inventory of prime Keaton titles, many in the form of 35mm negatives. He also had the undeniable advantage of his business association with Keaton himself, which lent a certain moral authority to the moves he made on their behalf.

While Friedman was passively deriving income from licensing the rights to films produced by Keaton Productions, whether or not they were still under copyright, Rohauer was actively creating new opportunities for some of the same titles and deriving income for himself and Keaton. At some point, it appears that Keaton made a direct appeal to Irving Berlin, who, apart from Nicholas Schenck, was the principal surviving shareholder of Buster Keaton Productions. Berlin directed his attorney, Abe Berman, to ask that Sheldon Abend of the American Play Company, an agency that represented the interests of many playwrights, meet with Friedman at Berman's office to "arrive at a productive formula wherein both Buster Keaton, as an individual, and Buster Keaton Productions, Inc., would merge certain rights of theirs which would create a new and vendible Buster Keaton film package for both television and theatrical exhibition." In other words, a merger that would combine the two warring factions for their mutual benefit and, expressly, for Keaton's.

On March 12, 1963, Rohauer wrote Buster and Eleanor from West Germany: "*College, Paleface,* and *The Goat* opened here in Munich last Friday to rave reviews and packed houses. It is even a bigger success than *The General.* . . . Buster is the hottest property in Germany." He added: "Good news from Sheldon Abend. Friedman will make the merger and I am trying to sew this up before the NBC show *Salute to Buster Keaton* [*sic*] goes on the air. All of Buster's big films will be used on the show including *The Navigator* which Friedman is giving his approval. So shortly it will be one big happy family."

In May, Buster told columnist Hedda Hopper that the Russians had not only bought *The General* but had paid cash for it. Meanwhile, in the U.S., Paul Killiam, a former lawyer and newsman who had amassed a vast collection of silent films—and who owned his own 35mm print of *The General*—incorporated scenes from it into his theatrical compilation, *The Great Chase.* Then Robert Youngson, still acting under the license Friedman had granted him, released *30 Years of Fun,* his fourth amalgamation of silent clips that covered filmed comedy from the gay nineties through the roaring twenties and included scenes from *Cops, Day Dreams,* and *The Balloonatic,* all films that had fallen into the public domain. Youngson was inclined to play by the rules as he understood them, while Killiam would be a thorn in Rohauer's side for years to come.

Keaton's vow to give up touring lasted all of two years. Eleanor, who said she had her fingers crossed, knew the lure of live audiences was more than he could resist. In May 1963, he committed to the Barnes-Carruthers State Fair Tour, which was booked into a circuit of seven midwestern and southern fairs over the months of August and September. With him consistently would be bandleader Warren Covington, with whom he would perform the dueling sketch he last did with Paul Whiteman, and variously, at the larger grandstand venues, Rosemary Clooney, the Smothers Brothers, big band vocalist Johnny Desmond, and country star Molly Bee. "This," said Keaton, "is the first time I've ever done this type of entertainment. . . . But I love it, and it's easy work. I'm on fifteen minutes a night and it's all over until the next night. I never had it so good."

The tour came to a somber conclusion at the Alabama State Fair in Birmingham just days following the 16th Street Baptist Church bombing that killed four children and injured seventeen others. A member of the company, Don Logay, remembered "an armed military escort to our hotel in Birmingham." The company was advised to remain in place other than for actual performances. "We would be picked up promptly at 6 p.m. and driven to do our show," said Logay. "We would be returned to the hotel the same way." It was under such tense circumstances that Keaton observed his sixty-eighth birthday on October 4 by cutting into a seven-layer cake, colored red, white, and blue, with a penknife. Instead of making a little speech in the tent that served as his backstage dressing quarters, he simply looked from one guest to the next with his hands outstretched in a gesture of appreciation.

While he was touring the fair circuit in the American heartland, the twenty-fourth annual Venice Film Festival was celebrating Buster Keaton on film with a ten-program retrospective of his features and shorts, assembled from the holdings of George Eastman House, the Cinémathèque Française, and the Italian film library in Milan. Titled "The Golden Years of Buster Keaton," the silent features, each accompanied by a two-reeler, were shown in the mornings, but because of the anticipated demand for seats, repeat showings were added at a smaller venue in the evenings. In a lackluster year for the fest, in which the most enthusiastic reaction to any American entry was for Shirley Clarke's *The Cool World,* the Keaton season was a standout. "As a result of word of mouth, the audiences increased daily," Gene Moskowitz reported, "and on the final showing of *Steamboat Bill, Jr.,* there was standing room only in the theater. Adult reaction was as definite and significant as that of the moppets who had never before seen, or even heard of, Keaton, and the comedy antics of the star delighted youngsters and oldsters alike. There was general agreement among all viewers that Keaton displayed more comic invention almost forty years ago than many stars or producers display today."

Back home, the Keatons attended the world premiere of *It's a Mad, Mad, Mad, Mad World* at the Cinerama Dome on November 7, 1963, as well as the gala ball that followed. Buster had already seen the picture and they both enjoyed themselves, even though Eleanor had a terrible cold.

"It's one of the times we stood out in the lobby ahead of time and talked to Hedda Hopper for a while," she said. "Because she looked at me and she says, 'What's the matter with you?' And I said, 'I've got a head cold I may die from, or wish I would die from.' She says, 'You look it.'"

The film was hailed as a surefire hit, a comic masterpiece, and Stanley Kramer was celebrated as having pulled off a near impossibility. "Three things are important in films," Keaton said. "Number one is the story. Number two is the star, the attraction. Number three is the director."

Mad World was written by the American-born screenwriter William Rose and his wife, Tania. It was Rose who was responsible for some of the best British comedies of the 1950s, including *The Ladykillers,* which Keaton considered a perfect comedy construction. What doubtless impressed him most about *Mad World* was how Kramer and Rose were able to sustain a three-hour picture with as much physical comedy as verbal.

"In our day," Keaton said, "there was tremendous competition in our field. Today there is none. Jerry Lewis remains on top . . . but Jerry doesn't have Chaplin, Lloyd, [Lloyd] Hamilton, and half a dozen others on his heels . . . with Laurel and Hardy coming on apace to reach truly great heights. If our comedy is acceptable today, if the critics rave and the fan letters come in, I think it has been taken for granted that we have contributed to something more than early movies. The laughter of the world?"

. . .

With the release of *Mad World,* Keaton entered the busiest period of his later life, a stretch of time that would scarcely last two years. On television, he made his first Ed Sullivan appearance in six years, played a guest suspect—a fashion mogul with laryngitis—on *Burke's Law,* and, with Gloria Swanson, offered a boisterous take on the first meeting of Marc Antony and Cleopatra on *The Hollywood Palace.* At the Los Angeles Sports Arena, he wrote, developed, and rehearsed comedy material for a new edition of *Ice Capades.* ("I tried to convince the boys to be comedians first and skaters second, but I failed.") And then there were commercials for Minute Rub, for Ford Econoline Vans, for United States Steel and others.

"Those commercials are jimdandies. I got paid twice for the Ford job, once for each time it will be shown. Some of the others pay each time they appear, and that adds up nicely."

A standout was another of Keaton's rare dramatic turns, that of a French clown in an episode of the Desilu series *The Greatest Show on Earth.* "You're All Right, Ivy" was built around a triumvirate of veteran circus performers put out to pasture and a girl's zeal for returning them to the center ring. Joan Blondell was a trick roper in her younger years, Keaton the wistful Pippo, and Joe E. Brown an Irish sword swallower.

"Pippo's in the prop department now," Blondell's character explains to young Ivy. "He used to be a Pierrot clown, but the big thing these days is Charlies. Now they keep us old-timers around as souvenirs. You know—kind of mementos of times gone by."

In an elegant miniature, Keaton, in whiteface, mimes a high-wire act with a paper parasol. Yet circus boss Jack Palance won't let them perform after Ivy (Lynn Loring) has encouraged them, causing them to turn away from her. Once she has left, they remain clustered under the deserted big top. Uttering "Please" and "Permit me" in French, Pippo scurries into the ring and bows, hands outstretched, and begins to explain himself in mime. Brown, seated behind Palance, interprets for him:

"I'm only one man, and I'm very small and insignificant . . . and rather homely," he indicates as he covers his face, "but I see a flower among the thousands, or a star among the millions, and I begin to think: Perhaps I can smile in the sun like that flower, or shine forth like that star. And then one comes to me. From her I learn about the flower and the star and a lot of other things, too. I am great now that I have learned. I am ready to show myself to the world."

He acts these things out, dropping to his knees prayerfully, and raising his arms beseechingly as he moves about the ring. "But the world does not applaud. A few laugh scornfully . . . I see that I am really very small and insignificant." He folds sadly. "She lied to me out of pity . . . only now I am unhappier than ever, for now I can no longer dream. . . . The flower wilts in the heat of the day. The star burns out and I am alone." He drops back to his knees, his hands folded in his lap. "All alone . . ."

It is a powerful scene, Chaplinesque in a sense, though thoroughly at one with Keaton's character and the mien of the sad Pierrot clown, his eyebrows exaggerated, his lips painted into a permanent frown, his expressive body informally clad

Keaton and Joe E. Brown during the filming of "You're All Right, Ivy," the final episode of the Desilu TV series The Greatest Show on Earth.

in a workman's jumpsuit. For Jack Palance, "You're All Right, Ivy" marked his debut as a director, an assignment concurrent with the series' cancellation after a single season. It must have been bitterly disappointing when "Ivy" went completely unnoticed by the press and the Television Academy, and that it came at the very end of a series that had begun with such outsize expectations. For Keaton it was one of his peaks as an actor, an unforgettable role, and for Palance, an artist and poet as well as an actor, it was the only time in his life that he ever tried directing anything.

Keaton took to giving interviews at home, where he enjoyed showing off the modest spread and all its embellishments. When NBC's *Here's Hollywood* featured him in 1961, the segment began with a shot of the model train hauling hot dogs and drinks into the backyard. With him was his current Saint Bernard, whose name, naturally, was Elmer. (Actually, at Eleanor's insistence, Elmer Jr., or simply Junior.) The same year, Charles Witbeck of King Features Syndicate paid a call and toured the house, particularly the playroom with its pool table, baseball bats, framed photos, and Oscar. ("They gave me that after I'd made my good pictures," Keaton explained.) The Canadian Broadcasting Corporation's Fletcher Markle came to film an interview for the series *Telescope* and staged it in the backyard, Eleanor in a tree swing as Buster and Markle sit down for coffee. Since they were being filmed for Canadian television, Keaton recalled that he played Mike Shea's in Toronto when it was an upstairs theater.

"That pretty much makes you the dean of Hollywood film stars," Markle suggested. "Pretty near," Keaton responded. "I don't know of anybody that passes me. In other words, I'm older professionally than Francis X. Bushman, Maurice Chevalier, Charlie Chaplin, Mary Pickford, Ed Wynn . . ."

He similarly reminisced when England's Penelope Gilliatt arrived to do a feature for *The Observer*. "He stands rather like a Victorian boy," she recorded, "with his chest out and his hands in his pockets. He is sixty-eight, but his body and his neat, vigilant movements still look very like the photographs of him when he played his first professional date, aged three, as the Human Mop in vaudeville. . . . He has bronchitis very badly but he still smokes all the time, using a long cigarette holder that juts out of his mouth like a bowsprit. We looked at his grapes and his apricots and the barn in the middle of the land, a red barn with pulleys on it like the beautiful rigging in *The Navigator*. . . . While he was talking, he kept having to walk away and bend over with his hands on his knees in a terrible fit of coughing. He ignored it stonily, as he ignores danger in his films."

The only time Samuel Beckett ever came to the United States was to make a film with Buster Keaton. It wasn't originally planned that way. The untitled short was to be one of three gathered into a portmanteau feature titled *Project One,* the other two authors being Harold Pinter and Eugène Ionesco. The entire project had been in the works for more than a year, and a company called Evergreen Theatre, Inc., an unlikely partnership between Grove Press and Four Star Television, had been formed to produce it. Beckett had conceived his portion of the feature as possessing "a stylized comic reality akin to that of a silent movie" and thought in terms of Chaplin or Zero Mostel for it. Chaplin, however, was inaccessible and Mostel was unavailable. Then the preference became actor Jack MacGowran, who had appeared in no fewer than nine Beckett works, including the first English-language production of *Endgame*. Small and elfin, with a face as distinctive—though certainly not as well known—as Keaton's, MacGowran was on Beckett's wavelength in a way Keaton could never be, and it was the loss of MacGowran to a stage commitment that occasioned a last-minute appeal to Keaton and, in England, to Alec Guinness.

The director was Alan Schneider, who had directed the first American production of *Waiting for Godot* with Bert Lahr but who had never directed a movie.

"Alan Schneider had directed me in *Who's Afraid of Virginia Woolf?*" said James Karen, "and Jack MacGowran couldn't make it. They were desperate, they had to start shooting, and I said to Schneider, 'Well, how about Buster Keaton?' Because I was always looking for a *Les Enfants du Paradis* kind of thing, a Pierrot for him late in life, and I thought it would be wonderful. And of course, he had turned down *Waiting for Godot*."

It is unclear whether Keaton was solicited for the original production of *Godot* that Schneider directed in 1956, or the subsequent Broadway production staged more successfully by Herbert Berghof. Both starred Lahr as Estragon and, in New York, E. G. Marshall as Vladimir. Somebody, possibly Beckett himself, envisioned Keaton as Lucky, slave to the brutish Pozzo, and one day a script arrived.

Typically, Buster asked Eleanor to read it: "I said, 'I can't make any sense out of this thing. I have no idea what it's about. All I know is that you don't speak until you have the last speech in the show, and it's about two or three pages long. It's a great long speech that you'll have to memorize thoroughly. I don't know that it makes any sense to me. I don't know if it will make any sense to you. All I can tell you is that you'd better read at least part of this to see if you can figure it out.' And he says, 'No thanks . . . Call Ben [Pearson] and say we won't do it.' I called Ben and I said, 'I don't like it, and from what I've told him he doesn't like it, so he says to tell him, "No."' And that was the end of that."

According to Karen, Beckett was sore because of the earlier rejection and didn't want Keaton for what was to become known as *Film*. "Then they got desperate, they had to go. And I got Schneider to talk to him on the phone. I got on and I said, 'Buster, you gotta do it. It doesn't matter what it reads like. You gotta do this. These are great people.'" (Schneider, Karen added, was not.)

Schneider made his first trip to Hollywood to meet with Keaton, who he concluded, erroneously, lived in the distant past. "Keaton had read the script and was not sure what could be done to fix it up," Schneider wrote. "His general attitude was that we were all, Beckett included, nuts." A fee of $5,000 for an eight-day shoot assuaged any concerns Keaton had; he would do it for the money alone.

Beckett arrived in New York on July 10, 1964, and was immediately flown to the East Hampton home of producer Barney Rosset, the owner of Grove Press, for a series of production conferences with Schneider and others. Keaton arrived in town a couple of days later.

"Beckett stayed with Schneider in Dobbs Ferry," Karen recalled, "and I was living with my first wife, Susan Reed, in West Nyack, New York. I had a big 1936 dual cowl phaeton Packard, and I would start out in the morning and go over to Dobbs Ferry. Buster was living with us, and we would drive over, cross the bridge, and pick up Schneider and Beckett and go touring New York. It was a marvelous time. Buster was showing Beckett all of New York . . . Lüchow's, for instance. He'd say, 'Oh, that's the theatre my father and I worked in in 1903 down here . . .'

"Once we were down in the Village and we were eating, I think at O. Henry's. There was a little deck where you could eat outside and it was summer. We were sitting there having a little lunch, the shrubs were masking us, and when we finished we stood up above the level of the shrubs [and were suddenly visible to the people on the sidewalk]. There were a hundred people out there who had heard that Sam Beckett and Buster Keaton were there, and when we stood up they went into the slow European clap. Nobody said a word. Nobody said, 'Can I have your autograph?' They just stood, quietly. It was one of the great tributes, just a wonderful moment."

It soon became apparent to Karen that Beckett really didn't know Keaton's work, even though he remembered seeing some of his films as a boy in Dublin. Karen called documentarian Willard Van Dyke, who arranged a private showing at the Museum of Modern Art. "I took my son, who was then about six years old, to see the films. And Beckett said, 'Here, you know, your name is Reed.' Reed said, 'Yes sir.' And Beckett said, 'Well, I only read in French. You read the titles for me.' So Reed sat on Beckett's lap and read the subtitles. All I could think of was myself doing it for my father. And I remember Reed said when we left, 'Is Mr. Beckett an actor?' I said, 'No, no, no. He's a writer.' He said, 'Oh, he must write wonderful things for children.'"

Filming began on July 20 in the shadow of the Brooklyn Bridge, where Beckett, in his quest for a "memorable wall," found one in a state of near collapse that was marked for demolition. Since there was no sound or dialogue required—other than a solitary "ssh!"—there were no worries about getting a clean soundtrack amid the weekday traffic and the crush of onlookers that included the French filmmaker Alain Resnais. Yet nothing seemed to go right, and there were countless delays. It was hot and humid, and Keaton

Samuel Beckett, director Alan Schneider (with cap), and Keaton during the making of Film *in New York City.*

was required to wear a heavy overcoat with his face covered as Schneider grappled with rookie problems like wobbling dollies, strobe effects, and pans that wouldn't match.

"All he did was to turn Buster loose on this horrible, dangerous—looked like a bombed-out street corner," said Susan Reed, who was in the opening shots with her husband. "The fact that Buster didn't turn an ankle or fall or cut himself or hurt himself . . . The heat was unbearable, and they had just a little hut for him to dress in, a little *tiny* trailer. We never got inside that I recall. Nothing for us. And no ice water, no nothing." She became convinced that Schneider was completely out of his depth. "Nobody knew what was expected of us. Alan, who had gone through that Actors Studio training and, I thought, knew about motivation, inner life, all those things, just guided us to walk toward the camera and make faces. It was the most external kind of direction I ever had, and by that time we were so hot and angry . . . I thought it was the Emperor's New Clothes. I thought there's really no content. They're just abusing, taking advantage of a great face, a great body, a great character. You know, they just turned the camera on him and had him run through the rubble."

Quickly, Keaton earned Schneider's grudging respect. "He was totally professional: patient, unperturbable, relaxed, easy to tell something to, helpful, there. . . . He never complained for a single moment when we asked him, for some reason or other, to run along that obstacle course of a wall over and over again in the boiling heat. Nor did he object when we kept adding obstacles that would have bothered a steeplechase expert. Or nag when something went wrong with something, which happened at least sixty percent of the time, or when we didn't do something the way he did it in 1927."

Beckett told *The New York Times* the film was about a man's self-perception, while Keaton conceded he wasn't too sure what the hell it was about. "What I think it means," he offered helpfully, "is a man may keep away from everybody but he can't get away from himself."

Some twenty years later, Beckett offered a fuller explanation in a conversation with Kevin Brownlow: "It's about a man trying to escape from perception of all kinds—from all perceivers—even divine perceivers. It's an idea from Bishop Berkeley, the Irish philosopher and idealist. 'To be is to be perceived.' *Esse est percipi.* The man who desires to cease to be must cease to be perceived. If being is being perceived, to cease being is to cease to be perceived."

After the difficult and unsatisfactory location work, much of which had to be scrapped, the company adjourned to a small studio on the Upper East Side to work on the film's principal interior. In the author's conception, Keaton is "O" and the camera is "E." All perception belongs to E other than O's perception of the tattered room and its few contents. O covers a mirror with a dark blanket. He puts the cat out. He puts the dog out and the cat runs back inside. He covers a birdcage. He covers a goldfish bowl. He tears up pictures. He perceives eyes everywhere. And in the end he comes face-to-face with himself.

"His movement was excellent—covering up the mirror, putting out the animals—all that was very well done," Beckett said. "To cover the mirror, he took his big coat off and asked me what he was wearing underneath. I hadn't thought of that. I said, 'The same coat.' He liked that. The only gag he approved of was the scene where he tries to get rid of the animals. He puts out the cat and the dog comes back, and he puts out the dog and the cat comes back. That was really the only scene he enjoyed doing."

Production took nine days; longer than it should have. Capturing the action with the cat and the dog alone consumed most of one day. And the irony of the thing escaped no one. As Schneider admitted, "Buster (and almost everybody on the crew) made a few corner-of-the-mouth remarks about his face being his livelihood all these years and here these idiots were knocking themselves out to avoid seeing it."

It all seemed deliberately oblique and amateurish, and Keaton was glad to be done with it. "He hated every minute of it," said Eleanor. "He'd just show up with his clothes on and they'd say, 'Okay, now you sit there and you do this, and you look at the cat and do the thing, and you turn that doorknob. . . .'" So he did *exactly* what they told him to do. He didn't do one whit less or one whit more than what he was told, because he didn't know what he was doing. They were so pleased with it; you wouldn't *believe* how pleased they were."

29

The Railrodder

WHILE BUSTER KEATON was making *Film* in New York City, Raymond Rohauer was in London arranging for a season of Keaton pictures in association with the British Film Institute. Given the outstanding success of the Keaton series at the Cinémathèque Française, Rohauer said he would be presenting a similar season in Paris with France's Jacques Tati (*Mr. Hulot's Holiday*) as co-sponsor. And with Tati's Specta Films, he claimed he was acquiring the rights to the Educational Pictures library, which would give him control of about a thousand shorts, including the sixteen two-reelers that Keaton made for the company.

Having gone to school on the Keaton inventory, Rohauer relinquished the Coronet Theatre and began extending his reach into other legacies. With him in London, for instance, was Hal Roach, who was there for the launching of a season of his own at the National Film Theatre. Rohauer's association with Roach was similar to the one he had with Keaton in which he would try to unravel years of tangled business dealings and regain worldwide control of the Roach library, which included the Laurel and Hardy and early Harold Lloyd comedies. He announced that he had acquired the Mack Sennett estate as well, which gave him control, he claimed, of all Sennett film and property rights, and was doing the same with the movies of Harry Langdon, dealing, in Langdon's case, with the comedian's widow, Mabel.

The Keaton pictures were still foremost among Rohauer's business activities, in no small part because Keaton, unlike Langdon, was still alive and, unlike Lloyd, still in the game. And while Keaton's compulsion to keep working was based partly on a need for income, there was also a restlessness within him that drove him to stay active, stay engaged, stay relevant.

"I drive by sometimes and talk to some of the old-timers," he said of the Motion Picture Country House, which was ten minutes from the Keaton home in Woodland Hills, "but it makes me so sad I don't do it often. They live in the past; I don't. One Easter Sunday I went to a party at Mary Pickford's house. Everybody from silent films was there. I tried to have fun, but I discovered we had nothing to talk about. Some of them had never heard a Beatles record. They hadn't kept up with the times."

Rohauer encouraged him to stay out in the world, and particularly to put himself in front of younger audiences who may have never heard of him but who might take to his old pictures the way they did in Europe. If the Beckett project had the effect of exposing him to the art house crowd, Keaton's next job was aimed squarely at the fifteen-to-twenty-five age group, which, according to some estimates, represented roughly two-thirds of all ticket sales. American International Pictures, which had gained prominence in the fifties with drive-in fare, created a new genre in 1963 with an inexpensive comedy titled *Beach Party*. Veteran actors Bob Cummings and Dorothy Malone were top billed, but the real stars of the picture were teen singing idol Frankie Avalon and *Mickey Mouse Club* alumna Annette Funicello. Lightweight and colorful, the film was the biggest hit in AIP's history, spawning sequels at the rate of two or three a year. *Muscle Beach Party* and *Bikini Beach* followed in 1964 with Avalon and Funicello starring and comedians like Buddy Hackett and Don Rickles mixed in.

The formula varied with the fourth entry in the series, *Pajama Party*. For the first time, Don Weis would be directing instead of William Asher, and paired with Annette Funicello would be Disney's Tommy Kirk. With Frankie Avalon's absence—he was shooting *I'll Take Sweden* with Bob Hope—it was thought wise to punch up the supporting cast, and so Elsa Lanchester, Dorothy Lamour, and William Bendix* were added. It was screenwriter Deke Heyward's idea to bring Keaton on, and Heyward created the character of Chief Rotten Eagle expressly for him.

"I had used him when I was doing *The Faye Emerson Show* way back when," Heyward explained, "and we became friendly. I regarded him as a wild genius that nobody really appreciated."

Added at the last possible moment was a gorgeous blonde named Bobbi Shaw, who was teamed with Keaton as a Swedish moll who spoke no English. He worked out bits of physical business with her, teaching her how to do things like a double take.

---

* When Bendix fell ill, he was replaced by Jesse White.

Keaton serenading Bobbi Shaw in his dressing room while the two were appearing in Pajama Party *(1964).*

"Buster taught me comic timing," she said. "I just thought he was a wonderful, sweet old man. I didn't realize who he was. It's like saying, 'Hey, Charlie Chaplin, teach me comedy.' But I knew nothing."

They also took to lunching together in Keaton's tiny dressing room on the Producers Studio lot. "His wife used to come into the dressing room and bring his lunch. And she called him 'sir.' Now, I don't know if they were kidding around, but it struck me as odd. I said, 'Buster, why is your wife calling you sir?' He said, 'Well, I trained her well.'"*

Written in two weeks, Deke Heyward's script was serviceable, but much of the comedy depended on broad, simplistic dialogue, and there was little Keaton could do to break free of it. The lines given to Rotten Eagle were often seasoned with the surfer exclamation "cowabunga," while Bobbi Shaw, apart from one scene, was limited to answering "ja" to anything asked of her. They were still seen together throughout the film, and Keaton would entertain her in the afternoons by showing her rope tricks and card tricks and serenading her with his ukulele.

"Elsa Lanchester was in the movie," Shaw remembered. "Elsa had a little crush, an attraction to me. And Buster was the one who really set her straight. It was all very friendly and fun, but he definitely took me under his wing. So here's the little guy in the funny hat, and he was really my guardian angel."

"I was in the animation department at the National Film Board," recalled Gerald Potterton. "I had dabbled a bit in live action before I made *The Railrodder*. I was a bit of an amateur actor, buggering around, and [I loved] sight

---

* James Karen laughed when he heard this story. "She was pissed because he had a girl in his dressing room," he said.

gags. I always liked all that because it's part of the animation genre. . . . I think originally the idea was a kind of animation thing. I was going to work one morning, and I saw the head of a guy shoot across an overpass over the highway. I discovered he was on one of those little track cars. They're motorized, very noisy, no muffler, so you could always hear them even if you couldn't always see them. What a way that would be to go across Canada from coast to coast! So I thought a bit and I did a few little drawings, thinking originally of it as an animation thing, maybe with the head of a character stuck onto the animation drawings and messing around with illustrations and live action, mixing the two.

"I think at that point the director of production, Grant McLean, who was quite a tough character, said, 'Well, look, if you want to do that, there's some money left in the government kitty now for the end of the fiscal year. Why don't you shoot it live?' And then somebody said, 'Wow, that's an amazing thought.' And somehow Buster's name came up. I said, 'Is he still alive?' Someone said, 'Well, sure, we just saw him in *Mad, Mad World.*' We looked around for his agent, and discovered that he was actually, at that moment, in Manhattan working on that Alan Schneider film, that Beckett thing. So it came about. I'd written down like a half page sort of idea for a story about this character jumping into the Thames in London and popping up in Nova Scotia and finding one of these machines and sweeping right across the country. Of course, no dialogue or anything."

Potterton and his producer, Julian Biggs, traveled to New York, where a meeting with Keaton in his suite at the St. Moritz stretched to three hours. "He opened the door, a big smile on his face, very sort of gruff voice. There was the usual racket out there on Central Park South, where the hotel was. We couldn't hear each other speak. He stuck his head out the window and yelled 'Quiet!' in a very loud voice." It was the evening of July 22, and Buster had just spent his third full day being directed by Alan Schneider and Samuel Beckett as if he were a mechanical doll. Potterton's story, conceived without him in mind, was for a nine-minute short titled *The Traveling Man.* Already committed to *Pajama Party,* Keaton welcomed the prospect of a silent comedy that wasn't already carved in stone.

"I had seen *The General,*" said Potterton, "and he was part of my boyhood list of wonderful, crazy silent-film actors. They were all there—Chaplin and Larry Semon, Ben Turpin and, of course, Keaton. I think the whole thing I loved about him was that single little guy against the planet."

Unwittingly, Potterton had followed Keaton's own formula for story development. The single typewritten sheet described a strong start and a good finish, while the middle was left to take care of itself. For Buster, it must have seemed like a deliverance.

"He seemed to be very enthusiastic for the idea," said Julian Biggs, "and discussed at great length with Gerry the various possibilities for incorporating his personal kind of comedy into the film."

Keaton committed to a five-week shoot, commencing once the job for American International was done. Owing to the trouble of dealing with government approval for Eleanor's expenses, he told the men it would be all right to skim $250 off the top of his weekly rate and write a contract for her to act as his personal makeup and wardrobe mistress.

Keaton finished with *Pajama Party* on September 1, 1964, and arrived in Montreal two days later. His first full day was given over to learning how to pilot the Canadian National's newly purchased track car, freshly painted and equipped with towing hooks, a task that took him all of fifteen minutes. In addition to the speeder, Canadian National also made a new International Travelall—a combination highway and track vehicle—available for filming. The "hy-track," as it was called, was equipped with both tires and flanged guide wheels, enabling the camera crew to make traveling shots from either a road or the tracks as needed. The evening was given over to *The General,* which attracted nearly everyone at the NFB.

"We had a beautiful print," Potterton said, "and Eldon Rathburn, who actually wrote the score for *The Railrodder*—he was our main composer at the National Film Board—played the piano on the stage. We had this great screening, and I remember sitting next to Buster and he had tears in his eyes." At the film's conclusion, the entire audience—staff, management, their families and children—stood and gave its maker a long and heartfelt ovation. "He was generally a man of few words, a very modest chap. He sort of stood up and thanked everybody in his own way. It was a lovely time."

After a day of filming at the railyard at Côte-Saint-Luc, the *Railrodder* company left for Halifax to shoot the opening scenes of the picture. Accompanying Potterton's crew of seven, which included the Keatons, was a three-man documentary team headed by cinematographer John Spotton. It would be Spotton's job to cover the filming of the 35mm Eastmancolor production in black and white with a shoulder-mounted 16mm camera.

"The camera John used was actually built by the National Film Board," said his assistant David de Volpi. "The Film Board was never able to do anything about it because it basically had an Arriflex movement in it. But it was the first wireless sync camera in the world."

Keaton and director Gerald Potterton confer during the making of The Railrodder *(1965).*

In Halifax, the crew was housed at the Nova Scotian Hotel, adjacent to the municipal railway station on the city's waterfront. There was a press conference upon their arrival, and time for a deep-sea-fishing trip.

Having made a matte shot of Keaton to be matched with footage of a stunt double dropping off Westminster Bridge and into the Thames, Potterton was now ready to stage Buster's emergence from the chilly waters of the North Atlantic and his discovery of a speeder on a seemingly deserted stretch of track.

"I was desperately trying to dream up a little business concerned with his hat," he recalled. "I suggested that as he wades onto the beach, he removes the hat and looks up to see the offending seagull who had possibly just dropped a small present. He said, 'No thanks. Leave that kind of stuff to Peter Sellers.' That incident led quickly to a short discussion of his rule number 2: *no* cartoon gags. It was clear, as I got to know him more, how much he loved working out things that were, first of all, funny, but humanly possible to enact. Hence, the magic of the collapsing bridge in *The General* and the life-threatening house facade collapsing around his little body in *Steamboat Bill, Jr.*"

On the return trip, the company stopped off at Levis to get a shot of Buster and the speeder traveling along with the Quebec City skyline in the background. In Montreal, the Keatons explored the underground shopping mall at Place Ville Marie and viewed the early rushes. It was in Montreal that the Canadian National's special car *Bedford* was placed into service for their use, a private seven-compartment affair with a commodious lounge and kitchen area.

"He was spoilt rotten," Potterton chuckled. "We had two guys, Jack and Nick, who had been on the Royal Tour for the Queen and Prince Philip— they were the Queen's personal chef and butler. So the food and the service were great."

Care had to be taken throughout to identify locations that could be photographed from Canadian National tracks, but that wasn't always possible. At Wakefield, Quebec, permission was sought from Canadian Pacific to film on a picturesque curved track that had a road right beside it for traveling shots, and on the Interprovincial bridge between Hull and Ottawa, the only possible location to take in the Parliament buildings. In Ottawa, Keaton welcomed the press to the lounge of the *Bedford*, moored at Union Station, before the company moved on to Rivers. Earlier, in comments released by the Film Board, he had twitted the locals in Rivers by likening the trestle gag to be staged there to the burning bridge collapse in *The General*. He had not seen the actual site, he said, only photos.

"Just looking at those pictures brought back a lot of fond memories," he mused. "I hope we can achieve some shots at Rivers which will be as memorable, in their way, as that shot in *The General*." But then he added: "Please be sure to let the people of Rivers and officials of the CN know that their bridge is safe. Once in a lifetime is enough to wreck a beautiful structure of that kind."

A small farming town, Rivers rolled out the red carpet for its visiting band of filmmakers, the biggest thing, by general consensus, that had ever happened there. The local cinema booked *When Comedy Was King*, and the mayor invited the Keatons and the Film Board crew to a Saturday-night reception at his home. Keaton, in return, proposed hosting the mayor and his wife and the president of the chamber of commerce and his wife for dinner aboard the *Bedford*. He also managed to borrow a portable TV set from an appliance store so that he could watch baseball.

"His energy level was very good until that one day when I changed the bridge gag," said Potterton. "I tried to straighten it out as best we could, but that day, I remember particularly, was quite a cold day. He was coughing really badly, and he did cough up some blood. I hadn't realized—none of us realized—that he was that sick. He shouldn't have been smoking, shouldn't have been drinking any beer, but he liked the odd beer and he had that little cigarette holder with the supposed safety filter thing in there. Eleanor smoked all the time too, so that didn't help."

The festivities on Saturday night were particularly elaborate, with the Rivers District Boys Pipe Band braving the cold and forming an honor guard for the guests as they arrived at the mayor's house. Following the reception, the Keatons were honored guests for a wild duck and turkey dinner in the basement of the Masonic hall. Before the seventy-five or so guests, the mayor conferred framed certificates designating both Buster and Eleanor as Manitoba Voyagers. The mayor also presented them with a rustic key to the town. All was captured by John Spotton's ever-present camera.

"We got so used to him with that 16mm shoulder holster, it got to be his second head," said Eleanor. "It got to where you ignored it. We were sitting around one day and I said, 'The first time I'm in the shower and I see that damn lens peeked over the shower door, you have had it! I'm gonna kill ya!' I said it with all our troupe there, and everybody laughed."

On Monday, it was time to move on to Jasper. "We'd get to where we were going," Eleanor remembered, "and they'd disconnect us off the train, shove us onto a siding, and we'd stay there two or three days or however long it took. We had a couple of railroad men with us at all times to divert traffic. And whenever they finished shooting, they'd wire the railroad and say, 'We're ready to leave.' And the next train that came by, whether it was passenger or freight train, would stop long enough to hook us on, and away we'd go to our next stop." As the idea for the gag with the rolling duck blind took shape, Keaton knew he couldn't halt filming for half a day to go off and dress the speeder with tree branches. Given the limited crew, there was only one person who had the time and flair to take on the job.

"[It was] bitter cold, half raining, half snowing," said Eleanor, "and I spent one whole damn morning out there putting that greenery on chicken wire with pieces of wire, and my fingers were bleeding. They were way down, ten miles down the track shooting something else, but they needed this for the afternoon. And then when they got back for lunch, the prop man went in and reinforced a few more things with his pliers and his strong hands that I couldn't do. But we weren't allowed to pick a leaf. We had to go to the park ranger station, explain exactly what we wanted, *why* we wanted it, what we were going to do with it, how much we would need, and then the rangers went out and cut it and brought it to us. You could get arrested for cutting one leaf!"

Keaton spent his sixty-ninth birthday making some spectacular traveling shots in Fraser Canyon, zooming over a huge trestle, the Fraser River far below, the crew shooting from the Trans-Canada Highway above. A party took place that night aboard the *Bedford*, which was stopped on a siding at the unincorporated Gold Rush town of Boston Bar, the men all in neckties, the champagne flowing freely, the evening's contractually stipulated duck bagged by camera assistant Bob Nichel. Gerry Potterton stood and offered a toast: "On behalf of the National Film Board, I would like to wish you many happy returns of the day, October the fourth, nineteen hundred and sixty-four. Also, the Queen sends her regards."

Keaton took a sip of champagne and assumed an Irish brogue. "Thank you, Mr. Chairman," he said. "I'm not very good at public speaking, but to show you me heart's in the right place, I'll fight any man in the house." Among the gifts that night: a model steam engine.

Filming concluded in Vancouver on October 9, a Japanese man emerging from the surf at White Rock, studying a sign pointing eastward, and taking off on the speeder as Buster, just a few feet away, is admiring the view. He starts, inclined to give chase, then thinks better of it. As the new rider disappears into the distance, he begins the long trudge home with the same resolve he has always shown, whether building a boat, assembling a house, outrunning the law, or proving himself to the girl he loved. There would be more films to come in the new year, but nothing nearly as satisfying, nor as intensely personal, as this charming farewell to the screen.

The year 1964 didn't end with *The Railrodder*. Keaton had scarcely arrived back in California when he was tapped for an upcoming episode of *The Donna Reed Show*, his second time guesting on the long-running family sitcom. As Andy Turner, an auto mechanic who also does body work, he was turned loose in the garage of a service station, gracefully rolling between car and work bench on a creeper, getting himself caught up in masking tape, and mistakenly answering the phone with a paint gun, spraying one whole side of his face. As he finished with the Reed appearance, he was back on the big screen in a variety of forms. *It's a Mad, Mad, Mad, Mad World* was still at Hollywood's Cinerama Dome, where it had played to more than a million people; Robert Youngson's latest compilation, *M-G-M's Big Parade of Comedy*, was highlighting footage from *The Cameraman;* and *Pajama Party* was in release, prompting his casting in the next entry in the series, *Beach Blanket Bingo*, for which he was also retained as special comedy consultant.

. . .

"He'd come to me once a year," said Eleanor, "the week before Christmas, and say, 'Give me a check.' I'd give him one and he'd tell me to sign it. 'You can sign it,' I'd say. 'You're on the account.' He didn't even want to get that involved. Money didn't interest him. If he had enough to buy what he wanted, he didn't care."

He still needed the work, even if he didn't need the money. Whatever free time he had was filled by commercials: two for United States Steel, one for Budweiser, two for Pure Oil, a whole week's worth for Seneca Apple Juice in New York City. For Keaton, work had become a compulsion, something akin to breathing, and although he talked of retiring, nobody took him very seriously.

"I could retire mighty easy," he told Bob Thomas, but his public wouldn't let him. It was, Thomas reasoned, the Keaton revival, the reemergence of his classic comedies in Europe and the U.S. that kept the demand for his services at a low boil. "No doubt retiring to the San Fernando Valley sounds appealing to him, but the compulsion to make people laugh seems stronger."

In January, American International announced a slate of eighteen releases for 1965, nine of which were to be produced in house, more than half aimed at the so-called youth market. One on the schedule, *The Chase,* was nothing more than a title, an idea inspired by the phenomenal success of *Mad World.* Details, however, began to emerge. Keaton would star in the picture, which, in an homage to the great comedies of the twenties, would be entirely silent, save for music and effects. As a broad parody of the James Bond adventures, the story would have Buster mistaken for a master disguise artist and counterspy named James Blonde, who would ultimately foil the plot of a female spy who kidnaps a famous monument and holds it for ransom. Filming would be spread over three continents, the surrounding cast would include dozens of well-known comedians, and the whole enterprise would be timed for release on Keaton's seventieth birthday. It was an ambitious plan for a man who had been in show business since the turn of the century, but Buster seemed up to the challenge and Eleanor knew better than to try to dissuade him. By the end of the month Elsa Lanchester had been added to the cast, and Keaton hinted at a scene to Hedda Hopper in which he would encounter his thirty-year-old self in a clip from *The General.* Retitled *The Big Chase* to avoid conflicting with a picture Sam Spiegel was producing, it

Eleanor and Buster at the 1965 funeral of Stan Laurel.

was considered a go until the death on February 23, 1965, of Stan Laurel at the age of seventy-four.

Some three months earlier, Gerry Potterton had come to California on the promise that Keaton would introduce him to Laurel. Potterton so loved Laurel and Hardy that he had named one of his sons Oliver Stanley. "When the door of the apartment opened, there was the one and only sitting, smiling away in his wheelchair. His first words to his old pal were, 'Gee, Buster, it sure is good to see yer . . .'" And a little later Keaton pointed out that he had been filming up in Canada, and said to Stanley, 'And guess who directed it?' Laurel asked politely, 'Who, Buster?' And the latter pointed at me and replied, 'THAT!'"

Laurel's passing took a lot out of Keaton. Films of the funeral at Forest Lawn show a man on the verge of tears, lost in a cloud of grief. Dick Van Dyke concluded his eulogy that day with the anonymous "A Prayer for Clowns":

> *God bless all the clowns.*
> *Give them a long, good life,*
> *Make bright their way—they're a race apart.*
> *Alchemists most, who turn their hearts' pain,*
> *Into a dazzling jest to lift the heart.*
> *God bless all clowns.*

"I'm getting tired," Keaton, in a familiar refrain, told columnist Dick Kleiner. "I don't want to work so much anymore. I'm sixty-nine and I've been working since 1899. I think I've earned the right to be lazy." Quietly, *The Big Chase* was dropped from the AIP schedule, and Keaton went back to piecework—a commercial in Salt Lake City, a guest shot on a Jonathan Winters special, a commitment to producer Joe Pasternak to attend the Academy Awards. He also sat down to play cards with the syndicated bridge authority Alfred Sheinwold.

"It's disconcerting," Sheinwold conceded, "to play against a man who fires the perfect card back at you without stopping for breath or moving a muscle of his face." At the conclusion of their game, the doorbell rang and Eleanor opened the door to a pair of nine-year-old boys who wanted to know if Buster could come out to play.

"The sixty-nine-year-old comedian grinned at us and went out to play baseball with his friends. Bridge is a wonderful game, but the love of Keaton's life is really baseball."

Keaton also sat for an interview with Don Alpert of the *Los Angeles Times,* a long meandering conversation. His voice was raspy ("It used to be baritone. Now it's a gravel bass"), but the subject matter stretched from vaudeville to the beach pictures. What was it, Alpert wanted to know, that made audiences laugh at his stone-faced countenance?

"I go back to a very old saying," Keaton responded. "A comedian does funny things. A good comedian does things funny. Here's your comparisons. You haven't got a better laugh-getter than Bob Hope. But Hope is a talker. When it comes to action he's lost. With the newcomers, one of the naturals is Dick Van Dyke. He has that knack of doing things funny. Cantor was a great entertainer. So was Jolson. But they were completely lost when it came to action. I've laid eggs as well as anybody else. Some dandies. But it wasn't so expensive in our independent days. We owned our own cameras, our own prop department, our own trucks, everything."

Asked about modern films, he said he didn't see too many of them. "But I was put back on my heels when I saw *Tom Jones.* Why, that was a dirty movie. And Peter Sellers in *A Shot in the Dark* was too. Even if censorship had permitted me to do those things, still I wouldn't have. I think they've gone way too far. I never did a smutty bit of business in my life. My father drove that home to me. The lowest form of comedy is vulgarity."

He had done practically everything there was to do in show business. What was left? "I was going to try to get into an opera because I've been in everything else. In Europe I was in a circus. As a kid I was Little Lord Fauntleroy and Little Alfie in *East Lynne.* Musical comedy. Straight dramatic roles. But I haven't done opera. Now, if we can only figure out something, I might sell the idea to the Met."

In April, Keaton began work on another beach picture, *How to Stuff a Wild Bikini,* as a tropical witch doctor called Bwana. Upon completion of his scenes with Bobbi Shaw, Frankie Avalon, and an unbilled Elizabeth Montgomery, American International announced that he would travel to Italy to star in a wartime comedy titled *Two Marines and a General*. A month later, word came that he would appear in a second European-based feature, *Pop Goes the World*, with Groucho Marx, Stanley Holloway, and a grouping of international singing stars headed by Petula Clark. When he joined the cast of AIP's *Sergeant Deadhead*, again with Frankie Avalon, it was abundantly clear he was still willing and eager to work. "I keep getting crazy offers from Europe," he said.

When Hedda Hopper interviewed him in May, she got him talking about his family and home life. He had surrendered his position as honorary mayor of Woodland Hills after three two-year terms but still did promotional chores for civic-minded groups like the Kiwanis Club. She asked him about his sons.

"They both live in Santa Monica and drop by all the time," he told her. "The older has four children and the younger, two. My grandchildren wreck the joint every time they come. A couple of the kids are around that age and perfect setups for shotgun weddings."

Did he ever see Natalie? "No. I've never seen her."

Had he and Eleanor celebrated twenty-five years of marriage yet? "That will be on May twenty-ninth."

Where was he taking her? "Well, there's a nightclub here in Woodland Hills—with bowling alley connected. Maybe I'll take her there."

There was another set of Ford commercials in July, coming on the heels of a mini-remake of *Cops* he did for them the previous year. Then, with Keaton's departure for Italy looming, Ben Pearson landed him a starring role in the film version of *A Funny Thing Happened on the Way to the Forum*, which was set to start filming in Spain. A walking encyclopedia of theatrical lore, Pearson knew the role of the elderly, befuddled Erronius, created on Broadway by Raymond Walburn, was ideal for Keaton and limited to a few key scenes. He sought out the Los Angeles–based producer Melvin Frank and made his pitch.

"I had to work hard to sell him," Pearson said. "When it came to *Forum*, I practically had to break Mel Frank's arm to put him in the goddamned picture."

In July, Keaton recorded a version of the park bench skit he perfected at the Cirque Médrano for a well-intentioned but ill-conceived TV special called *Salute to Stan Laurel*. It was the first and only time he worked on-camera with Lucille Ball, who was grateful to have the chance.

"I agreed," she said, "even though I knew it was not right for me, because I also knew I'd never have another chance to work with him. He was terribly ill, and I didn't think he'd last through the day."

Though he was crowding seventy, no one on the set that day recognized Keaton as an old man. The sketch included an oft-repeated gag in which Buster, searching the floor of a telephone booth for change, doesn't notice that Lucy has entered the same enclosure. As he stands, she rides his shoulders through the top of the booth, a stunt he repeated several times for rehearsals and tape. It all ended with him being dragged

With Lucille Ball in Salute to Stan Laurel *(1965).*

offstage by the collar, tipping his hat to Lucy as he goes.

"The collar dug into Buster's throat and nearly choked him," *Life's* David Zeitlin said in a dispatch. "He fell into a paroxysm of coughing, and the spasm continued for ten minutes or so. . . . The attack was violent and stubborn. Buster sat in a chair and his wife ministered to him. Then they reworked the mechanics of the gag so that the cop [Harvey Korman] would grab Buster by the coat collar instead of the shirt collar. It worked better next time."

In Ball, Zeitlin knew that Keaton had found his perfect partner. "As they worked, Buster engineered each gag quietly, without fuss, the business with the flowers, the thing where he feigns blindness, thus allowing him to walk into Lucy and snitch a kiss, using a painter's easel as a blind for the old shell game, the gag in which he slides up to the lass on the park bench, finally gets his arm around her, only to have her move away to the chewing gum machine at the critical moment, leaving him grabbing air. The skit was one fine touch after another, but Buster was the first to say, 'There are no new sight gags. I've done 'em all before.'"

Eleanor was present throughout. He suffered from chronic bronchitis, she explained. "He hacks and coughs a lot. He smokes too much. But now he's smoking filter cigarettes through filters. Aside from that, he's fine."

He was also quite round, maybe twenty pounds overweight for a man of his age and height. "I'd rather have him fat than in the funny farm for having given up cigarettes and all the good food. If he wants to be fat, he's entitled."

Keaton himself was more to the point in addressing the paunch: "All beer and laziness," he said ruefully.

After nearly a month's delay, the Keatons flew to New York on August 25 and sailed for Italy the following day. Meanwhile, Hedda Hopper was reporting that she had seen *The Railrodder* at the Berlin Film Festival and thought it better than the featured films. *Film* was set to be shown at the annual fest in Venice, and then both pictures were to be gathered for the opener of the New York Film Festival under the collective title *Buster and Beckett,* accompanied by a rare screening of *Seven Chances.* Keaton made it to Venice for the September 4, 1965, showing of *Film,* but he was not well.

"He was so ill," said Eleanor. "He was sick as a dog. . . . He wasn't holding down food very well. He had no energy or strength left."

He appeared twice that day, the first time for a morning press conference at which he finally saw what Beckett and Alan Schneider had wrought. As Pearl Sheffy of the *Montreal Gazette* reported, "Two hundred critics from two dozen countries, most of whom were apathetic about the film, leapt to their feet when Keaton ambled on stage and roared for ten solid minutes."

After a few preliminaries, Keaton stood and began talking extemporaneously, saying he was in Italy to play a general—a notion that brought a loud cheer from the crowd—and that he would then go to Spain for *A Funny Thing Happened on the Way to the Forum.* "I've had several other offers but couldn't take 'em. No time to spare."

His expectations were low for the gala screening that evening. The picture was very stark and arty and grim. "I never did find out what it was all about," he said. "Beckett was always on the set, and once I asked him, 'How do you get all these crazy ideas? Is it because you had Welsh rarebit the night before?' He just smiled and walked away."

The capacity audience at the Palazzo del Cinema was rife with anticipation, as many had warm memories of the festival's Keaton season of two years back. The clapping began as the Keatons made their appearance at the front row of the balcony and took their seats. People turned and noticed, and as more of them did so, the applause grew louder and more insistent until the entire room was on its feet.

Acknowledging the cheers of the international audience at the 1965 Venice Film Festival.

"Buster Keaton . . . was given an ovation the like of which I have not witnessed in all my years of covering film festivals," wrote Francis Koval. "Even the most sedate journalists stood on their seats to cheer."

Somebody nudged Buster, and he looked genuinely surprised, as if to say: *For me?* Finally, he stood and bowed.

"He cried at the ovation he got in the theater. . . . It was a standing ovation that went on and on and on," Eleanor said.

The picture that brought Keaton to Italy, a co-production between AIP and producer Fulvio Lucisano's Italian International Films, was renamed *War Italian Style,* a play on *Divorce Italian Style,* the title of a popular import of recent vintage. Nothing, however, could salvage Keaton's miscasting as a German officer during the Second World War, and a poor script, co-written by Lucisano, only compounded the problem. Keaton did what he could to enliven the picture, but had little help from director Luigi Scattini, whose principal job was to manage the comedy team of Franco and Ciccio, a sort of Italian Abbott and Costello. The addition of actress Martha Hyer and comic heavy Fred Clark was supposed to make the film more palatable to American audiences, but the essential cheapness of the thing reminded Eleanor of *El Moderno Barba Azul,* the impoverished Mexican picture Buster made in 1946.

Work on *War Italian Style* fell behind schedule, and production didn't wrap until late on September 17, a Friday night. The Keatons flew to Madrid on Saturday, costume fittings took place on Sunday, and Buster was on the set of *A Funny Thing Happened on the Way to the Forum* on Monday.

"He thought he had asthma . . . and what became apparent early on was that he was not going to be able to do much running," said director Richard Lester. "Since his part was to run around the seven hills of Rome, we thought we were in some trouble, and I hired a stunt double who was a National Hunt jockey called Mick Dillon to double Keaton in long shot. Now to end up with Keaton speaking and somebody else doing the moves is perhaps getting it round the wrong way. He'd been offered the part on Broadway, and there was an argument over whether they should have him or not, and it never came to anything."

Zero Mostel, who was starring in the movie as he had on Broadway, considered it a pleasure to be working with Keaton, whom he first met in 1942. "A touching man. A lovely man," he said. "Once, at M-G-M, I saw a man with a great big grin on his face and I didn't know who it was. Then suddenly he stopped smiling and it was Keaton."

Eleanor could see that her husband was exhausted, and fretted the weather would aggravate his bronchitis. "It rained and fogged, and half the picture looks like it's got very artistic lighting. It's because they finally had to shoot in the fog to get something on film." Keaton grew close to Mostel and Jack Gilford, while Phil Silvers kept to himself, brooding over the size of his part.

"His wife protected him a lot," Mostel said of Keaton. "One day there was a howling gale and he slipped out to my caravan. 'The wind's blown her away,' he said."

Dick Lester, who revered Keaton and loved his great silent comedies, feared he wasn't using him to full advantage. "We had one wonderful day which I engineered, taking a second unit and going into an empty field outside Madrid with Buster in costume, and I said, 'If you have any ideas, anything you'd like to do . . . We'll sit under this tree and think up some gags, and if we can put them into the film, I'll try to shoehorn them in.' That's a concept which is, I'm sure, very far from his way of working, where everything seemed to be beautifully planned and economic. Certain setups appear in the final film, but they are more in terms of his running round the seven hills of Rome, just physical attitudes that we caught him doing. He did a few odd gags; nothing spectacular came out of it, I regret to say."

*With Phil Silvers,
Jack Gilford, and
Zero Mostel on the set
of* A Funny Thing
Happened on the
Way to the Forum
(1966).

The film was based at the Samuel Bronston studios, where Mel Frank and United Artists had established offices and taken over two stages. Frank initially had wanted to use the Roman Forum exterior Bronston had built for *The Fall of the Roman Empire,* but weather and creditors had left it in ruins.

"Our Rome isn't the gold and glorious type," he said in resignation. "Ours is the 'Little Rome around the corner from the Forum.' If you walked around the corner from the streets on the glamourous Bronston set, you'd find the kind of streets we want to use."

Most of Keaton's scenes were made on the mammoth studio lot at Las Matas, where he was exposed to the elements—wind, rain, and temperatures in the low fifties—while in a ragged purple toga that left him, as Eleanor put it, "half-naked." Mercifully, his work on the picture was confined to seven days on the schedule.

"It was written in the script," said Lester, "that he was running along in the woods and a series of chariots just miss him, and he says, 'Ah, the most refreshing climate in the whole world.' And started off again. And I thought of an ad lib: He should do that and go straight into a tree. So I said, 'Do you think this would be a good idea?' And he said, 'Yes, that would be fine.' I said, 'What do you need, Buster?' He said, 'Well, where are you going to put your camera?' I showed him. He stood behind me and looked at the tree and he said, 'I want two makeup sponges and eighteen inches of black cotton.' I thought: *This is professionalism.*

"Every yard between the camera and the tree he made a little mark. He took his hat and shoved the makeup sponges between his hat and his head, took the cotton and pulled it underneath his hair and tied it to the hat so the hat wouldn't fall off, and said, 'Okay, let's do it.' Turned the camera over.

Chariot goes through. Buster runs in, says the line, and goes straight into the tree. I said, 'That was perfect, Buster . . . Buster . . . ?' What he'd forgotten was that he no longer had the ability, with his eyesight going, to see his marks. And went straight into the tree on the wrong side of the hat and had almost knocked himself out. He'd got all the makeup sponges down one side and he'd missed them completely. And there he was . . . All the sense of how to do it was there, but the body was weak."

If Buster Keaton never appeared in another picture, at least he knew he'd go out on a solid laugh, flat on his back, just as he entered almost half a century earlier, felled not by a sack of flour this time, but by a tree. Several days later, on the eve of his seventieth birthday, he was feted at a testimonial luncheon in Madrid that gathered more than fifty of Spain's leading figures in theater, literature, film, and music, plus doctors, lawyers, government officials, press. Many of the attendees spoke elaborate tributes.

"He brought the light of fine comedy to us through his films," said one. "The hours of simple happiness he has given us can never be repaid," offered another. "His unsmiling face has brought tears of laughter to our eyes and undying smiles that remain in our hearts," yet another proclaimed. He was, said *Variety*'s Hank Werba, "praised to tears," and, sniffling occasionally, he could only respond by saying, "Thank you. Thank you. Thank you."

Their next stop was Toronto, via New York, where Keaton had committed to making another short film, this one to be directed by John Sebert, the stills photographer on *Ten Girls Ago*. "The whole thing was my idea," said Sebert. "I had wanted to get into film, and I made a deal with an art house in Toronto that wanted to get into the film business. If I would do some fashion stuff for them, I could then pursue doing some film work. They had a client, the Construction Safety Associations of Ontario, and we did a bunch of commercials for them. Then, about six months after that, they said they wanted to do a little film. I was the only one who knew anything about film in the company. I had spent two days doing nothing but photographing Buster [on *Ten Girls Ago*], and I got to know him fairly well. So when this project came up on construction safety, a thirty-minute film, I thought: *My god, a perfect opportunity—Buster on a construction site.* So I sold the idea to the construction safety people; they really couldn't have cared less what I did. Then I went ahead and talked to Buster."

It qualified as an industrial, and Sebert had to make do with a minuscule budget. "We had $25,000," he remembered, "which was not very much." From Spain, Eleanor had cabled Sebert, but he never saw it. "He was very busy. He was in Europe doing *Funny Thing Happened on the Way to the Forum.* I called, then Eleanor got on the phone and said, 'Didn't you get my telegram?' I said, 'No.' She said, 'Well, Buster can't do it. He's just not well enough.' Oh, my god. This is just what you love to hear. I was talking to Eleanor and then Buster came back. We had the whole thing set up, how much he was going to make and all that stuff. . . . He said to Eleanor, 'Look, these guys [Sebert and writer Paul Sutherland] have put a lot into this. Let's go and do the thing.' So they did, but it came very close to not getting done."

Keaton with director John Sebert in Toronto during the filming of The Scribe.

Keaton's resolve was likely more than a simple act of friendship for a man he knew and liked. He now had a real need to keep moving, to keep working, to outrun this thing that was pursuing him. They arrived in Toronto on October 3, and immediately Buster went to work. The scene was the construction site of a new government building complex that would come to be known as the MacDonald Block. Under the title *The Reporter,* the film would present Keaton scouring the job site for safety hazards. "The one thing Buster kept saying to me was, 'It isn't *funny.*' I'd say, 'Yeah, I know, Buster, but we have a guy who's paying for this. He wants to get these things in.' But he did help a lot, getting things in. We'd set up a thing like pushing a wheelbarrow. And he'd say, 'Let's do it *this* way.' A lot of that was improvised."

On the night of October 4, 1965, producers Ann and Kenneth Heeley-Ray gave a seventieth birthday party for Keaton at their home outside of the city. It was a fleeting interlude of warmth during what was otherwise a challenging shoot for a man with chronic bronchitis.

"The construction site was a mudbath," said Sebert, "cold and miserable." They also had to work in and around the actual construction as it was happening. "Eleanor was right—he really was not well enough to do the thing. We didn't realize that. In the middle of a shot he'd start coughing and we'd lose a half hour. The cough went on for four or five minutes and then he'd have to rest a bit. Then he'd bounce back up again."

Sebert took the liberty of having a double on hand, an old friend of his in a duplicate wardrobe named Larry Reynolds. "Buster never complained once. He never complained about anything. He did everything we asked him to do. Every time we were going to use Larry as the stand-in, he'd say, 'I can do that.' He was willing. We were more concerned than he was. He did a lot of his own stuff, but some of the things were a bit dangerous. There was one shot where Larry got pulled up in the air [on the hook of a crane]. Buster said, 'I'll do that.'" The picture was completed within the space of two weeks, and even Eleanor admitted that he had a good time making it. They left for home on October 17, but the flight didn't go well. "I got him on a plane," she said, "and he started having breathing problems. The stewardess gave him an oxygen mask." He was taken off the plane in a wheelchair. At home, Eleanor called the doctor, who ordered X-rays the following morning. Once the films had been taken, the doctor said, "When he gets dressed, hospital. Now."

"Okay," said Eleanor, "we'll stop by the house and get some clothes and whatever."

"*Now*," he emphasized. "Then you go back and worry about the clothes and the toothbrush."

In the surgery that was performed on October 19, Keaton's lymph nodes were removed. "One lung is totally gone," the doctor told Eleanor. "He's only got part of the second lung. He's got anywhere from one week to three months."

On November 2, Hedda Hopper received a postcard from a reader: "I haven't read anything about Buster Keaton's illness in the papers, so I thought you might like to know that he came home from the hospital last week and is very ill with a chest complication. He probably won't recover."

Hopper checked with Eleanor, who told of the miserable working conditions in Spain and Toronto. Then Buster came on the line.

"I aged five years before that operation," he told her. "A guy came in to prepare me. He shaved under my arm and my entire chest—for a minor operation. I thought they were going to cave in my entire chest. I'm laying for that guy. I've got a special custard pie and I'm gonna haunt him."

Hopper reported: "Buster Keaton is okay now, but had a rough go when he got home from picture-making abroad."

Keaton was diagnosed with small-cell carcinoma of the lungs, a particularly aggressive form of cancer that is more prevalent in men than women and almost invariably linked to smoking. "It's what they call 'the black cancer,'" Eleanor said in a 1975 interview. "It's the most rapid and the most treacherous; when it starts it's like wildfire. There's like five grades of malignancy, and that was the fastest and the worst. He had none of it in April, and by November [the lungs were] practically gone." And Buster, she confirmed, didn't realize how sick he was. "He thought he had bronchitis. And the doctor says, 'Don't tell him any different. Bronchitis he understands. He's bad enough off now without scaring him to death on top of it.'"

He was feeling well enough to do a photo shoot for New York–based Levy's rye bread on December 15. Levy's agency, Doyle Dane Bernbach, sent a photographer and an art director to the house, dropped a seamless background, and shot a series of pictures of Buster in his familiar vest, tie, and pork pie hat holding a corned beef sandwich. The famous campaign, with the tagline "You Don't Have to be Jewish to Love Levy's Real Jewish Rye," targeted subway riders and was so popular the posters themselves became collector's items.

Keaton also relished the prospect of a job at CBS. "Bus was in the hospital," said Bill Cox, "and that was the day they told us that he couldn't live. He was telling me that Danny Kaye had called him. Danny was having trouble with his television series, because Harvey Korman's the greatest second banana in the world, [but he was] stealing scenes from him, catching flies in the background. . . . [Bus said], 'Don't get rid of Harvey. Harvey's great. What you need is the direction of . . .' " Danny said, 'Will you direct me next season?' That's really what he was looking forward to when he died—directing Danny Kaye."

"They put him on a real horrible course of chemotherapy," said Eleanor, "and it looked like it was working. He was breathing better and the cancer was shrinking." The doctor ordered new X-rays every week or two.

"God, this medication's working," the doctor told her. "He could have a couple of years, he's getting so much better."

Through it all, Buster kept smoking, and he kept having the dreadful coughing attacks that left him struggling for breath. "Then it went on the move. It metastasized. While the lungs were getting better, it was moving around, going somewhere else."

In time, he seemed to acknowledge the seriousness of his condition. "How are we financially?" he asked Eleanor.

"Fine," she replied. "Why?"

"Well, I don't think I'm getting well as quickly as I think I should."

"Don't worry about it. We've got enough money to last as long as it takes."

He whiled away the hours playing cards, solitaire by himself, bridge whenever visitors stopped by. Jane Dulo was there every week, Louise Keaton drove out most weekends; Bill Cox and his wife, Lee, were often around; and Jim Talmadge frequently came out by himself, sometimes bringing the family on Sundays.

Keaton began experiencing headaches and a stiff neck during the last week of January 1966. Sunday, January 30 was relatively quiet, with Jane Dulo and Louise and the usual afternoon bridge game. Both Eleanor and Jane noticed something erratic in Buster's scoring, which had always been so fiercely precise. They quit the game around five so that Louise could drive home before dark. Eleanor and Jane went into the kitchen to fix dinner, leaving Buster to his solitaire. They were in the kitchen when they heard something, the struggling sounds of what they discovered was a seizure.

"His cancer had metastasized," said Eleanor, "and gone to his brain."

She called the doctor and an ambulance was dispatched. A second seizure took place at the hospital in front of the doctor, who thought he had suffered a stroke. A series of scans confirmed that he hadn't, but they still held him under observation until around noon the following day. Meanwhile, Eleanor called Jim Talmadge and had him come and get the pool table out of the den. In its place she had a hospital bed delivered. "I brought him home, and he sat at the bridge table. I said, 'Have you had any lunch?' He said, 'No.' And he was just a little bit off, his speech was a little off. And he was just barely dragging one leg. He sat at his table there and he got more and more irrational. Now he wants to fight; he doesn't care about what or who."

He could finally see where all of this was leading. He hated being sick, and was now in a rage over it. He would not go gentle.

His nurse, a man known as Chick, called the doctor, wondering if he should administer a sedative.

"Hit him with everything you've got," the doctor instructed.

But Keaton wouldn't let anybody touch him.

"He just kept walking," Eleanor said. "He would not sit down. He was terrified by then."

Chick gave him pills. Chick gave him injections. Nothing seemed to have any effect.

"He got angry at me because I kept walking behind him all the time for fear he'd fall down the steps [between the den and the living room]. And he was just a horror, [an] absolute horror. . . . It took something like two hours before he started winding down enough to quit fighting it, because he knew if he ever lay down he wouldn't get up. He knew that."

Unable to stand any longer, he sat down on the couch, rambling and defeated.

"Do you think you could stretch out and have a little nap now?" Eleanor asked.

"Yeah," he replied. "I guess so." He was wobbly on his feet, and it took both Eleanor and Chick, one on each side, to walk him the few steps over to the bed.

Drained of all strength, he was asleep in moments.

30

Something Like a Genius

BEING RELATIVELY NEW ON THE SCENE, the night nurse didn't want to wake Eleanor the next morning. Instead, he phoned Chick at home and asked him to do it. So Chick dragged himself out of bed, got dressed, and came in an hour early.

"He's gone," said Eleanor before Chick could utter a word.

It was Tuesday, February 1, 1966. The doctor had given Buster Keaton three months at the outside, and he surpassed that prognosis by two weeks. For one final time he had double-crossed his audience.

Eleanor called Jim Talmadge; his brother, Bob; and Louise Keaton. Buster's death was not unexpected, but in the confusion that followed, others were left to get the news over the radio. Jane Earl was in Fresno with her husband, composer-arranger Dee Barton, when she heard, and she phoned her sister, Ruth, who was with their parents in Whittier, to say she was on her way.

"My gosh . . . ," Ruth said when she reached Eleanor, because she had been planning to visit. "Buster had said, 'Come out and I'm going to teach you how to play bridge.' He threatened us for years, and I hadn't learned to play bridge. It would have taken three or four days or a week, and I had my bags packed."

As Buster Keaton's final director, John Sebert felt an understandable pang of guilt. "I think we shortened his life somewhat," he admitted in 2014. "We had no idea how sick he was. He was willing to do anything, and when people are willing to do it, you take advantage of them. So I do feel kind of badly. I was in Mexico when I heard he died, and I thought: *Jesus, did we do that?*"

Raymond Rohauer was in England on business and had the news broken to him by a British critic who had heard it on the radio. "I'm sorry to tell you that Buster is dead," was the way he put it.

"Is it *confirmed*?" snapped Rohauer.

James Karen was living and working in New York and his son, Reed, heard it first. He left a message for his father to call him when he was finished at the studio. "Reed was eight years old," he recalled. "I said, 'Reed, what is it? I'm through.' He said, 'You really through?' I said, 'Yeah.' He said, 'Are you comin' home?' I said, 'Yeah.' He said, 'Well, I have terrible news. Our Buster, we lost him today.'"

Ruthie made it to Woodland Hills in record time and was first on the scene. Eleanor had already decided that Buster should be interred at Forest Lawn, Hollywood Hills, and the cemetery sent a limousine. On the ride over, the two women brainstormed the kind of music Buster would want.

"Gracie Allen had only died about three weeks before," Eleanor remembered, "and George [Burns] had spent something like $25,000 on the funeral, the mausoleum, the crypt. . . . And we talked about how *outrageously* stupid something like that was, even if they were wealthy."

So when she faced the "mingy little mortician" she called Mr. Whipple, she was loaded for bear: "Now I'll tell you one thing right off the top. We are not going to spend one penny over $3,500. I don't care how you do it—that's the top I will blow on this thing because I think it's so stupid."

The man remained professionally solemn throughout. "He takes us up to this big room with all the caskets and says, 'Now I will leave you alone to browse.' I said, 'We'll take that one,' and I walked out before he could." On the matter of music, he was suitably distressed when they specified Louis Armstrong's recording of "Hello, Dolly!" He gave them a list of more appropriate selections, and on it they found three or four, such as the Lord's Prayer, that weren't, as Eleanor put it, "too objectionable." But various renderings of Jerry Herman's hit tune remained mandatory, and on the way home the women smiled, knowing that it was what Buster would have wanted.

Jimmy Karen phoned Eleanor when he got home: "She was very businesslike. She had taken care of everything, and she was all set. It was another chapter. That's the way she was. I mean, she *adored* him. She would do anything for him. But she was cut-and-dry. She said, 'We're going to take care of Father, give him a good sendoff. Can you get out?' I said, 'I can't get out.' I was working; I was in a show at the time."

Director Jack Donohue, a good friend from the M-G-M days, asked Eleanor's permission to bring a rosary to the mortuary, and she said, "Of course." And Eleanor's sister, Jane, wanted to take a deck of cards, so Eleanor gave her one.

"When he was ready to be buried," Eleanor said, "he had a rosary in one pocket and a deck of cards in the other. So he was set for whichever direction he was going."

Every major media outlet in the world carried the news of Buster Keaton's death. *The New York Times* printed a formal obituary as well as two separate appreciations by Bosley Crowther. *Life* reprinted James Agee's words. The *San Francisco Examiner* mourned him on its editorial page as "a genius of the slapstick; a glum-visaged toy of events that picked on him; a brilliant star."

One voice that could not come forth was Keaton's old friend and co-star Hedda Hopper, who died suddenly of double pneumonia, aged eighty, on the same day as he. In England, Dilys Powell said she had never loved another star as she had loved him. "There was a kind of purity in the line of all his movements; I don't know how else to describe it. To my grief I never saw him in the flesh, never spoke to him." And in the pages of *The Observer,* Kenneth Tynan recalled the young, beautiful Buster Keaton. "If Chaplin was the greatest lyrical comic, this was the greatest stoic; and we live, of necessity, in a stoical age."

The funeral took place on Friday, February 4, at Forest Lawn's Church of the Hills, a colonial affair that was filled to its 158-seat capacity. Notable attendees included Donald O'Connor, Benny Rubin, Andy Clyde, Chester Conklin, Babe London, and Faith Holden. The eulogy was again given by Dick Van Dyke, who framed Keaton as a man who "manufactured the sweetest sound in the world—laughter." He spoke of Keaton's love for his modest plot of land in Woodland Hills, his garden and dogs and the chickens he kept. "Buster Keaton was possessed with the comic spirit. Comedy was not his profession. It was his point of view. . . . Who else is there now? What other face can have the look of Buster Keaton?"

Interment followed in the cemetery's Court of Valor. The will, which left everything to Eleanor, was entered into probate on June 24, 1966. Apart from the property in Woodland Hills and a collection of rentals, all of which they owned jointly, the estate, including a 1966 Cadillac sedan, anticipated royalties on *My Wonderful World of Slapstick* and the Rudi Blesh book, resid-

Eleanor Keaton is escorted from Forest Lawn's Church of the Hills by funeral director Gene Westlund on February 4, 1966. Robert Talmadge walks behind them.

uals on reruns of *Route 66, Donna Reed, Twilight Zone,* and *Greatest Show on Earth,* and all cash on hand, was valued at $18,590.

"You know, Buster was amazing," Richard Lester said in an interview with *Film Quarterly.* "He was dying in Spain and he knew it. I guess we all knew it. His part in *Forum* is mostly running. We had to shoot in short takes. He'd finish a sequence racking and coughing, looking a hundred years old. But his legs were magnificent. Once we had the stunt man do a scene where a chariot just misses Erronius. Something went wrong and the stunt man was knocked down. That blow would have killed Buster. After the stunt man was taken away to the infirmary, Buster said he wanted to do the scene. I held my breath, but Buster went through the maneuver in one take and did it perfectly. That was a loss. A very big loss."

Following its first public showing at Venice, where it received the Film Critics Prize, *Film* was given its American premiere at the New York Film Festival, wedged in between *The Railrodder* and *Seven Chances.* From his balcony seat at Philharmonic Hall, Alan Schneider dreaded the experience. "The professional film festival audience of critics and students of film technique started laughing the moment the credits came on, roaring at that lovely grotesque close-up of Buster's eyelid. I could hardly stand it. A moment later they stopped laughing. For good. All through the next twenty-two minutes they sat there, bored, annoyed, baffled, and cheated of the Keaton they had come to see. What the hell was Beckett? At the end they got up on their hind legs and booed. Lustily. I thought of Godard and Antonioni and a few others at Cannes; wept, and ran."

Its best audiences came with European festivals, and it did receive a measure of respect in France and Germany, where it was awarded special prizes just for being the strange and awkward thing that it was. In comparison, *The Railrodder* and its companion piece, *Buster Keaton Rides Again,* fared much better. Keaton saw *The Railrodder* when Gerry Potterton brought a print to Toronto while he was shooting with John Sebert. "We showed it at a private screening for him," he said, "and at the end of it he said, in that gruff voice of his, 'Beautiful scenery.' That's all he said."

Buster, Potterton could tell, liked it a lot, but, according to Eleanor, he didn't like *Keaton Rides Again.* "It caught him laughing and kicking up a storm, and he didn't think that kind of thing should be in the film. They caught him being *him* instead of the character, and he didn't think the world should see him like that. . . . He didn't squawk about it to anybody but me. I thought it was great; I loved it."

The Railrodder was shown theatrically in Montreal in December 1965, and more widely beginning September 1966 when it was paired with such varied fare as *Goldfinger* and *Born Free.* On the festival circuit, it won awards in Montreal, Brussels, Berlin, Locarno, and Philadelphia, and was warmly received in Moscow, New York, and San Francisco. *Buster Keaton Rides Again* made its Canadian television debut on October 16, 1965. While intended primarily for TV, the NFB's Grant McLean was so pleased with it he ordered 35mm blowups for possible art house bookings in the United States and Europe. At the San Francisco International Film Festival, it picked up a silver trophy in the Factual category, and gathered similar awards in Milan, Melbourne, Venice, New York, and Montreal, where it collected both a Genie and, later, a First Prize at the Montreal International Film Festival.

Keaton didn't live to see his final performance in the picture that became known as *The Scribe,* but in a tribute to him, a clip from the film was shown publicly for the first time on the CBC public affairs series *This Hour Has Seven Days.* Aired on February 20, 1966, this glimpse constituted the most exposure it would receive in any form for decades. In March, it was one of twenty-three films accepted for the Directors Guild of Canada's annual festival, and by September it was available for rental from Association Films, but few prints managed to circulate or, for that matter, survive. Even the Construction Safety Associations of Ontario disposed of its single print once a mediocre video transfer had been made. Occasionally someone would ask John Sebert if they could watch his copy, but it was in such poor condition he denied even having one. It wouldn't be until the film's video release as an extra on Kino's 2013 edition of *College* that it would finally gain a substantial—and appreciative—audience.

Keaton's final suite of commercials, which he found time to make while in Spain, were for a lemon-lime soft drink called Teem, Pepsi-Cola's answer to 7-Up in the sixties and seventies. Assembled into sixty, twenty, and ten-second spots, they were part of a campaign to position Teem as a cocktail mixer, but were only seen in scattered markets in the Midwest. By then, Keaton had appeared in so many TV commercials that the ad industry's Clio Award for Best Spokesman was renamed in his honor. The winner of the first "Buster" that year was Keaton's old friend Bert Lahr.

As Buster Keaton's life wound down, Rudi Blesh finally got serious about finishing his book. "You know those boxes of typewriter paper that are this deep?" asked Eleanor, holding her hands apart. "He brought it to the St. Moritz in New York—single spaced! The box was so full he couldn't hardly get the lid on. And every word's a gem. He would not allow an editor to cut one word. And they said, 'Okay . . .' So he took it home and sat on it for ten years until he got really hungry, and then he allowed an editor to cut it down to size. Because God knows it probably would have been a book that thick."

Blesh found a willing publisher in Macmillan and did a long-distance phone interview with Eleanor to sketch in the final years. ("He wasn't interested in sound pictures," she said, "he was only interested in silent pictures.") In a miracle of timing, the New York–based publisher announced the book, titled simply *Keaton,* on January 31, the day before its subject died on the opposite coast.

"He made me read the galleys," said Eleanor. "I read 'em, I made what corrections I could find, like correcting dates and wrong spellings. And there was so much trash in it. He took liberties. Buster would sit and tell him a story, with a smile, and by the time he got through putting it on paper it wasn't funny anymore. That kind of thing. Well, there's no use starting to argue when it's in galleys. So all you do is the best you can with the corrections."

Keaton was published in May 1966 and sold out an initial printing of twenty-five hundred copies. The reviews were solid, and the publisher got behind it with display advertising when it was sent back to press for a second time and then a third. At about the same moment the Blesh book was making its appearance, a last interview with Keaton, done at Venice with John Gillett and James Blue, surfaced in the winter issue of *Sight & Sound*, an event celebrated by David Robinson in the *Financial Times*.

"A few weeks ago at seventy he cheerfully crashed headfirst into a tree and did a beautiful backward fall to create a gag for Dick Lester. Through this sort of single-mindedness he made gags and films and his own sort of poetry. He was something like a genius. But he was a sweet clown as well. Buster was one of the great filmmakers; but he was also that short, slight figure, stumping around with the funny walk in which his feet seemed to strike the ground with the dubious challenge of a blind man's stick; or breaking into a run that turned him into a complex of little piston rods. His face was formal and beautiful, but not quite inscrutable, for there was not a thought went through his ingenious head that did not flicker there for a fraction of a second. He had grown older, of course, and stouter, and his smooth face had turned to crumpled leather; but at seventy not much else had changed. . . . At the end of his life he was once again appreciated at his rare worth."

With Buster Keaton's passing, another Buster Keaton replaced him—the immortal one captured so perfectly on film in the dizzying years of his youth when the movies were new and the horizons infinite. If the middle years represented times of struggle, there was a sense of contentment to the third act of Keaton's life, the awards and festivals and the gradual rediscovery of the Keaton canon as prints surfaced and audiences celebrated. Wherever he went in the last decade of his life, he was respected, honored, and acclaimed. All that needed to happen now was to put the films back before the public, a body of work virtually unique in the annals of film, and let them make their own eloquent case for the man who made them.

Keaton's death also changed the dynamic between his widow and Raymond Rohauer. Formerly in the background, Eleanor Keaton now assumed her husband's role in the functioning of Buster Keaton Productions and whatever moral authority that passed to her as the next in line of succession. She had the Keaton name, but she was not Buster Keaton, nor had she been present at the creation of the films Rohauer sought to control. As far as business was concerned, she and Rohauer found themselves joined at the hip, both wishing to be free of the other but bound by a series of decisions made back when the path to preserving Keaton's legacy was first set. They were, in other words, stuck with each other and would make the best of it, Eleanor for Buster's sake, Rohauer for his own.

Rohauer had long since established a reputation for being a slippery character, someone who always saw to his own interests above all else. And it helped that he looked the part of a doughy, second-rate accountant who inspired a level of distrust from the very first handshake.

"He was a slithery person," said James Karen. "He had the wettest handshake I've ever had in my life. I shook his hand one time—the only time I ever shook his hand—and I actually took rubbing alcohol after and washed my hands. There was something dreadful about the touch of his skin. But look what he did. He was mad as a hatter about film, he was over the edge. He would show up in a snowstorm to a house where he thought they were showing a picture, dressed all in his long, black coats and stuff, but the Keaton pictures would not exist today were it not for him."

Had Rohauer and Keaton never met, it would have been up to Leopold Friedman and Robert Youngson to gather and curate Keaton's silent comedies and put them out before the public—not a promising prospect. Even Keaton himself, at least initially, couldn't see the value of thirty-year-old movies. That it took a degree of chicanery on Rohauer's part to make that happen doesn't diminish the importance of what he accomplished. Was he using Keaton to legitimize his own ambitions toward power and ownership? Undoubtedly. Was Keaton nonetheless an unwitting beneficiary? Considering the scope and permanency of his reputation more than half a century after his death, the answer would have to be yes.

Rohauer's struggle with Leopold Friedman and the heirs to the various stockholders of the original Keaton organization continued during Keaton's final illness and long past his death. In October 1965, while Keaton was completing work on *The Scribe,* Herbert Schwab of Bautzer, Irwin & Schwab presented Friedman with a proposed agreement that specified the transfer of all rights to Rohauer for the sum, to be paid within one year, of $250,000. Complications arose and the one year stretched to several, forcing Friedman and Rohauer into an uneasy alliance in which Friedman and his associates would share in revenues derived from the promotions Rohauer engineered, an arrangement that would bring them $100,000 as their share of a deal with Specta Films, which had also agreed to pay $75,000 for the rights to *The Navigator* and *Seven Chances* in Germany, Austria, and Switzerland.

This didn't mean that Friedman stopped asserting his rights over the films that were still under his control until Rohauer was paid in full. In 1963, he had written to the Motion Picture Academy and demanded the return of the prints acquired in the James Mason donation, the resulting back-and-forth continuing until after Keaton's death. In November 1966, Margaret Herrick finally decided to turn everything that remained over to Friedman's attorneys since the films were in such generally poor condition. The transfer, effected in March 1967, included complete prints of *The Saphead, The Play House, The Blacksmith, Battling Butler, The General, College,* and *Steamboat Bill, Jr.,* and partial prints of *Sherlock Jr., The Boat, My Wife's Relations,* and *The Paleface.*

Keaton's deal with Rohauer was that the younger man stood all expenses and Keaton took 50 percent of the profits. But in his quest to gain full control of the entire Keaton library, Rohauer reported no profits because he kept plowing revenues back into attorney fees, lab costs, and the purchase of Friedman's interests. And so with no guarantee of income or compensation, Eleanor climbed aboard the bandwagon in her husband's stead, traveling to Philadelphia in October 1966 to make the first of countless personal appearances, this one to bolster attendance for a four-matinee Keaton homage at the city's Museum of Art. That same month, *A Funny Thing Happened on the Way to the Forum* was released, once again putting Keaton in front of first-run audiences, his presence, in the words of *Variety,* summoning "nostalgia for the silent master, already assuring the film a slot in the archives."

Originally set to go out to theaters on August 10, 1966, *War Italian Style* was instead paired with another weak American International release, *Trunk to Cairo,* and the dual bill was held until January 1967, giving *War* the unintended distinction of being Buster Keaton's last feature-length motion picture. In playing his Rommel-like role in silence, with the exception of a single "Thank you" at the end, Keaton came off as disengaged and unnatural, the poorly dubbed soundtrack keeping the audience at arm's length throughout. The one advantage to the five-month delay for *War Italian Style* was that virtually no one saw it, not even Eleanor, who was unaware of the two lonely Southern California drive-ins that gave it a week's booking apiece in the dead of winter.

The year 1967 also marked the release of Charles Chaplin's final film, the misbegotten *A Countess from Hong Kong,* which he wrote and directed, and in which he played a memorable cameo. Chaplin was severely wounded by the critical and commercial failure of the film, which starred Marlon Brando and Sophia Loren, and withdrew to his home in Switzerland. "The reaction to *A Countess from Hong Kong* was very, very bad," said his daughter Geraldine. "At that age [seventy-eight] he just didn't have the energy to bounce back. I know from my mother's diaries that he was completely devastated, and so was she.

"I came to the house once with [the Spanish writer and director] Carlos Saura, who was very taken with Buster Keaton. So at dinner he started to go on and on about Keaton, how wonderful he thought he was, what a great filmmaker. My father got smaller and smaller in his chair. He was so hurt, it looked as if someone had stabbed him. He became very quiet, didn't say a word through the rest of dinner. Afterwards, we're sitting by the fire and talking about other things now. My father was looking at the fire, still not talking. Then he looked Carlos in the eyes and said, 'But I was an artist. . . . And I gave him work.' He'd been thinking about it all during dinner."

In January 1968, a retrospective season of Keaton's films opened at the National Film Theatre in London, where it continued for nearly a month. The organizers, who boasted it was the first comprehensive showing of his silent works, were reportedly presenting it in an anti-Chaplin spirit, which the *Morning Star*'s Nina Hibbin considered a pity: "Their campaign to prove Keaton 'greater than Chaplin' strikes me as decidedly quaint."

The New York Times reported audiences that were large and enthusiastic. "Crowds are pouring to the National Film Theatre," Eric Rhode reported in the BBC's *Listener*, "making every performance of the Buster Keaton season look like a gala; predictably, it's turned out to be one of the great film events of the decade."

The NFT's season was sanctioned by Raymond Rohauer, who had developed a knack for attention-grabbing promotions, abetted by a growing demand for Keaton's pictures as the stark reality of his death settled in. It was a demand fed equally by discovery and regret, and the reappraisals came from all directions. Rhode wrote about him repeatedly, as did Andrew Sarris, Dilys Powell, and Penelope Gilliatt. Briefly, Robert Youngson contemplated a film on the order of his Laurel and Hardy compilations called *The World of Buster Keaton,* and David Robinson wrote an entire book on Keaton's films, the first of its kind, for the influential Cinema One series.

Meanwhile, Rohauer's forced alliance with Leopold Friedman resulted in Friedman growing more aggressive, the two men pursuing a scorched-

Raymond Rohauer and Leopold Friedman in a rare moment of comity.

earth policy against perceived infringers. In April 1967, Friedman filed suit against the Museum of Modern Art and its film library, seeking "estimated" damages of $2,900,000 and the return of prints the collection had held for decades. A few months later, Rohauer warned the newly constituted American Film Institute that if it didn't take steps to protect the rights of the owners of copyrights, literary rights, negatives, and prints in assembling its collection, its archives program "may fall on its face." By then, Friedman was threatening the National Film Board for using an unauthorized clip from *The General* in *Buster Keaton Rides Again,* a legally unenforceable matter given the film's copyright history that nonetheless caused Rohauer to fly to Ottawa in October 1968 to meet with the Film Board and the Canadian Department of Justice. Rohauer was also threatening to sue the British Film Institute based on the prints they held, and was anticipating yet another suit against New York's Channel 13, which had televised *The General* in 1965 using MoMA's print.

Rohauer was, by this time, film curator and program director for Huntington Hartford's Gallery of Modern Art in New York. Still, he doggedly worked toward his goal of owning the complete catalog of the Keaton pictures Joe Schenck produced, and in 1970 he finished paying the sum of $250,000 plus interest and got the assignment of rights he had long coveted. In celebration, he mounted a comprehensive five-week festival at New York's Elgin Cinema, lacking only the two shorts that had escaped his grasp, *Hard Luck* and *The Love Nest*. Announcing his intention of touring the festival nationwide, Rohauer scored prime coverage in both *Time* and *Newsweek*.

Friedman turned his attention to disposing of the only remaining asset of the dissolved corporation, the 25 percent share of the profits due him and the other stockholders on *The Cameraman, Spite Marriage,* and the seven talking features Keaton made for Metro-Goldwyn-Mayer between 1930 and 1933. Friedman went to M-G-M and offered to buy the films, two of which were in the public domain, for $300,000 or, if preferred, Metro could buy him out for $100,000. This went nowhere until Rohauer offered Friedman $50,000 for all his rights as "trustee in liquidation," meaning for the 25 percent owed annually by M-G-M and, after conferring with the former stockholders, Friedman agreed. So in April 1971, thirteen years after he first met Buster Keaton, and five years after Keaton's death, Raymond Rohauer owned the works.

More books and retrospectives followed. With full ownership now his, Rohauer proceeded to cement his grip on the Keaton materials, deliberately circulating poor prints of the ones in copyright so that they would yield bad copies if surreptitiously duplicated, and altering those in the public domain so that he could claim protection for his "revisions." In fact, trims and alterations became so habitual to him that, over time, they afflicted every Keaton two-reeler he owned. Whole scenes were removed, intertitles rewritten, gags eliminated or rendered ineffective, all toward the goal of being able to identify the source of an unauthorized copy. "Rohauer used to tell me that he appreciated having 'some decomposition' in films," said Edward Watz, "since this was like fingerprints that identified the 'Rohauer version' in the event someone duped his print."

Rohauer was also derided for the cheap soundtracks he imposed on the Keaton films, new elements he could copyright that also made them more viable in commercial settings. During a festival that took place in New York in 1981, philosopher and author Douglas P. Lackey wrote to the *Village Voice* in exasperation. "What was perhaps most impressive about the new soundtracks was the incredible variety of devices called forth to sabotage Keaton's work," he complained. "Some of the prints (*High Sign, One Week,* and—so help me—*The General*) were accompanied by a mad assortment of pops, crashes, squeaks, and toots which perpetually interrupted the flow of images and shattered the dreamlike universe created and the world lost with his move to M-G-M and the onset of sound. Others (*Sherlock Jr.,* etc.) blared forth a succession of old jazz 78s, one after the other with no reference to the action. Still others (*Steamboat Bill, Jr.*) sported newly commissioned pseudo-Dixieland scores which produced, after half an hour, that peculiar vibrating nausea which I have previously experienced only when riding the Seventh Avenue IRT."

As if the desecration of Keaton's art weren't enough, Rohauer also developed a way of portraying himself as the white knight in the sad story of Keaton's final years. "Rohauer wanted to be known as the man who made Buster Keaton a star again; he told me as much," said Watz, who was in his employ from 1977 to 1981. "Rohauer often told people that Keaton was illiterate, didn't communicate well, was glum, had little self-worth, and lost his creative ability due to an alcohol-soused brain. I heard him say this many times whenever we'd meet someone who asked him what Buster was like. The effect on listeners was supposed to be a 'Thank God you came along!' response."

Rohauer's assertions were frequently met with pushback, privately if not publicly, intimidation being his primary weapon of choice. Eleanor Keaton disliked and feared him, but never said anything against him on the record. After a typically self-aggrandizing interview published in 1970 in *Variety*, Rohauer's nemesis, Paul Killiam, requested equal space for a response: "Rohauer actually owns only the merest handful, at best, of clean-cut original silent film 'copyrights' (no Fairbanks, no Griffith, few Keatons, and maybe one Sennett, for example), but simply keeps making these claims and having lawyers write threatening letters. We thought the industry was beginning to catch on. . . . Despite the skills of the long and constantly changing list of lawyers he has retained, Rohauer has never, to the best of our knowledge (and we know the field well), actually gone to court, as he again pledges to do in the *Variety* interview, against such alleged 'violators' of films to which he holds 'copyrights.'"

Over the years, other takedowns appeared. In 1975, critic and historian John Baxter published "The Silent Empire of Raymond Rohauer" in the *Sunday Times Magazine*. "If an Oscar is ever given for the greatest achievement in infuriating the motion picture community," it began, "its first recipient will almost certainly be a pudgy fifty-year-old New Yorker named Raymond Rohauer. In the eyes of most fans of the cinema, Rohauer is to the movies what Dr. Jekyll is to medicine." Somewhat more kindly, William K. Everson titled his own essay for *Grand Street* "Raymond Rohauer: King of the Film Freebooters," crediting his subject with a "certain cavalier charm" that others might dispute. "Basically," Everson explained, "Rohauer operated under the principle of the Big Lie. He bent and used every loophole of the law to his own advantage—and when business opponents used the same loopholes, he descended on them with wrathful press releases and a battery of lawyers."

By the time of his death from AIDS in 1987, Rohauer had gained control of not only the Keaton library but those of Harry Langdon and Douglas Fairbanks, as well as nearly two hundred musical and comedy shorts distributed by Paramount Pictures, the Pendennis library that covered such British titles as *Forever and a Day, Storm in a Teacup,* and *St. Martin's Lane,* and the Tele-Pac library that boasted independent productions like *Hangmen Also Die!, It Happened Tomorrow,* and *Lured.* At the peak of his business activities, Rohauer claimed to own as many as twelve hundred movies, although his legitimate holdings were doubtless much fewer.

Eleanor Keaton moved on after the death of her husband, but he was never far from her thoughts. She leased out the place in Woodland Hills, not wanting to bother with gardeners and pool people, and moved into one of their rental properties, which suited her better in terms of space. Within a year she sold all her properties with the help of Harold Goodwin and moved to Costa Mesa, where, at the age of forty-nine, she opened a kennel and began raising Saint Bernards. At various other points she co-owned a pet shop in the San Fernando Valley, managed a bail bonds office with her sister, Jane, and volunteered as a docent a few days a week at the Los Angeles Zoo. In 1992, she became an honorary member of the Damfinos (later the International Buster Keaton Society), founded on Buster's ninety-seventh birthday by two sisters, writer-editor Patricia Eliot Tobias and actress Wendy Jolicoeur, and artists' representative Melody Bunting. In 1995 Eleanor presided over the Buster Keaton centenary and attended celebrations in Berlin, Rio de Janeiro, New York, and Los Angeles, and conferences in Iola, Kansas, near Buster's birthplace of Piqua, and in Muskegon, an annual event that continues to this day.

"As soon as I feel like it," Buster Keaton mused in 1963, "I'll turn the movies over to television. I don't know when this will happen, but one of these days I will. And let them stay on TV forever. I can think of no better way of letting the world know how much I loved it when I was around."

In 1995, it became possible to walk into a Barnes & Noble or a Tower Records and purchase a set of all of Buster Keaton's silent classics on home video, a remarkable development considering how difficult many of these films were to see during Keaton's lifetime. Collected as box sets under the title *The Art of Buster Keaton,* the nineteen shorts and ten features Keaton made for Joseph Schenck (plus *The Saphead*) were issued on VHS by Kino and on laser disc by Image Entertainment. (*The Cameraman* and *Spite Marriage* had already been released in the same formats by MGM/UA Home Video in 1991 and 1992, respectively.) The Schenck films made the transition to DVD in 2005, and to Blu-ray in 2011. Fulfilling Keaton's vow, all are also viewable, in differing versions and shades of quality, to audiences worldwide at no cost whatsoever, on YouTube.

Natalie Talmadge died in 1969 at the age of seventy-three. She had grown reclusive in her later years, lost in a haze of cigarette smoke and alcoholism. She suffered a stroke, and her son Bob moved her to a convalescent hospital in Santa Monica, near where he and his family were living at the time.

"I remember that when she was real ill she was in a rest home," said Melissa Talmadge, "and she did call me up and ask me if I would bring some Four Roses over to her. Nobody would let her have any, but I wasn't even old enough to buy liquor! We'd just go visit her when she was ill. I think my dad was very sad when she passed away; she was his mother. He was probably sadder than the kids, because we liked going to her house, but I don't think she was a real dynamic presence in our childhoods."

Natalie's remains were entombed in the Talmadge room at Hollywood Memorial Park, leaving the ebullient Constance as the only surviving sister.

After her last brief burst of notoriety in the late fifties, Mae Scriven disappeared from the scene, never to be heard from again. She still had plenty of time left, but exactly how she spent it is unknown. Did she keep her room at the Stratford Arms while working as a beautician? Or was she institutionalized as she once had been, lost to the scourge of dementia? Or did she settle down on a pittance of Social Security, talking occasionally of her past to whomever might listen and dropping the names of two of her erstwhile husbands, the other being Sam Fuller, who went on to a notable career as a director? Apparently she wasn't in touch with her family in California, and would not have known of the death of her twin brother in 1987. Still living under the name Jewel Steven, she died in Jamaica, Queens, in 1990 at the age of eighty-four.

Louise Keaton died of cancer in 1981. When she fell ill, Eleanor moved her out of her tiny Berendo Street apartment and into a board-and-care facility in the Valley, where she could visit two or three times a week.

"When Louise died," said Barbara Talmadge, "Eleanor phoned the mortuary to finalize plans for Louise's burial. The mortuary said, 'She's not here.' 'So what do you mean, she's not there? She was sent there.' 'We didn't receive her.' Now the search is on for Louise. . . . Louise is somewhere down near Redondo, somewhere over near the coast. They finally found her in a mortuary over there. Sent her back. Louise was cremated. Louise always wanted to be buried with her mother, so they bore a hole in the coffin, put a funnel there, and they poured Louise in with her mother. I remember Jim laughing his head off when Eleanor finally told him."

After the house on Victoria was sold in 1956, Harry Keaton transitioned to living on the streets of Los Angeles. "He had a lady friend [who] used to give him like one meal a day, or at least a couple of times a week she would give him a big meal," said Eleanor. "And he literally almost starved for a year or more."

Harry eventually relocated to San Diego, where, in 1959, he began tending bar at the El Toreador Motel in San Ysidro, three blocks from the Mexican border. When he turned sixty-five, Harry moved to the other side of the bar and, for tips, would sip a beer and regale tourists with stories of his famous brother and their times in vaudeville. In May 1983, he tripped while exiting a restaurant across the street from the motel, cracked his skull, and died at the age of seventy-eight. When his son, Harry Jr., arrived to clear out his father's room at the El Toreador, he found the old man had thirty-six hundred dollars in cash squirreled away in a Crown Royal pouch, more than enough to cover his cremation and burial in the plot to the left of his mother.

Eleanor Keaton was diagnosed with lung cancer in 1998, and the cancer spread to her back. James Karen and his second wife, actress-producer Alba Francesca, got her into the Motion Picture Country House and Hospital, and it was there that she died on October 19 at the age of eighty. "Eleanor was not a lady ever to go slowly," said the Earl twins at her memorial service. "She dashed every place she went. Every time we'd go to the hospital with her, the doctors and the nurses would say, 'Would you slow down?!' We'd practically have to sit on her and say, 'Eleanor, now cut it out!'"

In 1993, Eleanor took a visitor from New Zealand to Forest Lawn to see the grave of Buster Keaton. "I never come up here," she commented, "because he is not there." And she faced death with equanimity because she had the unshakable belief that she would be with him again. "Wherever he is, I'm going to join him," she said. "I'll join him wherever he went."

Did she see herself as a part of Buster? she was asked. "Yes," she answered. "He was the greater part of my life. So why not rejoin him?"

With her healthy contempt for the funeral industry, she specified that she wanted her remains to be cremated and her ashes scattered. She saw no point in slipping into the same grave as her husband—maybe funneled into the box as his sister Louise had been.

"Eleanor," wrote Kevin Brownlow, "was the least self-centered person I have met. And certainly the bravest. When cancer hit her, she behaved just like that heroic character from the Old West. I dropped in at her home in North Hollywood last October [1998] to say a quick goodbye on my way to the airport; she did a soft-shoe shuffle and whipped off her wig. It turned out to be a permanent goodbye—but it left a fond memory of a magnificent woman."

On a whim one day in 1986, Eleanor Keaton and Raymond Rohauer took a drive around the Seneca Heights section of Los Angeles where the Buster Keaton Studio once stood. Eleanor thought back to that day almost thirty years earlier when Ralph Edwards surprised her husband at the NBC studios in Burbank and ran through the story of his life on national television for the collective benefit of Comet Cleanser, Ivory Soap, and Crest Toothpaste. As he always did, Edwards brought the pageant to a close by enumerating all the loot they were giving the honoree for being a good sport. In Buster's case it started with a 16mm kinescope of the night's broadcast and a Bell & Howell projector on which to run it. Also thrown in was the 16mm movie camera Eleanor would use to photograph Buster's film within a play for *Merton of the Movies*. Then for her, a gold charm bracelet custom designed by Marshall Jewelers of New York "with each charm holding a memory you both share," as well as custom cuff links and a money clip for Buster. A Magnavox color television set would go to the Elks Lodge in Muskegon, and a small Wheel Horse tractor would be delivered to the Keaton farm in Woodland Hills. And then: "The Buster Keaton comedies made valuable contributions to the forward march of the motion picture industry. So, on Lillian Way in Hollywood, at the exact site of the old Buster Keaton Studio, Crest will have installed a bronze medallion to mark that spot for all time to come in your honor."

Edwards had come through with everything else on that list, but Eleanor had never personally gone to see the medallion Buster was promised. And after having combed the area, both she and Rohauer came to the conclusion that it had never been placed. True to form, Rohauer wrote a letter to Edwards, who was still in business and whose company, Ralph Edwards

Productions, was the producer of the current syndicated hit *The People's Court*. But, after thirty years, nobody in the office had any recollection of it.

"Now!" Edwards wrote in a memo to associate producer Dresser Dahlstead. "We *must* get a medallion on that property. Let's find out (1) who owns the property, (2) and then let's discuss the approach. I would think that any owner would allow us to insert a medallion somewhere, then get Eleanor and have some press on it. There has got to be a proper reason why the medallion was not placed, but it may not be too late yet."

The drive to have the medallion placed was long and frustrating. A marker was designed, various fees paid to the Board of Public Works, and insurance coverage was arranged. Then the city council failed to approve the project because the report was sent to the wrong district office. The whole thing was still in progress when Rohauer died in New York on November 10, 1987. Dahlstead kept at it, gaining written consent from Pacific Title and Art to install it on what was then a grassy plot between the sidewalk and the curb near the entrance to their parking lot. The approved wording went as follows:

BUSTER KEATON STUDIO
1920–1928
SITE OF THE ORIGINAL BUSTER KEATON
STUDIO THE BIRTHPLACE OF A UNIQUE
TYPE OF MOTION PICTURE COMEDY. HERE
THE GENIUS OF BUSTER KEATON MADE
HISTORY WITH PICTURES WHICH BROUGHT
LAUGHTER TO THE WORLD.

The placement ceremony took place at 12:30 p.m. on June 29, 1988. The city was represented by Rodri Rodriguez, vice president of the Los Angeles Cultural Affairs Commission, and a representative from Councilman Michael Woo's office. Eleanor was there in a dramatic royal-blue dress and sunglasses, posing for pictures with the new monument in the foreground. So were Bill Welsh, president of the Hollywood Chamber of Commerce; Johnny Grant, honorary mayor of Hollywood; Edwards, of course; Donald O'Connor; James Karen; Alba Francesca; Jane Dulo; and Leonard Maltin. The event went according to plan, although there was a quiet discomfort among some of the local historians and silent-film aficionados who were present.

It was only later that Eleanor learned what all the whispering was about, and she shook her head in dismay and laughed. It was the kind of well-meaning fiasco at the basis of many of the great Keaton comedies produced at the studio. It may even have been that Buster himself, from his perch in another dimension, engineered on a grand and lasting scale one final gag to leave the world with a laugh, a wink of the eye to anyone knowledgeable enough to know what they were seeing. For the new Keaton studio marker, three feet by four feet, with its two hundred bronze letters and numbers, installed in terrazzo and cement at a cost of more than $7,000, had been permanently and inalterably sunk . . . into the wrong corner.

God bless all clowns.

Acknowledgments

The first time I saw Buster Keaton was as a child watching Saturday-morning television. The show was called *Life with Buster Keaton,* and it was a strangely unfunny affair, an episode of a thirteen-week series originally filmed in 1951. Keaton was a private eye grimly roaming the waterfront, encountering an odd array of suspicious characters, including a bartender whose head wound up on a serving platter and a bizarre trio of puppets. Over a period of a few months, I'm sure I saw them all, which made me think I knew who Keaton was when he popped up briefly in *It's a Mad, Mad, Mad, Mad World.* Then came the *Beach Party* pictures, where he was more a presence than an active participant, and finally a documentary, *Buster Keaton Rides Again,* which opened my eyes to Keaton's rich history as a moviemaker. By then he was dead, but over the ensuing decades I was able to see a good sampling of his silent shorts and features.

There were also books, principally a biography by Rudi Blesh titled *Keaton,* published soon after his death, as well as a heavily ghosted autobiography called *My Wonderful World of Slapstick.* Others followed, so many, in fact, that I wondered if there was room for yet another when my editor suggested Keaton as a subject. I made inquiries, spoke with his family, and was universally encouraged to proceed. The result, after nine years, was accomplished only with the generous help of a number of individuals.

Chief among these was Patricia Eliot Tobias, one of the founders of the International Buster Keaton Society, more commonly known as the Damfinos, who urged me to write this book, and who pointed the way to a number of invaluable documents and primary source materials. Since Patty has consumed practically everything ever published about Keaton, I asked her to read the draft manuscript with the goal of poking as many holes in it as possible. This she did with exquisite attention to detail, and all of her comments and questions, including notes informed by her years as a New York–based copy editor, were wonderfully on point and gratefully received.

Melissa Talmadge Cox, Buster Keaton's granddaughter, has been of immense help as well, providing personal memories as well as photos and artifacts. Melissa fielded countless questions, always with grace and good humor, and arranged for multiple visits with her delightful mother, Barbara Talmadge, who married into the Keaton family in 1943 and whose memory is as razor sharp as her opinions. Getting to meet and spend time with them was one of the great pleasures of researching this book.

Kevin Brownlow has been a source of inspiration and encouragement for several generations of those who aspire to write about cinema. He generously allowed me access to his personal files on Keaton and, with the intrepid help of his wife, Caroline, made unedited transcripts of his interviews for his three-part documentary *Buster Keaton: A Hard Act to Follow* available for my use. Kevin also read this book in manuscript form and provided pages of helpful notes.

Bob Borgen, erstwhile president of the International Buster Keaton Society, kindly arranged for me to meet and interview Buster Keaton's brother-in-law, Walt Kelly, and Walt's son (and Eleanor Keaton's nephew) Rick Kelly. Bob also made me aware of Alan Hoffman, who once contemplated writing a book on Keaton himself and recorded a series of interviews in the mid-seventies. Alan not only gave permission for me to reference and quote from partial audio recordings in Bob's possession, but sent me the complete original tapes as well.

In tackling this project, I was fortunate that Buster Keaton had been readily accessible to interviewers throughout his life (as was his widow, Eleanor, who survived him by thirty-three years). Many of these encounters have been collected into the essential book *Buster Keaton: Interviews,* edited by Kevin W. Sweeney (Jackson: University Press of Mississippi, 2007), although I have gone back to the original sources wherever possible. In addition, I'd like to thank Bob Borgen for Irwin Allen's 1945 radio interview with Keaton; Ned Comstock for Keaton's 1962 summary of his career for the Hollywood Museum; John Slotkin for the 1961 radio interview recorded by his mother, Shirley Eder; the late Robert S. Birchard for his interview with actor Harold Goodwin; and Alan Hoffman for the interviews he recorded with Harold Goodwin, director Charles Lamont, and Eleanor Keaton. I'd also like to thank Lindsay Moen, Public Services Librarian, Special Collections and University Archives, University of Iowa, for having dozens of interviews recorded in the 1990s by Keaton biographer Marion Meade digitized for my use.

Randy Haberkamp, the senior vice president of preservation and foundation programs at the Pickford Center for Motion Picture Study, arranged for me to examine the Academy Film Archive's file on James Mason and his 1956 transfer of the contents of Buster Keaton's personal vault to the Academy of Motion Picture Arts and Sciences. This file was especially illuminating in documenting Raymond Rohauer's early efforts to copy and exploit the films, and I'm grateful to Randy for helping shed light on a famous but somewhat mysterious chapter in silent film preservation.

Karl Thiede, proprietor of the most impressive private library I've ever seen, has studied the financial aspects of the film industry for much of his life. His figures are not only authoritative but also revealing, and I'm always fortunate to have his insights in understanding the business side of a subject's story.

Ned Comstock, who retired from USC's Cinematic Arts Library about the same time I finished this book, has always been a great librarian as well as a great advocate for work of this nature. He was his usual essential self, and I am far from the only author who will miss him in the future.

The brilliant location detective John Bengtson has been a terrific help in identifying the locations used in the making of Keaton's silent shorts and features, many of which are explained and illustrated in his astonishing book *Silent Echoes* (Santa Monica, CA: Santa Monica Press, 2000). If a street or a landmark or a studio lot is mentioned in this book, chances are the information originated with John.

I especially want to thank historian and restoration archivist Paul Gierucki for the many courtesies and favors he did for me over the course of this book. Paul was always ready with an answer when I had a question concerning Roscoe Arbuckle, but he was also unfailingly helpful when I needed to see some Keaton rarity for which he was the only known source. He also gave priority to the scanning and preservation of the Damfinos' Rudi Blesh collection of manuscript materials and photographs for my benefit. I hope he'll consider this book adequate compensation for all the trouble I caused him.

David Weddle alerted me to his fascinating 2002 interview with Geraldine Chaplin, which originally appeared in *Variety*. He also referred me to the late Sam Dodge, whose collection and knowledge of silent film cameras helped me understand how Keaton obtained some of his amazing on-screen effects. And Sam's great friend and fellow collector Carroll Gray continued to answer questions after Sam's passing.

As she had for my previous biography of Mort Sahl, Leslie Lowe created expert transcriptions of the interviews I conducted for this book, as well as interviews done by others that came my way. Marc Wanamaker shared his memories (and some snapshots) of the original 1988 marker ceremony at the site of the Buster Keaton Studio on Lillian Way in Hollywood, Dr. Tracey Goessel contributed her analysis of the events leading to the 1921 death of Virginia Rappe, and author and historian Joe Adamson offered helpful comments and suggestions based on his own encyclopedic knowledge of film comedy.

From Europe, Edward Watz was gracious and forthcoming in his memories of Raymond Rohauer, for whom he worked for four years. Ed was also in possession of notes and photocopies made by the late Keaton biographer Tom Dardis, who was permitted access to the Metro-Goldwyn-Mayer studio archive in the 1970s. Ed's help enabled me to check and, in some cases, correct the error-prone Dardis' assertions in his 1979 book, *Keaton: The Man Who Wouldn't Lie Down.* Ed's a class act and a valued colleague.

In Muskegon, local historian Ron Pesch gave me a personal tour of the fabled Actors' Colony, where the Keatons had a home between the years 1909 and 1923. Ron patiently answered my many questions and permitted me access to his considerable collection of news clippings that covered not only the Keatons' time at Bluffton but virtually all the notable residents of the period. In Oregon, Lloyd Williams of the Cottage Grove Historical Society similarly provided a fascinating trip around the various sites associated with the filming of Keaton's 1926 masterwork *The General* that included a timely screening of the film itself.

I am particularly indebted to André D'Ulisse, archivist at the National Film Board of Canada, who researched and retrieved all existing paperwork relating to the production of *The Railrodder* and its companion documentary, *Buster Keaton Rides Again,* and provided me with scans. Bruce Goldstein read this book in manuscript form and contributed valuable notes. Cutler family genealogist Linda Neal was generous in sharing her remarkable research into the early years of Myra Cutler; her father, Frank Cutler; and her husband, Joe Keaton. Jack Dragga shared his extraordinary knowledge of *Ten Girls Ago* as well as his memories of Raymond Rohauer. And, from Ontario, Eryn Merwart, the current president of the Damfinos, shared her own research on *The Railrodder,* kindly delivered to me at the 2015 Buster Keaton convention in Muskegon by Binnie Brennan.

I'd also like to thank Michael Blake, John Cannon, Melissa Talmadge Cox, John McElwee, Karl Thiede, Patricia Eliot Tobias, Mark Vieira, and

Jordan Young for dipping into their private collections to offer images for inclusion in this book. Melanie and Andrew Kelly were, as always, gracious and knowledgeable hosts during my visits to England. And for various assists, comments, and courtesies, I am also indebted to Melody Bunting, Tap Duncan's great-granddaughter Michelle Drumheller, Rob Farr, Larry Harnisch, Leonard Maltin, Robert Moulton, Vergil Noble, Victoria Sainte-Claire, and Eileen Whitfield.

The Damfinos kindly granted me full access to photos, notebooks, and manuscript materials acquired from the estate of Rudi Blesh, Keaton's original biographer. Other primary sources essential to understanding Buster Keaton's life and work are held in a number of libraries and institutions, and I am grateful to the librarians and administrators who made this aspect of my work so rewarding.

Margaret Herrick Library, Academy of Motion Picture Arts and Sciences, Beverly Hills: Louise Hilton, Faye Thompson, and the outstanding staff of the Katharine Hepburn Reading Room. Louis B. Mayer Library, American Film Institute, Los Angeles: Mike Pepin. British Film Institute: Jonny Davies.

Cinematic Arts Library, University of Southern California, Los Angeles: Steve Hanson. Archives and Special Collections, Emerson College, Boston: Rosalie Gartner. Mohave Museum of History and Arts, Kingman, Arizona: Cathy Kreis. New York Society for the Prevention of Cruelty to Children: Joseph Gleason.

Paley Center for Media: Martin Gostanian (Beverly Hills) and Mark Ekman (New York).

San Francisco History Center, San Francisco Public Library. Regional History Collection, University of Southern California: Dace Taube. UCLA Film and Television Archive: Mark Quigley. Warner Bros. Archives, University of Southern California: Brett Service. Will Rogers Memorial Museums: Jennifer Holt.

A special note of thanks goes to the team responsible for the Media History Digital Library (mediahistoryproject.org) and that singular search and visualization platform known as Lantern.

There weren't many individuals left who could talk firsthand about Buster Keaton when I began work on this book. Fortunately, there were a few with whom I had talked for previous books who had valuable things to say about Keaton. These were Michael Anderson, who directed him in *Around the World in 80 Days;* Gene Fowler, Jr., who worked with him on *Tales of Man-*

hattan; Marshall Schlom, script supervisor on *It's a Mad, Mad, Mad, Mad World;* and Jules White, who directed Keaton in *Sidewalks of New York* and eight of the ten two-reelers he made for Columbia.

Those who met and in many cases worked with Keaton and were able to speak with me for this specific project include the late Frank Buxton, Dick Cavett, Bobbie Shaw Chance, David de Volpi, Dale Duffy, Jane Earl, Ruth Earl, Marsha Hunt, James Karen, Rick Kelly, Walt Kelly, John Lahr, Norman Lloyd, Harry (Keaton) Moore, Gerald Potterton, Elliott Reid, and John Sebert. Nicola Dantine shared memories of her uncle Joseph M. Schenck, and Bob and Minako Borgen recalled the Eleanor Keaton they knew.

I want to express my deep appreciation to Dr. Timothy Wilson and his colleagues at the St. John's Cancer Institute in Santa Monica for enabling me to finish this book when, at times, it seemed as if I might not. My editor, Victoria Wilson, proposed Keaton as a subject at a time when I had nothing else in mind, and it proved an inspired choice for me. This is the fourth book we have done together over a span of twenty-five years, and we've always seen eye to eye on everything from the first page to the last. I am grateful for her dedication, her support, and her extraordinary taste, and look forward to our collaboration continuing well into the future.

My wife, Kim Geary, has been a full partner in these books, and never more so than with this current one. Fortunately, she never issued one of those Keatonesque ultimatums ("Until you go out and get a real job . . ."), possibly to her own regret but never to mine.

James Curtis
Brea
June 2021

Notes and Sources

Frequently cited archives, collections, and libraries have been identified by the following abbreviations:

AMPAS Margaret Herrick Library, Academy of Motion Picture Arts and Sciences, Beverly Hills

BFI British Film Institute, London

BK Buster Keaton Collection, Margaret Herrick Library

BKS International Buster Keaton Society

EJM Edgar J. "Eddie" Mannix Ledger, Margaret Herrick Library

FOX 20th Century-Fox Script Collection at the Cinematic Arts Library, University of Southern California, Los Angeles

KA Keith/Albee Collection, University of Iowa Special Collections Repository, Iowa City

MM Marion Meade Buster Keaton Research Files, University of Iowa Special Collections Repository, Iowa City

MGM Metro-Goldwyn-Mayer Script Collection at the Cinematic Arts Library, University of Southern California, Los Angeles

NFB National Film Board of Canada Archives

NYPL Billy Rose Theatre Division, New York Public Library for the Performing Arts

PBH Paley Center for Media, Beverly Hills

PNY Paley Center for Media, New York

SPCC New York Society for the Prevention of Cruelty to Children

TMGM Turner/MGM Script Collection, Margaret Herrick Library

WB Warner Bros. Archives, School of Cinematic Arts, University of Southern California, Los Angeles

RIVERS, MANITOBA

7 "I was quite happy": Gerald Potterton to the author, via telephone, 2/2/2014.

7 "His pictures are motion pictures": Walter Kerr, *The Silent Clowns* (New York: Alfred A. Knopf, 1975), p. 212.

1 THE SMALLEST COMEDIAN

11 When Myra Cutler laid eyes: Myra Keaton told how she met Joe Keaton on the *This Is Your Life* radio broadcast of 10/26/1949.

11 The Bryants were drawn: Many details of Joe and Myra Keaton's early days come from

research conducted by Linda Neal, genealogist of the Cutler family, who generously shared them with me.

11 "Having been through the game": Sam M'Kee, *New York Telegraph,* undated clipping in the Keaton scrapbook (BK).

12 Joseph Hallie Keaton: In a 1929 interview, Buster Keaton detailed his parental background: "Father is of Irish and Scotch descent, and spent his boyhood in Indiana." Several generations of Keatons were born and reared in North Carolina, and according to *History of Vigo County, Indiana* (1891), Joe Keaton's great-grandfather Benoni Keaton (1783–1845) was of English descent. The tradition of naming the eldest male child Joseph began with Joseph Keaton (1745–1829), son of Zachariah Keaton of Pasquotank County, North Carolina. Buster said that his mother, Myra, was "of English and German parentage."

12 "well-stocked bar-room": *Terre Haute Weekly Gazette,* 6/28/1883.

12 "I was one of the fortunates": "Stage Career of 'Joe' Keaton," *Terre Haute Morning Star,* 5/30/1904.

13 "Fail and back": Rudi Blesh, "The Two Worlds of Buster Keaton," unpublished manuscript, p. 58 (BKS).

13 "five-cent sack": Blesh, "The Two Worlds of Buster Keaton," p. 59.

13 "in an acceptable manner": *Nebraska State Journal,* 12/17/1893.

13 "One day when I entered the hotel": "Stage Career of 'Joe' Keaton."

14 they were married: Marriage record, Saline County, Nebraska, 5/31/1894 (courtesy of Linda Neal). See also *New York Clipper,* 6/16/1894.

14 "We became regular medicine show actors": "Stage Career of 'Joe' Keaton."

14 "We had to live on the lot": *Los Angeles Times,* 4/27/1924.

14 Aullville, Missouri: The roster of Umatilla Indian Medicine Company No. 90 is from *The New York Clipper,* 7/20/1895.

15 utter fiction: Contrary to legend, Harry Houdini was not present at Buster Keaton's birth. At the time, the Keatons were clearly traveling with Frank Cutler's Mohawk Indian Medicine Company (a.k.a. the Cutler Comedy Company). Joe Keaton and Houdini were never partners in a show, and the great magician, being the proprietor and star of his own burlesque company, the American Gaiety Girls, was nowhere near Piqua. Previously, Houdini and his wife, Bess, had been on tour with the Welsh Brothers circus.

15 "That's the third accident": Rudi Blesh, *Keaton* (New York: Macmillan, 1966), p. 5.

15 "old Jack": *Iola Register,* 10/4/1895.

16 "His cradle was the till": "Buster Keaton," undated clipping in the Keaton scrapbook, circa 1904 (BK).

16 George A. Pardey: George Pardey's signature role was Toby Twinkle in Thomas and J. Maddison Morton's *All That Glitters Is Not Gold.* Pardey played Twinkle, the drunken Timothy Toodles, Rip Van Winkle, and other comedy favorites in repertory for nearly two decades. He began working the medicine circuits in the 1880s. Under Dr. Pardey's direction, the Umatilla Indian Medicine and Concert Company gave not only free shows designed to hustle product but also full-dress evening performances that often played to packed houses at a nickel a head. Typically leading off with a curtain raiser or a pantomime, the main attraction was the olio in which everyone did their specialties—magic, juggling clubs and tumbling, songs, instrumental solos, trapeze work. It all built up to a spectacle of a finish, anything from a boisterous pie-eating contest to three rounds of exhibition boxing with Joe Keaton squaring off against the bantamweight Topeka Kid.

16 "Gee whiz": "'Buster' Keaton," *New York Dramatic Mirror,* 1/23/1904. The story that credited Harry Houdini with the exclamation that gave the nickname "Buster" to the

Keaton infant first appeared in newspapers in 1921 as a blind item, presumably fed by a studio press agent. Since Buster Keaton embraced the story for the rest of his life, its origin was likely his own father, although Joe Keaton was not directly quoted. The story was repeated, with additional flourishes, as part of an official biography issued in 1924, possibly in support of *Sherlock Jr.* Yet twenty years earlier, in his bylined article for the *Terre Haute Morning Star,* Joe expressly credited the line to George Pardey. At the time of the utterance in 1896, Houdini was touring Canada with his wife, Bess.

16 "Buster": Although the Keatons never acknowledged it, at least one source says the midwife who delivered the baby, Mrs. Theresa Ullrich, claimed to have named him by remarking on how big he was at birth, "He's a buster!" Myra Keaton liked to say her son was given the name "Buster" a good five years before the Buster Brown cartoons first appeared, which is true. He was not, however, the first public figure to carry the name. Prominent in the New York media of the 1890s was Chauncey M. Depew, Jr. (1879–1931), whose doting father, then president of the New York Central Railroad and later a United States senator, nicknamed him "Buster."

16 "scuttling": Blesh, *Keaton,* p. 5.

18 "pair of shears": Blesh, *Keaton,* p. 21.

18 "Joe Keaton is a good impersonator": *Weir City Daily Sun,* 12/7/1896 (courtesy of Robert Moulton).

18 "Comedy Sketch Team": *New York Clipper,* 11/13/1897.

19 "Our impresario's great problem": *Variety,* 12/31/1920.

19 "Broke the record": Kenneth Silverman, *Houdini!!!* (New York: HarperCollins, 1996), p. 18.

19 "Acrobatic Double Songs": *New York Clipper,* 4/16/1898.

19 "Joe did his big acrobatic act": *Pittsburg Leader,* n.d., in the Robinson Locke collection (NYPL).

19 Joe spied the instrument: *Los Angeles Examiner,* 3/28/1928.

19 "When he gets to dancing": *Pittsburg Daily Tribune,* 7/16/1898.

20 "Buster, at times, would join us in a sketch": "Stage Career of 'Joe' Keaton."

20 Mrs. Altena Wolgamot: This incident was reported in the *Kinsley Graphic,* 4/28/1899. Buster also described being sucked out a window and down the street by a cyclone that day ("a clothes wringer, a peach tree, and a cyclone put me on the stage"), but neither the *Graphic* nor the *Kinsley Daily Mercury* reported a cyclone at any time during the month of April 1899. (J. T. R. Clark's German-American Vaudevilles Co. was in town April 17–30.) In the earliest trade article about Buster, engineered by his father in 1901, a cyclone is never mentioned. In January 1904, a similar biographical item in the *New York Dramatic News* doesn't mention one either. In Joe's career summary of May 1904, he has the fall down the flight of stairs, the finger injury, and the cyclone (blowing the child one block) happening during a single week in 1897. The following year, he has all three events taking place on the same day, with the twister now blowing the boy three blocks instead of just one. Buster himself recalled the cyclone for Rudi Blesh in the early 1950s and again in his own 1960 autobiography. This may, however, have been another of Joe's fabrications that Buster came to accept as genuine, as he had the crediting of Harry Houdini for his nickname.

21 landed a week's work: According to Blesh, the Keatons "all but starved" until they were given a chance to play Huber's. In reality, they played the Ocean View Theatre in Norfolk the week of September 18, 1899. They were open the week of September 25, during which time they traveled to New York, and were on the bill at Huber's the week of October 2.

21 "It ain't easy": Blesh, *Keaton*, p. 21.

21 an item in the *Clipper*: *New York Clipper*, 10/28/1899. According to Blesh, the Keatons had no work for six weeks following their stand at Huber's, but just two open weeks separated their time at Huber's and their week at Fall River. And by the time they opened at the Casto, they had secured the Pastor and Proctor bookings. Two open weeks followed, which were likely used to sharpen the new act. From the week of November 13 on, they were booked into February 1900.

22 "The gong just saved it": *New York Dramatic Mirror*, 11/17/1900. Joe Keaton recounted the events leading up to their debut at Tony Pastor's in this ad, which was written in verse. He dated their arrival in New York as "one year ago, to-day," which roughly coincides with their first appearance at the Atlantic Garden.

23 "Eccentric Tad": In vaudevillian slang, a "tad" was a young Irishman.

23 display ad commissioned: *New York Dramatic Mirror*, 9/22/1900.

23 "They were all talking": Blesh, *Keaton*, p. 27.

24 "grotesque comedy": *New York Clipper*, 2/10/1900.

24 "The Keatons do little": *New York Morning Telegraph*, 4/5/1900.

25 "When we went into this business": *Pittsburgh Daily Post*, 11/26/1903.

25 "Mr. and Mrs. Joe Keaton talk less": *New York Morning Telegraph*, 7/14/1900.

25 "The Keatons did too much talking": *New York Morning Telegraph*, 7/26/1900.

25 "All sorts of original step-dancing": *New York Dramatic Mirror*, 9/29/1900.

26 "Dockstader booked": "Buster Keaton," undated clipping in the Keaton scrapbook, circa 1904 (BK).

26 "a genuine Comedy Act": *New York Dramatic Mirror*, 11/3/1900.

26 spent the Christmas season: The quarter section of property northeast of Perry that Joe Keaton later claimed to have staked at the opening of the Cherokee Outlet was actually claimed in 1893 by a schoolteacher named Willard E. Merry. It was from Merry that Joe Keaton purchased the claim while acting as his father's agent. Joseph Z. Keaton filed a homestead application in 1894 and held the land for six years. In 1900, he acquired the two-bedroom house at 624 "G" Street (later Grove Street) in which he lived for the rest of his life. This was revealed in genealogical research by Linda Neal.

27 "Talk about getting comedy": *New York Dramatic Mirror*, 1/12/1901.

2 KEEP YOUR EYE ON THE KID

29 "One or two corrupt children": *New York Times*, 12/26/1879.

30 "The average child": *New York Times*, 9/1/1892.

30 "I had fought": "Stage Career of 'Joe' Keaton."

30 "I have a Son": Letter, Joe Keaton to the Gerry Society, 12/27/1900 (SPCC).

31 "In reply": Letter, Elbridge Gerry to Joe Keaton, 12/29/1900 (SPCC).

31 "I wish to state <u>again</u>": Letter, Joe Keaton to Vernon M. Davis, 1/5/1901 (SPCC).

32 Buster Keaton once told his elder son: Barbara Talmadge to the author, Cloverdale, CA, 11/2/2016.

32 "My father used to carry me": Elizabeth Peltret, "Poor Child!," *Motion Picture Classic*, March 1921.

33 "The Keatons proved": *New York Dramatic Mirror*, 3/23/1901.

33 "The curtain rose": Report by Officer Walton, 3/11/1901 (SPCC).

33 laughing hit of the bill: *New York Dramatic Mirror*, 4/6/1901.

34 "I am introducing": Letter, Joe Keaton to Harry Houdini, 4/17/1901 (Harry Houdini collection, Harry Ransom Center, Austin, Texas).

34 "The Keatons now number": *New York Morning Telegraph,* 4/13/1901.

35 "the low crowds": *Brooklyn Daily Eagle,* 5/12/1901.

35 "Tell little Bessie": Letter, Joe Keaton to Harry Houdini, 5/12/1901 (Harry Houdini collection, Harry Ransom Center, Austin, Texas).

35 "It was the non plus ultra": *Variety,* 1/5/1938.

36 "Buster is full of sarcastic sayings": *San Francisco Examiner,* 10/7/1901.

36 "Buster is easily the star": *San Francisco Call,* 10/8/1901.

36 "They say, 'Open the show' ": Blesh, *Keaton,* p. 59.

37 "barely up to the standard": *Los Angeles Evening Herald,* 10/29/1901.

37 "The best American plan hotels": Buster Keaton (with Charles Samuels), *My Wonderful World of Slapstick* (Garden City, NY: Doubleday, 1960), p. 24.

37 "I just watched": Keaton, *My Wonderful World of Slapstick,* p. 26.

38 "You'd call it pantomime": BK to UCLA professor Arthur B. Friedman, *Turning Point* radio/oral history interview, Los Angeles, 1/27/1956.

38 "All little boys": Keaton, *My Wonderful World of Slapstick,* p. 13.

39 "On the stage during his father's vaudeville turn": *Los Angeles Evening Herald,* 10/30/1901.

39 "Of the children": Unidentified clipping, n.d., Buster Keaton scrapbook (BK).

39 "I could take crazy falls": Keaton, *My Wonderful World of Slapstick,* p. 26.

39 "You see this pad": *Cleveland Plain Dealer,* 8/1/1906.

39 "Some other comedians": Keaton, *My Wonderful World of Slapstick,* p. 13.

40 "If something tickled me": Blesh, *Keaton,* p. 38.

40 "Most of the Gerry Society agents": Elsie Janis, *So Far, So Good!* (London: J. Long, 1933), p. 24.

41 "A man, a woman": Manager's report, Keith's Union Square, 12/15/1902 (KA).

41 "The Three Keatons are only two": *New York Morning Telegraph,* 1/15/1903.

42 "Buster was sore": *Portland Daily Advertiser,* week of 2/15/1904.

43 "They filed a complaint": Ibid.

43 "The law": Blesh, *Keaton,* p. 36.

43 "Buster is the kid": Keaton trade ad, *New York Clipper,* 4/18/1903. In 1903, Buster's standing as the youngest performer in vaudeville was eclipsed by James Francis Sully, age six, who began appearing with the Sully Family of sketch comedians.

44 "We wish to thank you": Letter, Joe Keaton to E. Fellows Jenkins, 4/8/1903 (SPCC).

44 "In reply": Letter, E. Fellows Jenkins to Joe Keaton, 4/10/1903 (SPCC).

44 "He is a very clever 'kid' ": Manager's report, Keith's Union Square, 5/18/1903 (KA).

46 "Mrs. Keaton's playing": *Boston Globe,* 5/26/1903.

46 "What do you think?": *New York Dramatic Mirror,* 8/22/1903.

3 BIG FROG IN A LITTLE PUDDLE

47 "The old man": James Karen to the author, via telephone, 8/23/2016.

47 "In his spic-and-span": *Indianapolis Morning Star,* 10/31/1903.

47 "One morning, I tried it": BK to Dean Miller, *Here's Hollywood,* audio excerpt, NBC, 1961 (PNY).

48 "Later, we hired a governess": *New York Post,* 7/3/1941.

48 "Every show's a different show": Ibid.

48 "He frequently surprises": *New York Dramatic Mirror,* 1/23/1904.

48 "It is seldom that such hearty laughter": *New York Dramatic Mirror,* 1/30/1904.

48 "After I was seven": Keaton, *My Wonderful World of Slapstick,* p. 14.

49 "[Buster] had a persistent habit": Undated clipping in the Keaton scrapbook, 1905 (BK).

49   "I rode the punches": Blesh, *Keaton*, p. 44.

49   "Yes, and I am still learning": *Portland Daily Advertiser*, week of 2/15/1904.

49   "I was just a harebrained kid": Christopher Bishop, "An Interview with Buster Keaton," *Film Quarterly*, Fall 1958.

50   "The food was good": Keaton, *My Wonderful World of Slapstick*, p. 43.

50   "So I was in ball teams": BK to Friedman.

50   "I am proud to inform": *New York Clipper*, 9/10/1904.

51   The "argus-eyed" agents: Undated clipping in the Keaton scrapbook, 1905 (BK).

51   "He told the court": *Albany Journal*, 2/18/1905.

52   "He enjoys his work": *New York Clipper*, 4/8/1905.

53   "At that time we had": Letter, BK to Arthur J. Siplon, Sr., 2/7/1955 (courtesy of Ron Pesch).

53   "What most burned up Pop": Keaton, *My Wonderful World of Slapstick*, p. 33.

54   "Neither Mom nor Pop was demonstrative": Keaton, *My Wonderful World of Slapstick*, p. 14.

54   "Another strong hit": *Variety*, 3/10/1906.

55   "The barber put the snippers": *Cleveland Plain Dealer*, 8/1/1906.

56   "My part alone": *New York Post*, 7/3/1941. A matinee performance of *Little Lord Fauntleroy* was given in Nashua, New Hampshire, on December 15, 1906. *East Lynne* was performed earlier in the week.

57   Louise Josephine Keaton: *New York Dramatic Mirror*, 11/10/1906.

57   "A big xylophone": Blesh, "The Two Worlds of Buster Keaton," p. 17.

57   "It is a treat": *Buffalo Courier*, 5/28/1907. This may be the first appearance in print of the adjective "Keatonesque," a word that was added to the *Oxford English Dictionary* in 2018. In this 1907 usage, it referred collectively to all the Keatons and not just Buster.

57   "His act runs": *New York Clipper*, 9/28/1907.

58   "Vaudeville is very rotten": Letter, Joe Keaton to Houdini, 5/12/1901.

58   "Buster Keaton is growing": *Boston Post*, 10/8/1907.

59   The Keatons were set: Details of the arrest of Joe Keaton are from *The New York Times*, 11/19/1907 and 11/28/1907; *New York Sun*, 11/19/1907; *Variety*, 11/23/1907; *New York Press*, 11/28/1907; and the archives of the New York Society for the Prevention of Cruelty to Children.

60   "The older of the three": Officer Obadiah Cunningham, report of investigation, case no. 216252, 11/18/1907 (SPCC).

4 NOT LIKE THE OLD MAN ANYMORE

62   "If nothing takes place": Postcard, Joe Keaton to Alva Keaton, 3/23/1908 (courtesy of Melissa Talmadge Cox).

62   "The doctors massaged": Keaton, *My Wonderful World of Slapstick*, p. 47.

63   "This property": *Muskegon Daily Chronicle*, 7/4/1908.

63   "There were about eighteen": Keaton, *My Wonderful World of Slapstick*, p. 40.

64   "The result": *Muskegon Daily Chronicle*, 10/10/1908.

64   able to claim six prime lots: Myra Keaton, who handled the family's finances, actually made the purchase.

64   "Isn't that what most children": Keaton, *My Wonderful World of Slapstick*, p. 14.

65   "I am getting the European fever": Letter, Joe Keaton to Houdini, 4/17/1901.

65   "I had $1,400 in cash": Joe Keaton, "Mr. Butt and Co.," *Variety*, 12/11/1909.

66   "Pop couldn't use me": Keaton, *My Wonderful World of Slapstick*, p. 61.

66 "Nine-tenths of the time": Blesh, "The Two Worlds of Buster Keaton," p. 79.

66 "They went very well": *Variety*, 7/24/1909.

67 "You actually scared the audience": Keaton, *My Wonderful World of Slapstick*, p. 62.

67 "I shall ask you": Joe Keaton, "Mr. Butt and Co."

67 "We could book up three years": *New York Clipper*, 7/31/1909.

67 "Coming back": Postcard, BK to Eddie White, n.d. (courtesy of Ron Pesch).

67 "bully and did everything": *New York Dramatic Mirror*, 8/7/1909.

67 "The day we sailed": Joe Keaton, "Mr. Butt and Co."

67 "couldn't have cost": BK to Arthur J. Siplon, Sr.

68 "Joe Keaton and his whole family": Manager's report, Keith's Philadelphia, 8/23/1909 (KA).

69 "rasping like a phonograph": *Harrisburg Telegraph*, 2/14/1910.

71 "I let him have the basketball": Blesh, *Keaton*, p. 77.

71 "I used to do a thing": BK to Fletcher Markle, *Telescope*, Canadian Broadcasting Co., 1964.

71 "The next five years": Blesh, *Keaton*, p. 77.

71 "In his efforts not to be violent": Unidentified clipping, 1910, in the Robinson Locke Collection (NYPL).

72 "By golly, we got here": *New York Telegraph*, 6/12/1910.

72 "Buster and Joe whooped it up": *Variety*, 9/10/1910.

72 "And they always told me": Blesh, *Keaton*, p. 80.

74 "Three in the front row": Blesh, *Keaton*, p. 46.

74 "Tighten up your ass": James Karen to the author, via telephone, 9/20/2016.

74 "He has to clear the orchestra pit": BK to Hugh Downs, *Today*, National Broadcasting Co., 4/26/1963 (PBH).

74 "My slapshoes": Blesh, *Keaton*, p. 47.

74 "The thought never entered his mind": BK to Downs. A month later, Yale students made the national news when they rioted at the nearby Hyperion Theatre after authorities cut short a racy performance by French singer-dancer Gaby Deslys.

75 "will never be satisfied": *Variety*, 9/10/1910.

75 "There was a bar": Keaton, *My Wonderful World of Slapstick*, p. 40.

75 "I used to fill her clothes": *Detroit Free Press*, 1/11/1961.

76 "This well-known family": Manager's report, Keith's Columbus, 3/25/1912 (KA).

76 "The same hit": Manager's report, Keith's Cleveland, 9/30/1912 (KA).

76 "He missed my hat": Blesh, *Keaton*, p. 80.

77 "Although Buster Keaton is": Manager's report, Keith's Philadelphia, 12/17/1913 (KA).

77 "In his hurry": Keaton, *My Wonderful World of Slapstick*, p. 69.

78 "in his old red sweater": Frank Scheide, "The Story of Mildred Millard," *The Keaton Chronicle*, Summer 1999.

79 "Gray avenue is still one": *Billboard*, 7/24/1915.

79 "I put a long pipe": Keaton, *My Wonderful World of Slapstick*, p. 42.

80 "Never in the history": *Muskegon Daily Chronicle*, 7/6/1915.

80 "every actor": *Muskegon Chronicle*, 7/6/1915.

80 "Any time that you leave the ground": BK to Markle.

80 "The act had to change": Blesh, *Keaton*, p. 80.

80 "It made it more understandable": Blesh, *Keaton*, p. 81.

80 "better than ever": *Billboard*, 4/15/1916.

81 "The Keatons were popular favorites": *Variety*, 4/28/1916.

81 "Pop could not stop talking": Keaton, *My Wonderful World of Slapstick,* p. 82.

81 "Beck ran": Blesh, *Keaton,* p. 82.

82 "Took five bows": *New York Clipper,* 5/20/1916.

82 "The entire profession": Keaton, *My Wonderful World of Slapstick,* p. 88.

82 "pick up a letter": Blesh, *Keaton,* p. 72.

83 "Three-a-day": Blesh, *Keaton,* p. 82.

83 "The intensely dramatic plot": *Winnipeg Free Press,* 10/3/1916.

83 "'Poor son-of-a-bitch'": Blesh, *Keaton,* p. 81.

84 "He would break down": Keaton, *My Wonderful World of Slapstick,* p. 89.

84 "As we say in the theatre": Blesh, *Keaton,* p. 82.

5 I CAST MY LOT WITH THE PICTURES

85 "Pop wasn't going to die": Keaton, *My Wonderful World of Slapstick,* p. 90.

86 According to the *Clipper*: *New York Clipper,* 2/12/1917.

86 It was sometime in March: Keaton always remembered that he was to go into the *Passing Show of 1917* when the opportunity to go with Roscoe "Fatty" Arbuckle presented itself. And although no Keaton contract exists in the Shubert Archive, a contemporary newspaper item confirms that Buster had "signed a contract with the new Winter Garden show." *New York Telegraph,* 2/12/1917.

86 "He wanted to know": Buster Keaton, "Why I Never Smile," *Ladies' Home Journal,* June 1926. See also *How I Broke into the Movies* by Sixty Famous Screen Stars (Hollywood: Hal C. Herman, 1930).

87 "I had no more idea": Keaton, "Why I Never Smile."

87 "ramshackle to a degree": Anita Loos, *The Talmadge Girls* (New York: Viking Press, 1978), p. 8.

88 "Roscoe—none of us who knew him": Keaton, *My Wonderful World of Slapstick,* p. 93. Other accounts have Keaton taking the camera apart himself. According to silent-era camera expert Sam Dodge, this would have been unlikely. "No novice could disassemble a [Bell & Howell] 2709," he said. "What would have been done is that you would open the door and remove the Unit I shuttle to show how the mechanism transported film." This is something Arbuckle would have been able to do.

88 "Not a scrap": Elizabeth Sears, "Fatty Off Guard," *Film Fun,* March 1916.

88 When they began shooting: Since an Equity contract allowed for up to five weeks of unpaid rehearsal, work on *The Passing Show of 1917* probably began in mid-March ahead of an April 17 opening in Pittsburgh. Buster's first day of filming with Roscoe Arbuckle was March 19, 1917.

88 "You only had to turn me loose": BK to Robert and Joan Franklin, Oral History Research Collection, Columbia University, November 1958.

88 "In those days, almost every comedian": Henry Gris, "A Brief Lesson on How to Make a Porkpie Hat," *The Keaton Chronicle,* Autumn 1994.

89 "Roscoe explained the technique": Paul Gallico, "Polyandry for All," *Esquire,* July 1954.

90 "From the first day on": Keaton, *My Wonderful World of Slapstick,* p. 93.

90 "I'd fallen in love": *Journal-News* (Nyack, NY), 5/18/1957.

90 "By the time I'm through": "'Fatty' Arbuckle Off the Screen," *Literary Digest,* 7/14/1917.

91 "The main ammunition": *Moving Picture World,* 4/28/1917.

91 opening scenes set at Churchill's famous: "It didn't fit into our comedy," Arbuckle explained, "and it was not as funny as I had expected it to be, and so it was thrown out."

92 "Everyone there was doing drawing-room pix": Blesh, *Keaton,* p. 96.

92   "He was one of the greatest friends": BK to Robert and Joan Franklin.

93   "I didn't know it at the time": BK to Tony Thomas, Woodland Hills, March 1960, included in *Voices from the Hollywood Past,* Delos Records, 1975.

93   "We just went down there": BK to Robert and Joan Franklin.

93   "There are many comedy points": *Exhibitors Herald,* 11/3/1917.

93   "We made about six pictures": BK to George C. Pratt, Los Angeles, 1958, in Marshall Deutelbaum, ed., *"Image" on the Art and Evolution of the Film* (New York: Dover, 1979), pp. 195–204.

93   "She was a very good worker": Peter Bogdanovich, *Allan Dwan: The Last Pioneer* (New York: Praeger, 1971), p. 42.

94   "During the few weeks": Margaret L. Talmadge, *The Talmadge Sisters* (Philadelphia: Lippincott, 1924), p. 41.

94   "Joe was no Rudolph Valentino": Loos, *The Talmadge Girls,* p. 28.

94   the Schenck brothers: Details of the brothers' early days in business are from *Variety,* 9/28/1906 and 4/9/1910, and from Henry F. Pringle, "Business Is Business," *The New Yorker,* 4/30/1932.

95   "He was nineteen years older": Loos, *The Talmadge Girls,* p. 29. Actually, Schenck was seventeen years older.

95   "I knew very well": Alan Hynd, "The Rise and Fall of Joseph Schenck, Part II," *Liberty,* 7/5/1941.

96   "She was the serious type": Talmadge, *The Talmadge Sisters,* p. 42.

96   "I was attracted to her": Keaton, *My Wonderful World of Slapstick,* p. 94.

97   "There are larger studios": *Motography,* 6/16/1917.

98   "You want to show The Three Keatons": Keaton, *My Wonderful World of Slapstick,* p. 90. Hearst opted for a series of animated shorts instead.

98   "I never had that thing": BK to Downs.

98   "In Long Beach": *Long Beach Press,* 10/17/1917.

98   "I've been making a living": *Muskegon Daily Times,* 6/5/1918.

100   "What we did to Fords": Blesh, "The Two Worlds of Buster Keaton," p. 161.

100   "No more tips": *Salt Lake Tribune,* 1/20/1918.

100   "that the average mentality": Keaton, *My Wonderful World of Slapstick,* p. 95.

102   "On the stage, even one": Keaton, *My Wonderful World of Slapstick,* p. 93.

102   "[Arbuckle] would turn you loose": BK to Pratt.

102   "I am interested in making good pictures": *Motion Picture World,* 6/30/1917.

102   "It has to be an old hat": Penelope Gilliat, *Unholy Fools* (New York: Viking Press, 1973), p. 50.

103   "Once you've got your realistic character": Gilliat, *Unholy Fools,* p. 48.

104   "miraculous": *Los Angeles Times,* 12/9/1917.

104   "He was hard as a brick wall": Blesh, *Keaton,* p. 98.

104   "Our latest picture": *Muskegon Chronicle,* 1/31/1918.

104   "hits a better comedy tempo": *Variety,* 1/25/1918.

104   "Nothing of the usual stuff": *Billboard,* 2/2/1918.

104   "sure fire hit": *Motography,* 2/9/1918.

104   "The star's best yet": *Motography,* 3/9/1918.

104   "About the best Arbuckle": *Motography,* 3/30/1918.

105   "lived in the camera": Blesh, *Keaton,* p. 105.

106   "The funniest-looking accident": Elizabeth Peltret, "It's a Hard Life!" *Photoplay,* December 1918.

107   "The big moment": Keaton, *My Wonderful World of Slapstick,* p. 140.

107   "excruciatingly funny": *Variety,* 3/22/1918.

108   "the best comedy": *Motography,* 2/9/1918.

108   "I never saw a better comedy": *Motion Picture News,* 4/27/1918.

108   "A better comedy": *Motion Picture News,* 3/30/1918.

108   "the director's idea": It should be noted that the version of *Moonshine* referenced here is the Lobster Films restoration issued on home video by Kino Classics. The intertitles were translated back into English from French cards and may not represent exactly what American audiences saw in 1918.

109   "the best of Arbuckle's": *Variety,* 6/28/1918.

109   "Oh, it's all right": *Variety,* 5/3/1918.

109   "a little overweight": *Variety,* 3/22/1918.

109   "Buster has joined the submarine service": *Variety,* 5/31/1918.

6 GETTING RESTLESS

112   "like an island": Media Mistley, "Cheering Up the Sad Sea Waves," *Photo-Play Journal,* November 1918.

112   "his pit bull terrier": Although the moviegoing public knew Luke as Roscoe Arbuckle's dog, he actually belonged to Minta Durfee, Arbuckle's wife, who received him as a gift from director Wilfred Lucas.

114   *A ring will soon be*: Blesh, *Keaton,* p. 113.

114   "My pants were too long": Keaton, *My Wonderful World of Slapstick,* p. 98.

114   "On mastering these subjects": Keaton, *My Wonderful World of Slapstick,* p. 97.

115   "If I rolled out": Keaton, *My Wonderful World of Slapstick,* p. 98.

115   "We had a wonderful eight or ten hours": Keaton, *My Wonderful World of Slapstick,* p. 99.

115   "The cooties we were to know": Keaton, *My Wonderful World of Slapstick,* p. 99. The word "cootie" was slang for louse or, in the plural, lice.

115   "There is always a draft": Keaton, *My Wonderful World of Slapstick,* p. 100.

115   "Because of my size": Peltret, "Poor Child!"

116   "[I got] just close enough": BK to Kevin Brownlow, 12/18/1964, in Kevin W. Sweeney, ed., *Buster Keaton Interviews* (Jackson: University Press of Mississippi, 2007), p. 207.

116   "Buster is fast winning": *Muskegon Daily Times,* 6/5/1918.

116   "I HEAR YOU ARE WORKING": *Los Angeles Examiner,* 3/28/1928.

116   "A feller up here": Joe Keaton, "The Cyclone Baby," *Photoplay,* May 1927.

117   "Joe hooks his foot": *Billboard,* 9/7/1935.

117   "Our division did a lot": BK to Robert and Joan Franklin.

118   "None of the carousing privates": Keaton, *My Wonderful World of Slapstick,* p. 103.

119   "Before I was overseas": Keaton, *My Wonderful World of Slapstick,* p. 104.

119   Now he was almost stone-deaf: In his datebook, Keaton recorded the formal diagnosis as acute otitis media, a painful ear infection.

119   "You look terribly peaked": Keaton, *My Wonderful World of Slapstick,* p. 105.

120   "He used to come home": Talmadge, *The Talmadge Sisters,* p. 133.

120   "I walked through that stage door": Keaton, *My Wonderful World of Slapstick,* p. 105.

120   "The mistake enabled": Keaton, *My Wonderful World of Slapstick,* p. 106.

122   "Arbuckle was that rarity": Keaton, *My Wonderful World of Slapstick,* p. 95.

122   "All my mechanical knowledge": *Los Angeles Evening Herald,* 10/28/1919.

123   "Buster was probably the original": Viola Dana to Kevin Brownlow in *Buster Keaton: A Hard Act to Follow,* Photoplay Productions, 1987.

124   "I like you": Blesh, "The Two Worlds of Buster Keaton," p. 149.

124 "The four of us": Stuart Oderman, *Roscoe "Fatty" Arbuckle* (Jefferson, NC: McFarland, 1994), p. 131.

124 "Venice was what we called": Oderman, *Roscoe "Fatty" Arbuckle,* p. 147.

125 "You only star in movies": *Los Angeles Evening Herald,* 10/28/1919.

126 "No entrances nor exits": *Los Angeles Evening Herald,* 11/3/1919.

126 "Arbuckle was one of the worst rough-houses": BK to John Schmitz, Woodland Hills, 5/20/1958 (BFI). Arbuckle weighed in the neighborhood of 260 pounds.

127 "It was a honey": BK to George C. Pratt, as quoted by Kevin Brownlow in "The Search for Buster Keaton," unpublished manuscript, p. 29.

JASPER, ALBERTA

129 "He's got such vitality": *Edmonton Journal,* 10/1/1964.

130 "There were certain gags": Potterton to the author.

130 "No, it's too simple": Gerald Potterton to Kevin Brownlow in interview footage shot for the documentary *Buster Keaton: A Hard Act to Follow* (1987).

130 "Of course, I was a bit impatient": Potterton to the author.

130 " 'Boy, that's going to take forever' ": Potterton to Brownlow.

131 "There was a time when": Ibid.

7 THE COMEDY SENSATION OF THE SCREEN WORLD

135 "I have all the money": *Variety,* 12/12/1919.

136 "The first thing Roscoe said": Bartine Burkett Zane, "The Buster Keaton I Knew," *The Keaton Chronicle,* Autumn 1996.

136 "Our practical jokes": Keaton, *My Wonderful World of Slapstick,* p. 112.

136 "We relied": Keaton, *My Wonderful World of Slapstick,* p. 113.

137 "Buster made his first entrance": *Variety,* 1/2/1920.

139 "the moving picture comedy": Keaton, "Why I Never Smile."

139 "I've never known anyone": Zane, "The Buster Keaton I Knew."

139 "They had a shot": BK to Brownlow, *Buster Keaton Interviews,* p. 208.

140 "His timing was fantastic": Zane, "The Buster Keaton I Knew."

140 "Not a titter": Blesh, *Keaton,* pp. 141–42.

141 "I'll do *Brewster's Millions*": Delight Evans, "West Is East," *Photoplay,* June 1920.

142 "The evening would begin": Joe Adamson, *Byron Haskin* (Metuchen, NJ: Scarecrow Press, 1984), p. 27.

143 "an earnest young man": Katherine Albert, "The Unknown Hollywood I Know, Part Two," *Photoplay,* November 1931.

143 "Don't know why": *Los Angeles Times,* 5/16/1920.

143 "I didn't pay enough attention": BK to Brownlow, *Buster Keaton Interviews,* p. 199.

143 "So I had a city lot": BK to Brownlow, *Buster Keaton Interviews,* p. 178.

144 "I suggested that I make only features": Keaton, *My Wonderful World of Slapstick,* p. 125.

144 The deal with Metro: Details of the contract between Comique Film Corporation and Metro Pictures Corporation are from the agreement between the two companies dated June 1, 1920.

145 "Both get laughs": Malcolm H. Oettinger, "Low Comedy as a High Art," *Picture-Play,* March 1923.

145 "I had my idea of comedy": *Los Angeles Times,* 11/17/1929.

145 "We used to meet": Edward F. Cline, "What's Become of the Keystone Kops?," *Los Angeles Times,* 7/10/1938.

147 "To lessen the impact": Keaton, *My Wonderful World of Slapstick,* p. 168.

148   "We built it on a turntable": BK to Brownlow, *Buster Keaton Interviews,* p. 185.
148   "I always wanted an audience": BK to Studs Terkel, WFMT Chicago, 9/5/1960.
150   "Two or three writers": "Happy Pro," *The New Yorker,* 4/27/1963.
151   "Put all your money": *Motion Picture News,* 8/21/1920.
151   "*Convict 13* gives ample proof": *Wid's Daily,* 8/22/1920.
152   "The combination of comic gifts": *Moving Picture World,* 9/4/1920.
152   "*One Week* starts Buster Keaton": *Buster Keaton Comedies,* Metro Pictures Corporation, September 1920.
153   "It is certainly great": *Moving Picture World,* 10/23/1920.
153   "This is a refreshing": *Variety,* 10/23/1920.
153   worldwide rentals: The total for *One Week* is from the library of Karl Thiede and the monthly revenue ledgers of Joseph M. Schenck Productions.
155   "Book the series": *Exhibitors Herald,* 11/20/1920.
156   "Shaving was a great time": BK to Markle.
156   "We always carried three men": BK to Brownlow, *Buster Keaton Interviews,* p. 175.
156   "I would shoot material": BK to Georges Sadoul, *Buster Keaton Interviews,* p. 153.
156   "Eddie was too kind-hearted": A. Edward Sutherland to Robert and Joan Franklin, 1959, Oral History Research Collection, Columbia University, p. 72.
156   "He'd be out there": John Gilliatt and James Blue, "Keaton at Venice," *Sight & Sound,* Winter 1965–66.
156   "I like long takes": Gilliatt, *Unholy Fools,* p. 53.
156   "We used to say one of the hardest things": BK to Pratt.
157   "He's the fellow": BK to Brownlow, *Buster Keaton Interviews,* p. 184.
157   "We used to study frames": BK to Robert and Joan Franklin.
158   "Buster Keaton in the not far distant future": *Motion Picture News,* 12/11/1920.
158   "Let's end the suspense": *Los Angeles Times,* 12/13/1920.
159   "Chaplin's just an automatic bum": BK to Downs.
159   "In our early successes": BK to Robert and Joan Franklin.
159   "I started out": Ibid.
160   "We constructed a tank": Harry T. Brundidge, *Twinkle, Twinkle, Movie Star!* (New York: E. P. Dutton, 1930), p. 211.
161   "There was something like": BK to Robert and Joan Franklin.

8 THE MOST UNIQUE AND ORIGINAL COMEDIAN

162   "badly constructed": *New York Times,* 2/20/1921.
162   "a bore": Malcolm H. Oettinger, "Tumbling to Fame," *Picture-Play,* December 1920.
163   "all gags and no sense": *Los Angeles Times,* 2/10/1929.
164   "Starring Muskegon's Own": Emma-Lindsay Squier, "He Really Can Smile," *Picture-Play,* July 1921.
164   "I am alone now": Keaton, *My Wonderful World of Slapstick,* p. 165.
164   "Some people seem to think": *Los Angeles Times,* 2/2/1921.
164   "There isn't anything to tell": *Los Angeles Herald,* 2/4/1921.
164   "war romance": *Muskegon Chronicle,* 2/5/1921.
165   "working a double": *Variety,* 2/11/1921.
165   "a slim little dark person": *Billboard,* 4/16/1921.
165   "She had only one objection": Keaton, *My Wonderful World of Slapstick,* p. 166.
166   "ingenious and irresistibly funny": *New York Times,* 3/20/1922.
166   "Such is the belief": *Los Angeles Herald,* 1/24/1921.

166 "Peg was still searching": Loos, *The Talmadge Girls,* p. 65.

166 "If Buster Keaton did make": *Nebraska State Journal,* 5/1/1921.

167 "We gotta bring this thing": Keaton, *My Wonderful World of Slapstick,* p. 166.

168 "It was difficult": Talmadge, *The Talmadge Sisters,* p. 173.

168 "Peg's smile": Anita Loos, *Cast of Thousands* (New York: Grosset & Dunlap, 1976), p. 34.

169 "Bride Natalie": *Los Angeles Herald,* 6/16/1921.

169 "I made eight comedies": Squier, "He Really Can Smile."

169 "I string all my stuff": Ibid.

169 Associated First National: Details of the contract between Comique Film Corporation and Associated First National Pictures are from the production agreement between the two companies dated August 1, 1921 (WB).

170 "During my vaudeville years": Keaton, *My Wonderful World of Slapstick,* p. 51.

170 "Thomas H. Ince presents": BK to Pratt. "A mild exaggeration," comments Kevin Brownlow. "Ince used his name as [Henry] Ford used his, to represent the product. What annoyed people in the industry was that he often took direction credit, even though he no longer directed."

170 "If we can't have falls and chases": Blesh, *Keaton,* p. 163.

170 "In comedy": *New York Telegraph,* 10/8/1922.

171 "Every move, song, and dance": Blesh, *Keaton,* p. 152.

172 "The camera used to shoot": Sam Dodge's comments are contained in e-mails to David Weddle, 5/17/2019, and to the author, 5/20 and 7/3/2019.

172 "it was hardest": Blesh, *Keaton,* p. 168.

173 "He would go by the sun": Gillett and Blue, "Keaton at Venice."

173 "My synchronizing was gotten": Blesh, *Keaton,* p. 168.

174 "I could have made the whole two-reeler": Gillett and Blue, "Keaton at Venice."

175 "A chimp as a headliner": Blesh, "The Two Worlds of Buster Keaton," p. 81.

176 "Buster Keaton starts off three laps": *Los Angeles Times,* 9/26/1921.

176 "It's too soon yet": Willis Goldbeck, *Motion Picture,* October 1921.

177 "I never cared a cent": *Los Angeles Times,* 8/8/1921.

177 "Los Angeles is the greatest motion": *Los Angeles Herald,* 10/26/1921.

179 "Mal was a great director": Mel Gussow, *Don't Say Yes Until I Finish Talking* (Garden City, NY: Doubleday, 1971), p. 36.

179 welcomed Sybil back: It has been suggested that Keaton brought Sybil Seely back so that *The Boat* could be combined with *One Week* to create a short feature, but this is unlikely since *The Boat* was made for First National release and Metro retained distribution rights to *One Week* for a period of five years.

179 "The manager of a theater": *New York Telegraph,* 10/8/1922.

180 "The main thing": James Bawden and Ron Miller, *You Ain't Heard Nothin' Yet* (Lexington: University Press of Kentucky, 2017), p. 11.

180 "She simply would not go straight down": BK to Pratt.

180 "We got that boat to slide down": BK to Brownlow, *Buster Keaton Interviews,* p. 190.

181 "Material was always": BK to Bob Quintrell, *Close Up: Three Comedians,* Canadian Broadcasting Co., April 1, 1962.

182 "We carried her": *Los Angeles Herald,* 9/10/1921.

183 "I was making a picture": Kevin Brownlow, *Hollywood: The Pioneers* (New York: Alfred A. Knopf, 1979), p. 108.

183 "Nobody is too busy": *Los Angeles Herald,* 9/12/1921.

184 "beauty parlor": *Los Angeles Times,* 9/18/1921.

184 "She would provide girls": Brownlow, *Hollywood: The Pioneers*, p. 109.

184 "We just couldn't work": *Los Angeles Times*, 9/15/1921.

185 "Mr. Dominguez talked": Keaton, *My Wonderful World of Slapstick*, p. 159.

185 "Arbuckle was not particularly glad": *New York Times*, 9/30/1921.

186 "We're all going right out home": *Los Angeles Herald*, 9/30/1921.

186 "What could you say": Blesh, *Keaton*, p. 180.

188 "Below the camera line": Ethel Sands, "A Fan's Adventures in Hollywood," *Picture-Play*, May 1922.

188 "I've never had the slightest fear": Brundidge, *Twinkle, Twinkle, Movie Star!*, p. 210.

189 "It is strange": Robert E. Sherwood, "The Silent Drama," *Life*, 6/1/1922.

190 Metro released *The Goat*: Rental figures for *The Goat* and *The Play House* are from the library of Karl Thiede and the monthly revenue ledgers of Joseph M. Schenck Productions. Keaton set the cost of *The Boat* at $22,000 in a 1960 interview with Ron Miller.

190 "You could write the whole plot": *New York Telegraph*, 2/21/1923.

190 "just ducking cops": BK to Downs. Among Keaton's influences, Kevin Brownlow suggests, were the French trick films he watched as a boy in vaudeville. "One, *La Course des Sergents de Ville* (Pathé, 1907; English title *The Policeman's Little Run*), has a dog who steals a policeman's hat, chased by a vast number of gendarmes through the streets of Paris, ending up at a police station, at the door of which the dog sits triumphantly wearing the gendarme's cap."

190 "Three hundred and fifty": BK to Downs.

191 "The director, a couple of": *New York Telegraph*, 2/21/1923.

191 "For any of our big rough-house scenes": BK to Terkel.

191 "We planned it to lead": Blesh, "The Two Worlds of Buster Keaton," p. 251.

192 "I tried to cut through": BK to Terkel.

192 "that's undercranked a little": BK to Downs.

193 "That poor horse": John Bengtson to the author, via email, 3/3/2018.

193 "one of the few": *New York Times*, 1/2/1922.

194 "The most unique and original": *Milwaukee Journal*, as quoted in *Moving Picture World*, 12/24/1921.

194 "more ingenious contrivances": *Atlanta Journal*, as quoted in *Moving Picture World*, 12/24/1921.

194 "The feature film": *New York World*, 3/6/1922.

9 SPOOLING COMEDY

195 "His position was that": *Los Angeles Times*, 11/19/1921.

195 "It is the consensus": *Variety*, 11/25/1921.

196 "Arbuckle appeared greatly disheartened": *Los Angeles Times*, 12/5/1921.

196 "This case has put quite a crimp": *Los Angeles Times*, 12/7/1921.

197 "It's heartbreaking work": *New York Tribune*, 11/27/1921.

197 "Buster Keaton, of the lugubrious": *Motion Picture News*, 9/30/1922.

197 "one of his funniest": *Exhibitors Herald*, 10/14/1922.

198 "Wild rumors": *Variety*, 12/16/1921.

198 "Taylor was the best fellow": *San Francisco Bulletin*, 2/2/1922.

198 "We are not rampant": *New York Times*, 2/12/1922.

199 "Each day I put in a certain number": *Los Angeles Times*, 12/10/1922.

199 "*My Wife's Relations*—that is": *Los Angeles Times*, 12/10/1922. Author David Yallop, in his book *The Day the Laughter Stopped*, suggests that Hart was targeted by Keaton because the cowboy star had attacked Arbuckle in the press. Hart, however, considered himself

a friend of Roscoe's. "People should remember that sin has no profession and not judge him until he has had a chance to tell his own story," Hart told the *Atlanta Constitution*. And in the *Detroit Free Press* he said that he did not believe that Arbuckle was guilty but added sadly that "he is deader than a doornail in the films."

201 "He had a big snow story": *San Francisco Chronicle*, 2/12/1922.

201 "For some reason he turned ham": BK to Terkel.

202 "I had a little trouble": Ibid.

203 "Acquittal is not enough": *New York Times*, 4/13/1922.

203 "Our contract with Arbuckle": *Los Angeles Times*, 4/13/1922.

203 "For this vindication": Ibid.

204 "They do this that the whole matter": *New York Times*, 4/19/1922.

204 "Gosh": *New York Times*, 4/20/1922.

204 "So far as he was concerned": Will H. Hays, *The Memoirs of Will H. Hays* (Garden City, NY: Doubleday, 1955), p. 361.

204 "Of course [Arbuckle] is innocent": *Variety*, 4/21/1922.

204 "I knew Arbuckle": Adolph Zukor to Robert and Joan Franklin, 1958, Oral History Research Collection, Columbia University.

205 "interesting": *Variety*, 3/24/1922.

205 "Keaton spent considerable pains": *Film Daily*, 3/26/1922.

205 "We shelved everything": BK to Pratt.

206 "the walls were bulging": Blesh, *Keaton*, p. 204.

207 "If I was hanging": Gussow, *Don't Say Yes Until I Finish Talking*, p. 31.

207 "Of all the movies I made": Virginia Zanuck to "Eliott," 11/24/1982.

208 "Nate is beginning to look": Loos, *The Talmadge Girls*, p. 129.

208 "some trouble between Keaton": *Variety*, 5/26/1922.

208 "I'm not sobbing": *Oakland Tribune*, 6/15/1922.

208 "He has nothing to do": Ibid.

208 "and walks around": *Muskegon Daily Times*, 7/1/1915.

209 The scenario was titled: Arbuckle's sale of *The Vision* was reported in *Variety*, 6/2/1922, and the *Oakland Tribune*, 5/19/1922. The change of title to *Day Dreams* was covered in *Moving Picture World*, 6/24/1922.

209 under Arbuckle's direction: Arbuckle's role as director of *Day Dreams* is described in the *Oakland Tribune*, 6/3/1922, and *Variety*, 6/30/1922. Renée Adorée confirmed working as "the leading lady of Buster Keaton under the direction of Roscoe Arbuckle" in Robert Florey, "Un Ménage d'Artistes à Hollywood: Tom Moore et Renée Adorée," *Cinémagazine*, 10/13/1922. Although it appears certain that Arbuckle directed portions of the picture, he did not shoot any of the location work in San Francisco, as any such activity would have attracted considerable press attention, and there is none to be found.

210 "I used to daydream": BK to Robert and Joan Franklin. *Day Dreams* is sometimes described as a three-reeler, but this is somewhat misleading. It was sold to exhibitors as a two-reeler, as were all the Keaton shorts, even though it was registered with the Copyright Office at a length of three reels. In the release chart in the April 7, 1923, issue of *Exhibitors Herald*, the film's length is given as 2,493 feet, making it the longest of all the Keaton releases but still shorter than a standard three-reel subject. "Buster Keaton finds it necessary to encroach on the third reel in order to tell what happens to him in *Day Dreams*, which First National will distribute" (*Exhibitors Trade Review*, 2/17/1923).

211 When First National exercised: Rental figures for *The Boat*, *The Blacksmith*, *The Frozen North*, and *The Electric House* are from the library of Karl Thiede and the monthly revenue ledgers of Joseph M. Schenck Productions.

211 "inconsiderate, unsympathetic": Charles Chaplin, *My Autobiography* (New York: Simon & Schuster, 1964), p. 295.
211 "Schenck showed this": Keaton, *My Wonderful World of Slapstick,* p. 172.
212 "something a lot better": Quoted in *Film Daily,* 7/14/1922.
212 "Buster Keaton is traveling high": *Motion Picture News,* 7/22/1922.
212 "Don't fail to wait": Quoted in *Motion Picture News,* 7/8/1922.
212 "Buster Keaton is irresistible": *Film Daily,* 7/2/1922.
212 "A great many kindly people": Robert E. Sherwood, "The Silent Drama," *Life,* 7/20/1922.
213 "That being the case": Keaton, *My Wonderful World of Slapstick,* p. 172.
213 "Comedy is best": *New York Telegraph,* 10/8/1922.
214 "with sheets of flame": *Berkshire Eagle,* 7/16/1960.

10 OUR HOSPITALITY

215 "A good time for": Blesh, "The Two Worlds of Buster Keaton," p. 256.
215 "The best of the three": Robert E. Sherwood, "The Silent Drama," *Life,* 11/16/1922.
216 "Terrible": *New York Telegraph,* 10/8/1922.
216 "Next I'm going back": Oettinger, "Low Comedy as a High Art."
217 "a perfect film face": Luke McKernan, "Just a Brixton Shop Girl," *The Keaton Chronicle,* Summer 2011.
217 "She is of the petite": *New York Times,* 12/2/1922.
217 "They have taken thousands": McKernan, "Just a Brixton Shop Girl."
218 "Margaret Leahy has natural ability": *New York Morning Telegraph,* 1/7/1923.
218 "I realize that stars": Ibid.
218 "I need a rest": *Oakland Tribune,* 8/16/1922.
218 "This money is seeking": *Variety,* 10/13/1922.
219 "It is not difficult": *New York Times,* 12/25/1922.
220 "What I did was just tell": BK to Pratt.
220 "Cut the film apart": Blesh, *Keaton,* p. 217.
221 "The cast for our two-reelers": Keaton, *My Wonderful World of Slapstick,* p. 130.
221 "Tell me from nothing": Blesh, *Keaton,* p. 149.
221 "I am going to show England": McKernan, "Just a Brixton Shop Girl."
221 "Miss Leahy was originally chosen": *Los Angeles Times,* 1/7/1923.
222 "It's just about a hundred times": *Los Angeles Times,* 1/14/1923.
222 "We didn't get William S. Hart": Bishop, "An Interview with Buster Keaton."
222 "We were knocking ourselves out": Blesh, *Keaton,* p. 213.
222 "It is only preliminary work": McKernan, "Just a Brixton Shop Girl."
223 "We built the sets": Of downtown Los Angeles' five urban tunnels, three were in existence in 1923. Keaton recalled shooting above either the Third Street or Broadway tunnel, but location detective John Bengtson has determined through visible landmarks in the film that he actually made his leap atop the double-bore Hill Street tunnel.
225 "Working with Buster Keaton": McKernan, "Just a Brixton Shop Girl."
226 "The scenes we threw": Blesh, *Keaton,* p. 218.
227 "The point of this comedy": Keaton, *My Wonderful World of Slapstick,* p. 194.
227 "Now, Buster accepted": Blesh, *Keaton,* p. 151.
227 hanging miniature: What was built of the Colosseum set reportedly cost $20,000.
228 "In that film I did take liberties": Gillett and Blue, "Keaton at Venice."
228 "I couldn't just run over": Ibid.
228 "She said that Buster Keaton": *New York Times,* 6/10/1923.

230 "Refined brutality": *Brooklyn Life*, 7/21/1923.

230 "All of us tried to steal": Peter Bogdanovich, *Who the Devil Made It* (New York: Alfred A. Knopf, 1997), p. 395.

230 "On *Our Hospitality* we had": Gillett and Blue, "Keaton at Venice."

230 "A dupe negative": BK to Brownlow, *Buster Keaton Interviews*, pp. 181–82.

231 "We did our own research": BK to Pratt.

231 "We don't know which event": *Los Angeles Times*, 6/2/1923.

231 "She loved her home": Eunice Marshall, "They Never Quit," *Screenland*, November 1923.

232 "She went to Lou Anger": *Los Angeles Times*, 6/22/1923.

232 "work very hard": McKernan, "Just a Brixton Shop Girl." Margaret Leahy soon returned to Los Angeles, where she married at least twice but never appeared in another movie. She was excoriated for her incompetence in Rudi Blesh's *Keaton*, published in July 1966. Whether she ever saw the book is unknown, but she reportedly burned her scrapbooks and took her own life the following year, at the age of sixty-four.

233 "They're naturally narrow-gauge": BK to Pratt.

234 "Once we started": BK to Robert and Joan Franklin.

234 "I don't know why": Margaret Reid, "The Child Who Was 'Abused,' " *Picture-Play*, February 1928.

234 melodramatic prologue: There is evidence this sequence was originally intended to serve as a flashback but that Keaton wisely moved it to the front of the film, where it gains power and expertly illustrates the deadly situation in which Willie finds himself.

234 "I use the simplest little things": Gillett and Blue, "Keaton at Venice."

235 "He was a good man": BK to Brownlow, *Buster Keaton Interviews*, p. 210.

235 "Buster is a 'wham' ": *San Francisco Chronicle*, 7/16/1923.

235 "in the rapids": Blesh, *Keaton*, p. 233.

235 "distinct screen fiasco": *Variety*, 8/16/1923.

238 "We had to build that dam": Gillett and Blue, "Keaton at Venice."

239 Much more serious: Details of the illness and death of Joseph H. Roberts are from the City of Los Angeles Death Certificate no. 9127, *Exhibitors Herald*, 11/10/1923, and *Nebraska State Journal*, 11/18/1923.

11 *THE NAVIGATOR*

241 "shied at it to a remarkable extent": *Variety*, 8/30/1923.

241 "On the Sunday night": *Variety*, 10/4/1923.

241 "the picture is really": *Billboard*, 9/8/1923.

241 "It was difficult to make him": *New York Morning Telegraph*, 10/21/1923.

242 "The kid is going to be": Margaret Warner, "How Buster Keaton Got That Way," *Movie Weekly*, 11/10/1923.

242 "Just came up": *San Francisco Chronicle*, 11/4/1923.

242 "The star hangs over": *Variety*, 12/13/1923.

242 "The best way to get a laugh": John Montgomery, *Comedy Films* (London: Allen & Unwin, 1954), p. 155.

243 "one of the most humorous": *Exhibitors Trade Review*, 12/1/1923.

243 "It is a genuine pity": *Billboard*, 12/22/1923.

243 delivering worldwide rentals: Figures for *Three Ages* and *Our Hospitality* are from the library of Karl Thiede.

243 "I ran around $225,000": BK to Herbert Feinstein, San Francisco, 10/6/1960, in *Massachusetts Review*, Winter 1963.

244 "Had Buster got the play rights": "Greenroom Jottings," *Motion Picture*, March 1924.

244 "I think the reason we started off": BK to Robert and Joan Franklin.

244 "'Ching Ling Foo'": Chinese illusionist Ching Ling Foo (1854–1922) was revered by Keaton. "There's the greatest magician I ever saw. The Great Lafayette and fellows like that did big showy illusions, but for honest-to-God magic no one ever touched Ching Ling Foo."

245 "That was the reason": Gillett and Blue, "Keaton at Venice."

245 "Roscoe was down": Keaton, *My Wonderful World of Slapstick*, p. 194.

245 "He told Roscoe": Oderman, *Roscoe "Fatty" Arbuckle*, p. 204.

246 "So we hire him": BK to Brownlow, *Buster Keaton Interviews*, p. 192. In a letter, Arbuckle told Minta Durfee Arbuckle that he had been "thrown in at the last minute to direct Buster's next picture and I have been very busy trying to get a story ready" (*New York Daily News*, 12/28/1927).

246 "There were never any problems": Oderman, *Roscoe "Fatty" Arbuckle*, p. 204.

246 directing Al St. John: In the 5/23/1924 issue of *Cinémagazine*, correspondent Robert Florey reported that Arbuckle "has directed two Al St. John comedies while Buster Keaton has been making *Sherlock Jr.*" (courtesy Kevin Brownlow).

247 "He looks a little thinner": *Billboard*, 11/25/1924.

247 "So then I went ahead": BK to Brownlow, *Buster Keaton Interviews*, p. 193.

248 "We built what looked": Bishop, "An Interview with Buster Keaton."

248 "All we needed was the exact distance": BK to Brownlow, *Buster Keaton Interviews*, p. 195.

248 "As I looked down": BK to Brownlow, *Buster Keaton Interviews*, p. 230.

249 man called Gillette: Keaton likely chose this name because the preeminent interpreter of Sherlock Holmes onstage was actor-playwright William Gillette (1853–1937).

250 "The control of the gas": BK to Brownlow, *Buster Keaton Interviews*, p. 202.

250 "Of course all my weight": Bishop, "An Interview with Buster Keaton."

251 "I had a headache": BK to Brownlow, *Buster Keaton Interviews*, p. 202.

251 "One of the main reasons": BK to Pratt.

251 "Keaton took in all the comment": *Variety*, 5/21/1924.

251 "We have never made a picture": BK to Pratt.

251 "Again Buster was not satisfied": *Variety*, 5/21/1924.

252 "We never paid the slightest attention": BK to Brownlow, *Buster Keaton Interviews*, p. 188.

252 "The best comedy": *Film Daily*, 5/11/1924.

252 "*Sherlock Jr.*, which is slightly": *Billboard*, 5/17/1924.

252 "about as unfunny": *Variety*, 5/28/1924.

252 "A good comedy drama": *Moving Picture World*, 3/7/1925.

252 The film would accumulate worldwide rentals: Rental figures for *Sherlock Jr.* are from the library of Karl Thiede.

253 "It had always occurred": Keaton, "Why I Never Smile."

253 "Well, we went to work": BK to Pratt.

253 "Now you go back": Bishop, "An Interview with Buster Keaton."

253 "So I tear up": BK to Friedman.

254 "I said, 'I've got'": BK to Brownlow, *Buster Keaton Interviews*, p. 192.

255 "For two whole days": *Los Angeles Times*, 5/25/1924.

255 "a fine little ship": E. B. White, "The Years of Wonder," *The New Yorker*, 3/13/1961. Previously, the *Buford* had been famous as the "Soviet Ark" used to deport 249 immigrant

radicals rounded up during the Palmer Raids conducted by the U.S. Department of Justice in 1919–20.

256 "The opening gag": BK to Pratt.

256 "I said to him, 'You don't' ": BK to Brownlow, *Buster Keaton Interviews,* p. 203.

257 "Nothing to do": BK to Robert and Joan Franklin.

257 "the camera withdraws": James Agee, "Comedy's Greatest Era," *Life,* 9/3/1949.

257 "We set the camera out": BK to Feinstein.

257 "We got a camera": BK to Brownlow, *Buster Keaton Interviews,* p. 209.

258 "In that particular period": Blesh, *Keaton,* pp. 252–53.

258 "We moved our generators": BK to Robert and Joan Franklin.

258 "Toward the end": *Variety,* 8/27/1924.

258 "A director can't do anything": BK to Brownlow, *Buster Keaton Interviews,* p. 203.

258 "But we found that when": Keaton, "Why I Never Smile."

258 "Well, we thought that would": BK to Pratt.

259 "Then I started fixing the leak": Reid, "The Child Who Was 'Abused.' "

259 "It was perfect": BK to Pratt.

259 cost of $385,000: *Variety,* 8/27/1924. In 1964, Keaton told Kevin Brownlow that *The Navigator* cost $220,000. "Our pictures always ran almost a third more in price than the dramatic pictures," he said.

259 "The two fish gags": Reid, "The Child Who Was 'Abused.' "

259 "didn't trust that preview": BK to Pratt.

260 "Could it be": Reid, "The Child Who Was 'Abused.' " Unwilling to let it go, Keaton had the school-of-fish gag inserted into the film's trailer, where, unhindered by context, it finally got the "out-and-out belly laugh" he always felt it would.

260 gross of nearly $26,000: Box office figures on *The Navigator* are from *Variety,* 10/15/1924 and 10/22/1924, and *Billboard,* 10/25/1924. Rental figures for the film are from the library of Karl Thiede. ("Played and paid" numbers in the monthly revenue ledgers of Joseph M. Schenck Productions show $588,749 in worldwide rentals for *The Navigator* as of December 25, 1926.)

261 "The laurels are again": *Los Angeles Times,* 11/9/1924.

12 FRIENDLESS

262 "Norma must be consulted": *Los Angeles Times,* 2/24/1924.

262 "Norma and Constance are as devoted": Samuel Goldwyn, *Behind the Screen* (New York: Doran, 1923), p. 225. It is interesting to note that when Peg Talmadge's book *The Talmadge Sisters* was published in November 1924, hometown reviewer George Currie made the following observation in *The Brooklyn Daily Eagle:* "Mrs. Talmadge is at great pains to inform the world that success has not spoiled her daughters; that they are, after all, only human clay; but the undercurrent throughout is a certain wonder that she, an Adam's rib, should have born such marvelous creatures as the Talmadges, *filles.* In this respect there is no reason to quarrel with her. The mother appears to like Constance most, Natalie least. It also appears that Norma did the most work to put the family up in electric lights. Which proves the Talmadge family is normal."

262 "we didn't dare photograph": Blesh, *Keaton,* p. 231.

263 "having got two boys": Blesh, *Keaton,* p. 236.

263 "I like to cook": *Buffalo Sunday Express,* 11/9/1924.

264 "The Muirfield place": Blesh, *Keaton,* p. 237.

264 "He carried no back banner": *Moving Picture World,* 8/2/1924.

265 "It is a singular fact": *Billboard,* 9/13/1924.

265 "six motion picture feature photoplays": Contract between Buster Keaton Productions, Inc., and Buster Keaton, September 1924.

265 "[It] was not a good story": BK to Pratt.

265 "local screwball": Blesh, *Keaton,* p. 258.

265 "the type of unbelievable farce": Ibid.

266 "experimenting with the possibilities": *Exhibitors Trade Review,* 8/16/1924.

266 a courtship exterior: Feature inserts in Technicolor, such as the opening 275 feet of *Seven Chances,* were becoming more common. Similar embellishments were added to *The Phantom of the Opera, The Merry Widow, Ben-Hur,* and *The Sea Beast,* among others. The next all-color feature produced in Hollywood would be Douglas Fairbanks' *The Black Pirate* (1926).

266 "I had an automobile": BK to Brownlow, *Buster Keaton Interviews,* pp. 195–96.

267 "You are the star": *Variety,* 9/24/1924.

267 "When you've got spots": BK to Feinstein.

268 "all shapes and forms": Ibid.

268 "we actually hired": Blesh, *Keaton,* p. 258.

269 "I went down to the dunes": Gillett and Blue, "Keaton at Venice."

269 "At least I was workin' ": BK to Friedman.

270 "When I've got a gag": Gillett and Blue, "Keaton at Venice."

270 "A LAUGHING RIOT": *Moving Picture World,* 3/7/1925.

271 "Joe was to be made president": Charles Chaplin, *My Autobiography* (New York: Simon & Schuster, 1964), p. 295.

271 the situation wasn't getting any better: As recalled by Eleanor Keaton in Oliver Lindsey Scott, *Buster Keaton: The Little Iron Man* (Christchurch, NZ: Buster Books, 1995), p. 174.

272 "It wasn't quite up": *Variety,* 3/18/1925. Box office figures on *Seven Chances* are from *Variety,* 3/25/1925, 4/22/1925, and 4/29/1925, and *Billboard,* 3/28/1925. Rental figures for the film are from the library of Karl Thiede. ("Played and paid" numbers in the monthly revenue ledgers of Joseph M. Schenck Productions show $513,991 in worldwide rentals for *Seven Chances* as of 12/25/1926.)

272 "It is the most uproariously funny": *New York Telegram and Evening Mail,* 3/16/1925.

273 Buster was inconsolable: Details of Captain's funeral are from *Los Angeles Times,* 4/7/1923.

273 "I'm on the side": Carl Hultberg, *Rudi (and Me)* (Middletown, DE: Ragtime Society Press, 2013), p. 67.

274 "about 400 head": *St. Petersburg Times,* 7/19/1925.

274 "I never had a more affectionate pet": Keaton, *My Wonderful World of Slapstick,* p. 142. Kevin Brownlow points out that Brown Eyes was also the name of the character played by Margery Wilson in Griffith's *Intolerance,* a favorite of Keaton's, and that Miriam Cooper's character in the same film was called the Friendless One. "Keaton loved to kid Griffith films," Brownlow says.

274 "didn't take her on location": Keaton, *My Wonderful World of Slapstick,* p. 142.

275 "We were really out in open country": BK to Pratt.

276 "I always preferred": Keaton, *My Wonderful World of Slapstick,* p. 142.

276 "I was going to do everything": Gillett and Blue, "Keaton at Venice."

277 "I brought 'em up": BK to Pratt.

277 "But then I thought that by goin' ": Ibid.

279 "tearing for his life": *Los Angeles Times,* 8/29/1926.

279 "We didn't dare speed them up": Blesh, *Keaton*, p. 264.

279 "because I'm known as frozen face": Gillett and Blue, "Keaton at Venice."

279 "Our mistake probably was that": Keaton, "Why I Never Smile."

279 "We didn't find out": Gillett and Blue, "Keaton at Venice."

281 "It seems rather silly": *Chicago Daily News*, 12/17/1925.

281 "Some parts I like": BK to Pratt.

281 *Go West* played: Box office figures on *Go West* are from *Variety*, 11/4/1925 and 11/18/1925. The library of Karl Thiede shows that worldwide rentals for *Go West* came to just under $600,000. ("Played and paid" numbers in the monthly revenue ledgers of Joseph M. Schenck Productions show $430,372 in worldwide rentals as of December 25, 1926.)

281 "I'm working on top": Gallico, "Polyandry for All."

282 "terrible flop when he tried": Keaton, *My Wonderful World of Slapstick*, p. 131.

283 "Saturday evening was picture night": *Bakersfield Californian*, 1/12/1926.

283 "I told the original story": BK to Pratt.

284 "That's the greatest battle": Unidentified clipping (courtesy of Patricia Eliot Tobias).

285 "We will never have": *Motion Picture News*, 3/20/1926.

13 THE GENERAL

286 "It cost only $33,000": Keaton, *My Wonderful World of Slapstick*, p. 181.

287 "Clyde Bruckman run into": BK to Pratt.

287 "Nothing I had ever heard": William Pittenger, *The Great Locomotive Chase* (Philadelphia: Penn Publishing, 1910), p. 22. The story of the Andrews raid was originally filmed as a one-reel subject produced by Kalem in 1911. Made near Jacksonville, Florida, *The Railroad Raiders of '62* was directed by Sidney Olcott.

288 "They lost the war": BK to Brownlow, *Buster Keaton Interviews*, p. 206.

288 The character he envisioned: Keaton's character in *The General* is actually an amalgam of the three men, led by the train's conductor, William A. Fuller, who pursued the stolen engine.

288 "The moment you give": Gillett and Blue, "Keaton at Venice."

288 "I went to the original location": BK to Brownlow, *Buster Keaton Interviews*, p. 179.

289 "A person has to work hard": *Eugene Guard*, 5/7/1926.

289 Back in Hollywood . . . Annabelle Lee: It should be noted that in Clyde Bruckman's draft script, Marion Mack's character was given the temporary name of Virginia, while Keaton's character was simply Buster. A major decision to be made during the titling process was to settle on the final names of the principal characters. Those names, Annabelle Lee and Johnnie Gray, have been used throughout for clarity.

290 "Buster was looking for": Richard J. Anobile, ed., *Buster Keaton's* The General (New York: Darien House, 1975), p. 13.

290 "Buster didn't say much": Ibid.

291 "The city of Marietta": *Eugene Morning Register*, 6/6/1926.

292 "We'd better have a dog or two": *Cottage Grove Sentinel*, 6/10/1926.

292 "The situation of the picture": Gillett and Blue, "Keaton at Venice."

293 "As he answered a reporter's questions": *Cottage Grove Sentinel*, 6/10/1926.

296 "the best thing we have": *Eugene Guard*, 7/3/1936.

296 "I staged it exactly": Gillett and Blue, "Keaton at Venice."

296 "The script they took": Marion Mack to Kevin Brownlow in interview footage shot for the documentary *Buster Keaton: A Hard Act to Follow* (1987).

298 a contract was let: Details of the events leading up to the destruction of the bridge and

the locomotive are from various issues of *The Cottage Grove Sentinel*, *The Eugene Guard*, *The Eugene Morning Register*, *The Corvallis Gazette-Times*, and *The Klamath Falls Evening Herald*. See also: *The Day Buster Smiled* (Cottage Grove: Eugene Print, 1998) in which the Cottage Grove Historical Society presents a collection of contemporary news items and articles from the *Sentinel*.

299 "It really knocked me down": Marion Mack to Kevin Brownlow in interview footage shot for the documentary series *Hollywood*, Photoplay Productions, 1979.

299 "I think I got that kiss": Anobile, *Buster Keaton's* The General, p. 14.

300 "I marched more there": Ronald Gilstrap to Kevin Brownlow in interview footage shot for the documentary *Buster Keaton: A Hard Act to Follow* (1987).

300 "Not satisfied to stand": *Eugene Guard*, 7/24/1926.

300 "He didn't direct much": Gregg Rickman, "Marion Mack 50 Years Later," *Cobblestone*, Summer 1977.

300 "There was an awful lot": Grace Matteson to Kevin Brownlow in interview footage shot for the documentary *Buster Keaton: A Hard Act to Follow* (1987).

302 realistic dummies: The *Cottage Grove Sentinel* published a report that Keaton himself had wanted to be the engineer on the Texas and leap clear of the engine as it fell, but that Natalie had nixed the idea. Grace Matteson recalled a rumor that one of the engineers was offered a hundred dollars to make the leap, but it seems unlikely that either idea was ever seriously considered.

302 "I was pulling them out": Gilstrap to Brownlow.

302 "Come on, gang": *Eugene Guard*, 7/24/1926.

303 "I'd just started to dance": Kieth Fennell to Kevin Brownlow in interview footage shot for the documentary *Buster Keaton: A Hard Act to Follow* (1987).

303 "When my picture ended": Gillett and Blue, "Keaton at Venice."

303 "Oh, the sparks!": Gene Woodward Barnes to Kevin Brownlow in interview footage shot for the documentary *Buster Keaton: A Hard Act to Follow* (1987).

304 "I had never worked": Anobile, *Buster Keaton's* The General, p. 15.

304 "I liked Mr. Keaton": Rickman, "Marion Mack 50 Years Later."

304 "One of the first gags": Anobile, *Buster Keaton's* The General, p. 15.

305 "The one that gave us the most trouble": Ibid.

305 "Some of the supposed indoor scenes": Anobile, *Buster Keaton's* The General, p. 16.

305 "There is not a prouder man": *Los Angeles Times*, 8/29/1926.

306 "rather jubilant": *Eugene Guard*, 8/30/1926.

306 "I had to handle it": Rickman, "Marion Mack 50 Years Later."

307 "There was a fellow called Al Boasberg": Ibid.

307 "Buster himself": *San Bernardino Sun*, 10/16/1926.

309 "Every gag": *Roseburg News-Review*, 11/15/1926.

14 *STEAMBOAT BILL, JR.*

310 "The thing that has impressed me": *Variety*, 10/20/1926.

311 "The problem of sites": *Los Angeles Times*, 6/13/1926.

312 *"Publicity man"*: *Oakland Tribune*, 2/2/1925.

312 "Not since the halcyon days": *Film Daily*, 8/26/1926.

313 "It was a two-story mansion": Keaton, *My Wonderful World of Slapstick*, p. 182.

314 "These old-world": Talmadge, *The Talmadge Sisters*, p. 168.

314 "I designed": Keaton, *My Wonderful World of Slapstick*, p. 182.

314 "I hope, Buster": Keaton, *My Wonderful World of Slapstick*, p. 183.

315 "Amusing": *Exhibitors Herald,* 1/8/1927.

315 mixed evidence: In his 1964 interview with Kevin Brownlow, Keaton estimated the cost of *The General* at "around $330,000," about $85,000 less than records indicate.

316 "Hardly a foot": *Brooklyn Daily Eagle,* 2/7/1927.

316 "*The General* is no triumph": *New York Sun,* 2/8/1927.

316 "The story is a burlesque": *Variety,* 2/9/1927.

316 "Keaton's previous picture": *Billboard,* 2/19/1927.

316 "somewhat mirthless piece": *New York Times,* 2/13/1927.

316 "The camera work is good": *New York Telegraph,* 2/8/1927.

317 "Such uncommon comedians": *Brooklyn Daily Eagle,* 2/13/1927.

318 "I hadn't because I'd been reading": Bishop, "An Interview with Buster Keaton."

318 "It is difficult": Robert E. Sherwood, "The Silent Drama," *Life,* 2/24/1927. *The General* was actually banned in Ohio after complaints that events surrounding the Andrews raid were depicted with "undue levity."

318 "Well, he was a little sensitive": BK to Pratt.

318 "ranked among the few genuinely great": Robert E. Sherwood, "The Silent Drama," *Life,* 12/10/1925.

318 The returns at the Capitol: Box office figures on *The General* are from *Variety,* 1/19/1927, 1/26/1927, 2/2/1927, 2/16/1927, and 3/23/1927. Domestic rental figures for the film are from the library of Karl Thiede and reflect producer settlement statements dating to December 28, 1935. Foreign rentals can be estimated at $348,131, which are the actual figures reported for the 1928 Keaton feature *Steamboat Bill, Jr.,* which was also distributed by United Artists. (According to Thiede, all known foreign rentals for Keaton's features, both silent and sound, fall within the same general range.) Worldwide rentals under this formula come to $834,596, with the producer's share amounting to $586,134. This yields a profit of $122,190 for Buster Keaton Productions, Inc., once the negative cost of $415,232 and United Artists Corporation distribution charges are deducted. See also David Weddle, "Show Us the Money," *The Keaton Chronicle,* Summer 2002.

319 "Buster was in the audience": *Los Angeles Evening Herald,* 3/12/1927.

319 "*The General,* especially recommended": *Los Angeles Record,* 3/12/1927.

319 "It was the title": Brownlow, "The Search for Buster Keaton," p. 126.

320 "Think it the best Keaton": *Exhibitors Herald,* 3/12/1927.

320 "Marion sold the idea": Keaton, *My Wonderful World of Slapstick,* p. 195.

321 "But then they didn't like the rushes": Marion Davies, *The Times We Had* (Indianapolis: Bobbs-Merrill, 1975), p. 111.

321 "an idiotic screen morsel": *Variety,* 2/16/1927.

322 "He didn't write nothing": BK to Brownlow, *Buster Keaton Interviews,* p. 175.

323 "absolutely useless": BK to Brownlow, *Buster Keaton Interviews,* p. 210. Brownlow points out that James W. Horne had directed some important features, such as *The Yankee Consul* (1924) with Douglas MacLean.

323 "I was called over": Harold Goodwin to Alan Hoffman, Woodland Hills, 10/29/1975 (courtesy of Alan Hoffman).

324 "Jimmy Horne—he was probably": Harold Goodwin to Robert S. Birchard, Woodland Hills, CA, 3/16/1976 (courtesy of Robert S. Birchard).

324 "But once he was on the job": Blesh, *Keaton,* p. 284.

324 "Well, Snitz Edwards": Goodwin to Birchard.

326 "fine old couples": *Variety,* 3/23/1927.

326 "I worked with Keaton": Brownlow, "The Search for Buster Keaton," p. 131.

327 "We knew from bitter experience": Bawden and Miller, *You Ain't Heard Nothin' Yet*, p. 16.

327 "I could not do the scene": Brundidge, *Twinkle, Twinkle, Movie Star!*, p. 209.

327 "We'd make five attempts": Goodwin to Hoffman.

328 "Chuck's story": Keaton, *My Wonderful World of Slapstick*, p. 203.

328 "Miss Byron has never worked": *Sacramento Bee*, 7/22/1927. Marion Byron did some extra work prior to working with Keaton, but *Steamboat Bill, Jr.* was her first prominent role in a picture.

329 "pretty young girls": *Sacramento Bee*, 7/18/1927.

330 "We're having a wonderful time": *Sacramento Union*, 8/15/1927.

330 "We're using panchromatic stock": In 1927, ordinary commercial film negative was sensitive to blues and blue-greens only. The colors green, yellow, and red hardly registered, so sets and makeups had to be designed accordingly. Orthochromatic stock was an improvement, sensitive to greens as well as blues and violets. But blue eyes still came out as "fish eyes" and yellows registered as black. Then Eastman introduced panchromatic film that was sensitive to the entire visible spectrum and recognized natural skin tones as well as the full tonal range of exteriors. In 1928, panchromatic stock displaced orthochromatic as the new industry standard.

330 "We obtained our source material": *Sacramento Bee*, 7/21/1927.

331 "They had this great old riverboat": Dean Reisner to Kevin Brownlow in interview footage shot for the documentary *Buster Keaton: A Hard Act to Follow* (1987).

331 "I'm sort of a long-lost son": *Sacramento Bee*, 7/22/1927.

331 "a mannish young person": *Sacramento Bee*, 8/1/1927.

332 "While *College* will undoubtedly prove": *Los Angeles Times*, 7/30/1927.

332 grossed nearly $30,000: Los Angeles figures for *College* are from *Variety*, 8/10/1927.

332 "I all but jumped out of my seat": Blesh, *Keaton*, p. 285.

332 "The prints—two hundred and fifty": United Artists records show that there were actually 132 prints of *College* in circulation.

332 "Prior to outfitting Keaton": Ira Price, *A Hundred Million Movie-Goers Must Be Right* (Cleveland: Movie Appreciation Press, 1939), p. 126.

333 "Now perhaps it sounds like conceit": Blesh, *Keaton*, p. 285.

333 "There'll be no more supervisors": Blesh, *Keaton*, p. 294.

15 GIVING IN

334 "So many times": Blesh, *Keaton*, p. 297.

334 "He was too big": Blesh, *Keaton*, p. 298.

335 "Take any program": BK to Brownlow, *Buster Keaton Interviews*, p. 187.

335 $879,323 in worldwide rentals: The figure for *Within the Law* is from the monthly revenue ledgers of Joseph M. Schenck Productions.

335 "You are right": Letter, Arthur Kelly to Sydney Chaplin, 4/10/1928 (Chaplin Archive).

336 Keaton's stature: M-G-M's star roster wasn't completely devoid of comedians. By virtue of its distribution of producer Hal Roach's short comedies, the company already had Max Davidson and Charley Chase delivering ten two-reelers apiece each season. Roach also had a new series of shorts starring Stan Laurel and Oliver Hardy. He was, however, not producing features at the time.

337 "We loaned [Keaton] out": Tom Dardis, *Keaton: The Man Who Wouldn't Lie Down* (New York: Scribner, 1979), p. 152. When Friedman says they "loaned" Keaton, he's referring to the percentage of the profits M-G-M agreed to pay Buster Keaton Productions in

exchange for making him available. When he says they loaned Arbuckle, he's referring to the company's 1920 arrangement with Famous Players.

337 "His crew loved him": Brownlow, "The Search for Buster Keaton," p. 131.

337 "Buster was a guy": Blesh, *Keaton*, p. 149.

338 "So Schenck told me": Gillett and Blue, "Keaton at Venice."

338 "I have traveled": *Sacramento Bee*, 8/23/1927.

338 "And a twister": Keaton, *My Wonderful World of Slapstick*, p. 205.

339 "Gabourie, a whiz": Keaton, *My Wonderful World of Slapstick*, pp. 204–5.

339 "The best new gag": Keaton, *My Wonderful World of Slapstick*, p. 205.

340 "First I had them build the framework": Gillett and Blue, "Keaton at Venice."

340 at the south end of the River Junction set: John Bengtson, *Silent Echoes* (Santa Monica: Santa Monica Press, 2000), p. 217.

340 "My father, who was": Reisner to Brownlow.

341 "Two extra women": Brundidge, *Twinkle, Twinkle, Movie Star!*, p. 209.

342 "As a gagman": Blesh, "The Two Worlds of Buster Keaton," p. 175.

343 "piece of stupidity": *New York Times*, 9/18/1927.

343 "This is partly attributable": *Los Angeles Times*, 9/18/1927.

343 gathering worldwide rentals: Figures for *College* are from the library of Karl Thiede.

343 "It must have taken either great courage": *Variety*, 10/19/1927.

343 "as macabre as the end": David Robinson, *Buster Keaton* (Bloomington: Indiana University Press, 1969), p. 156.

344 "Don't let them": Keaton, *My Wonderful World of Slapstick*, p. 202.

344 "He would never say a word": William Cox to Kevin Brownlow in interview footage shot for the documentary *Buster Keaton: A Hard Act to Follow* (1987).

344 "I explained that I wanted": Keaton, *My Wonderful World of Slapstick*, p. 202.

344 "I got myself thoroughly mixed up": Blesh, *Keaton*, p. 298.

345 "What is this thing?": Blesh, *Keaton*, p. 299.

345 "It is stated": *Variety*, 11/16/1927.

346 "The tip is out": *New York Daily News*, 11/19/1927.

346 "I gave in": Keaton, *My Wonderful World of Slapstick*, p. 202.

16 THE CAMERAMAN

347 "In taking this over": BK to Shirley Eder, syndicated radio interview, January 1961 (courtesy of John Slotkin).

348 "When we went down there": Goodwin to Hoffman.

349 Lipton proposed: Lew Lipton, "Buster Keaton Story," first rough draft, 11/28/1927 (MGM).

349 "The story itself": Keaton, *My Wonderful World of Slapstick*, p. 206.

350 "I played child parts": Robert Grau, *The Theatre of Science* (New York: Broadway Publishing, 1914), pp. 372–73.

350 a tintype photographer: Details on the development of *The Cameraman* are from various drafts of the screenplay in the Metro-Goldwyn-Mayer script collection at the Cinematic Arts Library, University of Southern California, and in the Turner/M-G-M script collection at the Margaret Herrick Library.

350 "I wasn't in trouble enough": BK to Feinstein.

351 would be titled *Snapshots*: On scripts, in the press, and on internal studio documents, the title is expressed as both *Snap Shots* and *Snapshots*. For clarity's sake I have standardized on the latter in the text.

351 "not enough comedy": *Variety,* 3/7/1928.

351 "It's the simplest story": BK to Pratt.

351 a Pathé: According to camera collector Carroll Gray, Keaton's camera in the picture is a vintage Prevost, not a Pathé. "Was the Prevost considered a good camera in 1910–1912? Yes it was. . . . Universal bought some sixteen of them . . . and yes, by 1928 it was considered seriously out-of-date," he says.

352 "The first shot": Keaton, *My Wonderful World of Slapstick,* p. 209.

353 At City Hall Park: The first days of filming in New York were covered in the *New York Sun.*

353 "Clyde Bruckman knew": Brownlow, "The Search for Buster Keaton," p. 145.

353 six scripted scenes: Details on the making of *The Cameraman* are from the daily production reports in the Metro-Goldwyn-Mayer collection at USC.

354 "I walked on": Blesh, *Keaton,* p. 303.

354 "You had to requisition a toothpick": Ibid.

354 "For a half hour": Blesh, *Keaton,* p. 304.

355 "Each bathhouse": Keaton, *My Wonderful World of Slapstick,* p. 211.

355 "The scene ran for four minutes": Keaton, *My Wonderful World of Slapstick,* p. 212.

356 monkey named Josephine: Years later, Keaton remembered the monkey's name as Josephine, but some contemporary press reports had the animal's name as "Chicago" and said that he was the same monkey who worked with Harold Lloyd in *The Kid Brother.* In 1952, the monkey, under the name Josephine, was featured in William Wyler's *Carrie.* See also: Ruth M. Tildesley, "The Temperamental Dumb," *Picture Play,* February 1929.

356 "Now here's the thinking": Goodwin to Birchard.

356 "You can't ever forget": Goodwin to Hoffman.

357 M-G-M advertised: *Santa Ana Register,* 5/18/1928.

358 Constance Talmadge's career: Her latest picture for First National, *Venus of Venice,* had returned just $60,574 in domestic rentals, a disastrous showing.

358 "All the social strata": *New York Daily News,* 11/19/1927.

358 Of Schenck's personal productions: Figures for these productions are from the library of Karl Thiede.

359 "more ups and downs": *New York Evening Post,* 2/18/1928.

359 "the last comedy": *Variety,* 5/16/1928.

359 "We cannot remember": These critical comments were summarized in *Film Daily,* 5/27/1928.

359 the resulting business was disappointing: Box office figures for *Steamboat Bill, Jr.* are from *Variety,* 5/30/1928 and 6/20/1928.

360 worldwide rentals to $723,400: Figures for *Steamboat Bill, Jr.* are from the library of Karl Thiede and reflect producer settlement statements dating to December 28, 1935.

361 "Can you speak Chinese": "Gossip of All the Studios," *Photoplay,* September 1928.

361 "Finally I said, 'Sedgwick wouldn't'": BK to Brownlow, *Buster Keaton Interviews,* p. 211.

362 "It was a western": Bogdanovich, *Who the Devil Made It,* p. 96. Although Dwan said he kept the Keaton stunt in as "a bit of atmosphere," it doesn't survive in the picture today.

362 "He loved to barbecue": Brownlow, "The Search for Buster Keaton," p. 132.

363 "Many others came uninvited": Keaton, *My Wonderful World of Slapstick,* p. 184.

363 "Keaton was a very quiet guy": Brownlow, "The Search for Buster Keaton," p. 131.

363 "I didn't seem to have any choice": BK to Pratt.

364 melodrama *West of Zanzibar:* Cost and rental figures for *West of Zanzibar* and *The Kiss* are from the Edgar J. "Eddie" Mannix ledger at the Margaret Herrick Library.

364 "We didn't shoot by no schedule": BK to Pratt.

364 Following the pattern: Details on the development of *Spite Marriage* are from various drafts of the screenplay at USC and the Margaret Herrick Library.

365 "One feels quite sorry": *New York Times*, 9/17/1928.

365 "undoubtedly one of the funniest": *Brooklyn Daily Eagle*, 9/18/1928.

365 Box office for the week at the Capitol: Box office figures for *The Cameraman* are from *Variety*, 9/26/1928 and 10/24/1928.

365 worldwide rentals of $797,000: Cost and rental figures for *The Cameraman* are from the library of Karl Thiede and the Mannix ledger.

366 Thalberg passed supervision: Although Weingarten claimed toward the end of his life that he produced *The Cameraman* as well as *Spite Marriage,* his name does not appear on any of the daily production reports for the film, which consistently identify Eddie Mannix as supervisor. Moreover, Weingarten married Sylvia Thalberg on June 2, 1928, while *The Cameraman* was still in production and would have presumably been on his honeymoon during a critical phase of the film's making.

366 M-G-M formalized: Letter, J. Robert Rubin to Joseph H. Moskowitz, 10/9/1928.

367 In October, Keaton signed over: Assignment, Joseph F. Keaton to Natalie T. Keaton, 10/30/1928. California was—and is—a community property state, so assigning a portion of one's income to a spouse would yield no obvious tax advantage.

367 "My wife was forever hearing": Keaton, *My Wonderful World of Slapstick*, p. 224.

367 "She couldn't act": Charles Francis, *Encounters: A Memoir* (Bloomington: iUniverse, 2014), p. 83.

367 "I remember the day": Tim McCoy, *Tim McCoy Remembers the West* (Garden City, NY: Doubleday, 1977), p. 238.

368 Keaton, who was rarely sick: Details on the making of *Spite Marriage* are from the daily production reports (MGM).

369 "a series of Rube Goldberg": Richard Schayer, *Spite Marriage;* continuity okayed by Irving Thalberg, 11/7/1928 (MGM).

370 superb physical comedy: After Keaton's death, Larry Weingarten made the ridiculous claim that he—and not Keaton—developed this scene and convinced a reluctant Buster to do it. This calls into question everything he had to say about Keaton in the multiple interviews he gave late in life.

370 "Buster came up": Helen Ludlam, "Yo Ho Ho! and a Buster Keaton Location," *Screen-land*, March 1929.

370 popular songs with an accordionist: Among the songs for which Edward Sedgwick wrote music and lyrics were "You Told Me to Go," "Just Remember," and "You Can't Fly Over Dixie."

371 Budgeted at $264,493: *Spite Marriage* was brought in at a negative cost of $282,215. These cost figures are from the library of Karl Thiede and the Mannix ledger.

MONTREAL, QUEBEC

373 "It was a great prop": BK to Brownlow, *Buster Keaton Interviews*, p. 190.

373 "He knew by the sound": Potterton to the author.

374 "he was the film director": Ibid.

375 "On that first day of shooting": Gerald Potterton, "Simply the Best," *The Great Stone Face* (New York: International Buster Keaton Society, 1996), p. 24. Although Potterton recalled the first day of filming as taking place in Halifax, the Film Board's camera reports confirm that the first day of filming took place in Montreal on September 5, 1964. The first shots in Halifax were made on September 8.

17 THE GAG DAY IS OVER

379   "*The Jazz Singer*": Scott Eyman, *The Speed of Sound* (New York: Simon & Schuster, 1997), p. 176.

380   "No talking picture": *Billboard*, 9/1/1928.

380   "I have never seen anything like it": *Exhibitors Daily Review*, 9/21/1928.

381   "Even those of us who are extreme": *New York Evening Post*, 3/23/1929.

382   "a cheap dull affair": Chaplin, *My Autobiography*, p. 324.

382   "Words can hardly tell of the relief": *New York Times*, 3/25/1929.

383   "*Spite Marriage* is a silent picture": *New York Evening Post*, 3/26/1929.

383   "Although the frozen-faced Buster": *New York Daily News*, 3/26/1929.

383   "a knockout for laughs": *Billboard*, 4/6/1929.

384   "I talked like a Dutch uncle": Blesh, *Keaton*, p. 311.

384   "sacrificed to emergency": *Variety*, 4/3/1929.

384   With the headwinds, domestic rentals: Rental figures for *Spite Marriage* are from the library of Karl Thiede and the Mannix ledger.

384   "The silent film": *New York Times*, 5/26/1929.

384   "He had quite a crush": Goodwin to Hoffman.

385   "I would give anything": *New York Times Herald*, 4/15/1929.

385   "Dorothy was sweet, funny": Francis, *Encounters*, p. 83.

385   "Buster was very sexy": Letter, Louise Brooks to Tom Dardis, 10/26/1977 (AMPAS).

386   "We talk when we're supposed to": BK to Markle.

386   "New York stage directors": Ibid.

386   Keaton counted twenty-two writers: Keaton, *My Wonderful World of Slapstick*, p. 208.

388   "The romance of picture making": Laurence Irving, *Designing for the Movies* (Lanham, MD: Scarecrow Press, 2005), p. 40.

388   "I don't think M-G-M knew": Brownlow, "The Search for Buster Keaton," p. 132.

388   "talkie mood": Brundidge, *Twinkle, Twinkle, Movie Star!*, p. 205.

388   "If Buster Keaton had been still": Lawrence Weingarten interview for the M-G-M/Louis B. Mayer Oral History Project, circa 1973 (courtesy of Karl Thiede).

388   "Right from the start of talkies": *Columbus Citizen-Journal*, 1/9/1961.

389   due to an equipment breakdown: Details on the making of *Free and Easy* are from the daily production reports (MGM).

389   "He rushed on the set": Blesh, *Keaton*, p. 303.

389   "Everything got so technical": Bart Williams, "Maaaaarvelous Darling . . . You Found Me," *The Keaton Chronicle*, Spring 2000.

389   "I don't think he enjoyed": Martha Jett, "He Was an Absolute Doll!" *The Keaton Chronicle*, Spring 2000.

390   "He thought that clown-face thing": Geraldine Hawkins, "The Friendship of Buster Keaton and Loyal Lucas," *The Keaton Chronicle*, Winter 1998.

390   Estimated at $439,782: Budget and cost figures for *Free and Easy* are from the library of Karl Thiede and studio summary sheets dated 3/2/1948 and 9/9/1957.

390   Keaton never said publicly: In later years, Keaton tended to conflate *Free and Easy*, which he mistakenly said in his autobiography "was among the company's biggest moneymakers of the year," with the film that followed it, *Doughboys*, which was far more profitable.

391   "I kept pleading": Keaton, *My Wonderful World of Slapstick*, p. 212. In his autobiography, Keaton has this discussion with Thalberg after *The Cameraman*, while Blesh, whose work with Keaton came a few years earlier, has it coming after *Free and Easy*.

391   "In writing this story": Willard Mack, *Fix Bayonets*, 1/8/1930.

392 With a budget: Budget and scheduling figures for *Doughboys* are from the library of Karl Thiede and studio summary sheets dated 2/27/1948.

392 "When darkness fell": Keaton, *My Wonderful World of Slapstick,* p. 72.

393 "Buster Keaton needed excitement": Blesh, *Keaton,* p. 321.

393 "I never liked the idiot cards": Keaton, *My Wonderful World of Slapstick,* p. 239.

393 "a noisy trip": *Los Angeles Times,* 4/12/1930.

394 "very much like that of Dante's Satan": *Hollywood Filmograph,* 4/19/1930.

394 It opened in New York: Box office figures for *Free and Easy* are from *Variety,* 4/16/1930 and 4/30/1930.

394 "strictly a routine programmer": *Variety,* 4/23/1930.

394 "just one of those things": *Film Daily,* 4/20/1930.

394 "Keaton in the talkies": *Brooklyn Daily Eagle,* 4/27/1930.

394 On the fifth day: Details on the making of *Doughboys* are from the daily production reports (MGM).

396 "I would say [on] *Doughboys*": Gil Perkins to Kevin Brownlow in interview footage shot for the documentary *Buster Keaton: A Hard Act to Follow* (1987).

396 "Audiences are still used to": *Film Daily,* 12/10/1929.

397 "YOU ARE FURTHER ADVISED": Telegram, Irving Thalberg to BK, 6/3/1930 (courtesy of Edward Watz).

397 "Without stars": Irving Thalberg to Nicholas Schenck, undated draft memo, circa 1932.

398 "It's just like the candymaker": Martin Regan, "Why I Can't Laugh," *Screen Mirror,* June 1930.

399 "While the comedian is away": *Los Angeles Times,* 7/16/1930.

399 "a riot of cross purposes": *Hollywood Filmograph,* 7/19/1930.

399 "It was abandoned": Gilbert Roland, "Wine of Yesterday," unpublished autobiography, pp. 285–87 (AMPAS).

400 "The picture is moderately amusing": *New York Daily News,* 9/20/1930.

400 "There is a mechanical": *New York Sun,* 9/23/1930.

400 "Keaton I got to know": Robert M. W. Vogel to Barbara Hall, Academy of Motion Picture Arts and Sciences Oral History, 5/11/1990, p. 152 (AMPAS).

401 negative cost of $572,557: Figures for *Doughboys* are from the library of Karl Thiede and the Mannix ledger.

401 "We were desperate": Dardis, *Keaton: The Man Who Wouldn't Lie Down,* p. 190.

401 "He really did not want": Sam Marx to Kevin Brownlow in interview footage shot for the documentary *Buster Keaton: A Hard Act to Follow* (1987).

402 "Farce comedy, as a rule": BK to Robert and Joan Franklin.

404 "We did one of our scenes": Grant Hayter-Menzies, *Charlotte Greenwood* (Jefferson, NC: McFarland, 2007), p. 110.

404 an astounding $36,967: Cost and scheduling figures for *Parlor, Bedroom and Bath* are from the library of Karl Thiede and studio summary sheets dated August 2, 1944.

404 "When Metro put Keaton": *The Film Spectator,* 4/11/1931.

405 "There I was": Blesh, *Keaton,* p. 314.

18 RUNNING AROUND LOOSE

406 "a strange little kid": Dorothy Manners, "The Girl Friend Makes Good," *Picture Play,* September 1924.

406 "I think I'm a little crazy": Margaret Reid, "Beauty and Bad Luck," *Picture Play,* December 1926.

406 "Two years off the screen": Ibid.

407 "She was no good": Goodwin to Hoffman.

407 "After working one day": Manners, "The Girl Friend Makes Good."

407 "Miss Key came back": *San Francisco Examiner,* 2/6/1931.

407 "Another attorney came": Ibid.

408 "She blew up": *Los Angeles Times,* 2/6/1931.

408 "Call up Mr. Keaton": *Los Angeles Examiner,* 2/5/1931.

408 boxing exhibitions: *Boston Globe,* 2/6/1931.

409 "Hollywood this morning": *Spokane Spokesman Review,* 2/6/1931.

409 "What a joke!": *Los Angeles Times,* 2/7/1931.

409 "all mixed up": When Keaton described the incident to Rudi Blesh some twenty-five years later, he conjured a story completely at odds with contemporary press accounts. "Somebody brought a girl, a bit player, to my bungalow for lunch. Late that afternoon [Willie Riddle] had gone, and I was there alone. She came back. 'I've decided,' she announced, 'to let you keep me.' 'Just dandy,' I said, 'and now, kid, I've got news for you. I'm not keeping you or anybody. Now flag your ass out of here quick.'" Kathleen Key died in 1954.

409 "They served my brother and I": James Talmadge to Patricia Eliot Tobias, Santa Ynez, CA, circa 1999 (courtesy of Patricia Eliot Tobias).

410 "There was no other girl": Keaton, *My Wonderful World of Slapstick,* p. 224.

410 "If she doesn't get it": Keaton, *My Wonderful World of Slapstick,* p. 225.

410 "Demand for comedies": *Variety,* 10/13/1931.

411 "It's too late": Keaton, *My Wonderful World of Slapstick,* p. 212.

411 "I read the story": Keaton, *My Wonderful World of Slapstick,* p. 239.

411 "The house chuckled": *Inside Facts of Stage and Screen,* 3/21/1931.

412 "They'd say, 'This is funny'": BK to Robert and Joan Franklin.

412 "I knew before the camera": Blesh, *Keaton,* p. 313.

413 "alternated telling me": Blesh, *Keaton,* p. 324.

413 "[Buster] was unhappy": Jett, "He Was an Absolute Doll!"

413 "have a whole group": William M. Drew, *At the Center of the Frame* (Lanham: Vestal Press, 1999), p. 165.

413 "Buster was an introvert": Jules White to the author, Sherman Oaks, CA, 4/9/1975.

414 "At the preview": Keaton, *My Wonderful World of Slapstick,* p. 240.

414 "The Keaton house": Louise Brooks to Tom Dardis, 4/7/1977 (AMPAS).

415 "I know of no woman": Blesh, *Keaton,* p. 327.

415 "I know my son": Ibid.

415 "It was all very gay": *New York Times,* 7/26/1931.

416 "That was an old trick": Weingarten interview for the Mayer Oral History Project.

416 "If they had known": Keaton, *My Wonderful World of Slapstick,* p. 236.

416 "entirely wrong": Blesh, *Keaton,* p. 325.

417 "In Buster Keaton's heyday": *Variety,* 11/17/1931.

417 "It came out such a complete stinker": Blesh, *Keaton,* p. 324.

417 "Buster used to have a group": Marx to Brownlow.

418 "He tried hard": Blesh, *Keaton,* p. 325.

418 "I make it a rule": Keaton, *My Wonderful World of Slapstick,* p. 242.

419 "a laughfest": *Hollywood Filmograph,* 1/23/1932.

419 "Durante just can't keep quiet": BK to Robert and Joan Franklin.

420 "There is some comedy of merit": *Variety,* 3/14/1932.

420 "I got to the stage": BK to Robert and Joan Franklin.

421 "Buster arrived": Marcel Oms, *Buster Keaton* (Lyon: Société d'Etudes, Recherches et Documentation Cinématographiques, 1964), p. 79.

421 "This is to advise you": Letter, Louis B. Mayer to BK, 4/8/1932 (courtesy of Edward Watz).

422 "He was drunk": Donald McNamara, "Lulu in Rochester: Self-Portrait of an Anti-Star," *Missouri Review,* Summer 1983.

423 badly scratched: Having declared bankruptcy in New York, Louise Brooks returned to Hollywood to look for work. On April 4, Myra Keaton told the *Los Angeles Times* that her son had suffered "a badly scratched eye in a scuffle with friends" and that a hemorrhage that developed was being treated with hot applications. "Sunday night I stayed at his home to apply hot towels to his eye; his sister was there Saturday for the same purpose."

423 "I don't care to make any trouble": *Los Angeles Examiner,* 4/5/1932.

423 "I just went to show": *Los Angeles Examiner,* 4/6/1932.

424 "It was just stubbornness": *Los Angeles Examiner,* 4/7/1932.

425 "This is a perfect story": Alexina Brune, synopsis of the novel *Footlights* by Clarence Budington Kelland, 2/9/1932 (MGM).

425 "Sound comedy": Dardis, *Keaton: The Man Who Wouldn't Lie Down,* p. 187.

425 "On the way out": Hawkins, "The Friendship of Buster Keaton and Loyal Lucas."

426 "was very much like the real Jimmy": Keaton, *My Wonderful World of Slapstick,* p. 237.

427 "We'll make the ship our floating home": *Oakland Tribune,* 6/28/1932.

428 "There isn't the remotest chance": *San Francisco Examiner,* 7/16/1932.

428 "I don't mind": *Los Angeles Examiner,* 7/18/1932.

429 Kathleen Key incident: From Paris, Kathleen Key sent word via *Variety* that she was "not too pleased at being dragged into [the] Buster Keaton divorce proceedings."

429 She also put the boat: Margaret Talmadge quickly arranged the sale of the yacht to Lynn Atkinson, a local contractor, for an undisclosed price.

429 "My husband was impossible": *Los Angeles Examiner,* 8/9/1932.

429 "Social engagements caused": *New York Daily News,* 8/9/1932.

429 "*Speak Easily* is another very funny": *New York Daily News,* 8/2/1932.

430 a profit of just $33,000: Figures for *Speak Easily* are from the library of Karl Thiede and the Mannix ledger.

430 "I think the audience started": Brownlow, "The Search for Buster Keaton," p. 133.

430 "Listen": William Collier, Jr., to Tom Dardis (courtesy of Edward Watz).

431 "I saw it begin": Blesh, *Keaton,* p. 321.

431 "I had as much fun": Keaton, *My Wonderful World of Slapstick,* p. 231.

432 "We would park it": *Los Angeles Herald-Examiner,* 6/7/1962.

434 "I was trying to drink away": Keaton, *My Wonderful World of Slapstick,* pp. 237–38.

434 "Most pathetic": Gilbert Roland, diary entry, December 1932 (AMPAS).

435 "Buster started it": *New York Daily News,* 1/14/1933. It's interesting to note that this wasn't the only time Joe and Buster got together to, in a sense, re-create the family act. In December 1917, Roscoe Arbuckle and his associates at Comique offered a seven-act Christmas show at several army camps in Southern California. Joe and Buster opened the live-entertainment portion of the show, which also featured Valerie Bergere, Arbuckle, Sophye Barnard, Lou Anger, and Alice Lake. Then, in November 1938, Joe, Buster, and Myra took the stage as The Three Keatons one final time during a performance of the Federal Theatre Project's vaudeville re-creation *Two-a-Day* at the Hollywood Playhouse.

435 Smelling smoke: *San Francisco Examiner,* 1/15/1933.

435 "That trailer": Marx to Brownlow.

436 "The picture needs plenty of trimming": *Hollywood Reporter,* 1/31/1933.

436 "for good and sufficient cause": Dardis, *Keaton: The Man Who Wouldn't Lie Down,* p. 225.

19 CRASH IN TO MY LIFE

437 Buster Keaton wept: Herb Howe, "Our Hollywood Boulevardier Denies Everything," *New Movie,* July 1933.

438 "Like so many old pinochle": Keaton, *My Wonderful World of Slapstick,* p. 185.

438 "I was anything but": Marx to Brownlow.

439 "is finished at M-G-M": *Hollywood Reporter,* 2/3/1933.

440 "When we returned, Dr. Martin": Keaton, *My Wonderful World of Slapstick,* p. 245.

441 married in Ensenada: In his 1979 biography, *Keaton: The Man Who Wouldn't Lie Down,* author Tom Dardis makes the claim that Mae Scriven had a previous alcoholic patient in comedian Joe E. Brown "who had required her services more than once. She had made strong efforts to land Brown, but he managed to slip through the net she had cast for him. Buster was not so lucky." Dardis gives no source for this, and it appears he simply made it up. There is no evidence that Brown (1891–1973) and Scriven were connected in any way, or that Brown was even an alcoholic. In fact, one former co-worker of the period recalled that Brown didn't drink at all. Moreover, he was unavailable for poaching, having married in 1915, a union that remained strong until his death in 1973. He was, by all accounts, a devoted family man. (Special thanks to Edward Watz.)

441 "I'm just out for a good time": *El Paso Herald-Post,* 2/28/1933.

442 "either kidding": *San Bernardino Sun,* 3/2/1933.

442 "By that time": Keaton, *My Wonderful World of Slapstick,* p. 241.

442 "I always thought that Buster": Marx to Brownlow.

442 business at the Capitol: Box office figures for *What—No Beer?* are from *Variety,* 2/14/1933 and 2/21/1933. Cost and rental figures are from the library of Karl Thiede and the Mannix ledger.

443 "Losing out at M-G-M": Keaton, *My Wonderful World of Slapstick,* p. 244.

443 "We tried to keep our marriage quiet": *El Paso Times,* 3/2/1933.

443 "I'll be around": *Los Angeles Times,* 3/4/1933.

443 "attempt to straighten out financial matters": *San Bernardino County Sun,* 3/19/1933.

443 "Of course we are not legally married": *Los Angeles Examiner,* 3/22/1933.

444 "She was the talk of the family": Glenn Scriven to the author, via telephone, 8/29/2017.

445 "Think of it": *Los Angeles Times,* 6/7/1964.

445 "I was determined": Keaton, *My Wonderful World of Slapstick,* p. 244.

445 "who insisted on getting": *Muskegon Chronicle,* 10/7/1933.

445 when Roscoe Arbuckle slipped: *Los Angeles Times,* 6/30/1933.

447 "Clyde Bruckman directed": Goodwin to Hoffman.

447 "Lloyd didn't know": BK to Brownlow, *Buster Keaton Interviews,* p. 175.

447 "I really started to hit the bottle": Keaton, *My Wonderful World of Slapstick,* p. 245.

448 "new flicker *Gland Hotel*": The idea of a *Grand Hotel* travesty was first raised as a blind item in Walter Winchell's column of October 24, 1932. The all-star drama and *Speak Easily* were both in wide release at the time. The proposed casting—ZaSu Pitts in Garbo's role, Keaton in place of John Barrymore's Baron, and Jimmy Durante as Kringelein—suggests that Keaton wasn't the source.

449 "do you have any friends": BK to Eder.

450 "nervous indigestion": *Los Angeles Times,* 9/23/1933.

452 "A personal appearance tour": *San Francisco Examiner*, 10/30/1933.

452 "It starts with three days": Keaton, *My Wonderful World of Slapstick*, p. 246.

453 a small volcano: *Variety*, 11/21/1933.

453 "Buster Keaton celebrating": *San Francisco Examiner*, 1/4/1934.

453 "A writer we had, Ernie Pagano": Charles Lamont to Alan Hoffman, Costa Mesa, CA, 11/7/1975 (courtesy of Alan Hoffman).

454 "Buster Keaton is ill again": *New York Daily News*, 2/9/1934.

454 rocky start: *The Gold Ghost* began filming on February 14, 1934.

454 He is Waddy: The unusual name of Keaton's character (not "Wally" as widely believed) is also a slang term for a cowboy or, as western historian Marshall Trimble clarifies, a "lower-class hired hand on horseback." Usually it is spelled "Waddie," but in a continuity script filed with the Copyright Office, the name is spelled with a "y." (Thanks to Joe Adamson, Paul Gierucki, and Rob Farr.)

454 "Let the others talk their heads off": *Ithaca Journal*, 3/5/1934.

454 "He was practically his own boss": Brownlow, "The Search for Buster Keaton," p. 172.

454 "He was a great joker": *Motion Picture Daily*, 4/4/1934.

456 "a finely executed": *Film Daily*, 3/28/1934.

456 "Buster Keaton is almost a forgotten story": *Variety*, 4/3/1934.

457 "I wish a half-dozen": *Motion Picture Herald*, 11/10/1934.

458 "Buster Keaton will take the loss": *San Francisco Examiner*, 6/1/1934.

458 unashamedly tearful: *Santa Rosa Press-Democrat*, 6/3/1934.

458 "He wrote that this covered my share": Keaton, *My Wonderful World of Slapstick*, pp. 251–52.

459 He scheduled debts: *Los Angeles Times*, 7/15/1934.

459 "A Los Angeles report": *New York Daily News*, 7/17/1934.

461 "There was trouble": Adrian Brunel, *Nice Work* (London: Forbes Robertson, 1949), pp. 176–77.

462 "a big American football type": Brownlow, "The Search for Buster Keaton," p. 170.

462 "being a very good boy": *Fresno Bee*, 10/14/1934.

462 "In between these professional mishaps": Keaton, *My Wonderful World of Slapstick*, p. 246.

463 "The Buster Keatons have stopped": *Glens Falls (NY) Post-Star*, 11/13/1934.

464 "I got so tired": *Salt Lake Telegram*, 8/22/1934.

464 Filling out the cast were Louise Keaton: Louise actually joined Educational before her brother, appearing for Charles Lamont in *Trimmed in Furs* in late 1933.

464 "Speaking behind the camera": Lamont to Hoffman.

465 "Picture contains a certain number": *Variety*, 1/22/1935.

465 "The two of us would work together": Lamont to Hoffman.

467 "When the festivities": *Los Angeles Examiner*, 7/19/1935.

467 "It is the most ridiculous thing": *Los Angeles Times*, 7/18/1935.

467 "Friends of my husband": *Los Angeles Examiner*, 7/22/1935.

468 "I don't want a divorce": *Los Angeles Examiner*, 7/19/1935.

468 "through Mrs. Keaton's association": *Los Angeles Examiner*, 7/30/1935.

468 judgment of divorce: Interlocutory Judgment No. D-134150, Superior Court of the State of California, 10/10/1935.

470 influenza: Details of Keaton's illness and admission to the hospital are from *Los Angeles Times*, 10/20/1935 and 10/21/1935.

470 "a very confused": *Motion Picture Daily*, 10/22/1935.

20 I'VE GOT LOTS OF TIME

471   "Buster Keaton is suffering": *Los Angeles Times,* 10/21/1935.

471   "I know I can help": Unidentified clipping, n.d. (NYPL).

471   "Darling—Please tell": *Los Angeles Examiner,* 10/23/1935.

471   "They won't release you": BK to Brownlow, *Buster Keaton Interviews,* p. 203.

472   "It all depends": *Los Angeles Times,* 11/2/1935.

472   "I'm not interested": Ibid.

472   "Apparently Buster wasn't suffering": *Los Angeles Examiner,* 11/2/1935.

474   "After taking that cure": Keaton, *My Wonderful World of Slapstick,* p. 247.

474   "every cut-out piece": Brunel, *Nice Work,* p. 178.

474   "The staging is cheap": Montgomery, *Comedy Films,* p. 157.

475   "This is a wholly funny": *Variety,* 3/25/1936.

476   brought an action: Details of the court battle between Natalie Talmadge Keaton and Joseph Frank Keaton are from various documents and filings in the Superior Court of the State of California in and for the County of Los Angeles, Case D-105469.

476   "boarding school": Affidavit, Joseph F. Keaton, 10/29/1936.

477   "The boys adored Buster": Louise Keaton to Tom Dardis (courtesy of Edward Watz). In 1936, producer David O. Selznick made tests of the Keaton boys for the roles of Tom and Huck in his anticipated production of *The Adventures of Tom Sawyer.*

477   "My mother was very vindictive": James Talmadge to Tobias.

477   "That was a prison": James Talmadge to Marion Meade, via telephone (MM).

477   "It is my belief that the persecution": Unidentified clipping, n.d. (NYPL).

478   "There is a claim": *Los Angeles Times,* 10/29/1936.

478   "In this action I am being persecuted": Unidentified clipping, n.d. (NYPL).

478   part of a trade: Ownership of the Keaton estate passed to restaurateur William H. Simon in 1933. Simon, a family friend and distant relation, was married to Fanchon Wolff of the brother-and-sister production team Fanchon and Marco.

479   "He had a subtle way": Goodwin to Hoffman.

481   "Schenck knew Buster": Ibid.

481   "Buster Keaton, former star": *New York Times,* 6/26/1937.

482   "Well, I guess that stuff": *San Francisco Examiner,* 12/18/1937.

483   "I grabbed him": Jules White to the author.

483   short comedies program: Two-reel comedies weren't the only short subjects distributed by Columbia Pictures in a typical season. There were also sixteen cartoons, called *Color Rhapsodies,* from producer Charles Mintz; twelve *Screen Snapshots;* twelve *World of Sports* subjects; six *Washington Parades;* and ten *Community Sings,* all one-reelers.

483   "All the shorts": Jules White to the author.

483   "Del, at Mack Sennett": Ed Bernds, in a tape-recorded recollection for Marion Meade, 6/16/1990 (MM).

484   "He was playing the ukulele": *Muskegon Chronicle,* 10/7/1995.

484   "Buster gave every indication": Bernds for Meade.

485   "The Marx Brothers—it was an event": BK to Fletcher Markle.

486   budgeted at $15,000: The exact cost of *Pest from the West* was $15,513, putting it $518 over its $14,995 budget. According to notes in the Jules White collection, all ten of Keaton's Columbia shorts were budgeted at around $15,000 each, and most took four or five days to shoot (AMPAS).

486   "Lousy": Revised treatment by Hilary Lynn, 12/9/1938 (FOX).

486   "We are going to write Buster Keaton": Darryl F. Zanuck, rough draft of notes, 4/26/1939 (FOX).

487 innocent fiction: The pie-in-the-face dates back to a time when Keaton was still in vaudeville. Its originator may have been Roscoe Arbuckle.

487 "I had the studio's bakers": Keaton, *My Wonderful World of Slapstick*, p. 254.

487 "was crazy about him": Scott, *Buster Keaton: The Little Iron Man*, p. 314.

487 "One of the funniest": *Film Daily,* 6/28/1939.

487 "Here is a comedy": *Motion Picture Herald,* 7/29/1939.

487 *Pest* accrued domestic rentals: Rental figures for *Pest from the West* are from the library of Karl Thiede. Domestic rentals for the 1948 reissue amounted to $26,100.

487 two months later: Domestic rentals for *Mooching Through Georgia* amounted to $20,000 on a cost of $15,532. It was never reissued.

488 "After all these years": *New York Times,* 10/22/1939.

488 "They were making a picture": Goodwin to Hoffman.

488 "The biggest surprise": *San Francisco Examiner,* 10/25/1939.

21 ONE OF THE SKELETONS IN THE M-G-M CLOSET

489 Born on Hollywood Boulevard: Eleanor Ruth Norris was born at the Garden Court Apartments on July 29, 1918.

489 "I was never young": *Los Angeles Times,* 10/29/1995.

489 was in *The Gay Divorcee*: Eleanor was one of the dancers in the "Let's Knock Knees" number.

489 put her under contract: Scott, *Buster Keaton: The Little Iron Man*, p. 306.

490 "The kids used to sit": Scott, *Buster Keaton: The Little Iron Man*, p. 309.

490 "My first impression": Eleanor Keaton to Patricia Eliot Tobias, July 1992, in *The Keaton Chronicle,* Winter 1999.

490 "I met the whole family": Scott, *Buster Keaton: The Little Iron Man*, p. 309.

490 "The whole family looked pretty much alike": Eleanor Keaton to Alan Hoffman, Los Angeles, 2/21/1976 (courtesy of Alan Hoffman).

491 "The reason I was given": Gil Perkins to Marion Meade, via telephone (MM).

492 "He said the first time": Scott, *Buster Keaton: The Little Iron Man*, p. 310.

492 "It was a gradual thing": Eleanor Keaton to Tobias.

492 "When Buster started": Jules White to the author.

493 "They were like the featured comics": Eleanor Keaton to Hoffman.

494 "That's a great piece": *Lancaster Eagle-Gazette,* 4/15/1940.

494 pulling domestic rentals: Rental figures for *The Spook Speaks* are from the library of Karl Thiede.

495 "I took the bull by the horns": Scott, *Buster Keaton: The Little Iron Man*, p. 317.

495 "It wasn't a boy": Scott, *Buster Keaton: The Little Iron Man*, p. 319.

495 "He was still beautiful": Scott, *Buster Keaton: The Little Iron Man*, p. 316.

495 "The doctor and the other friend": Scott, *Buster Keaton: The Little Iron Man*, p. 318.

496 "just a kind, gentle": John C. Tibbetts, "Life with Buster," *The Great Stone Face.*

496 "And I feel like smiling": *Los Angeles Times,* 5/23/1940.

496 "I have not smiled": *Los Angeles Examiner,* 5/23/1940.

496 "I wanted to finish up": *Los Angeles Times,* 5/30/1940.

496 "They were all busy getting drunk": Scott, *Buster Keaton: The Little Iron Man*, p. 321.

496 "The only practical thought": Scott, *Buster Keaton: The Little Iron Man*, p. 320.

497 "He used to come to our house": Eleanor Keaton to Marion Meade (MM).

498 "We wrote down the description": Al Rogell to Kevin Brownlow in interview footage shot for the documentary *Buster Keaton: A Hard Act to Follow* (1987).

498 "He not only did a great deal": Brownlow, "The Search for Buster Keaton," p. 189.

499 clever use of stock footage: According to Joe Adamson, the police chase in *So You Won't Squawk?* was derived from second-unit footage Del Lord directed for *She Couldn't Take It* (1935).

499 "This was my first good part": *Journal and Courier,* 5/13/1941.

500 "He giggles": *New York Post,* 4/3/1941.

500 "Because much of the talk": *Columbus Citizen Journal,* 1/9/1961.

500 "making money": Eleanor Keaton to Hoffman.

500 picture was finished: Schedule and cost figures for *She's Oil Mine* are from the Jules White Collection (AMPAS).

501 "I just got to the point": Keaton, *My Wonderful World of Slapstick,* p. 259.

502 "because there was a big war plant": Eleanor Keaton to Meade.

503 "the Fields sequence": Although it was popular with preview audiences, the Fields sequence was cut from the picture due to length. The episode was restored for the film's home video release in 1996.

503 "Buster was assigned an office": Gene Fowler, Jr., to the author, Los Angeles, 9/10/1997.

503 "I knew where he was": James Talmadge to Meade.

503 "From that day on": Keaton, *My Wonderful World of Slapstick,* p. 277.

503 Barbara Jane Tichenor: Once ranked fourteenth in the nation, Barbara Talmadge won her last tournament at the age of seventy-seven.

503 "I had some very strict parents": Barbara Talmadge to the author, Cloverdale, CA, 5/13/2014.

504 Walking away from Jules White: Income figures for 1941 and 1942 are from statement of total salary, Office of Economic Stabilization, 11/3/1942.

504 "I told him how I felt": Keaton, *My Wonderful World of Slapstick,* p. 259.

504 "It seemed to me": Blesh, *Keaton,* p. 349.

504 preparing to remake *Spite Marriage*: The remake, which starred Red Skelton and Eleanor Powell, was released as *I Dood It* (1943).

505 "I was doing magic tricks": Orson Welles introduction to *The General, The Silent Years,* WNET, 1971.

505 "a satire on the present": Sam Taylor, *Laurel and Hardy on the Home Front,* 7/12/1943 (USC). According to studio records, Keaton's time was charged to this production for a total of thirty-three weeks and five days beginning July 19, 1943, and ending March 11, 1944. He received no credit.

506 "Buster worked with Red Skelton": Ronald L. Davis, *Just Making Movies* (Jackson: University Press of Mississippi, 2005), p. 69.

506 "Red was trying to get out": Brownlow, "The Search for Buster Keaton," pp. 191–92.

507 "Abbott and Costello never gave": BK to Markle.

509 "You and I just met": BK radio interview with Irwin Allen, 1945 (courtesy of Bob Borgen).

22 A COMEDY SEQUENCE HERE AND THERE

510 "Joe was a wonderful character": Scott, *Buster Keaton: The Little Iron Man,* p. 325.

511 "The last time I went": Scott, *Buster Keaton: The Little Iron Man,* p. 340.

511 "She told me he had prostate cancer": Barbara Talmadge to the author.

512 "being destitute": M-G-M meeting summary, 4/3/1944 (courtesy of Edward Watz).

512 "He was a *leech*": Scott, *Buster Keaton: The Little Iron Man,* p. 323.

513 "Buster wrecked": Scott, *Buster Keaton: The Little Iron Man,* p. 324.

513 "I got Buster principally": Brownlow, "The Search for Buster Keaton," pp. 192–93.

514 "They assigned us": Richard Goldstone to Barbara Hall, Academy of Motion Picture Arts and Sciences Oral History, 1991–92, p. 206 (AMPAS).

514 "I built this thing": *San Francisco Examiner,* 5/11/1940.

514 "Just a purse": *Los Angeles Times,* 2/3/1946.

515 production of his play: The original title of the play was *The Dunes.* In 1937, it was registered with the Copyright Office as *Marooned in Mojave.* The ultimate title, *Lambs Will Gamble,* was a play on the name of the famed theatrical club the Lambs, which produced an annual charity performance known as a gambol.

515 "The Dunes must have been": Eleanor Keaton to Hoffman.

516 "It's from a story by Buster Keaton": *Pittsburgh Press,* 4/30/1946.

516 "The whole play": Eleanor Keaton to Hoffman.

516 "A third-rate agent": Brownlow, "The Search for Buster Keaton," pp. 194–95.

517 "As a comedy I must say": Brownlow, "The Search for Buster Keaton," p. 196.

518 "CLOSE SHOT": Buster Keaton, changes, *The Rich, Full Life,* 10/30/1946 (USC).

519 "He was a deliberate drunk": Walt Kelly to the author, Escondido, CA, 8/4/2016.

519 "Buster started to drink": Reisner to Brownlow.

519 "I had the idea of bringing": Brownlow, "The Search for Buster Keaton," pp. 206–7.

521 "He first comes on": *Variety,* 9/17/1947.

521 "When we got to Europe": Scott, *Buster Keaton: The Little Iron Man,* p. 343.

521 an act with four elephants: *Oakland Tribune,* 10/15/1947.

521 "Things were very scarce": Eleanor Keaton to Hoffman.

521 Keaton's salary: In *My Wonderful World of Slapstick,* Keaton remembered his 1947 salary at Cirque Médrano as $3,500 a week. It should be noted, however, that when he played the same venue again in 1952, *Variety* reported that his weekly rate was $1,500.

521 "The American Graves": Eleanor Keaton to Meade.

522 "deliberately dogged it": Arthur Marx, *Red Skelton* (New York: Dutton, 1979), p. 140.

522 "One was having Red": Keaton, *My Wonderful World of Slapstick,* p. 264.

523 "I was working": Lee Server, *Screenwriter* (Pittstown, NJ: Main Street Press, 1987), pp. 137–38.

523 "They wrote a whole chase": Perkins to Brownlow.

523 "Both sides cheer": Keaton, *My Wonderful World of Slapstick,* p. 264.

523 "These were the kind of things": Perkins to Brownlow.

524 splitting $5,000: Details of financial arrangements surrounding *April Showers* are from the studio production files (WB).

525 "Brightening the dialogue": Henry Ephron, *We Thought We Could Do Anything* (New York: W. W. Norton, 1977), p. 71.

525 "We were sitting home": Eleanor Keaton to Hoffman.

525 "Buster Keaton stops me": *Hollywood Citizen News,* 5/27/1948.

526 "And he didn't know how": Eleanor Keaton to Hoffman.

527 "Sounds easy": *Republican and Herald* (Pottsville, PA), 12/10/1948.

528 "See?": *Los Angeles Examiner,* 11/27/1948.

528 "He was just bored stiff": Eleanor Keaton to Hoffman.

528 Ed Sedgwick allocated to a remake: This was *Watch the Birdie* (1950).

529 one-day cameo: This was for the Technicolor musical *You're My Everything* (1949). Keaton is in just one shot.

23 DIGGIN' UP MATERIAL

530 "and three friends": Charles Brackett, Billy Wilder, D. M. Marshman, Jr., *Sunset Boulevard,* screenplay, 7/19/1949, p. 39.

530 "She looked well": Anthony Slide, ed. *It's the Pictures That Got Small* (New York: Columbia University Press, 2014), p. 373.

531   "I thought I was": *Muskegon Chronicle*, 6/9/1949.

531   "Most people don't know how": *Detroit Free Press*, 1/11/1961.

531   "There was a young man": *Muskegon Chronicle*, 10/7/1995.

531   "I must have eaten two dozen": Unidentified clipping, 8/6/1963.

532   "They organized a parade": *Detroit Free Press*, 1/11/1961.

532   "There were several moments": Frank Buxton, "Three Men (and Buster) on a Horse," *The Keaton Chronicle*, Autumn 1999/Winter 2000.

532   "Billy Miles, the director": Frank Buxton to the author, via telephone, 8/22/2014.

533   "At another point": Buxton, "Three Men (and Buster) on a Horse."

533   "We had great houses": Buxton to the author.

534   "We had one of the very first": Jim Talmadge to Tobias.

536   "One of the most delightful gifts": *Chicago Tribune*, 12/27/1949.

536   "It looked like something": *San Francisco Sunday Examiner & Chronicle*, 11/22/1970.

536   "When he did the 'Butcher Boy' fall": Brownlow, "The Search for Buster Keaton," p. 202.

537   "An old-timer came into his own": *Daily Variety*, 12/23/1949.

537   "One of the reasons": *The Times* (San Mateo, CA), 12/28/1949.

538   "The biggest thing": BK to Feinstein.

538   "And on future shows": *The Times* (San Mateo, CA), 12/28/1949.

538   "They were paying the writers": Goodwin to Hoffman.

539   "It's the quickest way": BK to Feinstein.

542   "Only when he toyed": *Variety*, 11/8/1950.

543   "I averaged two shows": Keaton, *My Wonderful World of Slapstick*, p. 274.

543   "He was going crazy": Scott, *Buster Keaton: The Little Iron Man*, p. 354.

544   "We shot that in one day": Goodwin to Hoffman.

544   "It didn't look up to date": BK to Terkel.

545   "They weren't spending": Tibbetts, "Life with Buster."

545   "one of the funniest": *Los Angeles Times*, 5/9/1951.

545   "These are the kind of film quickies": *Variety*, 5/16/1951.

545   "I could never get a hot meal": *Evening Standard*, 3/12/1954.

546   "Oh, old home week": BK to Friedman.

546   "He seemed astonished": Keaton, *My Wonderful World of Slapstick*, p. 271.

547   "Charlie was debating": Jerry Epstein to Kevin Brownlow in interview footage shot for the documentary *Buster Keaton: A Hard Act to Follow* (1987).

548   "His reserve was extreme": Claire Bloom, *Limelight and After* (New York: Harper & Row, 1982), p. 112.

548   "unconscious communication": Norman Lloyd to the author, via telephone, 1/15/2014.

549   "brilliantly alive": Bloom, *Limelight and After*, p. 112.

549   "I was with him every second": Epstein to Brownlow.

550   "He was ready to retire": Scott, *Buster Keaton: The Little Iron Man*, p. 346.

MONTREAL, QUEBEC

553   "The cameraman, Bob Humble": Potterton to the author.

24 ALONG CAME TELEVISION

560   "I gave Buster an option": Dardis, *Keaton: The Man Who Wouldn't Lie Down*, p. 273.

560   "I cannot consider": Letter, Leopold Friedman to Joseph Schenck (courtesy of Edward Watz).

560   "gleaned from the copyright": M-G-M interoffice memo, Mark Avramo to Leopold Friedman, 9/8/1952.

560 "all of the information": Letter, Harold J. Cleary to Joseph H. Moskowitz, 9/22/1952.
561 "With a million writers": *Chicago Tribune*, 6/22/1952.
562 "play Ben-Hur": Ibid.
563 "He clowned spontaneously": Gallico, "Polyandry for All."
563 "After that, nothing is definitely decided": *European News*, 1/6/1954.
564 "The ringmaster chased him": Billy Beck to Kevin Brownlow in interview footage shot for the documentary *Buster Keaton: A Hard Act to Follow* (1987).
564 "I shouted with laughter": Paul Gallico, "Circus in Paris," *Esquire*, August 1954.
564 "He suggested I get off the hook": Keaton, *My Wonderful World of Slapstick*, p. 273.
564 500,000-franc-a-week: This was about $1,428 in the United States at the time.
564 "It was my agent's fault": *The Times* (San Mateo, CA), 4/15/1954.
565 "I think he sued": Scott, *Buster Keaton: The Little Iron Man*, p. 351.
565 "I'll do it": *News Chronicle* (UK), 2/12/1954.
565 "It struck me as a beautiful idea": Don Lybarger, "A Beautiful Actor," *The Keaton Chronicle*, Spring 1996.
566 "He'd done a lot of TV": Ibid.
567 "B. met me": Rudi Blesh, "B.K. #2" notebook (BKS).
568 "He had long since given up": Eleanor Keaton to Hoffman.
568 "some medical school": Matthew Dessem, *The Gag Man* (Raleigh, NC: Critical Press, 2015), p. 225.
569 "ACT welcomed": *Variety*, 8/31/1955.
569 "Just bones": Eleanor Keaton to Hoffman.
569 "She drank a pint": Jim Talmadge to Tobias.
570 "We sent a cable": Scott, *Buster Keaton: The Little Iron Man*, p. 364.
570 "She was Buster's favorite": Barbara Talmadge to the author.
570 "From the moment they came over": Scott, *Buster Keaton: The Little Iron Man*, pp. 371–72.
570 "This is the story": Pitch script, *The Buster Keaton Story*, n.d. (AMPAS).
571 "Mike Todd called me": *Los Angeles Times*, 3/3/1957.
571 "It was bitter cold": Eleanor Keaton to Hoffman.
571 "I think there's been some mistake": Michael Todd, Jr., and Susan McCarthy Todd, *A Valuable Property* (New York: Arbor House, 1983), pp. 295–96.
572 "For a bit part": *Los Angeles Examiner*, 12/26/1956.
572 "There was no process": Michael Anderson to the author, via telephone, 10/23/2001.
572 "Just give me enough money": *Los Angeles Mirror-News*, 10/21/1955.
573 "Comedy is comedy": *Democrat and Chronicle* (Rochester, NY), 11/19/1955.

25 THE WORST THING EVER MADE
574 "Eleanor phoned us": Barbara Talmadge to the author.
575 "Yes, it was a tough time": *Ithaca (NY) Journal*, 1/6/1956.
576 "Buster Keaton called once": Pamela Mason to Marion Meade, via telephone (MM). In 1966, Kenneth Tynan revealed that, as a houseguest of the Masons, he was the one who answered the door when Keaton paid his call.
576 "It was about 1938": Bart Williams, "Rendezvous at the Italian Villa," *The Keaton Chronicle*, Spring 1998.
576 "a sort of gardener's cottage": Williams, "Rendezvous at the Italian Villa." The rotting structure was demolished soon after Williams' visit, but the vault remained.
577 "Not everything": *New York Herald Tribune*, 7/25/1956.
577 "He sold off": *New York Post*, 9/11/1956.

577 "A dilemma presented itself": Raymond Rohauer, "Buster Keaton and the Race Against Time, or Where Have All the Comedians Gone?" Notes for the National Film Theatre of London, 1968.

578 Metro's rights to *The Saphead*: There is some confusion over exactly what M-G-M retained in its vaults as of 1955. In 1962, handwritten notes on a copyright search made at the request of Julian Abele indicate that the studio still retained prints of *Battling Butler, The Goat, The Haunted House, The High Sign, Neighbors, The Scarecrow,* and *Seven Chances.*

578 "There was a bar": Scott, *Buster Keaton: The Little Iron Man,* p. 324.

580 "When I sold him this house": Goodwin to Hoffman.

580 "and Harry stayed": Eleanor Keaton to Meade.

581 "Gobel would get more laughs": *Santa Cruz (CA) Sentinel,* 10/10/1955.

581 "It all boiled down": Eleanor Keaton to Hoffman.

581 "Some of the prints": *New York Times,* 4/15/1956.

582 "You've got to learn": *New York Post,* 7/2/1956.

582 "Why don't we grain down": Donald O'Connor to Kevin Brownlow in interview footage shot for the documentary *Buster Keaton: A Hard Act to Follow* (1987).

582 "Donald did so much screaming": Eleanor Keaton to Hoffman.

583 "I worked with Buster": O'Connor to Brownlow.

584 "it's the worst thing": Scott, *Buster Keaton: The Little Iron Man,* pp. 368, 372.

586 "dumbfounded": Eleanor Keaton to Meade.

587 "Of course, it is no camera trick": BK to Pratt.

587 "He taught me": Stu Levin, "Donald O'Connor and Buster Keaton," *Blackhawk Film Digest,* August/September 1980.

587 "I'm a little dizzy": *Journal-News* (Nyack, NY), 5/18/1957.

587 "I was interviewed": Scott, *Buster Keaton: The Little Iron Man,* p. 373.

26 MERTON OF THE MOVIES

589 "I was born in 1923": James Karen to the author, Los Angeles, CA, 1/27/2014.

590 "He was kind of vague": Alan Harper to Marion Meade, via telephone (MM).

590 "There was a meeting": Karen to the author.

592 "Buster Keaton didn't draw": *Asbury Park (NJ) Press,* 9/8/1957.

593 "At one point": *Binghamton (NY) Press and Sun-Bulletin,* 8/6/1957.

593 "Buster Keaton is more than durable": *Chicago Tribune,* 8/21/1957.

594 "that the plaintiff married": Mae Elizabeth Keaton, Plaintiff, against Paramount Pictures Corporation, Defendant, 1957, Index No. 12264, New York County Clerk's Office.

595 "I lived in Hell": Jewel Steven, "I Am Being Blackmailed," *Confidential,* December 1958.

595 "You never do find out": *Chicago Tribune,* 8/30/1957.

596 "All the guys at Yale": Dick Cavett to the author, via telephone, 1/6/2017.

596 "The only thing I liked": *Arizona Republic,* 1/24/1958.

597 "We ended up shooting": Karen to the author.

599 "Keaton's sense of timing": *Los Angeles Times,* 10/9/1957.

599 "The vast difference": *Daily Variety,* 10/10/1957.

599 "It was badly publicized": Brownlow, "The Search for Buster Keaton," p. 219.

599 "I remember one time": Karen to the author.

600 "When it came time": *Variety,* 1/4/1978.

600 "I've got an idea": *Binghamton (NY) Press and Sun-Bulletin,* 8/6/1957.

600 "Hey, Lee": Edward Watz to the author, via email, 4/2/2018.

603 "We had been looking": Éric Rohmer, "Notre Couverture," *Cahiers du Cinéma,* August 1958.

603 "Mr. Keaton met me": The original English-language transcript is at the British Film Institute.

604 "It's rural": *Columbus (OH) Dispatch,* 1/5/1961.

605 "The chickens seem": *Los Angeles Herald-Examiner,* 2/2/1966.

605 "My favorite memory": Scott, *Buster Keaton: The Little Iron Man,* p. 375.

605 "It looked like a little red schoolhouse": Melissa Talmadge Cox to the author, Cloverdale, CA, 8/15/2014.

605 but her white stucco house: Natalie Talmadge's home at 18904 Roosevelt Highway was gutted by fire in 1943. She moved to this house at 916 Palisades Beach Road in Santa Monica sometime after the war.

606 "I have very fond memories": Melissa Talmadge Cox to the author, via email, 3/20/2016.

606 "We had a breakfast nook": Barbara Talmadge to the author.

607 "He came down": Scott, *Buster Keaton: The Little Iron Man,* p. 356.

608 "The first thing I did": Edward Watz to the author, via email, 3/25/2019.

609 "They intend to produce": Leopold Friedman to Irving Berlin, 5/13/1958 (Irving Berlin papers, Library of Congress).

27 *ONCE UPON A MATTRESS*

610 "We were kind of out of touch": Eleanor Keaton to Meade.

610 "He never talked": Scott, *Buster Keaton: The Little Iron Man,* p. 438.

611 "He wouldn't always get the right terms": Ben Pearson to Tom Dardis (courtesy of Edward Watz).

611 "What I don't understand": Karen to the author.

612 Rohauer conceived the fiction: In a 1976 interview with Keaton biographer Tom Dardis, Harold Goodwin was asked about the films Keaton supposedly kept in his garage. "What?" Goodwin responded. "Oh no, he didn't have any of those." Dardis: "Really? No nitrate copies of *The General, Cameraman, Navigator, The Three Ages,* all the shorts?" Goodwin: "No, none of that. He had a 16mm projector, so he might've rented some of the old films from a camera store, but he didn't own any."

Edward Watz once asked Eleanor Keaton if Rohauer's account of how he and Buster took Keaton's personal print of *Three Ages* to a lab to be copied was true. "She sort of twinkled her eyes, smiled, and said, 'Well, it makes a good story, doesn't it?'"

Rohauer promulgated many falsehoods concerning his relationship with Keaton, and key among them was his assertion that he and Keaton met in 1954. "Rohauer slipped once," said Watz, who was employed by Rohauer for four years, "and told me that he 'didn't know Buster' when *The Buster Keaton Story* was being made 'or I would have worked on Paramount to make safety copies of all his films.' I didn't point out the discrepancy to him—Buster being busy on the production in 1956 and heavily promoting it in 1957."

612 "They set it up": Scott, *Buster Keaton: The Little Iron Man,* p. 383.

613 "Keaton was in and out": N. C. Chambers, "The Industry's Third Oscarcast," *Films in Review,* May 1960.

613 "the most spontaneous": *Wilkes-Barre (PA) Times Leader,* 4/15/1960.

614 "It wasn't on the air": Scott, *Buster Keaton: The Little Iron Man,* p. 384.

614 "What the hell": *New York Post,* 2/2/1960.

614 "One day in a New York elevator": *Daily Variety,* 6/5/1957.

615 those distributed by First National: Because Robert Youngson was making *When Comedy Was King* for 20th Century-Fox release, he may have gained access to Joseph Schenck's personal print of *Cops,* which was stored at the studio.

617 "The success of Charles Chaplin": *Daily Variety,* 8/11/1960.

617 "They wanted me": BK to Downs. Until his third marriage, Keaton's hats had often been made by his mother. In 1940, Myra Keaton showed Eleanor how to make them, and she assumed the responsibility thereafter.

618 "They tried to get me": *Binghamton (NY) Press and Sun-Bulletin,* 9/17/1960.

618 "cleaned up a bunch": Patricia Eliot Tobias (with Woolsey Ackerman and Carol Bradshaw), "The Mattress Tour: The Next Best Thing to Broadway," *The Keaton Chronicle,* Summer 1997.

619 "Mr. Keaton is Mr. Keaton": *Chicago Tribune,* 9/2/1960.

619 "The thing that always impressed me": Tobias, "The Mattress Tour: The Next Best Thing to Broadway."

620 "It's a clean show": *San Francisco Examiner,* 10/9/1960.

620 "Somewhere along the line": *San Francisco Examiner,* 9/29/1960.

620 "I've had it": *Santa Cruz (CA) Sentinel,* 11/27/1960.

620 "All we know": BK to Eder.

621 "We were in the process": Allen Funt to Kevin Brownlow in interview footage shot for the documentary *Buster Keaton: A Hard Act to Follow* (1987).

623 "it's been a long time": *Columbus (OH) Dispatch,* 1/20/1961.

623 Losses were well in excess: Financial details on the national tour of *Once Upon a Mattress* are from *Variety,* 3/15/1961 and 10/25/1961.

623 "He said, 'Would you'": Scott, *Buster Keaton: The Little Iron Man,* p. 391.

623 "I'm going to stay home": *Buffalo Courier-Express,* 7/24/1961.

624 "They gave me a certain framework": *Alabama Journal,* 1/15/1961.

624 "Here's a legend": Marc Scott Zicree, *The Twilight Zone Companion* (New York: Bantam Books, 1982), p. 260.

625 "I realized later": Richard Matheson to Karen Herman, Hidden Hills, CA, 4/16/2002 (Archive of American Television, Academy of Television Arts and Sciences).

625 "A much older clown": *Variety,* 12/20/1961.

625 "weird and wonderful": *Los Angeles Times,* 12/15/1961.

625 "He was a happy person": Hawkins, "The Friendship of Buster Keaton and Loyal Lucas."

626 "it's a big job": *Santa Cruz (CA) Sentinel,* 11/27/1960.

626 "He had electric trains": Brownlow, "The Search for Buster Keaton," p. 187. These were O scale trains.

626 "I want you to look at": *White Plains (NY) Journal News,* 12/13/1961.

626 "For a while, Buster ate": *Columbus (OH) Citizen-Journal,* 1/9/1961.

626 "She did everything": Karen to the author.

626 "He was a project": Rick Kelly to the author, Escondido, CA, 8/4/2016.

627 "five-dollar bill": Eleanor Keaton to Hoffman.

627 "He came east": Karen to the author.

629 "I had never met a finer man": Keaton, *My Wonderful World of Slapstick,* p. 109.

28 THE LAUGHTER OF THE WORLD

632 "We've lost a good friend": *Los Angeles Times,* 1/12/1962.

632 "I was born in Trenton": *Elmira (NY) Advertiser,* 1/16/1962.

632 "We hit all the major cities": Tibbetts, "Life with Buster."

632   "Raymond and I": Tibbetts, "Life with Buster."

633   "We—Ray and I—were standing": Don McGregor, "An Interview with Eleanor Keaton," *Buster Keaton Film Festival Album*, 1982.

633   "In ten towns": BK as quoted by Georges Sadoul in *Buster Keaton Interviews*, p. 147.

633   "At a showing": *Los Angeles Times*, 10/29/1995.

633   "Nothing could be nicer": *Chicago Tribune*, 7/2/1962.

634   "I looked around": *Democrat and Chronicle* (Rochester, NY), 3/1/1962.

634   "They came to me": John Lahr, *Notes on a Cowardly Lion* (New York: Alfred A. Knopf, 1969), p. 225.

634   "There were budget constraints": John Sebert to the author, via telephone, 3/12/2014.

635   "I wonder how this movie": Joy Brown, "Three Clowns Make a Movie," *Weekend Magazine, Ottawa Citizen*, 5/19/1962.

636   "When we got home": Eleanor Keaton to Kevin Brownlow in interview footage shot for the documentary *Buster Keaton: A Hard Act to Follow* (1987).

636   "Buster had this idea of journeying": Cox to Brownlow.

637   "Keaton worked with me": George Maharis to the author, via telephone, 8/23/2015.

639   "When Buster worked": James Curtis, *Spencer Tracy: A Biography* (New York: Alfred A. Knopf, 2011), p. 808.

640   "He was not supposed to be drinking": McNamara, "Lulu in Rochester: Self-Portrait of an Anti-Star."

640   "When Keaton was in Rochester": Louise Brooks to Tom Dardis, 3/24/1977 (AMPAS).

640   Buster's bronchitis worsened: According to the newspapers, Keaton's stay at West Hills Doctors Hospital in Canoga Park lasted four days, not six.

641   "I was pretty proud": Brendan Gill, "Happy Pro," *The New Yorker*, 4/27/1963.

642   "It's not M-G-M": Hedda Hopper, BK interview notes, 5/2/1963 (AMPAS).

642   "sock reviews": *Variety*, 7/11/1962.

643   "arrive at a productive formula": Sheldon Abend to Leopold Friedman, 11/23/1962.

644   "is the first time": *Birmingham News*, 10/4/1963.

644   "an armed military escort": Don Logay, "Birmingham in 1963," *The Keaton Chronicle*, Summer 2000.

645   "word of mouth": *Variety*, 9/25/1963.

645   "It's one of the times": Scott, *Buster Keaton: The Little Iron Man*, p. 398.

645   "Three things are important": *Los Angeles Times*, 6/7/1964.

645   "there was tremendous competition": William Cahn, *Harold Lloyd's World of Comedy* (New York: Duell, Sloan and Pearce, 1964), p. 187.

646   "I tried to convince the boys": *Capital Times* (Madison, WI), 8/20/1964. The Ford commercial, shot in New York, featured Keaton being pursued by a squad of Keystone-like cops, one of whom was actor Paul Dooley.

647   "They gave me that": *White Plains (NY) Journal News*, 12/13/1961.

648   "He stands rather like a Victorian boy": *The Observer Weekend Review* (UK), 5/24/1964.

649   "Alan Schneider had directed me": Karen to the author.

649   "I said, 'I can't make any sense'": Scott, *Buster Keaton: The Little Iron Man*, p. 322.

649   "Then they got desperate": Karen to the author. It should be noted that Alan Schneider, in his autobiography, says it was Beckett's idea to seek out Keaton for the film.

651   "All he did": Susan Reed to Marion Meade, circa 1990 (MM).

651   "He was totally professional": Samuel Beckett, *Film* (New York: Grove Press, 1970), pp. 73–74.

652   "What I think it means": *New York Times*, 7/21/1964.

652   "It's about a man": Brownlow, "The Search for Buster Keaton," p. 245.

652   "His movement was excellent": Brownlow, "The Search for Buster Keaton," p. 246.

653   "He hated every minute": Eleanor Keaton to Hoffman.

29 *THE RAILRODDER*

655   "I drive by": *New York Times,* 10/17/1965.

655   "I had used him": Tom Weaver, *Return of the B Science Fiction and Horror Heroes* (Jefferson, NC: McFarland, 2000), p. 157.

655   "When Bendix fell ill": William Bendix died of pneumonia on December 14, 1964.

656   "Buster taught me": Bobbie Shaw Chance to the author, via telephone, 7/13/2015.

656   "I was in the animation department": Potterton to the author, via telephone.

658   "He seemed to be very enthusiastic": Julian Biggs to Ben Pearson, 7/27/1964 (NFB).

658   "The camera John used": David de Volpi to the author, via telephone, 3/6/2016.

659   "I was desperately trying": Gerald Potterton to the author, via email, 3/28/2014.

660   "He was spoilt": Potterton to the author, via telephone.

660   "Just looking at those pictures": *Rivers Gazette Reporter,* 9/17/1964.

660   "His energy level": Potterton to the author, via telephone.

661   "We got so used to him": Scott, *Buster Keaton: The Little Iron Man,* p. 403.

661   "We'd get to where we were going": Eleanor Keaton to Hoffman.

661   "[It was] bitter cold": Ibid.

663   "He'd come to me once a year": *Los Angeles Times,* 10/29/1995.

663   "I could retire": *New York World-Telegram & Sun,* 8/12/1964.

664   "When the door": Letter, Potterton to the author, 5/2/2014.

664   "I'm getting tired": *Eureka Humboldt (CA) Standard,* 3/22/1965.

665   "It's disconcerting": *Los Angeles Times,* 4/11/1965.

665   "I go back to a very old saying": *New York Journal-American,* 4/4/1965.

666   "I keep getting crazy offers": BK to Hopper, 5/12/1965.

666   "They both live in Santa Monica": *Los Angeles Times,* 5/15/1965.

666   "I had to work hard": Ben Pearson to Tom Dardis (courtesy of Edward Watz).

666   "I agreed": *New York World-Telegram & Sun,* 2/3/1966.

667   "The collar dug into Buster's throat": *Life* dispatch, David Zeitlin to Tommy Thompson, 2/1/1966 (AMPAS).

668   "He was so ill": Scott, *Buster Keaton: The Little Iron Man,* p. 409.

668   "Two hundred critics": *Montreal Gazette,* 11/18/1965.

668   "I've had several other offers": Gillett and Blue, "Keaton at Venice."

668   "I never did find out": *New York World-Telegram & Sun,* 8/12/1964.

669   "was given an ovation": Francis Koval, "Venice 1965," *Films in Review,* October 1965.

669   "He cried at the ovation": Scott, *Buster Keaton: The Little Iron Man,* p. 409.

670   "He thought he had asthma": Brownlow, "The Search for Buster Keaton," p. 258.

670   "A touching man": *The Guardian* (UK), 2/15/1966.

670   "It rained and fogged": Eleanor Keaton to Hoffman.

670   "His wife protected": *The Sun* (UK), 2/2/1966.

670   "We had one wonderful day": Brownlow, "The Search for Buster Keaton," pp. 258–59.

671   "Our Rome": *Daily Variety,* 8/18/1965.

671   "It was written in the script": Brownlow, "The Search for Buster Keaton," p. 259.

672   "He brought the light": *Edmonton Journal,* 11/13/1965.

672   "praised to tears": *Daily Variety,* 10/19/1965.

672   "The whole thing was my idea": John Sebert to the author, via telephone, 3/12/2014.

674 "I got him on a plane": Tibbetts, "Life with Buster."
674 "When he gets dressed": Eleanor Keaton to Meade.
674 "I haven't read": Postcard, Jane Thompson to Hedda Hopper, 11/2/1965 (AMPAS).
674 "I aged five years": *Los Angeles Times,* 11/10/1965.
675 "It's what they call": Eleanor Keaton to Hoffman.
675 "Bus was in the hospital": Cox to Brownlow.
675 "They put him on": Eleanor Keaton to Hoffman.
675 "God, this medication's working": Eleanor Keaton to Meade.
676 "How are we financially?": Tibbetts, "Life with Buster."
676 "His cancer had metastasized": Ibid.
676 "I brought him home": Eleanor Keaton to Meade.
676 "Hit him with everything you've got": Ibid.
677 "He got angry": Scott, *Buster Keaton: The Little Iron Man,* p. 415.
677 "Do you think you could stretch out": Scott, *Buster Keaton: The Little Iron Man,* p. 417.

30 SOMETHING LIKE A GENIUS
678 "My gosh": Ruth Silva to Marion Meade (MM).
678 "I think we shortened his life": Sebert to the author.
679 "Is it *confirmed?*": John Baxter, "The Silent Empire of Raymond Rohauer," *Sunday Times Magazine* (UK), 1/19/1975.
679 "Reed was eight years old": Karen to the author.
679 "Gracie Allen had only died": Eleanor Keaton to Meade. Gracie Allen actually died in August 1964.
679 "She was very businesslike": Karen to the author.
680 "When he was ready": Scott, *Buster Keaton: The Little Iron Man,* p. 417.
680 "There was a kind of purity": *Sunday Times* (UK), 2/6/1966.
680 "If Chaplin was the greatest": *The Observer* (UK), 2/6/1966.
681 "You know, Buster was amazing": George Bluestone, "Lunch with Lester," *Film Quarterly,* Summer 1966.
681 "The professional film festival audience": Beckett, *Film,* p. 93.
682 "We showed it at a private screening": Potterton to the author, via telephone.
682 "It caught him laughing": Eleanor Keaton to Hoffman.
683 "You know those boxes": Eleanor Keaton to Meade.
683 "He wasn't interested": Scott, *Buster Keaton: The Little Iron Man,* p. 438.
683 "He made me read the galleys": Eleanor Keaton to Hoffman.
684 "A few weeks ago at seventy": *Financial Times,* 2/4/1966.
685 "He was a slithery person": Karen to the author.
686 "nostalgia for the silent master": *Variety,* 9/28/1966.
687 "The reaction to": Geraldine Chaplin to David Weddle, 2002 (courtesy of David Weddle).
687 "Their campaign to prove": *Morning Star* (UK), 1/13/1968.
687 "Crowds are pouring": *The Listener,* 2/1/1968.
689 "Rohauer used to tell me": Edward Watz to the author, via email, 4/3/2019.
689 "What was perhaps most impressive": *Village Voice,* 9/16/1981 and 9/22/1981.
690 "Rohauer wanted": Edward Watz to the author, via email, 4/8/2019.
690 "Rohauer actually owns": *Variety,* 9/30/1970.
690 "If an Oscar": Baxter, "The Silent Empire of Raymond Rohauer."

690 "Rohauer operated under": William K. Everson, "Raymond Rohauer: King of the Film Freebooters," *Grand Street* 49.

691 "As soon as I feel like it": Henry Gris, "Buster Keaton's Sentimental Journey," *The Keaton Chronicle*, Autumn 2019.

692 "I remember that when she was real ill": Melissa Talmadge Cox to the author, via email, 3/20/2016.

692 "When Louise died": Barbara Talmadge to the author.

693 "He had a lady friend": Scott, *Buster Keaton: The Little Iron Man*, p. 324.

693 "Eleanor was not a lady ever to go slowly": *The Keaton Chronicle*, Winter 1999.

693 "I never come up here": Scott, *Buster Keaton: The Little Iron Man*, p. 417.

694 "was the least self-centered": *The Keaton Chronicle*, Winter 1999.

695 "Now!": Interoffice memo, Ralph Edwards to Dresser Dahlstead, 6/26/1986 (Ralph Edwards Papers, Department of Special Collections, UCLA).

696 into the wrong corner: The marker belonged on the southwest corner of Lillian and Eleanor, and studio historian Marc Wanamaker had given the organizers the correct location. "When I arrived around 11:30 a.m. to the site," Wanamaker remembered, "I was horrified that the plaque was placed on the NORTHWEST corner! I mentioned this quietly to the Ralph Edwards Productions publicist, and he was scared to death I would say something and ruin the event. . . . Eleanor Keaton was there to unveil the plaque. She did not know where the site was. It was up to historians like myself to tell the organizers where it was, but they were influenced by the Pacific Title and Art Studio people who heard it was on their property." The error was finally corrected in 2018 with the placement of a new plaque at the proper location by the International Buster Keaton Society.

List of Illustrations

Appendix I

FILM CHRONOLOGY

These films are listed in the order in which they were made, not in the order in which they were released. Where possible, credits are as they appear on-screen.

The Butcher Boy

A Paramount-Arbuckle Comedy presented by Joseph M. Schenck. Written and Directed by Fatty Arbuckle. Production: Comique. Distribution: Famous Players-Lasky. Release Date: April 23, 1917. Length: 2 reels. Cast: Fatty Arbuckle. (Uncredited: Al St. John, Josephine Stevens, Buster Keaton, Arthur Earle, Agnes Neilson, Luke.)

The Rough House

A Paramount-Arbuckle Comedy presented by Joseph M. Schenck. Written and Directed by Fatty Arbuckle. Production: Comique. Distribution: Famous Players-Lasky. Release Date: June 25, 1917. Length: 2 reels. Cast: Fatty Arbuckle. (Uncredited: Al St. John, Buster Keaton, Alice Lake, Agnes Neilson.)

His Wedding Night

A Paramount-Arbuckle Comedy presented by Joseph M. Schenck. Written and Directed by Fatty Arbuckle. Production: Comique. Distribution: Famous Players-Lasky. Release Date: August 20, 1917. Length: 2 reels. Cast: Fatty Arbuckle. (Uncredited: Al St. John, Buster Keaton, Alice Mann.)

Oh! Doctor

A Paramount-Arbuckle Comedy presented by Joseph M. Schenck. Written and Directed by Fatty Arbuckle. (Uncredited: Buster Keaton.) Production: Comique. Distribution: Famous Players-Lasky. Release Date: September 19, 1917. Length: 2 reels. Cast: Fatty Arbuckle. (Uncredited: Buster Keaton, Al St. John, Alice Mann.)

Fatty in Coney Island

A Paramount-Arbuckle Comedy presented by Joseph M. Schenck. Written and Directed by Fatty Arbuckle. (Uncredited: Buster Keaton.) Production: Comique. Distribution: Famous Players-Lasky. Release Date: October 29, 1917. Length: 2 reels. Cast: Fatty Arbuckle. (Uncredited: Buster Keaton, Al St. John, Alice Mann.)

A Country Hero

A Paramount-Arbuckle Comedy presented by Joseph M. Schenck. Written and Directed by Fatty Arbuckle. (Uncredited: Buster Keaton.) Production: Comique. Distribution: Famous Players-Lasky. Release Date: December 13, 1917. Length: 2 reels. Cast: Fatty Arbuckle. (Uncredited: Buster Keaton, Al St. John, Alice Lake, Joe Keaton.)

Out West

A Paramount-Arbuckle Comedy presented by Joseph M. Schenck. Written and Directed by Fatty Arbuckle. (Uncredited: Buster Keaton.) Production: Comique. Distribution: Famous Players-Lasky. Release Date: January 20, 1918. Length: 2 reels. Cast: Fatty Arbuckle. (Uncredited: Al St. John, Alice Lake, Joe Keaton.)

The Bell Boy

A Paramount-Arbuckle Comedy presented by Joseph M. Schenck. Written and Directed by Fatty Arbuckle. (Uncredited: Buster Keaton.) Production: Comique. Distribution: Famous Players-Lasky. Release Date: March 18, 1918. Length: 2 reels. Cast: Fatty Arbuckle. (Uncredited: Buster Keaton, Al St. John, Alice Lake, Joe Keaton, Charles Dudley.)

Moonshine

A Paramount-Arbuckle Comedy presented by Joseph M. Schenck. Written and Directed by Fatty Arbuckle. (Uncredited: Buster Keaton.) Production: Comique. Distribution: Famous Players-Lasky. Release Date: May 13, 1918. Length: 2 reels. Cast: Fatty Arbuckle. (Uncredited: Buster Keaton, Al St. John, Alice Lake, Charles Dudley.)

Good Night Nurse

A Paramount-Arbuckle Comedy presented by Joseph M. Schenck. Written and Directed by Fatty Arbuckle. (Uncredited: Buster Keaton.) Production: Comique. Distribution: Famous Players-Lasky. Release Date: July 8, 1918. Length: 2 reels. Cast: Fatty Arbuckle. (Uncredited: Buster Keaton, Al St. John, Alice Lake, Kate Price.)

The Cook

A Paramount-Arbuckle Comedy presented by Joseph M. Schenck. Written and Directed by Fatty Arbuckle. (Uncredited: Buster Keaton.) Production: Comique. Distribution: Famous Players-Lasky. Release Date: September 15, 1918. Length: 2 reels. Cast: Fatty Arbuckle. (Uncredited: Buster Keaton, Al St. John, Alice Lake, Glen Cavender.)

Back Stage

A Paramount-Arbuckle Comedy presented by Joseph M. Schenck. Written and Directed by Fatty Arbuckle. (Uncredited: Buster Keaton.) Production: Comique. Distribution: Famous Players-Lasky. Release Date: August 20, 1919. Length: 2 reels. Cast: Fatty Arbuckle. (Uncredited: Buster Keaton, Al St. John, Molly Malone, Jack Coogan, Charles A. Post.)

The Hayseed

A Paramount-Arbuckle Comedy presented by Joseph M. Schenck. Written and Directed by Fatty Arbuckle. (Uncredited: Buster Keaton.) Production: Comique. Distribution: Famous Players-Lasky. Release Date: October 26, 1919. Length: 2 reels. Cast: Fatty Arbuckle. (Uncredited: Buster Keaton, Molly Malone, Jack Coogan, Luke.)

The Garage

A Paramount-Arbuckle Comedy presented by Joseph M. Schenck. Written and Directed by Fatty Arbuckle. (Uncredited: Buster Keaton.) Production: Comique. Distribution: Famous Players-Lasky. Release Date: January 11, 1920. Length: 2 reels. Cast: Fatty Arbuckle. (Uncredited: Buster Keaton, Molly Malone, Harry McCoy, Daniel Crimmins, Luke.)

The High Sign

Presented by Joseph M. Schenck. Director: Buster Keaton. Production: Comique. Distribution: Metro. Release Date: April 12, 1921. Length: 2 reels. Cast: Buster Keaton, Bartine Burkett, Ingram B. "Cupid" Pickett, Al St. John.

The Saphead

Presented by Marcus Loew. Supervisor: Winchell Smith. Director: Herbert Blaché. Based upon the play The New Henrietta by Winchell Smith and Victor Mapes, adapted from The Henrietta by Bronson Howard. Scenario: June Mathis. Photography: Harold Wenstrom. Production and Distribution: Metro. Release Date: October 18, 1920. Length: 7 reels. Cast: William H. Crane, Buster Keaton, Odette Tyler, Carol Holloway, Irving Cummings, Jack Livingston, Beulah Booker, Edward Connelly, Edward Jobson, Edward Alexander.

One Week

Presented by Joseph M. Schenck. Directors: Buster Keaton, Eddie Cline. Writers: Buster Keaton, Eddie Cline. (Uncredited: Jean Havez, Joseph Mitchell.) Production: Comique. Distribution: Metro. Release Date: September 1, 1920. Length: 2 reels.

Cast: Buster Keaton. (Uncredited: Sybil Seely, Joe Roberts.)

Convict 13

Presented by Joseph M. Schenck. Directors: Buster Keaton, Eddie Cline. Writers: Buster Keaton, Eddie Cline. (Uncredited: Jean Havez, Joseph Mitchell.) Production: Comique. Distribution: Metro. Release Date: October 27, 1920. Length: 2 reels. Cast: Buster Keaton. (Uncredited: Sybil Seely, Joe Roberts, Joe Keaton, Eddie Cline.)

The Scarecrow

Presented by Joseph M. Schenck. Directors: Buster Keaton, Eddie Cline. Writers: Buster Keaton, Eddie Cline. (Uncredited: Jean Havez, Joseph Mitchell.) Production: Comique. Distribution: Metro. Release Date: December 22, 1920. Length: 2 reels. Cast: Buster Keaton. (Uncredited: Sybil Seely, Joe Roberts, Joe Keaton, Eddie Cline, Luke.)

Neighbors

Presented by Joseph M. Schenck. Directors: Buster Keaton, Eddie Cline. Writers: Buster Keaton, Eddie Cline. (Uncredited: Jean Havez, Joseph Mitchell.) Production: Comique. Distribution: Metro. Release Date: January 3, 1921. Length: 2 reels. Cast: Buster Keaton. (Uncredited: Virginia Fox, Joe Roberts, Joe Keaton, Eddie Cline.)

The Haunted House

Presented by Joseph M. Schenck. Directors: Buster Keaton, Eddie Cline. Writers: Buster Keaton, Eddie Cline. (Uncredited: Jean Havez, Joseph Mitchell.) Production: Comique. Distribution: Metro. Release Date: February 10, 1921. Length: 2 reels. Cast: Buster Keaton. (Uncredited: Virginia Fox, Joe Roberts, Eddie Cline.)

Hard Luck

Presented by Joseph M. Schenck. Directors: Buster Keaton, Eddie Cline. Writers: Buster Keaton, Eddie Cline. (Uncredited: Jean Havez, Joseph Mitchell.) Production:

Comique. Distribution: Metro. Release Date: March 16, 1921. Length: 2 reels. Cast: Buster Keaton. (Uncredited: Virginia Fox, Joe Roberts, Bull Montana.)

The Goat

Presented by Joseph M. Schenck. Directors: Buster Keaton, Mal St. Clair. Writers: Buster Keaton, Mal St. Clair. (Uncredited: Jean Havez, Joseph Mitchell.) Production: Comique. Distribution: Metro. Release Date: May 18, 1921. Length: 2 reels. Cast: Buster Keaton. (Uncredited: Virginia Fox, Joe Roberts, Mal St. Clair, Eddie Cline, Jean Havez.)

The Play House

Presented by Joseph M. Schenck. Directors: Buster Keaton, Eddie Cline. Writers: Buster Keaton, Eddie Cline. (Uncredited: Joseph Mitchell, Clyde Bruckman.) Production: Comique. Distribution: First National. Release Date: October 6, 1921. Length: 2 reels. Cast: Buster Keaton. (Uncredited: Virginia Fox, Joe Roberts.)

The Boat

Presented by Joseph M. Schenck. Directors: Buster Keaton, Eddie Cline. Writers: Buster Keaton, Eddie Cline. (Uncredited: Joseph Mitchell, Clyde Bruckman.) Production: Comique. Distribution: First National. Release Date: November 1921. Length: 2 reels. Cast: Buster Keaton. (Uncredited: Sybil Seely, Eddie Cline.)

Screen Snapshots

Producers: Jack Cohn, Louis Lewyn. Production: CBC Film Sales. Length: 1 reel. Release Date: January 5, 1922. NOTE: Keaton appears in views of the Talmadge sisters and their husbands.

The Paleface

Presented by Joseph M. Schenck. Directors: Buster Keaton, Eddie Cline. Writers: Buster Keaton, Eddie Cline. (Uncredited: Joseph Mitchell, Clyde Bruckman.) Production: Comique. Distribution: First National. Release Date: January 1922. Length: 2 reels. Cast: Buster Keaton. (Uncredited: Joe Roberts, Virginia Fox.)

Seeing Stars
Production and Distribution: First National.
Release Date: February 1922. Length: 1
reel. Cast: Charlie Chaplin, Buster Keaton,
Norma Talmadge, Constance Talmadge,
Jackie Coogan, Anita Stewart.
NOTE: Keaton impersonates a waiter during
a banquet at Los Angeles' Ambassador Hotel
at which the stars have united to form the
Independent Screen Artists' Guild.

Cops
Presented by Joseph M. Schenck. Directors:
Buster Keaton, Eddie Cline. Writers: Buster
Keaton, Eddie Cline. (Uncredited: Joseph
Mitchell, Clyde Bruckman.) Production:
Comique. Distribution: First National.
Release Date: March 1922. Length: 2 reels.
Cast: Buster Keaton. (Uncredited: Virginia
Fox, Joe Roberts, Eddie Cline.)

Screen Snapshots
Producers: Jack Cohn, Louis Lewyn.
Production: CBC Film Sales. Length: 1 reel.
Release Date: April 27, 1922. Keaton appears
with Norma and Constance Talmadge.

My Wife's Relations
Presented by Joseph M. Schenck. Directors:
Buster Keaton, Eddie Cline. Writers: Buster
Keaton, Eddie Cline. (Uncredited: Joseph
Mitchell, Clyde Bruckman, Thomas J.
Gray.) Production: Comique. Distribution:
First National. Release Date: May 1922.
Length: 2 reels. Cast: Buster Keaton.
(Uncredited: Kate Price, Joe Roberts, Monte
Collins.)

Screen Snapshots
Producers: Jack Cohn, Louis Lewyn.
Production: CBC Film Sales. Length: 1 reel.
Release Date: July 2, 1922.

The Blacksmith
Presented by Joseph M. Schenck. Directors:
Buster Keaton, Mal St. Clair. Writers: Buster
Keaton, Mal St. Clair. (Uncredited: Joseph
Mitchell, Clyde Bruckman.) Production:
Comique. Distribution: First National.
Release Date: July 1922. Length: 2 reels.
Cast: Buster Keaton. (Uncredited: Virginia
Fox, Joe Roberts.)

Screen Snapshots
Producers: Jack Cohn, Louis Lewyn.
Production: CBC Film Sales. Length: 1 reel.
Release Date: July 30, 1922.
NOTE: Keaton appears with Bull Montana.

The Frozen North
Presented by Joseph M. Schenck. Directors:
Buster Keaton, Eddie Cline. Writers:
Buster Keaton, Eddie Cline. (Uncredited:
Joseph Mitchell, Clyde Bruckman, Thomas
J. Gray.) Production: Buster Keaton
Productions. Distribution: First National.
Release Date: August 1922. Length: 2 reels.
Cast: Buster Keaton. (Uncredited: Bonnie
Hill, Joe Roberts, Sybil Seely, Eddie Cline.)

The Electric House
Presented by Joseph M. Schenck. Directors:
Buster Keaton, Eddie Cline. Writers: Buster
Keaton, Eddie Cline. (Uncredited: Joseph
Mitchell, Clyde Bruckman.) Production:
Buster Keaton Productions. Distribution:
First National. Release Date: October
1922. Length: 2 reels. Cast: Buster Keaton.
(Uncredited: Joe Roberts, Virginia Fox.)

Day Dreams
Presented by Joseph M. Schenck. Directors:
Buster Keaton, Eddie Cline. (Uncredited:
Roscoe Arbuckle.) Writers: Buster Keaton,
Eddie Cline. (Uncredited: Roscoe Arbuckle,
Joseph Mitchell, Clyde Bruckman.)
Production: Buster Keaton Productions.
Distribution: First National. Release Date:
November 1922. Length: 3 reels. Cast: Buster
Keaton. (Uncredited: Renée Adorée, Joe
Keaton, Joe Roberts, Eddie Cline.)

Screen Snapshots
Producers: Jack Cohn, Louis Lewyn.
Production: CBC Film Sales. Length: 1 reel.
Release Date: December 17, 1922.
NOTE: Keaton appears with Norma
Talmadge.

Screen Snapshots
Producers: Jack Cohn, Louis Lewyn.
Production: CBC Film Sales. Length: 1 reel.
Release Date: January 28, 1923.
NOTE: Keaton appears with the Talmadge
family.

The Love Nest

Presented by Joseph M. Schenck. Director: Buster Keaton. Writer: Buster Keaton. (Uncredited: Joseph Mitchell, Clyde Bruckman.) Production: Buster Keaton Productions. Distribution: First National. Release Date: March 1923. Length: 2 reels. Cast: Buster Keaton. (Uncredited: Joe Roberts.)

The Balloonatic

Presented by Joseph M. Schenck. Directors: Buster Keaton, Eddie Cline. Writers: Buster Keaton, Eddie Cline. (Uncredited: Joseph Mitchell, Clyde Bruckman.) Production: Buster Keaton Productions. Distribution: First National. Release Date: January 1923. Length: 2 reels. Cast: Buster Keaton. (Uncredited: Phyllis Haver.)

Three Ages

Presented by Joseph M. Schenck. Directors: Buster Keaton, Eddie Cline. Story: Jean Havez, Joseph Mitchell, Clyde Bruckman. Photography: Elgin Lessley, William C. McGann. Technical Director: Fred Gabourie. Production: Buster Keaton Productions. Distribution: Metro. Release Date: September 24, 1923. Length: 6 reels. Cast: Buster Keaton, Margaret Leahy, Wallace Beery, Lillian Lawrence, Joe Roberts, Horace Morgan, Blanche Payson, Lionel Belmore.

Our Hospitality

Presented by Joseph M. Schenck. Directors: Buster Keaton, Jack Blystone. Story: Jean Havez, Clyde Bruckman, Joseph Mitchell. Photography: Elgin Lessley, Gordon Jennings. Lighting: Denver Harmon. Art Director: Fred Gabourie. Production: Buster Keaton Productions. Distribution: Metro. Release Date: November 19, 1923. Length: 7 reels. Cast: Buster Keaton, Natalie Talmadge, Joe Roberts, Ralph Bushman, Craig Ward, Monte Collins, Joe Keaton, Kitty Bradbury, Buster Keaton, Jr.

Screen Snapshots

Producers: Jack Cohn, Louis Lewyn. Production: CBC Film Sales. Length: 1 reel. Release Date: December 16, 1923.

NOTE: Keaton appears with Wallace Beery.

Sherlock Jr.

Presented by Joseph M. Schenck. Director: Buster Keaton. Story: Jean Havez, Joseph Mitchell, Clyde Bruckman. Photography: Elgin Lessley, Byron Houck. Art Director: Fred Gabourie. Electrician: Denver Harmon. Production: Buster Keaton Productions. Distribution: Metro. Release Date: April 21, 1924. Length: 5 reels. Cast: Buster Keaton, Kathryn McGuire, Joe Keaton, Ward Crane, Erwin Connelly, Jane Connelly, Ford West, Horace Morgan.

Screen Snapshots

Producer: Jack Cohn. Production: CBC Film Sales. Length: 1 reel. Release Date: September 15, 1924.

NOTE: Keaton appears with the Talmadge family.

The Navigator

Presented by Joseph M. Schenck. Directors: Donald Crisp, Buster Keaton. Story: Clyde Bruckman, Joseph Mitchell, Jean Havez. Photography: Elgin Lessley, Byron Houck. Technical Director: Fred Gabourie. Electrician: Denver Harmon. Production: Buster Keaton Productions. Distribution: Metro-Goldwyn. Release Date: October 13, 1924. Length: 6 reels. Cast: Buster Keaton, Kathryn McGuire, Frederick Vroom, Clarence Burton, H. M. Clugston, Noble Johnson.

Screen Snapshots

Producer: Jack Cohn. Production: CBC Film Sales. Length: 1 reel. Release Date: November 1, 1924.

NOTE: Keaton appears with Joseph Schenck and Norma Talmadge.

Seven Chances

Presented by Joseph M. Schenck. Director: Buster Keaton. Adapted from the play by Roi Cooper Megrue. Screen Version: Clyde Bruckman, Jean Havez, Joseph Mitchell. Photography: Elgin Lessley, Byron Houck. Art Director: Fred Gabourie. Electrician: Denver Harmon. Production: Buster Keaton

Productions. Distribution: Metro-Goldwyn. Release Date: March 16, 1925. Length: 6 reels. Cast: Buster Keaton, T. Roy Barnes, Snitz Edwards, Ruth Dwyer, Frankie Raymond, Erwin Connelly, Jules Cowles.

Character Studies

Distribution: Educational Pictures. Release Date: November 20, 1927. Length: 1 reel. Cast: Carter De Haven, Buster Keaton, Harold Lloyd, Roscoe Arbuckle, Rudolph Valentino, Douglas Fairbanks, Jackie Coogan.

NOTE: In this privately produced novelty reel, Carter De Haven offers "a few makeup impressions of the world's greatest screen stars." The subject of each "impression" appears briefly in De Haven's place to put over the illusion, with ten-year-old Jackie Coogan's appearance finally giving the joke away.

Go West

Presented by Joseph M. Schenck. Written and Directed by Buster Keaton, "Assisted by Lex Neal." Scenario: Raymond Cannon. Photography: Elgin Lessley, Bert Haines. Art Director: Fred Gabourie. Electrical Effects: Denver Harmon. Production: Buster Keaton Productions. Distribution: Metro-Goldwyn-Mayer. Release Date: October 25, 1925. Length: 7 reels. Cast: Buster Keaton, Howard Truesdale, Kathleen Myers, Ray Thompson, Brown Eyes.

Screen Snapshots

Producer-Director: Ralph Staub. Production and Distribution: Columbia. Length: 1 reel. Release Date: May 1, 1926.

NOTE: Keaton appears with Norma Talmadge.

Battling Butler

Presented by Joseph M. Schenck. Director: Buster Keaton. Based upon the musical *Battling Butler* by Stanley Brightman, Austin Melford, and Douglas Furber, adapted for Broadway as *Battling Butler* by Ballard MacDonald. Screen Adaptation: Paul Gerard Smith, Al Boasberg, Charles H. Smith, Lex Neal. Photography: J. D. Jennings, Bert Haines. Technical Director: Fred Gabourie. Electrical Effects: Ed Levy. Production: Buster Keaton Productions. Distribution: Metro-Goldwyn-Mayer. Release Date: August 22, 1926. Length: 7 reels. Cast: Buster Keaton, Snitz Edwards, Sally O'Neil, Walter James, Bud Fine, Francis McDonald, Mary O'Brien, Tom Wilson, Eddie Borden.

The General

Presented by Joseph M. Schenck. Directors: Buster Keaton, Clyde Bruckman. Writers: Buster Keaton, Clyde Bruckman. Adaptation: Al Boasberg, Charles Smith. Photography: Dev Jennings, Bert Haines. Lighting Effects: Denver Harmon. Technical Director: Fred Gabourie. Production: Buster Keaton Productions. Distribution: United Artists. Release Date: February 5, 1927. Length: 8 reels. Cast: Buster Keaton, Marion Mack, Glen Cavender, Jim Farley, Frederick Vroom, Charles Smith, Frank Barnes, Joe Keaton, Mike Donlin, Tom Nawn.

NOTE: This film was inspired by the book *The Great Locomotive Chase* by William Pittenger.

College

Presented by Joseph M. Schenck. Supervisor: Harry Brand. Director: James W. Horne. (Uncredited: Buster Keaton.) Story: Carl Harbaugh, Bryan Foy. Photography: Dev Jennings, Bert Haines. Editor: Sherm Kell. Lighting Effects: Jack Lewis. Technical Director: Fred Gabourie. Production: Buster Keaton Productions. Distribution: United Artists. Release Date: September 10, 1927. Length: 6 reels. Cast: Buster Keaton, Anne Cornwall, Flora Bramley, Harold Goodwin, Snitz Edwards, Carl Harbaugh, Sam Crawford, Florence Turner.

Steamboat Bill, Jr.

Presented by Joseph M. Schenck. Director: Charles F. Reisner. (Uncredited: Buster Keaton.) Story: Carl Harbaugh. Photography: Dev Jennings, Bert Haines. Technical Director: Fred Gabourie. Production: Buster Keaton Productions. Distribution: United Artists. Release Date:

May 12, 1928. Length: 7 reels. Cast: Buster Keaton, Ernest Torrence, Marion Byron, Tom Lewis, Tom McGuire.

The Cameraman

Supervisor: Edgar J. Mannix. Director: Edward Sedgwick. (Uncredited: Buster Keaton.) Story: Clyde Bruckman, Lew Lipton. Continuity: Richard Schayer. Titles: Joe Farnham. Settings: Fred Gabourie. Photography: Elgin Lessley, Reggie Lanning. Editor: Hugh Wynn. Production and Distribution: Metro-Goldwyn-Mayer. Release Date: September 22, 1928. Length: 8 reels. Cast: Buster Keaton, Marceline Day, Harold Goodwin, Sidney Bracy, Harry Gribbon.

Spite Marriage

Supervisor: Irving Thalberg. (Uncredited: Lawrence Weingarten.) Director: Edward Sedgwick. (Uncredited: Buster Keaton.) Story: Lew Lipton. Adaptation: Ernest S. Pagano. Continuity: Richard Schayer. Titles: Robert E. Hopkins. Art Director: Cedric Gibbons. Photography: Reggie Lanning. Editor: Frank Sullivan. Production and Distribution: Metro-Goldwyn-Mayer. Release Date: September 22, 1928. Length: 8 reels. Cast: Buster Keaton, Dorothy Sebastian, Edward Earle, Leila Hyams, William Bechtel, John Byron.

Hollywood Revue of 1929

Supervisor: Harry Rapf. Director: Charles F. Reisner. Dances and Ensembles: Sammy Lee. Dialogue: Al Boasberg, Robert E. Hopkins. Photography: John Arnold, Irving G. Ries, Maximilian Fabian. Editors: William S. Gray, Cameron K. Wood. Art Directors: Cedric Gibbons, Richard Day. Production and Distribution: Metro-Goldwyn-Mayer. Release Date: November 23, 1929. Running time: 130 minutes. Cast: John Gilbert, Marion Davies, Norma Shearer, William Haines, Joan Crawford, Buster Keaton, Bessie Love, Marie Dressler, Cliff Edwards, Charles King, Stan Laurel and Oliver Hardy, Polly Moran. Masters of Ceremonies: Conrad Nagel, Jack Benny.

Free and Easy

Supervisor: Lawrence Weingarten. Director: Edward Sedgwick. Dances: Sammy Lee. Scenario: Richard Schayer. Adaptation: Paul Dickey. Dialogue: Al Boasberg. Photography: Leonard Smith. Editor: William LeVanway. Art Director: Cedric Gibbons. Production and Distribution: Metro-Goldwyn-Mayer. Release Date: March 22, 1930. Running Time: 93 minutes. Cast: Buster Keaton; Anita Page; Trixie Friganza; Robert Montgomery; Fred Niblo; Edgar Dearing; Gwen Lee; John Miljan; Lionel Barrymore; William Haines; William Collier, Sr.; Dorothy Sebastian; Karl Dane; David Burton. NOTE: This film was also released in a six-reel silent version. Estrellados (Spanish version of Free and Easy) Supervisor: George E. Kann. Director: Salvador de Alberich. Adaption and Dialogue: Salvador de Alberich. Cast: Buster Keaton, Raquel Torres, Don Alverado, Juan De Homs, Maria Calvo, Carlos Villarias. Buster Rutschet ins Filmland (German version of Free and Easy) Dialogue: Heinrich Fraenkel. Chi Non Cerca Trova (Italian version of Free and Easy).

The Voice of Hollywood

Producer-Director: Louis Lewyn. Production: Tec-Art. Distribution: Tiffany. Length: 11 minutes. 1 reel. Release date: April 18, 1930. Keaton appears with Raquel Torres.

Screen Snapshots

Producer-Director: Ralph Staub. Production and Distribution: Columbia. Length: 1 reel. Release Date: May 21, 1930.

Doughboys

Supervisor: Lawrence Weingarten. Director: Edward Sedgwick. Dances: Sammy Lee. Story: Al Boasberg, Sidney Lazarus. (Uncredited: Buster Keaton.) Scenario: Richard Schayer. Dialogue: Al Boasberg, Richard Schayer. Songs: Edward Sedgwick, Howard Johnson, Joseph Meyer. Photography: Leonard Smith. Editor: William LeVanway. Art Director: Cedric

Gibbons. Production and Distribution: Metro-Goldwyn-Mayer. Release Date: August 30, 1930. Running Time: 81 minutes. Cast: Buster Keaton, Sally Eilers, Cliff Edwards, Edward Brophy, Victor Potel, Arnold Korff, Frank Mayo, Pitzy Katz, William Steele, Edward Sedgwick.
De Frente, Marchen (Spanish version of *Doughboys*) Supervisor: George E. Kann. Director: Salvador de Alberich. Adaption and Dialogue: Salvador de Alberich. Cast: Buster Keaton, Conchita Montenegro, Juan de Landa, Romualdo Tirado.

The Voice of Hollywood
Producer-Director: Louis Lewyn. Production: Tec-Art. Distribution: Tiffany. Length: 10 minutes. Release Date: January 19, 1931. Keaton plays a brief scene at a new supper club in Culver City. Kenneth Harlan, Raquel Torres, Arthur Lake, Bert Wheeler, Robert Woolsey, June Clyde, and Monte Blue also appear.

Parlor, Bedroom and Bath
Supervisor: Lawrence Weingarten. Director: Edward Sedgwick. (Uncredited: Buster Keaton.) Based upon the play by Charles W. Bell and Mark Swan. Dialogue Continuity: Richard Schayer. Additional Dialogue: Robert E. Hopkins. Photography: Leonard Smith. Editor: William LeVanway. Art Director: Cedric Gibbons. Production and Distribution: Metro-Goldwyn-Mayer. Release Date: February 28, 1931. Running Time: 73 minutes. Cast: Buster Keaton, Charlotte Greenwood, Reginald Denny, Cliff Edwards, Dorothy Christy, Joan Peers, Sally Eilers, Natalie Moorhead, Edward Brophy, Walter Merrill, Sidney Bracy.
Buster se Marie (French version of *Parlor, Bedroom and Bath*) Supervisor: George E. Kann. Directors: Edward Brophy, Claude Autant-Lara. Adaption: Ivan Noe. Cast: Buster Keaton, Andre Luguet, Francoise Rosay, Jeanne Hebling, Andre Berley, Rolla Norman, Mona Goya, Lya Lys, George Davis.
Casanova Wider Willen (German version of *Parlor, Bedroom and Bath*) Supervisor: George E. Kann. Directors: Edward Brophy,

Paul Morgan. Dialogue: Paul Morgan. Cast: Buster Keaton, Paul Morgan, Egon von Jordan, Marion Lessing, Francoise Rosay, Leni Stengel, Gerda Mann, Karla G, George Davis, Wolfgang Zilzer.

The Stolen Jools
Supervisor: E. K. Nadel. Director: William McGann. Production: National Variety Artists (by arrangement and cooperation with Chesterfield Cigarettes). Distribution: National Screen Service. Release Date: April 1, 1931. Running Time: 19 minutes. Cast: Wallace Beery; Buster Keaton; Edward G. Robinson; Stan Laurel; Oliver Hardy; Polly Moran; Norma Shearer; Joan Crawford; William Haines; Victor McLaglen; Edmund Lowe; El Brendel; Warner Baxter; Irene Dunne; Bert Wheeler; Robert Woolsey; Richard Dix; Gary Cooper; Maurice Chevalier; Loretta Young; Douglas Fairbanks, Jr.; Bebe Daniels; Ben Lyon; Barbara Stanwyck; Frank Fay; Jack Oakie; Fay Wray.

Wir schalten um auf Hollywood! (*We Switch to Hollywood!*)
Supervisor: George E. Kann. Director: Frank Reicher. Manuscript and Dialogue: Paul Morgan. Photography: Ray Binger. Editor: Adrienne Fazan. Art Director: Cedric Gibbons. Production and Distribution: Metro-Goldwyn-Mayer. Release Date: July 1931. Running Time: 66 minutes. Cast: Paul Morgan, Buster Keaton, Ramon Novarro, Nora Gregor, Oscar Straus, Adolphe Menjou, Heinrich George, Dodge Sisters, John Gilbert, Egon Von Jordan, Albertina Rasch Ballet.
NOTE: In studio records, this film is identified as the German version of the unreleased *March of Time*.

Sidewalks of New York
Supervisor: Lawrence Weingarten. Directors: Jules White, Zion Myers. Story: George Landy, Paul Gerard Smith. Dialogue: Robert E. Hopkins, Eric Hatch. Photography: Leonard Smith. Editor: Charles Hochberg. Art Director: Cedric Gibbons. Production and Distribution: Metro-Goldwyn-Mayer.

Release Date: September 26, 1931. Running Time: 70 minutes. Cast: Buster Keaton; Anita Page; Cliff Edwards; Frank Rowan; Norman Phillips, Jr.; Frank LaRue; Oscar Apfel; Syd Saylor; Clark Marshall.
Buster Hat Nichts Zu Lachen (German version of *Sidewalks of New York*)
Buster Millionnaire (French version of *Sidewalks of New York*)

Splash! (*Sport Champions No. 1*)
Supervisor: Pete Smith. Directors: Jules White, Zion Myers. Production and Distribution: Metro-Goldwyn-Mayer. Release Date: October 3, 1931. Running Time: 9 minutes. Cast: Fred Cady, Larry "Buster" Crabbe, Jennie Cramer, Joy Crew, Oliver Hatch.
NOTE: According to M-G-M records, Keaton devoted one day to this short, in which he is briefly seen.

The Voice of Hollywood
Producer: Louis Lewyn. Production: Tec-Art. Distribution: Tiffany. Length: 1 reel. Release date: December 20, 1931.
NOTE: Keaton appears with Gilbert Roland.

The Passionate Plumber
Supervisor: Lawrence Weingarten. Director: Edward Sedgwick. Based upon the play *Her Cardboard Lover* by Jacques Deval. Adaptation: Laurence E. Johnson. Dialogue: Ralph Spence. Photography: Norbert Brodine. Editor: William S. Gray. Art Director: Cedric Gibbons. Production and Distribution: Metro-Goldwyn-Mayer. Release Date: February 6, 1932. Running Time: 73 minutes. Cast: Buster Keaton, Jimmy Durante, Polly Moran, Irene Purcell, Gilbert Roland, Mona Maris, Maude Eburne, Henry Armetta, Paul Porcasi, Jean Del Val, August Tollaire.
Le Plombier Amoureux (French version of *The Passionate Plumber*) Director: Claude Autant-Lara. Cast: Buster Keaton, Jimmy Durante, Polly Moran, Jeannette Ferney, Barbara Leonard.
Wer Andern Keine Liebe Gönnt (German version of *The Passionate Plumber*)

Chi La Dura La Vince (Italian version of *The Passionate Plumber*)

Screen Snapshots
Producer-Director: Ralph Staub. Production and Distribution: Columbia. Length: 1 reel. Release Date: April 18, 1932.

Speak Easily
Supervisor: Lawrence Weingarten. Director: Edward Sedgwick. Based upon the novel by Clarence Budington Kelland. Dialogue Continuity: Ralph Spence, Laurence E. Johnson. Photography: Harold Wenstrom. Editor: William LeVanway. Art Director: Cedric Gibbons. Production and Distribution: Metro-Goldwyn-Mayer. Release Date: August 13, 1932. Running Time: 80 minutes. Cast: Buster Keaton, Jimmy Durante, Ruth Selwyn, Thelma Todd, Hedda Hopper, William Pawley, Sidney Toler, Lawrence Grant, Henry Armetta, Edward Brophy.

Screen Snapshots
Producer-Director: Ralph Staub. Production and Distribution: Columbia. Length: 1 reel. Release Date: January 6, 1933.

Hollywood on Parade A-6
Producer-Director: Louis Lewyn. Production: Louis Lewyn Productions. Distribution: Paramount. Length: 10 minutes. Release Date: January 13, 1933.
NOTE: Keaton and Lew Cody are seen in and around Keaton's land yacht.

What—No Beer?
Supervisors: Frank Davis, Lou Edelman. Director: Edward Sedgwick. Story: Robert E. Hopkins. Screenplay: Carey Wilson. Additional Dialogue: Jack Cluett. Photography: Harold Wenstrom. Editor: Frank Sullivan. Art Director: Cedric Gibbons. Production and Distribution: Metro-Goldwyn-Mayer. Release Date: February 10, 1933. Running Time: 70 minutes. Cast: Buster Keaton, Jimmy Durante, Rosco Ates, Phyllis Barry, John Miljan, Henry Armetta, Edward Brophy, Charles Dunbar, Charles Giblyn.

Hollywood on Parade A-13

Producer-Director: Louis Lewyn.
Production: Louis Lewyn Productions.
Distribution: Paramount. Length: 12
minutes. Release Date: July 28, 1933.
Keaton sings a duet with Marion Mack
and introduces a pageant of movieland
couples that includes Mr. and Mrs.
Warner Baxter, William Powell and Carole
Lombard, and George Barnes and Joan
Blondell.

The Gold Ghost

Producer: E. H. Allen. Director: Charles
Lamont. Story: Ewart Adamson, Nick
Barrows. Adaptation and Continuity:
Ernest Pagano, Charles Lamont.
Photography: Dwight Warren. Production:
Educational Pictures. Distribution: Fox.
Release Date: March 16, 1934. Running
Time: 21 minutes. Cast: Buster Keaton,
Warren Hymer, Dorothy Dix, Joe Young,
William Worthington, Lloyd Ingraham,
Leo Willis.

Allez Oop

Producer: E. H. Allen. Director: Charles
Lamont. Story: Ernest Pagano, Ewart
Adamson. Photography: Dwight Warren.
Production: Educational Pictures.
Distribution: Fox. Release Date: May 25,
1934. Running Time: 20 minutes.
Cast: Buster Keaton, Dorothy Sebastian,
George Lewis, Harry Myers, the Flying
Escalantes.

Le Roi des Champs-Elysées (The King of the Champs-Elysées)

Producer: Seymour Nebenzal. Associate
Producer: John Blochert. Director:
Max Nosseck. Scenario: Arnold Lipp.
Dialogue: Yves Mirande. Photography:
Robert Le Febvre. Art Director: Jacques-
Laurent Atthalin. Production: Nero
Film. Distribution: S.A.F. Paramount.
Release Date: December 1934. Running
Time: 70 minutes. Cast: Buster Keaton,
Paulette Dubost, Madeline Guitty, Lucien
Callamand, Jacques Dumesnil, Pierre
Piérade, Gaston Dupray, Raymond Blot,
Colette Darfeuil.

The Invader

Producer: Sam Spiegel. Director: Adrian
Brunel. Story: Buster Keaton. Screenplay:
Edwin Greenwood. Photography: Eugen
Schuefftan, Eric L. Gross. Editor: Dan Birt.
Art Director: James Elder Wills. Production:
British & Continental Productions.
Distribution: Metro-Goldwyn-Mayer
Pictures, Ltd. Release Date: January 1936.
Running Time: 61 minutes. Cast: Buster
Keaton, Lupita Tovar, Esme Percy, Lyn
Harding, A. Malandrinos, Hilda Moreno,
Clifford Heatherley, Webster Booth.
NOTE: This film was distributed in the
United States by J. H. Hoffberg Co. under
the title An Old Spanish Custom.
Carambola D'Amore (Dubbed Italian version
of The Invader)

Palooka from Paducah

Producer: E. H. Allen. Director: Charles
Lamont. Story: Glen Lambert. Photography:
Dwight Warren. Production: Educational
Pictures. Distribution: Fox. Release Date:
January 11, 1935. Running Time: 20 minutes.
Cast: Buster Keaton, Myra Keaton, Joe
Keaton, Louise Keaton, Dewey Robinson,
Bull Montana.

One Run Elmer

Producer: E. H. Allen. Director: Charles
Lamont. Story: Glen Lambert. Photography:
Dwight Warren. Production: Educational
Pictures. Distribution: Fox. Release Date:
February 22, 1935. Running Time: 19
minutes. Cast: Buster Keaton, Lona André,
Dewey Robinson, Harold Goodwin.

Screen Snapshots

Producer-Director: Harriet Parsons.
Production and Distribution: Columbia.
Length: 1 reel. Release Date: March 15,
1935.

Hayseed Romance

Producer: E. H. Allen. Director: Charles
Lamont. Story: Charles Lamont.
Dialogue and Continuity: Glen Lambert.
Photography: Dwight Warren. Production:
Educational Pictures. Distribution: Fox.
Release Date: March 15, 1935. Running

Time: 20 minutes. Cast: Buster Keaton, Jane Jones, Dorothea Kent.

Tars and Stripes

Producer: E. H. Allen. Director: Charles Lamont. Story: Charles Lamont. Adaptation: Ewart Adamson. Photography: Dwight Warren. Production: Educational Pictures. Distribution: Fox. Release Date: May 3, 1935. Running Time: 20 minutes. Cast: Buster Keaton, Vernon Dent, Dorothea Kent, Jack Shutta.

The E-Flat Man

Producer: E. H. Allen. Director: Charles Lamont. Story: Glen Lambert, Charles Lamont. Photography: Dwight Warren. Production: Educational Pictures. Distribution: Fox. Release Date: August 9, 1935. Running Time: 20 minutes. Cast: Buster Keaton, Dorothea Kent, Broderick O' Farrell, Charles McAvoy, Si Jenks, Fern Emmett, Jack Shutta.

The Timid Young Man

Producer-Director: Mack Sennett. Photography: Dwight Warren. Production: Educational Pictures. Distribution: 20th Century-Fox. Release Date: October 25, 1935. Running Time: 20 minutes. Cast: Buster Keaton, Lona André, Stanley J. Sandford, Kitty McHugh, Harry Bowen.

La Fiesta de Santa Barbara

Producer-Director: Louis Lewyn. Photography: Ray Rennahan (Technicolor). Production: Louis Lewyn Productions. Distribution: Metro-Goldwyn-Mayer. Release Date: December 7, 1935. Running Time: 19 minutes. Narrator: Pete Smith. Cast: Eduardo Durant's Fiesta Orchestra and the Spanish Troubadours, Warner Baxter, Ralph Forbes, Buster Keaton, Andy Devine, Irvin S. Cobb, Joe Morrison, Ted Healy, Leo Carillo, the Fanchonettes, Garland Sisters, Kirby and De Gage, Dude Ranch Wranglers.

Three on a Limb

Producer: E. H. Allen. Director: Charles Lamont. Story: Vernon Smith. Photography: Gus Peterson. Production: Educational

Pictures. Distribution: 20th Century-Fox. Release Date: January 3, 1936. Running Time: 18 minutes. Cast: Buster Keaton, Lona André, Harold Goodwin, Grant Withers, Barbara Bedford, John Ince, Fern Emmett, Phyllis Crane.

Sunkist Stars at Palm Springs

Producer: Louis Lewyn. Director: Roy Rowland. Dialogue: John Krafft. Photography: Allen Davey, Aldo Ermini (Technicolor). Production: Louis Lewyn Productions. Distribution: Metro-Goldwyn-Mayer. Release Date: January 11, 1936. Running Time: 20 minutes. Cast: Edmund Lowe, the Fanchonettes, Hollywood Ingénues, Downey Sisters, Frances Langford, Walter Huston, Betty Furness, Jackie Coogan, Betty Grable, Buster Keaton, Johnny Weissmuller.

Grand Slam Opera

Producer: E. H. Allen. Director: Charles Lamont. Story: Buster Keaton, Charles Lamont. Photography: Gus Peterson. Production: Educational Pictures. Distribution: 20th Century-Fox. Release Date: February 21, 1936. Running Time: 21 minutes. Cast: Buster Keaton, Diana Lewis, Harold Goodwin, John Ince, Melrose Coakley, Bud Jamison.

Blue Blazes

Producer: Al Christie. Director: Raymond Kane. Story: David Freedman. Photography: George Webber. Production: Educational Pictures. Distribution: 20th Century-Fox. Release Date: August 21, 1936. Running Time: 19 minutes. Cast: Buster Keaton, Marlyn Stuart, Donald McBride, Earl Gilbert, Herman Lieb.
NOTE: This was the first of three shorts Keaton filmed for Educational in New York.

The Chemist

Producer-Director: Al Christie. Story: David Freedman. Photography: George Webber. Production: Educational Pictures. Distribution: 20th Century-Fox. Release Date: October 9, 1936. Running Time: 19 minutes. Cast: Buster Keaton, Marlyn

Stuart, Donald McBride, Earl Gilbert, Herman Lieb.

Mixed Magic

Producer: Al Christie. Director: Raymond Kane. Story: Arthur Jarrett, Marcy Klauber. Photography: George Webber. Production: Educational Pictures. Distribution: 20th Century-Fox. Release Date: November 20, 1936. Running Time: 17 minutes. Cast: Buster Keaton, Eddie Lambert, Marlyn Stuart, Eddie Hall, Jimmie Fox, Walter Fenner, Pass Le Noir.

Jail Bait

Producer: E. H. Allen. Director: Charles Lamont. Story: Paul Gerard Smith. Photography: Dwight Warren. Production: Educational Pictures. Distribution: 20th Century-Fox. Release Date: January 8, 1937. Running Time: 19 minutes. Cast: Buster Keaton, Harold Goodwin, Mathew Betz, Bud Jamison, Betty Andre, Louise Keaton.

Ditto

Producer: E. H. Allen. Director: Charles Lamont. Story: Paul Gerard Smith. Photography: Dwight Warren. Production: Educational Pictures. Distribution: 20th Century-Fox. Release Date: February 12, 1937. Running Time: 17 minutes. Cast: Buster Keaton, Gloria Brewster, Barbara Brewster, Harold Goodwin, Lynton Brent, Al Thompson, Bob Ellsworth.

Screen Snapshots

Producer-Director: Harriet Parsons. Production and Distribution: Columbia. Length: 1 reel. Release Date: February 19, 1937. Keaton is seen attending the world premiere of M-G-M's *Camille* in Palm Springs.

Love Nest on Wheels

Producer: E. H. Allen. Director: Charles Lamont. Story: William Hazlett Upson. Adaptation: Paul Gerard Smith. Photography: Dwight Warren. Production: Educational Pictures. Distribution: 20th Century-Fox. Release Date: March 26, 1937.

Running Time: 18 minutes. Cast: Buster Keaton, Myra Keaton, Al St. John, Lynton Brent, Diana Lewis, Bud Jamison, Louise Keaton, Harry Keaton.

Life in Sometown, U.S.A.

Producer: Jack Chertok. Director: Buster Keaton. Screenplay: Carl Dudley, Richard Murphy. Production and Distribution: Metro-Goldwyn-Mayer. Release Date: February 26, 1938. Running Time: 11 minutes. Narrator: Carey Wilson. Cast: Francis X. Bushman, Betty Blythe, King Baggot, Philips Smalley, Jules Cowles.

Hollywood Handicap

Producer: Louis Lewyn. Director: Buster Keaton. Production: Louis Lewyn Productions. Distribution: Metro-Goldwyn-Mayer. Release Date: May 28, 1938. Running Time: 10 minutes. Cast: The Original Sing Band.

Streamlined Swing

Producer: Louis Lewyn. Director: Buster Keaton. Screenplay: Marion Mack. Dialogue: John Krafft. Production: Louis Lewyn Productions. Distribution: Metro-Goldwyn-Mayer. Release Date: September 10, 1938. Running Time: 9 minutes. Cast: The Original Sing Band.

Screen Snapshots

Producer-Director: Harriet Parsons. Production and Distribution: Columbia. Length: 1 reel. Release Date: November 20, 1938.
NOTE: Keaton appears in this entry on how and why publicity photos are made.

Hollywood Hobbies

Producer: Louis Lewyn. Director: George Sidney. Story and Screenplay: Morey Amsterdam. Production: Louis Lewyn Productions. Distribution: Metro-Goldwyn-Mayer. Release Date: May 3, 1939. Running Time: 10 minutes. Cast: Joyce Compton, Sally Payne, William Benedict.
NOTE: Keaton is seen as a team member in the annual leading men versus comedians baseball game.

The Jones Family in Hollywood

Associate Producer: John Stone. Director: Malcolm St. Clair. Story: Joseph Hoffman, Buster Keaton. Screenplay: Harold Tarshis. Photography: Edward Snyder. Editor: Fred Allen. Art Directors: Richard Day, Mark-Lee Kirk. Production and Distribution: 20th Century-Fox. Release Date: June 2, 1939. Running Time: 61 minutes. Cast: Jed Prouty, Spring Byington, Ken Howell, George Ernest, June Carlson, Florence Roberts, Billy Mahan.

Pest from the West

Producer: Jules White. Director: Del Lord. Screenplay: Clyde Bruckman. Photography: Henry Freulich. Editor: Charles Nelson. Production and Distribution: Columbia. Release Date: June 16, 1939. Running Time: 18 minutes. Cast: Buster Keaton, Lorna Gray, Gino Corrado, Richard Fiske.

Mooching Through Georgia

Producer-Director: Jules White. Screenplay: Clyde Bruckman. Photography: John Stumar. Editor: Arthur Seid. Production and Distribution: Columbia. Release Date: August 11, 1939. Running Time: 19 minutes. Cast: Buster Keaton, Monty Collins, Jill Martin, Bud Jamison.

Quick Millions

Associate Producer: John Stone. Director: Malcolm St. Clair. Story: Joseph Hoffman, Buster Keaton. Screenplay: Joseph Hoffman, Stanley Rauh. Photography: Lucien Andriot. Editor: Harry Reynolds. Art Directors: Richard Day, Albert Hogsett. Production and Distribution: 20th Century-Fox. Release Date: August 25, 1939. Running Time: 60 minutes. Cast: Jed Prouty, Spring Byington, Ken Howell, George Ernest, June Carlson, Florence Roberts, Billy Mahan.

Hollywood Cavalcade

Producer: Darryl F. Zanuck. Associate Producer: Harry Joe Brown. Directors: Irving Cummings, Malcolm St. Clair. Based upon an idea by Lou Breslow. Story: Hilary Lynn, Brown Holmes. Screenplay: Ernest Pascal. Photography: Ernest Palmer, Allen M. Davey (Technicolor). Editor: Walter Thompson. Art Directors: Richard Day, Wiard B. Ihnen. Production and Distribution: 20th Century-Fox. Release Date: October 13, 1939. Running Time: 96 minutes. Cast: Alice Faye, Don Ameche, J. Edward Bromberg, Alan Curtis, Stuart Erwin, Donald Meek, George Givot, Eddie Collins, Buster Keaton, Ben Turpin, Chester Conklin, Hank Mann, Jed Prouty, Snub Pollard, Al Jolson, Mack Sennett.

Nothing but Pleasure

Producer-Director: Jules White. Screenplay: Clyde Bruckman. Photography: Henry Freulich. Editor: Arthur Seid. Production and Distribution: Columbia. Release Date: January 19, 1940. Running Time: 17 minutes. Cast: Buster Keaton, Dorothy Appleby, Beatrice Blinn.

Pardon My Berth Marks

Producer-Director: Jules White. Screenplay: Clyde Bruckman. Photography: Benjamin Kline. Editor: Mel Thorsen. Production and Distribution: Columbia. Release Date: March 22, 1940. Running Time: 18 minutes. Cast: Buster Keaton, Dorothy Appleby, Richard Fiske, Vernon Dent.

Screen Snapshots

Producer-Director: Ralph Staub. Production and Distribution: Columbia. Length: 1 reel. Release Date: March 29, 1940. A survey of sports venues around Los Angeles that are favored by the stars.
NOTE: Keaton, in a running gag, is seen as a spectator at all of them.

The Taming of the Snood

Producer-Director: Jules White. Screenplay: Ewart Adamson, Clyde Bruckman. Photography: Henry Freulich. Editor: Mel Thorsen. Production and Distribution: Columbia. Release Date: June 28, 1940. Running Time: 16 minutes. Cast: Buster Keaton, Elsie Ames, Dorothy Appleby.

The Spook Speaks

Producer-Director: Jules White. Screenplay: Ewart Adamson, Clyde Bruckman.

Photography: Henry Freulich. Editor: Mel
Thorsen. Production and Distribution:
Columbia. Release Date: September 20,
1940. Running Time: 18 minutes. Cast:
Buster Keaton, Elsie Ames, Don Beddoe,
Dorothy Appleby.

The Villain Still Pursued Her
Producer: Harold B. Franklin. Director:
Edward Cline. Screenplay: Elbert Franklin.
Additional Dialogue: Ethel La Blanche.
Photography: Lucien Ballard. Editor:
Arthur Hilton. Art Director: Louis Rachmil.
Production: Franklin-Blank Productions.
Distribution: RKO-Radio. Release Date:
October 11, 1940. Running Time: 67
minutes. Cast: Hugh Herbert, Anita Louise,
Alan Mowbray, Buster Keaton, Joyce
Compton, Richard Cromwell, Billy Gilbert,
Margaret Hamilton, Diane Fisher, Charles
Judels.

Li'l Abner
Associate Producer: Herman Schlom.
Director: Albert S. Rogell. Based upon
the United Features comic by Al Capp.
Story: Al Capp. Screenplay: Charles Kerr,
Tyler Johnson. Additional Dialogue: Ethel
La Blanche. Photography: Harry Jackson.
Editors: Otto Ludwig, Donn Hayes. Art
Director: Ralph Berger. Production: Vogue
Pictures. Distribution: RKO-Radio. Release
Date: November 1, 1940. Running Time:
78 minutes. Cast: Granville Owen, Martha
O'Driscoll, Mona Ray, Johnnie Morris,
Buster Keaton, Billie Seward, Kay Sutton,
Maude Eburne, Johnny Arthur, Walter
Catlett.

His Ex Marks the Spot
Producer-Director: Jules White. Screenplay:
Felix Adler. Photography: Benjamin Kline.
Editor: Mel Thorsen. Production and
Distribution: Columbia. Release Date:
December 13, 1940. Running Time: 18
minutes. Cast: Buster Keaton, Elsie Ames,
Matt McHugh, Dorothy Appleby.

So You Won't Squawk?
Producers: Del Lord, Hugh McCollum.
Director: Del Lord. Screenplay: Elwood

Ullman. Photography: Benjamin Kline.
Editor: Arthur Seid. Production and
Distribution: Columbia. Release Date:
February 21, 1941. Running Time: 16
minutes. Cast: Buster Keaton, Matt
McHugh, Eddie Fetherston.

Screen Snapshots
Producer-Director: Ralph Staub. Production
and Distribution: Columbia. Length: 1 reel.
Release Date: August 15, 1941.
NOTE: At a pool party hosted by Milton
Berle, Keaton schools Joan Davis in the art
of pie throwing.

General Nuisance
Producer-Director: Jules White. Screenplay:
Felix Adler, Clyde Bruckman. Photography:
Benjamin Kline. Editor: Jerome Thoms.
Production and Distribution: Columbia.
Release Date: September 18, 1941. Running
Time: 17 minutes. Cast: Buster Keaton,
Elsie Ames, Dorothy Appleby, Monty
Collins.

She's Oil Mine
Producer-Director: Jules White. Screenplay:
Felix Adler. Photography: Benjamin Kline.
Editor: Jerome Thoms. Production and
Distribution: Columbia. Release Date:
November 20, 1941. Running Time: 17
minutes. Cast: Buster Keaton, Elsie Ames,
Monty Collins, Eddie Laughton.

Forever and a Day
Producers and Directors: Rene Clair,
Edmund Goulding, Cedric Hardwicke,
Frank Lloyd, Victor Saville, Robert
Stevenson, Herbert Wilcox. Written by
Charles Bennett, C. S. Forrester, Lawrence
Hazard, and others. Editors: Elmo Williams,
George Crone. Production: Anglo-American
Productions. Distribution: RKO-Radio.
Release Date: March 26, 1943. Running
Time: 104 minutes. Cast: Victor McLaglen,
Herbert Marshall, Ray Milland, Anna
Neagle, Claude Rains, Jessie Matthews,
Charles Laughton, Sir Cedric Hardwicke,
Buster Keaton, Anna Lee, Patric Knowles,
Edward Everett Horton, Ida Lupino,
Brian Aherne, Merle Oberon, Nigel Bruce,

Elsa Lanchester, Roland Young, Robert Cummings, Donald Crisp.

San Diego I Love You

Producers: Michael Fessier, Ernest Pagano. Director: Reginald Le Borg. Story: Ruth McKenney, Richard Bransten. Screenplay: Michael Fessier, Ernest Pagano. Photography: Hal Mohr. Editor: Charles Maynard. Art Directors: John B. Goodman, Alexander Golitzen. Production and Distribution: Universal. Release Date: September 29, 1944. Running Time: 85 minutes. Cast: Jon Hall, Louise Allbritton, Edward Everett Horton, Eric Blore, Buster Keaton, Irene Ryan.

That's the Spirit

Producers: Michael Fessier, Ernest Pagano. Director: Charles Lamont. Story: Arnold Belgard. Screenplay: Michael Fessier, Ernest Pagano. Photography: Charles Van Enger. Editor: Fred R. Feitshans, Jr. Art Directors: John B. Goodman, Richard H. Riedel. Production and Distribution: Universal. Release Date: June 1, 1945. Running Time: 93 minutes. Cast: Jack Oakie, Peggy Ryan, June Vincent, Gene Lockhart, Johnny Coy, Andy Devine, Arthur Treacher, Irene Ryan, Buster Keaton, Victoria Horne, Edith Barrett.

That Night with You

Executive Producer: Howard Benedict. Producers: Michael Fessier, Ernest Pagano. Director: William A. Seiter. Story: Arnold Belgard. Screenplay: Michael Fessier, Ernest Pagano. Photography: Charles Van Enger. Editor: Fred R. Feitshans, Jr.; Charles Maynard. Art Directors: John B. Goodman, Martin Obzina. Alexander Golitzen. Production and Distribution: Universal. Release Date: September 28, 1945. Running Time: 84 minutes. Cast: Franchot Tone, Susanna Foster, David Bruce, Louise Allbritton, Jacqueline de Wit, Irene Ryan, Buster Keaton, Howard Freeman, Barbara Sears, Teddy Infuhr.

She Went to the Races

Producer: Frederick Stephani. Director: Willis Goldbeck. Story: Alan Friedman, De Vallon Scott. Screenplay: Lawrence Hazard. Photography: Charles Salerno. Editor: Adrienne Fazan. Art Directors: Cedric Gibbons, Preston Ames. Production and Distribution: Metro-Goldwyn-Mayer. Release Date: November 1945. Running Time: 86 minutes. Cast: James Craig, Frances Gifford, Ava Gardner, Edmund Gwenn, Sig Ruman, Reginald Owen, J. W. Kerrigan, Charles Halton, Chester Clute, Frank Orth.
NOTE: Keaton appears in a cameo as a bellhop.

God's Country

Producer: William B. David. Director: Robert Tansey. Screenplay: Robert Tansey. Photography: Marcel LePicard (Cinecolor). Editor: George McGuire. Art Director: Ed Jewel. Production: Action Pictures. Distribution: Screen Guild. Release Date: April 1946. Running Time: 62 minutes. Cast: Robert Lowrey, Helen Gilbert, William Farnum, Buster Keaton, Stanley Andrews, Trevor Bardette, Si Jenks, Estelle Zarco, Juan Reyes, Al Ferguson.

Equestrian Quiz (What's Your I.Q.? No. 11)

Producer: Pete Smith. Director: Buster Keaton. Screenplay: Dave O'Brien, Lew Harris. Editor: J. J. Durant, Jr. Production and Distribution: Metro-Goldwyn-Mayer. Release Date: May 18, 1946. Running Time: 10 minutes. Narrator: Pete Smith.
NOTE: Keaton directed a running gag in which Dave O'Brien learns how to saddle, mount, and ride a horse.

El Moderno Barba Azul (The Modern Bluebeard)

Producer: Alejandro Salkind. Director: Jaime Salvador. Story: Victor Trivas. Screenplay: Jaime Salvador. Photography: Agustin Jimenez. Editor: Rafael Ceballor. Production: Alsa Films S.A. First U.S. Showing: December 1949. Running Time: 98 minutes. Cast: Buster Keaton, Angel Garasa, Virginia Serret, Fernando Soto, Luis C. Barreiro, Jorge Mondragon, Oscar Pulido, Jose Elias Moreno.

NOTE: A dubbed sixty-nine-minute version of this film was released to the home video market in 1985 under the title *Boom in the Moon.*

Un duel à mort (A Duel to the Death)

Producers: René Bianco, Louis Lefait. Director: Pierre Blondy. Photography: Jacques Isnard. Music: Georges Van Parys. Production: Azur Films. Distribution: Les Films Cristal. Released 1948. Running Time: 24 minutes. Cast: Buster Keaton, Antonin Berval.

NOTE: Keaton developed this scene, inspired by the dueling sequence in *Passionate Plumber,* into a stage act for his 1947 engagement at the Cirque Médrano. This film is essentially a record of that act.

In the Good Old Summertime

Producer: Joseph Pasternak. Director: Robert Z. Leonard. Musical Sequences Directed by Robert Alton. Story: Miklos Laszlo, Samson Raphaelson. Screenplay: Albert Hackett, Frances Goodrich, Ivan Tors. Photography: Harry Stradling (Technicolor). Editor: Adrienne Fazan. Art Directors: Cedric Gibbons, Randall Duell. Production and Distribution: Metro-Goldwyn-Mayer. Release Date: July 29, 1949. Running Time: 102 minutes. Cast: Judy Garland, Van Johnson, S. Z. "Cuddles" Sakall, Spring Byington, Clinton Sundberg, Buster Keaton, Marcia Van Dyke.

You're My Everything

Producer: Lamar Trotti. Director: Walter Lang. Story: George Jessel. Screenplay: Lamar Trotti, Will H. Hays, Jr. Photography: Arthur E. Arling (Technicolor). Editor: James Watson Webb, Jr. Art Directors: Lyle Wheeler, Leland Fuller. Production and Distribution: 20th Century-Fox. Release Date: August 1949. Running Time: 94 minutes. Cast: Dan Dailey, Anne Baxter, Anne Revere, Stanley Ridges, Shari Robinson, Henry O'Neill, Selena Royle, Alan Mowbray, Robert Arthur.

NOTE: Keaton plays a self-referential cameo as a butler.

The Lovable Cheat

Producers: Richard Oswald, Edward Lewis. Associate Producer: Rosario Castagna. Director: Richard Oswald. Based upon the play *Le Faiseur* by Honoré de Balzac. Adaptation: Edward Lewis, Richard Oswald. Photography: Paul Ivano. Editor: Douglas Bagier. Art Director: Boris Leven. Production: Skyline Pictures. Distribution: Film Classics. Release Date: May 11, 1949. Running Time: 74 minutes. Cast: Charlie Ruggles, Peggy Ann Garner, Richard Ney, Buster Keaton, Curt Bois, Alan Mowbray, Iris Adrian, Ludwig Donath, Fritz Feld, John Wengraf, Otto Waldis, Edna Holland, Minerva Urecal, Helen Servis, Jody Gilbert, Judith Trafford.

Sunset Boulevard

Producer: Charles Brackett. Director: Billy Wilder. Screenplay: Charles Brackett, Billy Wilder, D. M. Marshman, Jr. Photography: John F. Seitz. Editors: Doane Harrison, Arthur Schmidt. Art Directors: Hans Dreier, John Meehan. Production and Distribution: Paramount. Release Date: August 1950. Running Time: 110 minutes. Cast: William Holden, Gloria Swanson, Erich von Stroheim, Nancy Olson, Fred Clark, Lloyd Gough, Jack Webb, Cecil B. DeMille, Hedda Hopper, Buster Keaton, H. B. Warner, Franklyn Farnum, Ray Evans, Jay Livingston.

Limelight

Director: Charles Chaplin. Screenplay: Charles Chaplin. Photography: Karl Struss. Editor: Joe Inge. Art Director: Eugene Lourie. Production: Celebrated Films. Distribution: United Artists. Release Date: February 6, 1953. Running Time: 143 minutes. Cast: Charles Chaplin, Claire Bloom, Nigel Bruce, Buster Keaton, Sydney Chaplin, Norman Lloyd, Andre Eglevsky, Melissa Hayden, Marjorie Bennett.

Paradise for Buster

Supervisors: H. M. Railsback, G. M. Rohrbach. Director: Del Lord. Story: J. P. Prindle, John Grey, Hal Goodwin. Photography: J. J. La Fleur, Robert Sable.

Editor: William Minnerly. Art Director: Edward C. Jewell. Production: Wilding Picture Productions. Distribution: John Deere and Company. First Regional Showings: November 1952. Running Time: 38 minutes. Cast: Buster Keaton.
NOTE: This film was the feature attraction at numerous John Deere Day events staged for farmers and their families throughout the Midwest.

The Misadventures of Buster Keaton
Producer: Carl K. Hittleman. Director: Arthur Hilton. Screenplay: Harold Goodwin. Photography: Jackson Rose. Production: Crown Pictures International. Distribution: British Lion Film Corp. Release Date: July 1953. Running Time: 63 minutes. Cast: Buster Keaton, Marcia Mae Jones, Harold Goodwin, Eleanor Keaton.

L'Incantevole Nemica (*The Enchanting Enemy*)
Producers: Dario Sabatello, Jules Borkon. Director: Claudio Gora. Story: Vittorio Metz, Marcello Marchesi. Screenplay: Edoardo Anton, Jean Bernard-Luc. Photography: Leonida Barboni. Editor: Stefano Canzio. Music: Raffaele Gervasio. Production: Orso Film (Rome), Lambor Films (Paris). Distribution: CEI-Incom. Release Date: December 10, 1953. Running Time: 87 minutes. Cast: Silvana Pampanini, Robert Lamoureux, Carlo Campanini, Ugo Tognazzi, Pina Renzi, Buster Keaton, Nyta Dover, Giuseppe Porelli, Nando Bruno.
NOTE: Keaton performs an abbreviated version of a scene he originally developed for American TV, and which became his Italian stage act. As an onlooker in a bakery, Buster tries his hand at working with bread dough.

Around the World in 80 Days
Producer: Michael Todd. Associate Producer: William Cameron Menzies. Director: Michael Anderson. (Uncredited: John Farrow, Michael Todd.) Based upon the novel by Jules Verne. Screenplay: James Poe, John Farrow, S. J. Perelman. Photography: Lionel Lindon (Todd-AO/Technicolor). Art Directors: James Sullivan, Ken Adams.

Editors: Gene Ruggiero, Howard Epstein. (Uncredited: Paul Weatherwax.) Production: Michael Todd Co. Distribution: United Artists. World Premiere: October 17, 1956. Running Time: 178 minutes. Cast: David Niven, Cantinflas, Robert Newton, Shirley MacLaine, Finlay Currie, Robert Morley, Ronald Squire, Basil Sydney, Noël Coward, Sir John Gielgud, Trevor Howard, Harcourt Williams, Martine Carol, Fernandel, Charles Boyer, Evelyn Keyes, José Greco and Troupe, Gilbert Roland, Luis Dominguin, Cesar Romero, Alan Mowbray, Sir Cedric Hardwicke, Melville Cooper, Reginald Denny, Ronald Colman, Robert Cabal, Charles Coburn, Peter Lorre, George Raft, Red Skelton, Marlene Dietrich, John Carradine, Frank Sinatra, Buster Keaton, Col. Tim McCoy, Joe E. Brown, Andy Devine, Edmund Lowe, Victor McLaglen, Jack Oakie, Beatrice Lillie, Glynis Johns, Hermione Gingold, John Mills, Edward R. Murrow.

The Buster Keaton Story
Producers: Robert Smith, Sidney Sheldon. Director: Sidney Sheldon. Screenplay: Sidney Sheldon, Robert Smith. Technical Advisor: Buster Keaton. Photography: Loyal Griggs. Editor: Archie Marshek. Art Directors: Hal Pereira, Carl Anderson. Production and Distribution: Paramount. Release Date: May 1957. Running Time: 87 minutes. Cast: Donald O'Connor, Ann Blyth, Rhonda Fleming, Peter Lorre, Larry Keating, Richard Anderson, Dave Willock, Claire Carleton, Larry White, Jackie Coogan.

The Adventures of Huckleberry Finn
Producer: Samuel Goldwyn, Jr. Director: Michael Curtiz. Based upon the novel by Mark Twain. Screenplay: James Lee. Photography: Ted McCord (Cinemascope/ MetroColor). Editor: Frederic Steinkamp. Art Directors: George W. Davis, McClure Capps. Production and Distribution: Metro-Goldwyn-Mayer. Release Date: June 17, 1960. Running Time: 107 minutes. Cast: Eddie Hodges, Archie Moore, Tony Randall, Patty McCormack, Neville Brand, Buster

Keaton, Judy Canova, Mickey Shaughnessy, Andy Devine, Josephine Hutchinson, Finlay Currie, Royal Dano, John Carradine, Sterling Holloway.

The Devil to Pay

Director: Herb Skoble. Script and Editing: Cummins-Betts. Video: Del Ankers, Fritz Roland. Art Directors: Peter Masters, Joseph W. Swanson. Production: Education Research Films/Rodel Productions, Inc. Distribution: National Association of Wholesalers. First Regional Showings: March 1960. Running Time: 27 minutes. Cast: Buster Keaton, Ralph Dunn, Ruth Gillette, Marion Morris, John Rodney.

NOTE: While this film was made with television in mind, it was more commonly shown to business and service groups, particularly chambers of commerce, to highlight the role of wholesaling in the "jet age of distribution."

The Home Owner

Director: Joe Parker. Script: Joe Parker. Photography: Leo Tover (color). Editor: Basil Wrangell. Narrator: Bob Hawk. Production: Skirball Productions. Distribution: John F. Long Company. First Showings: 1962. Running Time: 22 minutes. Cast: Buster Keaton.

NOTE: Made in 1961, this film showcases model homes in Arizona developer John F. Long's master planned community of Maryvale.

Ten Girls Ago

Producer: Edward A. Gollin. Director: Harold Daniels. Script: Peter Farrow, Diane Lampert. Songs: Sammy Fain, Diane Lampert. Photography: Lee Garmes (Eastman Color). Editor: Dave Nicholson. Production: Am-Can Productions. Distribution: Universal. Cast: Bert Lahr; Buster Keaton; Eddie Foy, Jr.; Dion; Jennifer Billingsley; Roselle Bain; Jan Miner.

NOTE: Filmed at Toronto International Film Studios, Kleinburg, during March–April 1962, this musical-comedy feature was never completed.

It's a Mad, Mad, Mad, Mad World

Producer-Director: Stanley Kramer. Screenplay: William Rose, Tania Rose. Photography: Ernest Laszlo (Ultra Panavision, Technicolor). Editors: Frederick Knudtson, Robert C. Jones, Gene Fowler, Jr. Production: Casey Productions, Inc. Distribution: United Artists. Release Date: November 7, 1963 (Roadshow), July 25, 1964 (General). Running Time: 190 minutes (Roadshow), 161 minutes (General). Cast: Spencer Tracy, Milton Berle, Sid Caesar, Buddy Hackett, Ethel Merman, Mickey Rooney, Dick Shawn, Phil Silvers, Terry-Thomas, Jonathan Winters, Edie Adams, Dorothy Provine, Eddie "Rochester" Anderson, Jim Backus, Ben Blue, Joe E. Brown, Alan Carney, Chick Chandler, Barrie Chase, Lloyd Corrigan, William Demarest, Selma Diamond, Peter Falk, Andy Devine, Norman Fell, Paul Ford, Stan Freeberg, Louise Glenn, Leo Gorcey, Sterling Holloway, Marvin Kaplan, Edward Everett Horton, Buster Keaton, Don Knotts, Charles Lane, Mike Mazurki, Charles McGraw, Cliff Norton, ZaSu Pitts, Carl Reiner, Madlyn Rhue, Roy Roberts, Arnold Stang, Nick Stewart, The Three Stooges, Sammee Tong, Jesse White, Jimmy Durante.

The Triumph of Lester Snapwell

Director: James Calhoun. Production and Distribution: Eastman Kodak. First Regional Showings: May 1963. Running Time: 21 minutes. Cast: Buster Keaton, Sigrid Nelsson, Nina Varela.

NOTE: Made in Rochester, New York, this film, covering photographic advances from the year 1868 to the present day, introduces the Kodak Instamatic line of cameras.

There's No Business Like No Business

Production: Interlock, Inc. Distribution: Maremont Corp. First Showings: 1964. Running Time: 15 minutes. Cast: Buster Keaton.

NOTE: Aimed at encouraging new business for mufflers and shock absorbers in the auto aftermarket, this film casts Keaton as a service station attendant who misses out on obvious sales opportunities.

Film

Producer: Barney Rosset. Director: Alan Schneider. Screenplay: Samuel Beckett. Photography: Boris Kaufman. Editor: Sidney Meyers. Art Director: Burr Smidt. Production: Evergreen Theatre. First Public Showing: September 4, 1965. Running Time: 17 minutes. Cast: Buster Keaton, Nell Harrison, James Karen, Susan Reed.

Pajama Party

Producers: James H. Nicholson, Samuel Z. Arkoff. Co-Producer: Anthony Carras. Director: Don Weis. Screenplay: Louis M. Heyward. Photography: Floyd Crosby (Pathécolor). Editors: Fred Feitshans, Eve Newman. Art Director: Daniel Haller. Production and Distribution: American International. Release Date: November 11, 1964. Running Time: 85 minutes. Cast: Tommy Kirk, Annette Funicello, Elsa Lanchester, Harvey Lembeck, Jesse White, Jody McCrea, Ben Lessy, Donna Loren, Susan Hart, Bobbi Shaw, Buster Keaton, Dorothy Lamour, Don Rickles, Frankie Avalon.

The Railrodder

Producer: Julian Biggs. Director: Gerald Potterton. Screenplay: Gerald Potterton. Photography: Robert Humble (Eastman Color). Music: Eldon Rathburn. Editors: Jo Kirkpatrick, Gerald Potterton. Production and Distribution: National Film Board of Canada. Release Date: October 1965. Running Time: 25 minutes. Cast: Buster Keaton.

The Fall Guy

Director: Darrel Bateman. Production: Evans Sight and Sound Productions. Distribution: United States Steel. First Showings: 1965. Cast: Buster Keaton, Bob Dahl.
NOTE: This is apparently one of two industrial shorts Keaton made in 1964 for U.S. Steel in Salt Lake City. Paul E. Gierucki of CineMuseum, LLC, has confirmed their existence with actor Bob Dahl, but no prints have surfaced.

Budweiser Beer Talk Report

First Showings: 1965. Length: 2 reels. Cast: Olan Soule, Joe E. Brown, Buster Keaton, Jackie Joseph, Johnny Carson, Ed McMahon, Fritz Feld, Alvy Moore.
NOTE: Intended strictly for Anheuser-Busch sales meetings, this film features an impressive array of TV personalities in brief cameos, including Keaton in a new one-minute Budweiser commercial. A recent discovery by Richard M. Roberts, who also rescued *The Home Owner* from certain extinction.

Beach Blanket Bingo

Producers: James H. Nicholson, Samuel Z. Arkoff. Co-Producer: Anthony Carras. Director: William Asher. Screenplay: William Asher, Leo Townsend. Photography: Floyd Crosby (Pathécolor). Editors: Fred Feitshans, Eve Newman. Art Director: Howard Campbell. Production and Distribution: American International. Release Date: April 15, 1965. Running Time: 98 minutes. Cast: Frankie Avalon, Annette Funicello, Deborah Walley, Harvey Lembeck, John Ashley, Jody McCrea, Donna Loren, Marta Kristen, Linda Evans, Timothy Carey, Don Rickles, Paul Lynde, Buster Keaton, Earl Wilson, Bobbi Shaw.

How to Stuff a Wild Bikini

Producers: James H. Nicholson, Samuel Z. Arkoff. Co-Producer: Anthony Carras. Director: William Asher. Screenplay: William Asher, Leo Townsend. Photography: Floyd Crosby (Pathécolor). Editors: Fred Feitshans, Eve Newman. Art Director: Howard Campbell. Production and Distribution: American International. Release Date: July 14, 1965. Running Time: 90 minutes. Cast: Annette Funicello, Dwayne Hickman, Brian Donlevy, Harvey Lembeck, Beverly Adams, John Ashley, Jody McCrea, Len Lesser, Bobbi Shaw, Marianne Gaba, Irene Tsu, Buster Keaton, Mickey Rooney, Frankie Avalon.

Sergeant Deadhead

Producers: James H. Nicholson, Samuel Z. Arkoff. Co-Producer: Anthony Carras.

Director: Norman Taurog. Screenplay: Louis M. Heyward. Photography: Floyd Crosby (Pathécolor). Editors: Ronald Sinclair, Eve Newman, Fred Feitshans. Art Director: Howard Campbell. Production and Distribution: American International. Release Date: August 18, 1965. Running Time: 90 minutes. Cast: Frankie Avalon, Deborah Walley, Cesar Romero, Fred Clark, Gale Gordon, Harvey Lembeck, John Ashley, Buster Keaton, Reginald Gardiner, Pat Buttram, Eve Arden, Romo Vincent, Donna Loren, Bobbi Shaw, Dwayne Hickman.

War Italian Style

Producer: Fulvio Lucisano. Director: Luigi Scattini. Story: Fulvio Lucisano. Screenplay: Franco Castellano, Pipolo. Photography: Fausto Zuccoli (Technicolor). Production: Italian International Films. Distribution: American International. Release Date: January 11, 1967. Running Time: 94 minutes. Cast: Buster Keaton, Franco Franchi, Ciccio Ingrassia, Martha Hyer, Fred Clark, Tommaso Alvieri, Barbara Loy, Alessandro Sperli, Alfredo Adami, Ennio Antonelli, Renato Chiantoni, Willy Colombini, Consalvo Dell'arti.

NOTE: The Italian version of this film was released in 1966 under the title *Due Marines e un Generale* (*Two Marines and a General*).

A Funny Thing Happened on the Way to the Forum

Producer: Melvin Frank. Director: Richard Lester. Based upon the musical by Burt Shevelove, Larry Gelbart, and Stephen Sondheim. Screenplay: Melvin Frank, Michael Pertwee. Photography: Nicolas Roeg (Color by De Luxe). Editor: John Victor Smith. Executive Art Director: Syd Cain. Production: Quadrangle Films S.A. Distribution: United Artists. Release Date: October 16, 1966. Running Time: 97 minutes. Cast: Zero Mostel, Phil Silvers, Buster Keaton, Michael Crawford, Jack Gilford, Annette Andre, Michael Hordern, Leon Greene, Roy Kinnear.

The Scribe

Executive Producers: Raymond Walters, James Collier. Producers: Ann and Kenneth Heeley-Ray. Director: John Sebert. Screenplay: Paul Sutherland, Clifford Braggins. Photography: Mike Lente (color). Editor: Kenneth Heeley-Ray. Production: Film-Tele Productions. Distribution: Construction Safety Associations of Ontario. First Showings: May 1966. Running Time: 29 minutes. Cast: Buster Keaton, Cecil Linder.

NOTE: Made in Toronto in October 1965, this was Keaton's final film appearance.

Appendix II

SIGNIFICANT TELEVISION APPEARANCES

Apart from commercials, Buster Keaton made hundreds of regional and national television appearances. Compiling a complete list of these would be a daunting, if not impossible, task. So this is a chronology of significant TV appearances Keaton made between the years 1948 and 1965.

George Pal Studio Tour
January 1948. (KTLA, Los Angeles) Host: Stew Wilson. Participants: George Pal, Carolyn Burke Adler, Buster Keaton, Ernst Fegte.
NOTE: This broadcast was to promote George Pal's upcoming production of *Tom Thumb,* in which Buster Keaton was to have played a featured role. This is Keaton's earliest known television appearance and possibly his TV debut.

Pantomime Quiz Time
November 8, 1949. (KTTV, Los Angeles) Producers: Mike Stokey, Bernie Ebert. Director: Philippe De Lacy. Host: Mike Stokey. Announcer: Ed Reimers. Regulars: Vincent Price, Gail Robbins, Hans Conried, Frank De Vol. Guests: Buster Keaton, Gale Storm, Vince Barnett, Marjorie Lord. Length: 30 minutes.
NOTE: *Pantomime Quiz Time* was also kinescoped for airing on WCBS in New York, where this episode was seen on November 22, 1949.

The Ed Wynn Show
December 8, 1949. (KTTV, Los Angeles) Producer: Harlan Thompson. Director: Ralph Levy. Writers: Hal Kanter, Leo Solomon, Seaman Jacobs. Music: Lud Gluskin. Announcer: Robert Le Mond. Cast: Ed Wynn, Buster Keaton, Virginia O'Brien. Length: 30 minutes.
NOTE: This appearance was heralded as Keaton's television debut, despite his earlier appearance on *Pantomime Quiz Time*. *The Ed Wynn Show* was also kinescoped for airing on WCBS and in fourteen other eastern and midwestern markets on a two-week delay.

The Buster Keaton Show
December 22, 1949–April 6, 1950. (KTTV, Los Angeles) Producer: Joe Parker. Director: Philippe De Lacy. Writers: Clyde Bruckman, Henry Taylor. Music: George Greeley. Announcer: Ed Reimers. Cast: Buster Keaton, Alan Reed, Leon Belasco, Ben Weldon, Dick Elliott. Length: 30 minutes.
NOTE: This initial series of live broadcasts endured a number of changes over its sixteen-week run. Joe Parker was replaced as producer by Al Manheimer, but then Parker returned to the show in March 1950. Writers who worked on one or more episodes, usually in collaboration with Clyde Bruckman, included Elwood Ullman, Ben Perry, Jay Sommers, and Harold Goodwin. Among those who appeared on the series were Robert Alda, Dorothy Sebastian, Sara Berner, Peter Leeds, Kay Erlenborn, Fritz

Feld, June Foray, Ruth Perrot, Dona Gibson, Harold Goodwin, and Harvey Parry.

Camel Comedy Cavalcade
June 15, 1950. (CBS, Los Angeles) Producer-Director: Ralph Levy. Writers: Hal Kanter, Frank Fox, Seaman Jacobs. Music: Lud Gluskin. Announcer: Robert Le Mond. Cast: Ed Wynn, Georgia Gibbs, the Keystone Cops (Chester Conklin, Heinie Conklin, Hank Mann, Snub Pollard, Tiny Ward), Buster Keaton. Length: 30 minutes.

Toast of the Town
November 5, 1950. (CBS, New York) Producer: Marlo Lewis. Director: John Wray. Music: Ray Bloch. Announcer: Art Hannes. Host: Ed Sullivan. Guests: Milton Berle, Buster Keaton, Nanette Fabray, Jack Whiting, Nat King Cole, Boys Town Choir. Length: 60 minutes.
NOTE: Keaton performed a sketch called "Goin' Fishin'."

Toast of the Town
November 12, 1950. (CBS, New York) Producer: Marlo Lewis. Director: John Wray. Music: Ray Bloch. Announcer: Art Hannes. Host: Ed Sullivan. Guests: Phil Spitalny's All Girl Orchestra, Arthur Lake, Buster Keaton, Eleanor Keaton, Jimmy Nelson. Length: 60 minutes.
NOTE: The Keatons performed the drunk scene from *Spite Marriage*.

The Garry Moore Show
November 13, 1950. (CBS, New York) Producer: Herb Sanford. Director: Clarence Schimmel. Announcer: Durwood Kirby. Cast: Garry Moore, Denise Lor, Ken Carson. Guest: Buster Keaton. Length: 60 minutes.
NOTE: Keaton made the first of many appearances with Garry Moore on this daytime version of Moore's CBS variety show.

4 Star Revue
November 15, 1950. (NBC, New York) Producer-Director: Coby Ruskin. Writers:

Nat Hiken, Billy Friedberg. Music: Dean Elliott. Announcer: Andre Baruch. Cast: Ed Wynn, Buster Keaton, Gertrude Niesen, Eddy Manson, Dick and Dot Remy, Duke Art. Length: 60 minutes.
NOTE: Keaton and Wynn reprised the "Butcher Boy" sketch they originally performed on Wynn's KTTV show a year earlier.

Toast of the Town
December 10, 1950. (CBS, New York) Producer: Marlo Lewis. Director: John Wray. Music: Ray Bloch. Announcer: Art Hannes. Host: Ed Sullivan. Guests: Jack E. Leonard, Mimi Benzell, Buster Keaton, Eddie Fisher, Jane Morgan. Length: 60 minutes.
NOTE: Keaton brought a bit of pathos to the show as a shabby Santa Claus hoping to find seasonal work.

Showtime U.S.A.
February 25, 1951. (ABC, New York) Producer: Vinton Freedley. Director: Howard Teichmann. Music: Nathan Kroll. Host: Vinton Freedley. M.C.: Eva Gabor. Guests: Beatrice Kay, Buster Keaton, Dorothy Stickney, Paul McGrath. Length: 30 minutes.
NOTE: Buster and Eleanor Keaton performed the park bench sketch he would later incorporate into his 1954 engagement at the Cirque Médrano.

The Buster Keaton Show
May 9–August 1, 1951. (KTTV, Los Angeles) Executive Producer: Carl K. Hittleman. Producer: Clyde Bruckman. Director: Arthur Hilton. Writers: Harold Goodwin, Ben Perry, Jay Sommers, Jack Harvey, Carl K. Hittleman. Photography: Jackson Rose, Karl Struss. Produced and Syndicated by Consolidated Television Productions. Cast: Buster Keaton, Marcia Mae Jones, Margaret Dumont, George Scott, James Blears, Leslie Holmes, Harold Goodwin, Harvey Parry, Dorothy Ford, Jack Reitzen, Philip Van Zandt, Eddie Gribbon, Crystal White, Steve Calvert, Eleanor Keaton. Length: 30 minutes.

Toast of the Town

September 2, 1951. (CBS, New York)
Producer: Marlo Lewis. Director: John
Wray. Music: Ray Bloch. Announcer:
Art Hannes. Guest Host: Dolores Gray.
Guests: Buster Keaton, Eleanor Keaton,
Henny Youngman, Bunny Briggs,
Jack Mann and Dick Dana. Length:
60 minutes.
NOTE: The Keatons performed the balcony
scene from *Romeo and Juliet*.

All Star Revue

November 10, 1951. (NBC, Los Angeles)
Producer: Hal Kemp. Director: Leo
Solomon. Writers: Hal Goodman, Bob
Fisher, Leo Solomon. Music: Lou Bring.
Cast: Ed Wynn, Dorothy Lamour, Buster
Keaton, Nicholas Brothers. Length: 60
minutes.
NOTE: Keaton performed a sketch set in a
bakery.

The Ken Murray Show

"Salute to Movietime, U.S.A." February 2,
1952. (CBS, Los Angeles) Producer: Ken
Murray. Director: Herb Sussan. Writers:
Royal Foster, Seaman Jacobs, Earl Brent.
Announcer: Nelson Case. Cast: Ken Murray,
Adolph Zukor, Buster Keaton, Ramon
Novarro, Ruby Keeler, Billy Gilbert. Length:
60 minutes.

Colgate Comedy Hour

March 2, 1952. (NBC, Los Angeles)
Producer-Director: Ernest B. Gluckman.
Cast: Donald O'Connor, Patricia Morison,
Broderick Crawford, Buster Keaton, Cecil
Kellaway. Length: 60 minutes.

I've Got a Secret

July 17, 1952. (CBS, New York) Producer:
Allan Sherman. Director: Franklin Heller.
Host: Garry Moore. Announcer: John
Cannon. Panel: Melville Cooper, Bill
Cullen, Jayne Meadows, Mrs. Laura
Hobson. Length: 30 minutes.
NOTE: Keaton made his first appearance
on this venerable network panel show.
His secret: "I threw a pie at Hedda
Hopper."

Life with Buster Keaton

December 4, 1952–February 26, 1953.
(WABD, New York) The thirteen episodes
of *The Buster Keaton Show* retitled and
syndicated by Crown Pictures International.

Douglas Fairbanks, Jr. Presents

"The Awakening" July 1954. (Dougfair
Corporation/Syndicated) Producer: Lance
Comfort. Director: Michael McCarthy.
Based upon the story "The Cloak" by
Nikolai Gogol. Teleplay: Larry Marcus.
Photography: Ken Talbot. Music: Bretton
Byrd. Host: Douglas Fairbanks, Jr. Cast:
Buster Keaton, James Hayter, Carl Jaffe,
Lynne Cole, Geoffrey Keen. Length:
30 minutes.

The Best of Broadway

"The Man Who Came to Dinner" by Moss
Hart and George S. Kaufman. October 13,
1954. (CBS, New York) Producer: Martin
Manulis. Director: David Alexander.
Adaptation: Ronald Alexander. Music:
David Broekman. Cast: Monty Woolley,
Joan Bennett, Reginald Gardiner, Bert Lahr,
William Prince, ZaSu Pitts, Buster Keaton,
Catherine Doucet, Margaret Hamilton,
Howard St. John. Length: 60 minutes.

Make the Connection

August 18, 1955. (NBC, New York) Producer:
Gil Fates. Announcer: Lee Vines. Host:
Gene Rayburn. Panel: Betty White, Gene
Klavan, Laraine Day, Eddie Bracken. Guests:
Buster Keaton, Harry Gribbon. Length: 30
minutes.

Eddie Cantor Comedy Theatre

"The Square World of Alonzo Pennyworth"
October 1955. (Ziv Television/Syndicated)
Host: Eddie Cantor. Cast: Buster Keaton,
Davidja, Lili Badalian, Alli Assan, Elcana
Beatti, Clarice Zadegian, Hari, Karoun
Tootikian. Length: 30 minutes.
NOTE: Keaton played a daydreaming travel
agent.

The Adventures of Mr. Pastry

July 1958. (Sapphire Film/Official Films)
Executive Producer: Hannah Weinstein.

Associate Producer: Sidney Cole. Director: Ralph Smart. (Uncredited: Buster Keaton.) Screenplay: Angus Macphail, Harold Kent. Music: Sydney John Kay. Photography: Gerald Gibbs. Editor: Inman Hunter. Length: 25 minutes.

NOTE: Made in July–August 1955, this was the pilot for a commercial series of thirty-nine episodes to be seen internationally. It didn't sell, but the film was transmitted in England in 1958.

Sunday Spectacular

"Show Biz from Vaudeville to Video" October 9, 1955. (NBC, Burbank) Producer: Ernest B. Gluckman. Director: Richard McDonough. Writer: Ken Englund. Music: Gordon Jenkins. Host: Art Linkletter. Cast: Groucho Marx, Beatrice Kay, Buster Keaton, Dennis Day, Bert Lahr, Eartha Kitt, Rosemary Clooney, Paul Gilbert, Melinda Marx, Jay C. Flippen, Harold Goodwin. Length: 90 minutes.

NOTE: Keaton was announced with a sign that read, "Buster Keaton formerly of the '3' Keatons." He disrupted a magician's act and they ended up trading whacks with a broom and a roll of paper, respectively, while the orchestra played "The Anvil Chorus."

Screen Directors Playhouse

"The Silent Partner" December 21, 1955. (NBC/Hal Roach Studios) Director: George Marshall. Story: Barbara Hammer, George Marshall. Teleplay: Barbara Hammer. Photography: Ed DuPar. Editor: Bert Jordan. Cast: Buster Keaton, ZaSu Pitts, Joe E. Brown, Evelyn Ankers, Jack Kruschen, Jack Elam, Percy Helton, Bob Hope. Length: 30 minutes.

The Martha Raye Show

March 6, 1956. (NBC, New York) Producer: Karl Hoffenberg. Director: Norman Lear. Writers: Norman Lear, Ed Simmons. Cast: Martha Raye, Rocky Graziano. Guests: Paul Douglas, Buster Keaton, Harold Arlen, Bill and Cora Baird Marionettes. Length: 60 minutes.

NOTE: Keaton and Raye reprise the act that Keaton and Charlie Chaplin performed in *Limelight*.

Lux Video Theatre

"The Night of January 16th" by Ayn Rand. May 10, 1956. (NBC, Burbank) Producer: Cal Kuhl. Director: Fred Carney. Teleplay: S. H. Barnett. Host: Otto Kruger. Cast: Phyllis Thaxter, Richard Shannon, Les Tremayne, Helen Westcott, Douglas Dumbrille. Members of the Jury: Mack Sennett, Buster Keaton, May McAvoy, Betty Bronson, Jack Mulhall, Viola Dana, Shirley Mason, Claire Windsor, Julia Faye, Gertrude Astor, Mary Carr. Length: 60 minutes.

It Could Be You

June 7, 1956. (NBC, Burbank) Producer: Stephen Hatos. Director: Stuart Phelps. Host: Bill Leyden. Announcer: Wendell Niles. Guest: Buster Keaton. Length: 30 minutes.

NOTE: Keaton made the first of several appearances on this daytime audience participation show from Ralph Edwards Productions.

Producers Showcase

"The Lord Don't Play Favorites" September 17, 1956. (NBC, Burbank) Producer: Hal Stanley. Director: Bretaigne Windust. Story: Patrick Malloy. Teleplay: Jo Swerling, Hal Stanley. Music and Lyrics: Hal Stanley, Irving Taylor. Cast: Robert Stack, Kay Starr, Dick Haymes, Buster Keaton, Louis Armstrong, Mike Ross, Oliver Blake, Barry Kelly, Jerry Maren. Length: 90 minutes.

This Is Your Life

April 3, 1957. (NBC, Burbank) Producer: Axel Gruenberg. Director: Richard Gottlieb. Writers: Paul Phillips, Mort Lewis. Host: Ralph Edwards. Subject: Buster Keaton. Guests: Louise Dresser, William "Mush" Rawls, Louise Keaton, Harry Keaton, Eddie Cline, Donald Crisp, Red Skelton, Eleanor Keaton, Donald O'Connor, Jim Talmadge, Bob Talmadge. Length: 30 minutes.

The Ed Sullivan Show

April 21, 1957. (CBS, New York) Producer: Marlo Lewis. Director: John Wray. Music: Ray Bloch. Announcer: Art Hannes. Host: Ed Sullivan. Guests: Marion Marlowe,

Roberta Sherwood, Bob Sweeney, Gale Gordon, Mitzi Green, Donald O'Connor, Buster Keaton, Don Murray, Charlotte Rae. Length: 60 minutes.

NOTE: Donald O'Connor, discussing his role in *The Buster Keaton Story*, appeared by remote from Los Angeles. Then Keaton, in New York, performed the old peddler woman stunt from *Sherlock Jr.* before a live audience.

The Rosemary Clooney Show

June 1957. (Maysville Corporation/Syndicated) Producer: Joseph S. Shribman. Director: Dik Darley. Writer: Tom Waldman. Music: Nelson Riddle. Cast: Rosemary Clooney, Buster Keaton, Gail Stone. Length: 30 minutes.

What's My Line?

September 1, 1957. (CBS, New York) Producer: Gil Fates. Director: Franklin Heller. Host: John Daly. Announcer: Hal Simms. Panel: Dorothy Kilgallen, Ernie Kovacs, Arlene Francis, Bennett Cerf. Mystery Guest: Buster Keaton. Length: 30 minutes.

You Asked for It

December 22, 1957. (ABC, Los Angeles) Producer: Cran Chamberlin. Director: Fred Gadette. Writers: Gomer Cool, Rick Mittleman. Host: Art Baker. Guests: Buster Keaton, Eddie Gribbon. Length: 30 minutes.

NOTE: Keaton made his first appearance on this long-running Sunday-night program by again performing the "Butcher Boy" sketch, this time with Eddie Gribbon.

The Betty White Show

February 12, 1958. (ABC, Los Angeles) Producer: Don Fedderson. Director: James V. Kern. Writers: George Tibbles, Si Rose, Seaman Jacobs. Music: Frank De Vol. Announcer: Tom Kennedy. Cast: Betty White, John Jacobs, Cornel Wilde, Charles Coburn, Sterling Holloway. Guests: Buster Keaton, Boris Karloff. Length: 30 minutes.

Playhouse 90

"The Innocent Sleep" June 5, 1958. (CBS, Los Angeles) Producer: Martin Manulis.

Director: Franklin Schaffner. Teleplay: Tad Mosel. Announcer: Dick Joy. Host: Raymond Burr. Cast: Hope Lange, John Ericson, Buster Keaton, Hope Emerson, Dennis King. Length: 90 minutes.

The Donna Reed Show

December 24, 1958. (ABC/Todon Briskin) Producer: Tony Owen. Director: Oscar Rudolph. Writer: Nate Monaster. Cast: Donna Reed, Carl Betz, Shelley Fabares, Buster Keaton. Length: 30 minutes.

NOTE: In his first of two appearances in this long-running series, Keaton played a hospital handyman who is recruited by Donna to play Santa Claus.

Breck Sunday Showcase

"After Hours" February 2, 1960. (NBC, New York) Producer-Director: Alex March. Teleplay: Tony Webster. Cast: Christopher Plummer, Sally Ann Howes, Buster Keaton, Philip Abbott, Paul McGrath, Natalie Schafer, Robert Emhardt. Length: 60 minutes.

NOTE: Keaton played an opening scene as a sidewalk Santa.

The Revlon Revue

"A 70th Birthday Salute to Paul Whiteman" March 24, 1960. (NBC, Burbank) Producer: Perry Lafferty. Director: Norman Jewison. Writer: Abe Burrows. Host: Mike Wallace. Cast: Paul Whiteman, Bing Crosby, Peggy Lee, Buster Keaton, Jack Teagarden. Length: 60 minutes.

NOTE: Keaton and Whiteman reprised the duel sketch they performed in *Newcomers of 1928*.

Candid Camera

December 18, 1960. (CBS, New York) Producer-Director: Julio DiBenedetto. Writer: Bill Jacobson. Hosts: Arthur Godfrey, Allen Funt. Guest: Buster Keaton. Length: 30 minutes.

NOTE: Keaton made the first of two appearances on this popular hidden-camera show. His sequence, in which he struggled with a sandwich and a bowl of soup, was filmed at a diner in Denver, Colorado.

The Scene Stealers

January 1962. (National Foundation/Syndicated) Producer: Edward A. Franck. Director: Jack Shea. Writer: Johnny Bradford. Photography: Loyal Griggs. Editor: George Boemler. Cast: Ed Wynn, Buster Keaton, Jimmy Durante, David Janssen, Rosemary Clooney, Jack Lemmon, Ralph Edwards, Fritz Feld, The Limeliters, James Garner, Jackie Cooper, Abby Dalton, Eartha Kitt, Dr. Frank Baxter, Roger Williams, Nanette Fabray, Dan Blocker, Lorne Green, Fabian, Dorothy Provine. Length: 60 minutes.
NOTE: This all-star appeal, shot at Paramount studios in June 1961, was made available free to more than four hundred stations nationwide as part of the 1962 March of Dimes campaign.

The Twilight Zone

"Once Upon a Time" December 15, 1961. (CBS/Cayuga Productions) Producer: Buck Houghton. Director: Norman Z. McLeod. Teleplay: Richard Matheson. Photography: George T. Clemens. Editor: Jason H. Bernie. Host: Rod Serling. Cast: Buster Keaton, Stanley Adams, James Flavin, Gil Lamb, Jesse White.

Medicine Man

"A Pony for Chris" Filmed January 1962. (ABC/Screen Gems) Producer-Writers: Jay Sommers, Joe Bigelow. Director: Charles Barton. Cast: Ernie Kovacs, Buster Keaton, Kevin Brodie, Richard Devon, Joe Higgins, Josip Elic, Alan Hewitt, Charles Tannen, Valerie Allen. Length: 30 minutes.
NOTE: CBS announced plans to air this film as part of a weekly series of unsold pilots called The Comedy Spot over the summer of 1962. Matters involving Ernie Kovacs' estate forced the network to cancel the showing.

Close-Up

"Three Comedians" April 1, 1962. (CBC, Toronto, Ontario) Producer: Ross McLean. Host: Frank Willis. Moderator: Bob Quintrell. Guests: Buster Keaton, Bert Lahr, Eddie Foy, Jr. Length: 30 minutes.

NOTE: Keaton made this appearance while in Canada shooting Ten Girls Ago.

Route 66

"Journey to Nineveh" September 28, 1962. (CBS/Lancer-Edling) Producer: Mort Abrahams. Director: David Lowell Rich. Teleplay: William R. Cox. Photography: Jack A. Marta. Editor: Harry Coswick. Cast: Martin Milner, George Maharis, Joe E. Brown, Buster Keaton, Jenny Maxwell, Guy Raymond, John Astin, Edgar Buchanan. Length: 60 minutes.

Mr. Smith Goes to Washington

"Think Mink" January 19, 1963. (ABC/Screen Gems) Producer: Hal Stanley. Director: Claudio Guzman. Writers: Howard Snyder, Jack Harvey. Cast: Fess Parker, Sandra Warner, Stan Irwin, Red Foley, Buster Keaton. Length: 30 minutes.

The Man Who Bought Paradise

January 17, 1965. (CBS, Los Angeles) Producer-Director: Ralph Nelson. Teleplay: Richard Alan Simmons. Music: Richard Shores. Cast: Robert Horton, Dolores Del Rio, Ray Walston, Walter Slezak, Cyril Ritchard, Buster Keaton, Paul Lukas, Angie Dickinson, Hoagy Carmichael. Length: 60 minutes.
NOTE: Recorded in January 1963 under the title Hotel Paradise, this ninety-minute comedy-drama about fugitives in a decaying South American hotel was the brainchild of CBS programming executive Hubbell Robinson, who planned four original productions over the 1963–64 season in an attempt to recapture the audience he originally built with Playhouse 90. But Hotel Paradise wasn't well received in sponsor screenings and, despite its star power, was shelved by the network. Retitled The Man Who Bought Paradise and trimmed to sixty minutes, it was finally aired in January 1965—a full two years after its making.

Today

"Buster Keaton Revisited" April 26, 1963. (NBC, New York) Producer: Al Morgan. Hosts: Hugh Downs, Jack Lescoulie, Pat

Fontaine. Guest: Buster Keaton.
NOTE: Keaton had previously appeared on
Today in 1956, 1957, and 1960. This was,
however, the only time the entire program
was devoted to him.

The Ed Sullivan Show
December 23, 1963. (CBS, New York)
Producer: Robert Precht. Director: Tom
Kiley. Music: Ray Bloch. Announcer: Art
Hannes. Host: Ed Sullivan. Guests: Tessie
O'Shea, Buster Keaton, George Kirby, Topo
Gigio, Frank Ifield, Dick Libertini and Paul
Dooley, The Burke Family. Length:
60 minutes.
NOTE: In his final appearance on the
Sullivan show, Keaton played a man trying
to get some time to himself on Christmas
Day.

Telescope
"Deadpan" April 17, 1964. (CBC, Ottawa,
Ontario) Producer: Robert Crone. Host:
Fletcher Markle. Subject: Buster Keaton.
Length: 30 minutes.

The Greatest Show on Earth
"You're All Right, Ivy" April 28, 1964. (ABC/
Desilu) Producer: Bob Rafelson. Director:
Jack Palance. Teleplay: William Wood. Cast:
Jack Palance, Joe E. Brown, Joan Blondell,
Buster Keaton, Lynn Loring, Stu Erwin, Ted
Bessell, Barbara Pepper. Length: 60 minutes.

Burke's Law
"Who Killed 1/2 of Glory Lee?" May 3, 1964.
(ABC/Four Star) Producer: Aaron Spelling.
Director: Don Weis. Teleplay: Harlan
Ellison. Photography: Chas E. Burke. Cast:
Gene Barry, Gary Conway, Regis Toomey,
Leon Lontoc, Dawn Wells, Eddie Quillan.
Suspects: Joan Blondell, Nina Foch, Anne
Helm, Betty Hutton, Buster Keaton, Gisele
MacKenzie. Length: 60 minutes.

The Hollywood Palace
June 6, 1964. (ABC, Los Angeles) Producer:
William O. Harbach. Director: Grey

Lockwood. Writers: Joe Bigelow, Jay Burton.
Music: Mitchell Ayres. Announcer: Dick
Tufeld. Host: Gene Barry. Guests: Juliet
Prowse, Jack Carter, Buster Keaton, Gloria
Swanson, The Swingle Singers. Length: 60
minutes.

Buster Keaton Rides Again
October 16, 1965. (CBC/National Film
Board of Canada) Producer: Julian Biggs.
Director: John Spotton. Photography: John
Spotton. Assistant: David de Volpi. Sound:
Barry Ferguson. Commentary: Donald
Brittain. Cast: Buster Keaton, Gerald
Potterton, Eleanor Keaton, Jo Kirkpatrick.
Length: 55 minutes.

The Jonathan Winters Show
"Jonathan and the Movies" March 29, 1965.
(NBC, Los Angeles) Producer-Director:
Greg Garrison. Narrator: Alexander Scourby.
Cast: Jonathan Winters, Buster Keaton,
Julie Newmar, Agnes Moorehead, Robert
Middleton, Fred Clark.

Salute to Stan Laurel
November 23, 1965. (CBS, Los Angeles)
Producer: Gene Lester. Director: Seymour
Berns. Writers: Charles Isaacs, Hugh
Wedlock, Allan Manings, Aaron Ruben,
Carl Reiner. Music: David Rose. Host:
Dick Van Dyke. Cast: Lucille Ball, Fred
Gwynne, Danny Kaye, Buster Keaton,
Leonid Kinskey, Tina Louise, Audrey
Meadows, Bob Newhart, Louis Nye,
Gregory Peck, Cesar Romero, Phil Silvers.
Length: 60 minutes.

Flashback
October 10, 1965. (CBC, Toronto, Ontario)
Producer-Director: Don Brown. Writer:
Alfie Scopp. Host: Bill Walker. Panel:
Allan Manings, Maggie Morris, Elwy Yost,
Lorraine Thomson. Guest: Buster Keaton.
Length: 30 minutes.
NOTE: Keaton made his final TV appearance
on this Canadian panel show while in
Toronto filming *The Scribe*.

Index

Pearl, Jack, 363, 463
Pearson, Ben, 549–50, 591, 600, 611, 614*n*, 649, 635, 666
Pearson, Pearl, 591
Peers, Joan, 402, 403
Pendleton, Nat, 493
Penney, Arthur, 118
Pépé le Moko, 503
Percy, Eileen, 218
Perkins, Gil, 396, 491, 523–24
Perrin, Nat, 523
Perry, Ben, 538
Pest from the West, 483–84, 486, 487
Peter Pan (1924), 328
Pialaglou, John, 164*n*, 231
Pickett, Ingram B. "Cupid," *138*
Pickford, Jack, 121
Pickford, Mary, 184, 222, 271, 285, 320, 380, 445, 494, 573, 648, 655
Pidgeon, Walter, 507
Pilgrim, The, 169
Pincher, Otto, 118
Pinter, Harold, 648
Piquo, Harry, 64
Pittenger, William, 287, 330
Pitts, ZaSu, 418, 575
Plastic Age, The, 322
Play House, The, 170–76, 178, 190, 193, 346, 426, 617, 686
Playhouse 90 (TV), 599, 602
Playthings of Desire, 446, 447
Plombier amoureux, Le, see Passionate Plumber, The
Plummer, Christopher, 615
Pocketful of Miracles, 623
Pollard, Snub, 575
Polly of the Circus, 434
Ponjola, 254
Pony Express, The, 329
Poor Little Rich Girl, The (play), 123
Pop Goes the World (story), 666
Potterton, Gerald, 3–7, 129–31, 373–75, 553–54, 656–62, 664, 682
Powell, Dilys, 680, 687
Powell, Eleanor, 490
Power, Tyrone, 580
Powers, Pat, 444
Powers, Rea John, 592

Powers, T. E., 75*n*
Prevost, Marie, 405, 410, 415
Price, Kate, 199
Princess and the Pea, The (story), 618
Private General, The, see General Nuisance
Proctor, F. F., 21, 24
Project One, see Film
Prosperity, 432
Prosser, W. W., 76
Puddin' Head, 499

Quarterback, The, 322
Quartet (1948), 569
Quick Millions (1939), 482
Quicksand, 581
Quinn, Paul, 170
Quirk, James, 196–97

Rae, Frank, 64
Raft, George, 466
Rag and Tag (play), 13
Railrodder, The, 3–7, 129–31, 373–75, 553–54, 656–62, 668, 681, 682
Rainer, Luise, 500
Raintree County, 599
Raitt, John, 598
Raymond, Guy, 636
Randall, Tony, 612
Rapf, Harry, 366, 368, 439
Rappe, Virginia, 182–83, 184, 185, 196, 202 and *n*
Rasch, Albertina, 489–90
Rathbun, Eldon, 658
Rawls, Ella, 451
Rawls, William "Mush," 450–51, 585
Rawlston, Zelma, 32
Raye, Mona, 586
Raymaker, Herman C., 229
Raymond, Guy, 636
"Raymond Rohauer: King of the Film Freebooters" (magazine article), 690
Rear Car, The (play), 432, 433, 434
Reckless Age, The, 266
Reckless Romeo, A, 91, 92
Red Mill, The, 320–21
Reed, Alan, 537, 538

A NOTE ON THE TYPE

This book was set in Adobe Garamond. Designed for the Adobe Corporation by Robert Slimbach, the fonts are based on types first cut by Claude Garamond (c. 1480–1561). Garamond was a pupil of Geoffroy Tory and is believed to have followed the Venetian models, although he introduced a number of important differences, and it is to him that we owe the letter we now know as "old style." He gave to his letters a certain elegance and feeling of movement that won their creator an immediate reputation and the patronage of Francis I of France.

Composed by North Market Street Graphics, Lancaster, Pennsylvania

Printed and bound by LSC Communications, Harrisonburg, Virginia

Designed by Maggie Hinders